Florian Frensch

The Social Side of Mergers and Acquisitions

GABLER EDITION WISSENSCHAFT

Florian Frensch

The Social Side of Mergers and Acquisitions

Cooperation relationships
after mergers and acquisitions

With a foreword by Prof. Dr. Hans Georg Gemünden

Deutscher Universitäts-Verlag

Bibliografische Information Der Deutschen Nationalbibliothek
Die Deutsche Nationalbibliothek verzeichnet diese Publikation in der
Deutschen Nationalbibliografie; detaillierte bibliografische Daten sind im Internet über
<http://dnb.d-nb.de> abrufbar.

Dissertation Technische Universität Berlin, 2006

D 83

1. Auflage April 2007

Alle Rechte vorbehalten
© Deutscher Universitäts-Verlag | GWV Fachverlage GmbH, Wiesbaden 2007

Lektorat: Brigitte Siegel / Anita Wilke

Der Deutsche Universitäts-Verlag ist ein Unternehmen von Springer Science+Business Media.
www.duv.de

Das Werk einschließlich aller seiner Teile ist urheberrechtlich geschützt.
Jede Verwertung außerhalb der engen Grenzen des Urheberrechtsgesetzes
ist ohne Zustimmung des Verlags unzulässig und strafbar. Das gilt insbe-
sondere für Vervielfältigungen, Übersetzungen, Mikroverfilmungen und die
Einspeicherung und Verarbeitung in elektronischen Systemen.

Die Wiedergabe von Gebrauchsnamen, Handelsnamen, Warenbezeichnungen usw. in diesem
Werk berechtigt auch ohne besondere Kennzeichnung nicht zu der Annahme, dass solche
Namen im Sinne der Warenzeichen- und Markenschutz-Gesetzgebung als frei zu betrachten
wären und daher von jedermann benutzt werden dürften.

Umschlaggestaltung: Regine Zimmer, Dipl.-Designerin, Frankfurt/Main
Gedruckt auf säurefreiem und chlorfrei gebleichtem Papier
Printed in Germany

ISBN 978-3-8350-0754-3

Foreword

The latest increase in numbers of mergers and acquisitions (M&As) and the latest increase in size of M&As raise the question, whether M&As can meet the expectations. This question is relevant in two ways, from an economic as well as from a social perspective. Despite its central economic importance, many mergers and acquisitions fall short of their objectives.

In his work, Florian Frensch sees cooperation relationships between employees and management of previously separate firms as the key success factor for the realization of synergies and thereby for the M&A success. Cooperation depends on different factors on the environmental, the firm, team and the individual level.

Grounded on extensive literature search, Florian Frensch investigates which individual factors of employees and which dyadic factors of relationship partners affect the cooperation between employees of previously separated firms.

With the help of social network analyses, Florian Frensch investigates cooperation relationships after M&A-transactions in two case studies. Unlike previous studies, he asks employees on the lower operative levels of the firm instead of using key informants in the management ranks. In order to use social network analysis in larger groups, Florian Frensch develops an innovative approach for gathering network data with the help of a dynamic computer based questionnaire, which allows him to conduct a full network analysis in a group with ~ 400 employees.

Two findings, I find especially remarkable: First, structural cooperation requirements and integration measures are powerful means to make employees cooperate after M&As. Potential integration barriers caused by lack of disposition of individuals or lack of similarity of employees thus can be addressed effectively. A second important finding is the fact that age does not matter when it comes to relationship formation. Especially in an aging workforce, this point is important as most practitioner guidelines for M&As focus on bringing together younger employees in integration measures.

Florian Frensch presents a very ambitious work both regarding the content as well as the methodology used. And his results really provide answers to the questions, how integration after mergers and acquisitions can be measured, explained and improved. Admittedly, it is not an easy reading. But the innovativeness of the questions asked and the richness of the results provide a rich fund for future work in the field and for practitioners who are responsible for PMIs. It truly is a contribution.

Professor Dr. Hans Georg Gemünden

Preface

The work has been accomplished, the book is vast. ... This has only been possible thanks to numerous small and big favors and support from many different individuals. And some of them, I want to mention at this point.

First, I want to thank Professor Gemünden. After having accomplished successfully a diploma thesis with him with lots of space for independent research, he offered me for the second time the opportunity to do what I wanted, while supporting me with his insights and contacts. I also want to thank Professor Schewe, who agreed to advise my work despite the fact that I am external to him in two ways: From another university as well as an external doctoral candidate.

I further want to thank anonymously the CEOs of two companies, whose social networks I investigated. Without the trust and the support of Mister W. from SpecMatCo and Mister M. from SoftCo, this research could never have been accomplished.
Also, I want to thank Katharina Hölzle, who helped me with numerous small and big favors to succeed as an external doctoral candidate in the mists of academia.
I want to thank Svenja Gamp for her translation support. Très francais! Also, I want to thank Bertram Meyer and Oliver Merkel, who worked themselves through preliminary stages of this thesis and whose comments and suggestions helped me tremendously to produce a decent piece of work. It was hard and I know it!

And certainly, all this would not have been possible without the support of my parents Monika and Hans-Heinrich, as well as my sister Stefanie. The three of you made me the person I am today.
Last but not least, I want to thank Eva Spies. You put up patiently with me during the entire process from start to end, you supported me and motivated me and made me a very happy man. I cannot thank you enough for all you do and all you are.

Florian Frensch

Contents – Overview

Foreword	V
Preface	VII
Contents – Overview	IX
Contents	XI
List of illustrations	XXIII
List of graphs	XXV
List of tables	XXVII
Executive summary	1
Summary of content	3
1. Introduction and formulation of research questions	15
2. Theoretical model	133
3. Empirical investigation	159
4. Empirical study at the first research site: SpecMatCo	191
5. Empirical study at the second research site: SoftCo	247
6. Discussion of results for research question "Who cooperates?"	369
7. Discussion of results for research question "Who cooperates with whom?"	413
8. Implications for practitioners	429
9. Academic contribution and implications for further research	439
References	447
Appendix I – IV	473

Contents

Foreword	V
Preface	VII
Contents – Overview	IX
Contents	XI
List of illustrations	XXIII
List of graphs	XXV
List of tables	XXVII
Executive summary	1
Summary of content	3
1. Introduction and formulation of research questions	15
1.1. Mergers and acquisitions – Importance for economies and firms	15
1.2. But still: Most mergers and acquisitions fail	17
1.2.1. Objective success measures	19
1.2.2. Subjective success measures	21
1.2.3. Summary of success rates of mergers and acquisitions	22
1.3. What are they? - Definitions of mergers and acquisitions	23
1.3.1. Degree of dependency of combinations of firms	24
1.3.2. Mergers of equals vs. takeovers	25
1.4. Why do they happen? Reasons for the occurrence of mergers and acquisitions	27
1.4.1. Contingency explanations	29
1.4.2. Psychological explanations	30
1.4.3. Value generation objectives	32
1.4.3.1. Synergy mechanism	37
1.4.3.1.1. Economic synergy mechanisms	37
1.4.3.1.2. Resource based synergy mechanisms	39
1.4.3.1.3. Transaction cost based synergy mechanisms	40
1.4.3.2. Synergy effects	40
1.4.3.3. Strategic growth objectives of M&A-transactions	42
1.4.3.3.1. Value creation through horizontal mergers and acquisitions	44
1.4.3.3.2. Value creation through product-extending mergers and acquisitions	45
1.4.3.3.3. Value creation through market-extending mergers and acquisitions	46
1.4.3.3.4. Value creation through vertical mergers and acquisitions	46
1.4.3.3.5. Value creation through diversification	47
1.4.3.3.6. Summary of strategic objectives	47

1.4.3.4.	Financial objectives of M&A-transactions	48
1.4.4.	Synergy potential and synergy effects	49
1.4.5.	Summary	49
1.5. Why do M&As fail? Success factors for M&A-transactions		50
1.5.1.	A process-based multi-level framework of M&A-success factors	64
1.5.1.1.	Process character of success factors of mergers and acquisitions	64
1.5.1.2.	Levels of analysis of success factors	69
1.5.2.	Strategy making	71
1.5.2.1.	Success factors on the environmental level	72
1.5.2.1.1.	Global economic situation	72
1.5.2.1.2.	Industry specific factors	73
1.5.2.2.	Success factors on the firm level	74
1.5.2.2.1.	Characteristics of the firm	74
1.5.2.2.2.	Strategic objectives	76
1.5.2.3.	Success factors on the individual level	80
1.5.3.	Selection of target	80
1.5.3.1.	Success factors for selection of targets on the environmental level	81
1.5.3.2.	Success factors for selection of targets on the firm level	82
1.5.3.2.1.	Relative size of an acquisition target	82
1.5.3.2.2.	Relatedness and combination potential	84
1.5.3.2.3.	Cultural differences	86
1.5.3.2.4.	Other factors on firm level	90
1.5.3.3.	Success factors for selection of targets on the group level	91
1.5.3.4.	Success factors for selection of targets on the individual level	92
1.5.4.	Structural decision	92
1.5.4.1.	Success factors on the firm level for the structural decision	93
1.5.5.	Negotiation and closing	97
1.5.5.1.	Firm level success factors	97
1.5.5.1.1.	Attitude	97
1.5.5.1.2.	Single bidder vs. multiple bidder	99
1.5.5.1.3.	Payment method – Cash vs. Stock	99
1.5.5.1.4.	Premium paid	99
1.5.6.	Planning and information gathering	101

1.5.7.	Preparation of integration	102
1.5.7.1.1.	Firm level variables	105
1.5.7.1.2.	Organizational detailing	105
1.5.7.1.3.	Characteristics of the integration process	107
1.5.7.1.4.	Communication	109
1.5.7.1.5.	Active integration measures	111
1.5.7.1.6.	Management interventions	112
1.5.8.	Integration implementation	113
1.5.8.1.	Environmental variables – The role of unions	113
1.5.8.2.	Firm level variables – Acculturation	114
1.5.8.3.	Group level variables	116
1.5.8.4.	Individual level variables	118
1.5.8.4.1.	Loss of identity	118
1.5.8.4.2.	Emotional reactions of employees	119
1.5.8.4.3.	Coping strategies	121
1.6.	Relevance of central constructs	123
1.6.1.	Summary of reviewed success factors	123
1.6.2.	Research questions of the present study	129
2.	Theoretical model	133
2.1.	Who builds cooperation ties?	134
2.1.1.	Demographic characteristics	135
2.1.1.1.	Age	135
2.1.1.2.	Gender	138
2.1.1.3.	Education level	139
2.1.2.	Firm related characteristics	140
2.1.2.1.	Rank	140
2.1.2.2.	Seniority	141
2.1.3.	Attitudes	142
2.1.4.	Reactions to mergers	142
2.1.5.	Integration measures	143
2.1.5.1.	Communication	143
2.1.5.2.	Active integration measures	144
2.1.6.	Structure	146
2.1.7.	Summary of research model: Who cooperates?	146

- 2.2. Who cooperates with whom? ... 148
  - 2.2.1. Demographic characteristics ... 151
    - 2.2.1.1. Age ... 151
    - 2.2.1.2. Gender ... 151
    - 2.2.1.3. Education level ... 152
    - 2.2.1.4. Education content ... 153
  - 2.2.2. Firm related characteristics ... 153
    - 2.2.2.1. Rank ... 153
    - 2.2.2.2. Seniority ... 154
  - 2.2.3. Attitudes ... 154
    - 2.2.3.1. Work related attitudes ... 154
    - 2.2.3.2. Reactions to mergers ... 155
  - 2.2.4. Controls ... 156
    - 2.2.4.1. Active integration measures ... 156
    - 2.2.4.2. Structural constraints ... 156
  - 2.2.5. Summary of the research model: Who cooperates with whom? ... 157
- 3. Empirical investigation ... 159
  - 3.1. Research sites ... 161
    - 3.1.1. First research site - SpecMatCo ... 162
    - 3.1.2. SoftCo ... 164
  - 3.2. Research design ... 166
    - 3.2.1. Experiment ... 166
    - 3.2.2. Quasi-experiment ... 167
    - 3.2.3. Pre-experiment and correlation analysis ... 169
    - 3.2.4. Research design for this study ... 170
  - 3.3. Type of data gathered ... 171
    - 3.3.1. Gathering of secondary data ... 171
    - 3.3.2. Gathering of non-reactive data ... 172
    - 3.3.3. Gathering of primary data ... 174
      - 3.3.3.1. Observation ... 174
      - 3.3.3.2. Interrogation ... 177
        - 3.3.3.2.1. Personal interrogation - Interviews ... 177
        - 3.3.3.2.2. Written interrogation - Questionnaires ... 181

3.4. Data gathering approach		181
3.4.1.	Social network analysis	182
3.4.2.	Ego-centered and dyadic networks	184
3.4.3.	Social network analysis in this research	187
3.4.3.1.	Social network analysis in the first research site	187
3.4.3.2.	Social network analysis in the second research site	187
3.5. Selection of the sample		188
3.6. Summary of research setup		188
4. Empirical study at the first research site: SpecMatCo		191
4.1. Time schedule of research		191
4.2. Sample details		192
4.3. Gathering of ego-centered network data		193
4.3.1.	Frequency of cooperation	194
4.3.2.	Importance of cooperation	194
4.3.3.	Strength of cooperation	194
4.3.4.	Quality of cooperation	194
4.4. "Who cooperates?" Operationalization of hypotheses 1 to 11		194
4.4.1.	Dependent construct: Cooperative behavior of employee	195
4.4.1.1.	Existence of ties	195
4.4.1.2.	Characteristics of ties: Frequency, importance, strength, and quality	195
4.4.2.	Independent constructs	197
4.4.2.1.	Demographic characteristics	198
4.4.2.2.	Firm dependent characteristics of employees	199
4.4.2.3.	Psychological factors affecting cooperation	201
4.4.2.4.	Integration measures	203
4.4.3.	Controls	206
4.5. Results for the research question "Who cooperates?"		207
4.5.1.	Demographic characteristics	212
4.5.1.1.	Dependent variables: Commitment and uncertainty	212
4.5.1.2.	Dependent variables: Cooperation	214
4.5.2.	Firm related characteristics	216
4.5.2.1.	Dependent variables: Commitment and uncertainty	217
4.5.2.2.	Dependent variables: Cooperation	217
4.5.3.	Psychological factors	219
4.5.3.1.	Dependent variables: Commitment and uncertainty	220
4.5.3.2.	Dependent variables: Cooperation	220

4.5.4.	Integration measures	223
4.5.4.1.	Dependent variables: Commitment and uncertainty	224
4.5.4.2.	Dependent variables: Cooperation	224
4.5.5.	Structural cooperation requirements	226
4.5.6.	Summary of results	227
4.6. Methodological limitations		231
4.7. Who cooperates with whom? Operationalization of hypotheses 12 to 22		233
4.7.1.	Dependent construct: Characteristics of cooperation relationships	233
4.7.2.	Independent constructs	233
4.7.2.1.	Demographic similarity	234
4.7.2.2.	Attitude similarity	234
4.7.2.3.	Participation in integration measures	235
4.7.3.	Controls	235
4.8. Results for the research question "Who cooperates with whom?"		236
4.8.1.	Demographic similarity	238
4.8.2.	Attitude similarity	239
4.8.3.	Participation in integration measures	240
4.8.4.	Structural cooperation requirements	242
4.8.5.	Summary of results	242
4.9. Methodological limitation of results		244
5. Empirical study at the second research site: SoftCo		247
5.1. Time schedule of research		247
5.2. Sample details		249
5.3. Gathering of relational data in the present research		250
5.3.1.	Existence of cooperation relationships between employees	257
5.3.2.	Frequency of cooperation of individuals	257
5.3.3.	Importance of cooperation	257
5.3.4.	Strength of cooperation	258
5.3.5.	Relationship with same firm or other firm	258
5.4. Structure of the results section		259
5.4.1.	Detailed presentation of results	259
5.4.2.	Summary of results	265
5.4.3.	Methodological limitations of the research	266
5.4.4.	Discussion of results	266
5.5. "Who cooperates?" Operationalization of hypotheses 1 to 11		267
5.5.1.	Dependent construct: Cooperative behaviors of an employee	267
5.5.1.1.	Existence of ties	270
5.5.1.2.	Characteristics of ties: Frequency, importance and strength	271

5.5.2.	Independent constructs	273
5.5.2.1.	Demographic characteristics	274
5.5.2.2.	Firm dependent characteristics of employees	275
5.5.2.3.	Psychological factors affecting cooperation	277
5.5.2.4.	Integration measures	281
5.5.3.	Controls	284
5.6. Results for the research question "Who cooperates?"		291
5.6.1.	Demographic characteristics	298
5.6.1.1.	Dependent variables: Commitment and uncertainty	299
5.6.1.2.	Dependent variables: Cooperation	300
5.6.1.2.1.	Age	302
5.6.1.2.2.	Gender	302
5.6.1.2.3.	Education level	303
5.6.2.	Firm related characteristics	304
5.6.2.1.	Dependent variables: Commitment and uncertainty	304
5.6.2.2.	Dependent variables: Cooperation	305
5.6.2.2.1.	Rank	305
5.6.2.2.2.	Seniority	306
5.6.3.	Psychological factors	308
5.6.3.1.	Dependent variables: Commitment and uncertainty	308
5.6.3.2.	Dependent variables: Cooperation	309
5.6.3.2.1.	Task orientation	309
5.6.3.2.2.	Responsiveness	311
5.6.3.2.3.	Commitment	312
5.6.3.2.4.	Uncertainty	312
5.6.4.	Integration measures	313
5.6.4.1.	Dependent variables: Commitment and uncertainty	313
5.6.4.2.	Dependent variables: Cooperation	314
5.6.4.2.1.	Degree of feeling informed	316
5.6.4.2.2.	Participation in integration measures	316
5.6.5.	Structural cooperation requirements	317
5.6.6.	Summary of results	317
5.7. Methodological limitations		321
5.8. "Who cooperates with whom?" Operationalization of hypotheses 12 to 22		325
5.8.1.	Sample of relevant relationships	325

5.8.2.	Dependent construct	326
5.8.2.1.	Existence of ties	327
5.8.2.2.	Frequency of existing ties	327
5.8.2.3.	Importance of existing ties	327
5.8.2.4.	Strength of existing ties	327
5.8.3.	Independent constructs: Similarity	328
5.8.3.1.	Demographic similarities	328
5.8.3.2.	Firm related similarities	329
5.8.3.3.	Similarity of psychological reactions of employees	329
5.8.4.	Additional variables	330
5.8.4.1.	Participation in integration measures	330
5.8.4.2.	Structural cooperation requirements	331
5.9.	Results for the research question "Who cooperates with whom?"	332
5.9.1.	Similarity of demographic characteristics	337
5.9.1.1.	Age similarity	338
5.9.1.2.	Gender similarity	338
5.9.1.3.	Education level similarity	339
5.9.1.4.	Education content similarity	340
5.9.2.	Similarity of firm-related characteristics	340
5.9.2.1.	Rank similarity	341
5.9.2.2.	Seniority similarity	341
5.9.3.	Similarity of attitudes	342
5.9.3.1.	Similarity of task orientation	343
5.9.3.2.	Similarity of responsiveness	343
5.9.4.	Similarity of reactions to mergers	344
5.9.4.1.	Commitment similarity	345
5.9.4.2.	Uncertainty similarity	345
5.9.5.	Participation in integration measures	346
5.9.6.	Controls	348
5.9.7.	Summary of results	348
5.9.8.	Comparison of new ties with old ties	357
5.10.	Methodological limitations of the research at SoftCo	364
6. Discussion of results for research question "Who cooperates?"		369
6.1.	Reactions of employees after mergers and acquisitions	370
6.1.1.	Effects of age on reactions	371
6.1.1.1.	Age and reactions at SoftCo	371
6.1.1.2.	Age and reactions at SpecMatCo	372
6.1.1.3.	Synopsis of effects of age on reactions	372

6.1.2.	Effects of gender on reactions	372
6.1.2.1.	Gender and reactions at SoftCo	372
6.1.2.2.	Gender and reactions at SpecMatCo	373
6.1.2.3.	Synopsis of effects of gender on reactions	373
6.1.3.	Effects of education level on reactions	373
6.1.3.1.	Education level and reactions at SoftCo	373
6.1.3.2.	Education level and reactions at SpecMatCo	374
6.1.3.3.	Synopsis of effects of education level on reactions	374
6.1.4.	Effects of rank on reactions	374
6.1.4.1.	Rank and reactions at SoftCo	374
6.1.4.2.	Rank and reactions at SpecMatCo	375
6.1.4.3.	Synopsis of effects of rank on reactions	375
6.1.5.	Effects of seniority on reactions	376
6.1.5.1.	Seniority and reactions at SoftCo	376
6.1.5.2.	Seniority and reactions at SpecMatCo	380
6.1.5.3.	Synopsis of effects of seniority on reactions	380
6.1.6.	Effects of task orientation on reactions	381
6.1.6.1.	Task orientation and reactions at SoftCo	381
6.1.6.2.	Task orientation and reactions at SpecMatCo	382
6.1.6.3.	Synopsis of effects of task orientation on reactions	382
6.1.7.	Effects of the degree of feeling informed on reactions	382
6.1.7.1.	Degree of feeling informed and reactions at SoftCo	382
6.1.7.2.	Degree of feeling informed and reactions at SpecMatCo	384
6.1.7.3.	Synopsis of effects of the degree of feeling informed on reactions	384
6.1.8.	Effects of participation in integration measures on reactions	385
6.1.8.1.	Participation in integration measures and reactions at SoftCo	385
6.1.8.2.	Participation in integration measures and reactions at SpecMatCo	385
6.1.8.3.	Synopsis of effects of participation in integration measures on reactions	386
6.1.9.	Summary for reactions of employees after mergers and acquisitions	386
6.2. Cooperation of employees after mergers and acquisitions		390
6.2.1.	Effects of age on cooperation	391
6.2.1.1.	Age and cooperation at SoftCo	391
6.2.1.2.	Age and cooperation at SpecMatCo	391
6.2.1.3.	Synopsis of effects of age on cooperation	391
6.2.2.	Effects of gender on cooperation	392
6.2.2.1.	Gender and cooperation at SoftCo	392
6.2.2.2.	Gender and cooperation at SpecMatCo	393
6.2.2.3.	Synopsis of effects of gender on cooperation	393

6.2.3.		Effects of education level on cooperation	393
	6.2.3.1.	Education level and cooperation at SoftCo	393
	6.2.3.2.	Education level and cooperation at SpecMatCo	394
	6.2.3.3.	Synopsis of effects of education level on cooperation	394
6.2.4.		Effects of rank on cooperation	394
	6.2.4.1.	Rank and cooperation at SoftCo	394
	6.2.4.2.	Rank and cooperation at SpecMatCo	395
	6.2.4.3.	Synopsis of effects of rank on cooperation	395
6.2.5.		Effects of seniority on cooperation	395
	6.2.5.1.	Seniority and cooperation at SoftCo	395
	6.2.5.2.	Seniority and cooperation at SpecMatCo	398
	6.2.5.3.	Synopsis of effects of seniority on cooperation	398
6.2.6.		Effects of attitudes on cooperation	399
	6.2.6.1.	Attitudes and cooperation at SoftCo	399
	6.2.6.2.	Attitudes and cooperation at SpecMatCo	399
	6.2.6.3.	Synopsis of effects of attitudes on cooperation	399
6.2.7.		Effects of commitment on cooperation	400
	6.2.7.1.	Commitment and cooperation at SoftCo	400
	6.2.7.2.	Commitment and cooperation at SpecMatCo	401
	6.2.7.3.	Synopsis of effects of commitment on cooperation	401
6.2.8.		Effects of uncertainty on cooperation	401
	6.2.8.1.	Uncertainty and cooperation at SoftCo	401
	6.2.8.2.	Uncertainty and cooperation at SpecMatCo	402
	6.2.8.3.	Synopsis of effects of uncertainty on cooperation	402
6.2.9.		Effects of participation in integration measures on cooperation	403
	6.2.9.1.	Participation in integration measures and cooperation at SoftCo	403
	6.2.9.2.	Participation in integration measures and cooperation at SpecMatCo	405
	6.2.9.3.	Synopsis of effects of participation in integration measures on cooperation	406
6.2.10.		Effects of structural cooperation requirements on cooperation	406
	6.2.10.1.	Structural cooperation requirements and cooperation at SoftCo	406
	6.2.10.2.	Structural cooperation requirements and cooperation at SpecMatCo	407
	6.2.10.3.	Synopsis of effects of structural cooperation requirements on cooperation	408
6.2.11.		Summary for cooperation of employees after mergers and acquisitions	408

7. Discussion of results for research question "Who cooperates with whom?"		413
7.1. Likelihood of existence of cooperation relationships		415
7.2. Intensity of cooperation relationships		418
7.2.1. Explanations for findings on intensity of cooperation relationships		420
7.2.1.1. Explanation 1: "Homophily only applies for existence but not for intensity of relationships"		421
7.2.1.2. Explanation 2: "Homophily increases over time"		422
7.2.1.3. Explanation 3: "There are fundamental differences between relationships within and between firms"		423
7.3. Summary for cooperation relationships after mergers and acquisitions		426
8. Implications for practitioners		429
8.1. Determine potential synergy effects		431
8.2. Identify cooperation requirements		433
8.3. Identify cooperation constraints		434
8.4. Identify and implement management levers to ensure cooperation		435
8.5. Relevance of findings for the evaluation of acquisition targets		436
8.6. Summary of implications for practitioners		438
9. Academic contribution and implications for further research		439
9.1. Contributions to M&A-research and implications for future research		439
9.2. Contributions to Socioemotional Selectivity Theory and implications for future research		442
9.3. Contributions to social network research and implications for future research		443
9.3.1. Methodological contributions		443
9.3.2. Contributions to social network research		444
9.4. Final remarks on the social side of mergers and acquisitions		446
References		447
Appendix I – IV		473

List of illustrations

Illustration 1: Worldwide merger and acquisitions over the last 100 years (BCG, 2004) 15
Illustration 2: Classification of company combinations adapted from Gerpott 1993 24
Illustration 3: Different reasons for the occurrence of mergers and acquisitions 29
Illustration 4: Two types of value generating M&A-transactions... 36
Illustration 5: Synergy mechanisms 37
Illustration 6: Synergy mechanism in different activities of the firm 41
Illustration 7: Ansoff's product-market strategies for business growth alternatives 43
Illustration 8: An integrative Merger and Acquisition Model (in parentheses: empirical evidence of relationships) (Larsson, & Finkelstein 1999: 5)......................... 62
Illustration 9: Success factors for M&A-transactions by Gerds (2000)................................. 63
Illustration 10: Activities and partial processes in the M&A-process (Lucks, & Meckl 2002: 59).. 65
Illustration 11: M&A-process and subsequent steps for the realization of the M&A-success 67
Illustration 12: Framework for a process-based macro-micro-macro model of M&A-success factors 70
Illustration 13: Value creation potential after Negotiation & closing phase........................ 100
Illustration 14: Acculturation model after Cartwright, & Cooper 1993b: 65...................... 115
Illustration 15: Summary of success factors in different stages of the M&A-process on different levels 124
Illustration 16: Summary of success factors that directly or indirectly relate to synergy realization... 126
Illustration 17: Central role of cooperation in the research framework 128
Illustration 18: Summary of constructs for the investigation of individual characteristics on cooperation... 135
Illustration 19: Summary of research model for research question "Who cooperates?" 147
Illustration 20: Summary of effects of homophily on cooperation after M&A-transactions 150
Illustration 21: Summary of Research model for research question "Who cooperates with whom?" 157
Illustration 22: Standard process from idea to distribution with Key Success Factors per business model... 163
Illustration 23: Simple and complex egocentered networks 184
Illustration 24: Dyadic network graph and network data in a matrix.................................. 186
Illustration 25: Main aspects of different research setups at SpecMatCo and at SoftCo 189
Illustration 26: Time schedule of research at SpecMatCo 192
Illustration 27: Time schedule of research at SoftCo 249
Illustration 28: First step: Selection of highest level organizational unit............................ 251

Illustration 29: Second step: Selection of functions and teams 252
Illustration 30: Third step: Selection of cooperation partners 253
Illustration 31: Fourth step: Detailed information on relationships with cooperation partners 254
Illustration 32: Fifth step: Evaluation of quality with cooperation partners. 255
Illustration 33: Example of other information as gathered with the help of the electronic questionnaire 256
Illustration 34: Effects of control variables based on departmental averages 261
Illustration 35: Different cases for the effects of the control variable 262
Illustration 36: Effect of structural cooperation requirements on dependent variable 263
Illustration 37: Different effect of structural cooperation requirements on dependent variable 263
Illustration 38: Three step analysis to determine effects of independent variables 265
Illustration 39: Out-degree, in-degree and bilateral relationships 268
Illustration 40: Formation of the sample of relationships to test homophily 326
Illustration 41: Effects of commitment similarity and sum of commitment on likelihood of existence of relationships 417
Illustration 42: Path to M&A-success 429
Illustration 43: Management measures based on the current study 431
Illustration 44: Use of findings in the iterative evaluation of acquisition targets 437
Illustration 45: Summary of investigated factors within research framework 440

List of graphs

Graph 1: Age distribution of sample 198
Graph 2: Education level of sample 199
Graph 3: Distribution of rank in the sample 200
Graph 4: Distribution of TimeInCompany and TimeInFunction 201
Graph 5: Percentage of employees participating in different integration measures 205
Graph 6: Average values for intensity of old and new relationships 244
Graph 7: Share of reciprocated relationships depending on frequency 268
Graph 8: Effects of response rate on potentially bilateral relationships 269
Graph 9: Age distribution of research sample 274
Graph 10: Highest level of education of respondents 275
Graph 11: Rank distribution of respondents 276
Graph 12: Distribution of time in company and time in function 277
Graph 13: Descriptive statistics of items for operationalization of factor "Feeling informed" 283
Graph 14: Percentage of employees participating in different integration measures 284
Graph 15: Actual cooperation strength as percentage of maximum cooperation strength at SoftCo 285
Graph 16: Age difference of existing and possible relationships 354
Graph 17: Number of new ties of respondents of SoftCo ranked by number of ties 369
Graph 18: Cooperation intensity depending on number of participated integration measures 403
Graph 19: Change of cooperation after participation in integration measures (compared to non-participation) 404
Graph 20: Cooperation intensity depending on number of participated integration measures at SpecMatCo 405
Graph 21: Effects of integration measures on cooperation at SoftCo 436

List of tables

Table 1: Summary of findings at SoftCo and SpecMatCo on commitment 8
Table 2: Summary of findings at SoftCo and SpecMatCo on uncertainty 9
Table 3: Summary of findings at SoftCo and SpecMatCo on cooperation 10
Table 4: Existence of new ties 11
Table 5: Synopsis of results for findings at SpecMatCo and SoftCo 12
Table 6: Results of Bamberger's (1994) review of M&A-studies 17
Table 7: Success rates of mergers and acquisitions 18
Table 8: Reasons for M&A-transactions from different authors 27
Table 9: Different types of synergies (1) 33
Table 10: Different types of synergies (2) 34
Table 11: Different types of synergies (3) 35
Table 12: Studies looking at success factors of mergers and acquisitions (1) 52
Table 13: Studies looking at success factors of mergers and acquisitions (2) 53
Table 14: Studies looking at success factors of mergers and acquisitions (3) 54
Table 15: Studies looking at success factors of mergers and acquisitions (4) 55
Table 16: Studies looking at success factors of mergers and acquisitions (5) 56
Table 17: Studies looking at success factors of mergers and acquisitions (6) 57
Table 18: Studies looking at success factors of mergers and acquisitions (7) 58
Table 19: Studies looking at success factors of mergers and acquisitions (8) 59
Table 20: Hypotheses for research question "Who cooperates?" for dependent variable "cooperation" 147
Table 21: Hypotheses for research question "Who cooperates?" for dependent variable "commitment" 148
Table 22: Hypotheses for research question "Who cooperates?" for dependent variable "uncertainty" 148
Table 23: Hypotheses for research question "Who cooperates with whom?" for dependent variable likelihood of "existence of relationship" 158
Table 24: Hypotheses for research question "Who cooperates with whom?" for dependent variable "intensity of relationship" 158
Table 25: Selected social network studies on different levels 183
Table 26: Sample composition of the first research site 193
Table 27: Measures for dependent variables 197
Table 28: Items to investigate attitudes and reactions to mergers 202
Table 29: Results of factor analysis on attitudes after M&A-transactions 203
Table 30: Items to measure the degree of being informed 204
Table 31: Items of SumInfoAggr and Cronbach's alpha of factor items 205
Table 32: Control variables for dependent variables 206

Table 33: Correlation matrix for variables for research question "Who cooperates" at SpecMatCo 208
Table 34: Full model for dependent variables commitment and uncertainty at SpecMatCo . 210
Table 35: Full model for all independent variables and cooperation as dependent variables at SpecMatCo 211
Table 36: Hypotheses concerning demographic characteristics of employees 212
Table 37: Partial model of effects of demographic characteristics on commitment and uncertainty 213
Table 38: Partial model with effects of demographic characteristics on different aspects of cooperation 215
Table 39: Hypotheses concerning demographic characteristics of employees 216
Table 40: Partial model of effects of firm related characteristics on commitment and uncertainty 217
Table 41: Partial model with effects of firm related characteristics on different aspects of cooperation 218
Table 42: Hypotheses concerning demographic characteristics of employees 219
Table 43: Partial model of effects of attitudes on commitment and uncertainty 220
Table 44: Partial model with effects of attitudes and reactions after mergers and acquisitions on different aspects of cooperation 222
Table 45: Hypotheses concerning integration measures 223
Table 46: Partial model of effects of integration measures on commitment and uncertainty 224
Table 47: Partial model with effects of integration measures on different aspects of cooperation 225
Table 48: Summary of factors influencing commitment at SpecMatCo 228
Table 49: Summary of factors influencing uncertainty at SpecMatCo 228
Table 50: Summary of factors influencing cooperation at SpecMatCo 229
Table 51: Full model for all independent variables and characteristics of cooperation relationships as dependent variables 237
Table 52: Hypotheses concerning demographic similarity of cooperation partners 238
Table 53: Partial model of effects of demographic similarity on cooperation 238
Table 54: Hypotheses concerning attitude similarity of cooperation partners 239
Table 55: Partial model of effects of attitude similarity on cooperation 239
Table 56: Hypotheses concerning the effects of integration measures on cooperation relationships 240
Table 57: Partial model for joint participation in integration measures 240
Table 58: Partial model of effects of types of getting to know each other on cooperation 241

Table 59: Summary of factors influencing intensity of new cooperation relationships at SpecMatCo 243
Table 60: Measures for dependent variables 273
Table 61: Items for operationalization of psychological factors 279
Table 62: Results of the exploratory factor analysis 280
Table 63: Results of the confirmatory factor analysis 281
Table 64: Items to measure the degree of being informed 282
Table 65: Results of the confirmatory factor analysis 283
Table 66: Formulas to calculate the cooperation measures on departmental level 290
Table 67: Correlation matrix for variables for research question "Who cooperates" at SoftCo 292
Table 68: Full model for dependent variables commitment and uncertainty 294
Table 69: Full model for all independent variables and cooperation as dependent variables with controls 296
Table 70: Full model for all independent variables and cooperation as dependent variables w/o controls 297
Table 71: Hypotheses concerning demographic characteristics of employees 298
Table 72: Partial model of effects of demographic characteristics on commitment and uncertainty 299
Table 73: Partial model with effects of demographic characteristics on different aspects of cooperation at SoftCo 301
Table 74: Hypotheses concerning demographic characteristics of employees 304
Table 75: Partial model of effects of firm related characteristics on commitment and uncertainty 304
Table 76: Partial model with effects of firm related characteristics on different aspects of cooperation 307
Table 77: Hypotheses concerning demographic characteristics of employees 308
Table 78: Partial model of effects of attitudes on commitment and uncertainty 308
Table 79: Partial model with effects of psychological factors on cooperation 310
Table 80: Hypotheses concerning integration measures 313
Table 81: Partial model of effects of integration measures on commitment and uncertainty 314
Table 82: Partial model with effects of integration measures on different aspects of cooperation 315
Table 83: Summary of factors influencing commitment at SoftCo 318
Table 84: Summary of factors influencing uncertainty at SoftCo 319
Table 85: Summary of factors influencing cooperation at SoftCo 321
Table 86: Correlation matrix for dependent variables existence of cooperation at SoftCo ... 333

XXIX

Table 87: Correlation matrix for dependent variables frequency, importance and strength of cooperation at SoftCo 334
Table 88: Full models without control variable for existence and characteristics of new cooperation relationships at SoftCo 335
Table 89: Full models with control variable for existence and characteristics of new cooperation relationships at SoftCo 336
Table 90: Hypotheses concerning demographic similarity 337
Table 91: Partial models of effects of similarity of demographic characteristics on cooperation relationships at SoftCo 338
Table 92: Hypotheses about effects of firm-related characteristics on cooperation relationships 340
Table 93: Partial models of effects of similarity of firm-related characteristics on cooperation relationships at SoftCo 341
Table 94: Hypothesis on the effect of work attitudes on cooperation 342
Table 95: Partial model of attitude similarity at SoftCo 343
Table 96: Hypotheses on the effect of reactions to M&A-transactions to cooperation 344
Table 97: Partial model of similarity of reactions to M&A-transactions 345
Table 98: Hypotheses on the effect of participation in integration measures on cooperation 346
Table 99: Partial model of effects of participation in integration measures at SoftCo 347
Table 100: Hypotheses on the effect of structural cooperation requirements on cooperation between employees 348
Table 101: Existence of new ties 349
Table 102: Characteristics of new ties 352
Table 103: Full model for existence and characteristics of new bilateral cooperation relationships at SoftCo 355
Table 104: Full model with control variable for existence and characteristics of old cooperation relationships at SoftCo 358
Table 105: Full model with control variable for existence and characteristics of new cooperation relationships at SoftCo 359
Table 106: Comparison of old and new relationships for the likelihood of existence of relationships 360
Table 107: Comparison of old and new relationships for the intensity of relationships 361
Table 108: Relationships between employees within the previously separated firms younger than 3 years 362
Table 109: Average values of commitment by seniority cohort at SoftCo 377
Table 110: Average values of uncertainty by seniority cohort at SoftCo 379

Table 111: Correlation matrix for items of InformationAgg of employees and their superiors 383
Table 112: Summary of findings at SoftCo and SpecMatCo on commitment 387
Table 113: Summary of findings at SoftCo and SpecMatCo on uncertainty 388
Table 114: Average cooperation strength by seniority cohort at SoftCo 396
Table 115: Average number of old and new cooperation relationships by seniority cohort at SoftCo 397
Table 116: Average cooperation strength of old and new cooperation relationships by seniority cohort at SoftCo 397
Table 117: Summary of findings at SoftCo and SpecMatCo on cooperation 410
Table 118: Intensity of cooperation relationships within and between previously separated firms at SoftCo and SpecMatCo 414
Table 119: Synopsis of results for findings at SpecMatCo and SoftCo 419
Table 120: Comparison of full models with control variable for intensity of new relationships within and between previously separated firms 423
Table 121: Potential synergy effects after mergers and acquisitions 432
Table 122: Synergy effects and resulting cooperation requirements 433
Table 123: Individual disposition for cooperation and integration barriers 434

Executive summary

Mergers and acquisitions are critical phenomena: From an economic perspective, M&A-transactions are increasingly frequent events, which reshape entire industries. From a firm perspective, M&A-transactions often represent the single most important economic decisions in the life of a firm, bearing great opportunities as well as great risks. From an employee perspective, M&A-transactions are a source of uncertainty and change.

Many M&A-transactions fail to create value. Although the main motive for mergers and acquisitions is the generation of synergies, often the synergy targets are missed and the M&A-transactions do not live up to the expectations.
Numerous studies investigate success factors for mergers and acquisitions. Despite a long list of studies, the knowledge on mergers and acquisitions is still limited. Key questions about success factors get contradictory answers. Other questions are yet to be resolved.

Based on an extensive literature review, I identify an important gap in the existing body of research on mergers and acquisitions: Many authors emphasize that cooperation between employees of the merging firms is the key to unlock synergy potentials. Cooperation thus is an important moderating variable for the realization of synergy effects. Despite its importance, previous studies always neglected cooperation. There is no study that explicitly investigates cooperation between employees of merging firms in the aftermath of an M&A-transaction.

This research makes an important contribution to filling this gap. Five research questions guide the research:
- **Who cooperates? What are antecedents and constraints of individual cooperation?**
- **Who cooperates with whom? What are antecedents and constraints of cooperation relationships?**
- **How do structural cooperation requirements influence cooperation after mergers and acquisition?**
- **How does communication affect cooperation?**
- **How do active integration measures affect cooperation?**

The findings clearly indicate that individual characteristics as well as similarity of employees have a strong impact on the formation of cooperation relationships. Some employees are more likely to build cooperation relationships with new colleagues than others. Also, in most cases, similar employees are more likely to cooperate with each other than dissimilar employees.

At the same time, the findings clearly indicate that structural cooperation requirements have a very strong impact on cooperation. Management interventions can further compensate for a lack of individual disposition for cooperation and help to overcome cooperation barriers based on dissimilarities of employees.

These findings bear important implications for practitioners as well as for future research:
Practitioners need to be aware that cooperation between employees of merged firms cannot be taken for granted. Some individuals are less likely to cooperate than others. Some employees of merging firms might not get along with each other as well as others. The present study is the first study to generate knowledge about such potential integration barriers. Knowledge about these integration barriers allows the focus of integration measures and thereby increased chances to succeed.

Researchers need to be aware that cooperation is the key to unlock synergies. Previous studies considered a number of success factors, which most likely do not affect the synergy potential but the cooperation between employees of the merging firms. For example, cultural differences are hardly affecting the synergy potential. Rather, they strongly affect the cooperation of employees of the merging firms.

By considering cooperation in future research on M&A-success factors, previously fuzzy or even contradicting results might be reconciled and sharpened. The consideration of cooperation as key moderating variable for the generation of synergy effects and thus for the M&A-success can reduce noise of previous findings and establish more clearly relationships between success factors and M&A-success.

Future research needs to replicate the present findings in other organizational settings. While the present study identifies a number of individual and dyadic level variables, future research needs to understand the relationship of group and firm level variables and cooperation in order to qualify the present findings. Such research increases the understanding of the social side of mergers and acquisitions.

Summary of content

Ad 1: Introduction and formulation of research questions

In the first part of this work, I introduce the phenomenon mergers and acquisitions by highlighting its frequent occurrence and its importance for economies, firms as well as individuals (see **1.1**).

Still, a review of previous studies shows that mergers and acquisitions are very risky endeavors. Most studies show that the majority of mergers and acquisitions fail (see **1.2**). This, of course, is curious: Why would firms engage in mergers and acquisitions if they most likely loose money with it?

In **1.3**, I first define the phenomenon more rigidly. According to this definition, mergers and acquisitions in this work are conjunctions of firms. Conjunctions of firms are characterized by a high level of bonding, abandonment of economical sovereignty, which implies that at least one of the partnering firms is in a superior position.

Then I review different motives for mergers and acquisitions in **1.4**. Previous studies show that there are different motives for mergers and acquisitions. Some authors point out that contingent factors cause firms to merge (see **1.4.1**). Other authors argue that it is mainly psychological characteristics of the top management of a firm that cause mergers and acquisitions (see **1.4.2**). Again other others put forward value generation objectives as key motivation for mergers and acquisitions (see **1.4.3**). Value generation, however strongly depends on synergy potential and on synergy effects of M&A-transactions. The literature shows different strategic objectives for the generation of synergy effects. Regardless of the strategic objective, synergy effects share the need for cooperation amongst employees of the merging firms.

Previous studies identified a number of success factors, which affect the actual performance of mergers and acquisitions (see **1.5**). By reviewing previous classifications of success factors, I develop an innovative process framework for the classification of success factors (see **1.5.1**). The process considers the process character of M&A-transactions and allocates success factors in the different phases of the process, in which they become contingent. In a second dimension, the framework considers the level of analysis of the success factors: Environmental, firm, group as well as individual level of success factors. For example, the degree of consolidation in an industry at the point in time of the M&A-transaction is an environmental level success factor. An individual level success factor is the motivation of the top management to engage in M&A-transactions.

The process model clearly shows that one of the major reasons for conflicting evidence of previous studies is endogeneity of success factors. Endogeneity means that events or decisions in early phases constrain success factors in later phases of the M&A-process.

Based on a comprehensive review of existing M&A-studies, the process framework shows that M&A-success depends on synergy realization. At the same time, many authors mention that synergy realization requires cooperation between employees of the merging firms.

A short case study supports this view: Cooperation in this case study is the key for the generation of synergies. Despite its importance for synergy realization, there are no empirical studies that explicitly address cooperation after mergers and acquisitions (see **1.6**).

Cooperation of employees needs to be understood on two different levels. First, it is individuals, which cooperate. Hence it is necessary to understand, which individuals are more likely to cooperate than others. Second, cooperation always involves at least two individuals. Hence it is necessary to understand, which characteristics of individuals make it more likely that they get along well with each other and form a cooperation relationship. Of course, cooperation after mergers and acquisitions does not happen in a purely voluntary space. Rather, there are strong structural cooperation requirements, which constrain employees to cooperate. At the same time, there often are management interventions such as active integration measures and communication that facilitate cooperation between employees of merging firms.

As a consequence, I formulate a number of research questions, which explicitly address success factors for cooperation:

- **Who cooperates? What are antecedents and constraints of individual cooperation?**
- **Who cooperates with whom? What are antecedents and constraints of cooperation relationships?**
- **How do structural cooperation requirements influence cooperation after mergers and acquisition?**
- **How does communication affect cooperation?**
- **How do active integration measures affect cooperation?**

Ad 2: Theoretical model

The research interest of this work is strongly phenomenon driven and less driven by theory building objectives. As a consequence, I review different academic fields and consolidate empirical findings as well as conceptional considerations in order formulate a number of hypotheses for answering the research questions.

In a first step, I address the question "Who builds cooperation ties?" (see **2.1**). A number of different groups of variables are considered for this question:

- Demographic characteristics of employees such as age, gender, and education level
- Firm related characteristics such as rank and seniority
- Attitudes of employees
- Reactions to mergers and acquisitions
- Integration measures such as communication as well as active integration measures
- Structural cooperation requirements, which constrain cooperation of employees.

In a second step, I address the question "Who cooperates with whom?" (see **2.2**). I mainly consider work, which has been done in the field of social network research. The main proposition of social network research is that individuals, that are similar to each other, are more likely to form relationships. This effect is called *homophily*. Based on previous studies, I formulate a number of hypotheses based considering:

- Similarity of demographic characteristics, such as age, gender, education content and education level
- Similarity of firm related characteristics, such as rank and seniority
- Similarity of attitudes, such as task orientation
- Similarity of reactions to the mergers and acquisitions, such as commitment and uncertainty

In addition to that, I consider participation in integration measures as well as structural cooperation requirements between departments of employees as variables affecting cooperation.

Ad 3: Empirical investigation

In the third section of this work, I present the research design for investigating the research questions. In a first step, I introduce the two research sites, in which data was gathered to quantitatively test the postulated hypotheses (see **3.1**). Both sites recently were integrated after an M&A-transaction.

In a next step, I elaborate on the choice of the right research design to answer the research question (see **3.2**). Due to the phenomenon under consideration, it is not possible to conduct an experiment. As a consequence, the chosen research design is a pre-experiment based on a correlation analysis in each of the sites.

In order to conduct the correlation analysis, it is necessary to collect data in both research sites. In **3.3**, I review different approaches to collect data and discuss, which of them is best suited to generate data necessary to answer the research questions, while at the same time conform to practical considerations such as access to the research site, time and financial constraints. I conclude that the gathering of primary data with the help of personal and written interrogation is best suited for answering the research questions.

Due to the specific characteristics of the construct under consideration, social network analysis is well suited as an approach to gather the data (see **3.4**). Based on different site specific constraints, I identify different approaches to gather network data in the first and the second research site. For the research at the first research site, I identify ego-centered network analysis as best method to gather data. For the second research site, I find dyadic network analysis as being best suited to gather data.

Last but not least, I lay out the criteria for the sample selection in both research sites (see **3.5**).

Ad 4: Empirical study at the first research site: specmatco

After having laid out the theoretical model and the research design, I present the detailed empirical studies at the two research sites. In chapter **4**, I present the research at the first research site. I present the time schedule of the research (see **4.1**), the details of the sample (see **4.2**) with its 39 participants, and the details of the ego-centered network analysis used for gathering the data (see **4.3**).

In the next step, I elaborate the operationalization of the constructs for the postulated hypotheses for the first research question "Who cooperates?" (see **4.4**). Based on a literature review, I identify items, which have been used in previous studies. Other constructs, which have not been considered in previous research, I operationalize based on explorative interviews.

Then I present the detailed results of the empirical investigation of the first research site (see **4.5**). In a first step, I present the results for the effects of independent variables on reactions of employees after mergers and acquisitions. In a second step, I present the results for the effects of independent variables on cooperation of employees after mergers and acquisitions.

After having presented the results, I briefly outline the limitations of the approach, which will be considered in later discussion of the results (see **4.6**).

In a next step, I operationalize the constructs used for testing the postulated hypotheses for the second research question "Who cooperates with whom?" (see **4.7**). Again, I present the findings, which result from the data gathered at the first research site (see **4.8**).

After having presented the results, I briefly show the limitations of the approach (see **4.9**).

Ad 5: Empirical study at the second research site: softco

Basically the same structure as in 4. is used for the presentation of the empirical study at the second research site in 5.

After having presented the time schedule of the research (see **5.1**), I elaborate on the details of the research sample (see **5.2**). In the second research site, I gathered data from 282 employees. Then I present the detailed approach for gathering relational data with the help of a computer-based questionnaire, which represents a methodological innovation in the field of social network research (see **5.3**).

Before starting to present the results, I briefly discuss the approach taken for the analysis of the data. For each set of independent variables, I consider the partial model, the full model without control variable as well as the full model with control variables. Based on these different analyses, it is possible to discuss the identified effects thoroughly (see **5.4**).

In a next step, I elaborate on the operationalization of the constructs used to test the postulated hypotheses for the first research question (see **5.5**). As in the first research site, I use items from previous studies for the operationalization of the considered constructs. In case some constructs have not been used before, I develop an operationalization based on results of exploratory interviews.

In **5.6**, I present the results from the data gathered at the second research site. Again, I first discuss the effects of the independent variables on reactions of employees after mergers and acquisitions. Then I discuss the effects of the independent variables on cooperation of employees.

After having presented the research design and the results from the empirical study, I briefly elaborate on the limitations of the research, which will be considered in the later discussion of the results (see **5.7**).

In a next step, I detail the research design for the second research question "Who cooperates with whom?" (see **5.8**). I first present the detailed characteristics of the sample of the considered relationships. Then I elaborate on the operationalization of the dependent and independent constructs used in the postulated hypotheses.

Then I present the results for the second research question at the second research site (see **5.9**).

Again I present the methodological limitations of the research based on the research design chosen (see **5.10**). These limitations will be used in the later discussion of the results.

Ad 6: Discussion of the results for research question "who cooperates?"

The discussion of the results is being conducted in two steps. In a first step, the results for the first research question are discussed (see **6**). In a second step, I present the results for the second research question (see **7**). For each group of variables, the results from the research at the first research site are compared to the results of the second research site.

As a starting point for the discussion, the effects of the independent variables on reactions after mergers and acquisitions are considered. Some of the main findings include that older employees are more committed than younger employees. This finding is opposite to the postulated effects. Also, higher ranked employees are more committed than lower ranked employees. However, many of the postulated effects are not confirmed and require further discussion. Table 1 summarizes the findings of effects of the independent variables on commitment after mergers and acquisitions.

Hypo-thesis	Independent variable	Dependent variable	Expected effect	SpecMatCo	SoftCo	Total
1c	Age	Commitment	-	Opposite	Opposite	✓
2	Gender	Commitment	0	Supp.	Supp.	✓
4b	Rank	Commitment	+	Supp.	Partly supp.	✓
5b	Seniority	Commitment	-	Not supp.	Not supp.	✓
6b	Task orientation	Commitment	0	Supp.	Not supp.	(.)
9a	Degree of feeling informed	Commitment	+	Not supp.	Supp.	(.)
10b	Integration measures	Commitment	+	Not supp.	Not supp.	✓

■ Supported	✓	Same effect
■ Not supp.	(.)	Different effect
■ Opposite	?	Contrary effect

Table 1: Summary of findings at SoftCo and SpecMatCo on commitment

A second interesting finding on reactions after mergers and acquisitions is that information clearly reduces uncertainty of employees. While most other independent variables yield insignificant results or results that differ between the first and the second research site, the finding on the effect of information on uncertainty is clear. Table 2 summarizes the findings.

Hypo-thesis	Independent variable	Dependent variable	Expected effect	SpecMatCo	SoftCo	Total
1c.1	Age	Uncertainty	-	Opposite	Not supp.	(.)
1c.2	Age	Uncertainty	+	Partly supp.	Not supp.	(.)
2	Gender	Uncertainty	0	Supp.	Supp.	✓
3b	Education level	Uncertainty	-	Not supp.	Supp.	(.)
4c	Rank	Uncertainty	-	Not supp.	Supp.	(.)
5c	Seniority	Uncertainty	+	Supp.	Not supp.	(.)
6b	Task orientation	Uncertainty	0	Supp.	Not supp.	(.)
9b	Degree of feeling informed	Uncertainty	-	Supp.	Supp.	✓
10c	Integration measures	Uncertainty	-	Opposite	Not supp.	(.)

■	Supported	✓	Same effect
■	Not supp.	(.)	Different effect
■	Opposite	?	Contrary effect

Table 2: Summary of findings at SoftCo and SpecMatCo on uncertainty

In a second step, the results for cooperation are presented. Many of the postulated effects can be found in both research sites. Besides other results, the clear positive effect of integration measures on cooperation is very interesting from a practitioner perspective. Also, it is remarkable that older employees are not less cooperative after M&A-transactions. Rather, it is seniority of employees, which reduces their cooperativeness. Table 3 summarizes the findings on the effects of the independent variables on cooperation intensity.

Hypo-thesis	Independent variable	Dependent variable	Expected effect	SpecMatCo	SoftCo	Total
1a	Age	Cooperation intensity	-	Opposite	Not supp.	(.)
1b	Age	Average intensity of ties	+	Not supp.	Partly supp.	(.)
2	Gender	Cooperation intensity	0	Partly supp.	Not supp.	(.)
3a	Education level	Cooperation intensity	+	Partly supp.	Mixed	(.)
4a	Rank	Cooperation intensity	+	Strongly supp.	Strongly supp.	✓
5a	Seniority	Cooperation intensity	-	Partly supp.	Strongly supp.	✓
6a	Task orientation	Cooperation intensity	+	Strongly supp.	Mixed	?
7	Commitment	Cooperation intensity	+	Partly supp.	Partly supp.	✓
8	Uncertainty	Cooperation intensity	-	Opposite	Partly supp.	?
10a	Integration measures	Cooperation intensity	+	Partly supp.	Strongly supp.	✓
11	Structural requirements	Cooperation intensity	+	Strongly supp.	Strongly supp.	✓

■	Supported	✓	Same effect
■	Not supp.	(.)	Different effect
■	Opposite	?	Contrary effect

Table 3: Summary of findings at SoftCo and SpecMatCo on cooperation

Ad 7: Discussion of results for research question "who cooperates with whom?"

Based on the methodological constraints at the first research site, it was not possible to investigate the likelihood of existence of cooperation relationships between employees. As a consequence, I highlight in **7.1** the findings of the second research site. It shows that similarity of different characteristics of employees increase the likelihood of them having a cooperation relationship. Table 4 summarizes the findings of the second research site.

Hypo-thesis	Independent variable	Dependent variable	Expected effect	Partial model	Full model w/o control	Full model with control	Total
12a	Similar age	Existence of relationship	+	Supp.	Supp.	Supp.	Supp.
13a	Similar gender	Existence of relationship	+	Supp.	Supp.	Not supp.	Partly supp.
14a	Similar education level	Existence of relationship	+	Supp.	Supp.	Not supp.	Partly supp.
15a	Similar education content	Existence of relationship	+	Supp.	Supp.	Supp.	Supp.
16a	Similar rank	Existence of relationship	−	Supp.	Supp.	Supp.	Supp.
17a	Similar seniority	Existence of relationship	+	Supp.	Not supp.	Not supp.	Partly supp.
18a	Similar work attitudes	Existence of relationship	+	Partly supp.	Partly supp.	Supp.	Partly supp.
19a	Similar commitment	Existence of relationship	+	Opposite	Not supp.	Opposite	Opposite
20a	Similar uncertainty	Existence of relationship	+	Supp.	Supp.	Supp.	Supp.
21a	Integration measures	Existence of relationship	+	Supp.	Supp.	Supp.	Supp.
22a	Structural requirements	Existence of relationship	+			Supp.	Supp.

Supported
Not supp.
Opposite

Table 4: Existence of new ties

In **7.2** I then discuss the findings on the effects of similarity of characteristics in intensity of cooperation relationships. One important finding of this research is the fact that while likelihood of relationships follows the homophily principle, intensity of cooperation relationships does not. This challenges the existing concept of homophily because it calls for a more dynamic explanation. A number of additional analyses of relationships within the firms confirm the need for a more dynamic concept of homophily. Table 5 summarizes the findings on the effects of homophily on intensity of cooperation relationships.

Hypo-thesis	Independent variable	Dependent variable	Expected effect	SpecMatCo	SoftCo	Total
12b	Similar age	Intensity of relationship	+	Not supp.	Not supp.	✓
13b	Similar gender	Intensity of relationship	+	Not supp.	Not supp.	✓
14b	Similar education level	Intensity of relationship	+		Partly supp.	
15b	Similar education content	Intensity of relationship	+		Opposite	
16b	Similar rank	Intensity of relationship	-		Opposite	
17b	Similar seniority	Intensity of relationship	+		Opposite	
18b	Similar work attitudes	Intensity of relationship	+	Mixed	Not supp.	(.)
19b	Similar commitment	Intensity of relationship	+		Opposite	
20b	Similar uncertainty	Intensity of relationship	+		Mixed	
21b	Integration measures	Intensity of relationship	0	Strongly supp.	Partly supp.	✓
22b	Structural requirements	Intensity of relationship	+	Partly supp.	Strongly supp.	✓

■ Supported	✓ Same effect
■ Not supp.	(.) Different effect
■ Opposite	? Contrary effect

Table 5: Synopsis of results for findings at SpecMatCo and SoftCo

Ad 8: Implications for practitioners

Based on the empirical findings of this research, it is possible to identify a number of actions for practitioners, which might help them to increase the likelihood of success of mergers and acquisitions. Based on the framework elaborated in 1.5, it is possible to identify cooperation requirements for the generation of anticipated synergy effects (see **8.1**, **8.2**). In a next step, it is possible to determine potential cooperation barriers between functions, which are required to cooperate (see **8.3**).

- Based on the findings, it is possible to determine, whether specific employees are more or less likely to cooperate. For example, more senior employees are less likely to cooperate than more junior employees.
- At the same time, it is possible to determine, whether employees of two departments, which are supposed to cooperate, will get along more or less well with each other. Depending on similarities of the employees, there might be reduced chances for smooth cooperation between departments from the very beginning of the integration.

Based on the findings, it is also possible to determine integration measures, which can help to overcome integration barriers and ensure that the integration is successful.

Hence the research emphasizes the need for focused integration measures. Especially those organizational parts, which are required to cooperate and which are likely to suffer from cooperation barriers should be targeted with integration measures (see **8.4**).

As integration measures are costly, early consideration of potential cooperation barriers as well as an evaluation of necessary integration measures might change the evaluation of acquisition targets (see **8.5**).

Ad 9: Academic contribution and implications for further research

The research yields contributions to different academic fields.

First, it contributes to the field of M&A-research (see **9.1**). By emphasizing the importance of cooperation as key moderating variable for the generation of synergies, and by investigating variables affecting cooperation, it sheds light on a neglected area in M&A-research. Future research is needed to confirm the findings of this research in different organizational settings. Also, it is necessary to establish empirically the link between cooperation and the generation of synergies. Further research also is needed to better understand the effects of firm-level variables on cooperation.

Second, the present research contributes to the development of Socioemotional Selectivity Theory (see **9.2**). Being one of the principal psychological theories to investigate the effects of age on commitment, uncertainty and cooperation of individuals, the findings of the present research challenge the theoretical predictions. Further research is required to understand how older employees behave in organizational settings, and to what extent theoretical predictions of Socioemotional Selectivity Theory can be transferred from general social settings to organizational settings.

Last but not least, the findings of this research provide important contributions to the field of social network analysis (see **9.3**). A first contribution to the field of social network analysis is the innovative electronic questionnaire used in the second research site. Its dynamic structure allows the gathering of dyadic network data in large groups, which previous approaches were not able to.

A second contribution concerns some clarification on the effects of individual characteristics on structural aspects of the social network and vice versa. Due to the cross-sectional setup of most social network analyses, and due to the low dynamics of social networks, which have been investigated longitudinally, it is hardly possible to determine, whether individual characteristics drive structural characteristics or vice versa. As the current research considers newly formed cooperation relationships between employees of merging firms, it is in the unique position to determine effects of individual characteristics on the formation of cooperation relationships. One important finding in this context is the need for a dynamic conceptualization of homophily. Obviously, existence and intensity of new and older cooperation relationships cannot fully be explained with the homophily principle. Further research is needed to clarify to what extent present assumptions of homophily have to be adapted to a more dynamic perspective.

1. Introduction and formulation of research questions

1.1. Mergers and acquisitions – Importance for economies and firms

Mergers and acquisitions matter. For entire economies, countries, industries as well as firms. The number of mergers and acquisitions strongly increased during the 90s and peaked in 1998 Since 1998, the number and the volume of mergers and acquisitions have declined. But still, the number of deals is higher than the peak of the last merger wave in the seventies.

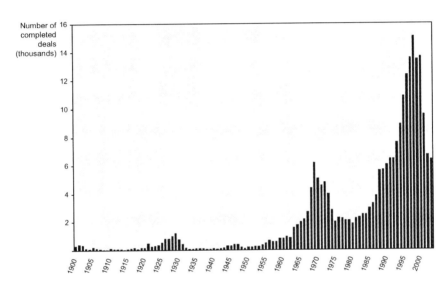

Illustration 1: Worldwide merger and acquisitions over the last 100 years (BCG, 2004)

The development of the numbers of mergers and acquisitions moved in waves. At least five different waves can be distinguished (Stearns, & Kenneth, 1996; Town, 1992):

1. The era of the Rockefellers: In the late 19th century, the first merger wave kicked off. In horizontal acquisitions, large companies such as Standard Oil strived for monopolistic market positions (Bittlingmayer, 1985)
2. The Golden 20s: In the 1920s, the merger wave was triggered by vertical acquisitions, especially in the automotive sector as well as in the steel industry and other industries. Already in its very first issue, the Harvard Business Review (1922) describes a case study on vertical integration in the copper industry.
3. The Age of the Conglomerates: At the end of the 1960s and beginning of the 1970s, huge conglomerates emerged. Strict antitrust laws in most developed countries limited

intra-industry growth options of firms. At the same time, the management paradigm of risk diversification emerged. As a result, firms started to become highly diversified conglomerates through mergers and acquisitions.

4. Consolidation in the 80s: A small M&A-wave rushed through the 1980s, when the Reagan administration relaxed the antitrust laws and the laws for taxation of gains from divesting firms, and Wallstreet discovered that money could be made by buying conglomerates, slicing them and selling them in small portions (Town, 1992).

5. Globalization and consolidation: Globalization and the new management paradigm of focus on core competences triggered strong consolidation tendencies in most industries. Berthold (2004) names a number of reasons for the merger wave in the 90s. He argues that increasing competition in home markets, new regional markets in Eastern Europe and Asia as well as privatization waves in most Western countries, globalization, technological changes and dynamization of the economy through shortened life cycles triggered the merger wave in the 90s.

Reseachers have offered different explanations for the appearance of the different merger waves. Bittlingmayer (1985) argues that changes in antitrust policy initiated by the Sherman Antitrust Law reduced the possibilities for firms to engage in cartels. Hence horizontal mergers were an efficient alternative to reinstall monopolistic market power.

Town (1992) argues that the literature has not found "an event that initiated two of the major movements: 1925:III – 1932:II and 1967:II – 1969:IV"[1] (Town 1992: 98). Rhodes-Kropf, Robinson, & Viswanathan (2005) argue that flawed valuation of stock markets drives M&A-activity. They argue that in times of strong stock markets, firms tend to engage in M&A-activity.

Merger waves are an aggregate economic phenomenon, which affects entire economies, countries and industry structures. M&A-transactions affect a significant percentage of the corporate assets of an economy. Cartwright and Cooper (1996: 2) claim that already in the 1980s, every fourth American employee had been involved in at least one M&A-transaction. At the same time, an isolated M&A-transaction often means a significant event in the life of a company. M&A-transactions often represent the largest single investment or divestment decision of a firm. They bind resources and strongly imprint the strategy of a firm for years. Due to the importance of M&A-transactions, they can determine the rise or fall of firms. Successful transaction can forge global players. Unsuccessful transactions can clear the way for ambitious competitors.

---

[1] Roman numbers indicate quarter of the respective year.

1.2. But still: Most mergers and acquisitions fail

Despite the significance of mergers and acquisitions for economies, countries, industries and acquiring companies, prior studies mostly show high failure rates of mergers and acquisitions. A recent study of The Boston Consulting Group (2003) analyzes 277 U.S.-American mergers and acquisitions between 1985 and 2000. They find that on the average, 64% of all mergers and acquisitions destroyed value at the time they were announced, and still 56% of all M&A-transactions had destroyed value after 2 years.

Most M&A-researchers find similar results. Bühner (1990a) claims that "In the majority of cases, acquisitions turned out to be unsuccessful" (Bühner, 1990a: 3). Sirower (1997) finds a failure rate of 65% of the major strategic acquisitions that he investigated. Agrawal, Jaffe and Mandelker (1992) find that on the average, acquirers suffered negative abnormal returns over a five year period of minus ten percent. Bamberger (1994), however, finds in a study on 397 acquisitions that managers classified only 20% of the M&A-transactions a failure or a complete failure.

In an extensive review, Bamberger (1994) summarizes 49 M&A-studies that use capital market and accounting based success measures. He finds that roughly 43% of the studies indicate that M&A-transactions are on the average successful (i.e. more than 50% of all transactions in the sample are successful), 39% indicate that M&A-transaction are on the average failures and 18% of the studies yield unclear results.

Type of study	Number of studies indicating success	Number of studies with unclear results	Number of studies indicating failure
Capital market studies USA			
• Tender offers	7	4	0
• Mergers	4	4	4
Capital market studies UK			
• Mergers	2	0	3
Capital market studies D	3	0	4
Accounting based studies USA	2	1	4
Accounting based studies UK			3
Accounting based studies D	3		1
Total	21	9	19

Table 6: Results of Bamberger's (1994) review of M&A-studies

In a more recent review of 8 studies, Gerds (2000) finds failure rates between 11 % and 53%, but also success rates between 36% to 68%. Dicken (2000) reviews studies from consulting companies and finds success rates between 44% and 50%. Simon (1999) finds in a study of his consulting company Simon-Kucher that more than 50% of all mergers showed a lower performance of stock market value development than the industry average.

Author	Year	Sample	Time period of sample	Success measure	Success rate
Kitching	1967	69 acquisitions	1960 - 1965	Financial results	72% of acquisitions are successful
Kitching	1974	90 acquisitions of U.S. multi-national companies, 305 acquisitions of European multi-national companies	1965 - 1970	Executive evaluation	U.S. multi-national companies: 50% European multi-national companies: 54%
Kusewitt	1985	128 firms with ~3.500 acquisitions	1967 - 1976	Return on assets (ROA) after 1 year	Average ROA: + 5.33%
Singh, & Montgomery	1987	105 large acquisitions (> 100 million)	1975 - 1980	Cumulative abnormal returns	Acquisition targets (Related: + 6.5%, unrelated: + 1.6%); Acquirer (related: + 1.8%, unrelated + 6.8%)
Lubatkin	1987	439 acquiring firms 340 acquired firms	1948 - 1979	Cumulative abnormal rate of return at 18 to 64 months time after an M&A-transaction	No significant effect
Lubatkin, & O'Neill	1987	297 large mergers	1954 - 1973	Systematic and unsystematic risk	Strong increase in unsystematic risk for all merger types
Porter	1987	3,788 acquisitions by 33 large U.S. companies	1950 - 1986	Divesture of acquisitions	74% of all acquisitions have been divested
Bühner	1990	90 German mergers and acquisitions	1973 - 1985	Abnormal returns 12 months after closing	Average abnormal returns: - 10%
Bühner	1990	110 German mergers and acquisitions	1973 - 1985	Return on capital employed, return on equity after 3 years	Average negative
Datta	1992	75 bidders and 79 targets	reports of the last 15 years	Prediction error	Bidder no effect Targets very positive
Agrawal, Jaffe, & Mandelker	1993	765 acquisitions	1955 - 1987	Cumulative abnormal returns up to 5 years after M&A-transaction	- 10% over a 5 year period
Bamberger	1994	397 acquisitions		Management classification on 5-point scale	20% failure or complete failure
Srinivasan, & Merchant	1997	120 acquisitions	1980 - 1987	Cumulative abnormal returns between 2 and 56 days after closing	Average abnormal returns: 0,0%
Sirower	1997	168 acquisitions	1979 - 1990	Different time periods	Failure rate: 65%
Haleblian, & Finkelstein	1999	449 acquisitions (> $ 10 million) by manufacturing firms	1980 - 1992	Abnormal returns (- 5 days to + 5 days of announcement	Average abnormal returns: 0,0%
Finkelstein, & Haleblian	2002	192 large acquisitions (> $ 10 million) by manufacturing firms	1970 - 1990	Abnormal returns (- 3 days to + 3 days of announcement	No significant effect

Table 7: Success rates of mergers and acquisitions

In Table 7, a selection of academic studies conducted in the last 40 years and their findings is presented. As can be seen, it is difficult to compare the findings, because sample size, industry as well as sample period differ widely. Also, researchers use different success measures, making it difficult to compare results.

Hogan, & Overmyer-Day (1994) differ between objective and subjective measures of M&A-success. Objective measures are measures of financial and market performance. Subjective measures are measures based on self-reported survey instruments that capture subjective information such as satisfaction, stress, or anxiety and job uncertainty.

1.2.1. Objective success measures

Objective measures are based on publicly available information. The advantage of using external information is that the information is readily available. As external information does not suffer from respondent's biases, it is possible to compare results from different studies based on external data. At the same, external information suffers from a lack of differentiation. External effects such as economic fluctuations, industry specific factors as well as firm specific factors such as other acquisitions, or divestures strongly affect the result and thus limit the explanatory power of external information.

Using objective success measures, researchers have studied the success of mergers and acquisitions in two different dimensions: strategic success and financial success.

Strategic success has been investigated by Porter (1987). He argues that success of an M&A-transaction needs to be considered based on its strategic effects. If an acquisition meets the requirements of a strategy, it becomes sustainably integrated in the acquiring firm. However, if an acquisition does not meet the strategic objectives of a firm, it will be resold. Porter (1987) finds in a study of 3,788 acquisitions by 33 large U.S. companies that 74% of all these acquisitions between 1950 and 1986 have been sold again within the time period considered. Hence, he argues, that the overwhelming majority of acquisitions are not strategically successful. This argumentation requires further discussion. First, acquisitions might be guided by short term interests. For example, it is possible to make acquisitions to get access to a specific technology. After having internalized the technology, it might be advisable to sell the firm again in order to save the integration effort. Second, the considered time period is very long. Firms might change their strategic objectives significantly over 30 years. Hence the effect of acquiring and selling firms might not only reflect strategic success but also changes in strategy. Therefore, Porter's (1987) findings are not conclusive to determine strategic success of mergers and acquisitions.

Financial success of mergers and acquisitions has been measured in many different studies. Ultimately, value creation is the core objective of firms. Hence value creation respectively financial success is a useful success measure for mergers and acquisitions. There are two different sources of data for financial success that have been used to identify success of mergers and acquisitions: Stock market data and accounting data of firms.

Stock markets react to the announcement of mergers and acquisitions. That means that stockholders evaluate the expected value creation or value destruction of acquisitions for acquiring firms and acquired firms. If they expect that an acquisition creates value for the acquiring firm, stock prices go up. If they expect that an acquisition destroys value for the acquiring firm, stock prices go down. Of course, only stock price developments that are unrelated to industry specific developments or stock market developments can be considered. These unrelated effects are called abnormal stock market reactions. Different time periods have been used before and after the announcement. For example, Agrawal et al. (1992) investigate the stock market effect before the announcement until five years after the announcement. Others such as Haleblian, & Finkelstein (1999) measure abnormal returns from 5 days prior to the merger until 5 days after the merger. This, however, assumes that stock markets react correctly to an announcement and anticipate all possible effects of an M&A. While long periods have the advantage of capturing long-term developments of an acquisition, they suffer from events happening after the merger.

While Agrawal et al. (1992) find in a study on 765 acquisitions that cumulative abnormal returns of acquisitions are -10% over a 5-year period, Haleblian, & Finkelstein (1999) find no effect. Similarly, Lubatkin (1987) finds in a study on 439 acquiring firms that there is no significant stock market effect at different points in time (18 – 64 months) after the M&A-transaction. Lubatkin, Srinivasan, & Merchant (1997) also find over periods of 2, 16, 56 days after an M&A-announcement no abnormal returns.

Bühner (1990a) investigates the stock market performance of 90 firms and finds that „Summarized, the results indicate that acquisitions do not yield increase of market value of the firms in the sample" (1990a: 45, own translation). In another study, Bühner (1990c) finds an average abnormal rate of return of -10% twelve months after the closing (Bühner 1990c: 300).

In a study of The Boston Consulting Group (2004), the authors find that while the majority of mergers fail, acquirers on the average create value. This is curious insofar, as the risk is seemingly high. But if a firm engages in many mergers and acquisitions, on the average, it might actually create money.

Consistent with the findings about financial performance, Lubatkin, & O'Neill (1987) find that M&A-transactions significantly increase the unsystematic risk of firms, while the systematic risks decrease. The systematic risk decreases, because mergers and acquisitions that follow a product or market extension objective reduce the systematic industry, respectively market risk in most cases. However, the unsystematic risk, which depends on firm characteristics, strongly increases, because some firms perform very well after mergers and acquisitions and some significantly loose after mergers and acquisitions. This, however, increases the unsystematic risk strongly.

The use of stock market information corresponds to financial theories that assume that markets correctly price the value of a firm and its strategy. According to this assumption, acquisitions will be evaluated correctly by stock markets, thereby representing the value potential.

Success measures based on accounting data use premerger and post merger accounting data. Common measures are return on assets, return on equity, EBIT, sales or profit of an acquiring firm. Kusewitt (1985) finds in a large scale study on 3,500 acquisitions that one year after an acquisition, the average ROA of acquiring firms increased by 5.33%. Kusewitt (1985) also finds that the market return of acquiring firm increases by 3.40% one year after the acquisition. Similarly, Bühner (1990a) investigates in a study on 110 German mergers and acquisitions the return on capital as well as the return on equity 3 years after an M&A-transaction. He finds that on the average, acquiring companies have deteriorating financial performance.

1.2.2. Subjective success measures

Subjective measures rely on information on a specific acquisition, provided by the acquiring firms. Subjective measures thus can capture acquisition specific results independently of other effects. Internal information of the firm about a specific M&A-transaction does not suffer from distorting effects, such as other events, industry or economic factors as do external measures. However, subjective measures suffer strongly from biases of the respondents. There are two main biases: Social desirability and attribution errors. It has been found that respondents often respond to questions according to what they perceive as socially desirable (e.g. Milholland 1964). Success is socially accepted. Failure is not. Insofar, it is likely that respondents have a tendency to evaluate a specific M&A-transaction more positively than the actual financial success would imply. Thus, social desirability might lead to systematic errors. Attribution errors are based on misattributions of respondents, i.e. the fallacious attribution of characteristics to an event or an individual (Kroeber-Riel, & Weinberg, 1996). Sources of attribution errors might be the halo-effect, primacy or recency effects. The halo-effect describes the effect that a dominant characteristic of an event, or an individual might affect the evaluation of other aspects of this event or this individual (Asch 1946). For example, if individuals perceive an M&A-transaction as successful in financial terms, it is likely that they will rate other success measures, such as effectiveness of team work, etc. as especially successful. The primacy effect describes the tendency of individuals to let first impressions guide all subsequent evaluations of an event or an individual. This effect is based on anchoring (Mussweiler, & Strack 1997). Anchoring means that individuals use a first data point as reference point for future evaluations. For example, if an M&A-transaction is assumed from the very beginning as a failure and it turns out less unsuccessful than assumed, individuals might evaluate it a success, because it exceeds their initial expectation. Recency effects, however, are based on cognitive effects, according to which more recent memories are more readily available for retrieval than older memories. This might lead to a stronger consideration of the recent history of a merger, for example, recent success stories or recent troubles, when evaluating the overall M&A-success.

Based on subjective measures, researchers have assessed different success measures of M&A-transactions. While some focused on the overall success, others more specifically assessed synergy realization or even partial objectives of mergers and acquisitions such as absenteeism.

Overall success has been assessed by Kitching (1974) in a study on 90 acquisitions by U.S. multi-national companies (MNC) and 305 acquisitions by European MNCs. Based on executive rating, Kitching (1974) finds that 50% of the U.S. MNCs and 54% of the European MNCs indicate that their acquisitions have been successful.

Datta (1991) investigates the performance of 173 acquisitions by asking key informants to rate performance along five performance criteria such as ROI, EPS, stock price, cash flow as well as sales growth using a 5-point Likert scale. Datta (1991) finds no significant effect for the bidders, however, the acquisitions targets are significantly positive.

Synergy realization has been investigated by Larsson, & Finkelstein (1999) They argue that "We reasoned that synergy realization is a conceptually advantageous measure of M&A performance and that synergy realization depends on the combination's potential, the degree of integration achieved, and the lack of employee resistance" (Larsson, & Finkelstein 1999: 2). They find that in a research on 61 case studies, that based on 11 items rated with a 3-point scale (synergy realization low = 0, moderate = 1, high = 2), firms scored with an average if 4.25, indicating relatively low synergies.

Synergy realization has also been assessed by Gerds (2000). He asked 59 external senior consultants to rate the degree of satisfaction of management with synergy realization for M&A-transactions. Gerds (2000) finds that 72% of the managers of a sample of 63 acquiring companies were very satisfied or satisfied.

1.2.3. Summary of success rates of mergers and acquisitions

While the overwhelming majority of studies show slightly higher failure rates than success rates, Lubatkin (1983) offers possible explanations, why mergers actually could create value despite poor empirical findings. Lubatkin (1983) argues that

"(1) Administrative problem may accompany merger and cancel out the benefits of merger.
...
(2) Methodological problems have prevented the empirically based studies from detecting the benefits. ...
(3) Only certain types of merger strategies benefit the stockholders of the acquiring firm" (Lubatkin 1983: 221ff).

These claims have been refuted by numerous studies on M&A-performance since 1986. Administrative problems nowadays are summarized in the research in integration problems. The possibility of methodological problems has been eliminated thanks to numerous studies based on different measures that all show similar results. The question whether some types of mergers and acquisitions might be more beneficial than others, and which acquisitions that might be has kept researchers ever since busy.

In a nutshell, it is possible to state that mergers and acquisitions are approximately equally likely to succeed and to fail. The variance of M&A-success is extremely high, which is reflected in the increase of unsystematic risk of acquiring firms after M&A-transactions. The variance also indicates that there are numerous different success factors strongly influencing the success of mergers and acquisitions.

In the following sections of this study, I will first narrow down the term mergers and acquisitions. Then I will discuss in detail different motivations for M&A-transactions. If M&A-transactions are such risky business, why would managers engage in mergers and acquisitions? Then I will discuss potential success factors that help explaining the success or failure of mergers and acquisitions.

Based on the analysis of the success factors, I will determine gaps in existing research on success factors on M&A-transaction. Based on these gaps, I will determine the research questions of this study.

1.3. What are they? - Definitions of mergers and acquisitions

There are numerous definitions for types of combinations of firms. Basically, "... combinations of firms are voluntary combinations of firms to form larger economic entities to do in parts or in total business together" (Möller 1983: 13). Similarly, Scheiter (1989: 6) points out that combinations of firms result from a union of economically and legally independent firms with the objective to follow a common economic objective. This implies at least some limitations to economic freedom to allocate the firm's resources. Others define combinations of firms as an acquisition of ownership rights of parts or the totality of an acquisition target through an acquiring company, with the help of an asset deal (transfer of assets to the acquiring company) or a share deal (transfer of equity to the acquiring company) with the result of a dominant influence of the acquirer over the acquisition target (compare Berthold 2004: 66ff).

A more comprehensive definition of combinations of firms is provided by a two-step classification framework (compare Pausenberger 1989, Gerpott 1993, Gerds 2000, Berthold 2004). In a first step, the classification differs between the levels of dependency of the partnering firms. Based on this step, cooperations and conjunctions of firms can be differentiated. In a second step, highly dependent firms are further classified according to the way accordance between the management teams of the partnering firms has been reached to comply with the agreement.

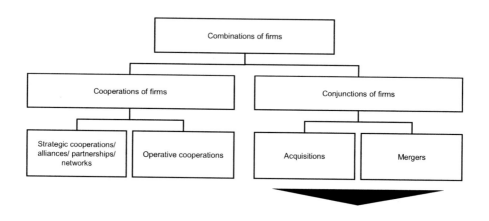

Illustration 2: Classification of company combinations adapted from Gerpott 1993

1.3.1. Degree of dependency of combinations of firms

The level of dependency between two firms describes the intensity of bonding, the degree, to which the entities are economically sovereign, whether there is a hierarchical order amongst the partnering firms and whether the partnering firms are free to end the relationship (compare Gerpott 1993). Based on this differentiation, it is possible to differ between cooperations of firms and conjunctions of firms[2].

According to Gerpott (1993) cooperations between firms are characterized by a low level of bonding, economic souvereignty of the partnering firms, equality of the partnering firms in

---
[2] The German language offers more a more detailed differentiation at this point. Gerpott (1993) speaks of "Unternehmenskooperationen", corresponding to cooperations and "Unternehmensverknüpfungen" corresponding to conjunctions. Similarly, Gerds (2000) differs between "Unternehmenskooperationen" and "Unternehmensvereinigungen".

taking decisions and the uni-lateral right to end the cooperation. Examples for cooperations between firms are alliances in research or sales, joint ventures, licensing agreements, as well as joint lobbies or cartels (compare Gerpott 1993: 39, Schubbe 1999: 39).

Conjunctions of firms are characterized by a high level of bonding, abandonment of economical souvereignity, which implies that at least one of the partnering firms is in a superior position. Conjunctions of firms can be further separated according to the way, accordance of the management teams between the partnering firms was reached.

1.3.2. Mergers of equals vs. takeovers

There are two possibilities for firms to form a conjunction. The first possibility is the rare case in which both firms enter as equally strong partners in the conjunctions. This case is referred to in literature as "merger of equals" (Gerds 2000: 10; Gerpott 1993: 30 ff). The second possibility is the case of one firm taking over another firm. The overwhelming majority of conjunctions of firms are initiated by the takeover of one firm by another[3].

Takeovers of one firm by another can be reached in two ways: Either the management team, respectively the owner(s) of one of the partnering firms convinces the owners of the other firm to form a conjunction, or they convince the management team of the partnering firms to agree to the conjunction. According to this logic, Sirower (1997) defines tender offer as offer of the acquirer to stockholders of the acquisition targets, whereas a merger results from an offer of the acquiring firm to the management of the acquisition target. Bühner (1990b: 6) points out that "Tender offers address directly the stockholders of the target company, with the offer, to acquire their shares for a price, which mostly exceeds the market value, within a certain period of time with the objective to control the firm." Mergers, however are negotiated directly with the management of the target company and their board of directors. The acquisition of stocks occurs only after the management teams reach agreement (Compare Bühner 1990b: 6). Hence Sirower (1997) and Bühner (1990b) suggest a differentiation of mergers and tender offers based on the addressee of the merger.

Other researchers argue that takeovers can be characterized by the degree of friendliness of the takeover. Buono, & Bowditch (1989) differ between friendly collaborative, laissez-faire and hostile contested situations. Hostile takeovers are takeovers, which are based on a tender offer of an acquiring firm. However, the management of the acquisition target strongly and actively opposes the takeover. Laissez-faire takeovers are takeovers, during which the management team of the acquisition target does neither engage in evaluations of the offer nor in activities to facilitate or hinder the acquisition. A friendly takeover is a takeover, in which

---

[3] The case of multiple buyers shall not be considered here. Also, the case of multiple acquisition targets shall not be considered, because each acquisition represents a single transaction, which can be separated from other acquisitions.

the management team of the acquisition target complies with the offer of the acquiring firm and recommends to the owners of the acquisition target to accept the offer of the acquiring firm. In this logic, a friendly takeover strongly corresponds to Sirower's (1997) definition of mergers.

Some authors criticize that the notion of "mergers" is frequently used for acquisitions although it should be reserved for mergers of equals. Others argue that the notion merger is reserved for the "… blending or fusing of two firms, rather than mere legal enjoinment or absorption of one firm into another" (Greenwood, Hinings, & Brown 1994: 240). Similarly, Koch (2000) distinguishes affiliation ("Angliederung") and fusion ("Verschmelzung/Fusion") as two different types of conjunctions. Differences in integration degrees, especially in terms of legal integration seem somewhat artificial as a classificatory dimension for conjunctions. Large companies often consist of hundreds or even thousands of different legal entities that are linked by different ownership structures. This indicates that the degree of integration is not bound to the legal structure but to the management structure[4]. Therefore, the degree of integration does not represent a suitable one-to-one definition of conjunctions.

As can be seen, the existing definitions of mergers and acquisitions are somewhat fuzzy. Therefore, I use the following definitions for the work in this paper:
The term *merger* is only used as mergers of equals, indicating the relative strength of the partnering firms. The term *acquisition* is reserved for takeovers.

In this paper, cooperation between employees of integrated companies will be central. In both forms of conjunctions of firms, mergers and acquisitions, cooperation is equally relevant. Thus the differentiation between mergers and acquisitions is mostly irrelevant. Therefore, I will mostly use the term *mergers and acquisitions* or *M&As*, or *M&A-transactions* in this work. If an argument is only valid for mergers of equals or for acquisitions, I will specifically mention it. In line with Sommer (1996), I argue that the differentiation between different types of conjunctions of firms can be better described with the help of attributes than with different terms. Hence a merger between equally strong partners is will be called merger of equals, and a takeover, which was agreed upon by the management team of the acquired company will be called a friendly acquisition or a friendly takeover.

---

[4] Management structure thereby describes the hierarchical structure of an organization, which contains organizational units as well as reporting lines.

1.4. Why do they happen? Reasons for the occurrence of mergers and acquisitions

There are different explanations, why mergers happen, and what potential reasons for M&A-transactions might be. In the following table, a selection of explanations from different authors is offered:

Author	Reasons for M&A-transactions
Bühner (1990c): 295, own translation	"The most important motives for conducting mergers and acquisitions are: …" • Market power, especially for horizontal mergers • Information advantage, which allows recognition of undervalued companies • Synergies, which allow an increase of performance • Inefficient management of the acquisition target • Financial advantages through tax advantages or lower cost of capital through risk diversification • Management interests such as prestige, power and recognition • Hubris of the top management • Free cash flows

Bamberger (1994)	• General acquisition motives
	  o Growth
	  o Capacity increase
	  o Risk diversification
	• Specific acquisition motives
	  o Time advantage compared to internal investment projects
	  o Acquisition of specific, non-tradeable resources
	  o The acquisition target is undervalued and an opportunity
	• Miscellaneous acquisition motives
	  o Motives of individuals, such as top manager hubris

Hayward, & Hambrick (1997)	• Synergies, • Poor performance of the management team of the acquisition target and • Hubris of the CEO of the acquiring firm.
Koegeler (1991)	• Risk diversification • Stagnation of markets • Usage of cash resources to diversify instead of further consolidation • Top-management desire for further growth • Realization of synergies.

Table 8: Reasons for M&A-transactions from different authors[5]

---

[5] For a more detailed review of merger and acquisition motives, see Bamberger (1994: 71). He offers a detailed list of different definitions of acquisition motives from twelve different authors.

Other authors point out that there are industry specific requirements leading to mergers and acquisitions (Haspeslagh, & Jemison 1991), that globalization leads to scale requirements (Galpin, & Herndon 1999), that acquisitions address best speed and cost considerations of growth (Marks, & Mirvis 1997c), that acquisitions allow an expansion of product and service range (Galpin, & Herndon 1999), and that acquisitions allow to leverage core competencies or technology changes (Slusky, & Caves 1991).

There are different approaches to classify reasons for mergers and acquisitions:

- Gutknecht, & Keys (1993) argue that "Not all mergers and acquisitions originate for the same reasons. A convenient classification is that of rescue, collaboration, contested situation, and raid" (Gutknecht, & Keys 1993: 26).
- Bamberger (1994) classifies motives into general, specific as well as miscellaneous motives.
- Bühner (1990a: 6ff) distinguishes between real and speculative motives.

    Real motives are based on the basic assumption that the firms are together more successful than separately. These motives can also be classified under synergies that primarily aim for market power increases and cost advantages. According to Bühner (1990a: 7), tax advantages also represent a real motive for a takeover. Another real advantage is the assumption that the acquiring management can manage the acquisition target better than its current management team.

    Speculative motives are based on the assumption that the real value of the target is not expressed in the market price.

In this paper, I choose a somewhat different classification for reasons why M&A-transactions happen. Depending on the epistemological level of the explanations, I differ between contingency theoretical models, psychological models and value creation models. Contingency theoretical models explain merger activity of a company or merger activity within an industry based on contextual variables that lead to M&A-activity. Psychological explanations, however, identify individual decision makers and their motives as primary drivers of mergers and acquisitions. Strategic explanations assume that the primary reason for the existence of firms is their ability to generate more value than markets, and which assume that activities of firms, respectively its (boundedly) rational decision makers always aim to increase its value (Coase, 1937; Bain, 1958; Simon 1957). According to strategic explanations, the primary reason for M&A-transactions is the aim to generate value.

The illustration below shows a summary of the different explanations why mergers and acquisitions happen. In parentheses, I indicate the chapter, in which I will elaborate on the different types of explanations:

Illustration 3: Different reasons for the occurrence of mergers and acquisitions

1.4.1. Contingency explanations

"The essence of the contingency theory paradigm is that organizational effectiveness results from fitting characteristics of the organization, such as its structure, to contingencies that reflect the situation of the organization" (Donaldson, 2001: 1). The paradigm is build on three types of contingency: (1) environmental contingency, (2) organizational size contingency and (3) strategic contingency. According to contingency theory, the structure of a firm depends on these factors: Environmental contingencies such as industry, industry structure, institutional environment build the context, to which the organization has to fit as well as possible to be effective (Lawrence, & Lorsch, 1967; Burns, & Stalker, 1961). Similarly, organizational structure depends on the size of a firm (Child, 1975). Strategic contingency implies that different strategic choices provide the context for internal organizational structure. For example, a diversification strategy works better in a divisional structure. A focused strategy requires a functional structure. "Because the fit of organizational characteristics to contingencies leads to high performance, organizations seek to attain fit" (Donaldson 2001: 2).

According to a contingency theoretical framework, M&A-transactions represent a vehicle to reach fit to contingencies. "Consistent with the framework for diversification, a merger contingency framework suggests that whether a firm gains or loses from merger is contingent on a number of conditions. These are its competitive strengths, the growth rate of its markets, and the degree to which these two achieve a logical or strategic fit with the competitive strengths and market growth rates of its acquired firm." (Lubatkin 1983: 218)

Similarly, Berthold (2004) names six different contingent factors that drive the current merger wave:

- Increased competition in domestic markets
- New regional markets respectively political changes
- Globalization
- Technological changes
- Increased dynamic of the economy
- Changes in ownership structures.

Bower (2001) differs between five different types of M&A strategies: (1) The overcapacity M&A, which aims to consolidate capacities in mature industries, (2) The geographic roll-out M&A, (3) the product or market extension M&A, (4) the M&A as R&D, and (5) the industry convergence M&A. Each of these M&As follows a specific logic and serves specific strategic objectives. Clearly, the overcapacity M&A as well as the industry convergence M&A follow a contingency logic.

A problem of contingency theory has always been the question how choice comes in. Contingency theory suffers from the "one best way" idea and does not consider motives, because actors only act according to external contingencies. According to a contingency theoretical framework, mergers and acquisitions simply happen, because a firm wants to fit to the firm's contingencies. This reduces the role of the decision makers within an organization to mere automats, which fulfill a fitting program. It is not even correct to speak of motives for mergers and acquisitions, because they are the result of a fitting automatism, which does not require motives.

1.4.2. Psychological explanations

While contingency theory excludes free will and decision makers from its consideration, psychological explanations for the occurrence of mergers and acquisitions focus on the role of the central decision makers: the managers.

Agency theory assumes that alignment of interests of principals (owners) and agents (managers) cannot be taken for granted (for a review on agency theory see Eisenhardt 1989a). "Management motives for the conduct of mergers are based on an agency conflict, which emerges from the separation of management and ownership of the firm. It is assumed that the management of the firm pursues own objectives and thereby not always act in the best interest of the owners" (Bühner 1990a: 19, own translation).

A starting point for explaining M&A-activity with the help of agency theory is provided by the free cash flow theory of Jensen (1986). He assumes that "Managers have incentives to cause their firms to grow beyond the optimal size. Growth increases managers' power by increasing the resources under their control" (Jensen 1986: 323). Managers therefore prefer to leave free cash flows in the company under their control instead of distributing it to shareholders. Acquisitions represent great opportunities to spend large amounts of free cash flow while at the same time increasing the sphere of influence of top managers of a firm (Bühner 1990a: 20; Jensen 1986).

There are two basic variations, why top managers behave in the way Jensen (1986) predicts: One is the hypothesis of size maximization of Malatesta (1983). Malatesta (1983) assumes that the management of a firm tries to increase its power and prestige with the help of corporate growth, regardless of the value of M&A-transactions for shareholders.

A second explanation is offered by Roll (1986), who assumes that top managers engage in M&A-transactions because they suffer from hubris. According to the hubris hypothesis, managers prefer to leave free cash flows within the companies, because they assume use them better than shareholders. Top managers engage in costly M&A-transactions because they assume they can create more value with an acquisition target than other potential acquirers, and certainly than the owners and management of the acquisition target. Bazerman, & Samuelson (1983) argue that in auction like situations, the winner always is the one with the most optimistic estimate of the real value of the acquisition target. This "winner's curse" increases with increasing numbers of bidders and with increasing uncertainty about the real value of the acquisition target. "Even if gains do exist for some corporate combinations, at least part of the average observed takeover premium could still be caused by valuation error and hubris. The left tail if the distribution of valuations is truncated by the current market price. To the extent that there are errors in valuation, fewer negative errors will be observed than positive errors" (Roll 1986: 200). Manager suffering from hubris tend to be overly optimistic and therefore engage into value destructive M&A-transactions (Roll 1986).

Hayward, & Hambrick (1997) investigate Roll's (1986) hubris hypothesis as one motive for deficient acquisitions and find strong support for it. Hayward, & Hambrick (1997) investigate three sources of hubris: recent organizational success, media praise for CEO, as well as CEO's self-importance. In a study on 106 M&As they show that managers suffering from hubris pay higher premiums for acquisition targets. The effects of CEO hubris are even stronger if the board of directors is weak and/or headed by the CEO. Hayward, & Hambrick (1997) state in the discussion of their results that it is unclear, whether frequent appearance of top managers in the media is an expression of a narcissistic disposition leading to hubris, leading to increased unsuccessful M&A-activities, or whether it could be the other way around.

As numerous studies show the lack of success of M&A-transactions, Bühner (1990d) argues that hubris might be at the core of reasons why so many M&A-transactions fail. Similarly, Lubatkin (1983) offers two explanations why mergers happen despite their low success rate: "(1) Managers make mistakes. […] (2) Managers may seek to maximize their own wealth at the expense of stockholder's wealth …" (Lubatkin 1983: 221).

However, this argument suffers from a number of problems: First, its logic is circular, meaning that if an M&A-transaction is successful, managers acted in the best interest of owners, and if an M&A-transaction is not successful, they did not. Second, it is not sufficient to take managerial action as null hypothesis for all other potential success factors of M&A-transactions. Third, it is empirically difficult to differ between effects of bounded rationality and effects of hubris.

In a nutshell, psychological explanations assume that mergers and acquisitions happen neither because firms have to engage in M&A-transactions nor because it generates value for the firm. Rather, psychological explanations assume that managers follow their own objectives. Hence success of mergers and acquisitions, i.e. value creation, should be unrelated to the motives of managers, because it was not their intention in the first place to create value but to follow their individual objectives.

1.4.3. Value generation objectives

"When managers outside the firm perceive more profitable uses for the firm's resources, they buy the firm from its owners (the shareholders) and reconfigure the acquired firm's resources, leading to improved efficiency and greater shareholder wealth" (Cannella, & Hambrick 1993: 138).

Kode, Ford and Sutherland (2003: 27) name three different approaches to create value: (1) through buying cheap, (2) through the creation or enhancement of deeper relationships and synergies, and (3) through managing the target better than the current managers.

Buying cheap is based on the assumption that there is an opportunity of buying an undervalued company (Bühner 1990a; Sirower 1997). Regardless of the current economical situation of the firm, speculative M&A-transactions assume that the stand-alone value of a firm is higher than its current market price. Without any post merger activities, "Value can be captured from the seller by identifying and acquiring firms whose market prices may be undervalued" (Haspeslagh, & Jemison 1991: 25). However, there is a chance that value might be shifted from future owners to the owners of the sold firm as well (Haspeslagh, & Jemison 1991: 26). Regardless of the outcome of value shifting during the M&A-transaction, "Value capture tends to be a one-time event, largely related to the transaction itself." (Haspeslagh, & Jemison 1991: 22f)

The other two ways for creating value through acquisitions are long term phenomena that results from managerial action and interactions between the firms. "It embodies the outcome of what many people refer to as synergy" (Haspeslagh, & Jemison 1991: 22ff). The expectation of synergies thus is a key driver for M&A-transactions. They "... are premised on the belief that the combined company will have greater value than the two companies alone. This added value is expressed as "synergy" between the firms, where $1 + 1 > 2$" (Mirvis, & Marks 1992: 69; compare also Kitching 1967: 92; Ansoff 1965: 75).

Sources and types of synergies have been investigated by a number of M&A-researchers. "Probably the most contested topic when dealing with acquisitions are synergy effects. [...] In general, the merger of two firms is accompanied by integration of economic activities at least in parts of the companies. The result of such combinations is a potential competitive advantage, called synergy effect" (Knop 1993: 80, own translation).

Sirower (1997) defines "... synergy as increases in competitiveness and resulting cash flows beyond what the two companies are expected to accomplish independently" (Sirower 1997: 6). More simply spoken, Seth (1990) argues that "Synergy exists in an acquisition when the value of the combined entity exceeds the sum of the values of the two combining firms" (Seth 1990: 432). According to these definitions, any value creation through acquisition can be labeled a synergy.

A general, system theoretical definition of synergies is offered by Fuller (1975), who claims that "Synergy is the behavior of integral, aggregate whole systems unpredicted by behavior of any of their components or subassemblies of their components taken separately from the whole" (Fuller 1975: 7). Koegeler (1991) more specifically defines synergies as the "laterally aligned collaboration between two or more companies in order to reach profitability and risk effects, which would not result from a simple addition" (Koegeler 1991: 5, own translation). Even more specific is Lubatkin (1983), arguing that "Related to strategic fit, synergy occurs when two operating units can be run more efficiently (i.e., with lower costs) and/or more effectively (i.e., with a more appropriate allocation of scarce resources, given environmental constraints) together than apart" (Lubatkin 1983: 218).

In this work, I define *synergies as positive or negative efficiency effects resulting from the partial or full integration of merging firms.*

In the literature, different types of synergies have been described:

Author	Synergy logic	Synergy description (type and source of synergy)
Knop (1993: 81, own translation)	Operational and financial synergies	• "Operative synergies result from the possibility to fuse company functions intra-industry takeovers" • "Financial synergy potential results independently of the industry of the merging firms."
Goold, & Campbell (1999)	Resource exploitation Market power, Transaction costs savings Strategic direction	Six sources of synergies: 1. Jointly used know-how 2. Jointly used resources 3. Pooled negotiation power with suppliers and buyers 4. Coordinated strategy to reduce competition 5. Vertical integration 6. Development of new businesses
Krüger (1988)	Market, Technology Know-how	• Market based synergies (from stronger penetration and/or from new geographic markets) • Technology based synergies (acquisition of new production sites, logistics systems, licenses as well as patents for new products) • Know-how based synergies (New transferable technological, management or geographic know-how)

Table 9: Different types of synergies (1)

Author	Synergy logic	Synergy description (type and source of synergy)
Bark, & Kötzle (2001)	Financial synergies Cost savings Know-how	• Fiscal synergy potential, which focuses on improved access to capital, lower cost of capital or debt, restructuring of assets, alternative financing methods • Product synergy potential, which focuses on consolidation of overheads, restructuring of purchasing, marketing and sales as well as accounting • Knowledge-based synergy potential, which are based on transfer of managerial know-how, systems as well as organizational structures • Market synergy potential, which are based on economies of scope and scale, as well as improved market power.
Olbrich, Alvis, & Reinke (1996: 301)	Centralization, capabilities transfer, and market coordination	• Synergies by fusion, which are based on centralization of activities • Synergies by transfer of capabilities, which includes transfer of management know-how, system transfer, as well as exchange of employees and production assets, • Synergies by coordination, which are based on regional coordination, market positioning as well as avoidance of competition
Koch (2000)	Functional logic	• Purchasing competence and market power • Optimization of production • Introduction of new service concepts • Strengthening of sales and marketing • Consolidation and downsizing of administrative functions
Möller (1983)	Activity logic	• Sales synergies • Purchasing synergies • Cost synergies • Investment synergies
Chatterjee (1986)	Financial, operating and market synergies	• Financial synergies • Operating synergies • Collusive synergies
Kitching (1967)	Market synergies and functional logic of cost synergies	• Market • Management • Administration • Human resources
Bradley, Desai, & Kim (1983)	Functional logic, resource logic, market logic	• Management • Scale effects • Production synergies • Collusive synergies • Complementary resources

Table 10: Different types of synergies (2)

Author	Synergy logic	Synergy description (type and source of synergy)
Lubatkin (1983: 218 ff)	Technical, market and financial logic	There are three basic kinds of synergies: • Technical economies (marketing and production economies, accumulated experience, scheduling economies, banking and compensation economies) • Pecuniary economies (market power through size) • Diversification economics (risk reduction)
Koegeler (1991: 42 ff)	Positive and negative synergies	Positive synergies • Reduction of competition • Reduction of doubled activities such as in sales or in R&D • Improved factor allocation through exchange of know-how, production capacity consolidation and increased specialization of assets • Increase in market power, which improves access to capital, lowers capital costs and improves the position for sales and purchasing Negative synergies • Dysfunctional effects in the HR-area, e.g. due to reduced motivation, higher attrition or lack of identity with the new entity • High cost of integration measures and lower productivity due to integration work • Market effects such as customer losses or reduced turnovers. Koegler (1991) points out that some companies prefer a diversified supplier base. In case of acquisition of a direct competitor, such customers may choose to look for a second supplier, which reduces sales with that customer. • Cost of compromise and inflexibility.
Sommer (1996: 64ff)	Positive and negative synergies	Positive and negative synergies based upon • Synergies through changes in resource allocation and • Synergies through know-how transfer
Ansoff (1965: 80ff)	Market, scale and investment	• Sales synergies (based on a coordinated approach in the markets) • Operating synergies (Improved production efficiency and higher purchasing power) • Investment synergies (synergies in the area of finance) and • Management synergies (synergies in administration and organization)

Table 11: Different types of synergies (3)

As can be seen, there is not one classification of synergies or one synergy logic. Rather, authors mix different conceptions of synergies. Some authors describe synergies according to the activity during which they are generated. Other authors describe more general synergies such as resource exchange or economies of scope, which are broad but not very specific. Again other authors describe single synergy effects such as dysfunctional effects concerning the motivation and the willingness for integration of employees due to identity losses.

In this work, I want to untangle the concept of synergies further to make it more transparent. I will distinguish synergy mechanism and synergy effects. Synergy mechanisms are grounded in general mechanisms of value creation, respectively of competitive advantage, such as scale curves, learning curves, risk diversification, market power as well as superior resources. Synergy effects, however, are manifestations of synergy mechanisms in different activities of the merged firm.

A basic premise for the generation of synergy effects is the integration of the merging firms. Depending on the integrated activities and the degree of integration, it is possible to distinguish two different ideal types of M&A-transaction: Strategic M&A-transactions and financial M&A-transactions. Illustration 4 shows the relationships between synergy effects and the type of M&A-transaction depending on the degree of integration. In parentheses, the chapters are indicated, in which I will elaborate on the different concepts.

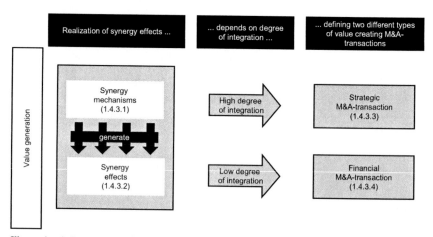

Illustration 4: Two types of value generating M&A-transactions

It is important to note that both, strategic as well as financial M&A-transaction are based on value generation objectives. However, as will be shown, they rely on integration of different activities as well as on different degree of integration.

1.4.3.1. Synergy mechanism

Looking at different schools of thought, it is possible to identify different basic sources of value creation for firms. Economics has offered two different sources of value: The first source is an increasing marginal utility of input factors with increasing scale of operations (Moore 1959). The second source of value is the competitive situation within an industry (Bain 1959).

With the emergence of the resource based view and the capabilities based view, the value of non-tradable resources has been recognized. Resource-based synergies are based on transfer of capabilities, resources and know-how.

A third source of synergies is based on transaction cost economics (Williamson 1975, 1979). According to transaction cost economics, market relationships between firms require safeguarding, which leads to transaction costs. M&A-transactions between firms can reduce transaction costs and thus generate synergy effects.

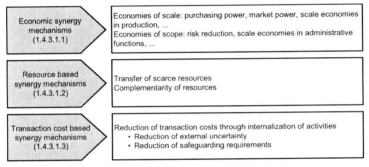

Illustration 5: Synergy mechanisms

1.4.3.1.1. Economic synergy mechanisms

Although today widely accepted, the discussion about economies of scale was heated, when the first authors brought up the idea that larger corporations might be more profitable and more efficient than smaller corporations. In 1951, Osborn insisted that economies of scale are actually diseconomies of scale and that empirical evidence indicates that small and medium sized firms are more profitable than large firms. Bain (1954) was one of the first to present statistical data to show the existence of scale curves and positive scale economies. Moore (1959) shows clear statistical evidence for the existence of scale economies, which, nevertheless were denied in a commentary of Schuman, & Alpert (1960). The outcome of the debate is clear: economic synergies are nowadays widely accepted.

Economic synergies can be distinguished in two different types: internal economic synergies and external economic synergies. Internal synergies are increases in efficiency based on improved relationship between input-output relations of factors. External synergies are based on market effects.

Internal economic synergies are based on increasing marginal utility of production factors with increasing scale. That means that with increased size of an operation, the output per input factor, respectively the efficiency of employed production factors increases. Economic synergies, according to Sommer (1996) are based on changes in resource utilization (better capacity usage, cross-usage of service units, sales units, etc.) There are different sources for scale effects. One is better usage of assets (Bühner 1990d: 1276). There is often a minimal scale of specific assets, which might be larger than the actual scale required. For example, a sales force requires a certain size to cover a geographic region, regardless of the sales volume. With increasing sales volume, at some point, the sales force is fully used. With further volume increase the sales, sales areas can be scaled down and thus travel time and thereby travel cost can be reduced. In the case of sales forces, it is possible that more sales with one product shows this effect. However, it is equally possible that more sales through addition of different products shows this effect as well. This means that not only scale of an operation but also scope of an operation can generate increases in factor efficiency. Accordingly, the literature on economic synergies differs between economies of scale and economies of scope.

"Economies of scale are economic advantages, which can result from an increase of size (through internal or external growth) of the operation and/or the increase of production capacities with simultaneous increase of output. [...] Economies of scope are economic advantages of a company, which accrue not due to scale but due to scope of its product range. They accrue if a company can produce a number of different products more cost efficiently than by specializing on one product only" (Koegeler 1991:5f ff, own translation).

While higher factor efficiency is one aspect of economies of scale and economies of scope, another aspect is the learning effect. Bühner (1990a: 12) points out that learning effects are based on the learning curve, according to which production cost decreases with increased cumulated production volume. Bühner (1990a:12) claims that empirical evidence shows that production cost decreases by 15% for each doubling of the accumulated production volume.

Economies of scale and economies of scope are not limited to the efficiency of production factors. They also influence the market power of firms. According to industrial economics or industrial organization (IO), concentration of an industry, respectively size of firms strongly affects the profitability and thereby the value creation potential of firms (Bain 1959; Porter 1980; 1985). Such market related economies of scale include advantages in purchasing production factors, advantages in selling goods to customers as well as advantages in financing the firm.

In purchasing, larger firms are able to negotiate lower prices (Goold, & Campbell 1999; Bark, & Kötzle 2001; Koch 2000; Möller 1983; Lubatkin 1983) thanks to increased market power. In sales, larger firms are able to raise prices (Goold, & Campbell 1999; Bark, & Kötzle 2001; Lubatkin 1983; Koegeler 1991) thanks to increased market power. This synergy effect is often called collusive synergies. In acquiring equity and debt, firms are able to negotiate lower prices, because scale reduces the risk of bankruptcy (Knop 1993). Economies of scope reduce the firm-specific risk through diversification and thereby the cost of capital (Seth 1990; Bühner 1990a).

In a nutshell, economies of scale and scope apply for both, company specific efficiency advantages and market related cost and price advantages.

1.4.3.1.2. Resource based synergy mechanisms

A second type of synergies is based on resources of merging firms. According to the resource based view of the firm (Wernerfelt 1984; Barney 1991; Teece, Pisano, & Shuen 1997) firms can gain competitive advantage and thereby create value through resources they use. Peteraf (1993) shows that competitive advantage from superior resources can be maintained if there is heterogeneity within an industry, ex post limits to competition, imperfect resource mobility and ex ante limits to competition. Resources or specific configurations of resources thus can lead to sustainable competitive advantage.

Resource based synergies thus are based on the transfer or joint use of superior resources from one of the partnering firms to the other partnering firms. Prahalad, & Hamel (1990) point out that superior core competences of a firm lead to competitive advantage. Such superior core competences can be used in larger or different businesses. M&A-transactions provide additional opportunities to exploit core competences on a larger scale, or in different businesses and thus create competitive advantage for the acquired businesses. Accordingly, Haspeslagh, & Jemison (1991) argue that "In our conception, synergy occurs when capabilities transferred between firms improve a firm's competitive position and consequently its performance" (Haspeslagh, & Jemison 1991: 22ff).

Such capabilities or resources can be tangible like human resources, specific production assets, or a superior technology. „Resource sharing involves the combination and rationalization of some of the operating assets of both firms" (Haspeslagh, & Jemison 1991: 29). A specific form of resource transfer concerns the transfer of financial resources, which allows diversified firms to attack more aggressively within specific markets (Bühner 1990d: 1277ff).

Resources can as well be intangible like a specific skillset, licenses or other knowledge-based resources. An example for intangible resource transfer is the application of general management skills from one firm in another firm in order to "... make another [firm] more competitive by improving the range or depth of its general management skills" (Haspeslagh, & Jemison 1991: 31). In addition, resource based synergies can result from a combination of resources of both firms, leading to superior performance. Liedtka (1998: 47) points out accordingly that "Synergy seeks to leverage the capabilities resident at the level of the individual business unit in order to create new institutional capabilities at the corporate level" (Liedtka 1998: 47).

Summarized, a resource based synergy mechanism is based on leverage of scarce resources of one firm in the other firm. A second resource based synergy mechanism is based on the complementarity of resources of merging firms, which together form a new superior set of resources.

1.4.3.1.3. Transaction cost based synergy mechanisms

A third basic mechanism of value creation can be economies in transaction costs. According to Williamson (1975), bounded rationality and opportunism require safeguarding of market transactions. Such safeguarding of market transactions is costly because transaction costs accrue. Three dimensions of a transaction, uncertainty, asset specificity and frequency, determine the height of transaction costs. Firms can avoid transaction costs by internalizing transactions. The most important transactions for a firm are the ones with suppliers and customers. If these transactions are characterized by high uncertainty, high asset specificity and/or high frequency, according to transaction cost economics, it is favorable for a firm to vertically integrate in order to reduce transaction costs (Bühner 1990d: 1277 – 1278).

1.4.3.2. Synergy effects

Synergy mechanisms are based on general value creation mechanism. In M&A-transactions, these mechanisms generate value in different activities of the merging firms. The actual value created thus is the sum of synergy effects. In this work, I define *synergy effects* as the effect of a synergy mechanism in a specific activity of the firm. A firm can be described as a bundle of activities, which in total form the firm's value chain (Porter 1980). In most firms, these activities are located in different organizational units or functions. Accordingly, Koegeler (1991) identifies potential synergies in the following functions.

- Sales and marketing
- Research and development
- Synergies in production
- Synergies in procurement and logistics
- Administration

- Financial synergies due to pooling of liquidity, tax effects, higher capital turnover (Koegeler 1991: 47 – 63).

Koegeler (1991) shows that in each of these functions different synergy effects can accrue. For example, synergies in administration can be generated through centralization of some administrative tasks. These synergy effects are based on scale effects, according to which an integrated unit can handle the same amount of transactions that the two previously separated units handled before with less people (compare also Bühner 1990d: 1277 – 1278). The synergy effect in administration based on scale economies thus is increased efficiency of employed human resources.

In previous studies, researchers found synergy effects in production, marketing, R&D, and administration based on economies of scale (Bain 1959, Lloyd 1976), vertical economies, respectively transaction cost economies in procurement and sales (Chandler 1977, Harrigan 1984, Williamson 1975), and economies of scope (Seth 1990). Researchers also found external synergy effects in procurement from purchasing power or in sales departments from market power (Caves, & Porter 1977; Chatterjee 1986, Scherer 1980), Again other researchers found managerial synergies from transferring complementary competencies or replacing incompetent managers (Davis, & Stout 1992; Lorsch, & Allen 1973). And again other researchers found financial synergies from risk diversification and coinsurance, which are based on scope of acquired firms. (Lubatkin 1983; Seth 1990). Last but not least, researchers found tax effects (Bühner 1990d: 1277 – 1278). Tax effects can either be based on the transfer of specific taxation capabilities of a firm such as a loss carried forward, or a specific tax regime based on international tax arbitrage.

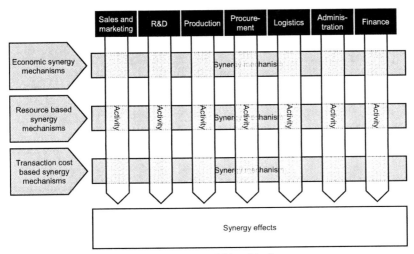

Illustration 6: Synergy mechanism in different activities of the firm

Illustration 6 summarizes how synergy mechanisms generate synergy effects in different activities of merged firms.

It is important to note that all synergies require at least to some extent the cooperation between the merging entities. For example, economies of scale in administration require the full integration of administrative activities of both firms in order to generate scale effects. At the same time, the generation of tax synergies only requires cooperation of finance departments of the merging entities. This implies that synergies in operative functions, such as sales, production, etc. require a high degree of integration, whereas the generation of financial synergy effects such as tax synergies or lower cost of capital require only little integration.

Depending on the targeted synergies, it is thus possible to differentiate two types of mergers and acquisitions: (1) M&A-transactions, which mainly pursue strategic growth objectives and (2) M&A-transactions, which mainly pursue financial objectives. While this differentiation necessarily bears some fuzziness, they differ in types of realized synergies and the necessary degree of integration of the activities of the merging firms. Strategic growth objectives usually require a high degree of operative integration of merging firms. Financial objectives, however, can be realized with limited degree of integration.

In the following paragraphs, I will investigate in further detail, how strategic growth objectives and financial objectives both aim for synergy realization. I will show the different synergy mechanisms, which contribute to the achievement of strategic respectively financial objectives.

1.4.3.3. Strategic growth objectives of M&A-transactions

Haspeslagh, & Jemison (1991: 27) note critically, that despite the prominence of value creation, „Value capture is not a sufficient motive for strategic acquirers" (Haspeslagh, & Jemison 1991: 27). Rather, it is strategic objectives of a firm that induce most of the M&A transactions.

Firms need to engage in strategic moves in order to create additional value or to retain their current value. "Just to retain its relative position, a business firm must go through continuous growth and change. To improve its position, it must grow and change at least 'twice as fast as that'" (Ansoff 1957: 113). Based on this assumption, Ansoff (1957, 1965) develops a two dimensional model to describe different product-market strategies as growth options for firms. As presented in Illustration 7, one dimension describes the development of new markets. A company can choose to further penetrate its current markets or to access new markets. The second dimension concerns the development of new products. A company can choose to continue producing their current product range or can move into related or unrelated technologies.

Within this framework, companies can choose different strategies for growth. Depending on the direction within the matrix, Ansoff (1957, 1965) differs between (1) penetration, which implies a stronger penetration of current product markets of a firm, (2) product development or product extension, which implies the addition of related or unrelated products or technologies to the current range of a firm, (3) market development or market extension, which implies entering new markets, such as new geographic markets or new customer segments, and (4) diversification, which implies to move into new markets and the addition of new products.

Products / Markets	Same products	New products
Same markets	Penetration	Product extension
New markets	Market extension	Diversification

Illustration 7: Ansoff's product-market strategies for business growth alternatives

The work of Williamson (1975) and Pfeffer, & Salancik (1978) extends the framework by adding vertical integration as one specific type of diversification. Vertical integration consists of either an extension in the supplier or in the buyer market of firms with new products.

Having decided about the strategic direction of the firm, there are two basic ways to realize it: with internal growth, respectively organic growth, or with external growth. Internal growth means that resources are acquired separately and then combined within the firm (Koegeler 1991: 13; Ansoff 1957; 1965). External growth means that firms acquire control over entire bundles of resources, i.e. firms (Koegeler 1991: 14; Ansoff 1957; 1965; Barney 1991).

External growth has a number of advantages over internal growth. Bühner (1990e) puts forward three main reasons to choose external growth through acquisitions. First, there is a time advantage in choosing acquisitions as a growth option over organic growth. Buying a bundle of resources, in the shape of a firm (Barney 1991; Wernerfelt 1984; Peteraf 1993) is much faster than buying single resources and combining them[6]. Second, acquisitions preserve mostly the current market structure. Market barriers can be avoided and excess capacities can be consolidated. Third, acquisitions of new products or technologies can be cheaper and faster than own developments. (Bühner 1990d: 1276; Bühner 1990a:1 ff) The latter rationale for

---

[6] Dierickx, & Cool (1989) describe in their work the differences between resources and capabilities. Resources are tradeable or at least potentially tradable goods, whereas capabilities are built over time within firms. Therefore, a firm is more than just a bundle of resources: It is a bundle of capabilities, which are formed around resources.

mergers and acquisitions implies that innovation can be acquired externally regardless of the strategic direction.

Mergers and acquisitions thus represent the vehicle for the implementation of a growth strategy. Mergers and acquisitions thus can be classified within Ansoff's growth matrix. Accordingly, Haspeslagh, & Jemison (1991: 33ff) distinguish three different types of impacts of acquisitions on corporate-level strategy

- Domain Strengthening.
- Domain Extension.
- Domain Exploration.

Similarly, Sommer (1996) argues that acquisitions are an instrument for realizing business strategies, which are derived from corporate strategy. Acquisition strategies according to Sommer (1996) have two effects on the current business: (1) Acquisitions to strengthen a business by strengthening the market position, strengthening of internal capacities such as low cost production capacities, and strengthening of know-how. (2) Related acquisitions help to expand a business and unrelated acquisitions help to develop a business.

Also Koegeler (1991: 1) argues that acquisitions help to increase national and international market shares (which corresponds to a penetration and a market extension strategy), access to new technologies, industries (which corresponds to a product extension strategy) and employees (which can be true for all types of acquisitions), diversify risk through diversification of the firms businesses, and secure the procurement with raw materials and semi-ready products (which corresponds to a vertical extension strategy).

Summarized, mergers and acquisitions can be triggered by different strategic growth objectives of firms. Depending on extension in existing or new products as well as extension in existing or new markets, different types of mergers and acquisitions can be distinguished. Vertical extension is a special type of extending in new markets and new products in supplier or buyer markets of the merging firm.

In the next paragraphs, I will investigate how different types strategic objectives of M&A-transactions can generate value. Therefore, I will identify synergy mechanisms as well as synergy effects for each type of strategic M&A.

1.4.3.3.1.   Value creation through horizontal mergers and acquisitions

„Usually, conjunctions are called horizontal, if the partnering firms produce same or similar products" (Berthold 2004: 65, own translation). Similarly, Bühner (1990b) claims that „Horizontal conjunctions of firms are done by companies that are operating with the same products within the same markets, meaning they are competing directly" (Bühner 1990b: 2, own translation).

A horizontal conjunction reinforces the market position, i.e. the market share of the integrated firm. A strong market position has advantages in negotiating with suppliers as well as with buyers (Bain 1959; Porter 1980). In addition to these synergy effects based on external scale economies, horizontal mergers can lead to a better cost structure based on internal scale economies. The better cost structure is the result of a number of synergy effects such as "…

- Specialization advantages, which result from possibilities of division of labor in larger organizational units
- construction technology related effects, according to which investment costs increase subproportionally with increases of capacities
- advantages, which result from a reduction of spare part volumes for production facilities thanks to central warehousing
- the principle of least common multiples, according to which consecutive production steps reach the lowest level of cost at their least common capacity multiple and
- economies due to lot sizes, as larger lots can be produced and set-up costs can be lowered"

(Bühner 1990a: 11 ff, own translation).

In a nutshell, horizontal acquisitions can generate synergy effects based on economic synergy mechanisms as well as on resource based synergy mechanisms.

1.4.3.3.2. Value creation through product-extending mergers and acquisitions

M&A-transactions that aim for product extension can also lead to synergy effects. "The empirical results indicate that value creation in related acquisitions is associated with economic efficiencies hypothesized to arise both from economies of scale and scope and from operating efficiencies, and with market power" (Seth 1990: 431). Bühner (1990a) points out that cost effects in production can result from transfer of learning effects between merging firms. "Especially the use of flexible production facilities, so called 'co-specialized assets' for the production of several products can lead to economies of scope" (Bühner 1990a: 13, own translation). Flexible production facilities can be used for the production of a large range of products. This allows merged firms to shift production between production facilities and thereby reach economies of scale through consolidation or specialization. Also, product extension can lead to synergy effects in the sales force. As the merging firms operate within the same market, it is possible to cross-sell products in case of disjunct customer bases, or to reduce the size of the combined sales force.

In addition to internal synergy effects, Bühner (1990a) argues that "Horizontal mergers with product extension lead to emergence or reinforcement of market power and to increases of market barriers, if transferable experience advantages from each of the core businesses can be used" (Bühner 1990a: 10). For example, a consumer goods company such as Procter & Gamble can profit from its 2003 takeover of Wella, as both firms share the same customers with different product ranges in the non-food business.

Summarized, product extending mergers can realize synergy effects based on economic synergy mechanisms as well as on resource based synergy mechanisms.

1.4.3.3.3. Value creation through market-extending mergers and acquisitions

Market extension can directly lead to synergy effects in the production of the integrated firms. As in the case of a related acquisition, production facilities can be consolidated or specialized, both leading to cost advantages in production (Knop 1993: 81; Krüger 1988).

An important external effect of market extension is the diversification of geographic markets. Different markets reduce the systematic risk of a firm and thereby lower its cost of capital (Lubatkin 1983). Another important source of synergy effects results from a specific type of external economies of scope. Firms operating in multiple markets can generate collusive synergies (Chatterjee 1986), which result from a multi-point competition logic: Rivaling firms that operate within similar markets are more likely to reduce competitive pressure within one specific market, if the competitors are confronted with each other in a number of other markets (Karnani, & Wernerfelt 1985).

In a nutshell, market extending mergers and acquisitions can generate synergy effects mainly through economic and resource based synergy mechanisms.

1.4.3.3.4. Value creation through vertical mergers and acquisitions

„Vertical mergers increase the vertical integration of a firm by taking over a customer or a supplier" (Bühner 1990b: 2, own translation). Similarly, Berthold (2004) defines that „The merger is vertical if there has been a kind of buyer-seller-relationship between the partnering firms and they thus seek integration along the value chain" (Berthold 2004: 65, own translation).

Vertical mergers and acquisitions mainly reduce market uncertainties, which results in lower transaction costs (Williamson 1975; Pfeffer, & Salancik 1978). These transaction cost savings include search- and information cost to gather prices and product characteristics of suppliers, cost for contract conclusion, as well as cost for quality control, and other costs such as administration and taxation (Bühner 1990a: 13). At the same time, vertical mergers can reduce warehousing costs and increase capital turnover as stocks can be reduced (Pfeffer, & Salancik 1978).

Vertical M&A-transactions thus mainly generate synergy effects based on transaction cost synergy mechanisms.

1.4.3.3.5. Value creation through diversification

M&A-transactions leading to diversification are conjunctions of firms that do neither operate in the same markets nor in the same industry. In the literature, authors often refer to this type of M&A-transaction as conglomerate. "In conglomerate conjunctions, partnering firms do not have any relatedness between their products and/or their markets" (Bühner 1990a: 5, own translation). Similarly, Bertold (2004) points out that „Conglomerate conjunctions are such between firms that have no commonalities" (Berthold 2004: 65, own translation).

Some conglomerate mergers and acquisitions might profit from better management. This corresponds to a transfer of scarce resources, i.e. management capabilities from one firm to the other firm. However, the main synergy effect in conglomerate mergers is based on specific risk reduction, which lower cost of capital. "In unrelated acquisitions, where such efficiencies [internal synergy effects] are not expected to be present, value creation occurs nevertheless, and is associated with the coinsurance effect" (Seth 1990: 431). This synergy effect is based on external economies of scope.

The coinsurance effect has been subject of an ongoing debate, in which opponents of conglomerate mergers and acquisitions argue that shareholders can achieve coinsurance effects better by diversifying their share portfolio, and that diversified companies create less value than a portfolio of focused companies (Prahalad, & Hamel 1990).

Despite the focus on financial synergy effects, Bühner (1990a: 14) points out that even in conglomerate mergers and acquisitions, reduction of overhead costs is possible. According to Bühner (1990a: 14) this reduction can mainly be realized in specific functions such as research and development, sales or in support functions that are not product related such as the Legal department or in IT. However, empirical support for this argument is missing (Seth 1990).

Summarized, diversification M&A-transactions generate synergy effects mainly based on economic and resource based synergy mechanisms.

1.4.3.3.6. Summary of strategic objectives

As has been shown, strategic objectives in mergers and acquisitions always aim for some sort of value creation. In principal, strategic objectives can be realized internally with organic growth or externally with conjunctions of firms. Ultimately, an M&A-transaction in this logic is only a vehicle to reach strategic objectives with specific advantages such as preservation of market structures and speed advantages. At the same time, mergers and acquisitions bear specific disadvantages such as integration effort as well as a potential mismatch of resource constellations of the partnering firms, which can be avoided in choosing organic growth over external growth.

It is important to note that strategic objectives in mergers and acquisitions require a significant degree of integration of the merging firms. Synergy effects in sales and marketing, production, R&D, procurement, logistics or administration mainly result from partial or full integration of these activities.

1.4.3.4. Financial objectives of M&A-transactions

Other motives for M&A-transactions directly seek value creation. In the existing research, financial motives represent one set of objectives that is independent of a corporate strategy or business strategy. These motives include financial objectives such as tax advantages (Bühner 1990a; Sommer 1996; Hughes, & Müller 1980) and lower cost of capital (Seth 1990).

Tax advantages can be a powerful motivation for mergers and acquisitions. On the one hand, it is possible that a firm can exploit an existing tax system (Sherman 1972). On the other hand, it is possible that governments manipulate the tax system in a way to encourage desired mergers and acquisitions.

Lower cost of capital is another motive for mergers and acquisitions. Lowering the firm specific cost of capital can be achieved by mere size, which reduces the specific risk of a firm by reducing the risk of bankruptcy. A second option to lower the costs of capital is by diversification, which, in the case of unrelated businesses, can reduce the firm specific risk, if the industry specific risks of the unrelated businesses share no covariance (Bark, & Kötzle 2001; Seth 1990).

A second type of financial objectives concerns the better management for the acquired firm (Bühner 1990a). These objectives are based on the assumption that the current management of the acquisition target does not exploit the full value creation potential of the acquisition target. By exchange of the management, value in the acquired firm can be created.

Financial objectives for M&A-transactions are somewhat difficult to separate from strategic objectives. Looking at the synergy effects and at the synergy mechanisms they use, financial and strategic M&A-transactions, especially conglomerate mergers are very much alike. However, there are two differences that are notable: (1) While strategic M&A-transactions follow a strategic logic and thus only represent the vehicle for the implementation of a growth strategy, financial M&A-transactions follow a simple value creation logic. (2) It is hard to imagine a strategic M&A-transaction, which does not imply at least partial integration of the activities of the partnering firms. Financial M&A-transactions, however, can be mostly based on ownership with hardly any integration between the partnering firms.

1.4.4. Synergy potential and synergy effects

As shown above, most objectives of mergers and acquisitions be it strategic objectives or financial objectives aim for synergy effects. Depending on the objective of a merger, the underlying synergy mechanism and the synergy effects may differ.

In discussing synergy effects, it is important to note that synergy effects do not accrue automatically after an M&A-transaction. Rather, it is necessary to differ between a synergy potential and realized synergies. "The potential of a synergy shall be […] the maximum value or factor load of a synergy" (Koegeler 1991: 5, own translation). Similarly, Larsson, & Finkelstein (1999) point out that "The various sources of synergy define a combination's potential, which in turn is as expected to affect the extent to which synergies will be realized in an acquisition" (Larsson, & Finkelstein 1999: 5). While the potential of a synergy is its theoretical maximum value, Koegeler (1991) argues that "The effect of a synergy […] shall be understood as degree of achievement of objectives" (Koegeler 1991: 5, own translation).

Sommer (1996) argues that there are synergy effects that can be captured in a short period of time, such as replacement of poor managers, tax or financial effects. Other synergy effects, however require more time if they are based on links between the merged companies.

1.4.5. Summary

As has been shown, there are three different explanations for the occurrence of mergers and acquisitions: contingency theoretical, psychological as well as value creation explanations. Cartwright, & Cooper (1993c) argue that "While the motives for merger are many - practical, psychological, or opportunist - the stated objective of all mergers and acquisitions is to achieve synergy or the commonly described "two plus two equals five" effect" (Cartwright, & Cooper 1993c: 57). Following their line of thought, I focus in this work on the value creation logic.

According to the value creation logic, expected synergy effects, i.e. the synergy potential of an M&A-transaction is the main driver for the occurrence of an M&A-transactions. Sommer (1996) points out that synergies are always based on the integration of the firms. "In general, a conjunction of firms comes along with at least partial integration of economic activities. This integration then generates a competitive advantage, which is called synergy effect" (Knop 1993: 80, own translation). Similarly, Olbrich et al. (1996) argue that synergies emerge in the course of acquisitions through co-action of participants of the acquisition (Olbrich et al. 1996: 300). Möller (1983) finds empirical support for this assumption. He finds a positive correlation between realization of synergies and degree of integration.

Based on the type of integrated activities and based on the degree of integration, it is possible to distinguish between two different types of value creating M&A-transactions: Strategic as well as financial M&A-transactions.

It is important to note that the combination of merging firms bears a synergy potential, which then has to be realized to become manifested in synergy effects. The key lever for realizing synergy effects is integration of the merging firms. Integration, however, requires cooperation of employees of the merging firms.

In 1.2, the success rate of mergers and acquisitions was found to be low, and it was stated that M&A-transactions are a risky business. In this section, motives for mergers and acquisitions were investigated. It turned out that managers in value creating M&A-transactions mostly have good intentions when engaging in mergers and acquisitions. Hence it is necessary to investigate the reasons, why so many mergers and acquisitions fail.

In the next sections of this paper, I will show that there are some obstacles in identifying synergy potential and later realizing synergy effects. I will review the literature on success factors, which have been found to affect the realization of synergy effects and hence the M&A-performance.

1.5. Why do M&As fail? Success factors for M&A-transactions

As has been seen above, mergers and acquisitions are a risky business. The odds, it seems, are rather high to suffer from severe losses when engaging into a merger or an acquisition. „Why some acquisitions fail and others succeed?" (Schweiger, & Walsh 1990: 47), i.e. the identification of success factors is therefore a question that has intrigued researchers since years.

Already in the 20s of the last century, economists were struggling with questions about success factors for merger success. In its very first issue, the Harvard Business Review printed a case study on a vertical integration in the copper industry and analyzed the success factors for such an acquisition (Harvard Business Review 1922: 11 – 15). The main success factor in this case study was the reduction of demand uncertainty from customers. Similarly, Edmonds (1923) describes tendencies in the U.S.-American car industry, which showed strong tendencies towards vertical integration except for the case of the General Motors Corporation, which back then followed a successful horizontal acquisition strategy. General Motors' secret of success was the right degree of integration for their acquisitions. Depending on expected synergies, General Motors integrated some firms while others remained independently and were managed from the General Motors Holding as separate divisions. Later, Learned (1930) investigates mergers in the cotton industry and finds that the main success factor for horizontal mergers is the time to full integration. According to his findings, slow integration, which allows customers to change their consumption habits, is more promising than fast integration. Learned (1930) also finds that vertical integration is especially successful in markets for branded products, because it allows to maintain a high quality standards. By controlling the full production chain, product quality can be better secured.

Some of these findings are still valid today and have been confirmed in some of the numerous studies that have been conducted ever since. For example, only recently, Zaheer, Castaner and Souder (2005) tackled the problem of the right degree of integration. They find that depending on the strategic merger objective, different degrees of integration are advisable.

The list of potential success factors for M&A-transactions is long. In a literature review of 15 books, Kode et al. (2003) find that by far the most heavily covered reason for M&A-failures is a lack of planning of integrating the firms and of integration problems, followed by too high payments of acquisition premiums. Sirower (1997) names four cornerstones that need to be considered for M&A-success: Strategic vision, operating strategy, systems integration and power and culture. Other authors emphasize stronger psychological success factors. Buono, & Bowditch (1989) identify six topics relevant for a better understanding of mergers and acquisitions:

- There are different types of mergers and acquisitions
- Merger events unfold in the course of a process
- Each M&A-transaction has psychological repercussions for the individuals involved
- There are cultural differences across firms
- There are different integrative mechanism that a firm can choose
- There is a relationship between employee attitudes and behaviors and organizational performance

Again others focus on the quality of the merger process. Scheiter (1989) points out that "Essentially, literature and practice names three reasons for the low chances for success of acquisitions: (1) No or insufficient planning of the acquisition by the acquiring firm (2) Errors in selecting and evaluating the acquisition target and (3) insufficient post merger management for the integration of the acquired firm" (Scheiter 1989: III, own translation).

In the table below, a sample of empirical M&A-studies of the last years is listed. For each study, the independent variables, the "success factors" as well as the dependent variables, the "success measures" of M&As are listed. In some cases, the dependent variable is not M&A-success but other variables that have been proved to be relevant for success of mergers and acquisitions. Further, the research logic for each study is listed. The research logic comprises the level of analysis and a first classification of success factors. Last but not least, a short description of the sample is provided.

Author	Success factors	Success measures	Sample
Kitching (1967)	- Size (+) - More than one integration (-) - Integration of production (-) - integration of financial resources (+) - Horizontal (+) - Concentric: (marketing, technology (-) - Conglomerate (.)	- Success	69 acquisitions (1960 – 1965)

Möller (1983)	- Size of target (+)
	- Acquisition type
	  o horizontal (+)
	  o vertical (+)
	  o marketing concentric (++)
	  o technical concentric (-)
	  o conglomerate (–)
	- Organizational culture (.)
	- Strategic planning (.)
	- Synergy expectation (+)
	- Objectives of acquirer
	- management controlled firm (+)
	- Evaluation of target (longer period +)
	- Degree of integration (+)
	- Key persons of integration phase (.)
		- Economic success	100 acquisitions
			(1970 – 1979)

Lubatkin (1987)	- Type of merger (.)
	  o Product concentric
	  o Horizontal and market concentric
	  o Conglomerate
	  o Vertical
		- Acquisition performance
		  o Acquirer
		  o Acquisition target
			439 acquiring firms
			340 acquired firms

Lubatkin, & O'Neill (1987)	- Relatedness	- Risk reduction
		  - unsystematic risk (increase independent of relatedness)
		  - systematic risk (-)
			297 larger mergers

Singh, & Montgomery (1987)	- Relatedness (+) (one or more of
	  o similar production technology
	  o similar science-based research
	  o similar products and/or markets)
	- Single bid acquisition (+)
		- Abnormal dollar value changes (stock market) of
		  o Acquiring firm
		  o Acquired firm
			105 acquisitions larger than US$ 100 M
			(1975 – 1980)

Table 12: Studies looking at success factors of mergers and acquisitions (1)

Author	Success factors	Success measures	Sample
Hitt, Hoskisson, Ireland, & Harrison (1989)	- Growth of acquirer through acquisition (-) - Leverage (-) - Diversification (-) - Size (-)	- Relative R&D intensity	191 mergers (1970 – 1986)

Bühner (1990c)	- Acquirer (-)
	- Acquired firm (+)
	- Diversification
	  o horizontal with product extension (.)
	  o vertical (.)
	  o horizontal w/o product extension (-)
	  o conglomerate (–)
	- Merger experience (+)
	- Relative size of target (-)
		- Abnormal stock market returns	90 German acquisitions
			(1973 – 1985)

Bühner (1990d)	- Acquirer (-)
	- Diversification
	  o horizontal with product extension (.)
	  o vertical (+)
	  o horizontal w/o product extension (-)
	  o conglomerate (-)
	- Merger experience (+)
	- Relative size of target (.)
		- EBIT/Assets
		- EBIT/Equity
			110 acquisitions
			(1973 – 1985)

Seth (1990)	- Economy of scale, economies of scope, operating efficiencies and market power in related acquisitions (+) - Coinsurance in unrelated acquisitions (+)	- Value creation	102 Tender offers (1962 - 1979)
Chatterjee (1991)	- Concentration of industry of acquirer (.) - Concentration of industry of acquired firm in vertical integrations (-)	- Acquirers standardized cumulative abnormal returns - Target's standardized cumulative abnormal returns	116 vertical mergers (1962 – 1979)
Datta (1991)	- Relative size - Differences in management styles (-) - Differences in size (.) - Differences in reward and evaluation systems (.) - Differences in management styles x integration degree (.) - Differences in reward and evaluation systems x integration degree (.)	- Acquisition performance (ROI, EPS, stock price, cash flow, sales growth)	173 acquisitions in the U.S. manufacturing industry

Table 13: Studies looking at success factors of mergers and acquisitions (2)

Author	Success factors	Success measures	Sample

Harrison, Hitt, & Ireland (1991)	· Differences
	  o Diff in capital intensity (+)
	  o Diff in Administrative intensity (+)
	  o Diff in Interest intensity (+)
	  o Diff in R&D intensity (+)
	· Controls: Relatedness
		· ROA	~ 1.100 acquisitions (1980 – 1989)

Hitt, Hoskisson, Ireland, & Harrison (1991)	· Acquisition activity (-) · Diversification (-) · Size of target of combined firm (+) · ROA (-)	· R&D intensity · Patent intensity	191 acquisitions (1970 – 1986)

Rentsch, & Schneider (1991)	· Size of the firm (large = positive, small = negative)
	· Motive of integration (survival = negative or growth = positive)
		· Postcombination expectations regarding
		  o Personal autonomy
		  o use of power
		  o postcombination sense of organizational morale
		  o identity
		  o feelings of job security
		  o career opportunities
			Scenario analysis method with 252 MBA students

Schweiger, & DeNisi (1991)	· Communication	· Perceived uncertainty (-) · Stress (-) · Job satisfaction (.) · Organizational commitment (+) · Perception of company's trustworthiness (+)	Field experiment Experimental plant: 75 employees, control plant 72 employees
Agrawal, Jaffe, & Mandelker (1992)	· Tender offer (.) · Point in time, from 1955 – 1984 (.) · Conglomerate vs. non-conglomerate (.)	· Stock performance (5 y post merger period)	937 mergers and 227 tender offers (1955 – 1987)
Chatterjee, Lubatkin, Schweiger, & Weber (1992)	· Perceptions of cultural differences of top management teams in acquisitions (-) · Buying firm's tolerance for multiculturalism (+) · Relative size of merging firms (.)	· Stock market performance	30 US M&As (1985 – 1987)
Cannella, & Hambrick (1993)	· Departure of top executives (-) · Acquisition relatedness (product market, customers) (no moderation effect) · Advancement of executives to top management team (+)	· Firm performance (7-point scale)	96 acquisitions (1980 – 1984)
Cartwright, & Cooper (1993b)	· Size of partnering company (-)	· Stress	Case study 157 middle managers in a merger

Table 14: Studies looking at success factors of mergers and acquisitions (3)

Author	Success factors	Success measures	Sample
Gerpott (1994)	· Premerger performance acquirer(.) · Premerger performance target firm (-) · Relative size of target (+) · Diversification (.) · Market similarity (.) · Readiness of target firm's management to continue in merged firm (+) · Age of top management team of target firm (.) · Importance of HR-questions with top management of target firm (+) · Implementation of cross-company integration teams (+) · Exchange of top management (+) · Participation of top management team of target firm in steering committees (+)	· Management retention	92 acquisitions -1988
Haunschild, Moreland, & Murrell (1994)	· Cohesion of groups (.) · Pre-merger performance (- enth., + bias)	· Enthusiasm · Ingroup/outgroup bias	Experiment with 46 groups
Pablo (1994)	· Need for strategic integration (Strategic task needs) (+) · Need for organizational independence of target (organizational needs (-) · Multiculturalism (-) · Power differential (-) · Compatibility of acquisition visions (-)	· Level of integration	56 acquisitions
Weber (1996)	· Perceived cultural differences of top management teams (by employees of acquired and acquiring firms) (-) · Autonomy removal of acquired top management team (-) · Commitment of acquired top management team (+)	· Effectiveness of integration process · Financial performance	73 US M&As (1985 – 1987)

Table 15: Studies looking at success factors of mergers and acquisitions (4)

Author	Success factors	Success measures	Sample

Hayward, & Hambrick (1997)	- CEO hubris
	  ○ acquiring firm's recent performance
	  ○ recent media praise for the CEO
	  ○ CEO's self-importance
	  ○ Composite measure of the three variables
	- Board inside control
	- Weak board
	- Premium paid
		- Premium paid
		- Acquisition performance
		(1 y cumulative abnormal security returns)
			106 large acquisitions

Krishnan, Miller, & Judge (1997)	- Complementarity of functional background of top management team (+) - Top management team turnover (-)	- Post acquisition corporate performance	147 acquisitions (1986 – 1988)
Lubatkin, & Srinivsan (1997)	- Relatedness of merger	- Total shareholder value (.) - Shareholder value for acquirer (.) - Shareholder value for acquired firm (.)	289 larger mergers (1980 – 1987)

Ramaswamy (1997)	- Dissimilarity of strategic characteristics (-)
	  ○ Dissimilar market coverage (.)
	  ○ Dissimilar operational efficiency (-)
	  ○ Dissimilar emphasis on marketing activity (-)
	  ○ Dissimilar client mix (-)
	  ○ Dissimilar risk propensity (-)
		- Performance (Post merger ROA)	46 mergers (92 firms) in the banking industry (1984 – 1990)

Sirower (1997)	- Acquisition premium (- always) - Relatedness (+ on the long run) - Cash (+ always) - Contested vs. uncontested (.) - Tender vs. Merger (.) - Relative size (+ on the short run, - on the long run) - Acquisition experience (.) - Diversification strategy (.)	- Stock returns (different time periods)	168 acquisitions

Table 16: Studies looking at success factors of mergers and acquisitions (5)

Author	Success factors	Success measures	Sample

Hayward, & Hambrick (1997)	- CEO hubris
	  o acquiring firm's recent performance
	  o recent media praise for the CEO
	  o CEO's self-importance
	  o Composite measure of the three variables
	- Board inside control
	- Weak board
	- Premium paid
		- Premium paid
		- Acquisition performance (1 y cumulative abnormal security returns)
			106 large acquisitions

Krishnan, Miller, & Judge (1997)	- Complementarity of functional background of top management team (+) - Top management team turnover (-)	- Post acquisition corporate performance	147 acquisitions (1986 – 1988)
Lubatkin, Srinivasan, & Merchant (1997)	- Relatedness of merger	- Total shareholder value (.) - Shareholder value for acquirer (.) - Shareholder value for acquired firm (.)	289 larger mergers (1980 – 1987)

Ramaswamy (1997)	- Dissimilarity of strategic characteristics (-)
	  o Dissimilar market coverage (.)
	  o Dissimilar operational efficiency (-)
	  o Dissimilar emphasis on marketing activity (-)
	  o Dissimilar client mix (-)
	  o Dissimilar risk propensity (-)
		- Performance (Post merger ROA)	46 mergers (92 firms) in the banking industry (1984 – 1990)

Sirower (1997)	- Acquisition premium (- always) - Relatedness (+ on the long run) - Cash (+ always) - Contested vs. uncontested (.) - Tender vs. Merger (.) - Relative size (+ on the short run, - on the long run) - Acquisition experience (.) - Diversification strategy (.)	- Stock returns (different time periods)	168 acquisitions

Table 17: Studies looking at success factors of mergers and acquisitions (6)

Author	Success factors	Success measures	Sample
Scheck, & Kinicki (2000)	· Perceived control (-) · Coping self efficacy (-) · Environmental conditions (+)	· Primary appraisal (+) (negative emotion, Coping strategy)	172 individuals in one firm
Krug, & Hegarty (2001)	· Positive (+) or negative (-) perception of merger announcement · Positive (+) or negative (-) interactions with the acquiring firm's top management team	· Decision to stay of top managers	273 managers

Larsson, & Lubatkin (2001)	· Two dimensions
	  o Autonomy removal
	  o Social control
	· Autonomy removal (high) x Soc. control = (++)
	· Autonomy removal (high) x Social control = (-)
	· Autonomy removal (low) x Social control = (+)
	· Autonomy removal (low) x Social control = (+)
		· Acculturation	50 M&As

Lubatkin, Schulze, Mainkar, & Cotterill (2001)	· Market effects
	  o Changes in market share (+)
	  o Increase in production cost (market) (+)
	  o Change in density (+)
	· Firm effects
	  o Relatedness (+)
		· Product performance	Nestlé/Carnation (73 products) and RJR/Nabisco (93 products)

Finkelstein, & Haleblian (2002)	· Similarity of industry environment of acquirer and targets (+)
	· Second acquisitions vs. first acquisitions (-)
	· Target to target similarity (.)
	· Controls
	  o Relative acquisition size (.)
	  o Stock considerations (Payment with stock) (.)
	  o Acquirer slack (financial resources of acquirer) (.)
	  o Attitude (friendly) (.)
	  o Acquirer performance (-)
		· Acquisition performance
		(Abnormal returns pre and post merger)
			192 large acquisitions by 96 acquirers (1970 – 1990)

Table 18: Studies looking at success factors of mergers and acquisitions (7)

Author	Success factors	Success measures	Sample
Schweiger, & Goulet (2002)	· Depth of cultural learning	· Cooperation (+) · Trust in management (u-shaped) · Perceived cultural understanding (+) · Level of communication (+) · Acceptance of combining cultures (.) · Perceived cultural differences (-)	Field experiment with 3 plants
Puranam, Singh, & Zollo (2003)	· Integration speed (-)	· Post merger product innovation	207 acquisitions by 49 acquirers
Weber, & Camerer (2003)	· Cultural differences (-)	· Group performance	Experiment with 11 sessions and 5 control sessions

Table 19: Studies looking at success factors of mergers and acquisitions (8)

As can be seen the list of researched success factors is long. In order to bring more clarity into this multitude of factors, Berthold (2004) classifies success factors for M&A-transactions according to different attributes of M&A-transactions, comprising;

- age (company, employees)
- industry
- nationality
- merger dynamics
- company goals
- similarity (concerning strategies, dynamic and objectives)
- homogeneity (concerning industry and nationality) and
- Process characteristics.

Being a mere list and not a systematic classification or framework, this summary requires further elaboration to yield analytical clarity and better understanding of success factors.

Möller (1983) suggests an alternative view with focus on contingent factors. He differs between environmental and firm-specific factors. "Environmental factors are on the one hand task and goal-specific, for example customers, suppliers, competitors of the firm and regulatory groups, on the other hand of more general nature, for example legal, political, economical, ecological and cultural conditions constraining the company. [...] The firm-specific factors shall be classified in structural and procedural elements. Structural elements are size of the two firms before the merger and the resulting size proportion, the industries of the two firms and the resulting merger type (horizontal, vertical, concentric, conglomerate), the type of firm control (owner controlled, management controlled), spatial distance between acquired and acquiring firm, organizational structure and the organizational culture of both firms" (Möller 1983: 61ff, own translation). Similar to Möller, Gerpott (1993) suggests a separation of success factors into (1) strategic-structural factors, (2) organizational-cultural factors and integration process and (3) employee-related factors. In the same tradition, Bamberger (1994) identifies a number of contingent factors responsible for the success of an M&A-transaction:

- Economic environment and industry group
- Context of acquiring company
- Context of acquired company
- Design of acquisition process

While Möller (1983) exclusively focuses on contingent factors, Gerpott (1993) and Bamberger (1994) explicitly mentions the design of the acquisition process as a deliberate design variable, considering individuals as relevant actors.

Other authors stress the importance of individual actors in mergers and acquisitions even stronger. For example, Goold, & Campbell (1999) argue that there are four main factors for failure of M&As: the overestimation of synergies, the belief that by enforcing cooperation, synergies will emerge, overestimation of own capabilities to make the integration happen, as well as an overly optimistic approach to generate synergies without considering risks.

Jemison, & Sitkin (1986a) point out that "Despite the diversity of these hypothesized motives, a single basic model – here called the choice perspective – has been fundamental to virtually all acquisition research. But mounting evidence that acquisitions do not reliably yield the desired financial returns suggests that the choice perspective may provide an incomplete view of acquisition processes and outcomes" (Jemison, & Sitkin 1986a: 145). Jemison, & Sitkin (1986a) thus call for an integration of contingency theoretical models of M&A-success as well as models of strategic management respectively decision making.

Summarized, there are numerous different approaches to classify success factors for mergers and acquisitions. A first deficit of the existing classifications, however, is a fuzziness concerning the level of analysis of the classified success factors. For example, Bamberger (1994) combines in his classification environmental factors with characteristics of the M&A-process. Interrelationships between success factors on different levels of analysis thus cannot be accounted for. Besides the neglect of level differences, the listed classifications have in common a rather static view on M&A-success factors. Different success factors, according to these classifications, are equally relevant for the M&A-success. Dynamic interrelationships between success factors, e.g. size of merging firms as well as reactions of employees and the M&A-success are not accounted for.

The importance of the dynamic of M&A-transactions, however has been recognized by other authors. For example, Scheiter (1989) argues that "… central determinants are the approach in the acquisition process, the compatibility of relevant behavioral determinants of the acquisition partners and the approach in the integration process" (Scheiter 1989: I).

Similarly, Larsson, & Finkelstein (1999) argue that by "Taking a broad process perspective, however, we believe it is possible to integrate the combination, integration, employee and performance issues into a comprehensive model that views M&A performance (conceptualized as synergy realization) as a function of combination potential, organizational integration, and employee resistance" (Larsson, & Finkelstein 1999: 3). Larsson, & Finkelstein (1999) thus create a simple model, in which the relationships between the main independent concepts are determined by a process nature of M&A-transactions, and which uses an estimate of synergy realization as the dependent success variable.

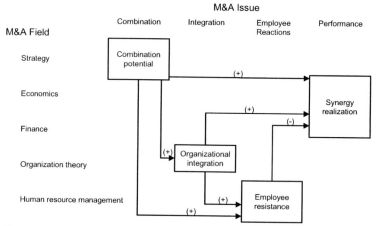

Illustration 8: An integrative Merger and Acquisition Model (in parentheses: empirical evidence of relationships) (Larsson, & Finkelstein 1999: 5)

As can be seen in the illustration above, Larsson, & Finkelstein (1999) integrate foci of different fields of M&A-research as well as different M&A-issues into one model. The interrelationships are determined by the process nature of an M&A-transaction. They find support for this model in a case survey research based on 61 case studies.

While Larsson's and Finkelstein's (1999) model accounts for the process logic of mergers and acquisitions, it is somewhat negligent in differentiating between different levels of analysis. Independent firm level variables are mixed with independent individual level variables to determine their effects on the dependent firm level variable synergy realization. Level problems, however, need to be accounted for carefully for proper theory building (compare Rousseau 1985 on issues of cross-level research).

A somewhat similar model is developed by Gerds (2000). Based on an extended situational logic (Kieser, & Kubicek 1992), Gerds (2000) integrates the integration context, integration objectives, integration layout, integration barriers and integration speed.

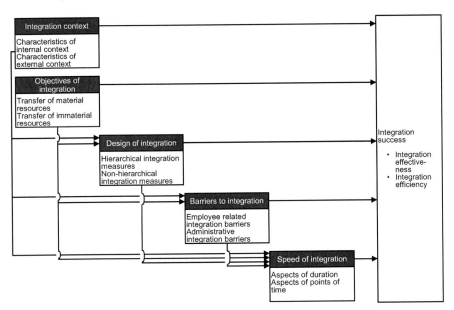

Illustration 9: Success factors for M&A-transactions by Gerds (2000)

Gerds' (2000) model also suggests to integrate concepts from different streams of research and to link them with a process logic. While Larsson, & Finkelstein (1999) follow to a large extent a contingency logic, in which organizational integration, respectively the integration degree represents the only managerial lever, Gerds (2000) adds the speed of integration as an additional choice variable that considers room for maneuver during the integration process. While Larsson, & Finkelstein (1999) use synergy realization as success measures, Gerds (2000) uses estimates of integration effectiveness and integration efficiency as success measures. As did Larsson and Finkelstein (1999), Gerds (2000) does not explicitly consider the cross-level issues arising from the different levels of the variables in his model.

Following Larsson, & Finkelstein (1999) and Gerds (2000), I will develop an integrative framework for success factors of mergers and acquisitions, which is based on a process logic. Using a process logic will allow the consideration of interrelationships of success factors as the M&A-process unfolds.

However, in addition to the process logic, I will differentiate between different levels of success factors. This will allow to consider interrelationships between success factors of different levels as well.

1.5.1. A process-based multi-level framework of M&A-success factors

1.5.1.1. Process character of success factors of mergers and acquisitions

In this work, *process* shall be understood as a series of interdependent events or activities that are structured by a sequential logic. Each event or activity of one phase bears consequences for subsequent events or activities. This influence of outcomes of one phase on subsequent phases is called endogeneity (Shaver 1998). Endogeneity indicates that depending on events, activities or choices in one phase, subsequent activities or choices as well as effects events become constrained. In the case of M&A-transactions, endogeneity causes that the synergy potential as defined in 1.4.4 is fixed in an early phase of the M&A-transaction. The actual synergy effects are generated in a later phase of the M&A-transaction. However, the synergy potential obviously constrains the synergy effects, which later can be generated. Realized synergy effects ultimately determine the M&A-success.

Choosing a process-model for the classification of success factors, it is necessary to define the different phases of the M&A-process. Sommer (1996) describes an ideal acquisition process, which comprises a planning phase, an acquisition phase (search and screening of acquisition targets, ending with the closing) and an integration phase. In a more differentiated model, Krüger (1988) identifies six relevant phases in the course of an M&A-transaction. He sees an initiation, a search, an evaluation, a contact and negotiation, a take-over or merger phase and last but not least a phase of coordinated action. Clearly, the emphasis of this model is on the activities before and during the takeover. The takeover phase is finished by the closing of the deal.

Buono, & Bowditch (1989) distinguish seven distinct phases in the process of an M&A-transaction:

- Precombination
- Combination planning
- Announced combination
- Initial combination process
- Formal physical-legal combination
- Combination aftermath
- Psychological combination.

Contrary to Kröger (1988), Buono and Bowditch (1989) thus focus on post closing activities. While the academic literature takes a more high-level approach to the description of the M&A-process, practitioners such as Lucks, & Meckl (2002) develop very detailed process model in order to help practitioners in each step of the M&A-process. They describe in detail core and support processes of an M&A-transaction. For each process, they describe main and peripheral activities.

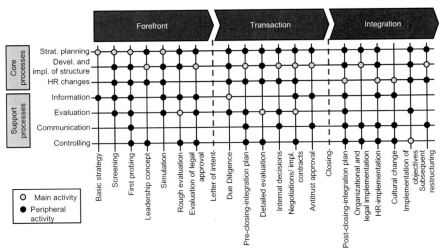

Illustration 10: Activities and partial processes in the M&A-process (Lucks, & Meckl 2002: 59)

In this research, I will use a process model, which represents a compromise between high level process models such as Sommer (1996) and very detailed practitioner process models such as Lucks, & Meckl (2002). Due to endogeneity, each process phase has implications for the subsequent process phases. Especially, the M&A-success, i.e. the realized synergy effects is determined by a number of different outcomes of each phase of the M&A-process. I will consider the following phases:

- Strategy making: Within this phase, the corporate and business strategy of a firm is formulated. The strategic objectives of the firm are defined and fixed. Also, in this phase, the decision to consider exogenous growth in the form of mergers and acquisitions is taken.

- Selection of target: The selection of the target is an iterative process. It comprises a screening of potential targets, a selection of targets, an evaluation of the synergy potential with the most interesting targets, as well as an iterative feedback loop, whether the acquisition target insures the realization of the strategic objectives.

  The selection of the target firm determines the synergy potential of an acquisition, i.e. the maximum possible amount of synergy effects that a conjunction of firms can generate.

- Structural decision: After a potential target is identified, first integration plans need to be made. In most M&A-transactions, at least some structural decisions are taken. For example, the degree of integration, i.e. which parts of the merging firms shall be integrated and how deep this integration shall be, is determined.

The degree of integration determines the share of the synergy potential that can be captured as well as the amount of integration efforts that will be required. The resulting potential for synergy effects will be called targeted synergy potential.

- Negotiation and closing: When the targeted synergy potential has been evaluated, negotiations with the management or the owners of the acquisition target start. Negotiations end with the closing, the signing of the takeover contracts. The results of the negotiations strongly determine the value creation potential of an acquisition. The price usually is higher than the stand-alone value of the acquisition target. The difference between price paid for an acquisition and the stand-alone value is called premium (Sirower 1997).

  The difference between the targeted synergy potential and the premium paid is the value creation potential of an acquisition. Ideally, this value creation potential is positive.

- Preparation of integration: After the closing, the partnering firms get full access to all relevant information necessary for the integration of the firms. While the legal situation in the pre-closing phases strongly restricts access to information, ownership of the acquisition target grants unlimited access to information. In this phase, the organizational detailing of the future organizational structure, the planning of the integration process as well as the preparation of integration measures are fixed.

- Integration implementation: After everything has been defined, the new integrated organizational structure is getting implemented.

  In the course of the implementation, the synergy effects are realized. Note that the gathered synergy effects depend on the synergy potential, the targeted synergy potential as well as on the decisions of the preparation phase, which synergy effects should be gathered with integration measures.

- Consolidation phase: In the consolidation phase, all changes that have been initiated during the implementation phase are solidified. The value creation of the M&A-transaction thus is finalized as the difference of premium paid and the realized synergy effects.

The process, which is formed by these phases will be called M&A-process in the following elaborations of this paper. Illustration 11 shows the different phases of the M&A-process as well as the different stages of endogenous value creation.

Illustration 11: M&A-process and subsequent steps for the realization of the M&A-success

Success factors for M&A-success can be allocated within this process model. Basically, there are two different allocation logics. According to a first logic, success factors are allocated within the phase, when they become effective or even virulent. For example, Buono, & Bowditch (1989) point out "... that cultural differences across the firms contributed to combination-related difficulties" (Buono, & Bowditch 1989: 57). According to this logic, cultural differences as one success factor would be allocated in the integration implementation phase. The second logic aims to allocate success factors according to a contingency logic: A factor might become contingent in an early phase of the M&A-process. That means, the characteristics of the factor are fixed in an early phase. The same factor, however, might become effective for M&A-success only at a later stage of the process. For example, in the moment that an acquisition target is selected, the culture of this acquisition target becomes contingent as well as the cultural differences between the acquirer and the acquiring firm. However, the actual cultural conflicts, as well as processes of acculturation manifest themselves only in a later phase of the M&A-process.

Several authors acknowledge this asynchronization. For example, in the case of organizational culture, authors such as Althauser, & Tonscheidt-Göstl (1999) or Krystek (1992) acknowledge that organizational culture becomes contingent in the moment of deciding upon an acquisition target, while the effects of organizational incompatibilities become salient much later. As a consequence, they suggest to conduct a "cultural due diligence" in selecting an acquisition target (e.g. Althauser, & Tonscheidt-Göstl 1999; Krystek 1992). With the help of a cultural due diligence, information about the culture and thus about potential cultural differences can be gathered in the forefront of an acquisition.

In this work, I choose an allocation of the according to the second logic, i.e. success factors in different phases of the M&A-process according to the point in time, when they become contingent and not when they become effective. There are two reasons for doing so:

1. Activities, decisions and outcomes in later phases of a merger and acquisition process are strongly determined by earlier activities, decisions and outcomes. For example, after a strategy has been decided upon, it represents the boundaries for the search of acquisition targets. If a business strategy aims to integrate vertically, the selection of

acquisition targets is constrained. Similarly, the success factors are constrained. For example, when evaluating potential synergies, there will be different potential synergies for vertical acquisitions than for horizontal acquisitions.

2. M&A-success is the result of a chain of succeeding activities. Each of these activities yields a specific type of success. I distinguish (1) synergy potential, (2) targeted synergy potential (3) value creation potential, (4) synergy effects and (5) the realized value creation. The synergy potential of an M&A-transaction is determined by the selection of an acquisition target. The choice of the integration degree determines the targeted synergy potential. The value of an acquisition target for the acquirer thus corresponds to the sum of the inherent or standalone value of the target and the synergy potential. During the negotiation and closing phase, the acquisition price is fixed. "…the final purchase price of a merger or an acquisition typically reflects both, the inherent value of a target business and its value to the buying or merging firm (i.e., combination value)" (Schweiger, Csiszar, & Napier, 1993: 54). The value potential of the M&A-transaction for the acquiring firm thus corresponds to the sum of inherent value and synergy potential minus the purchase price for the acquisition target. Taking this into consideration, the result of the negotiation and closing phase determines the value creation potential of an M&A-transaction. „The integration process is the key to making acquisitions work. Not until the two firms come together and begin to work toward the acquisition's purpose can value be created" (Haspeslagh, & Jemison 1991: 105). The integration of the two firms, i.e. the result of communication and transition phase thus determines the amount of synergy effects that can be realized and thus the realized value creation for the acquirer.

With the help of a process model, this staged realization of value from synergy potential to value creation potential and then realized value creation can best be described and success factors for each stage of the M&A-success can be defined.

The advantage of this allocation is twofold: On the one hand, it overcomes traditional conflicts between contingency and decision making theories. The argument put forward in this work is that at some point it is possible to influence some of the success factors of M&A-transactions. However, at a later stage, these success factors cannot be influenced anymore as they became contingent for succeeding activities.

The second advantage of this model is a clear disentanglement of M&A-success. So far, models did not capture the different stages of value creation in M&A-transactions. For example, numerous economic investigations have analyzed the effect of strategic objectives of M&A-transactions on M&A-success, e.g. what effect relatedness of merging firms has on the M&A-success. Results were often contradicting. The reason for these mixed findings is that these researchers only considered a small sample of the factors that influence M&A-success. By investigating relatedness, they looked at factors influencing the synergy potential of a transaction. Often, they skip the analysis of the structural decision on the synergy potential, of premiums paid during the negotiation and closing phase nor at the synergy that ultimately leads to value creation and thus to the long term evaluation in stock markets. In such empirical investigations, all the later success factors that influence value creation become in the best case noise or variance, reducing the correlations and their significance between measured constructs. In the worst case, if subsequent factors are interrelated and thus yield systematic effects, which have not been considered, these investigations yield fallacious results.

Summarizing, I will allocate the success factors of mergers and acquisition in the respective phase of the M&A-process, during which they become contingent. I will also describe the value creation implications these factors have in each phase of the M&A-process.

1.5.1.2. Levels of analysis of success factors

A second logic for the allocation of success factors is a Macro-Micro-logic. Macro-micro transitions are an important problem in social sciences. Coleman points out that "It is still another [thing] to construct models of the macro-to-micro and micro-to-macro processes. Quite clearly, some form of interdependence must be modeled [... if] the phenomena to be explained involve interdependence of individuals' actions, not merely aggregated individual behavior" (Coleman 1990: 22). Mealiea, & Lee (1979) point out that especially in contingency theoretical frameworks, the linkages between environment, system (size, technology, structure) and subsystems (functions, employees) need to be clearly defined in order to describe a system with a coherent logic. Similarly, Van de Ven (1976) points out that "A thorough assessment of complex organizations requires a theory and methods that cuts across macro (overall organization) and micro (work unit or department) levels of analysis. it is not obtained by either focusing upon aggregate structural characteristics of organizations as many researchers have done" (Van de Ven 1976: 65). Based on these considerations, Van de Ven (1976) concludes that "What is needed are theories and research which (a) identify and distinguish the relevant properties of macro and micro organization context, structure and process, (b) measure and compare the unique structural patterns of departments that are differentiated vertically and horizontally within the complex organization, and (c) examine how these differentiated components are linked together as a macro-organizational network" (Van de Ven 1976: 66).

Previous models of M&A-success factors did not address this level problem. Rather, they integrated environmental, firm-level and individual level variables within one model without discussing the macro-micro logic and the level problems that result from such models.

In the research model of this study, I will consider the level of the success factor under consideration. I will distinguish success factors on the environmental level of the firm. Environmental success factors, for example, are the general economic climate (e.g. Agrawal et al. 1992), the maturity of an industry (e.g. Bower 2001) or institutional contingencies (e.g. Kuranel 2005) of a firm. Furthermore, I will look at firm-level success factors, such as the strategic objective, choice of the target, structural decision, cultural differences as well as the quality of the activities in the selection and negotiation phases. I will look at group level variables such as social mechanisms after an M&A-transaction. Finally, I will look at individual level variables, which comprise different types of employee characteristics and reactions.

In the following illustration, the main elements of the framework can be seen. The numbers in the different fields indicate the chapters that each field will be dealt with in this work. If there is no number assigned to a field, the literature review did not reveal evidence of existing research covering success factors in this field. The arrows indicate that each of the success factors directly or indirectly affect M&A-success.

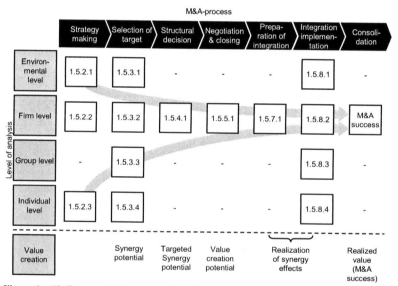

Illustration 12: Framework for a process-based macro-micro-macro model of M&A-success factors

It should be noted at this point that the M&A-process in this framework is an ideal-type process. „Although some consider it highly rational, the acquisition process is not neatly analytical and segmented" (Haspeslagh, & Jemison 1991: 41). There might be iterations and recursions, breaks and restarts during a real M&A-process. However, this does not change the logic of succeeding phases nor does it change the allocation of success factors within different phases of this process and on different epistemological levels.

The following sections of the first chapter of this work, I will use to fill the framework illustrated above. I will discuss each of the phases of the process. In each phase, I will allocate success factors for M&A-success, which I identify in an extensive literature review. I will show how these success factors interrelate and ultimately influence M&A-success.

At the end of the section, I will summarize the model and identify important gaps in the existing body of research. These gaps will be used to formulate the research questions for the remaining parts of this work.

1.5.2. Strategy making

Structure follows strategy. Strategy researchers such as Chandler (1962), Ansoff (1965), and Porter (1980, 1985) emphasize the importance of a strategy for actions within the firm. Although Mintzberg (1979) shatters the strategy paradigm with his concept of emerging strategy by pointing out that strategy never becomes implemented the way it is supposed to be, there is no real debate about the value of firms having a strategy.

There are two major schools of thought that describe the content of a strategy and the sources of competitive advantage. First, there is the positioning school (Porter 1980, 1985), which is grounded in industrial organization, and which proposes that competitive advantage is based on a favourable position within an industry. A strategy thus consists of the market position of a firm. Second, there is the resource based view (Barney 1987, 1991; Peteraf 1993), which proposes that superior resources lead to competitive advantages. According to the resource based view, firms should develop a strategy that achieves and secures resource superiority in order to achieve sustainable competitive advantage.

A strategy of a firm thus consists of two elements:
- Market strategy: A first element of a strategy is the market position that a company aims for. For example, Porter's Five Forces (Porter 1980, 1985) represent a framework to analyze the environment of the firm as a basis for the definition of the positioning of the firm.
- Organizational capabilities: A second element of a strategy concerns the capabilities of the firm (e.g. Wernerfelt 1984; Barney 1987, 1991; Dierickx, & Cool 1991). Capabilities concern the current strengths of the firm as well as necessary capabilities to succeed in the future.

In the course of the strategy development, different factors become relevant. First, the environment of the firm represents contingent boundaries for the firm (Meyer, & Rowan,

1977; DiMaggio, & Powell, 1983). Second, the current organizational setup is to some extent contingent. Proponents of the resource based view such as Wernerfelt (1984), Barney (1991), and Peteraf (1994) discuss the firm as a bundle of resources, which are the source of the competitiveness of a firm and starting point for strategic consideration. Others, such as Dierickx, & Cool (1989) emphasize the role of capabilities. Capabilities are grown abilities of the firm or a specific combination of resources of the firm. These capabilities are the real source of competitive advantage as they are non-tradeable, and very difficult to imitate. While resources at least in principal can be acquired in markets, the notion of capabilities emphasizes that they are non-tradable and require significant periods of time to build up. Hence the firm's current capabilities represent yet another set of contingencies for the firm.

Therefore, environmental factors as well as firm capabilities represent success factors in the strategy making phase. Based on these contingencies, a firm can define its strategic objectives.

In the following paragraphs, I will summarize research that investigates, which environmental factors, which firm characteristics and which strategic objectives facilitate, respectively hinder M&A-success, and which characteristics constrain further activities and decisions in the M&A-process.

1.5.2.1. Success factors on the environmental level

M&A-researchers have identified two different success factors for M&A-transactions in past research, which come into play in the strategy making phase. The first is the global economic situation at the time of the M&A-transaction. The second is the specific industry within which a firm is operating.

1.5.2.1.1. Global economic situation

Investigating the effects of the global economic situation on M&A-success, Bamberger (1994) finds in a research on 78 acquisitions that "In those years with growth rates of the real gross social product exceeding the median, there is a higher percentage of acquisitions with above average success" (Bamberger 1994: 193, own translation). In a more recent study, The Boston Consulting Group (BCG) finds the opposite in their 2003 study on M&A-transactions. In their study on 277 M&A-transactions in the U.S. from 1985 to 2000, BCG shows that the cumulative relative total shareholder return (RTSR) of mergers and acquisitions in weak economies on the average is 14.5% higher than the RTSR in strong economies. The RTSR considers the total industry specific shareholder return and subtracts them from the firm shareholder returns to calculate the relative total shareholder return.

A more detailed analysis helps to explain the differences in results: Both studies split years of weak and strong economies according to the median growth rate of the investigated time period. However, while Bamberger (1994) measures success with the help of key informants of acquirers that evaluate the success of an acquisition with the help of a Five-Point-Scale, which is a subjective measure. BCG (2003) considers the RTSR, which is an objective measure of M&A-success. Bamberger's data might suffer from a respondent bias. The bias could result from a misattribution of company success. In economic downturns, companies in general are less successful and vice versa. It is well possible that respondents misattributed company success to internal decisions, i.e. the acquisition, instead of environmental factors, i.e. the economic situation. There is no respondent bias in the results of the BCG study, because the measures are based on stock market data. Also, Bamberger (1994) only uses a firm-level success measure and does not control for industry effects or economic effects. BCG, however, uses the RTSR, which compares the performance of an acquiring firm with a relevant stock market index, thus controlling for market effects. In addition to the use of a subjective success measure, Bamberger (1994) does not use any additional independent control variables for his analysis, whereas BCG considers the premium paid in acquisitions as control variable. Due to the number of methodological weaknesses, the explanatory power of Bamberger's findings is limited.

A study by Agrawal et al. (1992) investigates 937 mergers and 227 tender offers over a time period from 1955 to 1987. They did not find differences in M&A-success measured as five year stock performance depending on the point in time at which the merger was conducted. Assuming that the economic climate differed within this period, the findings of Agrawal et al.indicate that economic climate has no effect on M&A-success.

Summarized, the findings on the effects of economic climate on M&A-success are mixed. Obviously, further research is required to clarify the findings.

1.5.2.1.2. Industry specific factors

In order to identify industry specific success factors, Sommer (1996) suggests the use of Porter's Five Forces Model (Porter 1980, 1985). Bower (2001) points out, how industry situations can constrain mergers and acquisitions. Bower differs between two types of industry situations affecting mergers and acquisitions. If there is overcapacity within an industry, horizontal mergers and acquisitions can help to reduce this overcapacity and thereby increase profitability. Bower (2001) points out that in order to be successful in an overcapacity related M&A-transaction, it is important to decide quickly, to avoid mergers of equals in order to avoid power struggles of the management, and to pay attention to similarity of organizational structures to succeed. The second type are mergers that follow industry convergence. In order to succeed in this situation, companies need to identify specific opportunities and focus on those solely. Other activities should remain separated.

Chatterjee (1991) investigates the effect of the concentration of the industry of the acquiring firm on the performance of acquisitions. In a study on 116 vertical mergers, she cannot find significant relationships between the concentration of the industry of the acquiring firm and the standardized cumulative abnormal returns.

In a study in 69 firms, Lubatkin, Schweiger, & Weber (1999) find that industry has no impact on the turnover of top managers. Low top management turnover has been shown in other studies as being important for the merger success (e.g. Krishnan, Miller, & Judge 1997). Bamberger (1994) finds similar results. He finds that looking at the industry of the acquirer, there is no significant effect on the success rate of mergers and acquisitions.

1.5.2.2. Success factors on the firm level

Two different types of firm level success factors have been investigated in prior research: One type consists of characteristics of the firm that might have an impact on M&A-success. The second type consists of the strategic objectives of a firm. These are constrained by environmental and firm specific factors. The strategic objectives for mergers and acquisitions mainly determine the direction of a merger as described earlier in 1.3.

1.5.2.2.1. Characteristics of the firm

Looking at characteristics of the acquirer that matter for M&A-success independently of the acquisition target, previous studies cover a number of different success factors. In the following paragraphs, I review a number of studies, which investigated the characteristics of the acquirer. I will look at the effects of size of the acquirer, the financial situation of the acquirer, the M&A-experience of the acquirer, the pre-merger performance of the acquirer, the decision making structure of the acquirer, and multiculturalism of the acquirer on M&A-success.

According to Gerds (2000), the size of the acquirer is an important success factor for M&A-transactions. He finds that the larger the acquirer, the better the integration effectiveness and integration efficiency. He argues that management slack and financial slack of larger firms explain the size advantages of acquiring firms.

Bamberger's (1994) research, however, generates opposite findings. He finds that acquisitions by smaller firms have a higher success rate than larger firms. He argues that the reason could be "... that larger companies often have acquisition departments, which derive their right of existence from the number of realized transactions, and which therefore are less selective in choosing promising projects than small firms are, who only go for attractive offers" (Bamberger 1994: 231; own translation).

Hence there is no clear evidence of the effects of the size of the acquirer on M&A-success. Different studies yield conflicting evidence.

Haleblian, & Finkelstein (1999) find that the pre-merger performance of acquiring firms increases the stock market returns for the acquirer. In a later study, Finkelstein, & Haleblian (2002) find by analyzing 192 large acquisitions by 96 acquirers between 1970 and 1990 that acquirer slack, i.e. the financial resources of acquirers have no effect on abnormal stock market returns.

Hitt et al. (2001), however, find in an in-depth-analysis of 24 acquisitions that financial slack increases merger success. Already in 1998, Hitt, Harrison, Ireland, & Best (1998) find that low debt position of the acquirer increase M&A-success measured as stock market returns. Bühner (1990a) finds in his study on German acquisitions, that a large amount of free cash flow leads to better M&A-performance than small amounts. At the same time, Haunschild, Moreland, & Murrell (1994) find that pre-merger performance of experimental groups (i.e. firms) show lower enthusiasm and higher ingroup-outgroup bias after having been merged with other groups (i.e. firms). This indicates that pre-merger performance of a firm can affect the motivation and willingness of employees to integrate in later phases.

Summarized, studies on the effects of pre-merger success on M&A-success yield mixed findings. Again, it is not clear, whether pre-merger success yields a positive or a negative effect on M&A-performance.

Another characteristic of the firm that has been investigated concerning its effect on M&A success is M&A-experience. While Haleblian, & Finkelstein (1999) argue that there is a U-shaped relationship between acquisition experience and merger success, Bühner find that there is a positive relationship between acquisition experience and stock market returns (1990c) respectively with accounting measures (1990d). Bamberger (1994), however, finds no significant correlation between acquisition success and acquisition experience.

Other researchers focus on organizational characteristics. Haspeslagh, & Jemison (1991) find that the decision making structure of strategic planning influences the ability to successfully merge companies. „We concluded that the nature of business planning and the way a corporate function is organized and manages the acquisition decision-making process can substantially affect the quality of acquisition justifications, the ability to handle multiple types of acquisitions, and the ability to learn from them" (Haspeslagh, & Jemison 1991: 101). Hence learning capabilities and planning processes are positively related to M&A-success.

As one element of the culture of the acquirer, Chatterjee, Lubatkin, Schweiger, & Weber (1992) find that the buying firm's tolerance for multiculturalism increases stock market performance. They argue that tolerance for multiculturalism enables employees of different cultural contexts to cooperate better and thus increase the M&A-performance. Similarly, Hayward, & Hambrick (1997) find that multiculturalism, i.e. the tolerance of the employees of the acquirer for cultural differences increases the success of acquisitions.

1.5.2.2.2. Strategic objectives

Strategic decisions usually should be based on an analysis of the external environment (e.g. Porter 1980, 1985) and the internal resources (e.g. Barney 1991) of the firm. Based on these analyses, firms can decide where to try their luck. According to Ansoff's strategy matrix (1957, 1965), the different strategic options for growth of a firm are consolidation or penetration of current markets, product or market extension as well as diversification in new products and new markets. An additional option for firms is to grow vertically by either growing upstream into the industry of their suppliers or by growing downstream into the industry of their customers (e.g. Pfeffer, & Salancik 1978; Williamson 1975).

Horizontal mergers
Horizontal mergers are mergers within the same markets and within the same industry. Horizontal mergers, according to Ansoff's logic serve to further penetrate current markets of the acquirer.

The findings on the performance of horizontal mergers are mixed. Kitching (1967) finds that horizontal mergers have the lowest failure rate of all merger types. In a later study, Möller (1983) finds that horizontal mergers and acquisitions are more successful than the average of mergers and acquisitions. Similarly, Bamberger (1994) finds that 70% of the horizontal acquisitions in his sample are successful, which is the highest success rate of all merger types. Lubatkin (1987), however, finds that horizontal and market-concentric mergers have no significant post-merger stock market effect for the acquirer. Even more negative about horizontal mergers is Bühner (1990c, d) who finds in two studies that horizontal mergers have a negative effect on abnormal stock market returns as well as on accounting measures.

Hence there is no clear evidence for success of horizontal mergers. Obviously, other, moderating variables are necessary to explain the seemingly contradicting evidence.

Vertical mergers
Vertical mergers are mergers that extend the product range of an acquirer either into the industries of their suppliers or in the industries of the customers.

Möller (1983) finds that vertical mergers are more successful than the average of mergers and acquisitions. Bühner (1990d,e) finds that vertical mergers have a positive effect on accounting based performance measures compared to average mergers and acquisitions.

Lubatkin (1987), however, finds that vertical mergers have no significant post-merger stock market effect for the acquiring firm.

In a study on 63 PMIs, Gerds (2000) finds that vertical integration yields negative integration efficiency. Integration efficiency thereby describes the input-output relation of activities in the integration process.

Chatterjee (1991) points out that vertical acquisitions are most beneficial for acquiring companies, if the acquirer comes from a concentrated market and the acquisition target is in a fragmented market.

Research on vertical mergers does not yield clear evidence of success or failure. Again, it seems that additional variables need to be considered to explain the mixed findings.

Product extension

Product extension mergers are mergers that add new products to the existing product portfolio of a firm.

Bühner (1990c, d) finds that horizontal mergers with product extension have a positive effect on stock market performance measures compared to other merger types. He argues that such careful diversification has most value creation potential, whereas horizontal integration without product extension signals industry consolidation, which often leads to price wars and thereby to rent erosion (Bühner 1990c: 306).

Lubatkin (1987) finds that product-concentric mergers have no significant post-merger stock market effect. And Kitching (1967) even finds that technology concentric mergers, which are operationalized similarly to product-concentric mergers, show increased failure rates compared to the average failure rate of mergers.

The empirical results show mixed findings on the success of product extension mergers. Again, additional variables are required to explain the failure or success of product extension mergers.

Market extension

There are not many studies that explicitly look at market extension. Rather, many studies operationalize horizontal mergers in a way that most market extension mergers would fall into that category. One study that explicitly investigates the success of marketing concentric mergers has been conducted by Kitching (1967). Kitching (1967) finds that marketing concentric mergers show increased failure rates compared to the average failure rate.

Diversification

Diversification according to Ansoff (1965) means that a firm extends its activities into new products and new markets. The potentially positive benefits from diversification are mainly financial synergies, such as coinsurance effects, risk diversification or tax effects (for details see 1.3).

Bamberger (1994) finds that conglomerate have the lowest performance of all M&A-types: Only 38% of the conglomerate mergers in his sample were successful. Bühner (1990c, d) also finds that conglomerate mergers have a negative effect on stock market as well as on accounting based performance measures. Compared to other merger types, conglomerate mergers are least successful (Bühner 1990c: 306). Similarly, Hitt, Harrison, Ireland, & Best (1998) find that diversification has a negative effect in acquisition success.

Kitching (1967) finds that diversification mergers do not show any significant increases in failure rates. Lubatkin (1987) also finds that conglomerate mergers have no significant post-merger stock market effect. However, Lubatkin (1987) finds that the acquired firms in these mergers experience significant pre-merger stock market gains.

Looking at other factors, affected by diversification, Gerpott (1994) finds no significant effect of diversification on retention of top management of the acquired firm after an M&A-transaction.

There is no clear evidence on success or failure of diversification of firms with the help of merger and acquisitions. Again, additional variables seem necessary to explain the mixed findings.

Relatedness

Some authors do not especially differ between market, product or vertical extension as three possible dimensions to extent the business of a firm. Rather, they build an aggregate measure of relatedness or similarity of firms and investigate its effect on merger success and other variables that indirectly influence merger success.

Cannella, & Hambrick (1993) investigate 96 acquisitions. They have two independent raters rate mergers according to customer and product similarities. According to similarity, mergers and acquisitions are categorized unrelated or related. Cannella, & Hambrick (1993) find no significant effect of relatedness on performance of the merged firm. While their method bears the risk of rater bias, Agrawal et al. (1992) find similar results in their study on the effect of conglomerate vs. non-conglomerate mergers on M&A-performance. Agrawal et al. (1992) operationalize non-conglomerate mergers according to American Standardized Industrial Classification (SIC) codes. Merging firms that have the same 4-digit SIC code are classified as non-conglomerate. Otherwise, they are considered conglomerate. Agrawal et al. (1992) find no significant effect of conglomerate vs. non conglomerate mergers on five year stock performance.

Similarly, Lubatkin et al. (1997) investigate relatedness measured by shared and different SIC codes of firms. They find no significant advantage of related mergers versus unrelated mergers based on different stock market performance measures.

While these researchers tried to identify the effect of relatedness on merger success, Gerpott (1994) investigates the effect of market similarity on retention of top manager in the aquired firm. Gerpott (1994) finds no significant effect of market similarity on retention of top management of the acquired firm after an M&A-transaction.

Other researchers, however, find that there is a positive effect of relatedness on merger performance. Haleblian, & Finkelstein (1999) find that relatedness of acquirer and the acquisition target yields positive effects on the stock market returns of the acquirer. Haleblian, & Finkelstein (1999) classify firms as related, if they share at least one 4-digit SIC code. Finkelstein, & Haleblian (2002) confirm these results in a second study on 192 large acquisitions. In another study, Sirower (1997) also finds that relatedness of mergers yields positive effects on stock market performance on the long run.

Looking at product performance, Lubatkin, Schulze, Mainkar, & Cotterill (2001) find that performance of products in merged companies is higher, if the products are related, i.e. when they are in the same product group as standardized by the SAMI –database.

Relatedness yields positive effects or no significant effects on merger performance. However, while the findings are not contradicting, they still show a mixed picture. Again, additional variables seem necessary to explain the success or failure of related mergers and acquisitions.

Summary

While it is not possible to evaluate, whether they met their strategic objective (i.e. product or market extension), the reviewed literature yields findings for the effects of different strategic objectives on the M&A-success.

Relatedness has been shown to either yield no significant effect or to have a positive effect on M&A-success.

The results on horizontal mergers are mixed. Although there are studies with positive results, there are others that indicate negative results. When looking at the sample size as an indicator of validity of the results, Lubatkin's (1987) study that has the by far largest sample with 439 acquiring firms. He finds no significant effects. Thus it is possible to assume that the other results show no clear tendency and that there is no correlation between horizontal mergers and merger success.

Summarizing the result of product extension mergers or product concentric mergers, again the findings are somewhat mixed. While some researchers find positive effects, others find non-significant or even negative effects.

Similarly, the findings on vertical mergers and acquisitions are mixed. Only Gerds (2000) finds that integration efficiency in vertical mergers is lower than in other mergers. This, however, might best be explained with the fact that vertical mergers are more difficult to integrate because there are only few similarities between the activities, markets and products. At the same time, vertical mergers have been found to either show insignificant or positive results.

While it is difficult to summarize the findings on market extension mergers, diversification shows rather clear results. As can be seen, studies either reveal negative or insignificant effects of conglomerate mergers on M&A-success. Hence it can be assumed that conglomerate mergers on the average rather show negative M&A-performance.

The different merger objectives all show mixed findings. According to the process logic of M&A-transactions, such mixed findings can be explained with the help of variables that become salient in later stages of the M&A-process. Obviously, knowing the merger objective is not sufficient to determine success or failure of M&A-transactions. There are other factors that later on in the process determine the success or failure of M&A-performance independent from the strategic objective of a merger.

1.5.2.3. Success factors on the individual level

Bühner (1990a) finds that acquirers that are managed by their owners show worse M&A-performance than companies, in which the management has ownership in the firm.

Hayward, & Hambrick (1997) investigate the hubris hypothesis of Roll (1986) and find that firms whose CEOs suffer from hubris show worse performance than firms with CEO without hubris. The effect is increased, if the board is weak.

Obviously, there is only a small number of studies, which investigate the role of individual level variables of the acquiring firm in the very early phases of the M&A-process. As will be shown later, most studies on individual level variables consider reactions of employees rather than contingent characteristics.

1.5.3. Selection of target

As the contingent factors of a firm, i.e. its environment and its firm characteristics, have been clarified and incorporated in the firm's strategy, the constraints for the choice of an acquisition target are set. Choosing an acquisition target determines a number of factors that influence the M&A-success and other aspects of an M&A-transaction.

It is important to note that according to the allocation logic chosen for putting together the research framework of this work, some of the characteristics of the selected target are not known at the point in time of the selection decision. Despite such lack of knowledge, these characteristics of the acquisition target become contingent with the selection of a target. For example, the acquisition target has a culture, which might not yet be known at the time of its selection. Only in rare cases, firms perform cultural due diligences (Krystek 1992). The main structural decisions are taken before closing the deal (Lucks, & Meckl 2002). In later stages of the M&A-process, it might turn out that the cultures between acquirer and acquisition target differ to some extent. The structural decisions form the basis for contact points or cooperation needs within the new structure. Cooperation between culturally different employees eventually leads to cultural conflict, which then must be resolved with the help of specific measures.

It is arguable whether these factors should be allocated in the strategy making phase or in the target selection phase of this research model. However, while the strategy details roughly the direction of an M&A-transaction, a specific M&A-target has numerous facets that cannot be captured with a strategy upfront. Studies on acquisition premiums indicate that the market for corporate control is a seller market (e.g., Sirower 1997). Because of this, chances are rather low that an acquisition target fully meets the ideal needs of a strategy.

In the following paragraphs, I will summarize a number of success factors that become contingent with the selection of a target. On the environmental level, there are a number of industry related factors such as concentration of the industry of the acquisition target that have been identified to be relevant. On the firm level, relative size as well as combination potential based on a detailed organizational analysis are important success factors. Also, culture of the acquisition target affects later M&A-success. On the group level, negative effects of group cohesion on M&A-performance are shown.

1.5.3.1. Success factors for selection of targets on the environmental level

While industrial organization (IO) economists have intensively investigated the effects of mergers and acquisitions on industry structure (e.g. Porter 1980, 1985; Bain 1959), there is only little research published in the management literature, which focuses on firm performance.

One example is Chatterjee (1991) who investigates the effects of concentration of the industry of the acquisition target on the M&A-performance. Chatterjee (1991) uses an industrial organization theoretical argument by evaluating how vertical integrations create value for acquiring and acquired firms. Based on IO-theoretical predictions, Chatterjee (1991) argues that acquirers from highly concentrated industries that acquire target firms from industries with lower concentration should pay lower premiums than acquirers from industries with low concentration buying firms in highly concentrated industries. Chatterjee (1991) confirms her hypotheses and finds that firms who vertically integrate gain most, if the industry of the acquisition target is fragmented. It should be noted that Chatterjee (1991) only considered the short term announcement effect measuring merger performance as cumulative abnormal returns until five days after the announcement.

In a study on product performance after mergers and acquisitions, Lubatkin et al. (2001) argue similarly based on a IO-theoretical basis. They find that changes in the market share in horizontal acquisitions have a positive effect on product performance. They also find that increased density in the market is beneficial for product performance. Both findings are based on the argument of increased market power, which leads to increased performance effects.

1.5.3.2. Success factors for selection of targets on the firm level

In the following paragraphs, I will investigate characteristics of the acquired firm on the firm level that have been found to influence M&A-success. A first characteristic that researchers found to be relevant is the relative size of an acquisition target. A second characteristic is the combination potential of the acquisition target. The combination potential determines the synergy potential of an acquisition target. Then I will discuss implications of the culture of the acquired firm and of cultural differences between acquirer and acquisition target. Furthermore, I will discuss effects of the industry, maturity and other firm specific characteristics of the acquisition target on the M&A-success.

1.5.3.2.1. Relative size of an acquisition target

Relative size of an acquisition target as a success factor has been researched in numerous studies. Sirower finds that "There is no consistent effect of the relative size of the acquisition on performance." (Sirower 1997: 82) On the short run, Sirower finds positive effects of larger relative size, on the long run, smaller relative size has a positive effect on merger success. On the other hand, Agrawal et al. (1992) could not find any evidence for size related performance effects. Finkelstein, & Haleblian (2002) argue that there might be a size effect, leading to larger acquirer gains if the target is relatively large. However, they cannot confirm that hypothesis. Similarly, Chatterjee, Lubatkin, Schweiger, & Weber (1992) find in a sample of 52 firms no significant effect of size on firm performance.

Kitching (1967), however, finds that relative size of the acquisition target improves the M&A-success. Kitching (1967) argues that the integration of merging firms requires changes on different levels of the firm. If the acquisition target is small, all structures of the acquirer are imposed on the target and the change requirements are very assymetrical. "The danger is that such action [organization structure changes] will create confusion at the subsidiary level and a lack of knowledge at the parent company level – two factors which help to explain the failures of these acquisitions" (Kitching 1967: 92). If the target is relatively larger, a more symmetrical change of acquirer and target is likely. Such assimilation of structures instead of an imposition of structures can help to consider business necessities business necessities of the acquired firm better and reduce the need for change in the acquisition target.

Möller (1983) also finds that acquisitions of large targets are more successful than acquisitions of small targets. He points out that one of the reasons for this finding could be that strategic preparation is a success factor for integrations, and that companies prepare more carefully the integration of large acquisition targets. Similarly, Bühner (1990d) also finds that large acquisitions (acquisition of firms whose nominal capital is larger than 4,6% of the nominal capital of the acquirer) are significantly more successful than small acquisitions. Bühner (1990d) argues that it could be the case that top management pays more attention to large acquisitions and therefore make sure that they succeed.

Shelton (1988) investigates 218 mergers and finds that increased relative size yields higher value creation for acquirers. Bamberger (1994) also finds that the probability of success is higher for acquisitions of large acquisition targets.

Larsson, & Finkelstein (1999) explain similar findings by arguing that with increased size of the firm, the combination potential of the two firms and thus the potential for synergies increases.

It is important to note that these results might underlie sample effects. Kusewitt (1985) finds that very small as well as very large acquisitions yield negative performance effects. He argues that acquisitions that are too small are not worth the effort, while larger acquisitions may be the case of "... biting off more than you can chew" (Kusewitt 1985: 162)

Other researchers rather look at effects of size differences on the reactions of employees in the merging firms. Cartwright, & Cooper (1993) find in a case study that employees of the smaller one of two firms that merged experience significantly higher stress than employees of the larger firm. They argue that potential sources of stress include loss of identity, job security, changes in personnel and work practices. In a merger situation, identity loss as well as changes in work practices are often more significant for the smaller merger partner.

Gerpott (1994) finds that the relative size of the acquisition target yields positive effects on management retention in the acquisition target. He argues that there are two possible explanations for this finding: First, if the acquisition target is significantly smaller than the acquirer, the acquirer is likely to have enough management reserve capacities to manage the acquired firm as well. For larger acquisition targets, such capacity is missing. Second, relatively larger acquisitions require more intense planning. Such planning requires continuous input from the top management team of the acquisition target. Therefore, the acquirer will create incentives to keep the top management team in order to secure them as information base.

Lubatkin, Schweiger, & Weber (1999) also investigate the effect of firm size on turnover of top managers in the acquired company. Lubatkin et al. (1999) argue that "... the executive may feel relatively unimportant, even insignificant in the new power structure." Therefore, they assume that smaller relative size of the acquired firm should lead to increased turnover of top managers of the acquired firm. However, their findings do not confirm this hypothesis.

Rentsch, & Schneider (1991) simulate in a scenario experiment the effects of size of merging firms on postcombination expectations of employees. They argue that "Because larger firms tend to dominate smaller organizations, employees in the larger organization are likely to have more positive and more realistic expectations if they expect to be dominant over the smaller organization following a combination. In contrast, members of the smaller organization combining with a larger organization who have realistic expectations are likely to develop less positive expectations for postcombination life; they will expect to be dominated" (Rentsch, & Schneider 1991: 236).

Summarizing, relative size of the acquisition target seems to be an important success factor: Studies in the financial success of M&A-transactions show higher success rates and higher and higher average performance for relatively larger acquisitions. Larger acquisitions receive more top management attention, are better planned, are more likely to undergo careful integrations and yield less detrimental effects on employees than relatively smaller acquisitions. There might be a negative performance for very large and for very small acquisitions, which does not show in all studies due to sample effects.

Obviously, size of merging firms have a significant effect on the reactions of employees in the implementation phase. If the relative size of the target is larger, the reactions of employees of the acquired firm are more positive.

1.5.3.2.2. Relatedness and combination potential

On the first view, the concept of relatedness resembles strategic merger objectives, i.e. horizontal, product extension, market extension conglomerate or vertical merger. However, it is on the second view that the differences become more obvious. While strategic objectives of a merger have a clear market perspective, the research investigating the relatedness of firms focuses on the resources of merging firms. Studies on relatedness of merging firms "…show that valuable insights can be gained by broadening the conceptualization and operational definition of relatedness by stepping beyond the bounds of mere product-market considerations" (Ramaswamy 1997: 699). More specific, Harrison, et al. (1991) argue that "A focus on specific resources rather than strategy types in the merger and acquisition research may better explain firm performance" (Harrison, Hitt, Hoskisson, & Ireland 1991: 173).

Barney (1986, 1988) points out that the combination of dissimilar resources in acquisitions can create more value than similar resources. He argues that "If any of these organizational attributes are unique and, when combined with a target, generate a more valuable cash flow than any other bidders can obtain when combined with a target, then the shareholders of these firms will obtain abnormal returns from acquisitions" (Barney 1988: 76).

Based on this assumption, Harrison, Hitt, Hoskisson, & Ireland (1991) investigate the rival hypothesis whether similarity or dissimilarity of resources of a firm create value. Based on a resource based perspective they "... assert that the possibility of uniquely valuable synergy is more likely to occur under dissimilar resource allocations rather than similar resource allocation patterns" (Hitt et al. 1991: 177). By analyzing a sample of roughly 1.100 acquisitions, they find that differences in capital intensity, in administrative intensity, in interest intensity as well as in R&D intensity increase the post merger ROA. In a later study, Hitt, Harisson, Ireland, & Best (1998) confirm these findings and show that complementary resources increase the acquisition success.

Ramaswamy (1997), however, finds the opposite. Ramaswamy (1997) investigates strategic similarities between acquirer and acquisition target. Strategic similarity exists, " ... if two firms exhibit very similar resource allocation pattern as measured across a variety of strategically relevant characteristics, they can be considered to be strategically similar" (Ramaswamy 1997: 699). Ramaswamy (1997) argues that each company has a dominant logic, which represents the manner of utilization of resources, and which co-evolved with the resources within a firm. If two firms with dissimilar resource allocation patterns merge, the dominant logic of one firm will be applied to the resources of the other firm. This leads to the risk of mismatch of dominant logic and resources and thus to inferior merger success. Ramaswamy (1997) finds support for his hypothesis: While dissimilar market coverage has no effect on merger performance, dissimilar operational efficiency, dissimilar emphasis on marketing activity, dissimilar client mix, as well as dissimilar risk propensity each reduce the post merger ROA.

An examination of Pablo (1994) identifies the source of the seemingly contradicting evidence of Harrison et al. (1991) and Ramaswamy (1997). She investigates strategic and organizational needs of acquisition targets. "... strategic task needs are defined by the degree to which the realization of intended synergies depends on the sharing or exchange of critical skills and resources", whereas "... the degree to which acquisition synergies depend on the preservation of a unique context-specific set of organizational capabilities defines organizational task needs" (Pablo 1994: 808). She finds that the integration degree depends on these two variables. High strategic task needs lead to high integration, whereas high organizational needs lead to little degree of integration. Hence the factors similarity and dissimilarity of factors cannot be seen independently of a specific context.

Larsson, & Finkelstein (1999) reconcile the seemingly contradicting effects of similarity and dissimilarity by further specifying what aspects of similarity and what aspects of dissimilarity might be beneficial and integrate them into a new concept name "combination potential". They "... conceptualize the combination potential of M&As in terms of both the strategic similarity and the strategic complementarity of operations of the joining firms" (Larsson, & Finkelstein 1999: 6). Larsson, & Finkelstein (1999) investigate in a case survey study the effect of combination potential on synergy realization. They argue that "The various sources of synergy define a combination's potential, which in turn is expected to affect the extent to which synergies will be realized in an acquisition" (Larsson, & Finkelstein 1999: 5). They define combination potential with a synergy based logic, according to which "… synergies can be achieved through both "economies of sameness" (from accumulating similar operations) and "economies of fitness" (from combining different, but complementary, operations)" (Larsson, & Finkelstein 1999: 6). They find that combination potential increases the degree of synergy realization.

The combination potential thus explains when acquisitions can create value. It is important to note that the assumed effects are based on a synergy logic. As described in 1.3 synergies can be based on different mechanisms: The combination potential of firms creates positive effects based on internal synergy mechanism. Strategic objectives of mergers and acquisitions, however, create positive effects based on external synergy mechanism.

The sum of the external synergy potential and the internal synergy potential together represent the synergy potential of an M&A-transaction.

1.5.3.2.3. Cultural differences

In the moment of selecting an acquisition target, an acquirer not only selects market synergies and resource complementarities but also the culture of the acquired firm. At this point in time, the culture of the selected firm has no effect on the firm performance. However, the potential cultural differences are fixed at the moment if the selection of a target. These potential cultural differences might lead to cultural conflicts, complex acculturation processes and integration problems in later stages of the M&A-process.

Cultural differences have been identified by numerous researchers as an important factor for M&A-success. Basically, there are two different streams of research: One stream of research investigates the effects of cultural differences in cross-national mergers (e.g. Weber & Shenker 1996; Very, & Schweiger 2001; Schweiger, Csiszar, & Napier 1993). The other stream of research investigates the effects of differences in organizational cultures in mergers and acquisitions (for a review see Stahl, & Voigt 2004). In this work, I will focus on organizational culture solely and not investigate the effects of national cultures any further.

Organizational culture has become one of the most prominent fields of research in organizational behavior. It was mainly a contribution of Pettigrew's famous 1979 article "On studying organizational cultures" that founded a new field of research. Ever since, organizational culture has gained importance in explaining behaviors of firms, respectively of employees within firms. As early as 1985, Duch (1985) already mentions the importance of organizational culture for firms. He argues that one of the key functions of culture is the affiliation it provides for employees. However, in a merger situation, this affiliation function might be lost. Other researchers, such as Cartwright, & Cooper (1993b) point out that "In particular, at the macro level, the issue of culture compatibility is frequently cited to be a potential source of human merger problems, and so ultimately of merger failure" (Cartwright, & Cooper 1993b: 330). Similarly, other researchers such as Hambrick, & Cannella (1993), Chatterjee et al. (1992), Weber, & Schweiger (1992), Nahavandi, & Malekzedah (1988), and Jemison, & Sitkin (1986) argue that organizational culture, and especially cultural differences play an important role in explaining M&A-success.

Despite its importance, Tetenbaum (1999) states that "One HR issue that plays a central role in the success or the failure of a merger is culture, an aspect that is vastly underrated in most mergers" (Tetenbaum 1999: 26). But not only practitioners seem to consider the topic relatively little. Berthold (2004) points out that while there seems to be general agreement that organizational cultures play an important role in explaining M&A-success, there are only few empirical studies on the subject.

Concepts of organizational culture

Organizational culture has been defined in many different ways. A classic definition is offered by Schein (1990):

> "Culture can now be defined as (a) a pattern of basic assumptions, (b) invented, discovered, or developed by a given group, (c) as it learns to cope with its problems of external adaptation and internal integration, (d) that has worked well enough to be considered valid and, therefore, (e) is to be taught to new members as the (f) correct way to perceive, think, and feel in relation to those problems" (Schein 1990: 111).

Schein (1990) points out that cultures consist of observable artifacts, values as well as basic underlying assumptions.

More detailed, Buono, & Bowditch (1989) define that "Objective culture refers to the artefacts and material products of a society. Subjective culture by contrast, is a group's 'characteristic way of perceiving the man-made environment', the rules and the group's norms, roles and values" (Buono, & Bowditch 1989: 136). An important element of culture is the way it is being transferred. Buono, & Bowditch (1989) point out that culture is rather learned than genetic or biological. They argue that culture is shared by people rather than idiosyncratic. Culture, according to them, therefore has a "... transgenerational and cumulative in that it is passed from one generation to the next. Finally, it is symbolic in nature and patterned (that is, organized and integrated) in our lives" (Buono, & Bowditch 1989: 136). Buono, & Bowditch (1989) summarize under organizational culture the organizational values, leadership styles, organizational heroes (i.e. role models), organizational myths and stories, organizational taboos, rites and rituals, as well as cultural symbols, which are part of the objective culture of an organization.

Other authors define culture similarly. For example, Althauser, & Tonscheidt-Göstl (1999) define organizational culture as „... the sum of shared beliefs, values and behavior patterns, which underlie the things that an organization values, supports and expects. It is visible in interactions, in procedures, in corporate identity, in leadership styles and communication behaviors" (Althauser, & Tonscheidt-Göstl 1999: 40, own translation). Similarly, Tetenbaum points out that "Culture refers to the norms, values, and beliefs the members of an organization maintain about the purpose of work and how they are expected to go about doing their work (Tetenbaum 1999: 26).

Krystek (1992) points out that there are different levels of cultures, which are relevant for an organizational culture. First there is private culture, which corresponds to the sum of cultural standards of an individual. Then there is the industry culture as a sum of industry wide standards. And then there is the societal culture, which is the sum of standards of a society, especially its political and economical system. Hence organizational culture is influenced and shares elements with all these different cultures. Krystek (1992) argues, that there are even different cultures within an organization. He argues that there might be different cultures in different parts of an organization or even in different departments. Similarly, Buono, & Bowditch (1989) argue that in most large companies, there is more than one unified organizational culture.

In this study, culture is defined as set of attitudes, beliefs, behaviours as well as artefacts, which are shared by a specific set of individuals. An effect of culture is an increased efficiency of interaction of individuals of a culture and a decreased efficiency of interaction of individuals of different cultures. Interaction is based on shared interaction symbols of verbal and nonverbal kind. Only if individuals share the same interaction symbolic, misunderstandings in interactions can be avoided. However, if there are cultural differences in interaction symbols, there is a risk of dysfunctional results even for simple interactions. Interactions between members of different cultures therefore have to be framed more carefully to avoid misunderstandings caused by a lack of shared symbols. Strong cultural differences can turn interactions quickly inefficient due to the ongoing efforts of framing interactions adequately. Coordination requirements might make integration of employees of different cultures more costly than beneficial.

There is an ongoing discussion in the academic literature, whether culture "is" or whether culture "is manageable". "One perspective, which is reflected in the popular literature, views culture as a managerial tool to create "strong" organizations. In contrast, a quite different orientation, characteristic of a growing body of empirical work, sees culture as something that is, an existential reality that can serve as a constraint to large-scale organizational change" (Buono, & Bowditch 1989: 17). Cartwright, & Cooper (1993a) point out that there might be some types of cultures that are easier to change than others. They argue that cultures that impose a high degree of individual constraint, such as power or role cultures, are less resistant to change than those which foster autonomy, such as task or person/support cultures" (Cartwright, & Cooper 1993a: 40)

Empirical findings

In an early study, Möller (1983) investigates leadership styles as one aspect of organizational culture. He finds that similarities in leadership styles increase the organizational success of M&A-transactions. However, in the same study Möller (1983) does not find significant effects of cultural differences on M&A-results.

Shrivastava (1986) investigates a number of case studies in order to identify main challenges in the post merger integration phase. He finds that "sociocultural integration" depends on cultural differences. Cultural differences, however, lead to dysfunctional merger outcomes.

Buono, & Bowditch (1989) analyze a series of case studies. They find that "... culture conflicts and clashes are often a significant determinant of merger- and acquisition related difficulties" (Buono, & Bowditch 1989: 162). They argue that cultural differences can lead to "... significant barriers and problems for the merged entity and its management" (Buono, & Bowditch 1989: 163).

Datta (1991) investigates at the example of 173 acquisitions in the U.S. manufacturing industry how differences in management styles, differences in reward and evaluation systems, and the moderation effect of the integration degree affect acquisition performance measured with accounting based measures. He argues that significant differences in management styles between merging firms can create cultural ambiguity, which leads to uncertainty about the dominating management style and thereby to increased anxiety, distrust as well as conflict on the level of employees. He further argues that "With reward and evaluation systems representing an important vehicle in reinforcing organizational culture, changes made to the existing system (or the imposition of a new system) after an acquisition are likely to elicit strong reactions" (Datta 1991: 285). He finds that while differences in management styles yield negative performance effects, differences in reward and evaluation systems show no effect on M&A-performance. His findings also cannot confirm a moderating effect of the degree of integration on the effects of cultural differences.

Chatterjee et al. (1992) investigate to what extent the perceptions of cultural differences of top management teams affect the stock market performance of mergers. Investigating 52 acquisitions, Chatterjee et al. (1992) find that perceptions of cultural differences between the merging firms indicated by the CEOs of the acquired firms are correlated with negative stock market performance. Chatterjee et al. (1992) also find that perceived tolerance of multiculturalism among the top management firm moderates the effect of cultural differences.

Bamberger (1994) finds in a study on 87 acquisitions that there is a significant relationship between cultural differences and M&A-success. He finds that "The results indicate a negative relationship between cultural differences and success rate. This means that the percentage of successful acquisitions is 50% if there are above average cultural differences. Little cultural differences, however, yield a success rate of over 70%" (Bamberger 1994: 271, own translation).

Weber (1996) investigates in 73 acquisitions the perceived cultural differences between top management teams. Unlike Chatterjee et al. (1992), Weber (1996) finds that perception of cultural differences between top management teams does not affect financial performance of the M&A-transaction. However, Weber (1996) finds that cultural differences significantly affect the effectiveness of the integration process. He explains these findings by the fact that "Merging firms cut costs and achieve synergy by integrating similar departments and functions, such as marketing, inventory, and so forth, especially in firms that share similar markets and products" (Weber 1996: 1185). Such integration bears the potential for conflict, if the members of merged firms have different organizational cultures.

In a second study, Weber, & Camerer (2003) investigate with an experimental research design the effects of culture after a merger. They find that cultural differences lead to reduced performance after the integration of experimental teams. "Overall, our results show that merged groups do considerably worse on average than the two separate premerger groups were doing immediately before the merger" (Weber, & Camerer 2003: 410). Weber, & Camerer (2003) argue that because of particular communication as well as interaction patterns of separate teams, the integration initially leads to misunderstandings and thus reduces the performance in the experimental task. They find it interesting that "In addition [to lowered performance], we also find evidence of conflict and mistaken blame arising from the differences in culture, pointing to a possible source for the high turnover rate following real mergers" (Weber, & Camerer 2003: 412). They find with the help of a questionnaire that members of the "acquired firm" blame those of the "acquirer firm" and vice versa.

It is important to note that all empirical studies show a negative effect of cultural differences on merger performance, and that this negative effect is explained with integration respectively cooperation problems between employees. At the same time, cooperation between employees has not been investigated empirically in these studies. Rather, it has been mentioned in the discussions as an important moderating variable.

1.5.3.2.4. Other factors on firm level

Researchers identified a number of other characteristics of a potential acquisition target that might affect the M&A-performance.

For example, Scheiter (1989) argues that the integration of an economically healthy company poses less integration problems than a company that has serious economic problems. Scheiter (1989) argues that doing two tasks at a time risks overstretching the flexibility of a firm and thereby might endanger the M&A-success.

Haspeslagh, & Jemison (1991) find "… research suggests that, at a more fundamental level, the significant differences among firms have more to do with the stage of the acquired business's development in both a market and an organizational sense than they do with pure size" (Haspeslagh, & Jemison 1991: 151). Similarly, Scheiter (1989) argues that "Young companies tend to be easier to integrate than 'midlife'-companies that are more advanced in their organizational life cycle" (Scheiter 1989: II; own translation)

In a scenario experiment, Rentsch, & Schneider (1991) investigate the role of the motive of the acquired firm. They test in a scenario analysis how the two motives 'growth' and 'survival' influence postcombination expectations. "These motives for combining affect how the employees from the two combining organizations will likely interact with each other, and what opportunities they can expect to have after the combination" (Rentsch, & Schneider 1991: 236). They find that survival results in more negative postcombination expectations than growth as a merger motive. Acquisition motives thus might yield effects on later cooperation of employees in integrated parts of the merged firm. Negative postcombination expectation hamper interaction between employees and vice versa.

1.5.3.3. Success factors for selection of targets on the group level

In an experiment with 46 groups, Haunschild, & Murrell (1994) investigate the effects of group cohesion on enthusiasm and on ingroup-outgroup bias. They hypothesize that based on social identity theory, group cohesion should reduce enthusiasm for an integration as well as increase the ingroup-outgroup bias. Both hypotheses are not supported by their experiment.

Krishnan, Miller, & Judge (1997) investigate how complementarity, i.e. differences in functional backgrounds affects the performance of M&As as well as management team turnover after a merger. They find that complementarity yields positive performance effects. They argue that "An acquisition represents a difficult and uncertain situation to the members of both firms. Having diverse functional skills among the top management during these situations enhances the search for information, makes the organization more innovative and provides the momentum for change" (Krishnan et al. 1997: 364). At the same time, they find that complementarity reduces top management turnover. They argue that the reason for this finding is that if there are complementary skillsets, the acquiring firm may be interested in retaining them because they cannot afford to loose the experience and the specific talents. Krishnan et al. (1997) also find that the lower the turnover of top management teams, the higher the performance of the acquiring firm.

Obviously, complementarity of skillsets of managers improves the integration of management teams. Complementarity thus might be a driver for improved cooperation of management teams.

1.5.3.4. Success factors for selection of targets on the individual level

Most studies on success factors of mergers and acquisitions on the individual level focus on general psychological reactions, such as uncertainty, stress, or motivation. However, psychological reactions only occur in later phases of the M&A-process. They are reactions to decisions, events and success factors that have been determined and fixed in earlier phases of an M&A-transaction. Only few studies have ever looked at characteristics of employees that have an effect on the merger performance, and that become contingent in the target selection phase similar to size of the acquisition target or culture of the acquisition target.

Berthold (2004) is one of the few authors who investigate characteristics of employees on the M&A-success. He finds that the average age of employees in a merger or an acquisition has a significant positive effect on the achievement of external goals.

Clearly, individual characteristics of employees should affect reactions after M&A-transactions. However, the literature review did not reveal other significant work on the effects of characteristics of employees, such as education, gender or other characteristics on M&A-success. There clearly is a deficit in understanding the effects of the characteristics of individuals in merging firms on M&A-success. While the importance of cultural characteristics of firms on M&A-success has been widely recognized, there seemingly is no understanding yet for the role of demographic characteristics of employees in merging firms on M&A-success.

1.5.4. Structural decision

After an acquisition target has been selected, the acquiring firm needs to decide, what to do with it. This question is closely linked to the future organizational structure of acquiring and acquired firm. Structural decisions determine what the structure of the merged company might look like. "Frequently cited dimensions of structure are its configuration, the balance between differentiation and structural integration, and the basis of structural authority" (Greenwood, Hinings, & Brown 1994: 241). Lucks, & Meckl (2002) point out that in most M&A-transactions, the main aspects of structural integration are fixed before closing.

M&A-researchers have investigated mainly one aspect of the structural decision in M&A-transactions: The degree of integration of the merging firms. In the following paragraphs, I will summarize existing research on the degree of integration, its dependencies on success factors that become contingent in earlier phases of the M&A-process and its effects on M&A-success and other relevant factors in the M&A-process.

1.5.4.1. Success factors on the firm level for the structural decision

As described above, the selection of an acquisition target constrains the synergy potential of an M&A-transaction. The combination potential of the acquisition target as well as the strategic objectives of the acquisition determine, what synergy effects can be expected and where they might be expected. The generation of synergies always implies that firms at least to some extent join forces, coordinate their activities and exchange knowledge (see 1.4.3.1). This requires an integration of their activities. "When two previously sovereign organizations come together under a common corporate umbrella, the result is a hybrid organization in which value creation depends on the management of interdependencies through the facilitation of firm interactions and the development of mechanisms promoting stability" (Pablo 1994: 805). The structural decision determines what elements of the merging firms shall be integrated, what the degree of integration is. Researchers identified a number of criteria, which can be used to choose the right integration.

There are different elements of firms that can be integrated. Pablo (1994) names functional activity arrangements, organizational structures as well as systems, and cultures as elements of firms that can be combined. Similarly, Sommer (1996) points out that "The integration of acquisition partners can be separated in three different fields: Integration of strategy, integration of structures and integration of culture" (Sommer 1996: 153, own translation). This means that integration is not limited to material objects. Rather material as well as immaterial objects such as strategies and cultures can both be combined in the course of an integration of firms.

Scheiter (1989) points out that integration in mergers and acquisitions is goal oriented as "… the fusion of systems, structures, resources and cultures of two firms serves an economic purpose" (Scheiter 1989: 7, own translation)

The degree of integration describes to what extent firms are being integrated. Haspeslagh, & Jemison (1991) differ between three levels of integration: absorption, preservation and symbiosis.

- „Absorption acquisitions are those in which the strategic task requires a high degree of interdependence to create the value expected but has a low need for organizational autonomy to achieve that interdependence. Integration in this case implies a full consolidation, over time, of the operations, organization, and culture of both organizations" (Haspeslagh, & Jemison 1991: 147).

- „In preservation acquisitions there is a high need for autonomy and a low need for interdependence among the combining firms. In such situations the primary task of management is to keep the source of the acquired benefits intact, because deterioration in the acquired (and sometimes acquiring) company's ways of managing, practices, or even motivation would endanger success" (Haspeslagh, & Jemison 1991: 148).
- „The third type of acquisition integration approach presents the most complex managerial challenges. Symbiotic acquisitions involve high needs for both strategic interdependence (because substantial capability transfer must take place) and organizational autonomy (because the acquired capabilities need to be preserved in an organizational context that is different from the acquirer's)" (Haspeslagh, & Jemison 1991: 149).

Similarly, Scheiter (1989) earlier describes three levels of integration as autonomy, partial fusion and full fusion. Buono, & Bowditch (1989) define the level of desired integration as the degree to which the PMI leads to total autonomy or to total absorption of the partnering firms. They differ between financial (low), strategic (moderate) and operational (high) integration of partnering firms.

Pablo (1994) uses a definition of level of integration that is based on the implied post-acquisition changes in the technical, administrative and cultural configuration of an organization that are linked to the integration of firms. According to her, "A low level of integration is conceptualized as one in which technical and administrative changes are limited to the sharing of financial risk and resources and the standardization of basic management systems and processes to facilitate communication. A moderate level of integration includes increased alterations in the value chain as physical and knowledge-based resources are shared or exchanged. Administrative changes at this level may include required selective modifications in reporting relationships and delegation of authority, with such structural changes necessitating reframing cultural bases of decision making. The highest level of integration is conceptualized as being quite inclusive, involving the extensive sharing of all types of resources (financial, physical, and human), generalized adoption of the acquiring organization's operating, control, and planning systems and procedures, and complete structural and cultural absorption of the acquired firm" (Pablo 1994: 807).

There are a number of criteria for deciding about the level of integration. Haspeslagh, & Jemison (1991) point out that the choice of the integration degree is a tradeoff between two dimensions. "The first dimension relates to the nature of the interdependence that needs to established between the firms to make possible the type of strategic capability transfer that is expected. The other dimension is associated with the need to preserve intact the acquired strategic capabilities after the acquisition" (Haspeslagh, & Jemison 1991: 139). Haspeslagh,

& Jemison (1991) suggest that based on the two central dimensions, a four field matrix can be created, which shows the appropriate level of integration.

Similarly, Pablo (1994) points out that strategic task needs, i.e. "... the successful sharing or exchange of the critical skills and resources that form the foundation for value creation" (Pablo 1994: 808) and organizational task needs, i.e. the preservation of any unique characteristics of an acquired firm that are a source of key strategic capabilities, indicate different levels of integration. While high strategic task needs result in a high degree of integration, high levels of organizational task needs result in a low degree of integration.

Empirical findings

The effects of different levels of integration on the M&A-performance have been investigated in several studies. Larsson, & Finkelstein (1999) investigate in a case survey study on 61 cases, how the degree of integration affects the realization of synergies. They argue that "Both the quantity and quality of organizational integration between joining firms should have a positive effect on synergy realization because little, or poorly-executed, interaction and coordination are unlikely to produce substantial joint benefits" (Larsson, & Finkelstein 1999: 6). They find that a higher degree of organizational integration leads to increased synergy realization. They also find that an increased combination potential increases the degree of organizational integration.

In an earlier study, Möller (1983) investigates the effect of organizational integration on merger success. He operationalizes the degree of integration with the help of four different levels of integration: (1) fully integrated, (2) some functions have been centralized, (3) joint planning, budgeting and controlling system, (4) not integrated. Möller (1983) finds that with higher degree of integration, mergers and acquisitions are more successful. At the same time, Möller (1983) finds that the degree of integration does not influence the degree to which expected synergy effects are reached. This indicates an interaction effect of synergy potential and integration degree. Expected synergies depend on the potential for synergies, and the realization of synergies depends on the integration degree of firms and the synergy potential of an acquisition.

Pablo (1994) investigates the performance effects of strategic needs and the level of integration chosen. She argues that high strategic task needs should lead to a high degree of integration in order to be able to capture the assumed synergy effects. Likewise, high organizational task needs should lead to a low degree of integration in order to preserve the stand-alone value of the acquisition target. Pablo (1994) finds that strategic task needs as well as organizational task needs strongly influence the level of integration chosen. The higher the strategic task needs, the higher the level of integration. The higher the organizational task needs, i. e. the need of the partnering companies to maintain their original core competencies to succeed in their business, the lower the degree of integration. It is interesting to note that

Pablo (1994) also showed that the level of integration is lower if acquiring CEOs support multiculturalism.

Zaheer, Castaner, & Souder (2005) investigate, how the realization of M&A-effects based on three different underlying sources of synergy: business similarity, product complementarity and geographic complementarity is affected by the degree of integration. Their definition of sources of synergy is based on Ansoff's (1965) classic growth vector matrix, which defines three elements of relatedness: (1) business relatedness, which refers to similarities in customers, distribution channels, products as well as technology and operations; (2) product complementarity, which refers to products, product portfolio and technology portfolio; (3) and regional complementarity, which refers to geographic scope and distribution channels. Zaheer et al. (2005) find that the degree of integration moderates the effect of the different dimensions of relatedness on M&A-performance. Especially in the case of business similarity and product complementarity, a high degree of integration is positive for the M&A-performance.

Puranam et al. (2003) find that there may be no such thing as the right degree of integration in order to realize synergies. In their research on 207 acquisitions of technology-based entrepreneurial firms by established firms, they find that there is an inherent conflict in integrating technology oriented acquisition targets. Low levels of integration lead to fast commercialization of products, because running processes are not disturbed. High levels of integration, however, lead to higher number of follow-ups. On the one hand, "Post-acquisition integration involves the alignment of incentives and the creation of communication channels by breaking down the internal boundaries between target and acquirer. Eventually, the objective is to create a shared culture between them, so that the target and acquirer are truly a single organization" (Puranam et al. 2003: 180). This, however, is time and cost intense and may lead to delays in product development in the acquired firms. On the other hand, a high level of integration allows full combination of the acquired firm's know-how with the know-how of the acquirer and thus should lead to long-term benefits. "Combining the arguments for the costs and benefits of integration, we can see why there is a trade-off between short-term (time-to market) and long-term (subsequent product pipeline development) performance" (Puranam et al. 2003: 181).

Hence the decision about the degree of integration of an acquisition target and the acquirer is a trade-off, whose cost and benefits need to be considered carefully in order to achieve M&A-success. „For resource sharing to create value, the benefits of sharing must outweigh these hidden costs of compromise" (Haspeslagh, & Jemison 1991: 108). This implies that the integration should focus on those elements of the merging firms that generate the highest synergies. All other elements of the firms should remain separated. This tradeoff makes a symbiotic degree of integration as defined by Haspeslagh, & Jemison (1991) likely.

The structural decision thus determines the synergy potential that is targeted in the integration of merging firms. As illustrated in 1.3, synergy effects are based on cooperation between employees of the merged firms. While the structural decision determines the targeted synergy potential, it is the subsequent cooperation within the integrated elements of the firms, which determine the generated synergy effects. A high degree of integration requires a high degree of actual cooperation and vice versa.

Clearly, the degree of integration determines the cooperation of employees within the merged firm. If there is no integration, it is most likely that employees do not cooperate. Synergy realization through structural integration only works if employees reflect the integration in their cooperation relationships.

1.5.5. Negotiation and closing

In the negotiation and closing phase, an acquirer makes an offer to buy the acquisition target that has been selected in the selection phase. Based on the results of the selection phase, the acquirer will offer a certain amount of money for the acquisition target and engage in the process of negotiation. The deal is closed, when the takeover agreement is signed.

Naturally, as the negotiation and closing are activities on the firm level, prior research focused on firm level success factors of this phase.

1.5.5.1. Firm level success factors

Researchers found a number of different factors on the negotiation and closing phase to be relevant on the success of the M&A-transaction. A first factor, which has been identified in prior research, is attitude of the takeover. The attitude of a takeover indicates, whether a takeover is friendly or hostile. A second factor is the presence of multiple bidders in the negotiation phase. A third factor is the payment either with cash or with stock. Last but not least, a fourth factor that has been investigated is the effect of premiums, of overpayment, on the M&A-success.

1.5.5.1.1. Attitude

The attitude of an acquisition indicates, whether the acquirer is well received by the acquisition target or not. Usually, attitude is defined on the top management level. In friendly transactions, top management teams of acquisition targets cooperate and suggest their stockholders or owners to comply with the offer of the acquiring firm. An unfriendly transaction, however, means that the top management actively defends the independence of a firm. They can do so by using "poison pills" (Lee, & Pawlukiewicz 2000), which increases premiums paid in acquisitions, or which lowers the attractiveness of the acquisition target. A very prominent example for poison pills is the acquisition of Mannesmann by Vodafone. Only shortly before the takeover, Mannesmann acquired Orange, another mobile phone provider at a very high premium. Due to anti-trust laws, it was clear that Vodafone would have to sell large parts of Orange after the acquisition of Mannesmann, which decreased Mannesmann's attractiveness. However, ultimately, it did not prevent the transaction. But the price paid for Mannesmann and the incurred loss due to the sale of Orange negatively affected the performance of the acquisition.

In concurrence with that, Hitt et al. (1998) find in a multiple case study on 24 acquisitions that friendliness has a positive effect on acquisition success. Similarly, Haleblian, & Finkelstein (1999) find in 449 acquisitions that attitude (friendly, neutral, or hostile) has a significant effect on the subsequent stock market returns of the acquiring firm. They find that friendly takeovers are more successful than unfriendly takeovers. However, in a 2002 study, Finkelstein, & Haleblian (2002) cannot confirm these results. Friendliness in this study has no significant effect on abnormal returns of the acquirer.

Hambrick, & Hayward (1997) investigate the effect friendliness on the acquisition premium paid in 106 acquisitions. However, they do not find significant effects of the attitude on the height of the acquisition premium paid.

Agrawal et al. (1992) investigate the effect of tender offers vs. mergers on stock performance after mergers. Tender offer is a public offer of the acquiring firm to the stockholders of the acquisition target. Usually, a tender offer indicates that the top management teams of the acquirer and the acquisition target do not negotiate directly and thus behave rather unfriendly. A merger indicates that the top management teams negotiated directly and the top management team of the acquisition target recommends the offer of the acquirer to the owners of the acquisition target. Agrawal et al. (1992) cannot find a significant effect of tender offer vs. merger. Similarly, Sirower (1997) finds that "Executing an acquisition through a tender offer versus a "friendly" merger has no independent effect in performance, nor is there a difference in the premium paid." (Sirower 1997: 82)

Friendliness of an M&A-transaction seems to be rather positive for the M&A-success. However, a number of studies show insignificant effects, indicating that attitude of a merger is not enough explain the M&A-performance. Rather, friendliness of a takeover seems to affect other variables in later stages of the M&A-process. For example, ingroup-outgroup reactions might depend on friendliness of a merger. Unfriendly M&A-transactions early might lead to a "we against them" attitude that later on translates into cooperation barriers. Again, success factors in early phases of the M&A-process seem insufficient to fully explain M&A-performance in later stages of the M&A-process.

1.5.5.1.2.   Single bidder vs. multiple bidder

In economic and finance research, the winner's curse is used to describe the phenomenon that in auction type situations, the winner is the one who is willing to pay most and thereby to get least out of an acquisition. The winner's curse even leads to overpayment and thus to negative performance effects.

In the market for corporate control, it therefore might make a difference whether an acquisition is contested or not. Sing, & Montgomery (1987) investigate in a sample of 105 acquisitions whether single bids vs. multiple bids have an independent effect on acquisition performance. They find that single bid acquisitions show higher abnormal dollar value changes in stock market value than multiple bid acquisitions.

This finding is confirmed by the study of Sirower (1997). "The presence of multiple bidders has a negative impact on performance, but this effect is independent of the negative effect of the premium." (Sirower 1997: 81)

1.5.5.1.3.   Payment method – Cash vs. Stock

Myers, & Maljuf (1984) argue that financing acquisitions with stock is equivalent to issuing stock. However, issuing stock suffers from an adverse selection process, because the aquirer would only pay with stock if he knew the stock was overvalued. This, however, should yield a strong signaling effect on the markets, which leads to worsening stock performance.

Haleblian, & Finkelstein (1999) investigate the independent effect of the share of payment in shares. However, they find no significant relationship between stock market returns and the payment method. Similarly, Hayward, & Hambrick (1997) find no effect of payment method on the stock market performance.

Sirower (1997), however, finds that "The use of cash for acquisitions results in better performance than the use of equity (stock)" (Sirower 1997: 81).

Payment method yields no clear effect on the M&A-performance. Seemingly, other factors need to be investigated to clarify the effect of payment method on performance.

1.5.5.1.4.   Premium paid

The premium in an M&A-transaction often is defined as overpayment over market value or stand-alone value of an acquisition target (Sirower 1998; Hayward, & Hambrick 1997).

In his book "The synergy trap", Sirower investigates in detail the effect of premiums paid on the performance of acquirers. Sirower (1997) argues that the payment of a large premium in most cases exceeds the synergy effects. Especially, he assumes that the payment of acquisition premiums implies "required performance improvements" by integration, which are difficult to achieve in today's hypercompetitive markets. In addition to that, time plays an important role: Due to the discount of future cash flows, depending on the cost of capital of a firm, it becomes increasingly difficult to regain the premium paid, if the expected synergy effects accrue further in the future. Sirower (1997) finds that "The level of the acquisition premium has a strong negative effect on performance across all twenty-eight measures of shareholder performance; the higher the premium, the larger the losses" (Sirower 1997: 81).

Hayward, & Hambrick (1997) investigate in 106 acquisitions the effect of CEO hubris on M&A-success. According to Roll's (1986) hubris argument, they expect that CEOs suffering from hubris pay higher premiums and higher premiums lead to worse M&A-performance. They find that CEO hubris increases premiums paid, and also that premiums paid significantly reduce the 1-year abnormal stock market returns.

Bamberger (1994) finds in a study on 87 acquisitions that self-indicated price sensitivity of the management in choosing the acquisition target leads to highest success rates. He argues that price sensitivity reduces the chance for overpayment and thus increases success rates.

The premium paid thus is a crucial element in constraining the value creation of an M&A-transaction. Illustration 13 shows how the different phases of the M&A-process determine the value creation potential, and how the Negotiation and closing phase have an important impact on the value creation potential.

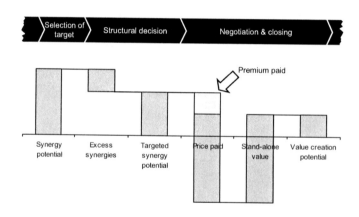

Illustration 13: Value creation potential after Negotiation & closing phase

In the selection phase, the synergy potential is fixed by the selection of the acquisition target. The structural decision then follows a trade-off between positive and negative effects of integration and thus determines the part of the synergy potential that shall be tapped by integrating the firms. Of course, the targeted synergy potential is equal or smaller than the synergy potential. In the negotiation and closing phase, the premium is decided upon. The value creation potential of an acquisition is fixed after the premium is paid. It corresponds to the difference of the sum of synergies and stand-alone value of an acquisition (assuming that the post acquisition stand-alone value does not suffer), and the premium paid. The value creation potential indicates the maximum possible value creation that can be achieved in an M&A-transaction. The realized value of an M&A-transaction is equal or smaller than this amount.

1.5.6. Planning and information gathering

While there are success factors in distinct phases of the M&A-process, the quality of planning and information gathering is an overarching issue that concerns all phases of the M&A-process. Especially in the stages that lead to a decision, most of the value creation potential of an acquisition becomes fixed within a relatively short period of time (Lucks, & Meckl 2002) and often on the basis of incomplete information. Therefore, the quality of planning and information gathering is an important determinant for all activities in the pre-merger phases.

„Despite managers' best intentions, however, acquisitions often do not live up to their hopes. Our research found that a major reason for these disappointments and failures lies in a series of problems that occur naturally during the acquisition decision-making process. These problems include fragmented decision making, escalating momentum, multiple motives, and ambiguous expectations" (Haspeslagh, & Jemison 1991: 77 ff).

The main danger of poor selection and poor evaluation is overpayment. As has been discussed above, the value creation potential of an acquisition target becomes fixed with the closing of a deal. If the premium paid for the acquisition target exceeds the tapped synergy potential, there is no post merger integration phase that can possibly win the deal. Therefore, Kode et al. (2003) argue that "Many acquisitions fail to create shareholder value for the buyer, not because of poor valuation techniques but through either a failure to evaluate synergies at all or through payment of excessive premiums relative to the potential synergies that could be realised from the merger." (Kode et al. 2003: 27) Therefore, Kode et al. (2003) conclude that "Without a proper analysis of synergies and a method to evaluate them, management will be hard pressed to deliver on their value creation mandate" (Kode et al. 2003: 27ff).

However, planning deficits in early stages of the M&A-process not only affect the outcome of the pre-merger phase. They also affect the outcomes of later phases. Scheiter (1989) argues that a strategically based takeover increases the probability of a successful integration. The basis for success thereby are concrete ideas of the acquirer about the value creation potential and the possibilities to realize it. Scheiter (1989) suggests that "A comprehensive evaluation of the behavioral determinants of the acquisition target, especially the management team, of the organizational cultures, the hierarchical structures as well as the product-market-dimension increases the probability for a successful integration" (Scheiter 1989: II).

Similarly, Koegeler (1991) argues that the development of a concrete integration concept before closing increases the probability of a successful integration.

Lucks, & Meckl (2002) point out that most of the structural decisions and most elements of the integration plan needs to be completed before closing, in order to really be able to evaluate positive and negative M&A-effects properly. Similarly, Goold, & Campbell (1999) argue that by considering realistically not only the potential but also the risks of integration, managers could avoid hunting every possible synergy effect and instead focus on preserving current successes and carefully developing future successes.

Empirical findings

Haspeslagh, & Jemison (1991) find in a multiple case study on 20 firms that the decision making process in the pre-merger phase underlies forces that are detrimental to merger success. "These forces included an overly deterministic view of the acquisition's purpose, destruction of value for the very people expected to create value for the shareholders, and a leadership vacuum" (Haspeslagh, & Jemison 1991: 135).

In an earlier study, Möller (1983) finds that the existence of a strategy increases significantly the generation of synergies in the production function. He also finds that with increasing time spent on the evaluation of the target, the success of an M&A-transaction increases.

Despite the importance of cultural and HR-issues in selecting the acquisition target, Hubbard (1999) finds that only a third of all due diligences considers HR-topics, and less than 10% of all acquirers conduct a serious HR-due diligence. This, according to Hubbard (1999) leads to significant information deficits in selecting an acquisition target and to later integration problems.

Greenwood, Hinings, & Brown (1994) investigate, whether there is a bias in selection and evaluation of an acquisition target. They assume that the top management team of an acquiring firm "… during the planning or 'courtship' stage of a merger attention focuses upon achieving a 'strategic fit' to the neglect of 'organizational fit'" (Greenwood, Hinings, & Brown 1994: 240). However, Greenwood, Hinings, & Brown (1994) find no support for the hypothesis that firms focus mainly on strategic fit and little on organizational fit during the courtship phase of the M&A-process.

Hitt, et al. (1998) investigate in a multiple case study on 24 acquisitions the independent effect of adequacy of target evaluation on the acquisition success. They find that inadequate target evaluation has a negative effect on the acquisition success.

1.5.7. Preparation of integration

Only recently, responsible managers started to pay attention to human as well as social aspects of mergers and acquisitions. "There are two basic reasons for which the human dynamics underlying organizational transformations are poorly managed. First, since technical issues generally have a "right- and wrong-way" mentality associated with them, managers often prefer to focus at that level. Errors tend to be relatively easy to find, and solutions can easily be formulated. Second, behavioural issues tend to be less concrete and easier to dismiss ante facto" (Buono, & Bowditch 1989: 13).

But not only practitioners discovered the importance for the human dynamics in mergers and acquisitions only recently. In 1986, Jemison and Sitkin suggested that pre-merger strategic fit is a necessary but insufficient explanation for M&A-performance, and that greater energy should be devoted to understanding issues of organizational fit, i.e. the processes of integrating two firms. Scheiter (1989) similarly complained about the lack of research in "people issues", which according to his view back then have only been little researched. Similarly, Gerpott (1993) points out that literature on mergers and acquisitions for long years focused on technical issues such as evaluation of targets, legal and tax issues as well as financial engineering. "Specifically, the economists have broadly examined the financial outcomes of M&As without considering how effectively these M&As have been implemented" (Schweiger, & Walsh 1990: 47). Since the end of the 80s, researchers discovered that existing explanations for high failure rates of mergers and acquisitions are insufficient. "Some mergers do fail because of financial and economic reasons. However, because of the myriad of questions about merger and acquisition success, attention has begun to shift toward human resource concerns, the cultural ramification of merger activity, management of the overall combination process, and specific efforts aimed at post-combination process, and specific efforts aimed at post-combination integration" (Buono, & Bowditch 1989: 10). Similarly, Schweiger, & Walsh (1990) argue that "... value creation depends greatly on the ability of managers to effectively combine the businesses" (Schweiger, & Walsh 1990: 47). Nowadays, it is widely accepted that the transaction itself does not suffice to get the expected benefits. Rather, it is the actions, and activities of managers and reactions and motivation of employees after an M&A-transaction that determine the performance of M&A-transactions (compare Haspeslagh, & Jemison 1991: 12; Cartwright, Cooper 1992: 5; Datta 1991: 283; Kirchner 1991: 64; Finkelstein 1986: 12).

One reason for a shift in attention lies in the change of the types of M&A-transactions. While the merger waves of the 60s and 70s were dominated by conglomerate mergers and acquisitions, changes in the antitrust policy initiated by the Reagan administration as well as a shifting management paradigm towards core competences (Prahalad, & Hamel 1990) lead to an increase of horizontal mergers. Cartwright, & Cooper (1993b) argue that "For in contrast to the 1960s, the current wave of merger and acquisition activity has involved horizontal-type combinations, resulting in the widescale integration of people and their organizational cultures" (Cartwright, & Cooper 1993b: 332). Haspeslagh, & Jemison (1991) offer a definition of integration: „Integration is an interactive and gradual process in which individuals from two organizations learn to work together and cooperate in the transfer of strategic capabilities" (Haspeslagh, & Jemison 1991: 106). Integrating firms, however, is more complex than adding a firm to a holding structure of a diversified firm. Blake, & Mouton (1985) point out that "Making two previously independent and often competing organizations into a single entity through a merger or acquisition is no simple task" (Blake, & Mouton 1985: 41). Established knowledge about M&A-transaction did not suffice to explain phenomena linked to horizontal mergers. "As the inadequacies of more traditional explanations of merger failure are being recognized, there is a significant revival of interest in the human aspect of the phenomenon and its role in determining merger outcomes" (Cartwright, & Cooper 1993c: 58). As a consequence, academic research increasingly focused on human aspects of mergers and acquisitions. Correspondingly, Mirvis, & Marks (1992) point out that the human factor in acquisitions is crucial. Similarly, Buono, & Nurick (1992) claim that "Most human resource (HR) researchers and practitioners involved in the merger and acquisition (M/A) process readily agree that the personal, interpersonal, group, and intergroup dynamics that follow the combination of two firms are significant determinants of merger success or failure" (Buono, & Nurick 1992: 19).

In the following years, significant research attention focused on human aspects of M&A-transactions. Increasingly, researchers from organizational behavior began to focus on the implications of M&A-transactions on human feeling, thinking and behaviors. Strategic M&A-research somewhat lost its dominant position to psychological M&A-research. This, as Cartwright, & Cooper (1993a) put it, reflects the changes in competences required for the implementation of a M&A-transaction: "Successful marriages are not solely made in a strategist's heaven – they require considerable and lengthy groundwork at the operational level" (Cartwright, & Cooper 1993a: 8). Similarly, Buono, & Bowditch (1989) conclude that "A merger or acquisition is ultimately a human process. Focused efforts on and sensitivity to what people are experiencing are necessary if managers hope to decrease the costs involved for both individual employees and the organization." (Buono, & Bowditch 1989: 133)

After the closing of a deal, merging firms can start with more detailed planning of the integration. Mostly, strategic decisions as well as basic organizational decisions have been taken at this point of the M&A-process already (Lucks, & Meckl: 2002). Strategic decisions comprise decisions about the market strategy, including branding, positioning of products and marketing approach, as well as decisions about the pursued business model. Basic organizational decisions comprise decisions about the scope and depth of the integration of the two firms.

Due to legal constraints, acquirers as well as merging firms only have limited access to information about the partnering firm before closing. After the closing, merging firms can fully exchange information. Based on this additional information, it might be necessary to revise some strategic and organizational decisions. In addition to that, the detailed information is used to plan the integration implementation. Despite such detailed information, "It is difficult of course, to totally prepare organizational members to accept and deal with all the transitions that can accompany a merger or acquisition" (Buono, & Bowditch 1989: 132). According to Buono, & Bowditch (1989), the main reason for such difficulties is the inherent complexity of human behaviors after mergers and acquisition. Therefore "Managers involved in a merger or acquisition should be aware of the impact that sudden changes in the psychological contract can have on employee satisfaction and commitment" (Buono, & Bowditch 1989: 131).

1.5.7.1.1. Firm level variables

Firm level variables in the preparation of an integration implementation can be different aspects. In this research, I focus on four different aspects. First, the organizational detailing needs to be determined before the integration of merging firms. The organizational detailing is constrained by the structural decisions taken in the forefront of an M&A-transaction. That implies that the integration degree of the merging firms is already known. However, the details, including manager appointments, structure of incentive and reward systems as well as detailed organizational processes and roles and responsibilities of different organizational departments need to be fixed after the closing.

A second aspect of an M&A-transaction that needs to be determined in the integration preparation is the structure of the integration process. Timelines for the integration process, different activities as well as responsibilities of actors need to be determined.

A third aspect that requires planning is the communication process. Due to the very nature of an M&A-process, information is distributed asymmetrically. Before closing, only few employees, sometimes only the top management team is informed about the merger plans. After the announcement of the deal, closing usually takes place quickly, and the information asymmetry needs to be equalized. This requires communication. Employees' perceptions and attitudes about the M&A-transaction are strongly shaped by the content, structure and sequencing of communication.

A fourth important aspect for the integration implementation is the planning of active integration measures. Active integration measures include all activities that directly influence the relationship building of employees.

1.5.7.1.2. Organizational detailing

While the company organization is usually easily defined, the definition of standard operating procedures easily gets neglected despite their high importance. Thus Dicken (2000) points out that the alignment of strategy and business processes is a central element for later integration of a firm.

There are different approaches to integrate organizational structures of firms. One approach is centralization of activities in one location. Sommer (1996) argues that centralization reduces the need for coordination between units, because all activities are centralized in one unit. Centralization can help to gather synergies based on economies of scale. At the same, Sommer (1996) points out that there are costs associated to centralization, such as coordination costs, costs of compromise and costs of inflexibility. In addition to these costs, centralization only reduces the need for coordination between units of one function. Centralizing activities within one function, however, directly affects cooperation between functions. For example, if firm A and firm B merge, and marketing of firm A and firm B gets centralized within one location A, and product management departments of firm A and firm B remain separated, the cooperation between product management and marketing changes. While product management of firm A still cooperates with marketing of firm A, product management of firm B has to develop new cooperation relationships with marketing of firm A. Such changes, however, increase cooperation and coordination needs between functions.

Koegeler (1991) describes another organizational approach to overcome communication barriers in research and development (R&D). He argues that by implementing steering committees for R&D across locations, know how transfer and coordination can be secured. Such committees also can help to reduce barriers between employees and reduces cultural differences within R&D-departments. Scheiter (1989) argues that the integration of the acquisition target into the planning and controlling systems of the acquiring firm, as well as formalization of communication systems and cooperation between organizational units increases the likelihood for a successful integration.

Krystek (1992) identifies a number of elements of organizational detailing that can facilitate the acculturation process of merging firms. Krystek (1992) argues that implementation of a new firm philosophy, new firm strategies as well as new management instruments and new forms of leadership can facilitate integration. He further argues that even architectural elements or office equipment can facilitate the acculturation process.

Reward and incentive systems have a key role for integrating merged firms. „Reward systems played an important role in developing a willingness work together by the ways in which they encouraged cooperation between the firms" (Haspeslagh, & Jemison 1991: 113). Similarly, - Dicken (2000) points out that alignment of salary and incentive systems is key for integration. If employees in merged firms shall be integrated, he argues, it is necessary to align individual behaviors of employees by aligning their incentives.

Although organizational detailing and its impact on integration of merging firms bears important implications on the integration of merging firms, it has received considerable little attention in the literature. One reason might be that the decline of the organizational design school lead to a shift of focus on other aspects of organizations. A second reason might be that organizational detailing bears implications for the integration long after the integration of merging firms is finished. Organizational detailing thus might be seen more independently of the M&A-transaction.

Despite its neglect in research, organizational detailing bears important implications for the integration of merging firms. Organizational details implements the desired degree of integration. At the same time, organizational details determines the amount of synergies needed and the cost of integration.

1.5.7.1.3. Characteristics of the integration process

While most authors agree upon the approximate structure of the integration process, i.e. the type of activities and their sequential order, there are highly different points of view on the speed of integration.

There are two different perspectives on the effect of speed of integration for the success of an M&A-transaction. The first perspective is based on financial reasoning and proposes that future synergies need to be generated as soon as possible in order to justify premiums paid. A second perspective is based in organizational behavior research, and assumes that speed of integration affects motivation and cooperation of employees and thus the generation of synergies, regardless of premiums paid.

A proponent of the first perspective, Sirower (1997) investigates how delaying the generation of synergies affects the required performance improvements. Sirower (1997) argues that even when only low premiums are paid, future synergies get discounted while premiums need to be fully paid. Waiting increases discounting and thus increases the required performance improvements.

Proponents of the second perspective reason differently. Dicken (2000) names speed of integration as one of the most important success factors of integration. Similarly, Lucks, & Meckl (2002) argue that speed is a very important aspect of the integration process to avoid uncertainties of employees as well as of customers. Uncertainties, according to their reasoning, represent significant risks, which endanger the success of an acquisition.

In an early study, Möller (1983) finds that "... fast reorganization is more promising than stepwise proceeding" (Möller 1983: 266, own translation). Möller (1983) finds that reorganizations after mergers and acquisitions that are accomplished within one year's time after closing are more successful than reorganizations that stretch over several years.

Scheiter (1989) argues that "Fast proceeding for integration (integration speed) of the acquired company increases the likelihood of successful integration, if the integration measures are right" (Scheiter 1989: III, own translation). Right integration measures, however might not always be possible, at maximum integration speed. For example, Meyer (2001) finds in two case studies that in integration processes, management has to make trade-offs between maximizing economic productivity and fostering relationships. Thus short-term success might depend on fast proceeding, long term success, however requires a more careful approach.

Similarly, Schweiger, & Walsh (1990) point out that "Proponents of the 'quick' approach argue that it is better to implement changes quickly so as to minimize the amount of uncertainty and ensuing trauma that employees must face. Proponents of the 'slow' approach suggest that a gestational period for studying, understanding and building empathy between members of the combining organizations is best" (Schweiger, & Walsh 1990: 72).

Koegeler (1991) promotes a differentiated approach to integration. Depending on considerations for each function of a company, the speed of integration needs to be determined. For examples, centralization allows quick improvements of cost positions in marketing and sales. At the same time, according to Koegeler (1991), fast integration of these activities might lead to market risks that endanger the success of an acquisition. Therefore, a slower centralization in marketing and sales increases the likelihood of success of an acquisition (Koegeler 1991: 228 ff). Yunker (1983) even recommends for some areas, such as personnel and benefits, that some five years are necessary to plan and implement necessary alignment and full integration.

Bamberger (1994) points out another constraint for the choice of integration speed. He argues that "If there is enough management time for the supervision of an acquisition target, the success rate [of M&A-transactions] is 70%, otherwise it is only 33%" (Bamberger 1994: 238, own translation). Similarly, Gerds (2000) finds that larger companies are generally more successful acquirer. Gerds (2000) argues that the reason is more management slack that can deal with the integration of an acquisition. Small companies have lower slack capacities and thus do not have enough resources to integrate an acquisition and thus make it a success.

Summarizing, the speed of the integration process bears implications for the amount of human resources, which can be invested in the implementation phase, for the quality of the implementation as well as for the social and individual processes. High integration speed reduces the time for employees to get to know each other carefully. Lack of mutual knowing each other might prevent cooperation and thus reduce the synergy effects.

1.5.7.1.4. Communication

Communication, according to Sommer (1996) can be defined as mutual exchange of information. Sommer (1996) distinguishes between competence related (vertical) and interdependency related (horizontal) communication. Sommer (1996) argues that vertical communication, which bounds employees by instruction can indirectly integrate different functions of a merged company and avoid competing activities. Zimmermann (2000) points out that such communication helps employees to identify with the targets of a merger or an acquisition, align information levels and avoid gossiping. Horizontal communication, however, is necessary to align activities on the operative level. Therefore, it is necessary not only to secure the vertical but also the horizontal communication.

Mergers and acquisitions are surrounded by uncertainties and ambiguities. "The primary intervention recommended for helping combat uncertainty is communication" (Schweiger, & Walsh 1990: 63). Similarly, Buono, & Bowditch (1989) argue that "Ambiguity in organizations is generally conceptualized in terms of the adequacy of information available to organizational members" (Buono, & Bowditch 1989: 102).

Zimmermann (2000) and Dicken (2000) points out the importance of communication to all stakeholders of the firm. Trzicky (2000) identifies even further stakeholders. Trzicky (1998) differs amongst others between owners, managers, employees as well as customers, capital markets, competitors and more distant institutions such as labor unions, the state as well as the abstract public opinion. All these stakeholders need to be addressed in the communication of the M&A-transaction. Similarly, Scheiter (1989) points out that communication to the market partners, i.e. suppliers and customers, is of paramount importance for the success of an M&A-transaction.

Balloun, & Gridley (1990) claim that uncertainty after the announcement of a merger is most detrimental for people working in the companies. Therefore, the implementation of a new purpose of the integrated firm, responsibilities and hierarchies as well as reduction of uncertainty for people on all levels is highly important. They argue that communication is key for implementing new purpose, clarifying power structures as well as informing people.

A general problem in M&A-transactions is the availability of information. At the moment of a merger decision, management rarely has all information in place that employees ask for. "Since the actual details of the merger or acquisition have to be worked out over a period of several months or even years after the combination, management rarely has accurate answers to employee questions" (Buono, & Bowditch 1989: 16). This, however, constrains the possibilities of communication significantly. Early uncertainties of details of an acquisition necessarily must reflect in uncertainties of communication and thus limits its uncertainty reducing effects.

While lack of availability of information constrains communication after M&A-transactions, Buono, & Bowditch (1989) moreover find that typical M&A-communication tries to hide things first, leaves employees in the dark and creates a lot of room for rumours and associated anxiety. "Virtually every case study of a merger or acquisition reports communication shortages at one point or another during the combination process" (Buono, & Bowditch 1989: 197). Therefore, Buono, & Bowditch (1989) suggest that the top management of a merged firm should communicate as open with employees as possible. "Accurate and honest responses to questions about these issues provide organizational members with a realistic assessment of what the merger or acquisition will mean for them personally and for the new organization" (Buono, & Bowditch 1989: 204).

As Buono, & Bowditch (1989) point out, effective communication needs to address individual information needs of employees. "Such communications should include information about both the changes that affect the company and the individual employee" (Schweiger, & Walsh 1990: 63). Similarly, Smidts, Pruyn, & Riel (2001) find that organizational identification depends on adequacy of the information received about the merger, and on the adequacy of the information received about the personal role of oneself.

In this way, communication bears positive effects in the integration process. Salecker, & Müller-Stewens (1991) point out that one of the effects of communication in the acquisition process is the avoidance of negative reactions of employees. Similarly, Ivancevich, Schweiger, & Power (1987b) argue that stress-avoiding and stress-reducing communication can limit dysfunctional outcomes of M&A-transactions.

Schweiger, & DeNisi (1991) investigate in a longitudinal field experiment the effect of communication on the reactions of employees. They find that communication of a realistic merger preview reduced or stabilized uncertainty, stabilized job satisfaction, and increased trustworthiness, honesty and caring. At the same time, communication did not have and effect on intentions to remain, performance as well absenteeism of employees.

Terry, & Callan (1997) also find mixed results for the effects of communication. They identify two coping strategies for adjustment to organizational change: One avoidant strategy and one problem-focused coping strategy. They find that management communication cannot influence the choice of these strategies. Instead, they find that high-self esteem reduces the chances of picking an avoidant strategy. Also, they find that appraised stress and appraised certainty do not influence the choice of coping strategy.

While communication seems to primarily affect attitudes about mergers and acquisitions, it does not directly affect cooperation. In the next paragraph, I will highlight active integration measures as an approach to directly facilitate the emergence of cooperation between merging firms.

1.5.7.1.5. Active integration measures

While communication during M&A-transactions aims to decrease information deficits of employees, active integration measures aim to directly initiate cooperation between employees of the merging firm. There are different types of active integration. A first type of integration measure consists of exchange of employees. Sommer (1996) defines exchange of employees as the assignment of employees from one firm in the mirroring departments of the other firm. A second type of integration measure is the organization of workshops visited by employees of both merging firms. Workshops are punctual meetings of a predefined group of employees with a predefined task. A third type of integration measure is the formation of integration teams. Unlike workshops, teams have an enduring structure for a limited time, shared goals and a joint responsibility for the work results (e.g. Hackman 1987: 322)

Exchange of employees serves different objectives. On the one hand, such exchanges aim to increase mutual understanding for the work styles and procedures of the partnering firms. By first-hand experiencing the operations of the partnering firms, employees might be better able to understand their partners. On the other hand, such exchanges aim to install social contacts between employees. They get to know their counterparts in the partnering firm and thus increase trust as well as cooperation. Gerpott (1993) finds that only 4,3% of a sample of 92 firms exchanged top managers. At the same time, he finds that on lower management levels, roughly 72% of the firms exchange managers.

Workshops have a somewhat different intention than exchange of employees. "The main purpose of combination-related workshops is to provide organizational members with ways to understand what is happening and regain some sense of control over their work lives and careers" (Buono, & Bowditch 1989: 207). By participating in the preparation of an M&A-integration, employees identify more strongly with the integrated organization and thus feel more committed.

Integration teams are the most frequent integration measure. Again, the objectives of integration teams are twofold. On the one hand, integration teams have to elaborate and finetune organizational details of the merged organization. Sommer (1996) points out that mutual coordination via communication is suitable for solving problems at hands. However, more complex problems require coordination of a larger number of employees, which can best be done in project groups or committees. On the other hand, integration teams represent nuclei for the integrated organization. The members of integration teams later might serve as relationship promoters that facilitate cooperation amongst different functions as well as between employees of the merging firms. Dicken (2000) thus points out that the formation of integration teams with employees from both firms is a key for later integration. Scheiter (1989) finds that integration teams are most effective, if personal continuity on both sides, from the acquirer as well as from the acquiring firm is guaranteed. Buono, & Bowditch (1989) argue that transition teams are an important source of integration because people that participate and shape some aspects of a merger or acquisition are rather willing to accept changes and to act as one company.

Buono, & Bowditch (1989) find in an investigation of two merging banks that strong task focus might lead to dysfunctional effects. They find that a failure to address interpersonal issues early on led to ethnocentric attitudes and defensiveness on the part of each banks' members. Therefore, they suggest that "…the potentially most effective team-building efforts between merging firms or an acquirer and its target can be accomplished through an eclectic combination of interactions focused on planning, work relations (individual and cultural), task procedures, and other legitimate task issue" (Buono, & Bowditch 1989: 218).

Assessing the importance, of active integration measures, Schweiger, & Weber (1989) find in a cross-sectional study of merging firms that managers rank social support workshops by far the most important integration measure (74% of the firms rated as important). A second important integration measure is the training of managers to deal with employees' concerns (40%). Stress management (14%), inoculation training (12%) and mourning (12%) workshops were not considered very important.

Integration measures reduce uncertainty. "The literature suggests that interventions, designed to help individuals and groups (i.e., work units) cope with uncertainty and change, may be useful in managing the stress and emotion" (Schweiger, & Walsh 1990: 67). Similarly, Schweiger, & Lee (1993) find in a later study that participation in an integration measure, during which employees had to interact with new colleagues, lowers the experienced job insecurity.

Active integration measures aim for the establishment of cooperation between employees of merging firms. As has been seen, they serve to install contact between employees, facilitate cooperation and, in most cases also fulfill a concrete task that is related to the M&A-transaction. Unlike communication, active integration measures thus do not aim to educate people about merger objectives. Rather, they aim for direct engagement of employees, providing them with the feeling of participation and providing them with opportunities to form contacts.

1.5.7.1.6. Management interventions

Integration, is an ongoing challenge for merging firms. „Many firms face serious difficulties in developing the willingness of people in both organizations to work together after the acquisition" (Haspeslagh, & Jemison 1991: 113). Therefore, isolated events such communication and active integration measures might not be enough. Rather, ongoing efforts by the management to facilitate cooperation and reduce dysfunctional outcomes of the integration are necessary. Gutknecht, & Keys (1993) point out that keeping up the morale in the acquired company is crucial for success in mergers and acquisitions. Therefore, survivors should always be treated well in order to integrate them successfully on the long run.

Buono, & Nurick (1992) argue that middle management plays a key role in the integration process. However, in order to allow them to cope with the situation, it is necessary "(1) helping these individuals to conceptualize and understand their sphere of influence; (2) facilitating their assessment of the potential opportunities that exist in ambiguous situations; and (3) gaining momentum from 'small wins'" (Buono, & Nurick 1992: 25).

Ivancevich, Schweiger, & Power (1987) argue that guidelines and interventions of managers can help to effectively manage merger stress. These are (1) prevention, which helps "... to reduce the actual stress-inducing merger events" (2) Reappraisal, which "... refers to changing initial cognitive appraisal of a situation by employees once a merger is underway" and (3) stress management and professional help, which helps those employees that are already stressed (Ivancevich, Schweiger, & Power 1987: 26).

1.5.8. Integration implementation

The implementation of the integration of merging firms bears effects on all levels. On the environmental level, unions react to the integration approach. On the firm level, cultural differences and the design of the integration process influence the acculturation process of the merging firms. On the group level, strong psychological reactions based on ingroup- and outgroup-reactions of employees influence the M&A-success. And on the individual level, loss of identity, emotional reactions of employees and coping strategies chosen by employees influence the success of mergers and acquisitions.

1.5.8.1. Environmental variables – The role of unions

As has been noted above, different stakeholders come into play during the integration of merging firms. Bryson (2003) considers the role of unions as one important external stakeholder on the integration of merging firms. in a case study on a banking merger, she finds that unions are helpful in raising issues during the implementation phase before they escalate. Acting as an early-warning system, unions thus can reduce frictions and dysfunctional tendencies in mergers and acquisitions. She points out that the management of the unions plays a crucial role in mergers and acquisitions: Unions can be very helpful during the M&A-process to get employees on board. At the same time, unions can initiate significant resistance to an M&A-transaction and thus negatively affect the success of mergers and acquisitions.

1.5.8.2. Firm level variables – Acculturation

In choosing an acquisition target, acquirers choose the cultural differences they have to deal with later. As has been described in 1.5.3.2.3, cultural differences have been found in some studies to yield detrimental effects on M&A-performance. Hence the process of bringing together employees from different organizational cultural settings deserves special attention.

"While there is a strong need for further research in this area, it would suggest that some form of culture audit of potential organizational marriage partners prior to any merger or acquisition decision would present essential and supplementary information to the customary financial and legal audits" (Cartwright, & Cooper 1993a: 40). The information gathered in a culture audit can be used to determine the degree of cultural similarity between two firms. Krystek (1992) claims that already during the screening of potential acquisition targets, cultural differences should be determined and considered. Potential elements of a cultural due diligence can be documents, visits and tours in the partnering firm, surveys as well as interviews (Krystek 1992: 547).

Althauser, & Tonscheidt-Göstl (1999) similarly point out the importance of gathering information on current organizational cultures. However, they further elaborate that based on the current organizational cultures, a target culture needs to be defined and paths from current to target culture need to be developed and implemented in integration workshops.

There are different views on the effects of cultural differences on the blending of organizational cultures after mergers and acquisitions. Buono, & Bowditch (1989) point out that there are different levels of cultural integration, which an acquirer can choose as a target result of a cultural integration. They differ between:

- Cultural pluralism, which means that there is no effort of aligning cultures. Instead, they coexist as cultural diversity
- Cultural blending, which means that different cultures merge to form a new culture that inherits traits of the merged cultures
- Cultural takeover, meaning that one of the cultures is completely erased and the dominant culture is the only supported and manifested model
- Cultural resistance, which emerges from a lack of understanding of cultural differences. Cultural resistance often leads to cultural conflict (Buono, & Bowditch 1989:143 ff).

Buono, & Bowditch (1989) develop a circular model of organizational culture change. The model is based on the assumption that behaviors, justifications as well as cultural communication form the culture of a firm. Managers seeking to create culture change can intervene in each of these activities. In addition to that, hiring and socialization of new employees as well as removal of members who deviate from the culture can support culture change. Hence Buono, & Bowditch (1989) assume that culture is manageable and should be actively managed after mergers and acquisitions.

While Buono, & Bowditch (1989) take a voluntaristic perspective to culture change, Cartwright, & Cooper (1993b) develop an acculturation model that describes the process and potential outcomes of two cultures coming together. Acculturation, according to Cartwright, & Cooper (1993b) is "... the resultant process of contact, conflict, and adaptation" (Cartwright, & Cooper 1993b: 65). Their acculturation contains "... four different modes depending on the extent to which members are satisfied with and value their existing culture and their evaluation of the attractiveness of the other culture" (Cartwright, & Cooper 1993b: 65).

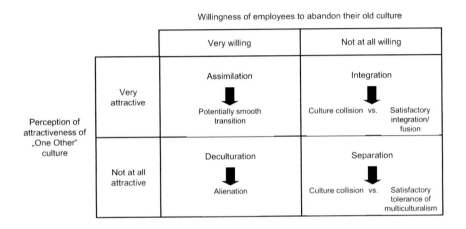

Illustration 14: Acculturation model after Cartwright, & Cooper 1993b: 65

Depending on the acculturation process, different outcomes for the acculturation process are likely. While assimilation leads to potentially smooth transition, separation either leads to lack of integration or to culture collision, both with potentially detrimental effects to M&A-success.

Schweiger, & Goulet (2002) regard the process of cultural integration from a learning perspective. According to them, "Learning about an organization's culture is learning not only how the organization functions but why it functions the way it does" (Schweiger, & Goulet 2002: Q1). They find that cultural learning is a key variable in the integration process to foster cooperation and communication between employees of merged firms. They find that integration measures that aim to increase knowledge and sensitivity about the partners' organizational culture help to increase levels of communication, trust in management as well as cooperation between the combined firms.

Scheiter (1989) points out that it is not necessarily the similarity of cultural characteristics of merging firms that determines the integration success. Rather, he argues, a general basic consensus is necessary as a common ground for cooperation. This is especially true for the management teams of both companies, their organizational cultures and the management systems. If this basic consensus does not exist, the likelihood of integration problems increases (Scheiter 1989: II).

Summarizing, acculturation is important to ease cooperation between employees of the merged firms. As culture provides the platform for cooperation, a lack of common culture increases the need for coordination and thus reduces the efficiency of cooperation.

1.5.8.3. Group level variables

One of the reasons for dysfunctional effects of cultural differences is the reinforcement of ingroup-outgroup tendencies between employees of the merged firm. Tenter, & Müller (2000) point out, that "Patterns of civilization ... frequently vary as a function of the social group, the respective ingroup that one is affiliated to, and other social groups, the outgroups, which also developed specific patterns of civilization" (Tenter, & Müller 2000, own translation). Such differences in organizational cultures can create an "us against them" feeling, which hinders integration significantly (Marks 1988). Similarly, Buono, & Bowditch (1989) describe that after an integration of firms, cooperation might suffer from integration barriers based on ingroup-outgroup effects: "Following the formal combination of two firms, there continues to be a high level of organizational instability, which may be compounded by a lack of cooperation between organizational members and a "we versus they" mentality between the groups." (Buono, & Bowditch 1989: 99)

The differentiation between ingroup and outgroup goes back to Sumner (1906). He uses these terms to describe feelings of sympathy, which members of the ingroup receive, and which members of the outgroup do not receive. Later, Sherif, & Sherif (1969) show in their famous summer camp experiments, how group affiliation strongly determines behaviors towards ingroup and ougroup members. According to Tajfel, & Wilkes (1963), social identity is based on the "minimal group paradigma" and the "social comparison". According to the minimal group paradigma, minimal differences between members of two groups suffice to develop ingroup-outgroup categorization and to develop group identity. Cultural differences can e perceived as differences between social groups. Cultural differences thus heighten social mechanisms, which have detrimental effects on integration of employees of merging firms. According to social comparison theory, social comparison plays an important role in forming a social identity of employees. Due to their need for positive identity, one's own group gets evaluated positively while other groups, outgroups, get evaluated negatively. However, such negative evaluation of outgroups hinder integration significantly. While cultural differences can be one trigger for ingroup-outgroup effects after M&A-transactions, there are other factors as well. Blake, & Mouton (1985) point out that one aspect leading to antagonism and even hostility might be that the merging organizations often have competed directly, and some management or marketing practices of the other firm have not been considered fair (Blake, & Mouton 1985: 42). Such ancient rivalry can provide additional background for ingroup-outgroup feelings.

Haunschild et al. (1994) apply social identity theory to mergers and acquisitions. In an experiment, they investigate, how cohesion of groups prior to a merger affects performance and ingroup-outgroup biases after mergers. They find that cohesion is unrelated with either of them. However, more successful groups show stronger ingroup-outgroup biases after mergers, indicating that cohesion of ingroups versus outgroups is an effect that takes place during an integration and not before an integration.

Similarly, Terry, & O'Brien (2001) confirm hypotheses based on social identity theory in a research on 120 employees of a newly merged firm. They find that for employees of the high status firm, ingroup bias is based on status relevant dimensions, whereas for low status firms, ingroup bias is based on status-irrelevant dimensions. This corresponds to the hypothesis, that group members always build their identity on strengths whereas strengths of others are devaluated.

While these psychological mechanisms are omnipresent, there are mechanism to overcome ingroup-outgroup categorizations and facilitate integration of firms after mergers and acquisitions. Haspeslagh, & Jemison (1991) suggest that "The quality of interface management therefore becomes a key to unlocking acquisition value. The presence of 'gatekeepers', who assume this role, the quality of the job they do, and the support top management provides for their task are vital, and often missing, ingredients" (Haspeslagh, & Jemison 1991: 156). These gatekeepers have different roles in facilitating integration after M&A-transactions. According to Haspeslagh, & Jemison (1991), "Gatekeeping involves three interrelated roles: filtering unwanted interactions, channeling acceptable ones, and fostering desirable ones" (Haspeslagh, & Jemison 1991: 175).

Active integration measures also aim to reduce ingroup-outgroup biases. For example, Allport (1954) points out that reduction of prejudices between groups is based on repeated face-to-face interactions. Hence the installation of implementation integration teams can help to reduce such prejudices, and thereby reduce stereotypes, which are referred to as ingroup-outgroup characteristics.

Obviously, dysfunctional group effects can threaten the integration of the merging firms significantly. Cooperation between employees of the merging firms requires a low level of ingroup-outgroup biases. Also, the biases might be overcome with the help of integration measures.

1.5.8.4. Individual level variables

A structural change such as an M&A-transaction, leads to consequences for individuals. "The actual or potential loss of organizational identity, job responsibilities, a valued co-worker, or even a work routine can create a number of uncertainties and ambiguities that can be quiet anxiety provoking and disruptive to people's lives" (Buono, & Bowditch 1989: 98). On the one hand, organizational structures are at disposition. On the other hand, feelings of job insecurity as well as sudden competition with new colleagues provoke fear and stress amongst employees. Ultimately, an M&A-transaction does not only concern decisions about structures, processes, evaluation and other activities of the M&A-process, it mainly concerns individuals that have to understand, cope and adjust the new situation. The individual level thus "… is more conducive to an understanding of how structure influences behaviour because it has the potential for describing structure in a way that reflects factors which an individual himself is likely to perceive about his place in the organization" (Rice, & Mitchell 1973: 56).

Despite the relevance of individual behaviors in M&A-transactions, Gerpott (1993) claims that employee related success factors have not been researched as frequently as strategic issues, issues about selection and evaluation as well as issues about organizational structures.

Buono, & Bowditch (1989) were amongst the first researchers to explore "… the "micro" side of mergers and acquisitions – employee reactions, expectations, and perceptions that emerge over the course of such large-scale organizational transformations" (Buono, & Bowditch 1989: 110). In their book "The Human Side of Mergers and Acquisitions", they describe at the example of case studies how mergers and acquisitions ultimately are a people question and have to be dealt with as such.

In the following paragraphs, I will highlight a number of different aspects of mergers and acquisitions that affect employees. In a first paragraphs, I will review loss of identity as a potential consequence after M&A-transactions. In a second paragraph, I will focus on reactions of employees to mergers and acquisitions. Uncertainty, fear as well as commitment to a merger are in the focus of this consideration. In a last paragraph, I will detail a few coping strategies that employees can choose. These vary between adaptation, resistance as well as exit.

1.5.8.4.1. Loss of identity

According to social identity theory, "… people's self evaluations are shaped in part by their group memberships" (Messick, & Mackie 1989). Based on self categorization and social comparison, individuals develop a social identity, which increases self esteem, and which provides a clear categorization of other individuals.

In an M&A-transaction, the social identity of employees is seriously threatened. Schweiger, et al. (1987) describe employees who indicated that after an M&A-transaction, "... they felt loss of identity and purpose: an anchor was taken from them. and this loss generated the type of trauma that Freud identifies in his general theory of neurosis" (Schweiger et al. 1987: 127). While social identity of all employees of the merged firm is threatened, it is mostly the employees from the smaller firm, who suffer identity loss. Identity loss, however, leads to stress. Therefore, Cartwright, & Cooper (1993b) find that employees from the smaller merger partner suffer from much higher levels of stress than the employees from the larger firm. "Having been employed in an organization in which their memberships were secure, they now find themselves "sold" as a commodity" (Blake, & Mouton 1985: 42). Suddenly, the social identity of employees gets devaluated. For years, their firm provided an aspect of their identity, which now is seriously threatened.

Rentsch, & Schneider (1991) investigate in an experiment how in mergers the size of the merging company (smaller, equal or larger), and the motive for combining (growth or survival) affects the postcombination expectations of employees. Growth as well as being part of the larger company should have positive effects on the social identity of employees and thus on postcombination expectations. Rentsch, & Schneider (1991) investigate postcombination expectations regarding personal autonomy, the use of power, post-combination sense of organizational moral/identity, feelings of job security and career opportunities. They find that the most positive expectations have persons in the larger companies when the motive is growth. The most negative expectations have persons in the smaller company when the motive is survival.

Similarly, Hui, & Lee (2000) find that organization-based self esteem has a moderating effect for the relationship between two independent variables (1) job insecurity and (2) anticipation of organizational changes, and three dependent variables (1) intrinsic motivation, (2) organizational commitment and (3) absenteeism. Organization based self-esteem, which is an aspect of social identity, moderates the effect, decreasing the effects of uncertainty on the dependent variables.

1.5.8.4.2. Emotional reactions of employees

Mergers and acquisitions are stressful events for employees of the merging firms. "A merger or acquisition can sufficiently transform the structures, cultures, and employment prospects of one or both of the firms such that they cause organizational members to feel stressed, angry, disoriented, frustrated, confused, and even frightened" (Buono, & Nurick 1992: 19). Especially employees of the acquired firm face stressful changes. Blake, & Mouton (1985) identify an number of issues for the employees of the acquired organization. First, they find that employees are afraid of a loss of autonomy. Second, employees are facing changes in reward and incentive systems, threatening them with income losses. Third, they are afraid of market separation, meaning that the acquiring firm separates the markets to avoid overlap. Fourth, the acquiring firm will exploit the technology of the acquired firm. Fifth, the acquired firm is afraid of being forced to introduce finance methods and systems, indicating a lack of trust. Corresponding to this, Schweiger, & Lee (1993) find in a study on employees in an acquired and an acquiring firm that employees in the acquired firm experience greater job insecurity than employees in the acquiring firm.

Cartwright, & Cooper (1993b) argue that one of the main stressors is the pressure to appear outwardly "merger fit", i.e. willing and able to change. This, according to Cartwright, & Cooper (1993b) might lead to long-term dysfunctional stress as a false impression may be created. "The merger may overtly appear to be progressing well leaving organizational leaders unaware of any underlying stress among employees" (Cartwright, & Cooper 1993b: 344). Especially middle management and line managers experience an M&A-transaction as particularly stressful. Cartwright, & Cooper (1993a: 8) argue that this is because the middle managerial groups carry most of the responsibility of making the merger work in practice.

Buono, & Bowditch (1989) distinguish three levels of ambiguity: (1) external or macro ambiguity, which refers to technological, market or socio-political ambiguity, (2) organizational or meso ambiguity, which refers to structural (reporting lines, organizational units) or cultural (what is right, what is wrong) ambiguity, and (3) individual or micro ambiguity, which refers to positional ambiguity about potential effects of M&As on job or status. They argue that ambiguity might lead to dysfunctional effects after mergers and acquisitions. "As a result of the uncertainty, ambiguity, tension, and anxiety that organizational combinations can cause, they are frequently associated with decreased organizational satisfaction and commitment, increased turnover and absenteeism, power struggles among those managers who stay, and poorer job-related attitudes and performance for a significant proportion of the new firm's work force" (Buono, & Bowditch 1989: 108). Similarly, Schweiger, & Lee (1993) find that higher job insecurity after organizational combinations is positively correlated with dysfunctional merger outcomes such as absenteeism and negatively associated with trust, organizational commitment and job satisfaction.

Commitment, however, has been found to be decisive for the success of an M&A-transaction. Weber (1996) finds that commitment of the top management team of the acquired company increases the effectiveness of the integration process. In the same study, Weber (1996) finds that commitment of the top management team of the acquired company also increases the financial performance of the integrated company. Similarly, Bamberger (1994) finds in an investigation of attitudes of the management that there is a significant relationship between the attitude of the management about the takeover and the acquisition success. Bamberger

(1994) finds that "It can be clearly seen that the percentage of successful acquisitions decreases with decreasing support by the management of the acquisition target" (Bamberger 1994: 279, own translation).

Balloun, & Gridley (1990) argue that there are two key measures to reduce dysfunctional uncertainty for employees of merging companies. First, the new purpose of the integrated firm, responsibilities and hierarchies as well as reduction of uncertainty for people on all levels is key for a successful integration. Second, they argue that communication is crucial for implementing new purpose, clarifying power structures as well as informing people.

Ivancevich, Schweiger, & Power (1987) develop a process model to describe the emergence and effects of stress in each merger phase. Invancevich, et al. (1987) assume that a merger event represents a possible source of stress. Employees based on individual characteristics engage in cognitive appraisal of the possible source of stress and respond to it. The merger stress outcome of this response then can be influence with the help of management measures. Ivancevich, et al. (1987) argue that it is possible to influence each element of the model. First, prevention can help to reduce the stressfulness of a merger event. Second, communication can help to influence the cognitive appraisal. Third, stress management and professional help can adjust the merger stress response and thereby reduce negative merger stress outcomes.

1.5.8.4.3. Coping strategies

For most employees, mergers and acquisitions just happen. They are left with the fact that their company merges with another company, regardless of their feelings or beliefs. Negative feelings or incongruent beliefs about the M&A-transaction lead to cognitive dissonance, and cognitive dissonance leads to stress. According to Festinger (1957), there are three basic strategies for coping with cognitive dissonance. First, employees can choose to leave the company if they find themselves in a state of cognitive dissonance. Second, employees might choose to change the causes of the cognitive dissonance by actively shaping the future design of the integrated firm. And third, employees might choose to simply change their beliefs and attitudes about the merger. In a nutshell, employees can choose to leave it, change it or love it. "Research, however, has indicated that, while organizational combinations in general tend to be accompanied with high levels of stress and anxiety, organizational members vary significantly in their ability to handle uncertainties and stresses involved" (Buono, & Bowditch 1989: 112). Depending on the perception of an M&A-transaction, Buono, & Bowditch (1989) suggest three different reactions to M&A-transactions:

- Irrelevant: Organizational members simply continue as before and do not assign specific emotions to the fact of being integrated. This reaction is frequently seen in lower ranks that experienced M&A-transactions before.

- Benign-positive: Employees reacting positively see mainly the opportunities of the integration.
- Stressful: Employees feel threatened by a pending combination, thinking that they might loose their jobs, status or influence.

Depending on the group of employees, different coping choices seem more likely. While top manager might be able to leave the company, because they can financially afford it, or because they can pursue outside opportunities, most employees do not have this choice. Only few employees have the chance to actively shape the future design of the merged company. Most of the decisions about the future structure are taken on the top level of the firm. Also, there is only limited space in implementation integration teams. Finally, changing beliefs and attitudes is a long lasting process. Therefore, a fourth coping strategy needs to be considered: Resistance to change. By simply denying necessary changes, employees avoid cognitive dissonance.

Several researchers have investigated employee turnover after mergers and acquisitions. Most of them investigated top management turnover after mergers and acquisitions. Blake, & Mouton (1985) point out that it might be especially hard for top managers of the acquired firm to cope with the new situation. "Often, top managers of organizations being acquired have not previously had organizational structures above them" (Blake, & Mouton 1985: 42). In the merged firm, however, they might significantly loose autonomy. Similarly, Weber (1996) finds that autonomy removal from the top management team yields a number of negative results: First, Weber (1996) finds that autonomy removal reduces the effectiveness of the integration process after an M&A-transaction. Second, financial performance of a merger suffers. Third, Weber (1996) finds that the commitment of top managers is significantly reduced.

Cannella, & Hambrick (1993) argue that "To strategy scholars, the success of acquisitions may hinge on the retention and integration of a competent management team in the acquired firm" (Cannella, & Hambrick 1993: 140). In their research on 96 acquisitions, they find "that the postacquisition departure of executives is harmful to postacquisition performance" (Cannella, & Hambrick 1993: 149). Cannella, & Hambrick (1993) also find that the postacquisition departure of more senior executives is more harmful for the post-acquisition performance than the departure of younger executives.

Researchers identified a number of factors that influence top management retention. Krug, & Hegarty (2001) find that top managers are less likely to leave, if they have (a) a positive perception of the merger announcement, (b) positive interactions with the acquiring company top managers following the merger and (c) if they have a positive perception of the long-term effects of the merger. Similarly, Gerpott (1994) finds that pre-merger discussions on top management retention reduce management attrition. He also finds that implementation of interfirm integration teams reduces management attrition. Gerpott (1994) shows that area specific exchange of top managers reduces management attrition.

Resistance to change is another coping strategy with negative consequences for the performance of an integration. Piderit (2000) points out that there are "three different conceptualizations of resistance to change: as a cognitive state, as an emotional state, and as a behaviour" (Piderit 2000: 785). All types of resistance are characterized by a refusal to accept new structures and work accordingly to them.
Larsson, & Finkelstein (1999) find that the degree of resistance depends on the degree of organizational integration. The higher the degree of organizational integration, the higher the resistance of employees is. Resistance, however, has been found by Larsson, & Finkelstein (1999) to reduce synergy realization.
Terry, & Callan (1997) identify two coping strategies for adjustment to organizational change: one avoidant strategy and one problem-focused coping strategy. They find that management communication cannot influence the choice of these strategies. However, they find that high-self esteem reduces the chances of picking an avoidant strategy. Also, they find that appraised stress and appraised certainty do not influence the choice of coping strategy. That means that social identity can influence the coping strategy chosen by employees.

While resistance has often been seen as a negative reaction of employees to mergers and acquisitions, social relationship researchers argue that resistance only describes the fact that individuals need time to adjust to a new situation. A mismatch between target behaviors and actual behaviors of employees in integrated firms thus might reflect further need for adaptation and not active resistance to change. Rushbult (1980a, 1980b) argues that the formation of new relationship requires initial relationship-specific investments that can only be placed over time. Hence the formation of cooperation relationships requires time and effort. Similarly, researchers dealing with organizational learning describe integration as a learning process, which lasts for a longer period of time (Very, & Schweiger 2001).

1.6. Relevance of central constructs

1.6.1. Summary of reviewed success factors

A summary of all success factors identified in the literature review is presented in Illustration 15. The relationships between these constructs, which have been identified above, have not been added to the illustration. There simply would have been too many of them.

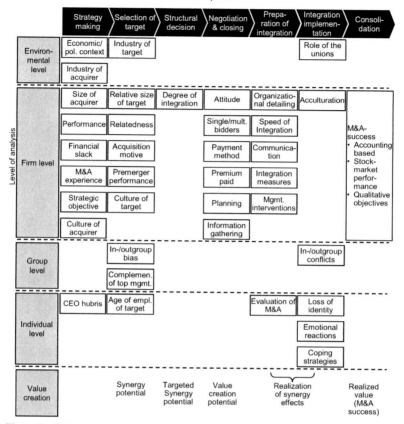

Illustration 15: Summary of success factors in different stages of the M&A-process on different levels

The literature review shows a trend in M&A-research from investigating pre-merger to investigating post-merger success factors. Ex ante explanations shifted over time from environmental and strategic factors to more structural factors such as size or integration degree. Ex post explanations over time increasingly focused on social and individual aspects of integration. Over time, the research models investigated in empirical studies became increasingly complex and focused more and more on the individual level.

A possible explanation for the shift of focus was dissatisfaction with strategic models, which proved unable to clearly identify success factors. Cartwright, & Cooper (1993c) elaborate that "There are many established models for assessing the financial health and strategic fit of a potential acquisition or merger partner. However, the criteria or framework by which to assess the likely culture fit between two organizations are vague and unelaborated" (Cartwright, & Cooper 1993c: 59).

The shift from pre-merger to post-merger and from environmental and firm-level to individual variables yielded interesting insights in the nature of M&A-success. As can be seen in the above model, M&A-success is the result of a number of different subsequent activities in an M&A-process. For each stage of the M&A-process, the value creation is illustrated. As can be seen, the selection of a target defines the synergy potential of an acquisition. The structural decision determines, which share of the potential synergy effects are aimed for. If there are reasons for leaving some potential synergy effects untapped, then the targeted synergy potential is smaller than the synergy potential. By paying the premium, the actual value creation potential of an M&A-transaction is fixed. As Sirower (1997) points out, the M&A-performance strongly depends on the synergy potential, on the premium paid, and on the integration process. If the premium paid is higher than the synergy potential, the value creation of the M&A-transaction is negative. Sirower (1997) calls this overpayment. If the synergies are realized too late, then the discounting of future synergistic gains increases the performance improvements required to pay back the premium. The realization of synergy effects depends on the effectiveness of the integration implementation after the closing. The realized value then corresponds to the value creation potential minus the synergy effects that have not been generated.

While activities and their results on each process step constrain subsequent activities and their outcomes, it is clear that by considering only success factors in early phases of the M&A-process, only little of the variance created by later activities can be explained. This might be one explanation for the mixed findings in earlier M&A-studies that focused on firm-level variables in the early stages of M&A-transactions.

It is important to note that the extensive literature hardly reveals studies, which explicitly investigate the realization of synergy effects. Despite the fact that value generation through realization of synergy effects is the main driver for financial and strategic M&A-transactions as described in 1.4.3, there are only very few studies investigating synergy realization. Most studies on success factors implicitly assume that the realization of synergy effects is necessary for M&A-success. Few authors explicitly mention the importance of synergy effects for M&A-success. Even fewer authors consider synergy realization empirically. As a notable exception, Gerds (2000) investigates in a study of 63 mergers and acquisitions the integration effectiveness of M&A-transactions. Integration effectiveness is measured as the degree to which the targeted synergies have been generated. Similarly, Larsson, & Finkelstein (1999) rate synergy realization as success measure in a sample of 61 case studies.

Literally all studies that investigated M&A-success considered synergy realization as a latent construct. That means that while many studies consider factors that influence the realization of synergy effects, most of them only focus on M&A-success directly, without considering the implicitly assumed synergy effects. Illustration 16 explicitly shows synergy realization as key construct for the M&A-success.

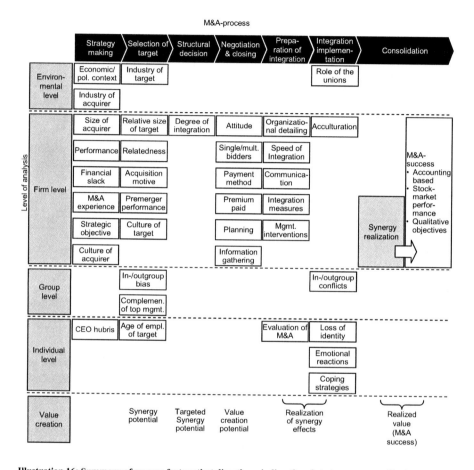

Illustration 16: Summary of success factors that directly or indirectly relate to synergy realization

The realization of synergies requires integration of economic activities of the merging firms. Integration requires cooperation between employees. There is no synergy realization without cooperation of at least some employees of the merging firms. Thus the formation of cooperation relationships is the necessary condition for all realization of synergies. Cooperation does not influence the synergy potential. However, it influences the realization of the synergy potential. Without cooperation, there is no synergy generation. With the right level of cooperation, there is full realization of the targeted synergy potential. Haspeslagh, & Jemison (1991) argue that the transfer of strategic capabilities is the main source of synergies. „Ultimately, the atmosphere necessary for capability transfer results from the stream of interactions between members of the two firms" (Haspeslagh, & Jemison 1991: 117).

Similarly, Pribilla (2000) argues that human capital is very important for the competitiveness of a company. Human capital is hard to imitate, and its value accrues only in daily interactions between employees of different functions and levels. Therefore, an M&A-transaction only generates value, if the human capital is integrated (Pribilla 2000: 378). Similarly, Buono, & Bowditch (1989) argue that psychological combination is the ultimate source of synergies and thus of M&A-performance. However, "… psychological combination is reached when there is renewed cooperation and intra- and inter-unit acceptance between the organizations" (Buono, & Bowditch 1989: 101).

Hence cooperation is the key moderating variable for the realization of synergies and thereby for the M&A-success.

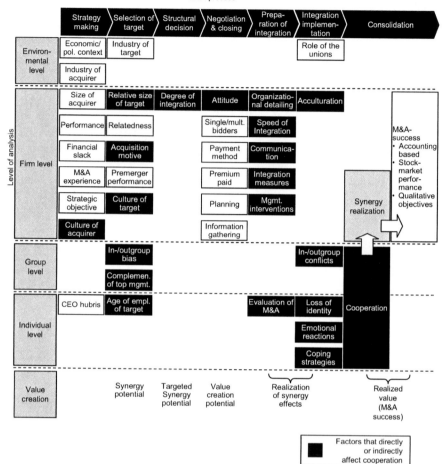

Illustration 17: **Central role of cooperation in the research framework**

Despite its importance as a key construct for the generation of synergies and thus for the M&A-success, cooperation after mergers and acquisitions has hardly been systematically researched.

As one of the few exceptions, Haspeslagh, & Jemison (1991) investigated integration in five case studies. They interviewed managers using an open interviewing technique. In the process of the research and later on, they used a grounded theory building approach to develop their framework (see Eisenhardt 1989b). However, they did not directly interrogate employees about their cooperation relationships, nor did they systematically gather information on it from key informants.

In a case study research on acquisitions of German companies in Poland, Piske (2002) investigates cooperation quality. Cooperation quality in his research is operationalized with the help of three factors that resulted from a factor analysis. The factors are (1) appreciation of the acquirer, (2) openness and trust, and (3) initiative. None of the items used for the factors captures aspects of cooperation. Rather, they capture attitudes about the acquiring firm.

Berthold (2004) investigates the effect of structural determinants and organizational culture on the success of mergers and acquisitions. In 56 acquisitions, he gathered information of key informants from both acquisition partners. On the average, 10 key informants per acquisition partner provided information, resulting in 1,240 respondents. Berthold (2004) measures integration with the help of four items and agreement to statements on a five point Likert scale. The items are

- "Many are missing a binding orientation in basic questions"
- "Executives in this organization always manage to give employees a clear orientation"
- "In this organization, everybody pulls together. There are no conflicts that seriously endanger cohesion"
- "Conflicts over factual issues hardly end in lengthy debates on principles"
(Berthold 2004: 42)

None of Berthold's (2004) items addresses cooperation directly. Rather, they capture cultural aspects of the integrated firm and the cooperation climate.

Summarizing, the literature review and the allocation of the investigated constructs reveals that the M&A-literature of the last years circles around the investigation of M&A-success as well as success factors, influencing M&A-success. M&A-success mostly is seen as value creation after the M&A-transaction.

Most researchers assume that M&A-success depends on the realization of synergies. Nevertheless, hardly any study investigates the realization of synergies. This implies that realization of synergies is mostly treated as a latent construct.

Researchers discussing synergies, point out the importance of cooperation for the realization of synergy effects. Numerous studies investigated the factors influencing the synergy potential. Cooperation is the key moderating variable for transferring synergy potential into synergy effects. However, hardly any research explicitly investigates cooperation after mergers and acquisitions and its antecedents. The research framework thus indicates a significant research gap in the field of cooperation after mergers and acquisitions.

1.6.2. Research questions of the present study

In this research, I focus on cooperation between employees after mergers and acquisitions. I explicitly investigate factors that influence the formation of cooperation after mergers and acquisitions. Cooperation is based on cooperation relationships of individuals. In order to understand the formation of cooperation relationships, it is thus necessary to investigate individuals and their motives as well as constraints for the formation of cooperation relationships. At the same time, it is necessary to investigate the relationships between individuals and the characteristics of relationships. Both, the individual and the dyadic perspective are necessary to understand how cooperation after M&A-transactions emerges.

Based on these considerations, the guiding questions of this research are:
- **Who cooperates? What are antecedents and constraints of individual cooperation?**
- **Who cooperates with whom? What are antecedents and constraints of cooperation relationships?**

I propose that on the individual level, there are a number of characteristics of individuals that affect cooperation behaviors. I will investigate these characteristics and determine, whether and to what extent they influence the cooperation behaviors of employees after mergers and acquisitions.

I further propose that on the dyadic level, the main motive for the formation of cooperation relationships is homophily, i.e. mutual attraction based on similarity of specific individual attributes. I will identify a number of characteristics of individuals that are object of homophily, and whose similiarity might facilitate the formation of cooperation relationships.

Cooperation within organizations is strongly constrained by the formal organizational structure. Hence it is necessary to understand, to which extend cooperation depends on the formal structure.

Therefore, an additional research question is:
- **How do structural cooperation requirements influence cooperation after mergers and acquisition?**

I propose that structural cooperation requirements will strongly influence cooperation after mergers and acquisitions. However, I also propose that structural requirements cannot fully explain individual cooperation.

Last but not least, it is important to know whether management actions can influence the cooperation of employees. I formulate two additional research questions to investigate the role of integration measures:
- **How does communication affect cooperation?**
- **How do active integration measures affect cooperation?**

I propose that both, communication and active integration measures have a direct and positive effect on cooperation.

In the second section of this work, I will review the psychological and sociological literature in order to identify characteristics that affect individual and dyadic cooperation. I further identify structural constraints such as integration measures as well as cooperation requirements between organizational units. Based on existing theories and empirical findings, I develop a set of hypotheses about the relationships of individual, dyadic and structural constructs and cooperation.

In the third section of this work, I will develop a research design to test the hypotheses. I will illustrate in detail the operationalization of the different constructs and present two empirical studies that have been conducted to test the hypotheses. Then I will present the results of the empirical study and discuss them in detail.

After having presented the results, I summarize the findings and reflect them based on previous studies and theoretical predictions.

Last but not least, implications for practitioners as well as for further research are presented.

2. Theoretical model

Cooperation is key for the generation of synergies. But what factors are key for cooperation? There is no unified theory of social relationships in general. Also, there is no theory for cooperation relationships in special. Rather, there many different rivaling and complementary theories that explain partial aspects of cooperation.

For example, Thibaut, & Kelley's Interdependence Theory (1959) posits that individuals engage in social relationships if they perceive them to be more valuable than a level of comparison, which is specific for each individual. Value of a relationship according to Thibaut, & Kelley (1959) is the difference of sum of benefits of a relationship and the sum of cost of that relationship. The level of comparison is defined by either past relationships or by an individual aspiration level. However, Thibaut, & Kelley (1959) remain silent about the evaluation of benefits and costs of a relationship. Also, they remain silent about possible dynamics of the level of comparison.

In the tradition of Thibaut, & Kelley (1959), Coleman (1990) argues in his Rational Choice Theory that individuals engage in relationships, if they perceive the expected gain of a relationship - that is the probability of the gain multiplied with the height of the gain - higher than the expected loss of a relationship. Coleman (1990) thus extends Interdependence Theory by arguing that trust is crucial in evaluating beneficiality of relationships: With increasing levels of trust, the probability of a gain is perceived higher, increasing the expected value of a relationship. But Coleman (1990) does not elaborate, how individual characteristics such as age, gender, or specific attitudes influence trust.

Carstensen (1992, 1993, 1995) presents in her Socioemotional Selectivity Theory an explanation how expansive and emotive motivations over the life-span of individuals change and thereby affect the propensity of individuals to engage in social relationships. But she does not consider aspects, which determine the characteristics of relationship partners that older employees select for relationships.

Emerson, & Cook (1978) elaborate with Social exchange theory a framework, according to which social relationships are primarily seen as exchange mechanisms, which allow utility maximizing individuals to maximize benefits and minimize costs by choosing specific relationships. Hence relationships are formed, if relationship partners profit from the characteristics of each other. But Social exchange theory hardly considers social mechanisms such as ingroup- or outgroup biases, that make it more or less likely to engage in relationships with individuals.

Tajfel (1985) focuses in his Social Identity Theory on mechanism such as self categorization, status and identity preserving activities that drive relationship building or adverse relationship building within and between groups. Ashforth, & Mael (1989) elaborate Tajfel's (1985) Social Identity Theory to describe social identity in organizations. However, neither Tajfel

(1982, 1985) nor Ashforth, & Mael (1989) elaborate how individual characteristics affect social identity.

This short overview on different theories that describe social relationships shows that there is no one theory that describes all aspects of social relationships in general and of cooperation relationships in specific. Rather there is a range of different theories that apply more or less depending on the phenomena described and the research interest.

The current research is strongly phenomenon driven. The focus of the work is not the generation of theories, theoretical frameworks, mid-range theories or frameworks for future theory building. Rather, the focus is on developing a better understanding of the complex phenomenon mergers and acquisitions, and especially on two aspects of mergers and acquisitions that have been identified to be crucial: Factors that influence cooperation on an individual level and factors that influence cooperation on a dyadic level. Therefore, I focus on two aspects of cooperation relationships:

- The characteristics of individuals that make it more or less likely that they engage in new cooperation relationships and that affect characteristics of cooperation relationships.
- Second, I focus on the characteristics of pairs of actors, that make it more or less likely that they form a relationship and that effect the characteristics of the relationships between actors

Corresponding to this objective of the present research, I will elaborate in the following chapters a research model that allows developing a set of testable hypotheses about the relationship of individual and dyadic factors and cooperation. In order to do so, I will draw from different social theories, as well as empirical findings on cooperation and social networks.

2.1. Who builds cooperation ties?

In the following paragraphs, I will highlight the effect of different individual characteristics on cooperation. The different individual characteristics are demographic characteristics, firm related characteristics, work attitudes, reactions to M&A-transaction as well as integration measures and structural effects. While demographic characteristics, firm related characteristics as well as attitudes are highly stable, reactions to M&A-transactions are more flexible and thereby affected by the other factors. Hence the research model assumes that demographic characteristics, firm related characteristics as well as work attitudes influence reactions to M&A-transactions. Also, integration measures are assumed to affect reactions to M&A-transactions. At the same time, all individual characteristics are assumed to affect cooperation. In addition to individual characteristics, structural cooperation requirements are assumed to affect individual cooperation. Therefore, structural cooperation requirements will be considered as a control variable in the model.

Illustration 18 summarizes the different constructs, which will be elaborated in more detail in the next paragraphs.

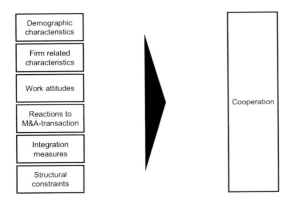

Illustration 18: Summary of constructs for the investigation of individual characteristics on cooperation

Each of these constructs and each of the illustrated relationships will be elaborated in detail in the following paragraphs. In order to do that, I will interpret theoretical predictions of different social theories and support these interpretations with diverse empirical findings of previous studies. Based on these interpretations, a number of hypotheses will be formulated for later empirical investigation.

2.1.1. Demographic characteristics

In this research, demographic characteristics comprise obvious characteristics of individuals that can easily be accessed in the course of a human resource due diligence. The factors are age of employees, gender as well as education level of employees.

2.1.1.1. Age

Carstensen's (1992, 1993, 1995) Socioemotional Selectivity Theory is one of the first theories that explicitly deals with the effect of age on perception, feelings and activities of individuals. According to the theory, individuals are motivated by "... two main classes of psychological goals: one comprises expansive goals, such as acquiring knowledge or making new social contacts; the second comprises goals related to feelings, such as balancing emotional states or sensing that one is needed by others" (Carstensen, Fung, & Charles 2003: 106). These two motives together represent the constellation that motivates social behavior throughout life.

Carstensen, Isaacowitz, & Charles (1999) argue that the prominence of these goals differs in different life phases. "The cardinal tenet of socioemotional selectivity theory is that the assessment of time plays a critical role in the ranking and execution of behaviors geared toward specific goals" (Carstensen et al. 1999: 167). While expansive goals are low in early childhood, they increase during adolescence and then steadily decrease over time until old age. At the same time, emotive goals are high during early childhood, decrease during adolescence and then rise again steadily until old age.

Carstensen et al. (1999) argue that depending on the perceived life time remaining, either knowledge or emotional motives dominate. "As people move through life, they become increasingly aware that time is in some sense 'running out'" (Carstensen et al. 1999: 165). This, according to their theory, has direct implications on age differences in social network composition as well as other aspects of feeling and behaviors. It is important to note that it is not necessarily age that drives the different prioritization of motives but rather the perceived future life span that matters. Carstensen et al. (1999) point out that the same prioritization of emotive goals can be seen in cases of severe sicknesses with reduced life expectation as well as in old individuals.

Carstensen et al. (1999) describe two main effects on behaviors. A first effect is the active shaping of social networks. "Age differences in social network size have been well-documented in social gerontology. Longitudinal and cross-sectional studies reveal far smaller social networks among older as compared with younger people" (Carstensen et al. 1999: 173). Carstensen et al. (1999) propose that older individuals tend to reduce their social networks while at the same time increasing the meaning of the remaining relationships.

A second effect is the emotional experience of events. "In addition, the theory suggests that the knowledge that time is limited has direct effects on emotional experience" (Carstensen et al. 1999: 169). According to them, older individuals cope better with uncertainty and tend to faster aim for emotional balance than younger individuals.

In an empirical study, Lansford, Sherman, & Antonucci (1998) investigate the theoretical predictions of Socioemotional Selectivity Theory. They find in line with the predictions that networks of older people tend to be smaller.

Lang, & Carstensen (2002) investigate the type of relationships that 480 older individuals engage in depending on age, respectively perceived future time. They find that younger people perceive their future to be open ended. Older people perceive their future time as more limited. "Individuals who perceived future time as being limited prioritized emotionally meaningful goals (e.g., generativity, emotion regulation), whereas individuals who perceived their futures as open-ended prioritized instrumental or knowledge-related goals" (Lang, &

Carstensen 2002). Accordingly, Lang, & Carstensen (2002) find that age reduces the size of personal networks, while at the same time, the meaning of single relationships increases.

In a different research, Finkelstein, Kulas, & Dages (2003) investigate age differences in proactive socialization strategies of newcomers in different organizational settings. They find that older individuals tend to engage less in information seeking behavior and build fewer relationships than younger newcomers.

In the case of an M&A-transaction, age thus should affect relationship building of employees. Based on the theoretical considerations and the empirical findings, it can be assumed that older employees build less cooperation relationships with new colleagues. Hence I hypothesize:

> Hypothesis 1a: Older employees have less cooperation relationships with new colleagues than younger employees after an M&A-transaction

At the same time, Carstensen et al. (1999) argue that older people focus their attention on fewer relationships. Therefore, the average intensity of relationships of older employees increases. Hence I hypothesize:

> Hypothesis 1b: Older employees have stronger relationships with new colleagues after mergers and acquisitions

Carstensen et al. (1999) further argue that older individuals focus more strongly on emotional goals. This, however, means that according to Socioemotional Selectivity Theory, older individuals should show less commitment to work objectives than younger employees. Kanfer, & Ackerman (2004) develop a model for describing the relationships between aging and work motivation. They propose that "The attractiveness of higher levels of effort declines with age" (Kanfer, & Ackerman 2004: 453). As a consequence, older employees should show less commitment to the M&A-transaction Hence I hypothesize:

> Hypothesis 1c: Older people will be less committed than younger people

Concerning uncertainty, it is difficult to assess the effects. "… for people who perceive time as more limited, the future seems less relevant and emotional meaning becomes more important. The strategy of focusing on emotions to handle stress may thus be used more often, and lead to more positive psychological outcomes" (Carstensen, Fung, & Charles 2003: 114).

Older individuals thus should be better able to cope with the event of an M&A-transaction and faster reach emotional balance, reducing feelings of uncertainty.

At the same time, empirical studies show that older people have more difficulties to cope with stressful and ambiguous situations. Haynes, & Love (2004) find in an investigation of 100 project managers that older project managers suffer more frequently from anxiety and stress than younger project managers. They argue that one of the reasons for that could be problems of older project managers to adopt new technology. An M&A-transaction represents a major source of change. If older employees are less flexible to adapt to new structures and systems, they might react with feelings of uncertainty. As there is no clear direction of theoretical predictions and empirical findings, I posit a rivaling hypothesis:

> Hypothesis 1d: 1: Older people are less uncertain than younger people
> 2: Older people are more uncertain than younger people

2.1.1.2. Gender

The effect of gender on cooperation is unclear. According to the gender hypothesis, researchers for many years sought differences between men and women in different fields. Empirical studies show mixed findings. Hyde (2005) investigates the gender similarity hypothesis in a review of 46 meta-analyses. She finds that in a wide range of researches, gender differences are very small. Hyde (2005) finds that by putting distribution curves of male and female individuals onto each other, 85% of distribution curves fully overlap, leaving a difference of only 15% of non-overlapping effect sizes. Simmons, King, Tucker, & Wehner (1986) investigate the effects of different personality traits on propensity to engage in cooperative vs. competitive behaviors. They find no gender specific difference in choosing cooperative or competitive behaviors for success. Similarly, Stackman, & Pinder (1999) investigate personal work networks of women and men. They find that expressive networks of women and men differ significantly, while instrumental networks are basically the same. Expressive networks comprise social relationships such as friendship, trust or social support. Instrumental networks comprise cooperation relationships, which are in the focus of this research.

According to these findings, it is reasonable to assume that after M&A-transactions, men and women show no difference in building cooperation relationships. Hence I hypothesize:

> Hypothesis 2: There is no gender difference in cooperation after mergers and acquisitions

2.1.1.3. Education level

Emerson, & Cook (1978) develop Social exchange theory as a grand theory to predict social structures based on individual motives of actors. Social exchange theory suggests that individuals pursue relationships in a self-interested fashion, optimizing benefits and minimizing costs. At the same time, social exchange only happens, if both relationship partners perceive a relationship as beneficial.

Education level usually should represent a value that individuals can exploit in their social relationships. At the same time, other individuals might especially seek cooperation relationships with well educated individuals. Based on these theoretical predictions, Klein, Lim, Saltz, & Mayer (2004) investigate the effect of individual characteristics on centrality in team networks over a period of five months. They investigate both, advice networks as well as friendship networks. They find that education leads to higher centrality within advice as well as friendship networks, supporting the prediction of Social exchange theory that valuable relationships should be more sought after than others.

In the case of an M&A-transaction, according to Social exchange theory, well educated individuals should build more cooperation relationships than poorly educated individuals all other things equal. Hence I hypothesize:

> Hypothesis 3a: Higher educated employees cooperate more than less educated employees

According to new institutionalists, higher level of education increases redeployability of knowledge assets (e.g. Meyer, & Rowan 1977; Williamson 1975). Higher redeployability, respectively lower asset specificity of knowledge assets significantly reduces the risks for employees to suffer from negative consequences of M&A-transactions. High asset specificity of knowledge assets means that in case of loss of employment, employees would experience significant value deterioration of their knowledge assets. For example, knowledge about firm-specific routines, technologies or standard operating processes might not be fully redeployable. While such knowledge within the firm has high value for the individual employee, it is worthless outside the specific firm environment.

In market transactions, Williamson (1975) suggests that transactions between firms requiring transaction-specific assets are safeguarded by higher costs. He argues that these costs are transaction costs. In intra-firm transactions, employees hardly can safeguard their firm-specific assets or capabilities. From a firm perspective, firm-specific knowledge assets of its employees do not have to be safeguarded. Employees, however, experience the situation differently. For them, an M&A-transaction potentially threatens their job and thereby the value of their firm-specific skills. Therefore, employees experience higher levels of uncertainty after M&A-transactions, if they have higher levels of firm-specific knowledge.

Higher levels of firm-specific knowledge, however, are most prominent amongst employees of lower education. Hence I hypothesize:

> Hypothesis 3b: Higher educated employees experience less uncertainty after M&A-transactions than lower educated employees

2.1.2. Firm related characteristics

Some characteristics of individuals are only defined in relation to the firm, they work in. Outside the firm, these characteristics loose significance. A first characteristic that is individual and related to the firm is rank. A second characteristic that is individual and related to the firm is seniority. Seniority is defined as the number of years that an individual spend within the company.

2.1.2.1. Rank

According to Social exchange theory, individuals seek relationships that are beneficial. Positional power within an organization provides the potential to distribute benefits to other individuals (e.g. Weber 1922; French, & Raven 1959). Therefore, higher rank should increase the number of cooperation relationships with employees.

At the same time, rank provides a structural basis for cooperation, creating opportunities for cooperation that other individuals do not have. Bovasso (1993) finds in the investigation of a merger of three firms that the upper management builds significantly more ties than middle management. Similarly, Schoennauer (1967) finds a higher level of integrative behaviors among upper management than in middle management.

Based on these theoretical considerations and empirical findings, I hypothesize:

> Hypothesis 4a: Higher ranked employees cooperate more with new colleagues

Schoennauer (1967) finds that upper management and middle management show different reactions to mergers and acquisitions. He finds that members of the upper management show a significantly higher level of agreement and commitment to the acquisition than lower management. Differences in incentive structures and responsibilities might cause these differences. Lower ranked employees often are not responsible for the integration and thus have less incentive to engage themselves in integrative behaviors. Higher ranked employees, however, mostly have responsibility for integration. Their performance is measured based on integration results. Festinger's (1962) Cognitive Dissonance Theory posits that on the long run, external constraints and thinking respectively acting converge. In the case of M&A-

transactions, this means that higher ranked employees show higher commitment than lower ranked individuals as the integrative pressure on them is higher. Hence I hypothesize:

> Hypothesis 4b: Higher ranked employees are more committed than lower ranked employees

Terry, & Callan (1997) investigate reactions of employees after mergers and acquisitions. They find that managers display lower levels of uncertainty than lower level employees. Similarly, Schoennauer (1967) finds that members of the middle management perceive a higher degree of uncertainty than upper management levels. Hence I hypothesize:

> Hypothesis 4c: Higher ranked employees feel less uncertain than lower ranked employees

2.1.2.2. Seniority

Professional identity is part of an individual's social identity. Tajfel, & Wilkes (1963) argue that social identity is based on the "minimal group paradigma" as well as the "Social Comparison Theory". According t0 the minimal group paradigma, smallest differences suffice to create ingroup-outgroup effects, i.e. different behaviors towards and feelings about members of the same group and members of another group. Social comparison then leads to a positive evaluation of the own group and to a negative evaluation of the other group. This self-esteem increasing mechanism is integral part of the creation of a positive concept of oneself.

Ashforth, & Mael (1989) develop a framework to apply Social Identity Theory to organizations. They argue that identification with an organization leads to ingroup and outgroup behaviors, categorizing others that are part of another organization as outgroup. Also, they argue that social identification leads to identity-preserving behaviors.

Social identity builds over time and becomes stronger with longer group affiliation (Hogg, & Williams 2000). According to this, social identity should increase with increased duration of affiliation to an organization or an organizational unit. Hence I hypothesize:

> Hypothesis 5a: The longer an employee work for a company, the less this employee cooperates with new colleagues

Social identity leads to identity preserving behaviors (Ashforth, & Mael 1989). High social identity thus should lead to avoidant coping strategies, reducing commitment to an M&A-transaction. Hence I hypothesize:

> Hypothesis 5b: Higher seniority of employees reduces commitment

Social identity is part of the self-concept of individuals. According to Social Identity Theory, events that threaten social identity are perceived as highly disturbing. Individuals react to threats to their social identity with feelings of uncertainty. An M&A-transaction represents a major disturbance of the organizational identity of employees. They are faced with the threat of loosing their identity. New organizational values, new systems as well as new skills thus threaten identity of employees and thereby lead to uncertainty. Hence I hypothesize:

> Hypothesis 5c: Higher seniority increases uncertainty

2.1.3. Attitudes

The effect of attitudes on integration after mergers and acquisitions is unclear. While there are many studies on the effects of attitudinal differences between employees, I could not identify studies that investigate the role of attitudes on cooperation behavior.

Generally, the leadership literature differs between task-oriented and people oriented leadership styles. Similarly, it is possible to define work attitudes of employees. Harrington (2002: J5) finds that task orientation of employees is positively correlated to network ties of individuals and to heterogeneity of groups. This indicates that task orientation of employees might increase cooperation after mergers and acquisitions. Hence I hypothesize:

> Hypothesis 6a: Higher task orientation leads to higher cooperation after mergers and acquisition

While task orientation strongly affects cooperation, it is unclear, how it might affect reactions after mergers and acquisitions. While the literature remains silent about possible reactions, exploratory interviews in the course of this study revealed that employees with high task orientation show all kinds of different reactions. Seemingly, other factors, than task orientation are responsible for the type of reactions showed. Hence I hypothesize:

> Hypothesis 6b: Task orientation should have no independent effect on uncertainty or commitment

2.1.4. Reactions to mergers

Demographic characteristics, firm related characteristics and attitudes of employees are rather stable. They should not vary too much after mergers and acquisitions. Reactions to mergers and acquisitions are more flexible and result directly from the M&A-transaction. In this research, I focus on two different reactions to mergers and acquisitions: Commitment and uncertainty.

According to findings of Schweiger, & DeNisi (1991) Commitment leads to proactive and positive coping strategies. In the case of an M&A-transaction, commitment thus should increase the number of cooperative behaviors. Hence I hypothesize:

> Hypothesis 7: Higher commitment increases cooperation after mergers and acquisitions

Uncertainty is frequently described as a feeling of lacking orientation, leading to negative appraisal of situations and to discomfort. Schweiger, & DeNisi (1991) find that uncertainty leads to avoidant coping strategies after an M&A-transaction. Hogg, & Terry (2000) argue that according to Social Identity Theory, subjective uncertainty should produce stronger identification with a work unit and thereby increase ingroup-outgroup biases, leading to decreased cooperation. Hence I hypothesize:

> Hypothesis 8: Higher uncertainty reduces cooperation after mergers and acquisitions

2.1.5. Integration measures

Integration measures aim to positively affect the integration of firms after an M&A-transaction. Based on the effect of integration measures, I differ between integration measures that aim to positively influence the perception of an M&A-transaction of employees and integration measures that actively create opportunities for employees to build cooperation relationships.

2.1.5.1. Communication

A first measure to improve cooperation that is taken during and after mergers and acquisitions is communication to and with the employees. Schweiger, & DeNisi (1991) find that communication directly affects uncertainty and commitment of employees. In a field experiment, they find that employees, which receive more and timely communication show more positive behaviors and choose more positive coping strategies after M&A-transactions. Similarly, Trzicky (2000: 55) argues that communication is the most important measure to reduce uncertainty and hostility of employees in mergers and acquisitions.

Communication is a complex process, which includes different parties and different process steps. Senders emit information, which needs to be transmitted, received and understood by receivers (Casstevens 1979). In each of these steps, there are potential disturbances, which reduce the correlation of effect as intended by the sender and actual effect of communication as shown by the receiver (Casstevens 1979).

In this research, I therefore do not focus on emitted communication. That means, I do not investigate discrete communication measures. Instead, I focus on the effects of communication: The degree to which employees feel informed. There is a theoretical and an epistemological reasoning leading to this choice: First, the communication process is very complex. Senders emit information that is received by receivers. According to communication theory, there are systematic and unsystematic disturbances of the transfer of information from senders to receiver. In order to understand the effects of discrete communication measures on individual behavior, it is thus not sufficient to investigate discrete communication measures but to investigate the effect of communication measures, the "feeling informed".

The investigation of communication measures as firm level variables and the effects of feeling informed as individual level variables require different levels of observation. In order to investigate communication measures, a number of different communication measures needs to investigated. In order to investigate the effects of communication, a number of individuals needs to be investigated. For example, Schweiger, & DeNisi (1991) investigate the effect of communication in a field experiment, in which some employees are deprived of communication and the effects on integrative behaviors is investigated in a case study approach. A quantitative study would require the research of multiple case studies to capture enough discrete communication measures. The focus of the present research is the individual level. Therefore, I focus solely on the effects of communication on the individual level.

Being informed should lower feelings of uncertainty of employees (Schweiger, & DeNisi 1991). As uncertainty is the result of lacking knowledge about a situation, information can reduce uncertainty directly. Also, information should increase understanding of the merger objectives and thereby increase commitment of employees.

> Hypothesis 9a: A high degree of feeling informed increases commitment of employees
>
> Hypothesis 9b: A high degree of feeling informed decreases uncertainty of employees

2.1.5.2. Active integration measures

In this research, active integration measures are those measures that actively bring employees of the different firms together and engage them into interaction or cooperation. Gerds and

Schewe (2004) find that soft integration measures, such as joint development of a shared vision or integration trainings have an important effect on integration of firms.

In exploratory interviews in the current research, I identified different types of integration measures that were used.

- Exchange of employees: Exchanging employees means temporary transfer of employees to locations of the other firms of an M&A-transaction. Temporary transfer can last from a few days to several weeks or even months. Typically, however, the transfer is rather short term. The objective of such exchanges is to allow employees to get to know practices, culture as well as their colleagues.
- Joint work in integration teams: The planning and the preparation of an integration of merging firms is the nucleus of later cooperation. Employees in integration teams can develop an in-depth understanding of the future organizational structure of the merged firm, understand the objectives of the M&A-transaction as well as get to know their new colleagues in intensive project work. Thereby, cooperation emerges, commitment increases and uncertainty decreases thanks to lots of first hand information as well as direct participation in designing the future organization.
- Visits of other locations: Visits of other locations are seen as a way to get to know new colleagues in their familiar environment. Visits to other locations can create a vivid representation of the new colleagues and their environment. Such visits provide opportunities to build cooperation ties based on face-to-face interaction. At the same time, uncertainty is reduced thanks to better knowledge of the new colleagues.
- Kickoff-meetings with the entire department: After the new structure has been fixed, many departments hold kick-off meetings with all employees. The objective of these meetings is to create a shared understanding of the new structure, specific responsibilities and future objectives. These meetings also serve to get to know the new colleagues.
- Integration trainings: In one of the research sites, specific off-site integration trainings have been organized for some employees.

Active integration measures are used as incentives for employees in order to increase commitment. At the same time, they aim to reduce uncertainty by reducing strangeness of new colleagues. Last but not least, integration measures aim to provide opportunities for relationship building. It is assumed that these relationships endure and form a platform for cooperation. Hence I hypothesize:

Hypothesis 10a: Participation in active integration measures increases cooperation with new colleagues

Hypothesis 10b: Participation in active integration measures increases commitment of employees

Hypothesis 10c: Participation in active integration measures decreases uncertainty of employees

2.1.6. Structure

Cooperation relationships are not deliberate relationships such as friendship relationships (e.g. Brass, & Burckhardt 1992, Laumann 1994; Ibarra 1992) or sexual relationships (e.g. Laumann 1994). Rather, cooperation after mergers and acquisitions is highly contingent on organizational structures. This means that structural cooperation requirements will strongly affect cooperation of employees. Stackman, & Pinder (1999) find that structural characteristics of organizations affect the structure of personal work networks of employees. For example, an employee in a coordination function will have to cooperate with many different employees in different functions, independent of her characteristics. Similarly, a researcher in the R&D-department can work highly independent of operating processes of the firm, which reduces the cooperation to colleagues within the same department as well as occasional cooperation with other departments.

After an M&A-transaction, structural requirements thus will strongly affect the cooperation of employees. Regardless of individual characteristics, structural constraints will have a strong effect on cooperation. Hence I argue:

Hypothesis 11: Structural cooperation requirements increase individual cooperation

2.1.7. Summary of research model: Who cooperates?

In the previous paragraphs, a number of independent constructs have been identified and the directionality of their effect on cooperation has been determined. In Illustration 19, the summary of the expected relationships between different constructs are indicated.

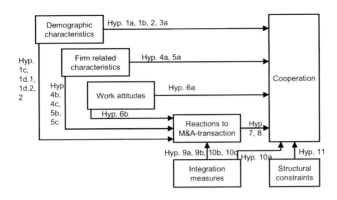

Illustration 19: Summary of research model for research question "Who cooperates?"

In Table 20, the different hypothesized effects for each independent variable on cooperation are listed. Expected effects are marked with "+" for positive effects, a "0" for insignificant effects and a "-" for negative effects. Only for the independent variable age, a differentiated hypothesis has been formulated concerning the total cooperation intensity and the average intensity of cooperation ties. As elaborated in 2.1.5.1, there is no hypothesis about the effect of the degree of feeling informed on cooperation intensity. Thus the degree of feeling informed is not listed.

Hypothesis	Independent variable	Dependent variable	Expected effect
1a	Age	Cooperation intensity	-
1b	Age	Average intensity of ties	+
2	Gender	Cooperation intensity	0
3a	Education level	Cooperation intensity	+
4a	Rank	Cooperation intensity	+
5a	Seniority	Cooperation intensity	-
6a	Task orientation	Cooperation intensity	+
7	Commitment	Cooperation intensity	+
8	Uncertainty	Cooperation intensity	-
10a	Integration measures	Cooperation intensity	+
11	Structural requirements	Cooperation intensity	+

Table 20: Hypotheses for research question "Who cooperates?" for dependent variable "cooperation"

In Table 21, the postulated effects for each independent variable on commitment are listed. As elaborated in 2.1.1.3, education level is not assumed to influence commitment of employees.

Hypo-thesis	Independent variable	Dependent variable	Expected effect
1c	Age	Commitment	-
2	Gender	Commitment	0
4b	Rank	Commitment	+
5b	Seniority	Commitment	-
6b	Task orientation	Commitment	0
9a	Deg. of feeling informed	Commitment	+
10b	Integration measures	Commitment	+

Table 21: Hypotheses for research question "Who cooperates?" for dependent variable "commitment"

In Table 22, the effects of the independent variables on uncertainty are listed. As elaborated in 2.1.1.1, a rival hypothesis has been formulated for the effect of age on uncertainty due to conflicting theoretical and empirical evidence.

Hypo-thesis	Independent variable	Dependent variable	Expected effect
1d.1	Age	Uncertainty	-
1d.2	Age	Uncertainty	+
2	Gender	Uncertainty	0
3b	Education level	Uncertainty	-
4c	Rank	Uncertainty	-
5c	Seniority	Uncertainty	+
6b	Task orientation	Uncertainty	0
9b	Deg. of feeling informed	Uncertainty	-
10c	Integration measures	Uncertainty	-

Table 22: Hypotheses for research question "Who cooperates?" for dependent variable "uncertainty"

After having elaborated the research model for the research question "Who cooperates?" I will develop in the next section the research model for the research question "Who cooperates with whom?". While the research model for the first research question focuses on the individual as unit of observation and unit of analysis, the research model for the second research question focuses on the relationship between two individuals as unit of observation and unit of analysis.

2.2. Who cooperates with whom?

It is one thing to identify individual level characteristics that affect cooperation. It is a second thing to identify characteristics on the dyadic level, which affect cooperation. The dyadic level is the level of the relationship. Identifying factors that affect the formation and characteristics of a relationship thus requires analysis of the relationships as well as the relationship partners.

Berscheid, & Reis (1998) point out that "… for two people to be in a relationship with each other, they must interact and, as a consequence of that interaction, each partner's behavior must have been influenced" (Berscheid, & Reis 1998: 199). Relationships cannot be described and analyzed without describing and analyzing both relationship partners.

In the present research, the formation of cooperation relationships after M&A-transactions is in the centre of interest. While the first contact between relationship partners is often caused by random or contingent factors, the formation of a relationship, i.e. the repetition of interactions between two relationship partners, is subject to motivational factors. "An individual's attraction to another is no doubt the most frequent cause of voluntary attempts to initiate interaction with that other" (Berscheid, & Reis 1998: 205). Attraction, however, can be caused by different effects. While physical attractiveness often plays a role for first contacts, "The most basic principle for attraction is familiarity. As opposed to the unfamiliar, familiar people usually are judged to be safe and unlikely to harm" (Berscheid, & Reis 1998: 205). In an early study, Byrne (1971) finds that attitudinal similarity is a strong driver of attraction. However, other researchers argue that it is not similarities but rather complementarities respectively dissimilarities that make individuals attractive for each other. "Both, similarity and dissimilarity have been assumed to be associated with interaction compatibility, often defined as the ratio of facilitating events to interfering and conflictful events on the partners' interaction, and thus with a positive emotional tenor to the relationship as well as satisfaction with it" (Berscheid, & Reis 1998: 207).

An extensive experimental literature in social psychology established that attitude, belief, and value similarity lead to attraction and interaction (for a review see Huston & Levinger 1978). Berscheid, & Reis (1998) thus conclude that "The weight of evidence is still in the side of similarity, however; evidence for complementarity is scarce" (Berscheid, & Reis 1998: 207).

The research of mutual attraction of individuals with similar characteristics has a long tradition. In the 1960s, psychotherapists carved the term "homophily" for the phenomenon. "Homophily is the principle that a contact between similar people occurs at a higher rate than among dissimilar people" (McPherson, Smith-Lovin, & Cook 2001: 416). McPherson et al. (2001) differs between two different types of homophily, depending on the focus of mutual attraction: "Status homophily includes the major sociodemographic dimensions that stratify society - ascribed characteristics like race, ethnicity, sex, or age, and acquired characteristics like religion, education, occupation, or behavior patterns. Value homophily includes the wide variety of internal states presumed to shape our orientation toward future behavior" (McPherson, Smith-Lovin, & Cook 2001: 419).

In the following paragraphs, I will highlight a number of different factors that have been found to play a role in predicting mutual attraction of individuals. Two aspects of status homophily will be considered: A first set of characteristics of individuals that can be the subject of homophily are demographic characteristics. I will focus on four types of demographic homophily: Age, gender, education level as well as education content. A second set of characteristics of individuals consists of firm related characteristics: Rank and seniority. In addition, two aspects of value homophily will be considered: work-related attitudes and reactions to M&A-transactions. Dissimilarities in these characteristics and attitudes will reduce cooperation after M&A-transactions. Cooperation will be considered as existence of cooperation relationships as well as intensity of cooperation. Intensity of cooperation contains aspects of frequency, of importance as well as strength of cooperation relationships. Later, in the empirical study, all these aspects will be investigated as different aspects of cooperation. At this point, however, no individual hypotheses for each aspect of intensity will be formulated, because there is not enough theoretical or empirical literature to ground such detailed hypotheses in.

Of course, the findings of homophily research cannot fully be transferred to cooperation relationships. As Berscheid, & Reis (1998) point out, first contact might be random or dependent on contingent factors, mutual attraction then is key for the formation of relationships. However, organizations, especially companies form strong constraints to individual behaviors such as cooperation. First contact after mergers and acquisitions is often induced on purpose. Also, formal organizational structures such as company organization as well as standard operating procedures constrain individual behaviors. Therefore, I will also consider participation of cooperation partners in integration measures and structural cooperation requirements. Illustration 20 summarizes the different constructs, which will be elaborated in more detail in the next paragraphs.

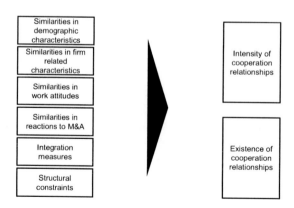

Illustration 20: Summary of effects of homophily on cooperation after M&A-transactions

2.2.1. Demographic characteristics

2.2.1.1. Age

Age homophily has been found to be an important factor for the formation of social relationships. Fischer (1977) finds that 38% of all Detroit men's close friends were within two years of their age; 72% were within eight years. Similarly, Verbrugge (1977) finds in an earlier study on friendships of 1,013 males in Detroit and 820 males and females in Germany high levels of age homophily. In yet another study, Marsden (1987) finds using data from the 1985 General Social Survey that age homogeneity in discussion relationships is very high.

McPherson et al. (2001) argue that age homophily in friendship networks is strongly based on life stage effects: Friendships are formed in school, during university studies, entering a new job or meeting young parents when kids go to preschool. These different life stage effects constrain opportunities of forming relationships with other individuals. "Age homophily includes a powerful baseline component" (McPherson et al. 2001: 424). At the same time, McPherson et al. (2001) identify homophily based on choice as a power driver for relationship choices. Such active choice of similar relationship partners they call "inbreeding homophily" (McPherson et al. 2001: 419).

Similarly, Carstensen (1992, 1993, 1995) offers a theoretical explanation of homophily based on Socioemotional Selectivity Theory. She assumes that motives and interests of individuals change over time. However, if that is the case, individuals of similar age have similar objectives and interests. Age thus indirectly forms a basis for homophily.

In firms, baseline effects leading to age homophily are less prominent. Mostly, firms have employees of different ages. That means that there are only few constraints to the choice of relationship partners. Hence inbreeding homophily should apply for firm settings. Hence I hypothesize:

> Hypothesis 12a: Employees of similar age are more likely to form cooperation ties after mergers and acquisitions.
>
> Hypothesis 12b: Employees of similar age build more intense cooperation relationships than employees of dissimilar age after mergers and acquisitions.

2.2.1.2. Gender

While gender of individuals might not affect the individual amount of cooperation behavior, gender homophily has been found to be an important predictor for the choice of relationship partners. Verbrugge (1977) finds strong gender homophily in friendship networks. While kin networks show more gender diversity, Verbrugge (1977) finds that non-kin networks are strongly gender homophilous.

Marsden (1987) examines interpersonal networks in which Americans discuss "important matters" (Marsden 1987: 122) based on the 1985 General Social Survey. He analyzes heterogeneity of discussion networks and finds that they are homogeneous concerning sex.

In organizational settings, Ibarra (1992, 1993a) finds that men tend to have more sex homophilous networks than do women, especially in establishments where they are a strong majority. Similarly, Reagans (2005) investigates the effects of interpersonal attraction based on homophily. He also finds a strong preference for relationships between same sex individuals. Hence I hypothesize:

> Hypothesis 13a: Employees of the same sex are more likely to form cooperation relationships after mergers and acquisitions.
>
> Hypothesis 13b: Employees of the same sex build more intense cooperation relationships after mergers and acquisitions.

2.2.1.3. Education level

Marsden (1987) finds in his study on the General Social Survey data that roughly 30% of personal networks are highly homophilous on education, with a standard deviation of less than one year of duration of education. Especially, the edge categories of extremely high and low education show the biggest inbreeding tendency (Marsden 1988). A possible explanation for this finding is the fact that a medium level of education allows the formation of relationships with higher as well as with less educated individuals, thus increasing the education level heterogeneity of personal networks of individuals with a medium level of education. Similarly, Laumann (1994) finds that in romantic relationships, partners often have a very similar education level.

Previously, Verbrugge (1977) shows similar effects for friendship networks. He finds that friendship networks tend to show high levels of education homogeneity. Similarly, Louch (2000) finds that relationships among individuals are more likely when they have the same education.

In organizational settings, McPherson et al. (2001) point out that white collar and blue collar occupations represent a significant integration barrier. Similarly, Reagans (2005) investigates the effects of interpersonal attraction based on homophily in a small firm. He also finds homophily amongst employees with similar education level. Hence I hypothesize:

Hypothesis 14a: Employees of similar education level are more likely to form cooperation relationships after mergers and acquisitions.

Hypothesis 14b: Employees of similar education level build more intense cooperation relationships with each other than employees of dissimilar education after mergers and acquisitions.

2.2.1.4. Education content

Not only the level of education has been found to play a role for homophilous relationships, but also the content of education matters. Verbrugge (1977) finds that homophily in friendship networks depends on occupation similarity.

In an organizational setting, Reagans (2005) similarly finds that there is homophily between employees that have knowledge overlaps. Similar education content leads to knowledge overlaps. Hence I hypothesize:

Hypothesis 15a: Employees with similar education background are more likely to form relationships than employees with a dissimilar educational background

Hypothesis 15b: Employees with similar education background build more intense cooperation relationships than employees with a dissimilar education background.

2.2.2. Firm related characteristics

2.2.2.1. Rank

In organizational settings, hierarchical structures strongly determine cooperation structures. That means that managers primarily cooperate with their subordinates, which are of different rank. Homophily in hierarchical structures therefore should not apply. Rather, it seems likely that rank differences lead to higher levels of cooperation. Therefore, opposite to the homophily principle, I hypothesize:

Hypothesis 16a: Employees of dissimilar rank are more likely to form cooperation relationships than employees of similar rank after mergers and acquisitions.

Hypothesis 16b: Employees of dissimilar rank are more likely to form strong cooperation relationships after mergers and acquisitions than employees of similar rank.

2.2.2.2. Seniority

Seniority of employees depends on the time spend within the company or within a specific department. In his research in interpersonal attraction, Reagans (2005) finds that same tenure increases homophily of employees. Therefore, I hypothesize:

Hypothesis 17a: Employees of similar seniority are more likely to form cooperation relationships than employees of dissimilar seniority.

Hypothesis 17b: Employees of similar seniority form more intensive cooperation relationships than employees of dissimilar seniority.

2.2.3. Attitudes

2.2.3.1. Work related attitudes

In research on attitude homophily, Verbrugge (1977) finds that relationships show a high level of similarity of political and religious preferences, indicating attitudinal homophily.

In an organizational setting, Klein, Lim, Saltz, & Mayer (2004) investigate the centrality of individuals in teams. Based on social exchange theory, as well as similarity-attraction theories, they investigate 900 individuals from 96 teams. They find that similarity of two attitudes – hedonism as well as tradition – leads to higher centrality of individuals, indicating attitudinal homophily.

Work related attitudes represent a specific type of attitudes. Work related attitudes determine how employees accomplish a task. Exploratory interviews revealed that differences in the way of doing things can represent barriers for cooperation. For example, if an employee is highly responsive, he might expect a similar behavior from other colleagues, he cooperates with. When cooperating with others, employees face strong interdependencies. The way how their colleagues perform their tasks affects the way they can perform their own tasks. Hence an employee with high responsiveness will cooperate rather with other employees with high responsiveness. Similar ways of doing things facilitate cooperation and thus should lead to higher levels of cooperation. Hence I hypothesize:

Hypothesis 18a: Employees with similar work attitudes are more likely to cooperate after mergers and acquisitions than employees with dissimilar work attitudes.

Hypothesis 18b: Employees with similar work attitudes build more intensive cooperation relationships after mergers and acquisitions than employees with dissimilar work attitudes.

2.2.3.2. Reactions to mergers

Reactions to an M&A-transaction strongly depend on the perception of an M&A-transaction and on the perceived adequacy of the reaction. Berscheid, & Rice (1998) argue that people tend to feel more attracted to people who see them as they see themselves. Similarly, people tend to feel more attracted to people who react similarly to themselves.

There are different possible reactions to M&A-transactions. Schweiger, & DeNisi (1991) describe two major reactions: commitment and uncertainty of employees. Commitment and uncertainty both yield results on the choice of a coping strategy (see also Buono, & Nurick 1992). Employees are more likely to engage in cooperation with other employees that share the same reaction to mergers, be it commitment or be it uncertainty. Hence I hypothesize:

Hypothesis 19a: Employees with similar levels of commitment are more likely to cooperate than employees with dissimilar levels of commitment.

Hypothesis 19b: Employees with similar levels of commitment build more intensive relationships than employees with dissimilar levels of commitment.

Hypothesis 20a: Employees with similar levels of uncertainty are more likely to cooperate than employees with dissimilar levels of commitment.

Hypothesis 20b: Employees with similar levels of uncertainty build more intensive relationships than employees with dissimilar levels of commitment.

2.2.4. Controls

2.2.4.1. Active integration measures

As described above, the necessary condition for the formation of relationships is the first contact. First contact, however, strongly depends on active integration measures. Employees that participate in integration measures are more likely to have first contact than other employees that do not participate in integration measures. Hence I hypothesize:

> Hypothesis 21a: If employees participate in integration measures, they are more likely to form cooperation relationships with each other after mergers and acquisitions.

However, as active integration measures only lead to the first contact and not to enduring attraction, I assume that integration measures do not have an effect on cooperation strength. Hence I hypothesize:

> Hypothesis 21b: There is no effect of participation in integration measures on strength of cooperation.

2.2.4.2. Structural constraints

As has been mentioned above, cooperation relationships in organizations are highly constrained by formal organizational structures. While inbreeding homophily determines deliberate relationships strongly, employees in organizational structures often have fewer opportunities to choose their relationship partners. Hence structural constraints should play an important role on the formation of cooperation relationships.

Therefore, I consider in this research the cooperation between two organizational units as a control variable in order to identify homophily effects between employees. Hence I hypothesize:

> Hypothesis 22a: The amount of cooperation relationships between two organizational units affects the probability of two individuals in each of the units to have a relationship.
>
> Hypothesis 22b: The strength of cooperation relationships between two organizational units affects the strength of relationships of two individuals in each of the units.

2.2.5. Summary of the research model: Who cooperates with whom?

In the illustration below, the expected relationships can be seen for the different kinds of similarity and the existence and intensity of cooperation relationships. Also, the influence of integration measures as well as of structural cooperation requirements can be seen:

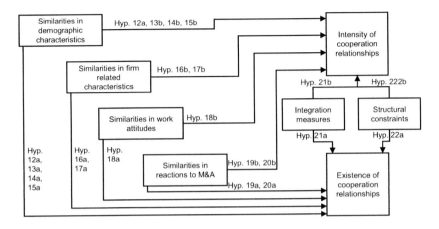

Illustration 21: Summary of Research model for research question "Who cooperates with whom?"

All but one hypothesis propose a positive relationship of similarity of a characteristic of two employees and the likelihood of existence of a relationship between these employees. The exception is similarity of rank. As cooperation across ranks is structurally constrained, and as employees hardly have a chance not to cooperate with their superiors, it is assumed that rank different yields a positive effect on likelihood of existence of a relationship between employees of different ranks. Table 23 summarizes the hypotheses about the effects of similarity of employees on the likelihood of existence of a relationship between them.

Hyp.	Independent variable	Dependent variable	Expected effect
12a	Similar age	Existence of relationship	+
13a	Similar gender	Existence of relationship	+
14a	Similar education level	Existence of relationship	+
15a	Similar education content	Existence of relationship	+
16a	Similar rank	Existence of relationship	-
17a	Similar seniority	Existence of relationship	+
18a	Similar work attitudes	Existence of relationship	+
19a	Similar commitment	Existence of relationship	+
20a	Similar uncertainty	Existence of relationship	+
21a	Integration measures	Existence of relationship	+
22a	Structural requirements	Existence of relationship	+

Table 23: Hypotheses for research question "Who cooperates with whom?" for dependent variable likelihood of "existence of relationship"

Corresponding to that, all but one hypothesis propose a positive relationship between similarities of characteristics of individuals and intensity of cooperation. Again, rank similarity is assumed to yield a negative effect on cooperation intensity. Also, participation in integration measures is assumed to have no independent effect on intensity of cooperation relationships, because it should only matter for the initiation of relationships but not for ongoing relationships. Table 24 summarizes the hypothesized effects.

Hyp.	Independent variable	Dependent variable	Expected effect
12b	Similar age	Intensity of relationship	+
13b	Similar gender	Intensity of relationship	+
14b	Similar education level	Intensity of relationship	+
15b	Similar education content	Intensity of relationship	+
16b	Similar rank	Intensity of relationship	-
17b	Similar seniority	Intensity of relationship	+
18b	Similar work attitudes	Intensity of relationship	+
19b	Similar commitment	Intensity of relationship	+
20b	Similar uncertainty	Intensity of relationship	+
21b	Integration measures	Intensity of relationship	0
22b	Structural requirements	Intensity of relationship	+

Table 24: Hypotheses for research question "Who cooperates with whom?" for dependent variable "intensity of relationship"

3. Empirical investigation

According to Popper (1959) hypotheses cannot be inductively verified. That means that no empirical study can prove a hypothesized relationship between variables. However, according to Popper (1959), hypotheses can be falsified. At the same time a positive result of a test can be interpreted as support for a hypothesis.

Empirical testing thus can achieve falsification respectively support of hypothesized relationships. In order to test hypothesized relationships, values of independent and dependent variables are collected. Qualitative analyses respectively statistical analyses help to determine the relationships between the considered variables.

When developing a research setup, it is important to consider the right level of observation and the right level of analysis for the research. The level of observation describes, on which level, the unit of observation is located. Units of observation can be very different things: actions, processes, events, as well as individuals, or larger social constructs such as groups, companies, or even countries. The level of analysis describes the level, on which the data is analyzed and statements are produced. For example, it is possible to gather information on companies within a specific industry. This is the level of observation. Based on this data, it is possible to make statements about the industry, such as growth rate of the industry, maturity of products, or profitability. This then is the level of analysis.

While it is well possible to aggregate units of observation to larger or more comprehensive units to analyze them, it is not possible to disaggregate units of observation to smaller units. For example, when gathering information about the vote in a specific local community, it is possible to make statements about this specific local community. However, it is not possible to make statements about single inhabitants within this community. Similarly, results on a certain level of analysis cannot be disaggregated to lower levels of analysis.

It is noteworthy that the source of data might not necessarily determine the level of observation. Key informants can provide information that describes a different level of observation than the individual level. For example, key informants can be used to gather information on companies. While they answer as individuals, the unit of observation is the company.

In the present research, three main questions are guiding the empirical investigation:
- Who cooperates after M&A-transactions?
- Who cooperates with whom after M&A-transaction?
- What is the impact of integration measures on cooperation after M&A-measures?

This puts certain boundaries to the choice of level of observation and level of analysis.

The level of analysis of the first question is the individual. In order to answer this question, it is necessary to gather data on cooperation on the individual level or even on a more detailed level. A more detailed level of observation could for example be specific activities of an actor, such as walking, writing and interacting. These specific activities could in a second step be grouped in different categories, and the cooperation category then could be analyzed to answer the research question.

The level of analysis in the second question is the dyad. "At the most basic level, a linkage or relationship establishes a tie between two actors" (Wasserman, & Faust 1994: 18). A dyad consists of a pair of actors and the tie between them. Dyadic analysis then can be used to generate insights about characteristics of the dyad, for example about the effect of similarity of two actors on the probability of existence and characteristics of a tie between these two actors.

The level of analysis in the third question can be both, on the level of the individual or on the level of a dyad. For example, it is possible to examine, how participation in an integration measure affects the cooperation of an individual actor. It is equally possible to investigate, whether the joint participation of actors in an integration measure increases the probability of existence of a tie between them.

Based on these considerations, it is obvious that for the present research, data needs to be gathered on the individual level. The individual level data then can be analyzed on the individual level respectively on the dyadic level. This bears a few important implications for the research setup of this research:

- The unit of observation has to be the individual. It is impossible to use key informants to gather information about cooperation of third individuals.
- A large number of individuals and their cooperation relationships need to be observed. In order to make sure that dyads can be gathered, it is necessary that these individuals potentially cooperate. That means that individuals within one firm need to be interrogated. Hence the sample of this study needs to consist of a large number of individuals within one firm
- Firm level variables cannot be considered quantitatively. Firm level variables can only be investigated, if the sample of different firms is sufficiently large. However, as the unit of observation in this study is the individual, the investigation of a large number of firms would require the investigation of a very large number of individuals, because in each firm, a sufficiently large number of individuals would have to be investigated. This is not possible in the context of this study.

Data on the level of the individual can be gathered in one or in several firms. By investigating employees from several firms within one sample, a large number of firm-level variables need to be considered as control variables. For example, the type and the characteristics of the

M&A-transaction strongly affect the cooperation relationships of employees and therefore need to be considered. This, however, increases the number of investigated variables and thus makes the research design very complex. The number of required cases increases strongly as the number of control variables increases. Therefore, gathering individual level data within one firm is more appropriate in this research.

Data on the level of the dyad can most meaningfully be gathered within one firm, because otherwise, only isolated relationships can be gathered, because no information on relationship partners is available. At the same time, the same effects as for individual level data apply: By investigating dyads of different firms within one sample, firm level variables need to be considered, making the research design very complex.

As a consequence, the date for this research has been gathered two research sites, which have been investigated with the help of two similar but distinct research designs. As firm level variables cannot be controlled for, the results need to be qualified with the help of information on the firm level variables. Thereby, potential effects of firm level variables can at least be qualitatively considered.

In the following paragraphs, I present the two research sites, which I investigated in order to test the postulated hypotheses. Then I describe different formal aspects of the research, and I clarify the exact content of the research. Formal aspects and content of the research need to be designed to test the research questions and the derived hypotheses in an appropriate manner.

Formal aspects are relevant for the structure and the process of the research. First, the research design needs to be determined. The research design determines the logic for testing the hypothesized relationships. Then the type of data needs to be determined, which is used for the testing. Finally the sample needs to be determined, that means the type of units of observation and the number of units of observation.

The content of the research mainly concerns the selection and the operationalization of the constructs which have been formulated in the hypotheses.

After having presented the two research sites, I will present the research setup of the current research, including research design as well as operationalization for the different research sites.

3.1. Research sites

In the following descriptions of the research sites, I highlight a number of firm-level variables. As individuals are in the center of interest of this study, I investigate a large number of individuals in two distinct M&A-transactions. As a consequence, I can describe and test in detail variables on the level of the individuals. However, it is impossible to generate statistically grounded results on the firm level. Nevertheless, some background information for the research sites is necessary for a qualified discussion of the results and potential firm level effects that influence individual behaviors of the employees.

3.1.1. First research site - SpecMatCo

The first research site is an international special material producer, which I will call SpecMatCo in the remainder of this document. The products of the firm are sold to customers coming from many different industries. The firm has approximately 2800 employees and a turnover of € 330 million[7]. It has ten different production sites and sales companies in all major European, Asian and American markets.

The merged firms had operated both in the same industry. In an international horizontal merger of equals, the top management of the firm pursued three main strategic objectives:

- Bundle the activities of both firms in order to develop a stronger position in the multi-point competition with the main competitor. Each of merged the firms was highly specialized in a number of small niches and had dominant market positions in these niches. However, each firm was significantly smaller than the main competitor, when defining the industry more broadly. By pooling its activities, they strengthened their market positions in some niches. At the same time, they occupied together a larger number of niches, giving them more resistance to eventual attacks of the main competitor.
- Pool production capacities and development knowledge in order to secure future growth options and the necessary capacities.
- Save cost, especially through using the extended production network to allocate each product to the production site best fitted for the production, and by merging sales companies.

The two firms implemented the new integrated structure approximately 15 months before the research. The new structure was based on a customer-oriented logic. While the former organizational structures were focused on products, the new structure put customer needs and thereby industries in the center of the organizational structure.

Despite operating in the same industries, the firms had slight differences in their business models. While they operated in almost every market as direct competitor with similar products chasing the same customers, Firm A had a stronger pull-oriented business model, whereas Firm B had a stronger push oriented business model. That means that Firm A generated a large share of its turnover with specialties, i.e. customized products that were produced to order. An order for a customized product usually comprises a drawing with all technical details such as geometry of a product and the material of a product. Also, customers ask for a price and a delivery date. In the pull business model, speed in deciding on the orders

---

[7] The key figures of the firm have been altered in order to ensure anonymity of the firms.

of the customers is crucial. The sales force of Firm A was relatively small, because it generated most of its sales from the pull business model, which requires only little active sales activities.

Firm B, however, generated a larger share of its turnover with standard products. Standards are catalogued products. Standards are produced to stock and sold from stock.

In the illustration below, the main process from product idea generation to distribution is shown. The activities on each step of the process are shown. Also, the key success factors in the process are shown. Looking at the high level process of the firms, it becomes clear that success factors in each business models differ widely.

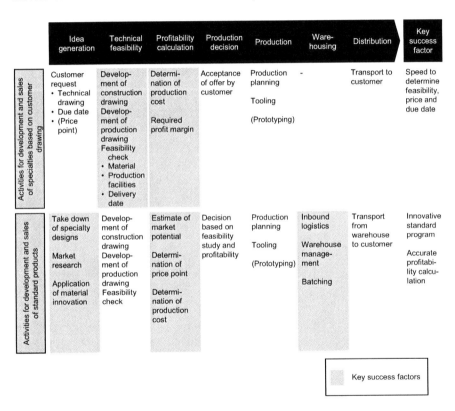

Illustration 22: Standard process from idea to distribution with Key Success Factors per business model

As can be seen, success factors differed widely between the firms. As a consequence, the organizational structures differed and the roles and responsibilities of the mirroring functions differed strongly. For example, in Firm A, the product management was mainly responsible for dealing with orders for customized products from large customers. The product management of Firm B had full sales responsibility and headed a team of sales persons, developers as well as production planners. Product managers of Firm B needed to conduct detailed market analysis to identify the market needs for a standard product. Also, they had to engage in sophisticated planning in order to produce the right volumes. Such differences in activities, however, resulted in interfaces between functions of Firm A that were highly dissimilar to interfaces between functions of Firm B.

Headquarters and main production sites were in the same location for each firm. That means that until the M&A-transaction, the cooperation between production and product management was extremely tight. As a consequence, employees of both firms were used to operate in tight operative networks and only little according to formal structures.

Besides strategic and organizational differences of the merging firms, it needs to be noted that the merging firms had headquarters in different countries with different languages. A shift from the respective national languages to English as the company language was the consequence.

During the first months of the integration, the firms had engaged in a number of integration measures. All employees and workers of Firm A had visited the main location of Firm B and vice versa. In addition to that, the company had kicked off a cultural change program in order to agree upon and implement a new shared culture. In order to do so, they had organized workshops with the top management team, and with some of the key functions of the firm.

3.1.2. SoftCo

The second research site is a specialized IT-systems producer and IT-service provider, which I will call SoftCo in the rest of this work. The firm offers IT-systems as well as IT-services for two distinct customer groups in different but related industries. Accordingly, the company has two divisions that operate highly independent. The firm has approximately 1,300 employees and roughly € 80 million turnover per year[8]. The M&A-transaction only concerns one of the two divisions, with approximately 450 employees and a turnover of € 35 million. It has operations in two different countries with a strong focus on the German market.

SoftCo had operated originally as an IT-service provider for a large number of customers. Due to technological changes, the business model of SoftCo is threatened on the long-run, i.e. within the next 10 years following the M&A-transaction. SoftCo assumed that IT-systems could be able to internalize their core service business on the long-run based on technological innovations and a shift of industry standards and industry structures. As a consequence, SoftCo decided to engage in the market for IT-systems, serving the same customer base as before and internalizing future rivals in order to secure its long term survival. Therefore, SoftCo acquired two IT-systems producers, who were direct competitors before the

---

[8] The key figures of the firm have been altered in order to ensure anonymity of the firms.

acquisition. Both acquired firms sold a self-developed complex software solution and a range of hardware components. They both offered extensive maintenance services, generating a significant percentage of their turnover. The software solutions they offered were grown software packages that both were on the market since more than 10 years. Regular updates and regular addition of new functions sufficed to win new customers. However, both firms were too small to take the next level of software development. That means that both firms did not have the capacities to develop an entirely new software solution for their customers.

Hence the M&A-transaction of SoftCo is a product concentric acquisition of two future rivals, serving the long-term survival perspectives of SoftCo and the acquired firms. The strategic objectives were threefold:

- In a short term perspective, the acquirer aims to ensure consolidation of development capacities and develop a new software platform.
- In a mid term perspective, the acquirer aims to merge the current core business and the IT-software business in order to provide a new and unique value proposition to customers reflecting the technology convergence
- In a long term perspective, the acquirer aims to develop strong development capacities serving all different divisions

As a consequence, the integration of the firms is accomplished in two steps. 24 months before the research took place, the firms had shifted to a fully integrated organizational structure. Four main activities had been conducted in order to achieve full integration:

1. Standardization and restructuring. The organizational structure in the integrated division had been standardized. That means that in both acquired firms, the same mirroring organizational structures have been implemented. The organizational structure has been selected according to best practice logic. Also, the management has been integrated. Mirroring teams in one function are always headed by one manager. That means that the organization is fully integrated down to the lowest management level.

    Systems have been aligned. A number of island-systems have been replaced by an ERP-solution, which is implemented equally in both acquired firms.

    The social standards have been aligned. That means that incentives, working hours, ranks and positions as well as non-pecuniary standards such as free beverages and free snacks have been aligned.

2. Centralization of activities. Purchasing has been centralized. Also, the coordination of the maintenance teams has been centralized. The marketing of the firms has been integrated. The firm now offers three product brands under one umbrella brand.

3. Better management. By introducing efficient sales and ordering processes, some of the core processes of the integrated firms have been improved.

Incentive systems have been aligned as well as technological standards in the call-centers. Also, the software development process got standardized. All developers now have to use a common standard approach.
4. Development of a new product. Early on, the product development and the programming teams started to develop a new software platform. At the time of the research, the firm had started to train sales people and maintenance people on the new product. However, the product was not yet on the market at the time of the research.

It is necessary to note that the old products of the software firms continue to be sold. While the development activities for both products were significantly reduced, the sales, order processing and production activities were maintained. As a consequence, the organizational structure was organized as a matrix with a functional and a product dimension. The product dimension was collapsed in the product management and the software development teams.

The next step of integration will be the collapse of the product dimension in the matrix organization. The target structure then will be a divisional structure.

In order to facilitate integration, the senior management had initiated a number of integration measures. Amongst others, two large annual works outings had been organized. Also, regular exchanges of employees and visits of the other locations were initiated.

3.2. Research design

The research design is decisive to what extent hypothesized causal relationships can really be tested. There are three basic forms of research design:
- The experiment
- The quasi-experiment
- The pre-experiment and correlation analysis

(Singleton, Straits & Straits 1993).

3.2.1. Experiment

The most important characteristic of the experiment is the repeated measurement of the dependent variable and the systematic manipulation of the independent variable by the researcher. A standard experimental research design consists at least of three different steps. First, the dependent variable is measured. Then the independent variable is manipulated. Then again, the dependent variable is measured. For example, it is possible to determine the effect of chess classes on the concentration performance of pupils. At the beginning of the school year, concentration performance of pupils can be measured. After a year of chess classes, at the end of the school year, concentration performance can be measured again.

The quality of the experiment can be improved with the help of a control group. A control group contains units of observation that resemble the units of observation in the experimental group. The dependent variable of the control group is measured similarly to the experimental group. However, the independent variable is not manipulated. By comparing the results of the repeated measurement of the dependent variable, it is possible to identify the effect of the independent variable. The delta between the values of the dependent variables of experimental group and control group can be explained with the manipulation of the independent variable. The use of control groups is helpful, because it controls for additional effects, which in addition to the manipulation of the control variable can influence the value of the dependent variable. For example, in the chess class example, a year of classes, maturing another year or more specific influences such as a good math teacher, might have an effect on the concentration performance of pupils. However, by investigating a control group of pupils in the same age and with the same math teacher, the additional effects can be controlled for, and the relationship between independent and dependent variable can clearly be determined.

The advantage of experimental research designs is the possibility to determine causal relationships between independent and dependent variables very exactly. In addition to that, control variables can be determined and controlled for very well.

The disadvantage of experimental research designs is the low number of independent variables that can be manipulated. By manipulating several independent variables, the number of experimental groups and control groups increases quickly. More complex phenomena therefore can hardly be tested in experimental research designs. Another disadvantage of experimental research designs are problems of transferring findings to real world phenomena. Due to the artificial nature of the experiment, it is not obvious to transfer experimental findings.

Basically, there are two different ways to conduct experiments. There are laboratory experiments and field experiments. Laboratory experiments are executed in strongly controlled laboratory settings, which often tend to be artificial. Field experiments, however, are held in the field, i.e. in real life settings. Field experiments thus allow measurement and manipulation of variables in natural settings. While the laboratory experiment allows high levels of control of the investigated variables, the results are hardly transferable. The field experiment allows findings, which are better transferable to real life situation. At the same time the control of context variables is much more difficult than in the laboratory experiment. Another disadvantage of field experiments is a relatively high organizational effort.

3.2.2. Quasi-experiment

The quasi-experiment resembles the setup of an experiment strongly. After a first measurement of the dependent variables the independent variable changes. Then the dependent variables are measured again. Again, the relationship between independent and dependent variables can be captured very well. However, unlike in an experimental setting, the researcher cannot manipulate the independent variable in a quasi-experiment. Rather, the changes of the independent variable are exogenously induced. It might even be possible to form control groups, which are not treated with the change of the independent variable (Singleton, Straits & Straits 1993).

An important type of quasi-experimental research designs is the panel study. In a panel study, a selected group of individuals or units of observation is repeatedly investigated. Changes in characteristics are related with events, which happen between the measurements. Another important type is the cohort analysis. In a cohort analysis, members of the same cohort, i.e. a predefined group of individuals that at some point in time share the same relevant characteristics is selected and repeatedly investigated. In a cohort analysis, it is not necessary to repeatedly investigate the same units of observation. Rather, a sample of the cohort is investigated at each measurement time.

The quasi-experiment is very useful to investigate natural phenomena. It is possible to investigate independent variables that cannot or only insufficiently be manipulated in experimental situations. For example, it is almost impossible to have the characteristics of mergers and acquisitions as independent variables in an experimental design. The situation is too complex to simulate in the context of an experiment. In quasi-experiments, causal relationships between independent and dependent variables can be determined unequivocally, because the chronological order of changes in dependent and independent variables can be traced clearly. This allows clear conclusions about the existence, strength and direction of the causal relationship between independent and dependent variable. Especially dynamic phenomena can be investigated well with the help of quasi-experiments.

An advantage of quasi-experiments is the applicability in real world settings, i.e. in field settings. Causal relationships can clearly be determined due to the repeated measurement, which captures the temporal order of cause and effect. For example, the formation of cooperation relationships after mergers and acquisitions can clearly be measured with the help of quasi-experiments.

An important disadvantage of quasi-experiments is a limited reproducibility of the quasi-experiment. As the variation of the independent variable is exogenously induced and not manipulated by the researcher, it is almost impossible to repeat a quasi-experiment. Another problem of quasi-experiments is the exclusion of effects from other independent influences.

In panel studies, panel mortality is a significant problem. Panel mortality describes the fact that during the measurement period, some individuals depart from the panel. If the departure is fully random, there is no problem. However, if members of the panel depart because of systematic effects, such as specific characteristics, the results of the repeated measurement is systematically distorted (Laatz 1993). For example, after mergers and acquisitions, layoffs might change the age structure of employees. According to hypothesis 1c, increasing age is assumed to have negative effects on commitment of employees. If a panel shows an increase in commitment, while at the same time older employees depart from the company, the increase in commitment might results from the changes of the panel.

Another effect of panel studies is the panel effect. Due to the repeated measurement, members of the panel systematically change their behaviors. As a result, changes in the dependent variable might not result from changes of an independent variable but from a panel effect.

A problem of cohort studies is the determination of characteristics that clearly identify a cohort. Based on these characteristics, two independent samples of the same cohort need to be determined.

Another effect can be cohort effects, which deteriorate the generalization of results. For example, specific events might imprint a cohort in a way that makes it difficult to compare the effects of an independent variable on other cohorts.

Another disadvantage of quasi-experiments is the need for repeated measurement. Especially in business settings, repeated measurement is difficult to achieve. Control groups only rarely can be implemented.

3.2.3. Pre-experiment and correlation analysis

Correlative analyses are frequently used for research on complex phenomena in research settings where access is difficult. In a correlative analysis, independent and dependent variables are measured in one measurement. For each unit of observation, the values of the independent and the dependent variables are measured. The direction of the causal relationship is determined with the help of theoretically and/or empirically grounded considerations. The strength of the causal relationship is determined with the help of statistical analyses.

The advantage of correlation analysis is the easy application. One measurement time suffices to gather the required data. This makes correlation analysis especially appealing in business settings, where repeated measurement often is not applicable because of time constraints of employees or lack of motivation of the management. The results are quickly available, because the measured results can directly be analyzed. All relationships between the variables can be determined.

A disadvantage, especially in exploratory research is the impossibility to determine causal relationships empirically. Dynamic phenomena cannot be described empirically because one measurement does not inform about direction and momentum of developments. Especially in research on cooperation relationships after mergers and acquisitions, a snapshot of the current structure of relationships might fall short of an in-depth exploration of the relationships between independent and dependent variables.

3.2.4. Research design for this study

The research design of the present study is a correlative analysis. Despite advantages of a quasi-experimental design, practical constraints outbalance the advantages of a quasi-experimental design.

A quasi-experimental research design would be favorable for two main reasons:
- The formation of cooperation is a dynamic phenomenon. The formation of cooperation relationships takes a long period of time. Cross-sectional studies only allow a snapshot. However, it is unclear, whether the cross-sectional analysis shows a steady state, or whether it shows a transitional situation, which is not stable, and which therefore does not show stable causal relationships.
- M&A-transactions last over longer periods of time. Therefore, the necessity of forming cooperation relationships builds up over time. Initially, first cooperation relationships are being formed in transition teams. After the completion of the integration phase, these relationships weaken significantly and might become irrelevant. At the same time, other cooperation relationships of the target structure of the company gain importance and converge to a steady state. With the help of repeated measurement, it is possible to identify convergence and determine a potential steady state. However, during the process of convergence, a snapshot picture shows integration that might be affected by random factors such as participation in integration measures or membership in an integration team.

Despite the cross-sectional design of this study, the research design can be interpreted as a quasi-experiment. Before the merger, there were no cooperation requirements and with a high likelihood no informal cooperation relationships between employees of the merging firms. After the independent event of the M&A-transaction, cooperation relationships could be formed. An imagined first measurement thus yields no relationships. After the M&A-transaction the relationships emerge. This corresponds to a quasi-experimental research design.

During the preparation of this research, several companies indicated that repeated measurement would be impossible because of the high effort for employees to provide the necessary data. While two firms complied with a cross-sectional approach, it was impossible to win them for a longitudinal study. The reason for their reluctance is the sensitivity of the employees after mergers and acquisitions. Any additional measure or impact, such as a scientific data gathering is perceived as a disturbance in a situation that is critical anyway. The period after an M&A-transaction usually is characterized by high anxiety and uncertainty (Schweiger, & DeNisi 1991; Hogg, & Terry 2000). The responsible top executives feared that repeated measurement could damage the organizational climate and the motivation of employees.

3.3. Type of data gathered

The research design determines the points in time at which data is gathered. In a second step, though, it is necessary to determine the type of data to be collected and the method of gathering them.

Basically, there are two different types of data: Primary data and secondary data. Primary data is data that is collected especially for the testing of the hypotheses of a study. Secondary data is data that has been gathered previously to the study with other intentions, and which is recycled to test a given set of hypotheses.

In the following paragraphs, in reverse order, I will go into the details of secondary data and then on primary data. In looking at primary data, I will consider a special type of primary data gathering: The gathering of non-reactive data. Later I will have a detailed look at the gathering of primary data via observation and interrogation. Then I will describe the data gathering approach in the two studies used in this research.

3.3.1. Gathering of secondary data

Using secondary data for testing hypotheses in an empirical research does not require the generation of new data. Rather, existing data, which has been gathered independently from the study and previously to the study can be used. Friedrichs (1980) correspondingly defines that "The secondary data analysis is a method to analyze existing material (primary data) independently of the original purpose and context of the gathered data" (Friedrichs 1980: 353, own translation). Similarly, Bortz, & Döring (2003) point out that "The analysis of already existing (raw) data with new methods or with another question is called secondary data analysis" (Bortz, & Döring 2003: 374, own translation). Secondary data thus can be data from previous studies that dealt with a similar question. However, it can also be data that has been gathered in a different context, such as yearbooks, special reports, statistics or annual reports of firms.

The use of secondary data is often significantly less time consuming and less resource intensive than the gathering of primary data. Bortz, & Döring (2003) correspondingly claim that " Data gathering is often very time consuming and expensive. Therefore, it is often little economical, if rich datasets are only used by one person – or one research team" (Bortz, & Döring 2003: 374). As secondary data is readily available, researchers only have to build a data set to run the analyses they need to answer the research questions.

It is necessary, though, to carefully check the validity of secondary data. Validity here describes the usability of secondary data to answer the research question at hand. As the data has been gathered originally with a different intention respectively with a different objective, it is possible that the secondary data is not suited for operationalization of the research constructs. For example, success of a company can be operationalized in different ways. Sales, sales growth, profit, EBIT, EBITDA and other measures can be used. However, depending on the question, the usefulness of these secondary data differs widely.

Another problem in using secondary data is the lack of knowledge about the quality of the data. If a researcher gathers primary data, she knows very well the limitations of the data and thus can qualify the findings and show limitations of the research. When using secondary data, weaknesses of the data are mostly unknown.

There is no secondary data for the research questions of this study. As there is no known study that deals explicitly with cooperation relationships after mergers and acquisitions, there is no data that could be recycled. Some practitioners might have data on cooperation in small teams after mergers and acquisitions. However, to the knowledge of the author of this study, there is no dataset that investigates cooperation as well as individual and dyadic variables, which could be used for answering the research questions.

3.3.2. Gathering of non-reactive data

"The collective term 'non-reactive methods' (unobtrusive measures, non-reactive research, nonintruding measures) describes data gathering methods, whose execution does not effect individuals, events or processes" (Bortz, & Döring 2003: 325, own translation). As early as 1966, Campbell, Schwartz, & Sechrest (1966) have put together a set of empirical studies with different data gathering methods, which all have in common that researcher and unit of observation are never in contact with each other. That means that neither the researcher influence the unit of observation nor vice versa.

One form of non-reactive data gathering is the content respectively document analysis. This analysis uses "… objectivations of human behaviors" (Laatz 1993: 207). "Document analysis means that investigated items represent certain units of observation" (Laatz 1993: 207, own translation). Documents can be written documents such as letters, files. Documents can also be non-written items such as pictures, photos, buildings and other manifestations of human activity. Content analysis, in contrast, deals with material that is used for communication (Laatz 1993: 208). Content analysis collects the content of documents and analyzes it. Content and document analysis both are based on readily available material, which can be analyzed according to specific criteria in order to generate the data necessary for a study (Laatz 1993: 209). Examples of documents that can be used in content analysis are signs, information boards, archives, sales statistics, diaries, meeting protocols, emails, quick dialing memories, meeting lists and itemized telephone bills. For example, Hayward, & Hambrick (1994) analyze annual reports to determine the hubris of CEOs.

Another form of non-reactive data gathering methods is trace analysis. Trace analysis investigates traces of all forms. For example, in museums, visitors leave traces in from of exhibits that are particularly famous. Also, it is possible to find out favorite seats in public settings.

For the research of cooperation relationships there are a number of different ways to use non-reactive data gathering methods. For example, quick dialing memories can be used as an indicator for the most important telephone contacts. Similarly, email logs can be used to determine email-traffic and thus relationships of written communication. With the help of meeting lists, formal interaction can be determined.

A great advantage of non-reactive data gathering methods to collect data on cooperation relationships is the unobtrusiveness of the data collection. The collection of data is temporally and locally decoupled from the individuals under consideration. The individuals do not notice the investigation and thus cannot react to it. Hence the risk of respondent bias is completely eliminated. Another advantage can be the availability of longitudinal data. For example, email logs or itemized telephone bills can capture interactions and thus relationships over longer periods of time.

There are three major problems with non-reactive methods in the research of relationships:

- The content of a relationship is unclear. While it is possible to gather information on existence and with some methods even on frequency of interaction, it is hardly possible to determine the importance, the content and the quality of cooperation. For example, it is not possible, whether two individuals that attended the same meeting really cooperate, or whether they only happened to be in the same meeting.

  Email traffic similarly can be used to track communication relationships. However, it is a very complex task to analyze the content of emails. The mere amount of emails makes it difficult to code emails according to content (Keila, & Skillicorn 2005). As emails only represent a fraction of human communication, it is possible that important cooperation relationships are not even tracked. For example, in an open-plan office, talk with each other. They do not need to send emails. An email-analysis thus would neglect these cooperation relationships completely. Also, a large percentage of email traffic is generated by putting individuals on "cc:". However, informing individuals does not imply any cooperation relationship.

- Fit of available non-reactive data and the research question is a second problem of non-reactive data. There are only few types of non-reactive data available. However, a research question often requires very specific operationalization of researched constructs. For example, when capturing cooperation, there are different forms of cooperation. Some employees might prefer personal and direct communication. Others use the phone for all aspects of cooperation. Again others might prefer email. And again others use comment fields in ERP-systems.

Operationalizing cooperation and measuring it with the help of non-reactive data thus would require measuring all different types of communication. Otherwise, the operationalization of cooperation would necessarily be incomplete.

- The legal situation is unclear. There are massive problems with protection of privacy. Especially in Germany, it is literally impossible to use email traffic as a method of data collection. The same is true for quick dialing memories. They are often used for storing private numbers as well.

In the present research, it was the latter aspect of non-reactive data that was decisive for not using it. In preparation talks of this research, representatives of the research sites had severe concerns of gathering non-reactive data.

The only non-reactive data that could have been gathered would have been meeting lists. However, in the preparation talks, it turned out that meeting lists are often incomplete. Also, there is no central gathering of meeting lists. Only very small fragment of cooperation takes place in meetings. Hence any collection of meeting lists would have yielded an incomplete picture of the cooperation relationships within the firm.

3.3.3. Gathering of primary data

Primary data is such that is gathered especially for the investigation and the testing of the hypothesized effects to answer the research questions (Bortz, & Döring 2003: 374). There are different approaches to gather primary data. The two most important approaches are observation and interrogation of units of observation of a research, in this case of employees.

Observation means that researchers track visible behaviors with the help of scientific observation. Scientific observation is characterized by a high degree of standardization and objectivity. Interrogation, in contrast, captures subjective statements of respondents (Laatz 1993: 169).

In the following paragraphs, I will first describe observation and then interrogation as two approaches for gathering primary data in more detail.

3.3.3.1. Observation

Observation in a strict sense is the collection of information in a non-communicative process with the help of all possible ways of perception of the researcher (Laatz 1993: 169). The researcher can capture and document behaviors, statements, as well as tonality of respondents. The main difference between common and scientific observation is the focus and the methodological rigor of scientific observation (Laatz 1993: 169). Quantitative as well as qualitative observation techniques aim to avoid the typical subjectivity and anecdotal character of common observation by standardizing the approach, detailed documentation and intersubjective comparability of the observation criteria (Bortz, & Döring 2003: 262). Direct observation is locally and temporally limited through the reach of perception of the researcher(s) and complementary aids such as cameras.

There are different dimensions to distinguish different types of observation (Laatz 1993: 171):

- Standardization: Observation can be standardized to different degrees. Standardized observation usually is based on a number of predefined patterns of behaviors, which can be captured in an individual, spatial as well as temporal logic. That means that it is possible to describe what individual shows what activity at what point in time and in what location.

  The advantage of standardization of observation is a high degree of intersubjectivity of the gathered data. Different observers can be trained to work with a specific observation standard and thus generate highly reliable observations.

  An important disadvantage of standardized observation is the potential loss of observation. A standardized observation can only document activities or events that fit into one of the predefined categories. However, if central categories are missing, the validity of collected data is low.

  The disadvantages can be avoided with the help of detailed pre-studies. However, standardization always implies a reduction of complexity. More complex phenomena therefore can hardly be captured.

- Transparency: Observation can be open or hidden. Open observation implies that the observed individuals are informed about the observation. An example for open observation are the Hawthorne studies (Roethlisberger 1941). In the Hawthorne studies, a team of researchers investigated different environmental effects on the performance of workers. However, the results of the study were strange. When the researchers dimmed the light, the performance of the workers increased. When the increased the light, the performance of the workers increased as well. As a consequence, they found the "Hawthorne effect". The Hawthorne-effect indicates that individuals that are observed react to the observation. In the case of the Hawthorne studies, the workers indicated that they felt observed and thus increased their performance. Open observation thus might suffer from a respondent bias.

  Hidden observation, however, might be questionable from an ethical point of view. While it is obvious that reactivity of respondents can be avoided, there can be serious ethical and even legal problems in observing individuals without their knowledge.

- Role of the observer: Observation can be participative or non-participative. Participative observation can be further distinguished in active participation and passive participation. Participative observation means that the observer is physically present in an observation situation. For example, Barley (1990b) investigates the introduction of CT-scanners in the radiology department of two hospitals. Barley (1990b describes in detail how he participated in meetings, how he was around all day in the setting. He describes, how he went "native" after a short period of time. Going native means becoming part of the setting that the researcher observes. While Barley (1990b) never participated in the activities of the settings, he describes that after a short period of time, employees perceived him as a colleague with special tasks.

Non-participative observation is frequently used in marketing research. For example, a group of individuals can be observed through hidden cameras or one-sided mirrors.

The advantage of participative observation is the possibility to be in the situation and thus capture the situation holistically. At the same time, there is a severe threat of influencing the behaviors of individuals. Also, participative observation requires special competencies and training of the observer. As the span of attention of an observer is limited, she can only capture a small fraction of the characteristics of a specific situation.

The advantage of non-participative observation is the possibility to use several observers, which each can focus on one aspect of behavior or on one individual. Moreover, it is possible to use media that allows a temporal decoupling of the observation and the analysis. Last but not least, non-participation of the observer reduces the influence of the observer on behaviors of observed individuals.

An important disadvantage of non-participating observation is the limitation to specific settings. For example, one-sided mirrors can only be used in special settings, which do not correspond to natural settings.

A central disadvantage of observation is the lack of introspection. Observation stands in a strong behaviorist tradition but excludes the inner processes of individuals completely. The observation of behaviors does not allow drawing any conclusions about motivations of individuals.

All forms of observation have in common that the observer has a central role for the gathering and coding of observed information. This increases the threat of a researcher bias, i.e. a systematic distortion of results due to subjectivity of the observer. With the help of systematic training, standardization and temporal decoupling of observation and analysis, it is possible to reduce the researcher bias. Nevertheless, the central role of the observer in the data gathering process needs to be considered.

Another general disadvantage of observation as a data gathering method is the enormous effort to collect the data. As observation time is hardly incompressible, the observation of many different situations is extremely time intense.

Especially for the investigation of cooperation relationships, observation is difficult to use. On the one hand, the number of actors that need to be observed is very high. On the other hand, a cooperation relationship can only be observed over a longer period of time. A relationship consists of interactions between individuals (Berscheid, & Reis 1998). That means that a relationship is a latent construct that manifests itself in repeated interactions between individuals. Such manifestations are scarce events. In order to capture all cooperation relationships of an individual, it thus would be necessary to observe that specific individual for a very long time. This makes observation practically impossible as a data gathering method for cooperation after mergers and acquisitions. Even parallelization of observation with the help of multiple observers cannot reduce the observation effort to a reasonable level. Observation therefore can only be used to capture cooperation of small groups in specific settings.

3.3.3.2. Interrogation

Interrogation helps to gather data in a communicative process (Laatz 1993: 103). The researcher asks questions and the respondent answers them. In contrast to observation, interrogation collects subjective data, which is based on information that respondents actively provide.

There are different dimensions to distinguish forms of interrogation (Bortz, & Döring 2003: 237; Laatz 1993: 103). The most important dimensions are degree of standardization, personal versus written interrogation, individual versus group interrogation, and degree of anonymity of the respondent.

In the following paragraphs, I will highlight personal vs. written interrogation as two main approaches of interrogation. Advantages and disadvantages of the approaches will be discussed. Then I will present the approach used on the two case studies of this research.

3.3.3.2.1. Personal interrogation - Interviews

Interviews or personal interrogation are characterized by their similarity to everyday communication processes (Laatz 1993: 108). Even standardized interviews are perceived as a social situation, as an interaction, in which the interviewee as well as the interviewer exchange information. This makes participation in a research much more attractive. Accordingly, Laatz (1993) points out that "Interviews […] are usually more effective in motivation the research sample. This positively influence the representativity of a research" (Laatz 1993: 108).

Interviews can be differed by the number of participating individuals. First, the number of interviewers can differ. Second the number of interviewees can differ. Interviews can be conducted by one interviewer, by an interviewer tandem or even in the form of a hearing, in which a group of individuals interrogate an interviewee (Bortz, & Döring 2003: 238). The usage of several interviewers can bear advantages, because several interviewers perceive more than one interviewer. Also, the interviewers can specialize on different roles during the interview. For example, one interviewer can focus on content, the other interviewer can focus on the process of the interview. Also, interviewers might focus on different content in an interview. The use of several interviewers is useful in expert interviews, which require high levels of attention to capture as much information as possible in a very limited period of time. A disadvantage of using several interviewers is the less intimate interview atmosphere. An interviewee might open up more in an interview with one interviewer, and one interviewer might have better possibilities to react emphatically to an interviewee. Also, the use of several interviewers increases the required resources.

According to the number of interviewees in an interview, single interviews and group interviews can be distinguished. Group interviews allow the consideration of a number of different individuals within one interview. The discussion of potential answers to questions might provide interesting information. Also, the answers are more objective than answers from single interviewees. A disadvantage of group interviews is the difficulty to control for social mechanisms such as group thinking, risky shifts or the dominance of single individuals, which might distort the results. Also, the complexity of a group interview situation is more difficult to control and to handle for an interviewer than a single interviewee. Last but not least, group interviews reduce the number of interviews significantly and thereby hamper a statistical analysis of the results due to reduced statistical significance.

Another dimension to distinguish interviews is the personal versus the telephone interview (Bortz, & Döring 2003: 238; Börtz 1984: 169). Telephone interviews are characterized by a limitation of senses of the interviewer. Hence the information density of telephone interviews is significantly lower than the information density of personal interviews. Also, telephone interviews can only be used for short interviews. The lack of information density requires additional focus, which makes it more difficult to conduct longer interviews for both, interviewer as well as interviewee. On the other hand, some interviewees can be easier be interviewed with the help of telephone interviews, because of availability restrictions and time contraints. Also, telephone interviews are much less expensive than personal interviews, especially, if traveling expenses apply.

A third dimension to distinguish interviews is the level of standardization. Interviews have a number of degrees of freedom that can on the one hand be used to improve the information extraction. However, on the other hand they might reduce the comparability of interview situations and thereby the comparability of the gathered data.

- The behavior of the interviewer has been found to strongly influence the results of an interview. It has been found that unemotional appearance has different effects on the interviewee and the information provided than emphatic and warm appearance (Choi,

& Comstock 1975). However, little standardization of the behavior of the interviewer might lead to interviewer biases.

- The order of the questions in an interview can lead to order effects. Open interviews offer the possibility to adjust the order of the questions in order to generate a natural interview situation, which corresponds more to a guided discussion than to an interview. However, such variation of the order of questions might lead to order effects.

Such order effects can be based on halo effects, first impression effects, last impression effects, anchoring effects as well as other distortions of the information provided. For example, Mussweiler, & Strack (1997) find that anchoring strongly influences the answers of respondents. They find that due to insufficient adjustment, conversational inference as well as numeric priming, individuals use anchor values as a reference point and adjust further answers to these anchor points.

- The exact wording of the questions can lead to different results. Single words and smallest modification can have systematic effects on the answers of interviewees. On the one hand, interview situations allow a rephrasing of questions in case of comprehension problems. On the other hand, such rephrasing always bears the risk of distortions of results. Systematic training of interviewers as well as predefined rephrasing can reduce the effects of changes in wording.

- Questions can be open or closed. Open questions imply that interviewees can answer to the question whatever they think is appropriate. Closed questions, in contrast, offer a selected number of answer categories that a respondent can choose from. Open questions can capture more complex answers and thereby generate higher validity of answers. At the same time, the comparability of answers to open questions is difficult and sometimes impossible. Closed questions, in contrast allow a high level of standardization and a high comparability of answers. At the same time, the information captured in the answer categories is limited. Open questions thus are useful in small sample, exploratory studies. Closed questions, however are useful in large sample studies, in which the answer categories have been extensively pretested to make sure that the relevant information can be captured within the given answer categories.

The flexibility of open and non-standardized interviews can yield more valid, better and richer information depending on the quality of the interviewer and the topic of the interview. High standardization, however, makes interviews more reliable and comparable. The level of standardization thus needs to be determined as a tradeoff of different research requirements, and of resources available (Laatz 1993: 106).

There are two general disadvantages of interviews. First, anonymity of respondents is very low. The interview as a social situation makes anonymity impossible. Hence respondents might reveal different information than they would reveal in anonymous situations. Especially questions that ask for potentially damaging information, such as evaluation of superiors, thoughts about changing the workplace or evaluation of a measure such as an M&A-transaction might be influenced by a lack of anonymity. A second general disadvantage is the influence of the interviewer on the interviewee. For example, when asking questions about gender issues, the gender of the interviewer, be it a man or a woman, always influences the answers of the interviewees.

In the present study, interviews or questionnaires can be used to gather the necessary data on cooperation relationships and characteristics of the individuals. As has been discussed above, observation and the use of non-reactive data cannot be used because of the need for direct information about cooperation relationships.

The advantage of gathering information on cooperation with the help of interviews is the possible qualification of cooperation. For example, conflicts, frictions, but also detailed content of relationships can be captured with the help of qualitative interviews better than with the help of a standardized questionnaire. Another advantage might be that information on cooperation relationships is highly sensitive. Anonymity is not possible. In interviews, it is easier to generate the trust necessary for employees to provide data about cooperation.

The disadvantage of interviews to gather data on cooperation relationships is the high number of interviews that need to be conducted in order to collect sufficient data on cooperation. As cooperation after mergers and acquisition is a dynamic phenomenon, the data gathering needs to be finished as quick as possible in order to avoid time effects. For example, when measuring cooperation 15 months after an M&A-transaction, a two month-data gathering period might yield other results for the first interviews than for the last interviews due to the effect of time passed.

In the present study, interviews were used to gather the data. In the first research site, data was exclusively gathered with the help of personal single interviews. The interviews were highly standardized. The order of the questions was fixed. Most questions were closed and offered scales or fixed choices as potential answers.

In the second research site too, a number of interviews were conducted. However, in addition to the data gathered in interviews, a large scale written interrogation was conducted. That means that in the second research site, interviews were used to gather background information on the M&A-transaction, in order to be better able to understand the data collected with the questionnaires.

3.3.3.2.2. Written interrogation - Questionnaires

Written interrogation is interrogation of respondents with the help of questionnaire that contain written questions, which are answered by the respondent without further help of an interviewer (Bortz, & Döring 2003: 253; Laatz 1993: 108).

Written interrogation can be done with the help of paper-based questionnaires and with the help of computer-based questionnaires. Paper-based questionnaires and computer-based questionnaires differ concerning the flexibility of the interrogation. In paper-based questionnaires, the scope and the structure of the questionnaire is fixed. The order of questions is fixed. While some questions might be optional, they are still visible to the respondent. Computer-based questionnaires, however, are more flexible, scope and structure can be manipulated. Also, questions can be shown or hidden. In addition to that, computer-based questionnaires are convenient for the researcher. Data can directly be saved to files, and then be further analyzed.

In addition to flexibility, computer-based questionnaires can offer additional information for questions, help functions, as well as rephrasing of questions, which are not possible for paper-based questionnaires.

Questions in written interrogation can be open or closed as in interviews. Open questions offer respondents the possibility to write a detailed answer. Closed questions offer predefined answer categories that a respondent can choose from.

In research on cooperation, written interrogation is well fitted to gather the necessary data. A large number of respondents can be interrogated with little investment of time and resources. Also, the gathered data can be analyzed with relative little effort (Laatz 1993: 109). Especially homogeneous groups of individuals can be interrogated at low cost (Bortz, & Döring 2003: 253). A significant disadvantage of written interrogation is the lack of control of the interrogation situation (Bortz, & Döring 2003: 253). Also, the richness of the gathered data is usually lower than in interviews. Especially, contextual information that increases understanding of the provided information can hardly be gathered.

In this research, I used a computer-based questionnaire for the investigation of the second research site. The main reason was a new way of operationalizing cooperation. With the help of a dynamic questionnaire, the construct could be better operationalized than with a paper-based version. For details, see 5.3.

3.4. Data gathering approach

As has been described above, cooperation relationships on the individual and on the dyadic level is the dependent construct of this research. Characteristics of individuals represent the independent constructs. Also, a number of controls are considered, especially, the effect of integration measures as well as structural requirements. Hence for each unit of observation, i.e. for each employee in the sample, data needs to be collected on the cooperation relationships, on individual characteristics, on participation in integration measures, and on structural cooperation requirements. In addition to that, data needs to be gathered on a dyadic level to test the homophily hypotheses. That means that for each relationship, information about similarity of the actors needs to be gathered.

A specific data gathering approach in social sciences is well suited to collect the required data: Social network analysis.

3.4.1. Social network analysis

Social network analysis is a very good method to gather and to analyze information on existence and characteristics of relationships, characteristics of actors and characteristics of dyads, i.e. of relationships partners. "The network concept is of remarkable simplicity and therefore quickly defined: It describes the fact that people are connected with others socially and provides for this fact a graphical illustration: Individual are illustrated as nodes that are connected with linkages to other nodes, which again represent individuals" (Keupp 1987: 11ff, own translation). Wasserman, & Faust (1994) argue that social network analysis is distinct from other research perspectives within the social and behavioral sciences, "... distinct because social network analysis is based on an assumption of the importance of relationships among interacting units" (Wasserman, & Faust 1994: 4). Sarason, Sarason, & Pierce (1995) point out that there are three different levels of analysis to research social relationships. First, there is the level of the individual. On this level, the individual and its characteristics are either seen as dependent on relationship characteristics or the relationship characteristics are seen as dependent on the individual characteristics. The second level is the level of the dyad. In this perspective, patterns of interaction of relationships or relationship specific behaviours are central. A third level of analysis is the level of the system. The systemic perspective investigates social systems with more than two actors. Investigations with this perspective focus on characteristics and behaviors of social systems of any size.

In the table below, social network studies with different levels of analysis are presented:

Author	Content of research	Perspective
Krackhardt, & Kilduff (1990)	Investigation of the relationship between proximity of actors in social networks and similarity of organizational cultural values of actors	Individual
Laumann (1994)	Investigation of the origin and position of close relationship partners within the social networks of individuals	Individual
Berscheid, & Ammazzaloroso (1999)	Type and content of relationships differed by frequency, diversity and strength	Dyadic
Spitzberg (1988)	Investigation on the structure and content of dating relationships	Dyadic
Barley (1990b)	Investigation of the effect of the introduction of a new technology (computer tomography) on the social structure of doctors and nurses in a hospital	Systemic
Mehra, Kilduff, & Brass (1998)	Formation of relationships amongst minorities	Systemic
Sha (1998a)	Formation of work and social ties after mass layoffs following a restructuring measure	Systemic

Table 25: Selected social network studies on different levels

Some researchers not only describe social network analysis as a research method to investigate social structures, but as a theoretical perspective on its own (e.g. Burt 1982, Berkowitz 1982, White 1994). Others again argue that social networks are only a construct without theory (Keul 1993: 48). Salancik (1995) claims that social network analysis might have theoretical potential. However, he points out that this potential has to be realized yet, proclaiming "Wanted: A good network theory of organization" (Salancik 1995: 345).

Without further exploring this discussion, I will use social network analysis in this research primarily for its potential to gather individual and relational data, which allows answering the research questions.

Social network analysis gathers information on actors and on relationships between actors. Actors can be any social entity, such as individuals as well as groups, companies or even countries. Relationship content strongly depends on the type of actor that is investigated. For example, while the content of a relationship between countries can be trade of specific products, it can be romantic relationships between individuals (e.g. Laumann 1994). Relationships between individual actors can be based on information flow (Sha 1998b; Brass, & Burkhardt 1992, 1993; Burkhardt, & Brass 1990; Krackhardt, & Porter 1986), advice (Sha

1998a; Ibarra 1993b, 1995; Stevenson, & Gilly 1991; Burt 1987), interaction (Tsai, & Goshal 1998; Barley 1990b), work (Tsai, & Goshal 1998; Ibarra 1992), or any other possible content of a relationship.

3.4.2. Ego-centered and dyadic networks

As elaborated above, the present research requires the collection of primary data gathered with the help of questionnaires used in written and personal interrogation. There are two different approaches to gather network data with the help of social network analysis. The first approach gathers data on ego-centered networks of individuals, the second approach collects dyadic network data.

Ego-centered networks are formed by a focal actor, 'ego' and other actors that are linked to ego, the 'alters'. There are different approaches to gather ego-centered network data. One approach is to ask respondents to indicate individuals to which they are connected by a predefined type of relationship, such as information flow, friendship, or cooperation. The result is a star with the focal actor as centre. Another approach is to ask ego about potential ties between alters that are connected to ego. This approach generates somewhat more complex networks. In addition to relational information, it is possible to gather data on characteristics of ego. Also, it is possible to ask ego to provide information about characteristics of alters.

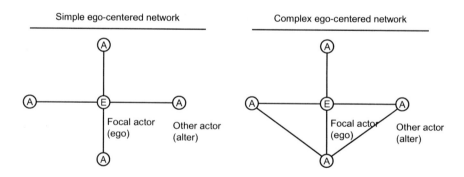

Illustration 23: Simple and complex egocentered networks

Ego-centered network data is often used, when the population under consideration is very large, and when it is only possible to gather information from a sample of this population. However, ego-centered network data suffers from potential respondent biases. There is no way to validate indicated relationships of ego. Also, there is no way to validate information provided about alters. From an epistemological perspective, providing information about oneself and providing information about others are two very different things. Both methods underlie biases. Providing information about oneself has been shown to underlie phenomena such as social desirability, which leads to indication of socially desirable information. Providing information about others underlies problems of observation biases, such as lack of attention, focus on dominant characteristics, halo-effects and other biases of social perception. Also, providing information about oneself allows introspection. Introspective data, however can be gathered for egos, but not for alters, because the respondent ego has no possibility for introspection of alters. For example, it is difficult to collect information about attitudes of alters with the help of ego-centered networks analysis.

In addition to that, the number of relationships indicated in an ego-centered network by an individual might depend on the time available to fill out the questionnaire or on its individual perception of the content of the relationship. Such opportunistic data provision needs to be controlled for. Usually, researchers limit the risk by asking egos to indicate a specific number of relationships. This however, bears a twofold risk: First, it might be possible that an individual has less relationships than the expected number. They then feel forced to indicate more relationships than they actually have. Second, for some individuals, the number of relationships is too low. The gathered network data then is incomplete.

The second approach, the collection of dyadic network data, generates data on all relationships between actors of a predefined population. In order to collect dyadic network data, all members of a selected population must be interrogated. A selected population is characterized by well-defined boundaries. For example, boundaries can be geographic boundaries, or membership or affiliation to a specific group. All members within this population are interrogated about all relationships they have to other members within the population. In addition to relational data, it is possible to gather information about actors. Based on the information provided by the respondents, the dyadic network data matrix can be formed. In the example below, each existing relationship is marked with a one in the dyadic network data matrix. Based on the network data, the network graph can be plotted.

Focal \ Alter	J. Kröger	R. Schmidt	S. Leetz	G. Zeit	T. Müller	H. Schulz	H. Rudolf	E. Soltz	R. Groß	H. Sieger	J. Graf
J. Kröger		1	1	1	1		1	1			
R. Schmidt					1	1		1			
S. Leetz				1					1		
G. Zeit									1		
T. Müller						1				1	
H. Schulz											
H. Rudolf										1	
E. Soltz											
R. Groß										1	
H. Sieger											
J. Graf											

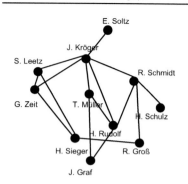

Illustration 24: Dyadic network graph and network data in a matrix

Based on the gathered information, it is possible to analyze the relationships between individual characteristics of an actor and her cooperative relationships. For example, it is possible to correlate the number of relationships an actor has with individual characteristics such as age or rank.

Also, it is possible to analyze dyads between each two individuals. Data on dyads is collected from each possible pair of actors in a population. For example, age similarity, i.e. the age difference between two actors, can be correlated with the existence of a relationship. In order to compute age similarity, information as indicated by both actors needs to be used.

There are two approaches to collect dyadic network data. One approach is, to provide all individuals within a given population with a list of names and ask them to choose relationship partners and provide additional information about the content of the relationships. A second approach is, to openly ask respondents to name their relationship partners, similarly to an ego-centered network analysis. While the first approach clearly suffers from methodological issues (how many names can you put on a list and get people to fill it out), the second approach suffers from some of the disadvantages of ego-centered network data.

There are many advantages of dyadic network data. First, it is possible to collect information about characteristics of all the actors. That allows analyses of similarity of actors without a potential observation bias. Second, it is possible to validate relationships between individuals. As both individuals indicate their relationships, it is well possible to validate the information given by one relationship partner with the information provided by the other relationships partner. A third advantage is the possibility of capturing the structure of a complete social network. For example, information about isolated actors, centrality of actors as well as other characteristics of nodes within a network can only be gathered with the help of a complete dyadic network.

A major disadvantage of dyadic network data is the need for personal information about cooperation relationships. Many people feel uncomfortable to indicate this information, especially, if quality of the relationship is asked as well. It is no secret that a dyadic social network analysis is a powerful tool to identify weak employees of a firm. Therefore, it is necessary to adjust the level of analysis on the level of groups with a minimum size.

In the first study, the level of analysis for all network graphs is a minimum group size of three. The level of analysis for all statistical analyses is the population.

In the second study, the level of analysis for all network graphs is a minimum group size of four. The level of analysis for all statistical analyses is again the population.

3.4.3.   Social network analysis in this research

Social network analysis is a very flexible data gathering approach. Depending on theoretical and practical considerations, it is possible to adapt the approach to meet the requirements of both, academic and practical considerations.

3.4.3.1.   Social network analysis in the first research site

In investigating SpecMatCo, the top management was concerned about the feelings and reactions of their employees to the research. Therefore, they wanted to limit the interrogation to a small sample of individuals in the firm. At the same time, the top management wanted to provide some anonymity to the employees: Cooperation relationships should be gathered anonymously.

As a result, an ego-centered network analysis was the method of choice. Data about individual characteristics as well as ego-centered network was collected from a small sample of employees.

3.4.3.2.   Social network analysis in the second research site

In investigating SoftCo, the top management was also concerned about the feelings and reactions of their employees. However, as the integrated structure had been implemented longer than in the case of SpecMatCo, the top management felt that a dyadic network analysis would not yield too much disturbance. It was possible to convince the top management as well as the worker's council that the anonymity problem would be handled in an appropriate manner. In a contract, the details of the approach were fixed. Amongst others, the level of analysis was fixed to a minimum group size of four employees. Also, the quality of single cooperation relationships could not be gathered.

As a result, a dyadic network analysis was the method of choice. Data about individual characteristics as well as dyadic network data was collected from the full population of the merged division of SoftCo.

In addition to that, a small sample of managers and employees was interviewed in order to gather qualitative data on the M&A-transaction as well as on cooperation relationships.

3.5. Selection of the sample

Choosing a sample for a research should always fulfill two criteria:
- The sample should be representative. That means that all relevant characteristics of individuals of the full population need to be reflected in the research sample. For example, if 40% of employees of a firm are female, however, the research sample only includes 10% female respondents, the results of the sample might be distorted.
- The sample size should be large enough. In order to yield statistically significant results, a sample should not bee too small. For exploratory analyses, a sample of 30 to 40 individuals might suffice. However, larger samples increase the likelihood of significant results.

For the investigation of cooperation after mergers and acquisitions, some additional aspects are relevant for the selection of a sample of individuals.
- The individuals should have the possibility to cooperate. By picking individuals that have no opportunity to cooperate with new colleagues, the results might be distorted.
- Only cooperation relationships should be considered that exceed a certain minimal strength. Occasional interaction does not qualify for a cooperation relationship.

When choosing a sample, it needs to be considered that the major characteristics of the sampled population is reflected in the sample. This can be done with the help of a stratified sample. Stratifying a sample implies that the major characteristics of individuals in the population are reflected in a similar percentage in the sample. For example, firm affiliation as well as gender and age are important characteristics of a population, which should be reflected in the sample.

3.6. Summary of research setup

The research setup in the two research sites differs to some extent. Both research setups are based on a pre-experimental research design. In both studies, the type of data gathered is primary data. However, while in the research of SpecMatCo primary data is gathered with the help of interviews, the research of SoftCo gathers primary data with the help of a computer-based questionnaire. In addition to the questionnaire, a number of exploratory interviews is conducted at SoftCo.

Also, the data gathering approach is different. In the research of SpecMatCo, data on ego-centered networks of the employees in the research sample is gathered. At SoftCo, a dyadic network analysis is conducted. This, however, bears consequences for the research samples in both research sites. While at SpecMatCo, it is possible to build a sample of the total population that is stratified in the main dimension, at SoftCo the full population needs to be investigated in order to be able to collect dyadic data.

In the table below, the main aspects of the different research setups at SpecMatCo and at SoftCo can be seen.

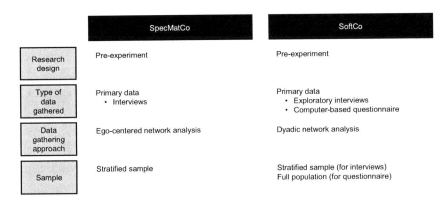

Illustration 25: Main aspects of different research setups at SpecMatCo and at SoftCo

The differences in the research setup bear consequences for the operationalization of the dependent and independent constructs of the postulated hypotheses, and for the results that can be generated with the help of these research setups.

In the following chapters of this study, I will elaborate the details and the operationalization of the research in both research sites, as well as the results for each research site. For each research site, I will present a short discussion of the results in order to show the limitations of the results and the constraints that are specific to each research site.

4. Empirical study at the first research site: SpecMatCo

In the next paragraphs, I will present the empirical study at SpecMatCo. In order to do so, I will first present the time schedule of the research. Then I will provide details about the research sample. Later I will describe the ego-centered network analysis, which was used to gather the data. In a first step, I will present the operationalization of the hypotheses for answering the first research question "Who cooperates?" and test the hypotheses with the help of the data gathered in the ego-centered network analysis. In a second step, I will present the operationalization of the hypotheses for answering the second research question "Who cooperates with whom?". Again, I will test the hypotheses with the help of the gathered data.

4.1. Time schedule of research

The research at SpecMatCo lasted for approximately five months. During that time, the research and all materials were prepared, the interviews were scheduled and conducted, the data was analyzed and presented to the firm.

After the initial contact had been made, the approach had to be adapted to the needs and wishes of the top management team. In a first step, all available internal information on the M&A-transaction was reviewed. Also, consulting firms responsible for the M&A-transaction and for the cultural integration after the transaction were interviewed to gather background information on the transaction. Based on the gathered information and based on the wishes of the top management team and the workers council, a cross-sectional study with one measurement, the sample size and the sample structure, as well as the detailed data gathering approach was fixed. The top management felt that it would be too risky to investigate the full population of the firm. In addition to that, the workers council insisted that the collected data should be anonymous. Hence there was no possibility to conduct a dyadic research network analysis. Therefore, the data was gathered with the help of a sample-based ego-centered network analysis.

In a next step, the interview guidelines had to be developed in English, French and German. For details of the interview guidelines, see Appendix I. In addition to that, memos for internal communication with senior management and with employees had to be developed, again in three different languages. After the approach was fixed, a written contract was developed, which determined the major elements of the analysis, such as anonymity, level of analysis to protect anonymity of employees, as well as handling of internal information that potentially could be gathered in the course of the study. All elements of the study were then approved in a meeting with the board.

In a next step, a schedule for the interviews and a travel plan were developed. Interviews were conducted in five different countries.

Then the interviews were conducted over a period of five weeks. As 90% of the interviews had been conducted in the first three weeks of the interview phase, data analysis already started at the beginning of the fourth month. The data analysis lasted more than six weeks.

One of the major obstacles during the analysis of the data was the lack of adequate software for analyses of network data on the departmental level. While UCINET is very useful for the analysis of dyadic network data on the individual level, it could not be used for analyses of ego-centered network data on an aggregate level. Hence all analyses on that level had to be run on self-programmed software. This, however, required a large share of the time for data analysis.

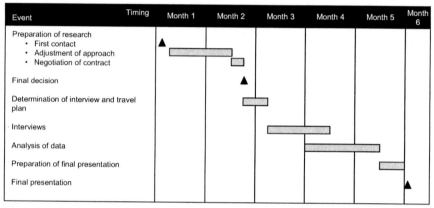

Illustration 26: Time schedule of research at SpecMatCo

4.2. Sample details

A total of 39 interview partners were selected in cooperation with the senior management and the Human Resources department. The sample covered an equal share of members of both firms, 20 of Firm A and 19 of Firm B. Only employees from the functions that correspond to the criteria presented in 3.5 were interviewed. Therefore, blue collar production workers were not considered as they do not have any contacts to their new colleagues. However, employees of the production planning have been considered. Three national sales companies have been investigated as well. In the following table, details of the sample are illustrated:

	All	Firm A	Firm B
Marketing	1	1	-
CF&A	2	1	1
Production planning	3	1	2
Logistics	3	2	1
Development	3	1	2
Product management	10	3	7
Customer service	6	3	3
Sales	11	7	4
	39	19	20

Table 26: Sample composition of the first research site

Five women have been interviewed. The share of roughly 13% of the sample corresponds to the percentage of female employees in the considered parts of the organization.

Of these 39 interview partners, three did not indicate ego-centered network data. The data of a fourth respondent cannot be used, as he made a transfer from his former location in his old firm to a location of the partnering firm. Hence the structural cooperation requirements strongly dominated his cooperation behavior. This case cannot be controlled for with the help of the control variable. Hence it was excluded from considerations concerning the ego-centered network data.

4.3. Gathering of ego-centered network data

With the help of an ego-centered social network analysis, were asked respondents to indicate their ten most important coworkers. These coworkers could be both, within their old firm or within the new firm. In addition to that, important coworkers could have entered the firm after the M&A-transaction and thus not belong to either of the two merged firms. Respondents thus indicated to which firm the important coworkers originally belonged, respectively whether they entered the firm after the M&A-transaction. Cooperation relationships with important coworkers that belong to the same firm are coded as old relationships. Cooperation relationships with important coworkers that belong to the other firm are coded as new relationships. Cooperation relationships with employees that entered the firm after the transaction are not considered.

For each relationship with an important coworker, frequency, importance and quality of the cooperation are gathered.

4.3.1. Frequency of cooperation

Respondents had to describe the frequency of interaction with their important coworkers by answering the question "How often are you in contact with this co-worker?" Possible answers were "Once per week" (=1), "Several times per week" (=2), "Daily" (=3), "Several times per day" (=4).

4.3.2. Importance of cooperation

Similarly, respondents had to indicate the importance of interactions with their most important colleagues by answering the question: "How important is this co-worker for the accomplishment of your work?" on a seven-point Likert-scale. The additional oral explanation to this item was "Not important (=1) means that you can accomplish the task without cooperation of this coworker. Very important (=7) means that delays or problems in cooperation with this coworker directly affect the outcome of your work".

4.3.3. Strength of cooperation

Based on frequency and importance of a cooperation relationship, the strength of that relationship is computed as the product of the indicated Likert-values of frequency and importance. Hence the range of values of strength ranges between 1 and 28.

4.3.4. Quality of cooperation

Quality of cooperation with their colleagues was measured with the question "How is the quality of cooperation with this co-worker?" on a seven-point Likert scale. The additional oral explanation to this item was "Not good (=1) means that there are conflicts, and/or that it is unproductive, and/or slow, very good (=7) means that the relationship is efficient, and/or frictionless and/or unbureacratic".

4.4. "Who cooperates?" Operationalization of hypotheses 1 to 11

In order to test the hypotheses 1 to 11, the dependent and the independent constructs need to be operationalized. Based on the gathered relational data, the dependent construct, i.e. cooperation of respondents can be operationalized. Independent constructs have been operationalized with the help of a number of items. The operationalization of both, dependent and independent constructs is described in detail in the following paragraphs.

4.4.1. Dependent construct: Cooperative behavior of employee

Based on the data gathered, it is possible to determine a number of different measures of cooperative behavior of an employee. Due to the exploratory nature of this research, a set of different measures is considered.

A first type of measures is based on existence of relationships as indicated in the ego-centered network analysis.

A second type of measures is based on the frequency, importance and quality of relationships as indicated in the ego-centered network analysis.

4.4.1.1. Existence of ties

Based on the results of the ego-centred network analysis, it is possible to determine for each of the respondents, how many of the 10 most important coworkers are colleagues from the old firm, and how many of them are colleagues from the new firm. The number of ties to new colleagues will be labeled NumNewTies, the number of ties to colleagues in the old firm will be labelled NumOldTies. The maximum number of NumNewTies as well as NumOldTies is limited by the maximum number of most important coworkers to 10 ties.

Based on the number of old and new ties, it is possible to determine a ratio for each of the respondents, which is based on the number of old ties divided by the sum of old and new ties. The ratio can take values between 0 and 1. A value of 1 indicates that an employee has no relationship with a new colleague amongst his 10 most important coworkers. A value of 0 indicates that an employee only cites new colleagues amongst his 10 most important coworkers. The ratio will be labeled ShareOldTies.

4.4.1.2. Characteristics of ties: Frequency, importance, strength, and quality

A second set of measures includes the more detailed information on frequency, importance, strength as well as quality of relationships as measured in the ego-centered network analysis.

Three different types of measures are computed for each respondent for frequency, importance, strength and quality. In the following paragraphs, the computation of the different measures is presented at the example of frequency:

- Sum of frequency for new relationships (SumFreqNew). The measure for new relationships indicates the absolute amount of cooperation frequency with new colleagues. The higher this value, the more frequent the cooperation between a respondent and new colleagues is.
- Ratio of the sum of frequency of old relationships and the sum of frequency of old and new relationships (ShareOldFreq). This ratio indicates regardless of the absolute

frequency, whether a respondent has a strong bias towards old colleagues, or whether a respondent equally cooperates with old and new colleagues. While a frequency ratio of 1 indicates that a respondent only names colleagues from the old firm as important coworkers, a ratio of 0.5 indicates that the cooperation frequency is equally distributed amongst colleagues from the old firm and new colleagues. A ratio of 0 indicates that a respondent names exclusively new colleagues as important coworkers.

- Average frequency of relationships with new colleagues (AvFreqNew). The average value for old and for new relationships helps to determine, whether differences in sums or in the ratio of frequency of old and new relationships depend on the mere number of cooperation relationships with old and new colleagues, or whether there is a systematic tendency to cooperate on the average more with old or with new colleagues. For example, based on the cooperation structure, an employee might only have few contacts with new colleagues. That means that the sum of frequency with new colleagues is low. Also, the ration of the sum of frequency of old relationships to the sum of frequency of all relationships is close to 1. However, maybe the employee cooperates very tightly with these few new colleagues, Then the average frequency of the new relationships might be very high.

In order to consider a potential systematic answer bias affecting the average values of respondents, I also compute the delta value between average value for old and for new relationships as a further variable (DelAvFreq).

In Table 27, the different measures can be seen. While dark grey boxes indicate that a measure cannot be computed in a meaningful manner, the light grey boxes indicate that these measures will not be considered as dependent variables, because old relationships are not in the focus of this research. Nevertheless, variables in the light grey boxes will also be computed in order to compute the composed measures.

	Existence of ties	Frequency	Importance	Strength	Quality
Old relationships	NumOldTies	SumFreqOld	SumImpOld	SumStrenOld	
New relationships	NumNewTies	SumFreqNew	SumImpNew	SumStrenNew	
Ratio old relationship to all relationships	ShareOldTies	ShareOldFreq	ShareOldImp	ShareOldStren	
Average characteristics of old relationships		AvFreqOld	AvImpOld	AvStrenOld	AvQualOld
Average characteristics of new relationships		AvFreqNew	AvImpNew	AvStrenNew	AvQualNew
Delta Average Old and New Ties		DelAvFreq	DelAvImp	DelAvStren	DelAvQual

Table 27: Measures for dependent variables

Hence different aspects of cooperation are operationalized based on the existence of relationships and based on the relationship characteristics frequency, importance, strength as well as quality with the help of different measures. That means that a total of 16 dependent variables will be considered in the following analyses. The different measures all capture specific aspects of cooperation. Later results need to be interpreted according to the differences in explanatory power of these dependent variables.

4.4.2. Independent constructs

There are several factors that influence cooperative behaviors of employees. As postulated in section 2 of this work, a first set of factors influencing cooperative behaviors of employees are demographic characteristics. Demographic characteristics include age, gender and the education level of employees. A second set of factors influencing cooperative behaviors are characteristics of employees that are dependent on the firm. These factors comprise rank as well as seniority of an employee. A third set of factors are of psychological nature. These psychological factors comprises reactions of employees to the M&A-transaction and work-related attitudes. A fourth factor, which affects cooperative behaviors of individuals are integration measures. In the following paragraphs, the operationalization of these independent constructs will be elaborated.

4.4.2.1. Demographic characteristics

Age. At the beginning of each interview, each respondent was asked to indicate his or her age in years. In the following illustration the age distribution of the respondents is shown in classes of ten years, ranging from 20 to +50 years. The variable age is coded as age in years.

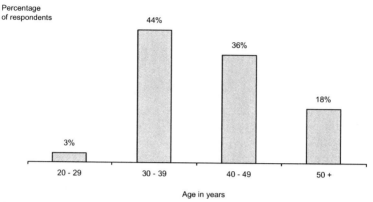

Graph 1: Age distribution of sample

Gender. Five of the interviewed employees were women, 34 of the interviewed employees were men. Gender of female respondents is coded as 1. Gender of male respondents is coded as 0.

Education. The interviewees were asked to indicate their highest level of education. Six different answers were given. These answers are: Secondary school, completed apprenticeship, master craftsman, studies, diploma, doctoral degree. Based on the description of the content of the master craftsman education, I treat master craftsman and studies as comparable levels of education. Hence there are five different levels of education, which are coded with 1 (= secondary school), 2 (= completed apprenticeship), 3 (= master craftsman, studies), 4 (=diploma) and 5 (= doctoral degree).

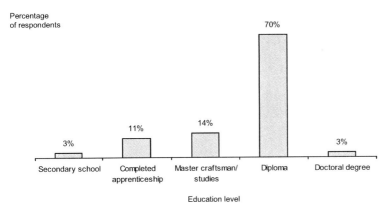

Graph 2: Education level of sample

4.4.2.2. Firm dependent characteristics of employees

Firm related characteristics of employees comprise characteristics of employees that only exist in relation to the firm they are working in. For example, outside the firm, employees do not have the rank, they have inside the firm. Similarly, time in department is related to the firm. Outside the firm, the seniority of an employee is zero.

Rank. All respondents had to indicate the department, in which they work, and the position, which they own. Based on the organizational chart of the integrated firm four levels of rank can be distinguished at SpecMatCo. The lowest level is the operative level (= level 1), or the non-managerial level. The highest level is the level of the board (= level 4). Each respondent is assigned to one level based on the following criteria: Managers are assigned to the management level they belong to according to the organizational chart. The management level is determined by starting at the top of the organizational chart, i.e. the board level) and then going down into the divisions and functions. Non-managerial employees are assigned to the lowest level of the organization, even if their direct supervisor is a third or fourth level manager. For example, personal assistants, who are directly reporting to the board are assigned to the first level, although they report directly to a fourth level managers. The reasoning for this assignment is based on two considerations. First, it is important to understand the hierarchical structure of the management. Therefore all managing employees are ranked top down. Second, the work on the operative level, the level on which the operative work of the firm is done, differs significantly from managerial tasks. In order to account for this difference, managerial is separated clearly from non-managerial staff.

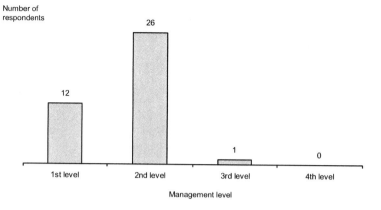

Graph 3: Distribution of rank in the sample

The lowest level of rank is coded with 1, the highest with 4. In the research sample, members of the first, second and third rank have been interviewed. In the illustration above, the rank of the employees in the sample are illustrated.

Seniority. Time in company has been studied in two different ways. First, respondents were asked to indicate the time they work within the main function, they are currently working in. This variable is labeled TimeInFunction. Second, employees were asked to indicate the time they work at the company, they are currently working in. This variable is labeled TimeInCompany. The twofold operationalization is based on the assumption that cooperation develops over time, and that stability of the cooperation context increases cooperation intensity. That means that the longer an employee works in the same function, the more stable her relationships should be. In the following illustration, the distributions of the variables TimeInCompany and TimeInFunction are illustrated.

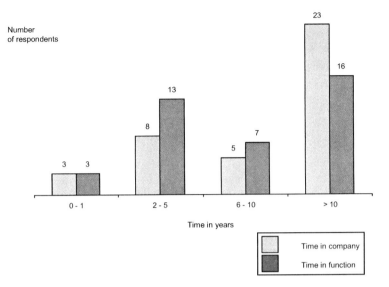

Graph 4: Distribution of TimeInCompany and TimeInFunction

More than half of the respondents worked for more than 10 years in the company. For further analyses, I operationalize seniority of employees with the variable TimeInFunction for two reasons: From a conceptual point of view, the cooperation requirements of employees are strongly dominated by the function they work in and not by the firm they work in. As it is hypothesized that the flexibility of cooperation networks of an employee decreases with increased age of cooperation relationships, TimeInFunction is more appropriate to capture the effects of seniority on relationship formation after mergers and acquisitions, because it is directly related to the age of cooperation relationships. From a methodological point of view, TimeInFunction is more favorable, because the variable has a higher variance than TimeInCompany, which is useful for statistical analyses.

4.4.2.3. Psychological factors affecting cooperation

As postulated in hypotheses 6 to 8, reactions of employees as well as attitudes of employees to an M&A-transactions are assumed to play a role in building relationships. Due to the exploratory nature of this first research, I use a number of common items that have been used in previous organizational culture studies as well as in studies on attitudes about mergers. Based on these items, relevant factors are determined and their effects on the cooperative behavior of the respondents.

In the research, three different preferences of employees about work styles have been investigated. The first preference, task orientation, has been identified based on previous studies as a relevant variable for cooperation styles of employees. A second, stress preference and a third, preference for democratic leadership have been measured at the request of the management of SpecMatCo (see questionnaire in Appendix I). However, they have not been considered in the scientific analysis of this work.

In order to measure the task orientation of respondents, an item from Hofstede's cultural survey (1980) has been used. Respondents had to indicate their preference for "Clearly defined area of responsibilities with clear tasks" based on a 7-point Likert-scale with 1 = "It is not at all important to have" and 7 = "It is very important to have". This variable is called "ClearTasks".

In addition to work attitudes, reactions after mergers and acquisitions have been measured. A first reaction that might affect cooperative behavior is uncertainty. In order to operationalize uncertainty, I use a number of items from Hofstede's (1980) operationalization of uncertainty avoidance, as well as of Schweiger, & DeNisi (1991).

A second attitude that might affect cooperative behavior is commitment, respectively job satisfaction. Again, I use items that are inspired by Schweiger, & DeNisi (1991).

Items used in previous studies	1 = I disagree, 7 = I fully agree	Item Name
Hofstede (1980): Uncertainty avoidance	At work, I feel nervous and tensed	Nervousness
	I would like to work the rest of my working life at SpecMatCo	RestOfLife
	Rules in a company should not be broken, even if an employee thinks, it is for the best of the company	Rules
Schweiger, & DeNisi (1991): Uncertainty	The merger meant additional work and stress	M&A-Stress
	The merger threatens jobs in my department	JobUncertainty
Schweiger, & DeNisi (1991): Positive attitude, job satisfaction	Since the merger my work is more fun than it used to be	WorkFun
	I am very happy with my career perspectives at SpecMatCo	CareerHappy

Table 28: Items to investigate attitudes and reactions to mergers

Using these 7 items, I conduct a factor analysis to confirm the two factors "uncertainty" and "commitment". The results are illustrated in the table below. It shows that the item "Rules" does not load on any of the factors. Seemingly, rule orientation is not connected to neither uncertainty nor commitment after mergers and acquisitions. Also, the variable "WorkFun" has a very low factor load (0.5) on the factor "commitment" and thus drives down the Cronbach's alpha of the factor "commitment". Investigating the items of the factor "commitment", it shows that the items "RestOfLife" and "CareerHappy" capture general long-term commitment with the employment at SpecMatCo, while "WorkFun" is specifically related to the M&A-transaction. Thus "WorkFun" might capture different aspects of commitment. In this research, I focus on long-term effects of mergers and acquisitions on commitment. Therefore, I exclude "WorkFun" from the factor commitment. Last but not least, the factor analysis shows that Hofstede's factors cannot be confirmed. "RestOfLife" is not an item of the factor "uncertainty" but an item of the factor "commitment".

Hence two factors are generated to capture reaction to the M&A-transaction: uncertainty with three items and a Cronbach's alpha of .671 and commitment based on two items with a Cronbach's alpha of .624.

Factor name	Item	Variable name	Factor loads	Cronbach's Alpha
Uncertainty	"At work, I feel nervous and tensed"	Nervousness	.786	
	"The merger meant additional work and stress"	M&A-stress	.735	
	"The merger threatens jobs in my department"	JobUncertainty	.742	.671
Commitment	"I would like to work for the rest of my working life for SpecMatCo"	RestOfLife	.781	
	"Since the integration, my work is more fun than it used to be"	WorkFun	(.500)	
	"I am very happy with my career perspectives at SpecMatCo"	CareerHappy	.825	.624 (.501)

Extraction method: Principal component analysis
Roation method: Varimax with Kaiser Normalization

Table 29: Results of factor analysis on attitudes after M&A-transactions

A possible explanation for the lack of fit of the variable "Rules" to the factors indicating reactions to mergers and acquisitions might be its attitudinal character. Hence I use "Rules" explorative as an additional item to operationalize work attitudes. Hence "Rules" and "ClearTasks" represent two items to capture the effect of work attitudes on the cooperation of respondents.

4.4.2.4. Integration measures

Integration measures can be distinguished in two different types of activities. A first type of activities comprises communication, which aims to increase the level of feeling informed. A second type of activities comprises measures that directly engage interaction between employees of the formerly separated firms.

As has been discussed earlier in this work, I do not focus on discrete communication measures, but on the effect of feeling informed. The reason is twofold: first, according to communication research, emitting communication does not necessarily imply that it is received and understood by the addressees (Pauly, 1977). Feeling informed captures the effect of communication, not the communication measure as such nor the reception and understanding of communication. Hence it captures the root of the effect of information on feelings and behaviors of employees. And second, it is impossible to assess the effect of company-wide communication measures in a case study on one firm. Company-wide communication measures are firm level phenomena. Their research requires a sample of many firms.

Based on this consideration, a number of different items have been developed to capture the degree to which employees in the merged firm feel informed.

Item	Name of item
"At each point in time of the integration, I had sufficient information"	EnoughInfo
"I was not always clear about what the merger meant for me"	PersonalConsNotKnown
"During the integration process, I often did not know, where we were heading"	DirectionNotKnown

Table 30: Items to measure the degree of being informed.

Respondents were asked to indicate to what degree they agree with the statements about being informed on a 7-point Likert scale with 1 = "I disagree" and 7 = "I fully agree".

Based on these three items, an aggregated variable was formed, which captures the degree feeling informed of the respondents. In order to do so, I first recoded the variables PersonalConsNotKnown and DirectionNotKnown inversely. Then I used a factor analysis with a principal component analysis to identify one factor labeled SumInfoAggr. The factor loads as well as Cronbach's alpha is indicated in the table below:

Factor name	Item	Variable name	Factor loads	Cronbach's Alpha
Degree of feeling informed	"At each point in time of the integration, I had sufficient information"	EnoughInfo	.787	
	"I was not always clear about what the merger meant for me"	PersonalCons-NotKnown	.827	
	"During the integration process, I often did not know, where we were heading"	DirectionNotKnown	.685	.637

Extraction method: Principal component analysis
Roation method: Varimax with Kaiser Normalization

Table 31: Items of SumInfoAggr and Cronbach's alpha of factor items

Based on exploratory interviews in the forefront of the research, different integration measures have been identified, in which some of the employees participated. The graph below shows the different integration measures under consideration and the percentage of employees that participated.

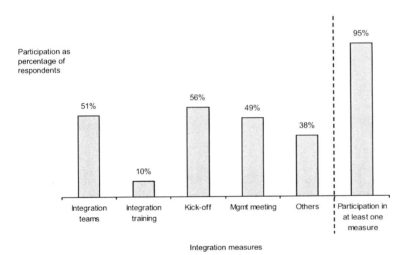

Graph 5: Percentage of employees participating in different integration measures

As can be seen, most of the respondents participated at least in one integration measure. More than half of the employees participated in integration teams, indicating a high level of involvement in the integration. Seemingly, many departments held a joint kick-off as a starting point for the integrated structure.

4.4.3. Controls

When looking at factors that affect the cooperation of employees with others, it is important to note that cooperation relationships are not entirely subject to characteristics of the individual. They are not fully deliberate. Rather, the formal structure of a firm strongly influences whether an employee cooperates little or much. For example, while developers may work for days without cooperating with other employees, coordination functions that receive customer orders and coordinate their timely fulfillment have to cooperate very frequently with different functions of the company. It is thus important to consider the cooperation requirements on a departmental level as a control variable for individual cooperation.

For each dependent variable, a specific control variable is computed to control for structural cooperation requirements. In Table 32, the control variables are listed.

	Existence of ties	Frequency	Importance	Strength	Quality
Old relationships	DepNumOldTies	DepFreqOldTies	DepImpOldTies	DepStrenOldTies	
New relationships	DepNumNewTies	DepFreqNewTies	DepImpNewTies	DepStrenNewTies	
Relation old relationship to all relationships	DepRatOld	DepRatFreqOld	DepRatImpOld	DepRatStrenOld	
Average characteristics of old relationships		DepAvFreqOld	DepAvImpOld	DepAvStrenOld	DepAvQualOld
Average characteristics of new relationships		DepAvFreqNew	DepAvImpNew	DepAvStrenNew	DepAvQualNew
Delta of average characteristics of relationships		DepDelAvFreq	DepDelAvImp	DepDelAvStren	DepDelAvQual

Table 32: Control variables for dependent variables

In this study, I asked interviewees to act as key informants and specify the existence, the frequency, importance and quality of cooperation between their team, respectively their department and other departments of the firm, even if the respondent himself did not cooperate with this department. Thereby, cooperation relationships on departmental level could be gathered. For each respondent, I determine the number of existing relationships of his team and teams of the other firm, respectively of their own firm. The number of relationships with departments of the old firm is labeled DepNumOldTies. Similarly, the number of relationships with departments of the new is labeled DepNumNewTies. These two variables will be used as controls for the dependent variables that measure the existence of ego-centered network ties with the respondent. Similarly, I label the sum of cooperation frequency with departments of the old firm DepFreqOldTies, respectively with departments of the new firm DepFreqNewTies. For importance and strength of the ties, the same measures are computed, and these measures are labeled in a similar manner.

Also, the average quality on departmental level is computed for relationships between the team of the respondent and other teams. The variable for relationships between the team of the respondent and teams of the old firm is called DepAvQualOld. The variable for relationships between the team of the respondent and teams of the new firm is called DepAvQualNew.

4.5. Results for the research question "Who cooperates?"

Based on past empirical findings and based on existing theories, a number of hypotheses have been postulated in the second part of this work to answer the research questions.

The operationalization of the research constructs allows testing of all hypotheses with the data gathered at SpecMatCo. In Table 33, the correlations between the independent as well as the dependent constructs are shown. For each variable, the first line indicates the Pearson's correlation coefficient. The second line indicates the 2-sided significance. The third line indicates the number of cases considered for the computation. A number of different independent variables have been identified, which should affect the dependent variables uncertainty and commitment as well as cooperation. The variables have been grouped into four groups of variables: demographic characteristics, (2) firm related characteristics, (3) attitudes and reactions to the merger and (4) integration measures. Structural cooperation requirements have also been considered as control variable for the analyses of the independent variables.

In the next table, the full model for the different operationalizations of cooperation is presented:

Correlation matrix for variables

	GenderQuant	EducationLevel	Rank	TimeInFunction	RuleOrientation	ClearTasks	Commitment	Uncertainty	InformationAgg	IntegrationAgg	NumNewTies	ShareOldTies
Age	-0,40* 0,01	0,06 0,72	0,20 0,22	0,29 0,07	-0,04 0,83	-0,12 0,48	0,24 0,15	0,26 0,12	-0,31 0,05	0,13 0,44	0,13 0,44	-0,14 0,41
GenderQuant		0,02 0,92	-0,24 0,14	0,15 0,38	-0,06 0,74	-0,01 0,98	-0,05 0,77	-0,04 0,80	-0,13 0,43	-0,08 0,63	-0,08 0,64	0,10 0,57
EducationLevel			0,19 0,24	0,12 0,46	0,13 0,44	-0,32 0,05	0,25 0,14	0,27 0,11	-0,20 0,22	0,25 0,13	-0,09 0,59	0,13 0,46
Rank				0,18 0,27	-0,05 0,77	0,06 0,72	0,38* 0,02	0,23 0,16	0,07 0,69	0,32 0,05	0,18 0,30	-0,17 0,31
TimeInFunction					-0,13 0,46	-0,05 0,75	0,18 0,30	0,32 0,06	0,04 0,81	0,14 0,40	0,22 0,19	-0,20 0,25
RuleOrientation						-0,04 0,81	0,04 0,83	0,18 0,29	-0,03 0,85	0,19 0,25	-0,11 0,52	0,10 0,57
ClearTasks							-0,06 0,71	-0,16 0,35	0,25 0,14	0,09 0,61	0,44** 0,01	-0,48** 0,00
Commitment								0,00 0,99	-0,02 0,90	0,06 0,73	0,23 0,18	-0,18 0,28
Uncertainty									-0,27 0,11	0,12 0,47	0,34* 0,04	-0,31 0,06
InformationAgg										0,14 0,39	0,21 0,21	-0,24 0,16
IntegrationAgg											0,06 0,75	-0,05 0,78
NumNewTies												-0,98** 0,00
ShareOldTies												
SumFreqNew												
ShareOldFreq												
AvFreqNew												
DelAvFreq												
SumImpNew												
ShareOldImp												
AvImpNew												
DelAvImp												
SumStrenNew												
ShareOldStren												
AvStrenNew												

* 2-sided significance at the 0.05-level   1st line: Pearson's correlation
** 2-sided significance at the 0.01-level   2nd line: Significance (2-sided)

Table 33: Correlation matrix for variables for research question "Who cooperates" at SpecMatCo

for research question "Who cooperates?"

SumFreqNew	ShareOldFreq	AvFreqNew	DelAvFreq	SumImpNew	ShareOldImp	AvImpNew	DelAvImp	SumStrenNew	ShareOldStren	AvStrenNew	DelAvStren
-0,02 / 0,90	-0,18 / 0,28	-0,20 / 0,29	-0,13 / 0,49	0,12 / 0,48	-0,14 / 0,41	-0,04 / 0,83	-0,03 / 0,86	-0,01 / 0,95	-0,18 / 0,29	-0,16 / 0,40	-0,13 / 0,49
-0,08 / 0,65	0,16 / 0,35	-0,05 / 0,78	0,30 / 0,11	-0,02 / 0,93	0,08 / 0,64	0,23 / 0,23	-0,09 / 0,65	-0,04 / 0,82	0,15 / 0,39	0,03 / 0,87	0,27 / 0,16
0,03 / 0,86	0,01 / 0,98	0,13 / 0,49	-0,24 / 0,20	0,00 / 0,99	0,04 / 0,83	0,29 / 0,11	-0,35 / 0,06	0,08 / 0,64	-0,05 / 0,76	0,22 / 0,25	-0,28 / 0,13
0,21 / 0,22	-0,24 / 0,16	0,35 / 0,06	-0,46* / 0,01	0,25 / 0,14	-0,23 / 0,18	0,48** / 0,01	-0,45* / 0,01	0,26 / 0,12	-0,27 / 0,11	0,47** / 0,01	-0,53** / 0,00
0,14 / 0,42	-0,09 / 0,61	-0,16 / 0,41	0,38* / 0,04	0,23 / 0,18	-0,18 / 0,29	0,02 / 0,92	-0,04 / 0,84	0,14 / 0,40	-0,08 / 0,64	-0,14 / 0,47	0,30 / 0,10
-0,05 / 0,76	0,06 / 0,71	0,15 / 0,44	-0,10 / 0,61	-0,11 / 0,52	0,12 / 0,50	0,03 / 0,89	0,12 / 0,54	-0,06 / 0,73	0,08 / 0,63	0,12 / 0,54	0,00 / 0,99
0,23 / 0,17	-0,38* / 0,02	-0,21 / 0,26	0,01 / 0,96	0,41* / 0,01	-0,48** / 0,00	0,10 / 0,61	-0,16 / 0,41	0,22 / 0,20	-0,39* / 0,02	-0,19 / 0,31	0,00 / 1,00
0,23 / 0,18	-0,24 / 0,16	0,11 / 0,56	-0,25 / 0,18	0,28 / 0,10	-0,20 / 0,25	0,24 / 0,20	-0,09 / 0,66	0,25 / 0,14	-0,24 / 0,16	0,13 / 0,51	-0,16 / 0,39
0,45** / 0,01	-0,36* / 0,03	0,39* / 0,03	-0,23 / 0,22	0,38* / 0,02	-0,36* / 0,03	0,29 / 0,12	-0,32 / 0,09	0,48** / 0,00	-0,40* / 0,02	0,42* / 0,02	-0,27 / 0,14
0,18 / 0,29	-0,20 / 0,26	-0,03 / 0,87	-0,07 / 0,71	0,16 / 0,37	-0,20 / 0,24	-0,16 / 0,39	0,09 / 0,65	0,15 / 0,37	-0,19 / 0,28	-0,07 / 0,70	-0,10 / 0,60
-0,11 / 0,51	0,01 / 0,94	-0,19 / 0,32	0,06 / 0,76	0,07 / 0,69	-0,10 / 0,54	0,20 / 0,29	-0,37* / 0,05	-0,09 / 0,62	-0,03 / 0,88	-0,07 / 0,73	-0,04 / 0,82
0,85** / 0,00	-0,93** / 0,00	0,20 / 0,28	-0,39* / 0,03	0,96** / 0,00	-0,97** / 0,00	0,18 / 0,35	-0,14 / 0,46	0,83** / 0,00	-0,91** / 0,00	0,16 / 0,41	-0,32 / 0,08
-0,80** / 0,00	0,92** / 0,00	-0,15 / 0,44	0,37* / 0,04	-0,92** / 0,00	0,98** / 0,00	-0,14 / 0,47	0,12 / 0,53	-0,78** / 0,00	0,90** / 0,00	-0,10 / 0,61	0,31 / 0,10
	-0,89** / 0,00	0,59** / 0,00	-0,50** / 0,01	0,82** / 0,00	-0,79** / 0,00	0,18 / 0,34	-0,06 / 0,76	0,98** / 0,00	-0,88** / 0,00	0,47** / 0,01	-0,38* / 0,04
		-0,41* / 0,02	0,65** / 0,00	-0,88** / 0,00	0,91** / 0,00	-0,15 / 0,43	0,13 / 0,49	-0,87** / 0,00	0,99** / 0,00	-0,32 / 0,09	0,55** / 0,00
			-0,68** / 0,00	0,25 / 0,18	-0,16 / 0,41	0,34 / 0,07	-0,12 / 0,51	0,63** / 0,00	-0,42* / 0,02	0,93** / 0,00	-0,60** / 0,00
				-0,40* / 0,03	0,42* / 0,02	-0,28 / 0,14	0,32 / 0,09	-0,51** / 0,00	0,67** / 0,00	-0,65** / 0,00	0,95** / 0,00
					-0,96** / 0,00	0,47** / 0,01	-0,36 / 0,05	0,86** / 0,00	-0,89** / 0,00	0,30 / 0,11	-0,36 / 0,05
						-0,32 / 0,09	0,35 / 0,06	-0,80** / 0,00	0,92** / 0,00	-0,17 / 0,37	0,41* / 0,03
							-0,77** / 0,00	0,36 / 0,05	-0,25 / 0,18	0,62** / 0,00	-0,35 / 0,06
								-0,20 / 0,30	0,28 / 0,14	-0,38* / 0,04	0,53** / 0,00
									-0,88** / 0,00	0,57** / 0,00	-0,43* / 0,02
										-0,37* / 0,05	0,61** / 0,00
											-0,63** / 0,00

A first set of hypotheses postulates effects of demographic characteristics, firm related characteristics, attitudes and integration measures on reactions to the merger. A second set of hypotheses postulates tests effects of all four groups of variables on cooperation.

In the following table, the full model for testing the first set of hypotheses is presented:

Dependent variable: Commitment and uncertainty		
	Commitment	Uncertainty
Standardized Beta		
Demographic characteristics		
Age	.304	.197
Gender	.172	.046
Education level	.196	-.026
Firm related characteristics		
Rank	.357**	.100
TimeInFunction	-.011	.218
Attitudes		
RuleOrientation	.086	.228*
TaskOrientation	-.006	-.120
Integration measures		
InformationAgg	.113	-.370***
SumIntegration	-.129	.239
Model statistics		
Total df	35	35
R^2	.243	.448
Adjusted R^2	-.019	.257
F	.926	2.344

**** Significant at a 0.01-level (2-sided)
*** Significant at a 0.05-level (2-sided)
** Significant at a 0.10-level (2-sided)
* Significant at a 0.15-level (2-sided)
Note: Pairwise exclusion of incomplete cases

Table 34: Full model for dependent variables commitment and uncertainty at SpecMatCo

The full model for the dependent variables commitment and uncertainty shows that demographic characteristics have no significant effect on reactions after M&A-transactions. Rank as one of the firm related characteristics has a significant effect on commitment. Rule orientation leads to high uncertainty. Information can significantly reduce uncertainty.

Full model with all independent variables and all operationalizations of cooperation

Standardized Beta

	NumNewTies	ShareOldties	SumFreqNew	ShareOldFreq	AvFreqNew	DelAvFreq	SumImpNew	ShareOldImp	AvImpNew	DelAvImp	SumStrenNew	ShareOldStren	AvStrenNew	DelAvStren	AvQualNew	DelAvQual
Demographic characteristics																
Age	.294	-.530***	.344	-.692****	-.271	-.249	.210	-.489***	-.178	.152	.275	-.629****	-.257	-.187	-.115	.170
Gender	.103	-.245	.189	-.254*	-.033	.002	.146	-.247	.245	-.128	.220	-.228*	.066	-.018	.012	.079
Education level	-.133	.230	-.162	.171	-.091	-.186	-.039	.118	.213	-.336*	-.066	.050	.026	-.297**	.195	-.258
Firm related characteristics																
Rank	-.088	-.072	.135	-.236*	.515***	-.499***	-.007	-.134	.450**	-.308*	.204	-.260**	.616****	-.529****	.156	-.189
TimeInFunction	-.016	.030	-.102	.176	-.234	.617***	-.030	.104	-.171	.235	-.123	.227**	-.277	.592****	-.059	.252
Attitudes																
RuleOrientation	-.132	.011	-.011	.010	.136	.033	-.155	.118	-.089	.332*	-.054	.117	.043	.173	-.071	.072
TaskOrientation	.497****	-.316**	.336**	-.181	-.274	-.026	.491****	-.328***	.199	-.301*	.311*	-.225**	-.195	-.073	-.190	-.114
Reaction																
Commitment	.213	.108	.113	.197	-.002	-.086	.267	.120	.145	-.063	.138	.177	-.013	-.011	.134	-.152
Uncertainty	.260	.063	.144	.173	.282	-.298	.345	.003	.332	-.546***	.256	.056	.381*	-.463***	.196	-.195
Integration measures																
InformationAgg	.170	-.198	.084	-.200	-.042	-.287*	.150	-.193	-.040	-.099	.114	-.244**	.024	-.402***	.166	.332
SumIntegration	.125	-.333*	.064	-.318**	-.228	.291*	.080	-.369***	-.025	-.072	.029	-.289**	-.215	.286*	-.103	-.102
Controls																
(Respective Control)	.113	.502***	.343**	.685****	.113	.204	.060	.576****	.135	.038	.270	.686****	.150	.159	.278	-.024
Model statistics																
Total df	34	34	34	34	28	28	34	34	28	28	34	34	28	28	28	28
R^2	.466	.579	.391	.691	.446	.678	.449	.663	.518	.589	.380	.758	.555	.697	.267	.396
Adjusted R^2	.174	.350	.058	.522	.031	.437	.149	.478	.157	.280	.041	.625	.221	.470	-.283	-.058
F	1.598	2.524	1.175	4.098	1.075	2.809	1.496	3.600	1.434	1.909	1.122	5.729	1.662	3.073	.485	.872

**** Significant at a 0.01-level (2-sided) ** Significant at a 0.10-level (2-sided)
*** Significant at a 0.05-level (2-sided) * Significant at a 0.15-level (2-sided)

Note: Pairwise exclusion of incomplete cases

Table 35: Full model for all independent variables and cooperation as dependent variables at SpecMatCo

In the following paragraphs the hypotheses for each group of variables are separately discussed. In addition to the full models presented in Table 34 and Table 35, I also consider the partial models for each group of variables.

4.5.1. Demographic characteristics

Three different demographic characteristics have been investigated: Age, gender, and education level. In the following table, all postulated hypotheses concerning these characteristics are listed:

Hypothesis 1a:	Older employees have less cooperation relationships with new colleagues than younger employees after an M&A-transaction
Hypothesis 1b:	Older employees have more intensive relationships with new colleagues after mergers and acquisitions
Hypothesis 1c:	Older people will be less committed than younger people
Hypothesis 1d:	1: Older people are less uncertain than younger people 2: Older people are more uncertain than younger people
Hypothesis 2:	There is no gender difference in cooperation after mergers and acquisitions
Hypothesis 3a:	Higher educated employees cooperate more than less educated employees
Hypothesis 3b:	Higher educated employees experience less uncertainty after M&A-transactions than lower educated employees

Table 36: Hypotheses concerning demographic characteristics of employees

4.5.1.1. Dependent variables: Commitment and uncertainty

In the following table, the effects of demographic characteristics on commitment and uncertainty of employees are presented:

Independent variable: Demographic characteristics		
	Commitment	Uncertainty
Standardized Beta		
Demographic characteristics		
Age	.292*	.440***
Gender	.074	.157
Education level	.217	.219
Model statistics		
Total df	35	35
R^2	.130	.225
Adjusted R^2	.049	.152
F	1.596	3.095

**** Significant at a 0.01-level (2-sided)
*** Significant at a 0.05-level (2-sided)
** Significant at a 0.10-level (2-sided)
* Significant at a 0.15-level (2-sided)
Note: Pairwise exclusion of incomplete cases

Table 37: Partial model of effects of demographic characteristics on commitment and uncertainty

As can be seen, age positively affects both, commitment as well as uncertainty. The full model only shows an insignificant positive effect of age on commitment. The finding in the partial model is opposite to the hypothesized effect. Hence hypothesis 1c is not supported.

At the same time, the partial model in Table 37 shows high levels of uncertainty for older employees. The full model only shows insignificant findings for the effect of age on uncertainty. The different findings can be explained to some extent with interaction effects of seniority and the degree of feeling informed. The degree of feeling informed shows a significant negative effect in the full model. Table 33 shows a strong negative correlation of age with the degree of feeling informed. This might create a spurious positive effect of age in the partial model, which vanishes in the full model, when the degree of feeling informed is considered. The rival hypothesis 1d.1 thus is partly supported. Seemingly, older employees experience higher levels of uncertainty after mergers and acquisitions.

The partial model in Table 37 as well as the full model in Table 34 show no significant effects of gender on commitment and uncertainty, supporting hypothesis 2.

Education level also has not been found to affect commitment or uncertainty of employees after mergers and acquisitions. While hypothesis 3b postulated that higher educated employees should feel less uncertainty because they experience lower levels of fear to loose their jobs, the effect cannot be confirmed.

4.5.1.2. Dependent variables: Cooperation

In Table 38, the effects of demographic characteristics on cooperation are presented. According to this analysis, hypothesis 1a cannot be confirmed. Older employees obviously form more new ties (NumNewTies), cooperate more frequently with new colleagues (SumFreqNew) and have a lower share of cooperation frequency (ShareOldFreq), importance (ShareOldImp) and strength (ShareOldStren) with their new colleagues. It is important to note that the increase of overall frequency (SumFreqNew), importance (SumImpNew) and strength (SumStrenNew) of cooperation with new colleagues stems from an increased number of new relationships (NumNewTies) and not from an increased average frequency of cooperation (AvFreqNew), or an increased average importance of cooperation (AvImpNew) in cooperation relationships with new colleagues. While Socioemotional Selection Theory predicts that older employees should show less overall cooperation, less cooperation relationships and higher intensity of existing cooperation relationships, these predictions cannot be confirmed with the partial model.

The full model in Table 35 shows less significant results. However, an increase of age still leads to a lower share of cooperation relationships with old colleagues (ShareOldTies) and, as a consequence, to a lower share of frequency (ShareOldFreq), importance (ShareOldImp) as well as strength (ShareOldStren) of cooperation with old colleagues. That means that older employees are less biased to cooperate with new colleagues and have a more balanced cooperation portfolio. While younger colleagues show a higher share of cooperation with colleagues of the old firm, older colleagues do not have such preferences.

A summary of the findings on the effects of age on cooperation thus shows that older people have more relationships with new colleagues a lower share of relationships with old colleagues. At the same time, the average characteristics of their relationships with new colleagues do not differ from the relationships of their younger colleagues. Hence hypotheses 1a and 1b are not supported.

	Independent variables: Demographic characteristics															
	NumNewTies	SharedOldties	SumFreqNew	SharedOldFreq	AvFreqNew	DelAvFreq	SumImpNew	SharedOldImp	AvImpNew	DelAvImp	SumStrenNew	SharedOldStren	AvStrenNew	DelAvStren	AvQualNew	DelAvQual

Standardized Beta

Demographic characteristics																
Age	.346**	-.530***	.338**	-.404***	-.142	-.081	.338**	-.321**	.042	-.018	.333**	-.389***	-.100	-.054	.020	-.004
Gender	.090	-.067	.091	-.014	-.090	.263	.159	-.077	.241	-.082	.152	-.022	.005	.243	-.036	.061
Education level	-.189	.224	-.102	.099	.109	-.222	-.080	.115	.285*	-.355**	-.007	.025	.202	-.271	.290*	-.389***

Model statistics

Total df	34	34	34	34	28	28	34	34	28	28	34	34	28	28	28	28
R²	.127	.137	.101	.162	.027	.143	.097	.096	.138	.134	.091	.144	.048	.145	.087	.154
Adjusted R²	.042	.053	.014	.081	-.090	.040	.009	.008	.034	.030	.003	.061	-.066	.043	-.023	.053
F	1.502	1.634	1.166	2.003	.229	1.392	1.105	1.093	1.332	1.294	1.039	1.734	.422	1.418	.793	1.521

**** Significant at a 0.01-level (2-sided)
*** Significant at a 0.05-level (2-sided)
** Significant at a 0.10-level (2-sided)
* Significant at a 0.15-level (2-sided)

Note: Pairwise exclusion of incomplete cases

Table 38: Partial model with effects of demographic characteristics on different aspects of cooperation

Gender shows no effect on cooperation in the partial model. Hypothesis 2 thus is supported in the partial model. However, the full model shows that women have a lower share of cooperation with old colleagues (ShareOldTies). This indicates that, similar to older employees, women are more open to cooperate with their new colleagues and integrate them in their cooperation portfolio. Hence hypothesis 2 is only partly supported.

Education level also shows some effects on cooperation. The partial model shows that higher educated employees differ less between old and new relationships concerning importance of relationships (ShareOldImp). Also, higher educated employees show less quality differences between old and new relationships (DelAvQual). The full model supports these findings weakly. Obviously, higher educated employees are less likely to follow "we against them"-stereotypes. By judging importance and quality of cooperation relationships with new colleagues more similarly to importance and quality of cooperation relationships with old colleagues, they show more openness. However, this does not translate in absolute increase of the sum of frequency or the sum of new ties. Hence hypothesis 3a is partly supported.

4.5.2. Firm related characteristics

Two different firm related characteristics of employees have been investigated: rank and seniority, respectively time spent in the current function. In the following table, all postulated hypotheses concerning these characteristics are listed:

Hypothesis 4a:	Higher ranked employees cooperate more with new colleagues
Hypothesis 4b:	Higher ranked employees are more committed than lower ranked employees
Hypothesis 4c:	Higher ranked employees feel less uncertain than lower ranked employees
Hypothesis 5a:	The longer an employee work for a company, the less this employee cooperates with new colleagues
Hypothesis 5b:	Higher seniority of employees reduces commitment
Hypothesis 5c:	Higher seniority increases uncertainty

Table 39: Hypotheses concerning demographic characteristics of employees

4.5.2.1. Dependent variables: Commitment and uncertainty

Table 40 shows the effects of firm related characteristics on commitment and uncertainty:

Independent variable: Firm related characteristics		
	Commitment	Uncertainty
Standardized Beta		
Firm related characteristics		
Rank	.357***	.168
TimeInFunction	.105	.284**
Model statistics		
Total df	35	35
R^2	.152	.125
Adjusted R^2	.100	.072
F	2.946	2.364

**** Significant at a 0.01-level (2-sided)
*** Significant at a 0.05-level (2-sided)
** Significant at a 0.10-level (2-sided)
* Significant at a 0.15-level (2-sided)
Note: Pairwise exclusion of incomplete cases

Table 40: Partial model of effects of firm related characteristics on commitment and uncertainty

The partial model shows strong support for hypothesis 4b. Higher ranked employees are more committed than lower ranked employees. At the same time, the results of the partial model do not support hypothesis 4c. These findings are supported by the full model in Table 34. Higher ranked employees do not feel less uncertain than lower ranked employees.

Seniority, respectively time spent in a function has no effect on commitment of employees as predicted in hypothesis 5b. At the same time, the partial model supports hypothesis 5c, according to which uncertainty increases with seniority of employees. The full model in Table 34 shows no significant effects of seniority on commitment or uncertainty. Hence hypothesis 5b is not supported. Hypothesis 5c is partly supported.

4.5.2.2. Dependent variables: Cooperation

In Table 41, the effects of rank and seniority on cooperation are presented in the partial model. As can be seen, rank and seniority have no significant effect on the number of ties that are formed with new colleagues (NumNewTies). However, rank significantly increases the average frequency of cooperation relationships with new colleagues (AvFreqNew). Also, rank significantly increases the average importance of cooperation relationships with new colleagues (AvImpNew), leading to increased average strength of cooperation relationships with new colleagues (AvStrenNew).

Independent variable: Firm related characteristics

	NumNewTies	ShareOldties	SumFreqNew	ShareOldFreq	AvFreqNew	DelAvFreq	SumImpNew	ShareOldImp	AvImpNew	DelAvImp	SumStrenNew	ShareOldStren	AvStrenNew	DelAvStren	AvQualNew	DelAvQual
Standardized Beta																
Firm related characteristics																
Rank	.124	-.530***	.237	-.234	.397***	-.547****	.207	-.191	.489****	-.468***	.309**	-.275*	.515****	-.597****	.247	-.334**
TimeInFunction	.193	-.161	.098	-.014	-.270*	.501****	.184	-.133	-.068	.038	.086	.002	-.253*	.420****	-.052	.207
Model statistics																
Total df	34	34	34	34	28	28	34	34	28	28	34	34	28	28	28	28
R²	.061	.048	.074	.056	.193	.453	.090	.063	.232	.215	.112	.075	.283	.444	.059	.130
Adjusted R²	.002	-.011	.016	-.003	.131	.411	.033	.005	.173	.154	.057	.018	.228	.402	-.013	.063
F	1.040	.811	1.284	.955	3.103	10.769	1.584	1.077	3.923	3.550	2.022	1.304	5.129	10.400	.819	1.944

**** Significant at a 0.01-level (2-sided)   ** Significant at a 0.10-level (2-sided)
*** Significant at a 0.05-level (2-sided)   * Significant at a 0.15-level (2-sided)

Note: Pairwise exclusion of incomplete cases

Table 41: Partial model with effects of firm related characteristics on different aspects of cooperation

The same effect can be found for average cooperation quality: Higher ranked individuals show a lower delta between the quality of old and new relationships (DelAvStren). While not having more new cooperation relationships (NumNewTies) or more frequent new cooperation (SumFreqNew), higher ranked individuals seem to differ much less in cooperating with colleagues in the old firm and with new colleagues. This finding is supported by the full model in Table 35. Only the difference between the average quality of old and new relationships (DelAvQual) is not significant in the full model. Hence hypothesis 4a is partially supported.

At the same time, seniority of employees increases the difference between average frequency of old and of new relationships (DelAvFreq). More senior employees do have as many new relationships (NumNewTies) as their junior colleagues. However, senior employees hardly cooperate with their new colleagues (AvFreqNew). Therefore, the average cooperation frequency in cooperation relationships with new colleagues is much lower than the average cooperation frequency of more junior employees (DelAvFreq). As a consequence, the strength of old cooperation relationships of more senior employees is higher than the strength of their new cooperation relationships (DelAvStren). This finding is also supported by the full model in Table 35. Hypothesis 5a is thus partially supported.

4.5.3. Psychological factors

Two different work related attitudes have been investigated in the research on SpecMatCo: rule orientation as well as preference for well specified tasks, respectively task orientation. While it was possible to formulate a hypothesis based on previous findings for the effect of task orientation, rule orientation as a variable has been considered exploratively. Hence there is no hypothesis for the effect of rule orientation on reactions after M&A-transactions, respectively on cooperation.

In addition to these attitudes, two possible reactions after mergers and acquisitions have been investigated: commitment and uncertainty. In Table 42, the postulated hypotheses are listed:

Hypothesis 6a:	Higher task orientation leads to higher cooperation after mergers and acquisition
Hypothesis 6b:	Task orientation should have no independent effect on uncertainty or commitment
Hypothesis 7:	Higher commitment increases cooperation after mergers and acquisitions
Hypothesis 8:	Higher uncertainty reduces cooperation after mergers and acquisitions

Table 42: Hypotheses concerning demographic characteristics of employees

4.5.3.1. Dependent variables: Commitment and uncertainty

In the following table, the effects of firm related characteristics on commitment and uncertainty are presented:

Independent variable: Attitudes		
	Commitment	Uncertainty
Standardized Beta		
Attitudes		
RuleOrientation	.045	.226
TaskOrientation	-.072	-.202
Model statistics		
Total df	35	35
R^2	.007	.095
Adjusted R^2	-.053	.040
F	.124	1.728

**** Significant at a 0.01-level (2-sided)
*** Significant at a 0.05-level (2-sided)
** Significant at a 0.10-level (2-sided)
* Significant at a 0.15-level (2-sided)
Note: Pairwise exclusion of incomplete cases

Table 43: Partial model of effects of attitudes on commitment and uncertainty

In line with hypothesis 6b, task orientation does not have an effect on commitment or uncertainty. The full model in Table 34 supports this finding.
According to the partial model, rule orientation does not have a significant effect on uncertainty. However, the full model in Table 34 shows that higher rule orientation leads to increased uncertainty after mergers and acquisitions. A possible explanation of this finding might be the significant changes in organizational structures, processes, norms, and social networks. These changes evoke transitional structures, which are fuzzy and unclear. Rule oriented employees might suffer from such fuzziness and react with higher levels of uncertainty than other employees, for whom rules are less important.

4.5.3.2. Dependent variables: Cooperation

In the following table, the effects of attitudes and reactions after mergers and acquisitions on cooperation are presented in the partial model.
In the partial model, task orientation shows very strong effects on cooperation: The number of new ties (NumNewTies) is significantly higher. As a consequence, the sum of frequency (SumNewFrew), of importance (SumNewImp) and of strength (SumNewImp) of highly task oriented employees is higher than for others. Also, the share of old relationships

(ShareOldTies), as well as the share of frequency (ShareOldFreq), of importance (ShareOldImp) and of strength of cooperation (ShareOldStren) with old colleagues is lower for highly task oriented employees. Hence the more individuals prefer clearly defined tasks, the more they cooperate with new colleagues. The results of the partial and the full model strongly support hypothesis 6a.

Rule orientation, however, shows only very weak effects on cooperation. Employees with high rule orientation differ more strongly in the average importance they assign to new and to old relationships (DelAvImp). Seemingly, relationships with former colleagues are seen as more important than with new colleagues. In the full model in Table 35, however, high rule orientation shows no significant effects on different aspects of cooperation.

		Independent variable: Attitudes and reactions															
		NumNewTies	SharedOldties	SumFreqNew	SharedOldFreq	AvFreqNew	DelAvFreq	SumimpNew	SharedOldImp	AvImpNew	DelAvImp	SumStrenNew	SharedOldStren	AvStrenNew	DelAvStren	AvQualNew	DelAvQual
Standardized Beta																	
Attitudes	RuleOrientation	-.150	-.530***	-.044	.085	.160	-.080	-.170	.167	-.069	.245	-.082	.124	.076	.052	.021	.009
	TaskOrientation	.552****	-.574****	.383***	-.493****	-.229	-.022	.529****	-.593****	.197	-.276*	.347***	-.507****	-.155	-.056	-.231	-.028
Reaction	Commitment	.255**	-.201	.265*	-.255*	.039	-.233	.319***	-.226*	.281*	-.163	.293**	-.261**	.089	-.169	.203	-.223
	Uncertainty	.328***	-.303**	.322**	-.300**	.166	-.141	.394***	-.385***	.387***	-.522****	.391***	-.365***	.292	-.273	.116	-.289
Model statistics																	
Total df		34	34	34	34	28	28	34	34	28	28	34	34	28	28	28	28
R²		.373	.365	.239	.305	.139	.082	.408	.426	.205	.299	.265	.345	.153	.088	.125	.121
Adjusted R²		.289	.281	.137	.212	-.004	-.071	.329	.349	.073	.182	.167	.258	.011	-.064	-.020	-.026
F		4.453	4.314	2.353	3.285	.969	.535	5.164	5.566	1.550	2.561	2.705	3.957	1.080	.579	.860	.826

**** Significant at a 0.01-level (2-sided) ** Significant at a 0.10-level (2-sided)
*** Significant at a 0.05-level (2-sided)   * Significant at a 0.15-level (2-sided)

Note: Pairwise exclusion of incomplete cases

Table 44: Partial model with effects of attitudes and reactions after mergers and acquisitions on different aspects of cooperation

In the partial model in Table 44, commitment shows a number of positive significant effects on cooperation: Higher commitment increases the number of new ties (NumNewTies), the sum of frequency (SumNewFreq), importance (SumNewImp) and strength (SumNewStren) of cooperation with new colleagues. At the same, highly committed employees show a lower share of cooperation with old colleagues (ShareOldTies). Obviously, commitment leads to more proactive cooperation behaviors. However, while the partial model shows strong effects of commitment on cooperation, the full model shows no significant effects. This confirms the assumed dependence of commitment of other independent variables such as firm-related variables or integration measures as postulated in the research model. In the full model, the effects of commitment vanish as these variables are considered. Hence hypothesis 7 is partly supported.

Opposite to the predicted effect of hypothesis 8, higher uncertainty leads to more new cooperation relationships with new colleagues, higher frequency as well as higher importance and strength of cooperation with new colleagues. The full model weakly supports this finding. Hence hypothesis 8 is not supported.

4.5.4. Integration measures

A number of different integration measures have been considered. First, the effects of information on the respondents have been investigated with different items. Second, the effects of participation in different active integration measures have been considered.
In the following table, the postulated hypotheses are listed:

Hypothesis 9a:	A high degree of feeling informed increases commitment of employees
Hypothesis 9b:	A high degree of feeling informed decreases uncertainty of employees
Hypothesis 10a:	Participation in active integration measures increases cooperation with new colleagues
Hypothesis 10b:	Participation in active integration measures increases commitment of employees
Hypothesis 10c:	Participation in active integration measures decreases uncertainty of employees

Table 45: Hypotheses concerning integration measures

4.5.4.1. Dependent variables: Commitment and uncertainty

In the following table, the effects of the degree of feeling informed and participation in active integration measures on commitment and uncertainty are presented:

	Independent variable: Integration measures	
	Commitment	Uncertainty
Standardized Beta		
Integration measures		
InformationAgg	-.074	-.474****
SumIntegration	.113	.365***
Model statistics		
Total df	35	35
R^2	.015	.285
Adjusted R^2	-.045	.242
F	1.057	6.576

**** Significant at a 0.01-level (2-sided)
*** Significant at a 0.05-level (2-sided)
** Significant at a 0.10-level (2-sided)
* Significant at a 0.15-level (2-sided)
Note: Pairwise exclusion of incomplete cases

Table 46: Partial model of effects of integration measures on commitment and uncertainty

According to the partial model, the degree of feeling informed as well as participation in integration measures have no effect on commitment of employees. This finding is confirmed by the findings in the full model as presented in Table 35. Hypotheses 9a and 10a thus are not supported.

However, there is a significant effect of the degree of feeling informed on uncertainty. Employees that feel well informed perceive less uncertainty than employees that feel poorly informed. This finding also is confirmed by the full model as presented in Table 35. Thus hypothesis 9b is supported.

The partial model shows a significant positive effect of participation in integration measures on uncertainty. That means that employees, who participate in integration measures experience higher levels of uncertainty than employees who participate in less or in no integration measures. This finding is not supported in the full model. Nevertheless, the effects shown in the partial model are opposite to hypothesis 10b.

4.5.4.2. Dependent variables: Cooperation

In Table 47, the effects of integration measures on cooperation are presented in the partial model.

Independent variable: Integration measures

	NumNewTies	SharedOldTies	SumFreqNew	SharedOldFreq	AvFreqNew	DelAvFreq	SumImpNew	SharedOldImp	AvImpNew	DelAvImp	SumStrenNew	SharedOldStren	AvStrenNew	DelAvStren	AvQualNew	DelAvQual
Standardized Beta																
Integration measures																
InformationAgg	.074	-.530***	-.044	-.051	-.150	-.011	.008	-.060	-.229	.149	-.076	-.033	-.172	-.050	-.069	.420***
SumIntegration	.230	-.198	.239	-.182	-.024	-.019	.246	-.267*	.268	-.389***	.248	-.228	.071	-.086	-.015	-.278*
Model statistics																
Total df	34	34	34	34	28	28	34	34	28	28	34	34	28	28	28	28
R^2	.065	.062	.055	.040	.025	.001	.061	.082	.098	.149	.060	.056	.030	.012	.005	.205
Adjusted R^2	.007	.003	-.004	-.020	-.050	-.076	.003	.024	.029	.084	.001	-.003	-.045	-.064	-.071	.143
F	1.120	1.058	.929	.661	.330	.008	1.048	1.420	1.418	2.283	1.013	.950	.396	.153	.072	3.344

**** Significant at a 0.01-level (2-sided) ** Significant at a 0.10-level (2-sided)
*** Significant at a 0.05-level (2-sided) * Significant at a 0.15-level (2-sided)

Note: Pairwise exclusion of incomplete cases

Table 47: Partial model with effects of integration measures on different aspects of cooperation

In the partial model, the degree of feeling informed has almost no effect on the cooperation. Only the difference of the quality of old and new relationships (DelAvQual) is higher for high degrees of feeling informed. However, as there is no significant effect of the degree of feeling informed on the average quality of new relationships (AvQualNew), this finding indicates that employees with better cooperation quality with old colleagues if they feel better informed. The full model in Table 35 shows a number of additional effects: Employees who feel well informed have cooperation relationships with their new colleagues that have a more similar average cooperation frequency (DelAvFreq) and the share of cooperation strength of old relationships (ShareOldStren) is lower and the differences between average strength of old and new relationships (DelAvStren) are smaller.

This means that well informed employees do not necessarily engage in more cooperation relationships (NumNewTies). However, within the new relationships they have, they cooperate frequently (AvFreqNew) and strongly (AvStrenNew).

The number of integration measures, in which an employee participates, affects some aspects of cooperation. The partial model shows that participation in integration measures reduces the differences of importance (DelAvImp) and of quality of relationships (DelAvQual) with old and new colleagues. The full model shows this effect even more strongly: The share of old ties (ShareOldTies) decreases, the share of frequency of cooperation with old colleagues (ShareOldFreq) as well as the difference of average cooperation frequency between old and new relationships (DelAvFreq) decreases. The same effects are found for importance (ShareOldImp, DelAvImp) and for strength of cooperation (ShareOldStren, DelAvStren). Seemingly, participation in integration measures helps employees to develop cooperation relationships with their new colleagues that are very much like the cooperation relationships they have with old colleagues. That means that integration measures facilitate the emergence of cooperation "normality". Hence hypothesis 10a is partly supported.

4.5.5. Structural cooperation requirements

Structural cooperation requirements have been considered in all regression analyses as control variable. Respondents indicated as key informants the cooperation of their departments with other departments. Based on number of cooperation relationships, on frequency, importance, strength and quality of cooperation between the department of a key informant and other departments, the structural cooperation requirements have been computed as department level control variables. Significant effects of the control variable thus indicate that the cooperation relationships of employees and their most important coworkers are in line with the cooperation requirements of their departments.

The full model in Table 35 shows a number of significant effects of structural cooperation requirements. Cooperation requirements show a strong effect on the share of old ties and on the share of frequency, of importance and strength of cooperation with old departments. This indicates that if a department has a lower share of cooperation requirements with old departments, employees similarly show a lower share of cooperation relationships with old colleagues. At the same time, the number of new ties, the sum of frequency, of importance and strength of cooperation of employees is not affected by the structural cooperation requirements. Individual cooperation thus is not directly influenced. The absolute cooperation indicators do not change. However, structural cooperation requirements significantly affect the relative cooperation indicators. Hypothesis 11 thus is partly supported.

4.5.6. Summary of results

In the following tables, the results presented above are summarized. For each hypothesis, the number of the hypothesis, the independent and the dependent variable are indicated. Also, the direction of the expected effect is indicated.

In Table 48 and Table 49, the results for the regression analyses to determine the effects of the independent variables on commitment and uncertainty of employees are presented for both the partial and the full model. Three different results are possible:

- Supported: Indicates a significant statistical support for the hypothesized effect
- Not supported: Indicates a non-significant effect
- Opposite: Indicates a significant statistical effect opposite to the hypothesized effect.

The total evaluation then indicates whether the results of the partial and the full model both show support (=supported), one shows support, one shows no support (= partly supported), one shows support and one shows the opposite of the postulated effect (= mixed) and one or both show the opposite of the postulated effect (= opposite).

Summarizing the results of the findings at SpecMatCo, a number of findings are remarkable.

In Table 48 the summary of the factors influencing commitment is presented. Obviously, hardly any of the investigated independent variables have a significant effect on commitment. While the null hypotheses on the effects of gender and of task orientation on commitment are supported, only rank shows a significant positive effect on commitment, supporting hypothesis 4b. Higher ranked employees thus show more commitment than employees in the lower ranks.

Older employees are more committed than younger employees as findings in the partial model indicate. This finding is opposite to the postulated effects.

Hypo-thesis	Independent variable	Dependent variable	Expected effect	Partial model	Full model	Total
1c	Age	Commitment	-	Opposite	Not supp.	Opposite
2	Gender	Commitment	0	Supp.	Supp.	Supp.
4b	Rank	Commitment	+	Supp.	Supp.	Supp.
5b	Seniority	Commitment	-	Not supp.	Not supp.	Not supp.
6b	Task orientation	Commitment	0	Supp.	Supp.	Supp.
9a	Degree of feeling informed	Commitment	+	Not supp.	Not supp.	Not supp.
10b	Integration measures	Commitment	+	Not supp.	Not supp.	Not supp.

Legend: Supported / Not supp. / Opposite

Table 48: Summary of factors influencing commitment at SpecMatCo

At the same time, Table 49 shows that older employees are somewhat more uncertain than their younger colleagues, supporting hypothesis 1c.2. As predicted in hypothesis 5c, higher seniority leads to higher uncertainty. As older employees often are with the company for a long time, uncertainty is even doubled for these employees, potentially leading to dysfunctional reactions. However, the level of feeling informed reduces uncertainty effectively.

Hypo-thesis	Independent variable	Dependent variable	Expected effect	Partial model	Full model	Total
1d.1	Age	Uncertainty	-	Opposite	Not supp.	Opposite
1d.2	Age	Uncertainty	+	Supp.	Not supp.	Partly supp.
2	Gender	Uncertainty	0	Supp.	Supp.	Supp.
3b	Education level	Uncertainty	-	Not supp	Not supp.	Not supp.
4c	Rank	Uncertainty	-	Not supp.	Not supp.	Not supp.
5c	Seniority	Uncertainty	+	Supp.	Supp.	Supp.
6b	Task orientation	Uncertainty	0	Supp.	Supp.	Supp.
9b	Degree of feeling informed	Uncertainty	-	Supp.	Supp.	Supp.
10c	Integration measures	Uncertainty	-	Opposite	Not supp.	Opposite

Legend: Supported / Not supp. / Opposite

Table 49: Summary of factors influencing uncertainty at SpecMatCo

It is notable that participation in integration measures increase uncertainty in the partial model. While the effect is insignificant in the full model, it still shows the same direction.

Cooperation has been operationalized with a number of different variables. Number of ties, frequency, importance, strength and quality of cooperation have been measured and different variables have been computed based on these measures. In Table 50, all measures are summarized as intensity of cooperation. Also, the different findings for partial as well as for the full model are summarized. Cooperation intensity is judged with the help of different in different evaluations:

- Strongly supported: Most or all of the regression analyses for the different variables of cooperation support the hypothesis
- Partly supported: Some of the regression analyses support the hypothesis
- Not supported: The results of the regression analyses do not support the hypothesis
- Mixed: The regression analyses yield some results supporting the hypothesis and other results that are opposite to the hypothesized effects
- Opposite: The regression analyses yield results that are opposite to the hypothesized effects.

In the following table, the effects of the independent variables on cooperation are summarized.

Hypo-thesis	Independent variable	Dependent variable	Expected effect	Partial model	Full model with control	Total
1a	Age	Cooperation intensity	-	Opposite	Opposite	Opposite
1b	Age	Average intensity of ties	+	Not supp.	Not supp.	Not supp.
2	Gender	Cooperation intensity	0	Strongly supp.	Not supp.	Partly supp.
3a	Education level	Cooperation intensity	+	Partly supp.	Partly supp.	Partly supp.
4a	Rank	Cooperation intensity	+	Strongly supp.	Strongly supp.	Strongly supp.
5a	Seniority	Cooperation intensity	-	Partly supp.	Partly supp.	Partly supp.
6a	Task orientation	Cooperation intensity	+	Strongly supp.	Strongly supp.	Strongly supp.
7	Commitment	Cooperation intensity	+	Strongly supp.	Not supp.	Partly supp.
8	Uncertainty	Cooperation intensity	-	Opposite	Opposite	Opposite
10a	Integration measures	Cooperation intensity	+	Partly supp.	Partly supp.	Partly supp.
11	Structural requirements	Cooperation intensity	+		Strongly supp.	Strongly supp.

Table 50: Summary of factors influencing cooperation at SpecMatCo

Looking at the effects of different independent variables on cooperation in Table 50, a number of findings are noteworthy. First, age does not show the postulated negative effects on cooperation intensity. Even the opposite is the case: Older employees cooperate more intensively than their younger colleagues. At the same time, cooperation relationships of older employees are equally intense as the relationships of their younger colleagues. Seemingly, older employees are more integrative after mergers and acquisitions than their younger colleagues. Especially, older employees differ less between colleagues from the old firm and new colleagues.

Female gender shows in the full model some significant positive effects on cooperation. This is opposite to the hypothesized effect. According to the findings, women are more open to cooperate with new employees.

A third interesting finding is that higher educated individuals differ less between cooperation relationships with colleagues from the old firm and new colleagues. Corresponding to the hypothesized effects, higher education level lets employees behave more integrative.

A fourth interesting finding is that rank has the postulated effect on cooperation: Rank increases intensity of cooperation. It is important to note that the effect is significant in the full model. Hence, other characteristics of individuals that might be correlated to rank, such as education level or higher degree of feeling informed are not responsible for the finding.

A fifth finding of the research is that seniority increases the difference between old and new relationships. While employees of high seniority are very well connected amongst old colleagues, they do not expand their cooperation relationships to the new firm. Rather, they preserve their old networks.

A sixth finding that deserves attention is the positive effect of task orientation on cooperation intensity. Obviously, work related attitudes do have an effect on cooperation.

Similarly, the strong effect of commitment on cooperation intensity in the partial model is noteworthy. It shows that commitment does increase cooperation after mergers and acquisitions. However, at the same time, the result shows that commitment depends to a high degree on other independent variables. Hence in the full model, the effect of commitment drops below the significance level.

Uncertainty shows an effect opposite to the predicted effect. In the partial as well as in the full model, uncertainty shows a positive effect on cooperation intensity.

Participation in integration measures shows a positive effect on cooperation. In partial as well as in the full model with control variable, participation in integration measures shows some positive effects on cooperation intensity. However, the effects are rather weak.

Last but not least, the structural cooperation requirements show significant effects. However, the effects are limited to the relative share of new cooperation relationships in relation to old cooperation relationships.

4.6. Methodological limitations

There are a number of methodological limitations, which have to be considered in order to discuss the results appropriately. Basically, limitations can be separated in limitations of the data gathering approach and limitations of the operationalization of the research constructs. Limitations of the data gathering approach research comprise limitations of the sample, of the use of key informants and of the use of the ego-centered network analysis.

A first limitation of the data gathering approach is the small sample size. As a rule of thumb in multiple regression analyses, the number of independent variables n should not exceed a tenth of the number of investigated cases (Bortz 1999). In the present research, this proportion cannot be maintained for the full models. Due to the small size, only a very limited number of significant effects have been generated. Even relatively strong effects have not been found to be statistically significant because of the small sample size.

A second limitation of the data gathering approach, which is also related to the sample is the low number of female participants in the research. Gender effects are based on the information provided by five women only. Due to the small number of female participants, there is a significant risk that one female participant can influence the findings strongly. An undetected sample bias might be the consequence. Hence gender specific results based on the information provided by the female respondents need to be considered very carefully.

Another limitation linked to the sample, is the low variance of the sample participants concerning the education level. As presented in Graph 2, 70% of the employees are in the same education level. Due to the small sample size, the effect of an individual thus alters the results strongly.

A fourth limitation represents the lack of variance of the variable "participation in integration measures". Almost all respondents participated in integration measures. Assuming that the effect of integration measures between individuals who did not participate in integration measures and individuals who did participate in integration measures, and assuming that the marginal effect of integration measures decreases strongly after the first integration measure, the research cannot capture the main effects of integration measures.

Another limitation of the data gathering approach is the use of key informants to indicate cooperation requirements on the departmental level. When key informants are used in a research, the underlying assumption is that the key informants possess the necessary knowledge to provide information about a supra-individual entity. In this case, the supra-individual entity is the department of an individual. That means that a key informant is assumed to possess largely objective information about the unit of observation. As has been elaborated in 3.3.3.1, it is very difficult to observe cooperation relationships of others, because cooperation relationships are only visible in the moment of a cooperation interaction. Cooperation of a department corresponds to the sum of all cooperation relationships of all employees within that department. Due to the difficulties of observation of cooperation relationships on the individual level, a key informant is hardly able to indicate the cooperation on the level of the department with high validity.

In addition to the problem of getting valid information from key informants, the usage of respondents as respondents of individual level information and as key informants for departmental level information bears the risk of an intra-respondent bias: A respondent might answer the questions about departmental cooperation similar to his own cooperation. Du to subjectivity and the limitations of perception of cooperation relationships of others, such a bias is very likely.

A further limitation, which needs to be considered, is the fact that respondents have been asked to indicate cooperation relationships on the departmental level to all other departments. However, on the individual level, respondents were only asked to indicate cooperation to the ten most important coworkers. Weak cooperation relationships thus are considered on the departmental level, however they are not considered on the individual level. In case there is a bias of strong relationships being rather old cooperation relationships and weaker relationships being rather new cooperation relationships, the lack of consideration of weak relationships on the individual level leads to systematic distortions of the results.

The operationalization mainly suffers from two limitations. First, the use of single item measurement of work attitudes of respondents bears the risk of conceptual poverty of the construct. In future research, attitudes should be measured with several items in order to capture a construct and not only a single item.

Second, the use of a factor analysis to determine and confirm the reactions to mergers and acquisitions, uncertainty and commitment, limits the validity and reliability of the results. Another research site, or even another sample at the same research site might result other factors. A more conceptual and theory driven approach for the measurement of attitudes would be helpful to avoid this risk and to ensure the validity and reliability of the findings.

These limitations need to be considered in the following discussion of the results. Also, the limitations need to be addressed in further studies.

4.7. Who cooperates with whom? Operationalization of hypotheses 12 to 22

In order to test hypotheses 12 to 22, the dependent and the independent constructs need to be operationalized. Based on the relationship data gathered with the ego-centered network analysis, the dependent constructs, i.e. the characteristics of cooperation relationships can be operationalized. Independent constructs have been operationalized with the help of a number of additional items. The operationalization of both, dependent and independent constructs is described in detail in the following paragraphs.

4.7.1. Dependent construct: Characteristics of cooperation relationships

For each relationship with alters (i.e. the most important coworkers) indicated by ego (i.e. the respondents in the ego-centered network analysis), a number of different characteristics of intensity of cooperation has been gathered. First, information on the frequency of cooperation in each relationship has been gathered with the help of a four-point scale (see Appendix I). Second, importance of a cooperation relationship has been indicated by the respondents on a seven-point scale (see Appendix I). Based on these two variables, a third variable, strength, is computed for each relationship as the product of the scores of frequency and importance. Last but not least, the quality of each relationship had to be indicated.

For each relationship, respondents had to indicate the former company of the relationship partner. Hence it is possible to determine, whether an indicated relationship was newly formed after the merger between new colleagues, or whether an indicated relationship is old and existed already before the merger. Relationships with important coworkers, which entered the firm after the merger, are not considered.

4.7.2. Independent constructs

The core hypothesis to answer the question "Who cooperates with whom?" is the principle of homophily. According to the homophily principle, similar employees are more likely to cooperate with each other than dissimilar employees.

The ego-centered network analysis bears significant hindrances to operationalize similarity of employees. The information provided about the relationship partners is fully subjective. Subjective information, however might underly strong respondent biases. For example, the homophily principle not only indicates that we tend to feel more attracted by similar others, but also that we perceive others that are close to us often to be more similar than they actually are. One explanation for this is the avoidance of cognitive dissonance in relationships (Festinger 1962). While individuals in a relationship might actually have different

233

characteristics, especially concerning attitudes or other characteristics that are not subject to direct observation, the differences might be neglected to avoid conflicts. Another explanation for a respondent bias is the ingroup-outgroup bias, which leads to identification with others based on shared traits (Tajfel, & Wilkes 1963). Individuals might focus on similarities more than on dissimilarities to maintain the ingroup-perception of significant others. Based on the research setup, it is impossible to eliminate a potential respondent bias. The information about relationship partners thus cannot be validated.

Nevertheless, an ego-centered network analysis can be used to collect information about the relationship partner. In this research, I focused on similarity of age, gender, as well as on similarity of two different types of attitude. In addition to that, I asked how respondents got to know the alter significant coworkers.

4.7.2.1. Demographic similarity

Age similarity. A first demographic similarity is the similarity of age. In order to test for age similarity, respondents were asked to indicate the approximate age of the relationship partners. Four different categories were used: 20 to 29 (= 1), 30 to 39 (= 2), 40 to 49 (= 3) and 50 or older (= 4). All respondents had to indicate their own age. Their own age was classified in the same age categories. Based on the age of the respondent and the indicated age of the relationship partner, it is possible to compute the similarity. The value of the difference of the age category of the respondent and the age category of the indicated relationship partner is a good measure for similarity. The range is between 0 and 3. I inverted the variable in order to get an increase of similarity from 0 (= minimum similarity) to 3 (= maximum similarity).

Gender similarity. For each relationship partner, the respondents were asked to indicate the gender. Also, respondents were asked to indicate their own gender. Hence it was possible to determine gender similarity for each relationship. Different gender of respondent and relationship partner was coded with 0, same gender of respondent and relationship partners was coded with 1.

4.7.2.2. Attitude similarity

As has been described above, psychological constructs such as attitudes can hardly be indicated for others. Introspection is needed, respectively systematic observation of behaviors of employees over long time periods. Therefore, respondents were not asked to describe the attitudes of their important coworkers. As a substitute for gathering information about the attitudes of the important coworkers and comparing them with the attitudes of the respondents, I chose to ask respondents about the perceived similarity of attitudes of the respondents and the important coworkers. Two different aspects of attitudes have been investigated:

- Work attitude similarity. For each relationship with an important coworker, the respondents were asked to indicate their degree of agreement with the statement "Concerning work, I have the same attitudes as this coworker". On a five-point Likert scale, respondents could indicate 1 (= not true) to 5 (= exactly true).
- General attitude similarity. For each relationship with an important coworker, the respondents were asked to indicate their degree of agreement with the statement "Outside work, I see things differently from this coworker". On a five-point Likert scale, respondents could indicate 1 (= not true) to 5 (= exactly true). That means that a low value indicates a high degree of similarity and vice versa. In order to get increasing values for increasing similarity of general attitudes, I inverted the variable. A value of 1 indicates low similarity, a value of 5 indicates high similarity of general attitudes.

4.7.2.3. Participation in integration measures

Respondents were asked how they got to know their most important coworkers. They could choose from a list of cooperation measures, which has been determined upfront in exploratory interviews. They could choose between: (1) joint participation in integration trainings, (2) joint kick-off meeting, (3) joint management meetings, and (4) other integration measures. Respondents could indicate several integration measures, if they participated in several integration measures together with the most important coworker. If an employee and the most important coworker participated in one of these integration measures, it was coded with 1. If they did not participate, it was coded with 0. The sum of participation then was formed. Hence the maximum value for the variable participation in integration measures is 4, the minimum value is 0.

4.7.3. Controls

Structural cooperation requirements might affect the choice of important cooperation partners as cooperation in companies is usually highly constrained by formal cooperation requirements.

For each relationship, respondents had to indicate the position that the important coworker had. They had to indicate all three levels of the organization: division, business unit as well as subordinate organizational units. However, due to anonymity reasons many respondents chose not to provide this information openly. Only the division can be clearly determined for most relationships. As a simple proxy for cooperation requirements, I use membership in the same division as control variable for cooperation requirements. Usually, cooperation requirements are high within the same divisions and lower between divisions. Hence if the respondent and a relationship partner were in the same division, structural cooperation requirement was coded with 1, otherwise, it was coded with 0.

4.8. Results for the research question "Who cooperates with whom?"

Based on past empirical findings and based on existing theories, a number of hypotheses have been postulated in the second part of this work to answer the research question "Who cooperates with whom?".
Based on the operationalization of the research constructs in the study at SpecMatCo, not all hypotheses could be considered. The use of an ego-centered network analysis made testing of several hypotheses impossible:

- With the help of the ego-centered network data, it is not possible to investigate the existence or non-existence of ties. Only a small sample of all employees indicated their relationships, and these employees only indicate their ten most important coworkers. Hence it is impossible to state whether a relationship does not exist, or whether it simply was not captured in the data gathering of the ego-centered network analysis due to methodological restrictions. Hence hypotheses 12a, 13a, 14a, 15a, 16a, 17a, 18a, 19a, 20a, and 21a cannot be tested.
- Similarity of education level and similarity of education background could not be considered. Early exploratory interviews showed that respondents hardly know, what education level, respectively what education background their important coworkers have. As the data on the important coworkers was gathered anonymously, it was impossible to track the important coworkers and find out their education level and education background later on. As a consequence, hypotheses 14b and 15b cannot be tested.
- While respondents were asked to indicate the position of the important coworkers, the data gathered was incomplete and inconsistent. Hence rank could not be determined for most important coworkers. Therefore, rank similarity has not been considered. Hence hypothesis 16b cannot be tested.
- Early exploratory interviews revealed that respondents hardly can estimate the seniority of their new important coworkers in the other firm. Hence this information was not gathered. Therefore, similarity of seniority could not be investigated. Hence hypothesis 17b cannot be tested.
- Reactions after mergers and acquisitions can hardly be indicated for others. First, psychological constructs are difficult to access. As has been described above, the investigation of psychological constructs requires either systematic observation over

longer periods of time, or introspection. Therefore, respondents were not asked to indicate reactions to the M&A-transaction of their important coworkers. Hence similarity of reactions could not be considered.

As a consequence, only hypotheses 12b, 13b, 18b as well as 21b could be tested. Hypothesis 22b has been tested indirectly by considering whether employees work in the same division or not.

The effects of these independent variables on intensity (i.e. frequency, importance, strength as well as quality) of new cooperation relationships have been tested. In Table 51, the results for the full model are presented.

	Summary of full models with control variable			
	Frequency	Importance	Strength	Quality
Standardized Beta				
Demographic characteristics				
Age similarity	.017	.004	-.027	.114
Gender similarity	-.107	-.074	-.120	.053
Attitudes				
Work attitudes similarity	-.067	.146	-.014	.593****
General attitudes similarity	.123	.172	.187	.204***
Participation in integration measures	-.104	.068	-.069	-.031
Controls				
Same division	.301***	-.084	.214**	-.021
Model statistics				
Total df	74	74	74	74
R^2	.125	.089	.084	.500
Adjusted R^2	.048	.008	.004	.456
F	1.622	1.103	1.045	11.338

**** Significant at a 0.01-level (2-sided)
*** Significant at a 0.05-level (2-sided)
** Significant at a 0.10-level (2-sided)
* Significant at a 0.15-level (2-sided)
Note: Pairwise exclusion of incomplete cases

Table 51: **Full model for all independent variables and characteristics of cooperation relationships as dependent variables**

In the full model, similarity of demographic characteristics does not show any significant effects on characteristics of cooperation relationships with important coworkers. Attitude similarity has a strong effect on quality of cooperation. Joint participation in integration measures also does not influence the cooperation between respondents and their important coworkers.

Being in the same division of the company positively affects the frequency and strength of cooperation relationships. However, it does not affect importance as well as quality of cooperation relationships.

In the following paragraphs, the hypotheses for each group of variables are separately discussed. In addition to the full model presented in Table 51, I also consider the partial models for each group of variables.

4.8.1. Demographic similarity

Two different aspects of demographic similarity have been investigated: Age similarity as well as gender similarity. In the following table, the postulated hypotheses concerning age and gender similarity and their effects on cooperation are listed:

| Hypothesis 12b | Employees of similar age build more intense cooperation relationships than employees of dissimilar age after mergers and acquisitions |
| Hypothesis 13b: | Employees of the same sex build more intense cooperation relationships after mergers and acquisitions |

Table 52: Hypotheses concerning demographic similarity of cooperation partners

In the following table, the effects of demographic similarity on the different characteristics of cooperation relationships are presented:

		Independent variable: Demographic similarity			
		Frequency	Importance	Strength	Quality
Standardized Beta					
Demographic characteristics					
	Age similarity	-.008	.032	-.034	.135
	Gender similarity	-.019	-.035	-.027	.096
Model statistics					
Total df		74	74	74	74
R^2		.000	.002	.002	.026
Adjusted R^2		-.027	-.025	-.026	-.001
F		.015	.086	.064	.976

**** Significant at a 0.01-level (2-sided)
*** Significant at a 0.05-level (2-sided)
** Significant at a 0.10-level (2-sided)
* Significant at a 0.15-level (2-sided)
Note: Pairwise exclusion of incomplete cases

Table 53: Partial model of effects of demographic similarity on cooperation

The partial model shows no significant effects of age or gender similarity on aspects of intensity of cooperation. These results are supported by the full model in Table 51. Hence hypotheses 12b and 13b are not supported by the results. Similarity of demographic characteristics shows not independent effect on any aspect of cooperation intensity.

4.8.2. Attitude similarity

Two different types of attitude similarity have been investigated: Similarity of work attitudes as well as similarity of general attitudes. In the following table, the postulated hypothesis is listed:

Hypothesis 18b:	Employees with similar work attitudes have cooperation relationships of higher intensity than employees with dissimilar work attitudes.

Table 54: Hypotheses concerning attitude similarity of cooperation partners

In the research on SpecMatCo, respondents were not only asked to indicate similarity of work attitudes but also similarity of general attitudes. In the following table, the effects of attitude similarity on the different characteristics of cooperation relationships are presented:

	Independent variable: Attitude similarity			
	Frequency	Importance	Strength	Quality
Standardized Beta				
Attitudes				
Work attitudes similarity	-.107	.181*	-.033	.574****
General attitudes similarity	.111	.136	.158	.237****
Model statistics				
Total df	75	75	75	75
R^2	.015	.069	.022	.484
Adjusted R^2	-.012	.044	-.005	.470
F	.567	2.713	.831	34.276

**** Significant at a 0.01-level (2-sided)
*** Significant at a 0.05-level (2-sided)
** Significant at a 0.10-level (2-sided)
* Significant at a 0.15-level (2-sided)
Note: Pairwise exclusion of incomplete cases

Table 55: Partial model of effects of attitude similarity on cooperation

The partial model indicates that similarity of work and general attitudes has no effect on frequency, importance and thus strength of cooperation. However, both similarity of work attitudes as well as similarity of general attitudes have significant effects on the quality of cooperation relationships. The higher the attitude similarity of cooperation partners is, the higher the quality of that cooperation relationship is. The findings are fully supported by the full model in Table 51. Hence hypothesis 18b is partly supported.

It is important to note that similarity of attitudes has been measured subjectively. That means that respondents were asked whether they perceive their coworkers to have similar attitudes or not. While subjectivity of data in ego-centered networks has already been recognized as a problem, it is important to note that the problem is especially virulent when attitudes of others are indicated.

4.8.3. Participation in integration measures

Respondents were asked during what integration measures they got into contact with their important new coworkers. As described in 4.7.2.3, four different options have been offered to respondents to describe how they got to know an important coworker. In the following table, the postulated hypotheses about the effects of integration measures on cooperation are listed:

Hypothesis 21b:	There is no effect of participation in integration measures on intensity of cooperation relationships

Table 56: Hypotheses concerning the effects of integration measures on cooperation relationships

Table 57 shows the effects of joint participation in integration measures on cooperation.

	Independent variable: Participation in integration measures			
	Frequency	Importance	Strength	Quality
Standardized Beta				
Participation in integration measures	-.170*	.113	-.107	.094
Model statistics				
Total df	75	75	75	75
R^2	.029	.013	.011	.009
Adjusted R^2	.016	.000	-.002	-.005
F	2.202	.963	.851	.658

**** Significant at a 0.01-level (2-sided)
*** Significant at a 0.05-level (2-sided)
** Significant at a 0.10-level (2-sided)
* Significant at a 0.15-level (2-sided)
Note: Pairwise exclusion of incomplete cases

Table 57: Partial model for joint participation in integration measures

Frequency of a cooperation relationship according to this finding is negatively correlated with the participation in integration measures. This indicates that integration measures have an effect, opposite to the postulated effect in hypothesis 21b.

A first possible explanation for this finding might be the type of integration measure that the respondents participated in: As shown in Graph 5 on page 205, the most frequent integration measure at SpecMatCo has been the joint kick-off in the department, followed by management meetings and work in integration teams. Looking at the effects of the different integration measures on intensity of cooperation sheds some light on the findings in Table 57. In the following table, the effects of different types of getting to know new colleagues in integration measures are presented:

	Independent variable: Participation in integration measures - Details			
	Frequency	Importance	Strength	Quality
Standardized Beta				
Participation in integration measures				
Integration training	-.127	-.038	-.125	-.090
Joint kick-off	-.214**	-.117	-.179*	-.056
Management meeting	.087	.196*	.099	.170
Other integration measures	-.074	.279***	.032	.229**
Model statistics				
Total df	75	75	75	75
R²	.063	.087	.043	.067
Adjusted R²	.011	.036	-.011	.015
F	1.202	1.696	.801	1.284

**** Significant at a 0.01-level (2-sided)
*** Significant at a 0.05-level (2-sided)
** Significant at a 0.10-level (2-sided)
* Significant at a 0.15-level (2-sided)
Note: Pairwise exclusion of incomplete cases

Table 58: Partial model of effects of types of getting to know each other on cooperation

Seemingly, a joint kick-off is not a very effective integration measure. Getting to know new colleagues in a joint kick-off even reduces frequency and the strength of cooperation. A possible explanation for this finding is the lack of participation in joint kick-offs. The exploratory interviews at SpecMatCo revealed that joint kick-offs usually contained the proclamation of a number of decisions on the future structure of a department. Hence participation of employees was very limited.

Management meetings at the same time are an effective integration measure to increase the perceived importance of coworkers. However, an alternative explanation for the relationship of management meetings and the perceived importance of coworkers might be caused by the fact that in management meetings only higher ranked coworkers participate. However, higher ranked individuals usually are perceived to be more important than lower ranked individuals.

Hence the positive effect of management meetings on importance of coworkers could be the result of the structurally given composition of the audience of management meetings.

In the interviews, respondents mentioned that some departments initiated extra integration measures, which were more informal than the listed measures. Further research also needs to investigate more closely, what "other integration measures" might be and what their effects on cooperation of employees are.

Hence hypothesis 21b is partly supported. Except for the effect of participation in integration measures on frequency, all effects are insignificant.

4.8.4. Structural cooperation requirements

As can be seen in Table 51, being in the same division has a significant positive effect on frequency and strength of cooperation within cooperation relationships with important coworkers. Importance and quality of cooperation relationships are not affected. Thus hypothesis 22b is partly supported.

4.8.5. Summary of results

In the following table, the results presented above are summarized. For each hypothesis, the number of the hypothesis, the independent and the dependent variable are indicated. Also, the direction of the expected effect is indicated.

In Table 59, the results for the regression analyses to determine the effects of the independent variables on the intensity of new relationships are indicated. Intensity of a relationship comprises frequency, importance, strength as well as quality of cooperation of a relationship. For the results of the partial model, two different results have been found:

- Not supported: None of the regression analyses for frequency, importance, strength as well as quality of cooperation support the hypothesis.
- Partly supported: Some of the regression analyses for frequency, importance, strength as well as quality of cooperation support the hypothesis.

For the results of the full model and the summary of both models, the same results have been found.

Hypo-thesis	Independent variable	Dependent variable	Expected effect	Partial model	Full model	Total
12b	Similar age	Intensity of relationship	+	Not supp.	Not supp.	Not supp.
13b	Similar gender	Intensity of relationship	+	Not supp.	Not supp.	Not supp.
18b	Similar work attitudes	Intensity of relationship	+	Partly supp.	Mixed	Mixed
21b	Integration measures	Intensity of relationship	0	Partly supp.	Strongly supp.	Strongly supp.
22b	Structural requirements	Intensity of relationship	+		Partly supp.	Partly supp.

Legend: Supported / Not supp. / Opposite

Table 59: Summary of factors influencing intensity of new cooperation relationships at SpecMatCo

As can be seen, there are hardly any effects of the independent variables on intensity of cooperation.

Neither age similarity nor gender similarity influence the intensity of a relationship. Despite strong support of homophily in previous studies, the formation of new cooperation relationships after mergers and acquisitions seems to follow other mechanisms than relationships that have been investigated in previous studies on homophily.

Similarity of work attitudes as well as similarity of general attitudes have a strong effect on quality of new cooperation relationships. However, they do not affect frequency, importance and strength of a new cooperation relationship. Unfortunately, it is difficult to evaluate that finding: Attitudes are psychological constructs, which cannot be directly observed. A respondent only can deduce from observed behaviors of an important coworker what attitudes this coworker might have. Such observation is highly subjective. Especially, there is a severe risk that high cooperation quality is perceived to be the consequence of similar attitudes. Hence the finding should be carefully interpreted.

A third interesting finding is the fact that participation in integration measures does not seem to affect the intensity of a cooperation relationship between two employees. A more detailed look at the single integration measures shows that joint kick-offs even have a negative effect on frequency of cooperation. At the same time, management meetings and other integration measures show a strong effect on intensity of cooperation relationships, especially on importance and quality of cooperation relationships. Such mixed findings require further examination. Further research is required to understand in detail the effects of different integration measures on cooperation between employees of merged firms.

4.9. Methodological limitation of results

As has been mentioned several times, the ego-centered network analysis used at SpecMatCo suffers from a number of methodological limitations, which first explain some of the findings and second, which limit the validity and the reliability of the findings.

The main finding of the study is the strong effect of similarity of work attitudes and general attitudes on quality of cooperation. Other similarities hardly show effects on intensity of cooperation. However, this finding suffers from a number of limitations, which need to be considered for further interpretation of the results:

- Asking respondents to indicate their ten most important coworkers neglects all relationships that are less important. Especially after mergers and acquisitions, relationships have to slowly grow. A comparison of frequency, importance, strength as well as quality of old and new relationships with important coworkers in Graph 6 shows that old relationships on the average are more intense:

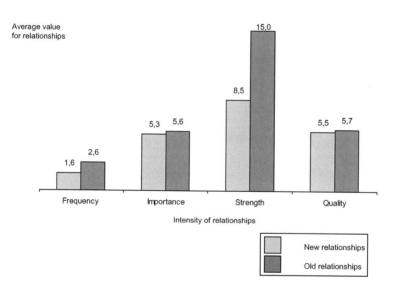

Graph 6: Average values for intensity of old and new relationships

Assuming that an employee does not only have ten cooperation partners, it is likely that the ego-centered network analysis systematically neglects new relationships and thus distorts the results.

A second limitation of an ego-centered network analysis is the limited variance of intensity of the relationships. The question for the ten most important coworkers necessarily yields only intensive relationships. Other relationships are not considered.

This, however limits the variance of the dependent variables, leading to insignificant results.
- The operationalization of similarity of attitudes has been done with a single item. Results on variables that were operationalized with a single item suffer from validity as well as from reliability problems.
- The concept similarity of work attitudes and quality of cooperation are conceptually close. That means that high correlation between the variables might be caused by a covariance problem, as both variables at least to some extent measure a similar phenomena.

Future research has to consider these limitations and operationalize attitudinal similarity based on multiple items and based on information of both cooperation partners. Also, all existing cooperation relationships need to be gathered in order to have enough variance of the dependent variables and in order to avoid systematic distortion of the sample.

5. Empirical study at the second research site: SoftCo

5.1. Time schedule of research

The research at SoftCo lasted for approximately five months. During that time, the research and all materials were prepared, the electronic questionnaire was developed, interviews were scheduled and conducted, the data was analyzed and extensively presented in several meetings to different audiences in the firm.

After the initial contact had been made, the approach had to be adapted to the requirements of the firm. In a first step, all available internal information on the M&A-transaction was reviewed. In close contact with the top management team, the status quo of the integration and the organizational structure were identified and documented.

Based on the available data, and based on the first discussions with the top management team, the research sample was focused and a first research design was developed:

- The research sample should comprise all employees of the merged division of the firm except for some support functions as described above.
- The research design should be based on a cross-sectional study.
- With the help of a dyadic network analysis, data on all employees and their cooperation relationships in the merged division should be gathered.
- In addition to a dyadic network analysis with the help of an electronic questionnaire, a series of interviews should be conducted to capture additional background and qualitative information about the M&A-transaction.

The discussion with the workers' council was crucial in the process of preparing the research: In German firms, the workers' council represents and protects the operative employees of the firm. Hence all empirical investigations concerning this level needs to be approved. As dyadic network analyses require personalized data, anonymity of employees needs to be guaranteed. It was agreed upon with the workers' council that the researcher acted as a trust center. The information provided by the employees would be sent directly to the researcher. No personalized data would ever be revealed to anyone by the researcher. Also, the researcher guaranteed that there would be no analyses of groups smaller than three individuals in order to protect single employees from potentially negative consequences of the results. In addition to these agreements concerning later data handling and data analyses, quality as one characteristic of cooperation relationships should only be gathered on the department and on the management level. The workers' council thus wanted to avoid a 360°-evaluation of operative employees with the help of the survey.

While the adjustment of the approach was still going on, first beta-versions of the electronic questionnaires were programmed. As the tool to gather the data was as important to the workers' council and to the top management team as the content of the questionnaire and the later data treatment, the questionnaire and its structure and design were integral part of the adjustment of the research design to the needs and wishes of the research site.

All elements concerning data gathering, data handling as well as data analysis and later confidentiality were fixed in a contract.

The final version of the electronic questionnaire was tested before using it. Three employees filled out a first version of the questionnaire, noting technical difficulties as well as problems of understanding and time constraints. As a result, the questionnaire was adapted to its final version.

After seven weeks of preparation and adjustment, the final decision on the research has been taken in the third week of March.

Directly after the positive discussion with the workers' council, the scheduling of the first interviews had started, first with the management team and later with operative employees of all departments.

Shortly after the first interviews with the highest management level, the participation of SoftCo in the study was communicated to all employees. At the same time, all participants received the questionnaire as a file with detailed instructions to fill it out and a general communication about the research.

The interviews and the gathering of data with the electronic questionnaire were conducted in parallel. After four weeks of interviews and three weeks of parallel data collection with the questionnaire, the data gathering was finished and the data analysis started.

As an integral part of the conditions for the research, a number of communication measures were fixed in order to feed back the results of the study to the employees. First, a meeting with the workers' council was held to discuss the results. Second, the main results were communicated to all employees in the concerned division. Third, an article on the research and its results was published in the company newspaper. In this way, employees outside the researched division also were informed about the research.

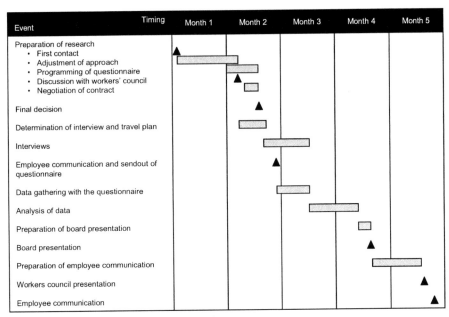

Illustration 27: Time schedule of research at SoftCo

5.2. Sample details

SoftCo has three divisions. Two of them were not affected by the merger. These divisions have not been considered in the course of this study.

Two samples have been formed for investigating the third division: one sample for the interviews and a second sample for the interrogation with an electronic questionnaire.

The sample of interviewees contained 39 employees as in the first research site. However, this time, all first line managers, and most second line managers have been interviewed in 20 interviews. The remaining interviews were conducted with employees from the operative level.

The second sample for the written interrogation comprised the full population of the merged divisions except for two functions: the CF&A functions (controlling, finance and accounting), as well as the human resources department. In the first research site, it has been found that these support functions hardly play a role in operative processes. Therefore, cooperation frequency with these functions is very low. At the same time, employees of these functions have to cooperate with literally every function and almost every employee from time to time. Therefore, the gathering of information on these functions is (a) not relevant for the operative cooperation and (b) hardly feasible, because employees in these departments have numerous very weak cooperation relationships.

The top management levels, i.e. the board members as well as the heads of the main functions were excluded from filling out the questionnaire as well, as they were interrogated in the course of the interviews. The top management levels comprise 11 employees.

Also, employees that were in maternity protection or who suffered from long-term sicknesses were not considered. That left 366 employees in the research sample.

Of these 366 employees, 282 employees filled out the questionnaire, corresponding to a response rate of 77%. In the course of the discussion with the workers' council, it was agreed upon communicating to the employees that they could skip questions if they felt not comfortable answering. Also, some of the questions did not apply for employees that entered the firm after the M&A-transaction took place. As a result, some of the questionnaires are not completely filled out. Therefore, the number of answers to a specific question might vary. In the statistical analyses, the number of valid answers is therefore indicated if necessary. In order to account for this offer to the participants of the research the regression analyses in this research have been conducted with pairwise deletion of incomplete cases.

5.3. Gathering of relational data in the present research

Relational data in the research at SoftCo was gathered with the help of an electronic dyadic network analysis. As has been described above, a full dyadic network analysis requires interrogating the full population. Each respondent indicates relationships to each other respondent within the research sample. There are two ways for gathering the information on relationships: First, a respondent freely recalls all relationship partners. Second, a respondent selects all relationship partners from a list with all members of the researched population. The first approach has the advantage of being relatively lean and simple. However, at the same time, respondents might have problems recalling relationship partners. The second approach reduces the risk of not recalling a relationship partner. At the same time, a complete list with all names of a given population can easily be very long. In the case of the present study with a full population of 366 employees, the list can be easily 10 to 15 pages long. On the average, each respondent indicated relationships with 25 employees. Working through a list with 366 employees to pick 20 to 30 cooperation partners is highly inconvenient and requires too much time for a research in a time-sensitive business setting.

The electronic questionnaire offers new possibilities to combine both, the advantages of the recall method and of the list selection method: In a top-down approach, respondents select in a first step the highest organizational units they cooperate with. Then, within the selected organizational units, respondents select the lower units, they cooperate with. From these lower units they select from a list of team members their actual cooperation partners.

In the electronic questionnaire, used for the research at SoftCo, respondents first indicated the main departments they cooperate with on a regular basis, i.e. more than once per month (see Illustration 28). A graphical interface offered them a selection of the organizational units of the highest organizational level as boxes similar to an organizational chart. When picking one of the organizational units, the boxes changed color to indicate the selection.

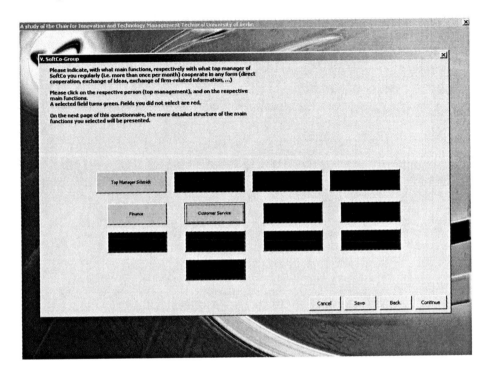

Illustration 28: First step: Selection of highest level organizational unit

After having chosen the highest level organizational units, a new page of the electronic questionnaire was automatically generated and shown (see Illustration 29). This new page only contained the selected highest organizational units and their subunits down to the team level again as a graphical interface. Respondents again could pick the functions and teams they cooperate with by clicking on the respective boxes.

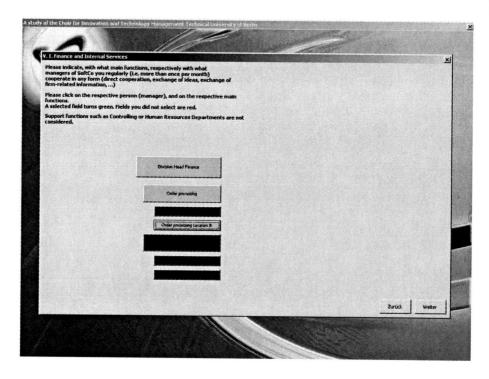

Illustration 29: Second step: Selection of functions and teams

In a next step, all members of the teams and functions that were selected were presented in a list (see Illustration 30). On the average, this list contained less than 50 to 60 names, leaving the respondents with a long list of employees to choose their cooperation partners from. Respondents had to choose only those employees with whom they cooperate with on a regular basis. This allowed to further reduce the number of relationship partners to a short list.

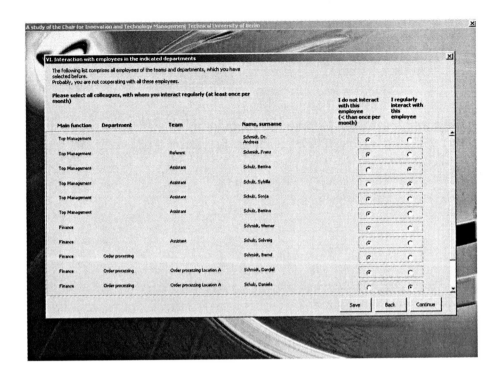

Illustration 30: Third step: Selection of cooperation partners

For the relationships with partners of this short list then, respondents were asked to indicate several details about the relationships (see Illustration 31). This short list, however, was significantly shorter than the full list of names. At the same time, it does not bear the risk of missing important cooperation partners.

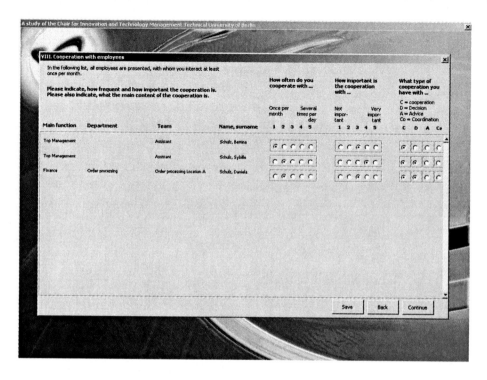

Illustration 31: Fourth step: Detailed information on relationships with cooperation partners

As has been described, quality of relationships could only be gathered for relationships on the management level and on the departmental level. Quality with single operative employees could not be gathered. Therefore, another list was generated with all managers and department and team names, which were selected in step one and two (see Illustration 32).

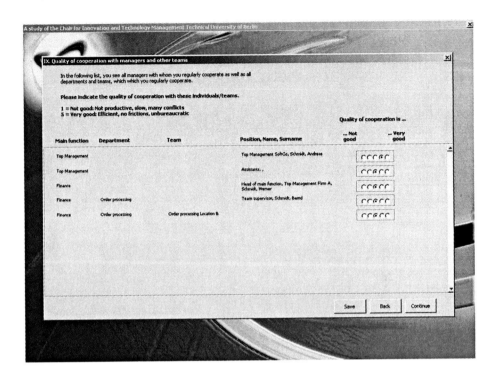

Illustration 32: Fifth step: Evaluation of quality with cooperation partners.

Other information was gathered as well with the questionnaire. For example, data on demographic characteristics of the employee, attitudes or judgements were gathered with the electronic questionnaire as well (see Illustration 33).

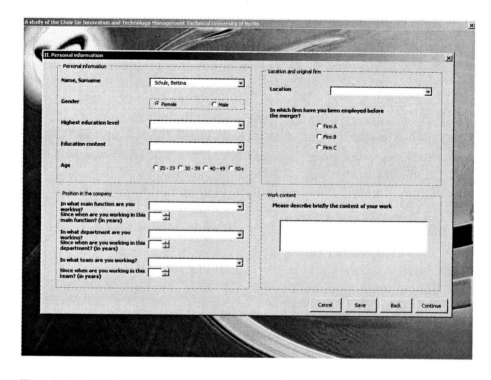

Illustration 33: Example of other information as gathered with the help of the electronic questionnaire

The electronic questionnaire was based on Microsoft's Excel. It was programmed in Visual Basic. Upfront, it was secured that all employees were able to fill out the questionnaire. The electronic questionnaire was tested on different versions of Excel on different computers of SoftCo. Seven programmers within the research population worked on Linux-computers. It was secured that they had access to Microsoft-computers with Excel installed in order to be able to fill out the questionnaire.

Besides advantages for treating large samples, the computer-based network analysis had advantages for collecting the data and for later data treatment. First, the filled out questionnaire was sent automatically as an email to the researcher. There were no delays and no postal charges. Second, the data was gathered with the help of closed questions and automatically stored in a file. That means that respondents had no possibility to choose invalid answers.

In the following paragraphs, the details of the collection of relational data with the help of the electronic questionnaire will be elaborated The different items that were used for the data collection are presented. First, the existence of ties was determined. Then characteristics of existing relationships were gathered.

5.3.1. Existence of cooperation relationships between employees

In a first step, information on the existence of cooperation relationships between any two employees of the relevant population was gathered.
All individuals in the researched population of the three merged firms were asked to indicate the colleagues they cooperate with. The following question and answer scale was used:
"Please select all colleagues you regularly deal with (at least once per month).
- *I do not deal with this colleague (less than once per month)*
- *I regularly deal with this colleague".*

5.3.2. Frequency of cooperation of individuals

An important characteristic of an existing relationship is its intensity. There are different ways of measuring the intensity of a relationship. A frequently used approach is to interrogate about the frequency of interactions between two individuals (e.g. Tsai & Goshal 1998; Ibarra 1995; Rice & Mitchell 1972). Frequency of cooperation in the current research is operationalized based on the following question and answers:
"Please indicate for each colleague and supervisor, how often you cooperate with them.
- *1 = Once per month*
- *2 = Once per week*
- *3 = Several times per week*
- *4 = Once per day*
- *5 = Several times per day."*

5.3.3. Importance of cooperation

Another important dimension of cooperation that has been investigated in numerous studies is the importance of a relationship (e.g. Ibarra 1992, 1995). There are relationships that have a high frequency. However, the content of these relationships might be irrelevant. For example, in a business setting, I might frequently call the secretary of my supervisor to get in touch with the supervisor. Probably, I talk to the secretary more often than to the supervisor. However, the relationship with the supervisor is much more important than the relationship with the secretary. In order to address this dimension of cooperation, importance of a relationship is also considered in the present research. Respondents were given the following text and answer scales:

> "Cooperation with colleagues can be of different importance. Please indicate the importance of cooperation with the colleagues and supervisors you selected.
> The following answers are possible:
> 1 = Cooperation with ... is not important. I can accomplish my tasks without cooperation with ...
> 5 = Cooperation with ... is very important. Problems or delays in the cooperation with ... directly affects the results of my work."

5.3.4. Strength of cooperation

Looking at ideal types of cooperation relationships, it is possible to qualitatively differ between relationships to same-level coworkers and relationships to supervisors, as well as between cooperation that deals with standard task and cooperation that deals with exceptional tasks. Interviews with the employees in the merged firm revealed that there might be considerably little cooperation with supervisors. However, when there is cooperation, it is highly important. Similarly, interviews revealed that there are relationships that are exclusively used to handle exceptions. For example, when there is a technical problem that cannot be resolved by the service units, it might be necessary to ask directly in the engineering department for help. Such exceptional cases are rare, but at the same time, they are extremely important.

While it is possible to consider effects of hierarchy by controlling for rank, it is not possible to differ between relationships for exceptional and standard tasks based on the gathered data.

Therefore, I created an aggregate measure based on frequency of cooperation and importance of cooperation. In order to capture both, frequent as well as important relationships with one measure, I simply multiply the scores for frequency and importance as indicated by the respondents. This computed measure, I call strength of a relationship.

Of course, both frequency as well as importance of a relationship are highly correlated to the strength of a relationship. Nevertheless, it allows the comparison of relationships that are either very frequent or very important in the same analysis. As both scales equally consist of five points, the effects of frequency and importance on strength have similar weights.

5.3.5. Relationship with same firm or other firm

The central question in this research is how employees after mergers and acquisitions cooperate with their new colleagues. Hence another important dimension of a relationship is whether it is a relationship with a colleague from their "old firm", i.e. within the previously separated firms, or whether it is a relationship with the "new firm(s)", i.e. between the previously separated firms.

In this research, all respondents indicated the firm they worked for before the M&A-transaction. In case they entered the firm after the M&A-transaction took place, they indicated the name of the firm they are most strongly affiliated to. Such affiliation can be based on location, on product affiliation (e.g. specific responsibilities for one brand or one product in sales), or on legal affiliation based on the work contract. The determination of the affiliation of employees was facilitated by the fact that the three firms still represented individual legal entities. Most employees therefore had work contracts with one of these three legal entities, even if they entered the firms a long time after the M&A-transaction.

This information was validated with the help of personnel lists from human resources that were provided by the firm. Based on information about firm affiliation of all employees, and based on the indicated names of relationship partners, it is possible to determine whether a relationship is based on cooperation between colleagues within the same previously separated firm or whether it is based on cooperation between colleagues of formerly separated firms. Hence each indicated relationship can be classified in "old" and "new" relationships. In the following paragraphs, I will use "old" relationships for relationships of employees that can be assigned to one of the merged firm, even if they entered the firm after the M&A-transaction took place. "New" relationships then are such that link employees, which originally worked in different firms before the M&A-transaction took place.

5.4. Structure of the results section

With the help of the data gathered at SoftCo, two research questions will be treated in the results section. The results sections for both research questions follow the same structure. The results of the empirical investigation will be elaborated in four different steps: First, the results will be presented in detail. Second, the results will be summarized briefly. Third, the methodological limitations will be laid out. Last but not least, the results will be discussed based on the findings and the methodological limitations.

In the following paragraphs, I will briefly elaborate on the different steps.

5.4.1. Detailed presentation of results

For each research question, three different types of statistical models will be analyzed. First, for each set of independent variables, the partial models for each dependent variable will be analyzed. For example, the partial model for demographic characteristics comprises the independent variables "Age", "Gender" as well as "Education level". The dependent variables comprise all 16 dependent variables as defined in Table 60. Second, for each dependent variable used to operationalize cooperation, the full model will be analyzed, comprising all independent variables except for the control variable. The control variable differs corresponding to the dependent variable as described in 5.5.3. In a third step, for each dependent variable, the full model with control variable will be analyzed.

Depending on the significance of the effects of the independent variables in the different types of analyses, the results can be interpreted. Based on the effects found three groups of independent variables can be formed:

- A first group consists of all independent variables, which consistently show significant effects in all three types of analyses.
- A second group consists of all independent variables, which consistently show insignificant effects in all types of analyses.
- A third group consists of all independent variables, which show significant effects in one type of model and insignificant effects in another type of model.

While the results of the first two groups of variables can be directly interpreted, the third group requires additional consideration:

If an independent variable shows significant effects in the partial model and insignificant effects in the full model without control variable or vice versa, it covaries with other independent variables. If the independent variable A shows significant effects in the partial model and insignificant effects in the full model, it covaries with another independent variable B, which has a strong independent effect on the dependent variable in the full model and has not been considered in the partial model together with variable A. When considering variables A and B jointly, the significant effect of A vanishes. Similarly, if an independent variable A shows no significant effect in the partial model and a significant effect in the full model, it covaries with another independent variable B, which has no independent effect on the dependent variable. In the presentation of results, the potential covariation will be identified for later discussion.

The significance differences between full model without control variable and full model with control variable require more detailed interpretation due to the nature of the control variable. Basically, there are two different effects of structural cooperation requirements, which can change the significance of an independent variable from the second to the third type of analysis. First, the cooperation requirements of departments can differ. As presented in Graph 15, the department average of cooperation varies strongly between different departments. For example, "Trainers" cooperate much less than employees in the "Sales support"-department. As a consequence, an employee with an individual disposition for high levels of cooperation might work as a "Trainer" and thus cooperate much less than another employee with an individual disposition for low levels of cooperation, who works in the "Sales support"-department. Second, the averages characteristics of employees within different departments can differ. For example, in some departments, there are mostly men, while in other departments, there are mostly women working. Different cooperation requirements between departments with mostly male employees and departments with mostly female employees can affect the results and change the significance of independent variables if the control variable is considered. Based on these considerations, it is possible to differ between four different cases, depending on similarity of averages of dependent and independent variables in different departments. In the following graph, the different cases are listed:

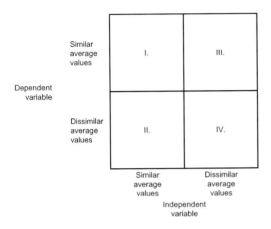

Illustration 34: Effects of control variables based on departmental averages

For each of these cases, it is possible to identify the possible differences of the significance of an independent variable between the second and the third model. While the cases I. to III. show differences of one of the two average values, case IV. is most complex, as differences of both averages are possible.

In Illustration 35, the first three cases are presented based on exemplary data. In each of the graphs, the x-axis shows the values of the independent variable and the y-axis shows the values of the dependent variable. Two different departments are considered with 20 employees each. The small circles represent pairs of characteristics of employees in the respective departments. The large circles represent the average values for each department. The first row of graphs indicates the effects on the level of significance (e.g. 0 ➔ +), if there actually is an effect of the independent variable on the dependent variable. It makes no difference, whether the effect is positive as in the exemplary illustration or negative. In case of negative effects, the direction of the effect becomes inversed. The second row of graphs indicates the effects on the level of significance if there is no effect of the independent variable on the dependent variable.

For example, in case II, the cooperation requirements between the two departments differ significantly. Employees of department 1 generally have a higher level of cooperation than employees of department 2. However, the average values of the independent variable do not differ between the departments. E.g. if the independent variable is gender, the share of male and female employees in these departments is similar. In case II., if there is a positive effect of the independent variable on the dependent variable, it would show regardless of the consideration of the control variable. Similarly, if there was a null effect of the independent variable on the dependent variable, the independent variable would show a null effect, regardless, whether departmental cooperation requirements were considered or not.

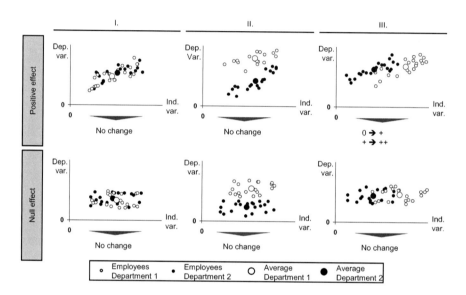

Illustration 35: Different cases for the effects of the control variable

As can be seen, the consideration of the control variable only changes the results in the third case. In case III, if there is a positive effect of the independent variable on the dependent variable, the significance of the effect increases. That means that non-significant effects of the full model without control variable can become significant effects if the control variable is considered. Also, significant effects can become even more significant if the control variable is considered. It is important to note that not only the departmental averages of the independent variable differ but also the structural cooperation requirements. Illustration 40 shows a more detailed analysis of case III. As can be seen, differences in departmental averages of the independent variable should result in differences of the departmental averages of the dependent variable if there are no differences in the structural cooperation requirements. However, if there are differences in the departmental averages of the independent variables and no differences in the departmental averages of the dependent variables as indicated in case III, there is an effect caused by structural cooperation requirements. Hence the significance changes of the effects of the independent variable in case III also result from differences in structural cooperation requirements between departments.

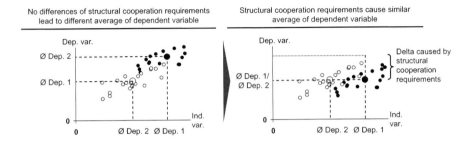

Illustration 36: Effect of structural cooperation requirements on dependent variable

In case IV, the departmental averages of both, independent and dependent variables differ. Four different constellations of the departmental averages are possible. In Illustration 37, the four different constellations and their effects on the significance of the effect of the independent variable on the dependent variable are presented.

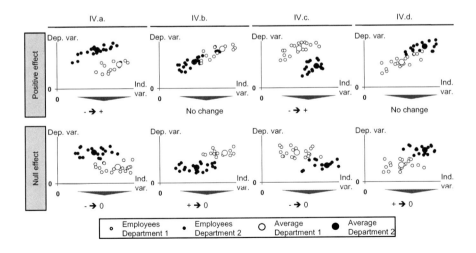

Illustration 37: Different effect of structural cooperation requirements on dependent variable

As can be seen, if there is a positive effect in case IV.b. and case IV.d., nothing changes. As discussed in Illustration 36, differences in departmental averages of independent variables lead to differences of departmental averages of the dependent variable.

The other cases require further attention. As can be seen, if there is a positive effect of the independent variable on the dependent variable, in case IV.a. and IV.c. the effects found in the full model without control variable can change direction and yet be significant in the full model with control variable.

Also, if there is no effect between independent and dependent variable, the full model without control variables might indicate a significant effect due to departmental effects. Only the full model with control variable can reveal the null effect.

Differences of significance of effects between the full model without control variable and the full model with control variable need to be interpreted carefully. Based on the analytic schema presented in Illustration 35 and Illustration 37, changes in significance of effects can be explained. It is important to note that the illustrations are ideal types. They serve as a first analytic schema. However, additional analyses are necessary to identify the departmental effects, isolate it and thus reveal the actual effect of independent variable on dependent variable. The differences of departmental averages of the independent variables need to be determined.

Based on these considerations, the three step analysis of the results allows a clear identification of the actual effects of independent variables on the dependent variables. The differentiation between partial model, full model without control variable and full model with control variable allows a clear interpretation of the findings. It is important to note that the analytic schema applies, regardless whether the results support a hypothesis or not. If the results show an effect, which is opposite to the postulated effect, it still can be discussed with the help of the scheme. Therefore, the case of an opposite effect is not considered in the above considerations.

In Illustration 38, the three different steps of analysis are summarized. Also, the interpretation requirements are presented.

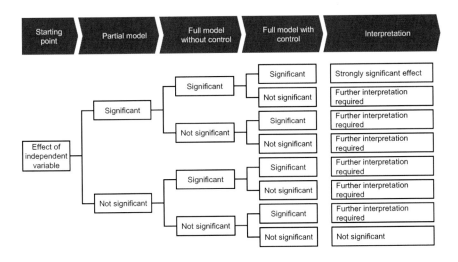

Illustration 38: Three step analysis to determine effects of independent variables

As the number of dependent variables is very high, there can be numerous changes of significance of effects between different models. A pragmatic focus thus is required in order to limit the scope of the analysis. Therefore, changes of significance of effects of independent variables will only be analyzed in detail, if effects on several dependent variables change.

In the results sections, first the results for the full models without control variable and the full models with control variable will be presented. Then, for each set of independent variables, the partial models will be presented. By first presenting the full models, they only need to be presented once and not several times in the course of presenting the results for the different sets of independent variables. The analysis then follows the three step schema as elaborated above.

5.4.2. Summary of results

In a next step, the detailed results will be summarized. For each independent variable, the effects shown in the partial, the full model without control variables as well as the effects shown in the full model with control variables will be summarized and evaluated. With the help of the summary, the later discussion of the results will be prepared.

5.4.3. Methodological limitations of the research

Limitations of the research approach need to be presented in order to understand their potential effects on the results and to identify methodological artefacts. In the section on methodological limitations, the characteristics of the sample and its potential effects on the findings will be discussed. Also, the limitations of the data gathering approach are presented. As has been discussed in 5.5.3, the control variable in this research requires further interpretation due to a potential covariance problem. Last but not least, the operationalization of the variables bears potential effects on the research findings, which need to be considered.

5.4.4. Discussion of results

Based on the presented results and the methodological limitations, the findings at SoftCo can be discussed and fed back to the hypotheses. If hypotheses are supported, the finding can be seen as a confirmation of previous findings and theoretical predictions. If the findings deviate from the postulated effects, the deviation needs to be discussed. The discussion first considers methodological limitations, which might be responsible for the findings. Second, it considers departmental variables, which might cause the effects found. The identified reasons for differing significance of effects between the full model without control variable and the full model with control variable will provide the necessary insights for this discussion. Third, a qualitative consideration of firm level variables will be presented. The use of firm level variables is difficult insofar, as the qualitative analysis of firm level variables stands in sharp contrast to the quantitative analysis of individual level and dyadic level variables. The validity and reliability of the qualitative findings is much more limited than the ones of the quantitative findings. The discussion thus might get a case study character, which is not intended. Fourth, if all explanations are insufficient, potential explanations from other bodies of research and other theoretical streams will be considered.

5.5. "Who cooperates?" Operationalization of hypotheses 1 to 11

In order to test the hypotheses 1 to 11, the dependent and the independent constructs need to be operationalized. Based on the gathered relational data, the dependent construct, i.e. the cooperation of respondents can be operationalized. Independent constructs have been operationalized with the help of a number of items.

In operationalizing the constructs, the experiences of the first research site have been considered. Therefore, some constructs are operationalized differently from the first research site, in order to include learnings from the first research site and thus improve the quality of the research. These differences later need to be considered in interpreting the results of both studies.

5.5.1. Dependent construct: Cooperative behaviors of an employee

Based on the information gathered above, it is possible to compute different measures for cooperation of an employee. Due to the exploratory nature of this research, several measures are considered.

A first type of measures considers the existence of ties to old and new colleagues. A second type of measure considers the intensity of cooperation relationships, which are frequency, importance, strength and quality of a relationship. For each type, absolute and relative measures will be computed.

There are different approaches to compute cooperation measures for an individual based on dyadic network data. In Illustration 39, the three main methods to measures relational data are presented. A first approach is to use the relational data as indicated by an employee. Relationships as indicated by an actor are called out-degree-relationships from the actor's perspective. This approach resembles an ego-centered network analysis with a sample that corresponds to the full population. All that has been said about biases of network data gathered with ego-centered network analysis applies for this approach as well.

A second approach is the use of relationships that were indicated by others. In order to determine the cooperation frequency of an actor i, all cooperation relationships with i that were indicated by other actors j, with $i \neq j$ and their frequency are used to compute the cooperation frequency. Relationships indicated by other actors are called in-degree-relationships from the actor's perspective. This approach eliminates the respondent bias.

Both, the first and the second approach use uni-lateral relationship data. That means that there is no validation whether a relationship of an actor i to an actor j is reciprocated by a relationship from actor j to actor i.

A third approach focuses on bilateral relationships. Bilateral relationships are all relationships that were indicated by both relationship partners.

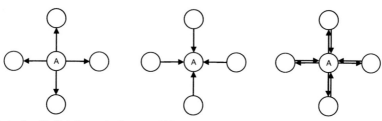

Illustration 39: Out-degree, in-degree and bilateral relationships

An advantage of using bilateral relationships is the validation of relationships by two independent actors. Bilaterally indicated relationships thus bear the highest validity. At the same time, not all unilateral relationships are considered. There is a significant risk that especially in large samples, a large share of the indicated relationships is not bilateral. Due to poor recall and due to the mere mass of potential cooperation relationships, respondents might indicate relationships that are not reciprocated. As can be seen in Graph 7, especially weaker relationships in the research sample at SoftCo tend to be unilateral. While 73% of cooperation relationships with the highest frequency are reciprocated, only 31% of the relationships with the lowest frequency are reciprocated. Using bilateral relationships thus would lead to a bias on strong relationships and not consider weak relationships.

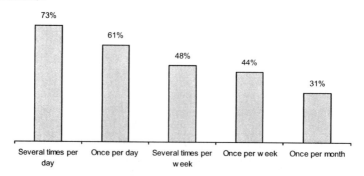

Graph 7: Share of reciprocated relationships depending on frequency

For the collection of dyadic data, information in individual characteristics from both relationship partners is required as well as relational data from at least one relationship partner.

Graph 8 shows this relationship and the linked problems. 7,029 ties were indicated by the 282 respondents. If all respondents in the research population had indicated relationships to all other respondents, the maximum number of ties would have been 133,590 unilateral ties. That means that only 5.2% of the possible relationships were indicated. Considering the response of 282 respondents out of the sample of 366 individuals, the maximum number of ties significantly decreases to 102,930 ties. However, as dyadic data requires information of both relationship partners, only relationships between the 282 respondents can be considered. Of the 282 respondents, only 266 indicated relational data. Hence the number of relationships, for which individual characteristics of both relationship partners is available decreases to 5,164 ties. That implies that roughly 27% of the indicated ties would not be considered.

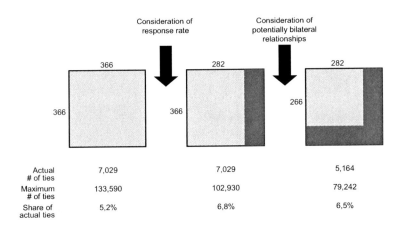

Graph 8: Effects of response rate on potentially bilateral relationships

In this research, unilateral indegree relationships are considered to compute measures of cooperation. That reduces potential respondent biases, while at the same time capturing weak relationships as well as relationships to actors that did not provide relational data.

Based on the characteristics of the indicated relationships, a number of different measures have been identified and computed for each actor. First, measures based on the existence of ties are computed. Then, measures based on the relationship characteristics frequency, importance and strength are computed. Last but not least, measures based on the quality of relationships are computed.

5.5.1.1. Existence of ties

A first measure for cooperation is the total number of relationships with old and with new colleagues. This number is helpful to see how many new relationships an employee i has formed with new colleagues j. At the same time, the number of old relationships indicates, to what extent an employee already before the merger has been well connected within the social network of the old firm. The number of old relationships will be labelled NumOldTies, the number of new relationships will be labelled NumNewTies. The maximum value of NumOldTies is limited by the number of employees of the old firm, whereas the maximum for NumNewTies is limited by the number of employees of the new firm.

Formula 1: Calculation of NumOldTies

$$NumOldTies_i = \sum_j r_{ij},$$ for all relationships r with actor i and actor j in the same firm with $r_{ij} = 1$ if j indicates a relationship to i and $r_{ij} = 0$ if j doesn't indicate a relationship to i

Formula 2: Calculation of NumNewTies

$$NumNewTies_i = \sum_j r_{ij},$$ for all relationships r with actor i and actor j in different firms with $r_{ij} = 1$ if j indicates a relationship to i and $r_{ij} = 0$ if j doesn't indicate a relationship to i

Based on the number of old and new ties of an employee i, it is possible to determine a ratio, which is based on the number of old ties divided by the sum of old and new ties. The ratio can take values between 0 and 1. A value of 1 indicates that an employee i has no relationships with new colleagues, whereas a low ratio indicates, that an employee i has most of her cooperation relationships with new colleagues. The ratio will be labelled ShareOldTies.

Formula 3: Calculation of ShareOldTies

$$ShareOldTies_i = \frac{NumOldTies_i}{NumNewTies_i + NumOldTies_i}$$

Hence a ration of 0.5 indicates that the relationship portfolio of an employee is well balanced between old and new cooperation relationships. Balanced relationship portfolio thus means that the share of old and new relationships is similar.

5.5.1.2. Characteristics of ties: Frequency, importance and strength

A second set of measures is based on more detailed information on frequency, importance, strength as well as quality of relationships as measured in the dyadic network analysis.
Three different types of measures are computed for each respondent:
- Sums of frequency (respectively importance or strength) for old and for new relationships. The measure for new relationships indicates the absolute amount of cooperation frequency with new colleagues. The higher this value, the more frequent the cooperation between a respondent and new colleagues is.

Formula 4: Sum of frequency of old relationships of an actor i

$$SumFreqOld_i = \sum_j f_{ij},$$ for the frequency of all relationships indicated by actors j with actor i, with actors j and actor i being in the same firm

Formula 5: Sum of frequency of new relationships of an actor i

$$SumFreqNew_i = \sum_j f_{ij},$$ for the frequency of all relationships of indicated by actors j with actor i, with actors j and actor i being in different firms

NumNewTies is highly correlated to SumFreqNew (as is NumOldTies to SumFreqOld).
- Ratio of the sum of frequency of old relationships (respectively importance or strength) and the sum of frequency of old and new relationships (respectively importance or strength). This ratio indicates regardless of the absolute strength, whether a respondent has a strong bias towards old colleagues, or whether a respondent equally cooperates with old and new colleagues. It is possible that some independent variables cause that employees have a low number of relationships. However, at the same time, they might have a high share of new relationships. Hence they are cooperative but with the help of the absolute values of number of relationships or sum of frequency of new relationships, their cooperativeness could not be captured. While a frequency ratio of 1 indicates that a respondent only names colleagues from the old firm as important coworkers, a ratio of 0.5 indicates that the cooperation frequency is equally distributed amongst colleagues from the old firm and new colleagues. A ratio of 0 indicates that a respondent names exclusively new colleagues as important coworkers.

Formula 6: Calculation of ShareOldFreq

$$ShareOldFreq_i = \frac{SumFreqOld_i}{SumFreqOld_i + SumFreqNew_i}$$

- Average frequency (respectively importance or strength or quality) of relationships with old and with new colleagues. The average value for old and for new relationships helps to determine, whether differences in sums or in the ratio of frequency of old and new relationships depend on the mere number of cooperation relationships with old and new colleagues, or whether there is a systematic tendency to cooperate on the average more with old or with new colleagues. For example, based on the cooperation structure, an employee might only have few contacts with new colleagues. That means that the sum of frequency with new colleagues is low. Also, the ratio of the sum of frequency of old relationships to the sum of frequency of all relationships is close to 1. However, maybe the employee cooperates very tightly with these few new colleagues, Then the average frequency of the new relationships might be very high.

In order to consider a potential systematic answer bias affecting the average values of respondents, I also compute the delta value between average values for old and for new relationships as a further variable.

Formula 7: Average frequency of old relationships of an actor *i*

$$AvFreqOld_i = \frac{SumFreqOld_i}{NumOldTies_i} \quad , \text{ for all actors } i$$

Formula 8: Average frequency of new relationships of an actor *i*

$$AvFreqNew_i = \frac{SumFreqNew_i}{NumNewTies_i} \quad , \text{ for all actors } i$$

AvFreqNew is highly correlated to SumFreqNew. The two variables NumFreqNew and AvFreqNew can be used to compute SumFreqNew. Hence two of the three variables are sufficient to compute the third variable.

In the table below, the different measures can be seen. While dark grey boxes indicate that a measure cannot be computed in a meaningful manner, the light grey boxes indicate that these measures will not be considered as dependent variables, because they are not in the focus of this research. Nevertheless, variables in the light grey boxes will also be computed in order to compute the composed measures.

	Existence of ties	Frequency	Importance	Strength	Quality
Old relationships	NumOldTies	SumFreqOld	SumImpOld	SumStrenOld	
New relationships	NumNewTies	SumFreqNew	SumImpNew	SumStrenNew	
Ratio old relationship to all relationships	ShareOldTies	ShareOldFreq	ShareOldImp	ShareOldStren	
Average characteristics of old relationships		AvFreqOld	AvImpOld	AvStrenOld	AvQualOld
Average characteristics of new relationships		AvFreqNew	AvImpNew	AvStrenNew	AvQualNew
Delta Average Old and New Ties		DelAvFreq	DelAvImp	DelAvStren	DelAvQual

Table 60: Measures for dependent variables

Hence different aspects of cooperation are operationalized based on the existence of relationships and based on the relationship characteristics frequency, importance, strength as well as quality with the help of different measures. That means that a total of 16 dependent variables will be considered in the following analyses. The different measures all capture specific aspects of cooperation. Later results need to be interpreted according to the differences in explanatory power of these dependent variables.

5.5.2. Independent constructs

There are several factors that influence cooperative behaviors of employees. As elaborated above, a first set of factors influencing cooperative behaviors of employees are demographic characteristics. Demographic characteristics include age, gender and education level of employees. A second set of factors influencing cooperative behaviors are characteristics of employees that are related tor the firm. These factors comprise rank as well as seniority of an employee. A third set of factors comprises psychological factors. A fourth factor, which affects cooperative behaviors of individuals are integration measures. In the following paragraphs, the operationalization of these independent constructs will be elaborated.

5.5.2.1. Demographic characteristics

Age. Instead of asking the age of respondents directly, I chose to develop a four point scale, on which employees could classify their age in ranges. The first range reaches from 20 to 29 years. The second range reaches from 30 to 39 years. The third range reaches from 40 to 49 years. The forth range covers all ages of 50 and more.

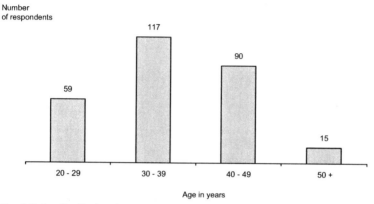

Graph 9: Age distribution of research sample

The reason to choose this approach was based on experiences made at the first research site. Respondents feel more confident indicating their age when choosing from a range instead of declaring their exact age.

Gender. In the questionnaire, respondents were asked to indicate their gender by crossing either male or female. According to 282 valid responses, 170 respondents (~ 60%) in the sample are male and 112 respondents (~40%) are female. Female respondents are coded as 1, male respondents are coded as 0.

Education. Respondents were asked to indicate their highest level of education. The possible answers ranged from "secondary school", "completed apprenticeship", "studies", "completed studies", "doctoral degree" as well as "others". The answer were coded automatically from 1 = "secondary School" to 5 = "doctoral degree". There was no number assigned to others. Out of 280 valid responses, only 15 respondents chose the option "others", corresponding to roughly 5% of the sample.

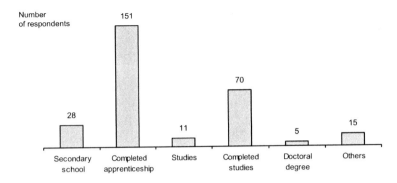

Graph 10: Highest level of education of respondents

5.5.2.2. Firm dependent characteristics of employees

Firm-related characteristics of employees comprise characteristics of employees that only exist in relation to the firm they are working in. For example, outside the firm, employees do not have the rank, they have inside the firm. Similarly, seniority is related to the firm.

Rank. All respondents had to indicate the department, in which they work and the position, which they own. Based on the organizational chart of the investigated firm, seven levels can be identified. The two highest levels are reserved for the management board. Four levels comprise the management levels of the firm. The lowest level is reserved for non-managerial employees. Each respondent are assigned to one level based on the following criteria: Manager are assigned to the management they belong to. Non-managerial employees are assigned to the lowest level of the organization, even if their direct supervisor is a fourth or fifth level manager. For example, secretaries, which are directly reporting to the board are assigned to the first level, although they report directly to sixth or seventh level managers. The reasoning for this assignment is based on two consideration. First, it is important to understand the hierarchical structure of the management. Therefore all managing employees are ranked top down. Second, the work on the operative level, the level on which the actual work of the firm is done, differs significantly from managerial tasks. In order to account for this difference, managerial is separated clearly from non-managerial staff.

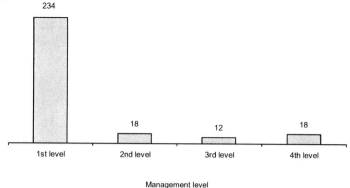

Graph 11: Rank distribution of respondents

A total of 234 respondents indicated that they are employed on the first level. This corresponds to a participation of ~75% of all first level employees. 100% of all second level managers and 75% of all third level managers and ~ 81% of all fourth level managers also participated in the study. In addition to that, interviews have been conducted with all fifth level managers, the level directly reporting to the board. However, these interviews did not generate sufficiently exhaustive relational data in order to consider it.

Seniority. Seniority affects cooperation in two ways: First, a firm identity increases ingroup outgroup sentiments and thus reduces cooperation between employees of previously separated firms. Second, relationships become increasingly stable over time. Stable relationships, however, are not easily switched, even if new potential cooperation partners from the previously separated firms are available for cooperation. In order to capture the first effect, the time that an employee worked for a company needs to be measured. In order to capture the second effect, the time that an employee has stable cooperation relationships around him, needs to be measured. Stable cooperation relationships depend on the position of an employee within the firm and thus of the time in a function.

Therefore, seniority has been operationalized in two ways: Time in company as well as time in function. In the following table, the values for time spent in company and time spent in function can be seen.

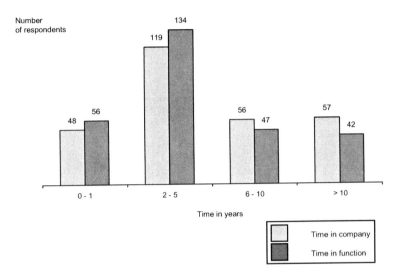

Graph 12: Distribution of time in company and time in function

As can be seen, employees spent less time in their current function than they spent time in the company. However, the difference is marginal. In order to reduce the number of independent variables, I only consider one of the variables. In the interviews at the first research site, it seemed that identification builds up very quickly while solidification of cooperation relationships takes more time. Hence it is sufficient to measure time in function as it captures the effect of firm identity sufficiently and specifically accounts for the effect of solidifying relationships.

5.5.2.3. Psychological factors affecting cooperation

In this study, I differ between two types of psychological factors that might affect cooperation: (1) Psychological reactions to mergers and acquisitions and (2) work related attitudes.

In the previous study, it was found that commitment as well as uncertainty affect cooperation after mergers and acquisitions. In the previous study, commitment was operationalized in a way to capture long term satisfaction and commitment to the firm. In this study, I chose to focus more strongly on the direct effects of the M&A-transaction. A first item, which has been discarded in the last study, interrogated about the work fun that employees felt since the merger. A second item interrogated, whether employees feel that the organizational culture has positively changed since the M&A-transaction. A third item asked about the wish of employees to continue working for the company for the rest of their life. Hence two of the three items focus on feelings related to the M&A-transaction. A fourth item, which originally had been considered, asked about satisfaction with career perspectives of employees. This item had to be dropped due to an intervention of the workers' council. The workers' council wanted to avoid that employees potentially indicate their dissatisfaction with their current positions. A fifth item had been included in the study: Employees were asked how their current spirit is. However, in later analysis, it was dropped, because the interviews revealed that employees answered to the question strongly depending on their moods and not depending on their general spirit.

Uncertainty has been found to be an important factor for the cooperation after mergers and acquisitions. In the present study, uncertainty again was operationalized with the help of several items. A first set of items addressed direct uncertainty reactions of employees: A first item, as in the previous study asked about job uncertainty in the department of the respondent. A second item asked about nervousness at work. A third item asked about additional stress due to the merger. In addition to the first set of items, a second set of items was introduced in the second study. In the course of the interviews at the first research site, respondents indicated that feelings of uncertainty lead to increased efforts to avoid negative impressions on new supervisors. New supervisors were expected to be more sensitive to negative impressions. At the same time, employees indicated that they felt that negative impressions would be punished more harshly than before the integration. Therefore, a second set of items investigated the relationship of employees to their supervisors asking whether employees felt confident to speak up to their supervisors. Also, employees were asked to indicate, whether they felt that critique lead to disadvantages.

In the previous study, work related attitudes have been found to strongly affect cooperation of employees. In addition to the empirical findings of the role of task orientation as well as rule orientation, it was found in the interviews that attitudes about the way of doing things in a company are most effective for cooperation between employees. A number of different items for measuring attitudes thus have been considered. First, the way of handling errors has been considered. Errors can be dealt with openly or in secret. Dealing openly with errors makes it easier to engage in the trial-and-error process of building cooperation relationships. A second factor is exactness and precision that employees aim for in their work. A third factor is the flexibility that employees apply to their work processes. A fourth factor is the responsiveness of employees. While error handling has been dealt with in some studies, process related attitudes have not been found to be considered in previous studies. Based on the interviews at the first research site, a number of aspects of attitudes about cooperation have been identified and translated into items.

In line with previous studies, respondents were asked to judge upon the statements that were generated to capture their attitudes and reactions (compare Hofstede 1984). Respondents could rate their level of agreement on a five point scale with 1 = "Do not agree at all" and 5 = "Fully agree".

In the following table, the items for the operationalization of the psychological factors can be seen.

Items used in previous studies	"Please indicate to what extent you agree to the following statements (1 = not at all, 5 = fully agree)"	Item Name
Commitment		
Adapted from Hofstede (1984)	I would like to work for the rest of my working life for this company	RestofLife
Adapted from Schweiger, Denisi (1991): Positive attitude, job satisfaction	"Since the integration, my work is more fun than it used to be"	MoreFun
	"After the integration, the organizational culture has positively changed"	PositiveCulture
Uncertainty		
Adapted from Schweiger, Denisi (1991): Stress and uncertainty	"The integration threatens jobs in my department"	JobUncertainty
	"The integration means additional work load and stress"	IntegrationStress
Adapted from Hofstede (1984): Uncertainty avoidance	At work, I feel nervous and tensed	Nervousness
Adapted from Hofstede (1984): Power distance	"Employees in my department do not openly oppose and criticize the supervisor"	NoCritique
Adapted from Keith, & Frese (2005)	"In my department, critique leads to disadvantages"	CritiqueDisadvant
Work related attitudes		
Adapted from Hofstede (1984)	"Rules in a company should not be broken, even if an employee thinks it is for the best of the company"	Rules
Adapted from Keith, & Frese (2005): Error handling	"If something in our department goes wrong, we learn from that and do not repeat the error"	LearnfromErrors
	"Smaller error in our department are rather brushed under the carpet"	DenyErrors
Exactness	"In our department, we plan carefully and exactly"	ExactPlans
	"An important criteria for the work in our department is exactness and precision"	ExactWork
Flexibility	"Good planning is key for success"	PlanningIsKey
	"In order to obtain good results, it is important to adjust processes to situation specific needs"	AdaptProcesses
	"We are always open for exceptions and changes of plans"	OpenForChange
Responsiveness	"When other departments need something from us, we react quickly and unbureaucratically"	QuickReaction
	"Speed is very important for all activities in our department"	SpeedMatters
	"Other departments sometimes have to wait, if we have to finish up something"	OthersWait

Table 61: Items for operationalization of psychological factors

With the help of an exploratory factor analysis, all items were grouped into four factors. Items that did not load on the four factors with the highest variance explanation were not considered any further. The results of the factor analyses are indicated below.

Item	1	2	3	4	5	6	7
RestOfLife	0,70						
MoreFun	0,74						
PositiveCulture	0,78						
ExactPlans		0,70					
ExactWork		0,73					
DenyErrors		-0,54	(0,47)				
LearnFromErrors		0,57					
JobUncertainty			0,71				
NoCritique			0,70				
CritiqueDisadvant			0,65				
Nervousness	(-0,43)						
IntegrationStress							
QuickReaction				0,60			
SpeedMatters				0,68			
Rules					0,80		
AdaptProcesses						0,87	
OpenForChange						0,42	
OthersWait							0,77
PlanningIsKey							-0,56
Explained variance	12,0%	11,3%	10,7%	7,9%	6,7%	6,3%	6,1%

Method of extraction: Principal component analysis
Method of rotation: Varimax
This rotation converged after 16 iterations

Table 62: Results of the exploratory factor analysis

As can be seen, the first factor comprises all items that were used for operationalizing commitment. The factor commitment thus is confirmed.

The second factor comprises the error handling items as well as the items for exactness. A high score for this factor thus means that individuals avoid errors and care strongly for exactness and precision. This factor thus is labeled task orientation. It needs to be noted that the factor differs from the single item construct used in the research at SpecMatCo.

The third factor consists of items that were used to operationalize uncertainty. However, as can be seen, two items that were originally used for the operationalization did not load on the factor. The first item is the perceived M&A-stress. A possible explanation for this is the fact that between M&A-transaction and measurement, significantly more time has passed than at SpecMatCo. Probably, the M&A-stress at SoftCo is over. As the item interrogates about the status quo, it does not capture any present M&A-stress at the time of the measurement. The second item that did not load is nervousness. It seems that nervousness in the large sample research does no longer match the factor uncertainty.

A fourth factor that was identified comprises the items fast reaction to requests of other departments as well as the importance of speed for activities within the department. This factor can be interpreted as responsiveness.

The other factors were not considered.

Hence the two hypothesized factors were mostly confirmed. Based on the analysis of the items for work related attitudes, two additional factors were identified that are further considered.

In confirmatory factor analyses, the factor loads and Cronbach's alpha were computed for all four factors. The factor loads differs from the factor loads generated in the exploratory factor analysis on all items.

Commitment		Task orientation		Uncertainty		Responsiveness	
Item	Factor Load	Item	Factor Load	Item	Factor Load	Item	Factor Load
PositiveCulture	0,80	LearnFromErrors	0,73	NoCritique	0,80	QuickReaction	0,77
RestOfLife	0,76	DenyErrors	-0,61	CritiqueDisadvant	0,79	SpeedMatters	0,77
MoreFun	0,80	ExactPlans	0,78	JobUncertainty	0,67		
		ExactWork	0,67				
Explained var.	61,9%	Explained var.	49,4%	Explained var.	56,9%	Explained var.	59,0%
Cronbach's alpha	.69	Cronbach's alpha	.65	Cronbach's alpha	.62	Cronbach's alpha	.30

Table 63: Results of the confirmatory factor analysis

Due to the small number of items, Cronbach's Alphas are very low. While the results for the Cronbach's Alpha yield satisfying results for the factors Commitment, Task Orientation and Uncertainty, the factor Responsiveness has a very low alpha. One explanation for this is the use of two items for this factor only. Another reason is its relative weakness in explaining the total variance of the items. For later interpretation of results, the quality of the factor Responsiveness needs to be considered.

5.5.2.4. Integration measures

Integration measures can be distinguished in two different types of activities. A first type of activities comprises communication, which aims to increase the level of feeling informed. A second type of activities comprises measures that directly engage interaction between employees of the formerly separated firms.

As has been discussed earlier in this work, I do not focus on discrete communication measures, but on the perception of employees of feeling informed. The reason is twofold: first, according to communication research, emitting communication does not necessarily imply that it is received and understood by the addressees. Feeling informed captures the effect of communication, not the communication measure as such nor the reception and understanding of communication. Hence it captures the root of the effect of information on feelings and behaviors of employees. And second, it is impossible to assess the effect of company-wide communication measures in a case study on one firm. Company-wide communication measures are firm level phenomena whose research requires a sample of many firms.

Based on these considerations, four different items have been developed to capture the degree to which employees in the merged firm feel informed. The first two items focus on general information, while the later items focus on individual-specific information.

Type of being informed	Item	Name of item
Generally informed	"At each point in time of the integration, I had sufficient information"	EnoughInfo
	"I know the objectives of the integration"	ObjectivesKnown
Specifically informed	"I always knew, what the integration meant for me personally"	PersonalConsKnown
	"I always knew, where we were heading in the process"	DirectionKnown

Table 64: Items to measure the degree of being informed.

While the items EnoughInfo, PersonalConsKnown and DirectionKnown have been used in the research on SpecMatCo already, the item ObjectivesKnown has been newly introduced. In the interviews at the first research site, many employees claimed that despite all the information they get, they are missing the big picture, i.e. the overall concept for the M&A-transaction. Hence I added an item about the knowledge of the objectives of the merger. Compared to the research at SpecMatCo, the two items PersonalConsKnown and DirectionKnown were formulated positively. In the interviews at the first research site, some respondents had problems to understand negatively formulated sentences. Therefore, these items were positively reformulated.

Respondents were asked to indicate to what degree they agree with the statements about being informed on a 7-point Likert scale with 1 = "Is not the case" and 7 = "Is very much the case". The descriptive statistics of these items are listed in the tables below:

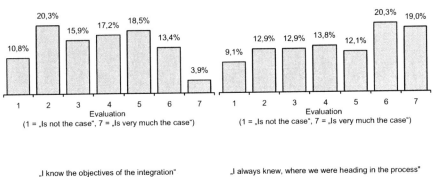

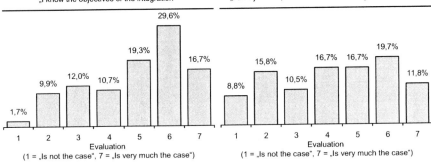

Graph 13: Descriptive statistics of items for operationalization of factor "Feeling informed"

In Table 65, the results of the confirmatory factor analysis for the factor InformationAgg are presented. The factor loads are all equally high as is the explained variance. As a consequence, Cronbach's alpha for InformationAgg is very high.

Factor name	Item	Variable name	Factor loads	Cronbach's Alpha
InformationAgg	"At each point in time of the integration, I had sufficient information"	EnoughInfo	0,79	
	"I know the objectives of the integration"	ObjectivesKnown	0,83	
	"I always knew, what the integration meant for me personally"	PersonalCons-Known	0,83	
	"I always know where we were heading in the process"	DirectionKnown	0,87	.85

Extraction method: Principal component analysis
Roation method: Varimax with Kaiser Normalization

Table 65: Results of the confirmatory factor analysis

Based on exploratory interviews in the forefront of the research, different integration measures have been identified, in which employees participated. The graph below shows the different integration measures under consideration and the percentage of employees that participated.

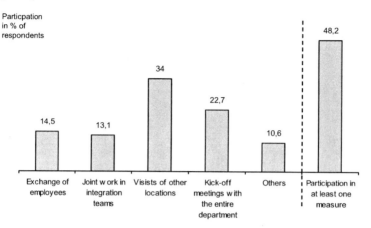

Graph 14: **Percentage of employees participating in different integration measures**

Compared to SpecMatCo, the integration measures show some differences. First, SoftCo arranged exchanges of employees. That means that employees of different departments worked for periods from a couple of days to several weeks at locations of the partnering firms. Second, SoftCo arranged visits to other locations. Many employees visited other location in order to get to know the physical, cultural and business environment of their new colleagues. SoftCo did not offer integration trainings for its employees.

As can be seen, the most frequently used integration measures are visits of the other locations. In total, almost half of the respondents participated in at least one integration measure. This ratio, however, is significantly lower than in the sample at SpecMatCo. At SpecMatCo the variance was too low to identify the effects of integration measures on cooperation properly. This problem should not exist at SoftCo.

5.5.3. Controls

When looking at factors that affect the cooperation of employees with others, it is important to note that cooperation relationships in companies are not entirely subject to characteristics of the individual. They are not fully deliberate as friendship relationships or romantic relationships. Rather, there are strong isomorphic forces, which affect the formation of cooperation relationships (Lazega, & Duijn 1997). The formal structure of a firm strongly influences whether an employee cooperates little or much. Within some departments, there is a lot of cooperation, while employees of other departments do not need to cooperate as frequently. Some departments have to cooperate a lot with other departments. Other departments have very few cooperation requirements with other departments.

In the graph below, the actual, measured cooperation strength within departments of the two acquired firms is illustrated. As has been described above, at SoftCo, most departments were maintained at the former location of Firm A and the former location of Firm B. For each of these mirroring departments, the cooperation strength within the departments is indicated as the ratio of the actual cooperation strength and the maximum possible cooperation strength within a department. Cooperation strength of a relationship is computed as the product of its frequency and its importance. The actual cooperation strength within a department is the sum of all indicated cooperation relationships within a department. The maximum cooperation strength is the sum of the maximum strength of all possible relationships within a department.

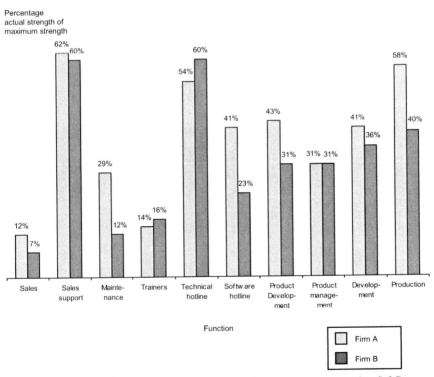

Graph 15: Actual cooperation strength as percentage of maximum cooperation strength at SoftCo

Different functions have different levels of cooperation strength within the function. For example, while sales employees cooperate very little, sales support employees cooperate very much within the departments. The finding bears some face validity: Sales employees in a regionally segmented sales organization do not have to cooperate frequently with their colleagues in other regions. However, sales support employees coordinate all processes within the organization. Hence they have to cooperate very tightly.

Obviously, the mirroring departments in Firm A and Firm B have similar cooperation levels within the departments. There are two prominent exceptions: First, the software hotline at Firm A cooperates more tightly than at Firm B. There are two explanations for this finding: First, the software hotline at Firm A is significantly smaller than at Firm B. As relationships require ongoing investments (Rushbult 1980a, 1980b) only a limited number of relationships can be maintained at any given point in time. In a small department, it is more likely that all or at least a higher percentage of all possible relationships with colleagues in the department can be maintained than in larger departments.

A second, more practical explanation might be the fact that the employees of the software hotline at Firm A are located within one room, facilitating cooperation. The same is true for the production workers. At Firm A, they are all located in one big open production hall, whereas production workers at Firm B are located in several separated rooms.

Nevertheless, it can be stated that different functions show different levels of cooperation strength. It can also be stated that different levels of cooperation strength depend of structural requirements that result from the activities within a given department and its role in the main processes of the organization.

It is not known, what the optimal level of cooperation within and between functions is. The question "What is the right level of cooperation?" will not be answered in the present research. Rather, I focus on reasons, why some employees cooperate more and others cooperate less. As has been pointed out above, the level of cooperation of an employee is strongly affected by the cooperation levels within her department. In order to find out, which factors influence the cooperation strength of employees, I thus cannot consider solely individual cooperation strength only, because it is too strongly affected by departmental cooperation requirements.

A departmental control variable is needed, which controls for the structural cooperation requirements on the departmental level. Such use of variables, which conform to different levels of analysis has been discussed in previous studies as "cross-level inference". „Broadly defined, cross-level inference occurs when relations among variables at one level are inferred from analysis performed at a different level. A straightforward example would be the use of departmental indices of work satisfaction and absenteeism in making inferences about relations between individual and absence from work" (Mossholder, & Bedeian 1983: 547). In organizational research, different cross-level phenomena have been investigated: For example, the relationship of group satisfaction and individual satisfaction respectively group absenteeism and individual absenteeism (Mathieu, & Kohler 1990), group job satisfaction and group absenteeism (Steel, Rentsch, & Hendrix 2002), group task satisfaction and individual job satisfaction (Mason, & Griffin 2005) have been investigated with the help of cross-level research designs. Similarly, in the present study, individual cooperation shall be controlled for departmental level cooperation requirements.

However, certain pitfalls in cross-level research need to be considered. "Not all phenomena can be easily separated into different levels of meaning. Consequently, it is important that a sound rationale exists for interpreting individual measures as functional surrogates of macro constructs" (Mossholder, & Bedeian 1983: 548).

From an empirical perspective, the results in Graph 15 provide a first indication that there are significant differences between average cooperation levels of different departments. Also, the findings indicate that specific functions have a specific level of cooperation requirement. Almost all functions show high similarity of the values for mirroring departments, providing validation for differential departmental cooperation requirements.

From a conceptual perspective, the organizational design school (e.g. Gailbraith 1974) posits that organizational structure determines the actual cooperation within organizations. Hence isomorphic forces of formal organizational structures should represent structural cooperation requirements for individual cooperation.

In a previous study at SpecMatCo, it proved to be methodologically difficult to assess the cooperation requirements between functions with the help of key informants. When asking managers about the cooperation requirements, they often are not enough into the details of the work flow to know the actual cooperation requirements. When asking employees on the operative level about cooperation requirements, it is well possible that the answer suffers from significant respondent biases. The respondent biases are caused by the fact that even in small departments, employees do not know in detail what their colleagues are doing and whom they are cooperating with.

Instead of using an independent measure of cooperation requirements, I use an aggregate measure of cooperation as departmental level control variable. Previous studies similarly use mean values of elements of social aggregates as supra-level independent variable. For example, Mathieu, & Kohler (1990) used group absence as one independent variable on individual absence. Of course, the use of such aggregate measures requires a high number of investigated supra-level units of analysis in order to generate satisfying levels of statistical significance.

"The two most commonly cited general analytic approaches for addressing cross-level inference procedures are (1) regression analysis and (2) analysis of covariance" (Mossholder, & Bedeian 1983: 549). In this study, I use regression analysis to determine the effects of individual and departmental effects on cooperation.

The regression model that is established to partition individual level effects $\beta_1 X_{1ij}, \beta_2 X_{2ij}, \ldots, \beta_n X_{nij}$ and aggregate level effects of the aggregate $\beta_{n+1}\overline{Y}_j$ is based on the following basic model:

Formula 9: Basic model for partition of individual level and departmental level effects

$$Y_{ij} = \beta_1 X_{1ij} + \beta_2 X_{2ij} + \beta_3 X_{3ij} + \ldots + \beta_{n+1}\overline{Y}_j + e_{ij}$$

, where $i = 1, 2, \ldots, k; j = 1, 2, \ldots, m$ and k is the number of employees in each department j and m is the number of departments.

In this model, Y_{ij} corresponds to the cooperation of an actor i, who works in department j. The individual effects $X_{1ij}, X_{2ij}, \ldots, X_{nij}$ correspond to the different independent variables such as age, gender, or education levdel as defined above. The coefficients $\beta_1, \beta_2, \ldots, \beta_n$ represent the regression coefficients for each independent variable as computed with the regression analysis. e_{ij} is the error term for each employee i in department j. The structural cooperation requirements correspond to the aggregate $\beta_{n+1}\overline{Y}_j$, which is computed as mean of the cooperation Y_{ij} for all employees i in department j.

In other words, I focus on deviation of cooperation of a specific employee from the average cooperation of employees within his department. Hence the question to be answered in this research is "What factors make employees cooperate more or less than other employees, when structural cooperation requirements are controlled for?"

The control variables are computed based on in-degree relationships of a department. For example, the variable DepNumNewTies indicates the average number of relationships between colleagues of previously separated firms that each employee in a given department has. DepNumNewTies is used as control variable for the analysis of the effects of the independent variables on the dependent variable NumNewTies.

Assuming that $K = \{E_1, E_2, \ldots, E_n\}$ is the set of employees in department k, DepNumOldTies$_k$ as well as DepNumNewTies$_k$ are computed according to the following formula:

Formula 10: Calculation of DepNumOldTies

$$DepNumOldTies_k = \frac{\sum_{i \in K} NumOldTies_i}{\sum_{i \in K}(1)}$$

Formula 11: Calculation of DepNumNewTies

$$DepNumNewTies_k = \frac{\sum_{i \in K} NumNewTies_i}{\sum_{i \in K} (1)}$$

Based on DepNumOldTies and DepNumNewTies, the average share of old relationship to the full amount of relationships for each employee in a department is calculated. The variable DepShareOldTies for a department k is used as control variable for ShareOldTies of all employees i in department k:

Formula 12: Calculation of DepShareOldTies for each department k

$$DepShareOldTies_k = \frac{DepNumOldTies_k}{DepNumNewTies_k + DepNumOldTies_k}$$

Similarly, the control measures for the characteristics of the relationships of an employee in department k are calculated:

Formula 13: Calculation of DepSumFreqOld for each department k

$$DepSumFreqOld_k = \frac{\sum_{i \in K} SumFreqOld_i}{\sum_{i \in K} (1)}$$

Formula 14: Calculation of DepSumFreqNew for each department k

$$DepSumFreqNew_k = \frac{\sum_{i \in K} SumFreqNew_i}{\sum_{i \in K} (1)}$$

The average strength of a relationship of employees in department k is correspondingly computed according to the following formulas:

Formula 15: Calculation of DepAvFreqOld for each department k

$$DepAvFreqOld_k = \frac{DepSumFreqOld_k}{DepSumOldTies_k}$$

Formula 16: Calculation of DepAvFreqNew for each department k

$$DepAvFreqNew_k = \frac{DepSumFreqNew_k}{DepSumNewTies_k}$$

The delta between the average frequency of old and new relationships of average employees in department k is thus computed according to the following formula.

Formula 17: Calculation of DepDelAvFreq

$$DepDelAvFreq_k = DepAvFreqOld_k - DepAvFreqNew_k$$

In the same way, the control variables for importance, strength and quality of cooperation are computed.

In the table below, the full list of control variables is listed. The control variables mirror the dependent variables precisely. That means that for each dependent variable, a specific control variable is used.

	Existence of ties	Frequency	Importance	Strength	Quality
Old relationships	DepNumOldTies	DepFreqOldTies	DepImpOldTies	DepStrenOldTies	
New relationships	DepNumNewTies	DepFreqNewTies	DepImpNewTies	DepStrenNewTies	
Relation old relationship to all relationships	DepRatOld	DepRatFreqOld	DepRatImpOld	DepRatStrenOld	
Average characteristics of old relationships		DepAvFreqOld	DepAvImpOld	DepAvStrenOld	DepAvQualOld
Average characteristics of new relationships		DepAvFreqNew	DepAvImpNew	DepAvStrenNew	DepAvQualNew
Delta of average characteristics of relationships		DepDelAvFreq	DepDelAvImp	DepDelAvStren	DepDelAvQual

Table 66: Formulas to calculate the cooperation measures on departmental level

These control variables are superior to the control variables used in the research on SpecMatCo insofar as they avoid the respondent bias of key informants by (1) using in-degree relationships only and (2) by using an aggregate measure and not a key informant measure. Nevertheless the control variables are suffering from a significant methodological weakness: In small departments, an individual employee strongly affects the cooperation of the entire department. Hence there is a significant risk of covariance of the dependent and the control variable. In order to reduce the risk of covariance, I calculated the control variable only for departments of four employees or more. That limits the covariance problem to a reasonable level.

In addition to the methodological weakness of the control measure, there is a notable conceptual weakness: While structural cooperation requirements on the departmental level are considered, there might equally well be structural cooperation requirements on the individual level. The interviews revealed that even in the smallest organizational units, employees have different roles, which imply different work activities and different cooperation requirements. Such individual level cooperation requirements, however, cannot be controlled for with the proposed control variable. This limitation needs to be considered in later discussions of the results.

5.6. Results for the research question "Who cooperates?"

Based on past empirical findings and based on existing theories, a number of hypotheses have been postulated in the second part of this work to answer the research questions. The operationalization of the research constructs allows testing of all hypotheses with the data gathered at SoftCo. In the following table, the correlations between the independent as well as the dependent constructs are shown. For each variable, the first line indicates the Pearson's correlation coefficient. The second line indicates the 2-sided significance. The third line indicates the number of cases considered for the calculation of the correlation coefficients.

Correlation matrix for variables

	GenderQuant	EducationLevel	Rank	TimeInFunction	TaskOrientation	Responsiveness	Commitment	Uncertainty	InformationAgg	IntegrationAgg	NumNewTies	ShareOldTies
Age	-0,15*	0,13*	0,17**	0,45**	0,07	-0,10	0,23**	-0,09	0,08	0,04	-0,02	0,05
	0,01	0,04	0,00	0,00	0,23	0,09	0,00	0,14	0,26	0,48	0,77	0,43
GenderQuant		-0,24**	-0,21**	-0,19**	0,07	-0,01	-0,03	0,01	-0,04	-0,18**	-0,02	-0,05
		0,00	0,00	0,00	0,28	0,85	0,68	0,92	0,60	0,00	0,73	0,41
EducationLevel			0,27**	0,11	-0,21**	0,05	0,00	-0,13*	-0,01	0,10	0,10	-0,18**
			0,00	0,07	0,00	0,46	0,97	0,05	0,87	0,12	0,10	0,00
Rank				0,19**	0,04	0,11	0,11	-0,17**	0,13	0,28**	0,40**	-0,35**
				0,00	0,55	0,08	0,09	0,01	0,05	0,00	0,00	0,00
TimeInFunction					-0,03	-0,05	0,06	0,00	-0,04	0,12*	-0,10	0,19**
					0,63	0,40	0,39	0,99	0,60	0,04	0,09	0,00
TaskOrientation						0,29**	0,28**	-0,29**	0,19**	0,07	0,06	0,02
						0,00	0,00	0,00	0,01	0,23	0,37	0,71
Responsiveness							0,12	-0,12	-0,05	-0,01	-0,06	0,06
							0,07	0,06	0,43	0,83	0,36	0,32
Commitment								-0,36**	0,43**	0,13*	0,17**	-0,17**
								0,00	0,00	0,05	0,01	0,01
Uncertainty									-0,18**	-0,04	-0,16**	0,18**
									0,01	0,50	0,01	0,01
InformationAgg										0,27**	0,15*	-0,19**
										0,00	0,03	0,01
IntegrationAgg											0,32**	-0,31**
											0,00	0,00
NumNewTies												-0,75**
												0,00
ShareOldTies												
SumFreqNew												
ShareOldFreq												
AvFreqNew												
DelAvFreq												
SumImpNew												
ShareOldImp												
AvImpNew												
DelAvImp												
SumStrenNew												
ShareOldStren												
AvStrenNew												
DelAvStren												
AvQualNewOut												

* 2-sided significance at the 0.05-level
** 2-sided significance at the 0.01-level

1st line: Pearson's correlation
2nd line: Significance (2-sided)

Table 67: Correlation matrix for variables for research question "Who cooperates" at SoftCo

for research question "Who cooperates?"

SumFreqNew	ShareOldFreq	AvFreqNew	DelAvFreq	SumImpNew	ShareOldImp	AvImpNew	DelAvImp	SumStrenNew	ShareOldStren	AvStrenNew	DelAvStren	AvQualNewOut	DelAvQualOut
0,00	0,02	0,10	-0,11	0,00	0,03	0,05	0,00	0,01	0,00	-0,02	-0,04	-0,04	0,034
1,00	0,70	0,13	0,07	0,96	0,66	0,46	0,97	0,89	0,98	0,80	0,53	0,63	0,653
-0,06	-0,02	-0,07	0,05	-0,04	-0,05	-0,04	-0,04	-0,08	-0,03	-0,14*	0,06	-0,06	0,083
0,36	0,70	0,27	0,44	0,48	0,45	0,59	0,56	0,21	0,67	0,04	0,31	0,39	0,266
0,06	-0,15*	-0,06	0,08	0,09	-0,17**	0,00	0,05	0,05	-0,13*	-0,01	0,08	0,02	0,053
0,32	0,02	0,40	0,18	0,16	0,01	0,99	0,43	0,41	0,03	0,89	0,20	0,82	0,491
0,35**	-0,34**	-0,02	-0,12*	0,43**	-0,36**	0,24**	-0,18**	0,36**	-0,34**	0,02	-0,05	-0,01	-0,139
0,00	0,00	0,71	0,02	0,00	0,00	0,00	0,00	0,00	0,00	0,70	0,33	0,91	0,061
-0,09	0,19**	-0,01	0,03	-0,09	0,20**	0,01	0,10	-0,08	0,18**	-0,05	0,05	-0,07	0,062
0,12	0,00	0,87	0,62	0,16	0,00	0,89	0,09	0,19	0,00	0,43	0,39	0,35	0,41
0,08	0,02	0,03	-0,08	0,07	0,01	0,09	-0,13*	0,08	0,00	0,08	-0,10	0,30**	-0,22**
0,21	0,79	0,65	0,21	0,26	0,81	0,19	0,04	0,17	0,95	0,24	0,09	0,00	0,003
-0,05	0,07	-0,02	0,05	-0,04	0,04	0,04	0,00	-0,05	0,05	-0,04	0,07	0,13	-0,061
0,39	0,27	0,83	0,40	0,50	0,49	0,60	0,98	0,43	0,38	0,57	0,28	0,08	0,42
0,19**	-0,17**	0,06	-0,09	0,17**	-0,15*	-0,07	-0,05	0,18**	-0,14*	0,02	-0,05	0,50**	-0,35**
0,00	0,01	0,38	0,18	0,01	0,02	0,33	0,46	0,01	0,03	0,76	0,42	0,00	0
-0,18**	0,14*	0,01	0,05	-0,18**	0,18**	-0,07	0,17**	-0,20**	0,14*	-0,07	0,07	-0,20**	0,055
0,00	0,03	0,86	0,41	0,00	0,00	0,32	0,01	0,00	0,02	0,30	0,27	0,01	0,482
0,11	-0,18**	-0,11	-0,13	,138*	-0,16*	-0,15	-0,09	0,10	-0,16*	-0,15	-0,09	0,28**	-0,121
0,10	0,00	0,15	0,06	0,04	0,02	0,06	0,17	0,15	0,02	0,06	0,16	0,00	0,145
0,33**	-0,34**	0,22**	-0,33**	0,32**	-0,34**	0,12	-0,26**	0,32**	-0,35**	0,14*	-0,25**	0,14	-0,05
0,00	0,00	0,00	0,00	0,00	0,00	0,09	0,00	0,00	0,00	0,04	0,00	0,06	0,502
0,95**	-0,74**	0,12*	-0,28**	0,98**	-0,74**	0,17**	-0,33**	0,92**	-0,71**	0,15*	-0,18**	0,17*	0,091
0,00	0,00	0,05	0,00	0,00	0,00	0,01	0,00	0,00	0,00	0,01	0,00	0,02	0,219
-0,72**	0,97**	-0,06	0,40**	-0,72**	0,98**	-0,01	0,45**	-0,67**	0,92**	-0,06	0,28**	-0,04	0,15*
0,00	0,00	0,35	0,00	0,00	0,00	0,93	0,00	0,00	0,00	0,33	0,00	0,54	0,044
	-0,75**	0,34**	-0,39**	0,96**	-0,73**	0,24**	-0,37**	0,99**	-0,74**	0,32**	-0,29**	0,17*	0,048
	0,00	0,00	0,00	0,00	0,00	0,00	0,00	0,00	0,00	0,00	0,00	0,02	0,515
		-0,24**	0,51**	-0,72**	0,97**	-0,09	,47**	-0,71**	0,98**	-0,20**	0,40**	-0,04	0,15*
		0,00	0,00	0,00	0,00	0,14	0,00	0,00	0,00	0,00	0,00	0,60	0,043
			-0,72**	0,16**	-0,11	0,36**	-0,20**	0,37**	-0,27**	0,74**	-0,48**	0,09	0,101
			0,00	0,01	0,05	0,00	0,00	0,00	0,00	0,00	0,00	0,24	0,194
				-0,30**	0,44**	-0,28**	0,76**	-0,39**	0,54**	-0,53**	0,84**	0,03	0,011
				0,00	0,00	0,00	0,00	0,00	0,00	0,00	0,00	0,73	0,88
					-0,74**	0,29**	-0,37**	0,95**	-0,72**	0,22**	-0,24**	0,17*	0,09
					0,00	0,00	0,00	0,00	0,00	0,00	0,00	0,02	0,226
						-0,17**	0,53**	-0,70**	0,97**	-0,15*	0,38**	-0,03	0,135
						0,01	0,00	0,00	0,00	0,01	0,00	0,64	0,069
							-0,75**	0,35**	-0,22**	0,49**	-0,39**	0,09	0,077
							0,00	0,00	0,00	0,00	0,00	0,24	0,325
								-0,39**	0,53**	-0,32**	0,72**	0,03	0,062
								0,00	0,00	0,00	0,00	0,73	0,405
									-0,73**	0,39**	-0,33**	0,16*	0,066
									0,00	0,00	0,00	0,03	0,376
										-0,29**	0,49**	-0,02	0,125
										0,00	0,00	0,83	0,09
											-0,74**	0,09	0,105
											0,00	0,23	0,177
												0,035	0,012
												0,637	0,868
													-0,62**
													0,00

It was hypothesized that a number of independent variables affect the psychological reactions after mergers and acquisitions as well as cooperation. The independent variables have been grouped into four groups of variables: (1) demographic characteristics, (2) firm related characteristics, (3) attitudes and reactions to the M&A-transaction and (4) integration measures.

A first set of hypotheses postulates effects of demographic characteristics, firm related characteristics, attitudes and integration measures on commitment and uncertainty after mergers and acquisitions. In the following table, the full model for testing the first set of hypotheses is presented:

Dependent variable: Commitment and uncertainty		
	Commitment	Uncertainty
Standardized Beta		
Demographic characteristics		
Age	.205****	-.049
Gender	.011	-.037
Education level	.010	-.166***
Firm related characteristics		
Rank	.008	-.120**
TimeInFunction	-.012	.037
Attitudes		
Task orientation	.160***	-.286****
Responsiveness	.112**	-.026
Integration measures		
InformationAgg	.392****	-.121**
SumIntegration	.004	.051
Model statistics		
Total df	210	210
R²	.277	.151
Adjusted R²	.244	.113
F	8.542	3.984

**** Significant at a 0.01-level (2-sided)
*** Significant at a 0.05-level (2-sided)
** Significant at a 0.10-level (2-sided)
* Significant at a 0.15-level (2-sided)
Note: Pairwise exclusion of incomplete cases

Table 68: Full model for dependent variables commitment and uncertainty

The full model for the dependent variables commitment and uncertainty shows that age has a very positive effect on commitment. At the same time, education level reduces uncertainty. Higher rank decreases uncertainty. Task orientation has a positive effect on commitment, while at the same time reducing uncertainty. Feeling informed strongly increases commitment, while at the same time reducing uncertainty. Participation in integration measures has no effect.

A second set of hypotheses postulates effects of all four groups of variables on different measures of cooperation.

Full model with all independent variables and all operationalizations of cooperation without controls

Standardized Beta		NumNewTies	SharedOldies	SumFreqNew	SharedOldFreq	AvFreqNew	DelAvFreq	SumImpNew	SharedOldImp	AvImpNew	DelAvImp	SumStrenNew	SharedOldStren	AvStrenNew	DelAvStren	AvQualNew	DelAvQual
Demographic characteristics																	
	Age	-.051	.029	-.031	-.004	.146**	-.151**	-.042	-.011	.063	-.052	-.026	-.043	-.018	-.067	-.151**	.137*
	Gender	.062	-.141****	.011	-.110**	-.066	.014	.040	-.139***	.000	-.059	-.012	-.112***	-.159***	.058	-.080	.103
	Education level	.023	-.120**	-.023	-.084	-.087	.137**	-.010	-.102*	-.067	.091	-.045	-.062	-.033	.102	.082	.036
Firm related characteristics																	
	Rank	.379****	.322****	.319****	-.301****	-.074	-.059	.410****	-.319****	.253****	-.148**	.328****	-.299****	-.007	-.004	-.096	-.160**
	TimeInFunction	-.184***	.271****	-.187****	.281****	-.117	.138**	-.177****	.293****	-.074	.161***	-.177****	.291****	-.110	.114*	-.036	.066
Attitudes																	
	Task orientation	.016	.072	.026	.064	.007	-.011	.020	.071	.105	-.061	.030	.057	.110	-.072	.195****	.042
	Responsiveness	-.137***	.114**	-.136***	.113**	-.019	.045	-.126**	.092*	-.023	.038	-.134***	.095*	-.110	.084	.010	.068
Reaction																	
	Commitment	.127**	-.120**	.159***	-.126**	.118	.000	.119*	-.095	.102*	-.081	.060	.138**	-.088	.082	.461****	.080
	Uncertainty	-.065	.088	-.090	.049	.013	.034	-.081	.102*	-.064	.150***	-.117**	-.074	.063	.020	.013	-.132*
Integration measures																	
	InformationAgg	-.040	-.015	-.105*	-.004	-.249****	.001	-.054	.013	-.214****	.020	-.116**	.014	-.277****	.008	.042	.035
	SumIntegration	.232****	-.253****	.270****	-.286****	.293****	-.331****	.228****	-.288****	.116*	-.255****	.262****	-.308****	.182****	-.250****	.068	
Model statistics																	
	Total df	210	210	210	210	179	210	210	210	175	210	210	210	175	210	152	147
	R²	.280	.322	.260	.302	.127	.153	.295	.327	.127	.143	.261	.297	.115	.097	.322	.205
	Adjusted R²	.241	.284	.219	.263	.069	.106	.256	.290	.068	.096	.220	.258	.056	.047	.269	.141
	F	7.050	8.589	6.357	7.825	2.214	3.269	7.567	8.804	2.162	3.018	6.385	7.633	1.939	1.943	6.074	3.187

**** Significant at a 0.01-level (2-sided)
*** Significant at a 0.05-level (2-sided)
** Significant at a 0.10-level (2-sided)
* Significant at a 0.15-level (2-sided)

Note: Pairwise exclusion of incomplete cases

Table 69: Full model for all independent variables and cooperation as dependent variables with controls

Full model with all independent variables and all operationalizations of cooperation

		NumNewTies	SharedOldies	SumFreqNew	SharedOldFreq	AvFreqNew	DelAvFreq	SumImpNew	SharedOldImp	AvImpNew	DelAvImp	SumStrenNew	SharedOldStren	AvStrenNew	DelAvStren	AvQualNew	DelAvQual
Standardized Beta																	
Demographic characteristics	Age	-.060	.010	-.028	-.031	.212***	-.170***	-.064	-.017	.035	-.037	-.039	-.049	.000	-.066	-.106*	.107
	Gender	.150***	.171***	.092**	-.164***	-.127***	-.021	.136***	-.176***	-.049	-.029	.087***	-.183***	-.180***	.036	-.081	.127**
	Education level	-.087**	.068**	-.122***	.067*	-.117**	.065	-.091***	.070*	.003	.070	-.118***	.062	-.024	.030	.093	.037
Firm related characteristics	Rank	.352***	-.267***	.326***	-.262***	-.108*	-.085	.385***	-.261***	.185***	-.120	.333***	-.253***	-.046	.001	-.071	-.116*
	TimeInFunction	-.043	.100***	-.078**	.137***	-.177***	.225***	-.031	.115***	-.010	.142**	-.064	.144***	-.113	.164**	-.044	.060
Attitudes	Task orientation	-.058	.025	-.086**	.019	-.046	-.023	-.081**	.034	.041	-.051	-.096***	.031	.054	-.062	.185****	-.149**
	Responsiveness	.004	-.063**	.001	-.072*	.076	-.003	.008	-.081**	.051	.011	-.005	-.084*	-.036	.039	.067	.027
Reaction	Commitment	-.044	.053	-.006	.048	.033	.032	-.025	.049	-.027	.038	.012	.047	.067	.018	.294****	-.309****
	Uncertainty	.013	-.013	.006	-.040	-.058	.079	.020	-.024	-.002	.121	.003	-.051	-.079	.077	.023	-.107*
Integration measures	InformationAgg	.068	-.051	.018	-.041	-.132**	-.017	.066	-.035	-.026	-.036	.009	-.031	-.178***	-.033	.015	.110
	SumIntegration	.169****	-.175****	.210****	-.178***	.209****	-.233****	.179****	-.217****	.067	-.241****	-.223****	-.215****	.135**	-.189****	-.018	.069
Controls	(Respective Control)	.758****	.819****	.775****	.783****	.634****	.446****	.756****	.766****	.676****	.266****	.768****	.707****	.371****	.392****	.495****	.490****
Model statistics	Total df	155	155	155	155	155	155	155	155	155	155	155	155	155	155	152	147
	R^2	.746	.851	.774	.786	.496	.496	.778	.781	.531	.208	.767	.684	.238	.521	.521	.425
	Adjusted R^2	.745	.839	.755	.768	.454	.454	.759	.762	.491	.141	.748	.658	.174	.480	.480	.373
	F	38.643	68.245	40.807	43.854	11.748	11.748	41.669	42.380	13.470	3.122	39.281	25.852	3.730	12.711	12.711	8.303

**** Significant at a 0.01-level (2-sided)   ** Significant at a 0.10-level (2-sided)
*** Significant at a 0.05-level (2-sided)   * Significant at a 0.15-level (2-sided)

Note: Pairwise exclusion of incomplete cases

Table 70: Full model for all independent variables and cooperation as dependent variables w/o controls

In Table 69, the full models with the effects of demographic characteristics, firm related characteristics, attitudes and reactions of employees as well as integration measures on cooperation are presented. Structural cooperation requirements are not considered in Table 69. In Table 70, structural cooperation requirements are considered in the full models with control variables.

The full model shows a number of significant effects of independent variables on the dependent variables, which were used to operationalize cooperation. All full models are highly significant. The different control variables have a very strong effect.

The variables commitment and uncertainty have hardly any effect in the full model, which confirms that they are strongly dependent on the other independent variables.

In the following paragraphs, the results for the hypotheses for each group of variables are separately discussed. In addition to the full models presented in Table 68 and Table 70, I also consider the partial models for each group of variables.

5.6.1. Demographic characteristics

Three different demographic characteristics have been investigated: Age, gender, and education level. In the following table, all postulated hypotheses concerning these characteristics are listed:

Hypothesis 1a:	Older employees have less cooperation relationships with new colleagues than younger employees after an M&A-transaction
Hypothesis 1b:	Older employees have more intensive relationships with new colleagues after mergers and acquisitions
Hypothesis 1c:	Older people will be less committed than younger people
Hypothesis 1d:	1: Older people are less uncertain than younger people 2: Older people are more uncertain than younger people
Hypothesis 2:	There is no gender difference in cooperation after mergers and acquisitions
Hypothesis 3a:	Higher educated employees cooperate more than less educated employees
Hypothesis 3b:	Higher educated employees experience less uncertainty after M&A-transactions than lower educated employees

Table 71: Hypotheses concerning demographic characteristics of employees

5.6.1.1. Dependent variables: Commitment and uncertainty

In the following table, the effects of demographic characteristics on satisfaction and uncertainty of employees are presented:

Independent variable: Demographic characteristics	Commitment	Uncertainty
Standardized Beta		
Demographic characteristics		
Age	.235****	-.084
Gender	.002	-.037
Education level	-.027	-.125**
Model statistics		
Total df	226	238
R^2	.054	.024
Adjusted R^2	.041	.011
F	4.255	1.891

**** Significant at a 0.01-level (2-sided)
*** Significant at a 0.05-level (2-sided)
** Significant at a 0.10-level (2-sided)
* Significant at a 0.15-level (2-sided)
Note: Pairwise exclusion of incomplete cases

Table 72: Partial model of effects of demographic characteristics on commitment and uncertainty

As can be seen, older employees are significantly higher committed than younger employees. This contradicts hypothesis 1c. According to Socioemotional Selectivity Theory, hypothesis 1c assumes that older people should feel less committed to their work, because older people increasingly accentuate emotionally satisfying activities outside work. However, the results strongly contradict this hypothesis. The full model in Table 68 fully confirms the findings of the partial model.

At the same time, age shows no significant effect on uncertainty after mergers and acquisitions. The full model equally shows no significant effects. Hence neither hypothesis 1d.1 nor hypothesis 1d.2 are supported.

There is no gender specific effect on uncertainty or commitment. Although there was no hypothesis about the relationship of gender and reactions to M&A-transactions, the finding confirms hypothesis 2, which postulates that gender has no specific effects on dependent variables.

In line with hypothesis 3b the partial as well as the full model shows that higher educated employees experience less uncertainty than employees with lower education levels. This confirms that higher educated employees experience less uncertainty because their knowledge is better transferable and less firm-related than the knowledge of less educated employees. An employee who learned everything "on the job" is more dependent on the firm and thus is more uncertain about loosing his job.

5.6.1.2. Dependent variables: Cooperation

In Table 73, the partial models of the effects of demographic characteristics on cooperation are presented. Demographic characteristics are age, gender as well as education level. In the following paragraphs, effects of each of these independent variables will be discussed.

Independent variables: Demographic characteristics

Standardized Beta	NumNewTies	SharedOldies	SumFreqNew	SharedOldFreq	AvFreqNew	DelAvFreq	SumImpNew	SharedOldImp	AvImpNew	DelAvImp	SumStrenNew	SharedOldStren	AvStrenNew	DelAvStren	AvQualNew	DelAvQual
Demographic characteristics																
Age	-.032	.061	-.014	.036	.102*	-.113**	-.018	.039	.047	-.012	-.006	.011	-.035	-.039	-.047	.040
Gender	.001	-.092*	-.044	-.058	-.081	.056	-.024	-.088	-.033	-.026	-.067	-.060	-.158***	-.079	-.069	.107
Education level	.107**	-.212****	.052	-.167****	-.091	.110**	.084	-.199****	-.015	.044	.035	-.148***	-.043	.103*	.007	.074
Model statistics																
Total df	263	263	263	263	209	263	263	263	205	263	263	263	205	263	176	171
R^2	.012	.046	.006	.027	.022	.024	.008	.039	.004	.003	.007	.021	.023	.014	.006	.014
Adjusted R^2	.000	.035	-.006	.016	.008	.012	-.003	.028	-.011	-.008	-.005	.010	.009	.003	-.011	-.004
F	1.013	4.173	.489	2.402	1.527	2.109	.738	3.554	.240	.263	.591	1.872	1.612	1.255	.357	.801

**** Significant at a 0.01-level (2-sided) ** Significant at a 0.10-level (2-sided)
*** Significant at a 0.05-level (2-sided) * Significant at a 0.15-level (2-sided)

Note: Pairwise exclusion of incomplete cases

Table 73: Partial model with effects of demographic characteristics on different aspects of cooperation at SoftCo

5.6.1.2.1. Age

There is no negative effect of age on number of cooperation relationships (NumNewTies). Hence hypothesis 1a cannot be confirmed.

However, hypothesis 1b is partly supported: The average frequency of new relationships of older employees is significantly higher than the average frequency of new relationships of younger employees (DelAvFreq). These findings are supported by the full model without control variable in Table 69 and the full model with control variable in Table 70. This corresponds to the predictions of Socioemotional Selectivity Theory, according to which older employees have less but more intense relationships.

Additionally, the full model without control variable and the full model with control variable show that the average quality of new relationship is slightly lower for older employees. However, the significance of this relationship is only weak. Hence hypothesis 1a is not supported. Hypothesis 1b is partly supported.

5.6.1.2.2. Gender

The partial model shows weak significant effects for gender, according to which women have a lower share of old ties (ShareOldTies), indicating that they have a more balanced portfolio of old and new relationships than men. Also, the partial model shows some weaker average strength of relationships (AvStrenNew) for women than for men.

However, the full model without control variables in Table 69 shows significant lower levels for the share of frequency (ShareOldFreq), the share of importance (ShareOldImp) as well as the share of strength of cooperation (ShareOldStren) for women. This indicates that female gender has covariance with a variable, which is correlated to cooperation. The correlation matrix in Table 67 shows that women mostly are working in lower ranks than men. As rank is positively related to cooperation, the consideration of rank in the full model without control variables reveals positive effects of female gender on cooperation.

The full model with control variables reveals even stronger effects: Women have more new relationships (NumNewTies), a higher frequency (SumFreqNew), importance (ImpFreqNew) and strength (StrenFreqNew) of new relationships. The full model confirms that the share of old ties (ShareOldTies) and thus the share of strength of old relationships (ShareOldStren) is lower. At the same time, women's relationships with new colleagues are of lower average frequency (AvFreqNew) and lower strength (AvStrenNew) than men's relationships. Women also have a higher difference in quality of old and new relationships (DelAvQual). Seemingly, they get along better with colleagues from their old company.

Two things are remarkable about these findings: First, the effects of the full model are stronger after controlling for structural cooperation requirements. When not controlling for structural cooperation requirements, women show that they have a more balanced relationship portfolio and that the cooperation frequency, cooperation importance as well as cooperation strength with colleagues from the old and from the new firm is more balanced. This indicates that women are less biased in cooperating with new colleagues. However, after controlling for structural cooperation requirements, it shows that not only the relative share of cooperation with new colleagues is higher for women but also the absolute value of ties, frequency and strength. This indicates that women predominantly work in departments that cooperate less with new departments. Therefore, the absolute effects show only after controlling for structural cooperation requirements.

Second, these findings are not supporting hypothesis 2. Obviously, there are gender differences in cooperation after mergers and acquisitions: Women cooperate differently than men after controlling for structural cooperation requirements. Women have more and at the same time on the average weaker relationships with new colleagues.

5.6.1.2.3. Education level

The partial model shows that employees with higher education have more relationships to new colleagues (NumNewTies). At the same time, their relationship portfolio is more balanced (ShareOldTies), i.e. they have a lower share of old ties in their relationship portfolio. Their share of frequency (ShareOldFreq), importance (ShareOldImp) and strength (ShareOldStren) of cooperation with old colleagues is lower.

In the full model without control variable some of the effects found in the partial model drop below the significance level. Obviously, covariance with other variables is responsible for the effects in the partial model. Looking at the correlation matrix in Table 67, rank can be identified as variable, which has a strong effect on cooperation and at the same time is highly correlated with education level. Rank thus creates a spurious effect in the partial model, which vanishes in the full models. Hence only little of the effects of education level on cooperation are independent of other variables.

The full model with control variable shows inverse effects of education: After controlling for structural cooperation requirements, education level shows negative effects on cooperation: Higher education leads to less new ties (NumNewTies), lower frequency (SumNewFreq), lower assigned importance (SumNewImp) as well as lower strength (SumNewStren) of new relationships. The average frequency of cooperation relationships (AvFreqNew) with new colleagues is lower. Obviously, there are some departments with highly educated employees with high cooperation requirements as described in Illustration 37 in case IV. Hence hypothesis 3a is not supported.

5.6.2. Firm related characteristics

Two different firm related characteristics of employees have been investigated: rank and seniority, respectively time spent in the current function. In the following table, all postulated hypotheses concerning these characteristics are listed:

Hypothesis 4a:	Higher ranked employees cooperate more with new colleagues
Hypothesis 4b:	Higher ranked employees are more committed than lower ranked employees
Hypothesis 4c:	Higher ranked employees feel less uncertain than lower ranked employees
Hypothesis 5a:	The longer an employee work for a company, the less this employee cooperates with new colleagues
Hypothesis 5b:	Higher seniority of employees reduces commitment
Hypothesis 5c:	Higher seniority increases uncertainty

Table 74: Hypotheses concerning demographic characteristics of employees

5.6.2.1. Dependent variables: Commitment and uncertainty

In the following table, the effects of firm related characteristics on commitment and uncertainty are presented:

Independent variable: Firm related characteristics		
	Commitment	Uncertainty
Standardized Beta		
Firm related characteristics		
Rank	.103*	-.179****
TimeInFunction	.037	.034
Model statistics		
Total df	241	250
R^2	.013	.031
Adjusted R^2	.005	.023
F	1.615	3.954

**** Significant at a 0.01-level (2-sided)
*** Significant at a 0.05-level (2-sided)
** Significant at a 0.10-level (2-sided)
* Significant at a 0.15-level (2-sided)
Note: Pairwise exclusion of incomplete cases

Table 75: Partial model of effects of firm related characteristics on commitment and uncertainty

The partial model in Table 75 shows a significant effect of rank on commitment. The full model in Table 68, however, does not show this effect. Obviously, rank has covariance with other variables, which have significant effects on commitment. The correlation matrix in Table 67 shows that rank is significantly correlated with age and the degree of feeling informed (InformationAgg). Hence the positive effect of rank on commitment in the partial model can be a spurious effect caused by the covariance of commitment with these two other independent variables. Hypothesis 4b is only partly supported.

According to the partial model in Table 75, rank has a negative effect on uncertainty. This finding is supported by the full model in Table 68. Hence hypothesis 4c is fully supported. Higher ranked employees feel less uncertain.

At the same time, seniority (TimeInFunction) does not have an effect on commitment. Hypotheses 5b, according to which higher identity with the old firm of more senior employees should lead to lower commitment is not supported. The finding is supported by the full model. Also, seniority does not have an effect on uncertainty. Again, the full model supports this finding. Hypotheses 5b and 5c thus are not supported.

5.6.2.2. Dependent variables: Cooperation

In Table 76, the partial models of the effects of firm related characteristics on cooperation are listed. Firm related characteristics comprise rank and seniority, measured as time spent in a function. In the following paragraphs, effects of each of these independent variables will be discussed.

5.6.2.2.1. Rank

Rank shows very strong positive effects on cooperation with new colleagues. Higher ranked employees have more new ties (NumNewTies) and a more balanced relationship portfolio (ShareOldTies). As a consequence, the frequency of cooperation (SumFreqNew), the importance of cooperation (SumImpNew) and the strength of cooperation (SumStrenNew) are higher for employees in higher ranks. In addition to that, the share of frequency of cooperation (ShareOldFreq), importance of cooperation (ShareOldImp) and the strength of cooperation (ShareOldStren) is lower for higher ranked individuals. It is notable, that higher ranked employees have significantly higher importance in average new relationships, indicating that new colleagues perceive them to be more important. Also, the cooperation quality (DelAvQual) of cooperation relationships with old and new colleagues is more similar for higher ranked employees. The full model without controls in Table 69 and the full model with controls in Table 70 strongly support these findings. Hence hypothesis 4a is strongly supported.

5.6.2.2.2. Seniority

Seniority, however shows strongly negative effects on cooperation with new colleagues. The partial model indicates that more senior employees have less new ties (NumNewTies), they have a lower cooperation frequency (SumFreqNew), assign less importance to new relationships (SumImpNew) and generally have a lower cooperation strength (SumStrenNew) with new colleagues. As a consequence, the relationship portfolio (ShareOldTies) as well as the share of frequency of cooperation (ShareFreqOld), importance of cooperation (ShareImpOld) as well as strength of cooperation (ShareStrenOld) is higher for old colleagues than for new colleagues.

The full model without control variables supports the findings of the partial model. However, the full model with control variable in Table 70 shows somewhat weaker effects than the partial model and the full model without control variables. There is no significant effect on the number of new ties (NumNewTies). As a consequence of that, there is no significant effect on the sum of importance of cooperation with new colleagues (SumImpNew), as well as the strength of cooperation with new colleagues. At the same time, the average frequency of cooperation relationships (AvFreqNew) with new colleagues decreases with increasing seniority.

Obviously, there are departmental structural cooperation requirements according to which more senior employees work predominantly in departments, which have lower cooperation requirements with new colleagues. However, still most of the effects of seniority on cooperation are significant. Therefore, hypothesis 5a is strongly supported.

Independent variable: Firm related characteristics

	NumNewTies	SharedOldties	SumFreqNew	SharedOldFreq	AvFreqNew	DelAvFreq	SumImpNew	SharedOldImp	AvImpNew	DelAvImp	SumStrenNew	SharedOldStren	AvStrenNew	DelAvStren	AVQualNew	DelAvQual
Standardized Beta																
Firm related characteristics																
Rank	.434****	-.404****	.382****	-.384****	-.021	-.129***	.462****	-.409****	.247****	-.202****	.390****	-.385****	.035	-.062	.005	-.156***
TimeInFunction	-.184****	.269****	-.166****	.257****	-.007	.054	-.172****	.273****	-.037	.141***	-.153****	.253****	-.060	.064	-.071	.091
Model statistics																
Total df	278	278	278	278	220	278	278	278	216	278	278	278	216	278	184	179
R²	.192	.194	.150	.176	.001	.017	.213	.200	.059	.050	.153	.175	.004	.006	.005	.027
Adjusted R²	.186	.189	.143	.171	-.009	.010	.207	.194	.050	.043	.147	.169	-.005	-.001	-.006	.016
F	32.820	33.306	23.281	29.576	.060	2.363	37.363	34.448	6.700	7.257	24.874	29.317	.431	.882	.445	2.492

**** Significant at a 0.01-level (2-sided)
*** Significant at a 0.05-level (2-sided)
** Significant at a 0.10-level (2-sided)
* Significant at a 0.15-level (2-sided)

Note: Pairwise exclusion of incomplete cases

Table 76: Partial model with effects of firm related characteristics on different aspects of cooperation

5.6.3. Psychological factors

Two different work related attitudes have been investigated in the research on SoftCo: Task orientation as well as responsiveness. In addition to these attitudes, two possible reactions after mergers and acquisitions have been investigated: commitment and uncertainty. In the following table, the postulated hypotheses are listed:

Hypothesis 6a:	Higher task orientation leads to higher cooperation after mergers and acquisition
Hypothesis 6b:	Task orientation should have no independent effect on uncertainty or commitment
Hypothesis 7:	Higher commitment increases cooperation after mergers and acquisitions
Hypothesis 8:	Higher uncertainty reduces cooperation after mergers and acquisitions

Table 77: Hypotheses concerning demographic characteristics of employees

5.6.3.1. Dependent variables: Commitment and uncertainty

In the following table, the effects of firm related characteristics on commitment and uncertainty are presented:

	Independent variable: Attitudes	
	Commitment	Uncertainty
Standardized Beta		
Attitudes		
Task orientation	.271****	-.278****
Responsiveness	.039	-.039
Model statistics		
Total df	241	250
R^2	.081	.085
Adjusted R^2	.073	.078
F	10.531	11.531

**** Significant at a 0.01-level (2-sided)
*** Significant at a 0.05-level (2-sided)
** Significant at a 0.10-level (2-sided)
* Significant at a 0.15-level (2-sided)
Note: Pairwise exclusion of incomplete cases

Table 78: Partial model of effects of attitudes on commitment and uncertainty

As can be seen, higher task orientation significantly increases commitment and significantly decreases uncertainty after mergers and acquisitions. This contradicts hypothesis 6b, which postulates no significant effect of task orientation on commitment. The full model in Table 68 supports the results of the partial model. It seems that employees, which strongly focus on exactness, precision and error elimination are more committed than other colleagues. Hypothesis 6b is not supported.

There were no specific hypotheses for responsiveness, as the factor resulted from an exploratory factor analysis. Nevertheless, it is interesting to note that responsiveness has no effect on uncertainty and in the full model a slightly positive effect on commitment.

5.6.3.2. Dependent variables: Cooperation

In Table 79, the partial models of the effects of psychological factors on cooperation after mergers and acquisitions are listed. Psychological factors comprise attitudes of employees as well as reactions of employees after mergers and acquisitions. Attitudes comprise task orientation as well as responsiveness. Reactions after mergers and acquisitions comprise commitment as well as uncertainty. In the following paragraphs, effects of each of these independent variables on cooperation will be discussed.

5.6.3.2.1. Task orientation

According to the partial models in Table 79, task orientation has positive effects on the quality of cooperation (AvQualNew). At the same time, task orientation has weak effects on the difference of importance of old and new relationships (DelAvImp). Also, the difference between average strength of cooperation relationships with old and new colleagues (DelAvStren) is slightly smaller for task oriented employees. Seemingly, stronger task orientation lets employees treat relationships with colleagues from the old and the new company as equally important.

Table 79: Partial model with effects of psychological factors on cooperation

	Independent variable: Attitudes and reactions															
	NumNewTies	SharedOldties	SumFreqNew	SharedOldFreq	AvFreqNew	DelAvFreq	SumImpNew	SharedOldImp	AvImpNew	DelAvImp	SumStrenNew	SharedOldStren	AvStrenNew	DelAvStren	AvQualNew	DelAvQual
Standardized Beta																
Attitudes																
Task orientation	.007	.089	.025	.069	.031	-.077	.015	.082	.100	-.105*	.031	.054	.088	-.117*	.170***	-.162***
Responsiveness	-.089	.070	-.092	.078	-.027	.084	-.077	.053	.012	.044	-.091	.066	-.071	.107*	.028	.014
Reaction																
Commitment	.133**	-.142***	.145***	-.155***	.074	-.068	.123**	-.118**	-.133**	.031	.122**	-.120**	-.017	-.017	.448****	-.350***
Uncertainty	-.126**	-.160***	-.132**	.111*	.044	.016	-.141***	.170***	-.088	.153***	-.156***	.123**	-.063	.043	.013	-.115
Model statistics																
Total df	236	236	236	236	192	236	236	236	189	236	236	236	189	236	165	161
R²	.048	.058	.058	.047	.007	.017	.050	.052	.025	.037	.059	.038	.014	.023	.274	.153
Adjusted R²	.032	.042	.042	.031	-.014	.000	.034	.036	.004	.021	.043	.022	-.007	.006	.256	.131
F	2.953	3.586	3.557	2.884	.314	.996	3.062	3.198	1.200	2.252	3.660	2.298	.0668	1.358	15.175	7.073

**** Significant at a 0.01-level (2-sided)
*** Significant at a 0.05-level (2-sided)
** Significant at a 0.10-level (2-sided)
* Significant at a 0.15-level (2-sided)

Note: Pairwise exclusion of incomplete cases

Table 79: Partial model with effects of psychological factors on cooperation

The full model without control variable shows weaker effects. Only the effects of task orientation on cooperation quality persist. Seemingly, there are some independent variables with significant effects on cooperation, which are correlated to task orientation.

The full model with control variable again shows two significant differences to the full model without control variables: Task oriented employees have a lower sum of cooperation frequency (SumFreqNew), of cooperation importance (SumImpNew) and of cooperation strength (SumStrenNew) than less task oriented employees. Obviously, there are some departments with high structural cooperation requirements, which are predominantly staffed with highly task oriented employees. The findings of the full models without control variable and the finding of the full models with control variable thus show mixed findings for the effect of task orientation. The findings for hypothesis 6a are mixed. Hence hypothesis 6a is not supported.

5.6.3.2.2. Responsiveness

Responsiveness only shows a weak positive effect on the difference of average strength of cooperation relationships (DelAvStren) with old and new colleagues. This indicates that more responsive employees have on the average stronger cooperation relationships with their old colleagues.

However, in the full model without control variable, responsiveness shows negative effects on the number of new relationships (NumNewTies), the sum of cooperation frequency (SumFreqNew), the sum of cooperation importance (SumImpNew) as well as the sum of cooperation strength (SumStrenNew). At the same time, the old cooperation relationships dominate the relationship portfolio (ShareOldTies) as well as the shares of old ties of the cooperation frequency (ShareOldFreq), of cooperation importance (ShareOldImp) and of cooperation strength (ShareOldStren).

In the full model with control variable, the effects for responsiveness change strongly compared to the full model without control variable. The number of new ties (NumNewTies), the sum of frequency (SumFreqNew), of importance (SumImpNew) and of strength (SumStrenNew) with new colleagues drops below the level of significance. At the same time, the share of old ties is lower for the number of ties (ShareOldTies), the cooperation frequency (ShareOldFreq), the cooperation importance and the cooperation strength (ShareOldStren), which is opposite to the findings in the full model without control variable.

This finding indicates that responsiveness actually has a positive effect on cooperation, however, highly responsive employees are predominantly working in departments with low cooperation requirements.

5.6.3.2.3. Commitment

In the partial model, commitment shows very strong positive effects on cooperation with new colleagues. Almost every measure for cooperation with new colleagues shows a positive relationship. The full model without control variables confirms this finding. Only the share of importance of old relationships (ShareOldImp) and the average importance of new relationships (AvImpNew) drop below the significant level.

At the same time, the full model with control variables shows no independent effect of commitment on cooperation except for cooperation quality. This indicates that departments with high cooperation requirements are predominantly staffed with highly committed employees. Seemingly, employees who work in departments, which cooperate strongly with new colleagues, perceive the changes of the organizational culture after the M&A-transaction as more positive than their employees in departments, which cooperate less. The same employees are happy to work for the rest of their lives at SoftCo and perceive that their work is more fun since the M&A-transaction. These findings raise the question, whether commitment is an independent variable or a dependent variable. The findings will be discussed later in detail. As commitment has strong and persistent effects on cooperation quality in the full model with control variable, hypothesis 7 is nevertheless strongly supported.

5.6.3.2.4. Uncertainty

In the partial model, uncertainty shows very strong negative effects on cooperation with new colleagues. Almost every measure for cooperation with new colleagues shows a negative relationship.

In the full model without control variable, many of these effects vanish. The effects of uncertainty on the number of new ties (NumNewTies), the sum of frequency of cooperation (SumFreqNew), the sum of importance of cooperation (SumImpNew) with new colleagues drop below the significance level. Also, the effects of uncertainty on the share of old ties (ShareOldTies) and the share of frequency of cooperation with old colleagues (ShareOldFreq) drop below the significance level. This indicates that uncertainty covaries with other independent variables, which have a stable effect on cooperation. In Table 67, uncertainty shows a negative correlation with the degree of perceived information (InformationAgg). At the same time, the degree of perceived information shows a negative effect on cooperation. Other independent variables are either positively correlated with uncertainty and negatively correlated with cooperation or vice versa, which creates a spurious negative correlation of uncertainty on cooperation in the partial model. In the full model, the spurious correlation vanishes and uncertainty shows a null effect. Hence the strong effect of uncertainty is an artifact of covariance with other variables. This finding is supported by the full model with control variable. In this model, uncertainty hardly shows any effect on cooperation. Hence hypothesis 8 is only partly supported.

5.6.4. Integration measures

Two different types of integration measures have been considered: First, the effects of communication, i.e. the feeling informed and second participation in active integration measures. Active integration measures comprise for example exchanges of employees between different locations, mutual visits of employees in mirror departments and integration trainings. The effects of these independent variables on psychological reactions of employees as well as on cooperation of employees has been investigated.

In the following table, the hypothesized effects are listed:

Hypothesis 9a:	A high degree of feeling informed increases commitment of employees
Hypothesis 9b:	A high degree of feeling informed decreases uncertainty of employees
Hypothesis 10a:	Participation in active integration measures increases cooperation with new colleagues
Hypothesis 10b:	Participation in active integration measures increases commitment of employees
Hypothesis 10c:	Participation in active integration measures decreases uncertainty of employees

Table 80: Hypotheses concerning integration measures

5.6.4.1. Dependent variables: Commitment and uncertainty

In the following table, the effects of the degree of feeling informed and of participation in integration measures on psychological reactions are presented:

Independent variable: Integration measures		
	Commitment	Uncertainty
Standardized Beta		
Integration measures		
InformationAgg	.431****	-.179***
SumIntegration	.012	.006
Model statistics		
Total df	211	213
R^2	.189	.032
Adjusted R^2	.181	.022
F	24.328	3.439

**** Significant at a 0.01-level (2-sided)
*** Significant at a 0.05-level (2-sided)
** Significant at a 0.10-level (2-sided)
* Significant at a 0.15-level (2-sided)
Note: Pairwise exclusion of incomplete cases

Table 81: Partial model of effects of integration measures on commitment and uncertainty

The partial model indicates that feeling informed (InformationAgg) increases the commitment and reduces uncertainty of employees significantly. This finding is supported by the full model in Table 68. Hence hypotheses 9a and 9b are strongly supported.

At the same time, participation in integration measures (SumIntegration) have neither in the partial nor in the full model an independent effect on commitment and uncertainty. While participation in integration measures shows a positive and significant correlation with commitment in Table 67, the effect vanishes in the partial model if the degree of feeling informed is considered as well. This indicates that integration measures increase the degree of feeling informed and thereby have a positive effect on commitment. However, the spurious effect vanishes in the partial model when participation and the degree of feeling informed are considered jointly. Hence hypotheses 10b and 10c are not confirmed.

5.6.4.2. Dependent variables: Cooperation

In Table 82, the partial models of the effects of integration measures on cooperation after mergers and acquisitions are listed. Integration measures comprise information, i.e. the degree of feeling informed and participation in active integration measures. In the following paragraphs, effects of each of these independent variables on cooperation will be discussed.

Independent variable: Integration measures

	NumNewTies	ShareOldTies	SumFreqNew	ShareOldFreq	AvFreqNew	DelAvFreq	SumImpNew	ShareOldImp	AvImpNew	DelAvImp	SumStrenNew	ShareOldStren	AvStrenNew	DelAvStren	AvQualiNew	DelAvQual
Standardized Beta																
Integration measures																
InformationAgg	.069	-.109**	.023	-.098*	-.181****	-.039	.056	-.077	-.190***	-.023	.009	-.071	-.197***	-.029	.256****	-.115
SumIntegration	.297****	-.284****	.323****	-.313****	.265****	-.139****	.302****	-.314****	.167**	-.252****	.321****	-.331****	.193****	-.237****	.068	-.019
Model statistics																
Total df	226	226	226	226	179	226	226	226	175	226	226	226	175	226	152	147
R²	.104	.109	.109	.124	.077	.110	.104	.118	.047	.067	.105	.127	.055	.061	.080	.015
Adjusted R²	.096	.101	.101	.117	.067	.102	.096	.110	.036	.059	.097	.120	.044	.053	.067	.001
F	12.988	13.752	13.709	15.924	7.378	13.818	12.974	14.961	4.245	8.057	13.115	16.367	5.075	7.264	6.500	1.093

**** Significant at a 0.01-level (2-sided)   ** Significant at a 0.10-level (2-sided)
*** Significant at a 0.05-level (2-sided)   * Significant at a 0.15-level (2-sided)

Note: Pairwise exclusion of incomplete cases

Table 82: Partial model with effects of integration measures on different aspects of cooperation

5.6.4.2.1. Degree of feeling informed

The partial model shows that feeling informed (InformationAgg) leads to a more balanced relationship portfolio with a higher share of new relationships and a higher share of cooperation frequency with new colleagues. Also, employees who feel better informed have a higher average cooperation quality (AvQualNew) with new colleagues. At the same time, the average frequency of cooperation relationships of well informed employees with new colleagues (AvFreqNew) is significantly lower than for employees who feel not as well informed. The same is true for the average importance of new relationships.

In the full model without control variable, the effects change: The effects of information on the share of old ties (ShareOldTies) and the share of frequency of cooperation with old colleagues (ShareOldFreq) are no longer significant. At the same time, the degree of feeling informed decreases the sum of cooperation frequency (SumFreqNew) with new colleagues and the sum of strength of cooperation (SumStrenNew) with new colleagues. The quality of cooperation relationships with new colleagues (AvQualNew) is no longer higher for well informed employees. Hence the full model without control variable shows effects opposite to the postulated effects. Covariance with other independent variables thus strongly influences the effects of information on cooperation in the partial model. Hence the findings for hypothesis 10a show mixed results.

Obviously, there are departments, in which employees feel very well informed, which have lower structural cooperation requirements than others. At the same time, employees in departments, which have strong cooperation requirements, feel poorly informed. Again, this finding bears the question, whether the degree of feeling informed is a dependent or an independent variable. This question will be discussed later.

5.6.4.2.2. Participation in integration measures

Participation in integration measures shows strongly significant effects on cooperation with new colleagues. Employees that participate in active cooperation measures have a higher number of new relationships (NumNewTies), a more balanced relationship portfolio with a lower share of old ties (ShareOldTies), the cooperation frequency with new colleagues is higher (SumFreqNew), the share of frequency with new colleagues is higher (ShareOldFreq) and the average cooperation frequency of relationships with new colleagues (AvFreqNew) is higher. The same is true for cooperation importance as well as cooperation strength. Only cooperation quality is not affected by integration measures. These results are fully supported by the full model without control variables and the full model with control variables. Hence hypothesis 10c is fully supported.

5.6.5. Structural cooperation requirements

Structural cooperation requirements have a very strong effect on cooperation of employees. While some of this effect is surely caused by the covariance problem, the high strength of the effect indicates that employees in a department have similar cooperation requirements, and these similar cooperation requirements are caused by structural and not by individual effects. Thus hypothesis 11 is strongly supported.

As can be seen, structural cooperation requirements not only have a strong effect on cooperation, they also constitute a meaningful control variable for the ANOVA-analyses. As the many examples show, there are significant differences of effects of independent variables on cooperation between the full model without control variable and the full model with control variable. The differences have face validity. This further supports the validity of the control variable and thus can be seen as a proof of quality of the measure.

5.6.6. Summary of results

In the following tables, the results presented above are summarized. For each hypothesis, the number of the hypothesis, the independent and the dependent variable are indicated. Also, the direction of the expected effect is indicated.

In Table 48 and Table 84, the results for the regression analyses to determine the effects of the independent variables on commitment and uncertainty of employees are presented for both the partial and the full model. Three possible results are possible:

- Supported: Indicates a significant statistical support for the hypothesized effect
- Not supported: Indicates a non-significant effect
- Opposite: Indicates a significant statistical effect opposite to the hypothesized effect.

The total evaluation then indicates whether the results of the partial and the full model both show support (=supported), one shows support, one shows no support (= partly supported), one shows support and one shows the opposite of the postulated effect (= mixed) and one or both show the opposite of the postulated effect (= opposite).

In Table 48, the summary for the factors influencing commitment is presented. Only gender, rank as well as the degree of feeling informed show the expected results. All other variables do not show significant results, respectively show effects, which have not been expected:

- Age has an effect on commitment opposite to the postulated effect. Older employees are especially committed to the merged firm.
- Seniority has no significant effect on commitment.
- Task orientation shows a significant positive effect on commitment. While there were no hypotheses postulated for the effects of responsiveness, it is notable, that responsiveness similarly shows a significant positive effect on commitment.

- Participation in integration measures has no significant effect on commitment.

Hence age, as well as rank, task orientation and the degree of feeling informed have a significant effect on commitment. The other variables, however, have no significant effect.

Hypo-thesis	Independent variable	Dependent variable	Expected effect	Partial model	Full model	Total
1c	Age	Commitment	-	Opposite	Opposite	Opposite
2	Gender	Commitment	0	Supp.	Supp.	Supp.
4b	Rank	Commitment	+	Supp.	Not supp.	Partly supp.
5b	Seniority	Commitment	-	Not supp.	Not supp.	Not supp.
6b	Task orientation	Commitment	0	Not supp.	Not supp.	Not supp.
9a	Degree of feeling informed	Commitment	+	Supp.	Supp.	Supp.
10b	Integration measures	Commitment	+	Not supp.	Not supp.	Not supp.

Supported
Not supp.
Opposite

Table 83: Summary of factors influencing commitment at SoftCo

In Table 84, the summary for the factors influencing uncertainty after the M&A-transaction at SoftCo is presented. Gender, as well as education level, rank and the degree of feeling informed show effects as predicted in the hypotheses in the second chapter of this work. However, the other variables do not show significant results, respectively show effects, which have not been expected:

- Age has no significant effect on uncertainty. None of the rival hypothesis is supported by the data.
- Seniority has no significant effect on uncertainty. The predictions derived from Social Identity Theory did not hold.
- Task orientation has a significant negative effect on uncertainty. Highly task oriented employees feel less uncertain than employees with low task orientation. Responsiveness shows no significant effect on uncertainty.
- Participation in integration measures has no significant effect on uncertainty.

Hypo-thesis	Independent variable	Dependent variable	Expected effect	Partial model	Full model	Total
1c.1	Age	Uncertainty	-	Not supp.	Not supp.	Not supp.
1c.2	Age	Uncertainty	+	Not supp.	Not supp.	Not supp.
2	Gender	Uncertainty	0	Supp.	Supp.	Supp.
3b	Education level	Uncertainty	-	Supp.	Supp.	Supp.
4c	Rank	Uncertainty	-	Supp.	Supp.	Supp.
5c	Seniority	Uncertainty	+	Not supp.	Not supp.	Not supp.
6b	Task orientation	Uncertainty	0	Not supp.	Not supp.	Not supp.
9b	Degree of feeling informed	Uncertainty	-	Supp.	Supp.	Supp.
10c	Integration measures	Uncertainty	-	Not supp.	Not supp.	Not supp.

Supported
Not supp.
Opposite

Table 84: Summary of factors influencing uncertainty at SoftCo

The degree of feeling informed thus reduces dysfunctional reactions to mergers and acquisitions. On the one hand, it increases commitment and on the other hand, it reduces uncertainty. Hence negative reactions after mergers and acquisitions can be reduced with the help of effective communication.

In Table 50, the results for the effects of the independent variables on cooperation are presented. Cooperation has been operationalized with a number of different variables. Therefore, in Table 50, a number of different evaluations for the partial and the full model are used to describe the effects of the independent variables on cooperation:
- Strongly supported: Most of the regression analyses for the different variables of cooperation support the hypothesis
- Partly supported: Some of the regression analyses support the hypothesis
- Not supported: The results of the regression analyses do not support the hypothesis
- Mixed: The regression analyses yield some results supporting the hypothesis and other results that are opposite to the hypothesized effects
- Opposite: The regression analyses yield results that are opposite to the hypothesized effects

Looking at the effects of demographic characteristics on cooperation, there are two remarkable findings. First, age has no significant effect on cooperation intensity, while at the same time yielding more intensive average cooperation relationships. Second, gender does have an effect on cooperation intensity: Women cooperate significantly more intensive with new colleagues than their male colleagues.

At the same time, education level shows mixed findings on cooperation intensity. In the partial model, education level shows a partial positive effect on cooperation intensity. However, in the full model without control, the effect vanishes, indicating a spurious correlation in the partial model caused by another independent variable. The full model with control then even indicates an opposite effect, indicating that some of the departments with high cooperation requirements mainly consist of employees with a higher education level.

Rank and seniority show the postulated effects. While higher rank has a positive effect on cooperation, seniority has a negative effect on cooperation.

The null effect for task orientation is not supported. Task orientation shows a While task orientation has no effect on number of cooperation relationships, frequency of cooperation, nor on importance of cooperation, it has a positive effect on quality of cooperation: Highly task oriented employees have a significantly higher cooperation quality with new colleagues.

Responsiveness, however, shows mixed results: In the partial model, there are no effects of responsiveness, it shows negative effects on cooperation in the full model without control variable and positive effect on the full model with control variable.

Commitment and uncertainty show significant effects on cooperation intensity. It is noteworthy, that the effects of commitment and uncertainty are very strong in the partial model. However, in the full model without control variables, the effects are much weaker, indicating that commitment and uncertainty strongly depend on other independent variables as discussed above. In the full model with control variables, the effects completely vanish except for a significant positive effect of commitment on quality of cooperation.

Integration measures yield very strong effects on cooperation intensity. Integration measures thus can be used as effective measure to initiate cooperation wherever it is necessary. At the same time, information even yields a negative effect on cooperation intensity. Mainly, well informed employees have much more intense relationships with old colleagues than with new colleagues.

Last but no least, structural cooperation requirements show very strong effects on cooperation intensity of individuals. In line with hypothesis 11, cooperation intensity to a large extent depends on structure and to a smaller extent depends on individual characteristics.

Hypo-thesis	Independent variable	Dependent variable	Expected effect	Partial model	Full model w/o control	Full model with control	Total
1a	Age	Cooperation intensity	-	Not supp.	Not supp.	Not supp.	Not supp.
1b	Age	Avr. intensity of ties	+	Partly supp.	Partly supp.	Partly supp.	Partly supp.
2	Gender	Cooperation intensity	0	Partly supp.	Not supp.	Not supp.	Not supp.
3a	Education level	Cooperation intensity	+	Partly supp.	Not supp.	Opposite	Mixed
4a	Rank	Cooperation intensity	+	Strongly supp.	Strongly supp.	Strongly supp.	Strongly supp.
5a	Seniority	Cooperation intensity	-	Strongly supp.	Strongly supp.	Strongly supp.	Strongly supp.
6a	Task orientation	Cooperation intensity	+	Partly supp.	Partly supp.	Mixed	Mixed
7	Commitment	Cooperation intensity	+	Strongly supp.	Strongly supp.	Partly supp.	Partly supp.
8	Uncertainty	Cooperation intensity	-	Strongly supp.	Partly supp.	Not supp.	Partly supp.
10a	Integration measures	Cooperation intensity	+	Strongly supp.	Strongly supp.	Strongly supp.	Strongly supp.
11	Structural requirements	Cooperation intensity	+			Strongly supp.	Strongly supp.

Supported
Not supp.
Opposite

Table 85: Summary of factors influencing cooperation at SoftCo

Obviously, factors that are influenced by isomorphic forces such as the firm's structure or by management measures show the strongest effects: rank and structural cooperation requirements are determined by the firm's structure. Management measures are responsible for participation in integration measures as well as the amount of information available in the firm.

Other factors such as age, education level as well as work related attitudes show no effect or mixed effects. There are only three factors affecting cooperation consistently, which are non-structural and non-management initiated: Gender, seniority, as well as task orientation. Women cooperate more intensively. More senior employees cooperate less. Highly task oriented employees have a higher cooperation quality.

5.7. Methodological limitations

Many of the conceptual limitations of the research at SpecMatCo listed in 4.9 have been considered in the research at SoftCo. The use of a full dyadic network analysis eliminated the problems, which were generated by the ego-centered network analysis at SpecMatCo:

- The sample contains 282 respondents. Bortz's (1999) rule of thumb that the number of independent variables should not exceed a tenth of the number of investigated cases is fulfilled for all models.

- The sample is well balanced concerning the participation of women. 112 respondents, corresponding to 40% of the respondents are female. Hence the validity of gender effects is secured.
- There is a high variance of participation in integration measures. Only some 50% of the respondents participated in one or more integration measures.
- The key informant problem does no longer exist. Department level variables have been operationalized with the help of aggregate measures. As a consequence, they do not suffer from key informant biases.
- Instead of single item measurement, attitudes and reactions have been operationalized with the help of several items each.
- The respondent bias in evaluating cooperation has been eliminated by the use of indegree relationships only. The cooperation of an actor i has been measured based on all cooperation relationships that other actors indicated to have with actor i.

However, there still are some methodological limitations, which need to be considered in order to qualify the later discussion of the results:

A first methodological limitation is the focus on one research site. Firm level variables cannot be considered quantitatively. That means that structural aspects or characteristics of the M&A-transaction can only be considered qualitatively. For example, effects of hostility or friendliness of a takeover on cooperation of employees cannot be investigated based on the research design of this study.

A second methodological limitation is the use of the top down electronic questionnaire. The use of a new data gathering approach always bears the risk of tool-related biases, which cannot be qualified due to the lack of experiences with the tool. A first problem related to the top-down approach of the electronic questionnaire is the required knowledge of the organizational structure. In the exploratory interviews, it showed that a small number of respondents did not properly know the organizational structure. These respondents thus struggled to find their cooperation partners, because they did not know the departments, in which their cooperation partners works. While the advantages of the electronic questionnaire in handling and its reduced complexity dominate, it needs to be noticed that a small number of relationships might not have been indicated because employees were unable to identify their cooperation partners.

This problem, however, is not considered to be very severe in the present case. The organizational structure under consideration was relatively small and simple. Hence most respondents should have been able to exhaustively identify their cooperation partners and indicate their cooperation relationships. Also, the exploratory interviews showed very few problems but hardly any failures. Hence the first usage of the electronic questionnaire should not have generated any specific biases of the gathered data.

A third methodological limitation, which needs to be considered in the discussion is the computation of the control variable. As has been mentioned several times, the use of a department-level control variable, which is based on aggregate dyadic-level measures, bears a number of important limitations for this research. In order to limit the covariance problem, only departments with four or more employees have been considered. This, however, produces a bias favoring larger departments in the analysis, because small departments are excluded.

Nevertheless, most departments have a significantly high level of diversity concerning the independent characteristics. Data of employees of a few departments might suffer from the covariance problem, however, most of the departments are sufficiently diverse. Also, in analyzing the data, the respective models always have been computed with and without control variable. Hence the effects of covariance of the control variable can be interpreted.

A fourth limitation of the research design is the factor analytic approach for the independent variables task orientation, responsiveness, commitment and uncertainty. While most items of the factors have been identified conceptually and confirmed in a confirmatory factor analysis some items have been identified in an exploratory factor analysis. This, however, implies a lack of theoretical foundation of the factors. The problem is especially virulent in the case of work attitudes, which represent new constructs that have not been investigated in previous studies. Some of the items have been validated by previous research. However, others have been determined based on exploratory interviews.

Last but not least, the differentiation between old and new relationships bears some methodological risks. As has been described, the research design corresponds to a pre-experimental design, which, due to its specific research question can be used to simulate a longitudinal study. Hence relationships of two different types have been gathered: Old relationships and new relationships. It is assumed that old relationships are relationships between employees within one of the previously separated firms. New relationships are relationships between employees of previously separated firms. However, it is not known, when the relationships have been formed. As a consequence, it is possible that an "old" relationship is younger than a "new" relationship. Also, within the new relationships, there might be relationships of different age. As described above, SoftCo has been integrated incrementally over a longer period of time. The integration process at the time of the research was still continuing. This, however, means that over time, more and more employees start to cooperate. Some of the new cooperation relationships thus might date back to the early phases of the integration while other new cooperation relationships are very recent.

A second, more conceptual problem is that there are different findings for old and for new relationships. As has been said, there are at least two different explanations for the findings:

First, the formation of a relationship is a dynamic process. Mature relationships therefore follow different mechanisms than new relationships. The exact mechanisms that affect intermediary stages of relationships need to be investigated in future research. A second explanation, however, might be that firm level variables or specific characteristics of the M&A-transaction are responsible for the differences between old and new relationships. In the course of this study, it cannot be clarified, to what extent either one or the other explanation apply.

Further longitudinal research on cooperation relationships is required to identify whether the differences of old and new relationships are the consequence of supra-individual variables, such as characteristics of the M&A-transaction, or whether there are different phases in the life of a relationship from initiation to maturation to termination.

5.8. "Who cooperates with whom?" Operationalization of hypotheses 12 to 22

The answer to the question "who cooperates with whom?" aims to find factors that affect the existence and the cooperation between two actors within the merged firm. As this research focuses on the new cooperation relationships after an M&A-transaction, I solely focus on relationships between employees that were not in the same firm before the M&A-transaction. Asking the question "who cooperates with whom?" additionally implies that the unit of analysis is no longer an individual but a pair of individuals. The dependent constructs as well as the independent constructs therefore are on the level of the dyad.

The control variables capture situational and structural effects that directly influence the existence and the strength of a relationship.

5.8.1. Sample of relevant relationships

As indicated above, a total of 377 employees were working regularly in the merged division at the time of the investigation. Of these 377 employees, 11 top managers were interviewed and not asked to fill out the questionnaire. That means that the questionnaire was sent to 366 employees. Of these 366 employees, 282 employees returned the questionnaire. That corresponds to a response rate of 77 %. Thereof, 272 employees provided information about the cooperation relationships they maintain within the merged firm, corresponding to a response rate of 74% of the interrogated employees.

A total of 7,029 relationships was indicated by 272 employees. Respondents could indicate relationships to all 377 employees in the merged division, except themselves. Hence the maximum theoretical number of relationships of the sample is 102,272. This means that 6.9 % of all possible relationships have been indicated and described. Roughly 81 % of all indicated relationships are amongst colleagues of the formerly separated firms, 19% with new colleagues.

In order to test similarity of relationship partners, however, it is only possible to consider the relationships between employees that provided personal information. That means that only relationships of the 272 employees, who indicated cooperation relationships to the 282 employees, who returned the questionnaire can be considered. This limits the maximum theoretical number of relationships to 76,432. The number of relationships indicated by the 272 employees to these 282 employees is 5,164. This means that 6.8 % of all possible relationships in the relevant sample have been indicated. Roughly 82 % of all relevant relationships are amongst colleagues of the formerly separated firms, 18 % with new colleagues.

In order to test homophily in newly formed relationships, only new relationships can be considered. That means that all relationships that are formed amongst employees of one of the three merged firms are not considered. 137 employees of the first firm indicated relationships. 146 employees of the first firm returned the questionnaire. 82 employees of the second firm indicated relationships. 83 employees of the second firm returned the questionnaire. 53 employees of the third firm indicated relationships and returned the questionnaire.

Amongst these employees of the different firms, 909 relationships were indicated of a theoretical maximum of 47,087 relationships. That means that only 1.9% of the possible relationships of the relevant sample were indicated.

Based on the indicated shares of old and new relationships in the full sample and the relevant sample, it can be assumed that there is no relevant systematic distortion by using the subsample for the test of homophily. Illustration 40 shows the construction of the subsample used for the test of homophily:

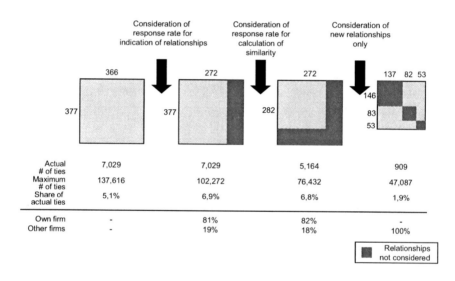

Illustration 40: Formation of the sample of relationships to test homophily

5.8.2. Dependent construct

As has been described above, actors are assumed to prefer cooperating with other actors that are similar to themselves. The principle of homophily states that similarity of actors should be positively related to both, existence as well as strength of cooperation relationships. Therefore, I will examine two dependent variables: The existence of ties as well as the strength of cooperation within existing ties.

5.8.2.1. Existence of ties

The basic characteristic of a relationship between two actors is its existence or non-existence. Between each two employees i and j of the merged firm, there is a relationship. However, only some of these relationships exist. As has been described above, in the sample of relevant relationships, there are 48,512 potential relationships. 909 of them were indicated by the respondents. It is assumed that all relationships that have not been measured do not exist. Each relationship that exists between any two actors in the sample is coded with 1, relationships that do not exist are coded with 0.
A relationship between two employees i and j is defined as relationship indicated by employee j to employee i.

5.8.2.2. Frequency of existing ties

For existing ties, respondents indicated the frequency of cooperation of that relationship. Frequency was measured with the help of a five-point scale with 1 = once per month, 2 = one per week, 3 = several times per week, 4 = daily, and 5 = several times per day. Accordingly, frequency is coded with values between 1 to 5.
It is important to note that only existing ties were considered. The sample of existing ties contains 909 relationships. The frequency thus never takes the value 0.

5.8.2.3. Importance of existing ties

For each tie, respondents indicated the importance of that relationship. Based on a five-point scale, they indicated the importance with 1 = not important and 5 = very important.
Again, only existing ties were considered. The sample of existing ties contains 909 relationships.

5.8.2.4. Strength of existing ties

According to the definition for the strength of a relationship given above, strength is calculated as product of frequency and importance of a relationship.
The effect of homophily on strength of relationships is only considered within the sample of 909 existing ties. That means that for these ties, strength is coded between 1 (minimal strength) and 25 (maximal strength).

5.8.3. Independent constructs: Similarity

The principle of homophily states that similarity between individuals increases the likelihood of a relationship between them, respectively the strength of that relationship.
There are three different types of similarity considered in this research. A first type of similarity considers similarities in demographic characteristics of employees. A second type of similarity considers similarities in firm related characteristics of individuals. A third type of similarity considers attitudes and reactions of the employees on the merger transaction.

5.8.3.1. Demographic similarities

The measurement of demographic similarity between two individuals in a dyad is based on similarity of age, gender, education level and education content.

Age similarity. Each respondent i indicated her age on a four point scale, each point representing an age range. 1 corresponds to 20 – 29 years, 2 corresponds to 30 – 39 years, 3 corresponds to 40 to 49 years and 4 corresponds to 50 and more years of age of respondents. Age similarity of an actor i and an actor j is simply calculated as the difference between indicated age ranges of these actors:

Formula 18: AgeSimilarity

$$AgeSimilarity_{ij} = -|Age_i - Age_j|, \text{ for each i, j in the relevant set of actors.}$$

Hence, *AgeSimilarity* is coded negatively. The highest possible value for *AgeSimilarity* is 0, the lowest possible value for *AgeSimilarity* is -3.

Gender similarity. Relationships can exist between employees of same or differing gender. GenderSimilarity for relationships between individuals of the same gender is coded 0, for individuals of differing gender, it is coded -1.

Education level. There are five different levels of highest education degree considered in the present research. Level 1 = Secondary school degree, 2 = completed apprenticeship, 3 = studies, 4 = accomplished studies and 5 = doctoral degree. The similarity of education level of two actors i and j is computed as:

Formula 19: EducationLevelSimilarity

$$EducationLevelSimilarity_{ij} = -|EducationLevel_i - EducationLevel_j|, \text{ for each } i, j \text{ in the relevant set of actors.}$$

Education content similarity. In addition to education, respondents indicated the main content of their education. There were three different education contents that respondents could choose from: "commercial", "technical" and "information and decision sciences". They also could indicate "others" as a fourth option. When partners in a relationship indicated the same of the three, "commercial", "technical", and "informatics", the education content similarity of a relationship was coded as 0, all other combinations were coded as -1.

5.8.3.2. Firm related similarities

Similarly to demographic similarities, firm related similarities are derived from the firm dependent characteristics of employees.

Rank similarity. For each dyad, the similarity of rank is computed. As defined above, there are seven different career levels within the firm. Two individuals have the same rank, if they are on the same level within the organization. Rank similarity is calculated according to the following formula:

Formula 20: EducationLevelSimilarity

$RankSimilarity_{ij} = -|Rank_i - Rank_j|$, for each i, j in the relevant set of actors.

Seniority similarity. The seniority of an individual i is measured as the time in the department. The similarity of seniority of two employees i and j thus is computed as follows:

Formula 21: SenioritySimilarity

$SenioritySimilarity_{ij} = -|Seniority_i - Seniority_j|$, for each i, j in the relevant set of actors.

5.8.3.3. Similarity of psychological reactions of employees

Based on an exploratory and confirmatory factor analysis, four relevant psychological factors have been identified, describing two work attitudes as well as reactions to the M&A-transaction.

For each of the factors, the similarity of two employees can be measured as the absolute value of the difference of their attitude scores according to the following formulas:

Formula 22: TaskOrientationSimilarity

$$TaskOrientationSimilarity_{ij} = -|TaskOrientation_i - TaskOrientation_j|$$, for each i, j in the relevant set of actors.

Formula 23: ResponsivenessSimilarity

$$ResponsivenessSimilarity_{ij} = -|Responsiveness_i - Responsiveness_j|$$, for each i, j in the relevant set of actors.

Formula 24: CommitmentSimilarity

$$CommitmentSimilarity_{ij} = -|Commitment_i - Commitment_j|$$, for each i, j in the relevant set of actors.

Formula 25: UncertaintySimilarity

$$UncertaintySimilarity_{ij} = -|Uncertainty_i - Uncertainty_j|$$, for each i, j in the relevant set of actors.

Based on these definitions of the independent variables, positive correlations of independent and dependent variables signify that with increasing similarity, the probability of existence, respectively the frequency, importance and strength of a relationship increases.

5.8.4. Additional variables

In addition to independent factors that might affect existence and strength of relationships between actors, there are other factors that facilitate the formation of such relationships. A first important factor is the participation in integration measures. A second factor is structural cooperation requirements. Both factors create opportunities respectively obligations for cooperation that are independently of homophily and thus make cooperation more likely.

5.8.4.1. Participation in integration measures

Respondents were asked to indicate different integration measures they participated in. It is assumed that if an individual i participated in an integration measure, it is more likely that between i and another individual j of the new firm a relationship emerges. If both participate in integration measures, it is even more likely that these individuals engage in cooperation. Hence, participation of both relationship partners in integration measures is coded as 2, participation of one partner is coded as 1 and if none of the relationship partners participated in an integration measures, it is coded as 0.

5.8.4.2. Structural cooperation requirements

As has been noted above, cooperation in firms is no deliberate activity. Rather, there are structural cooperation requirements caused by hierarchical structures as well as by process requirements.

In past research, structural cooperation requirements were hardly considered. Mostly, researchers only considered membership within the same main function or department. However, this operationalization only captures hierarchical structures. Cross-functional process-based cooperation requirements are not considered. Therefore, I choose to operationalize structural cooperation requirements based on the aggregate cooperation between departments.

For each dependent variable, there is a different control for structural cooperation requirements: As control for the existence of relationships, the ratio of the number of existing relationships between the departments of an individual i and an individual j divided by the number of the theoretical maximum of relationships between the two departments I and J is calculated:

Formula 26: ControlExistence

$$ControlExistence = \frac{\sum_j \sum_i Existence_{ij}}{\sum_j \sum_i 1},$$ for all $i \neq j$, with i in organizational unit k and all j in organizational unit l, and $Existence_{ij} = 1$ for indicated relationships from j to i and 0 for non-indicated relationships.

The maximum value of this ratio is 1, indicating that every possible relationship between two organizational units exists, and 0, indicating that there is no relationship between two organizational units. The ratio is defined for organizational units l of four employees or more. However, the ratio is defined for all organizational units k, regardless of the size of k. For example, if an organizational unit l of the size 5 indicates cooperation relationships with an organizational unit k of the size 1 (a manager), and 3 of the 5 employees in l indicate a relationship, the variable has the value 0.6. While there is a covariance problem for cases, in which there is either no cooperation between departments or cases, in which there is maximal cooperation between departments, this control measure indicates that for any two employees i of organizational unit k and j of organizational unit l, there is a certain probability that a relationship from j to i exists. For example, for each relationship there is a probability of existence of a certain percentage. If a relationship does not exist, there might be non-structural reasons such as homophily or participation in integration measures that initiated the relationship. If the probability of existence of ties between two employees is very low but a relationship exists, the existence of the relationship represents a strong deviation from the average probability of existence of a relationship. In a regression analysis, this stronger deviation will be reflected in a stronger impact on regression coefficients, which are calculated according to the least square method. Hence the control variable effectively control for structural cooperation requirements.

It is important to note that structural cooperation requirements as operationalized in this research do not reflect formal cooperation requirements as defined by a formal organizational structure such as organizational charts or organizational processes. Rather, it is assumed that formal cooperation requirements within or between two departments are strongly correlated to the actual cooperation between two departments. Hence for each employee, the average cooperation with other employees within the same or within another department can be calculated. This average cooperation is considered as cooperation requirement. Any deviation of this cooperation requirement is assumed to be caused by any of the independent variables.

As a control for the strength of existing relationships, the ratio of the sum of the strength of all relationships and the theoretical maximum strength of relationships between two departments I and J of the two employees i and j is computed:

Formula 27: ControlStrength

$$ControlStrength = \frac{\sum_j \sum_i Strength_{ij}}{\sum_j \sum_i 25},$$ for all $i \neq j$, with i in organizational unit k and all j in organizational unit l, and $Strength_{ij} = [1, 25]$ for indicated relationships from j to i.

As the maximum strength of a relationship is 25, the maximum strength of relationships between two departments corresponds to the sum of possible relationships multiplied with 25.

5.9. Results for the research question "Who cooperates with whom?"

Based on past empirical findings and based on existing theories, a number of hypotheses have been postulated in the second part of this work to answer the research questions. I investigate four different dependent variables in two different samples. First, I investigate the dependent variable "existence of relationships" between any two actors i and j with i and j being employees of different merged firms. The sample contains all relationships, existing and non-existing relationships between any two actors of different merged firms. Existing relationships are all relationships that have been indicated by the respondents. Second, I investigate the dependent variables "frequency", "importance" and "strength" of existing relationships. The second sample thus contains only existing relationships between any two actors of different firms.

In Table 86 and Table 87, the correlations between the independent as well as the dependent constructs are shown. For each variable, the first line indicates the Pearson's correlation coefficient. The second line indicates the 2-sided significance. The third line indicates the number of cases considered for the computation.

In Table 86, the correlations between independent variables and the dependent variable existence of relationships are presented. Many of the correlations are highly significant. At the same time, the correlations are very weak. This effect is caused by the large share of non-existing relationships and the small number of existing relationships. Nevertheless, the correlations show highly significant weak correlations, which provide a sound basis for testing the postulated hypotheses.

Correlation matrix for dependent variable existence of relationship

	Gender similarity	Education level similarity	Education content similarity	Rank similarity	TimeInDep similarity	TaskOrientation similarity	Responsiveness similarity	Commitment similarity	Uncertainty similarity	SumIntegration	Existence	Existence unilateral
Age similarity	.028**	-.027**	.011*	-.031**	.168**	.027**	.033**	.030**	.019**	.043**		.036**
	0,00	0,00	.017	0,00	0,00	0,00	0,00	0,00	0,00	0,00		0,00
Gender similarity		.025**	.096**	-.027**	-.005	-.005	-.016**	-.024**	.009	.056**		.034**
		0,00	0,00	0,00	.326	.312	.001	0,00	0,00	0,00		0,00
Education level similarity			.088**	.150**	-.013**	.062**	-.042**	-.046**	-.006	-.067**		.012*
			0,00	0,00	.006	0,00	0,00	0,00	.297	0,00		.011
Education content similarity				.012**	.034**	.022**	.004	-.01	-.007	-.008		.042**
				.007	0,00	0,00	.365	.071	.196	.099		0,00
Rank similarity					.099**	-.089**	-.080**	.024**	-.028**	-.173**		-.050**
					0,00	0,00	0,00	0,00	0,00	0,00		0,00
TimeInDep similarity						-.001	-.030**	-.067**	-.026**	.006		.009
						.805	0,00	0,00	0,00	.188		-.052
TaskOrientation similarity							.118**	.057**	.110**	.086**		.027**
							0,00	0,00	0,00	0,00		0,00
Responsiveness similarity								.032**	.025**	-.029**		.009*
								0,00	0,00	0,00		.044
Commitment similarity									.089**	-.035**		-.008
									0,00	0,00		.154
Uncertainty similarity										.005		.018**
										.371		0,00
SumIntegration												.077**
												0,00

| * | 2-sided significance at the 0.05-level | 1st line: | Pearson's correlation |
| ** | 2-sided significance at the 0.01-level | 2nd line | Significance (2-sided) |

Table 86: Correlation matrix for dependent variables existence of cooperation at SoftCo

In Table 87, the correlations between independent variables and the dependent variables frequency, importance and strength of cooperation are presented.

Correlation matrix for dependent variables frequency. importance and strength

	Gender similarity	Education level similarity	Education content similarity	Rank similarity	TimeInDep similarity	TaskOrientation similarity	Responsiveness similarity	Commitment similarity	Uncertainty similarity	SumIntegration	Frequency	Importance	Strength
Age similarity	.006	-.024	.073*	-.006	.095**	.031	-.025	-.02	.054	.014	-.019	.011	-.012
	.849	.486	.03	.867	.004	.37	.476	.604	.154	.681	.57	.743	.72
Gender similarity		.067	.027	.065*	.02	-.066	-.039	.019	.047	.057	.04	.039	.04
		.053	.419	.049	.557	.057	.26	.621	.204	.088	.228	.237	.229
Education level similarity			.110**	.195**	.137**	.015	-.089*	-.015	-.005	-.071*	.057	.008	.05
			.001	0	0	.67	.013	.705	.888	.039	.1	.824	.148
Education content similarity				.023	-.002	.002	-.019	-.064	.049	.039	-.064	-.026	-.058
				.498	.947	.944	.591	.099	.195	.247	.055	.435	.08
Rank similarity					.123**	-.091**	-.071*	-.053	-.133**	-.138**	.058	-.028	.039
					0	.009	.041	.169	0	0	.083	.398	.239
TimeInDep similarity						-.041	-.039	-.023	-.102**	-.093**	-.017	-.080*	-.028
						.235	.257	.55	.006	.005	.605	.016	.404
TaskOrientation similarity							-.013	-.041	.039	.100**	.004	0	.017
							.717	.295	.301	.004	.918	-.995	.635
Responsiveness similarity								.049	-.012	.034	-.008	.032	.011
								.202	.748	.324	.816	.36	.761
Commitment similarity									.205**	-.001	-.01	-.082*	-.067
									0	.987	.797	.034	.082
Uncertainty similarity										-.035	-.058	.052	-.035
										.35	.118	.165	.344
SumIntegration											.04	.056	.061
											.23	.09	.068
Frequency												.408**	.927**
												0	0
Importance													.672**
													0

* 2-sided significance at the 0.05-level
** 2-sided significance at the 0.01-level

1st line: Pearson's correlation
2nd line: Significance (2-sided)

Table 87: Correlation matrix for dependent variables frequency, importance and strength of cooperation at SoftCo

For each dependent variable, regression analyses have been conducted to test the effects of the independent variables. In Table 88, the results of the ANOVA-analyses for the full models without control variable are presented.

Summary of full models without control variable

	Existence	Frequency	Importance	Strength
Standardized Beta				
Demographic characteristics				
Similar Age	.030****	-.014	.023	-.005
Similar Gender	.024****	.045	.035	.042
Similar Education Level	.019****	.055	.011	.047
Similar Education Content	.038****	-.073**	-.028	-.067**
Firm related characteristics				
Similar Rank	-.038****	.061*	-.005	.053
Similar TimeInDep	.007	-.019	-.086***	-.034
Attitudes				
Similar TaskOrientation	.013***	.010	-.010	.019
Similar Responsiveness	.007	.002	.033	.019
Reactions to M&As				
Similar Commitment	-.005	-.003	-.091***	-.065**
Similar Uncertainty	.015****	-.059*	.057*	-.032
Participation in integration measures	.068*****	.051	.052	.067**
Model statistics				
Total df	30,931	668	668	668
R^2	.012	.019	.024	.021
Adjusted R^2	.011	.003	.007	.005
F	33.288	1.172	1.455	1.286

**** Significant at a 0.01-level (2-sided)
*** Significant at a 0.05-level (2-sided)
** Significant at a 0.10-level (2-sided)
* Significant at a 0.15-level (2-sided)
Note: Pairwise exclusion of incomplete cases

Table 88: Full models without control variable for existence and characteristics of new cooperation relationships at SoftCo

In Table 89, the results of the ANOVA-analyses of the full models with control variable are presented.

Summary of full models with control variable		Existence	Frequency	Importance	Strength
Standardized Beta					
Demographic characteristics					
	Similar Age	.023****	-.019	.021	-.008
	Similar Gender	.003	.030	.025	.025
Similar Education Level		.007	.046	.005	.038
Similar Education Content		.018****	-.086***	-.036	-.078***
Firm related characteristics					
	Similar Rank	-.018****	.073**	.004	.063*
Similar TimeInDep		-.006	-.029	-.091***	-.043
Attitudes					
Similar TaskOrientation		.017****	.014	-.009	.022
	Similar Responsiveness	.012***	.004	.035	.021
Reactions to M&As					
Similar Commitment		-.010**	-.008	-.093***	-.068**
Similar Uncertainty		.011**	-.058	.055	-.031
Participation in integration measures		.046****	.035	.042	.051
Controls					
Cooperation requirements		.449****	.361****	.197****	.359****
Model statistics					
Total df		24,816	530	530	530
R^2		.211	.148	.062	.149
Adjusted R^2		.210	.129	.040	.129
F		551.197	7.515	2.862	7.558

**** Significant at a 0.01-level (2-sided)
*** Significant at a 0.05-level (2-sided)
** Significant at a 0.10-level (2-sided)
* Significant at a 0.15-level (2-sided)
Note: Pairwise exclusion of incomplete cases

Table 89: Full models with control variable for existence and characteristics of new cooperation relationships at SoftCo

As can be seen, both, the full models without control variable and the full models with control variable show strong effects of the independent variables on the likelihood of existence of relationships. At the same time, they both show only weak effects on frequency, importance and strength of existing relationships.

The full models with control variable show strong effects of structural cooperation requirements on existence, frequency, importance and strength of relationships.

In the following paragraphs, I will discuss the findings for each group of independent variables. It should be noted that instead of formulating hypotheses for each characteristic of a relationship, the hypotheses formulated in section 2 of this work considered "intensity" as dependent variable. Intensity of a relationship comprises frequency, importance and strength of a relationship.

5.9.1. Similarity of demographic characteristics

The homophily principle assumes that similarity of individuals makes relationships between them more likely and stronger.
In the present research, four different aspects of demographic similarity have been considered: age, gender, education level as well as education content. A number of hypotheses based on theoretical and empirical findings have been postulated in section 2 of this work. The hypotheses are listed in Table 90.

Hypothesis 12a:	Employees of similar age are more likely to form cooperation ties after mergers and acquisitions.
Hypothesis 12b:	Employees of similar age build more intense cooperation relationships than employees of dissimilar age after mergers and acquisitions.
Hypothesis 13a:	Employees of the same sex are more likely to form cooperation relationships after mergers and acquisitions.
Hypothesis 13b:	Employees of the same sex build more intense cooperation relationships after mergers and acquisitions.
Hypothesis 14a:	Employees of similar education level are more likely to form cooperation relationships after mergers and acquisitions.
Hypothesis 14b:	Employees of similar education level build more intense cooperation relationships with each other than employees of dissimilar education after mergers and acquisitions.
Hypothesis 15a:	Employees with similar education background are more likely to form relationships than employees with a dissimilar educational background
Hypothesis 15b:	Employees with similar education background build more intense cooperation relationships than employees with a dissimilar education background.

Table 90: Hypotheses concerning demographic similarity

In Table 91, the partial models for the effects of demographic similarities on cooperation are presented.

Summary of partial models: Similarity of demographic characteristics

		Existence	Frequency	Importance	Strength
Standardized Beta					
Demographic characteristics					
	Similar Age	.035****	-.018	.010	-.011
	Similar Gender	.029****	.046	.042	.045
	Similar Education Level	.009**	.061**	.010	.054*
	Similar Education Content	.038****	-.074***	-.031	-.067**
Model statistics					
Total df		42,497	844	844	844
R^2		.004	.010	.003	.009
Adjusted R^2		.004	.006	-.002	.004
F		42.222	2.200	.554	1.820

**** Significant at a 0.01-level (2-sided)
*** Significant at a 0.05-level (2-sided)
** Significant at a 0.10-level (2-sided)
* Significant at a 0.15-level (2-sided)
Note: Pairwise exclusion of incomplete cases

Table 91: Partial models of effects of similarity of demographic characteristics on cooperation relationships at SoftCo

5.9.1.1. Age similarity

According to the results of the partial model in Table 91, employees of similar age are more likely to build relationships with each other than employees of dissimilar age. The full model without control variable and the full model with control variable support this finding. Hence hypothesis 12a is strongly supported.

At the same time, the partial model shows no significant effect of age similarity on intensity of cooperation relationships. This finding is supported by the models without control variable and the models with control variable. Hence hypothesis 12b is not supported. While age similarity plays an important role for the initiation of cooperation relationships, it does not affect the intensity of existing relationships.

5.9.1.2. Gender similarity

According to the partial model in Table 91, gender similarity has a positive effect on the likelihood of existence of cooperation relationships after mergers and acquisitions. This finding is supported in the full model without cooperation requirements.

However, the full model with control variable shows no significant effects of gender similarity on existence of cooperation relationships. This indicates that there are cooperation requirements between some departments, which are predominantly staffed with employees of the same gender. By controlling for the structural cooperation requirements between these departments, the effect of gender similarity vanishes in the full model with control variable. Hence hypothesis 13a is partly supported.

At the same time, the partial model indicates that gender similarity has no significant effect on aspects of intensity of relationships. Neither frequency, importance nor strength of relationships are affected by gender similarity. This finding is supported by the full models without control variables and the full models with control variables. Obviously, gender similarity does not affect the cooperation intensity of cooperation relationships, which have been formed after the M&A-transaction.

5.9.1.3. Education level similarity

According to the partial model in Table 91, similarity of education level has a positive effect on the initiation of cooperation relationships after mergers and acquisitions. This finding is supported in the full model without control variable.

However, the full model with control variable shows no significant effect of similarity of education level on existence of cooperation relationships. this indicates that there are cooperation requirements between some departments, which are predominantly staffed with employees of the same education level. By controlling for the structural cooperation requirements between these departments, the effect of similarity of education level vanishes in the full model with control variable. Hence hypothesis 13a is partly supported.

At the same time, the partial model indicates that similarity of education level increases the frequency and strength of cooperation in existing relationships. This finding is not supported in the full model without control variable. Obviously, similarity of education level is correlated with other independent variables, which have an independent effect on intensity of cooperation. The correlation matrix in Table 87 shows a significant correlation of similarity of education level with rank similarity. Rank similarity has a positive effect on intensity of cooperation relationships. As a consequence, the spurious effect of education level similarity on cooperation intensity vanishes in the full model if rank is considered. The full model with control variable also shows no significant effect of education level on intensity of existing cooperation relationships. Hence hypothesis 14b is partly supported.

5.9.1.4. Education content similarity

The partial model in Table 91 shows a significant positive effect of similarity of education content on the likelihood of existence of cooperation relationships between two employees. This finding is supported by the full model without control variable and the full model with control variable. Hypothesis 15a thus is strongly supported.

At the same time, the partial model shows a significant negative effect of similarity of education content on the frequency and the strength of cooperation in existing cooperation relationships. This indicates that employees cooperate more intensively with colleagues, who have a dissimilar education background. This finding is supported by the full model without control variable and the full model with control variable. While homophily of education content applies for the initiation of cooperation relationships, it obviously does not apply for existing cooperation relationships, which have been formed after the M&A-transaction. The findings for hypothesis 15b thus are mixed. Hypothesis 15b is not supported.

5.9.2. Similarity of firm-related characteristics

Similarities of two different firm-related characteristics have been under consideration: rank similarity as well as similarity of seniority. In the following table, the postulated hypotheses about the effects of similarity of firm-related characteristics on cooperation relationships are presented:

Hypothesis 16a:	Employees of dissimilar rank are more likely to form cooperation relationships than employees of similar rank after mergers and acquisitions.
Hypothesis 16b:	Employees of dissimilar rank build more intense cooperation relationships after mergers and acquisitions than employees of similar rank.
Hypothesis 17a:	Employees of similar seniority are more likely to form cooperation relationships than employees of dissimilar seniority.
Hypothesis 17b:	Employees of similar seniority form more intensive cooperation relationships than employees of dissimilar seniority.

Table 92: Hypotheses about effects of firm-related characteristics on cooperation relationships

In the following table, the partial models for the effects of similarities of firm-related characteristics on existence and characteristics of cooperation relationships are presented:

Summary of partial models: Similarity of firm related characteristics					
		Existence	Frequency	Importance	Strength
Standardized Beta					
Firm related characteristics					
	Similar Rank	-.051****	.060**	-.020	.042
	Similar TimeInDep	.014****	-.023	-.078***	-.032
Model statistics					
Total df		47,325	903	903	903
R^2		.003	.004	.007	.003
Adjusted R^2		.003	.002	.005	.000
F		63.805	1.741	3.072	1.146

**** Significant at a 0.01-level (2-sided)
*** Significant at a 0.05-level (2-sided)
** Significant at a 0.10-level (2-sided)
* Significant at a 0.15-level (2-sided)
Note: Pairwise exclusion of incomplete cases

Table 93: Partial models of effects of similarity of firm-related characteristics on cooperation relationships at SoftCo

5.9.2.1. Rank similarity

According to the partial model in Table 93, employees of dissimilar rank are more likely to build relationships with each other. This finding is supported by the full model without control variable and the full model with control variable. Obviously, employees are more likely to build cooperation relationships with their supervisors, respectively with their subordinates than with colleagues of the same level. Hence hypothesis 16a is supported.

At the same time, the partial model shows that employees cooperate more frequently with colleagues of the same level. This finding is supported by the full model without control variables and the full model with control variables. In the full model with control variables, there is also a significant positive effect of rank similarity on strength of cooperation relationships. Hence hypothesis 16b is not supported.

Obviously, employees of dissimilar rank are more likely to form a cooperation relationship with each other. At the same time, after having formed their cooperation relationships, they cooperate more intensively with employees of similar rank.

5.9.2.2. Seniority similarity

According to the partial model in Table 93, employees of similar seniority (TimeInDep similarity) are more likely to build relationships with each other. This finding is not supported by the full model without control variable. Obviously, similarity of seniority covaries with other variables, generating a spurious correlation, which vanishes in the full model. The correlation matrix in Table 86 shows that seniority similarity is highly correlated with age similarity. Obviously, employees of a similar age group often have a similar seniority. However, age shows a significant effect in the full model. The spurious effect of seniority vanishes in the full model without control variable as age is considered as well. This effect is supported in the full model with control variable as well. Hence hypothesis 17a is partly supported.

The partial model in Table 93 also shows that similarity of seniority reduces the importance of a relationship. That means that employees who are only shortly in the company perceive their more senior colleagues as especially important. At the same time, more senior employees perceive their less senior colleagues as especially important. This finding is supported by the full model with control variables. This is opposite to the postulated effect of hypothesis 17b. Hence hypothesis 17b is not supported.

5.9.3. Similarity of attitudes

Similarities of two different attitudes have been investigated in this research: similarity of task orientation as well as similarity of responsiveness. In the following table, the hypothesized effects on cooperation are illustrated. As these work attitudes have been identified with the help of a factor analysis, no specific hypotheses have been formulated upfront. In the interviews in the first research site, a number of work related attitudes have been identified that were used to formulate a number of items, which were then clustered to factors. In the interviews, similarity of these items has been seen to positively affect cooperation between employees. Hence the hypotheses assume a general positive effect on similarity of work attitudes.

Hypothesis 18a:	Employees with similar work attitudes are more likely to cooperate after mergers and acquisitions than employees with dissimilar work attitudes.
Hypothesis 18b:	Employees with similar work attitudes build more intensive cooperation relationships after mergers and acquisitions than employees with dissimilar work attitudes.

Table 94: Hypothesis on the effect of work attitudes on cooperation

In the table below, the results of the partial models of the effects of attitudinal similarity on existence and characteristics of relationships are presented:

Summary of partial models: Attitude similarity					
		Existence	Frequency	Importance	Strength
Standardized Beta					
Attitudes					
	Similar TaskOrientation	.027****	.005	-.004	.015
	Similar Responsiveness	.006	-.009	.032	.009
Model statistics					
Total df		44,371	827	827	827
R^2		.001	.000	.001	.000
Adjusted R^2		.001	-.002	-.001	-.002
F		17.354	.035	.419	.143

**** Significant at a 0.01-level (2-sided)
*** Significant at a 0.05-level (2-sided)
** Significant at a 0.10-level (2-sided)
* Significant at a 0.15-level (2-sided)
Note: Pairwise exclusion of incomplete cases

Table 95: Partial model of attitude similarity at SoftCo

5.9.3.1. Similarity of task orientation

According to the partial model in Table 95 similarity of task orientation has a positive effect on the likelihood of existence of a cooperation relationships. This finding is supported by the full model without control variables and the full model with control variables.

At the same time, similarity of task orientation shows no significant effect on intensity of existing cooperation relationships. This finding is supported by the full model without control variables and the full model with control variables.

5.9.3.2. Similarity of responsiveness

Similarity of responsiveness shows no significant effect on the likelihood of existence of cooperation relationships in the partial model. This finding is supported by the full model without control variable. However, the full model with control variable shows a significant positive effect of similarity of responsiveness on likelihood of existence of cooperation relationships. Obviously, there are some departments connected by structural cooperation requirements, which are staffed with employees of dissimilar responsiveness. By controlling for the structural cooperation requirements, the effect of similarity of responsiveness on likelihood of existence of cooperation relationships becomes significant.

At the same time, the partial model in Table 95 does not show any significant effects on intensity of existing cooperation relationships. This finding is supported by the full model without control variable and the full model with control variable.

Summarizing the effects of similarity of task orientation and the effects of similarity of responsiveness on cooperation, the findings show that hypothesis 18a is strongly supported. At the same time, hypothesis 18b is not supported.

5.9.4. Similarity of reactions to mergers

Employees show different reactions after mergers and acquisitions. In the present research, two different reactions of employees to mergers and acquisitions are considered: Commitment as well as uncertainty. Committed employees are satisfied with their job and with the firm and its new organizational culture. Uncertain employees suffer from job uncertainty and are afraid of speak up to their supervisors.

In the following table, the hypothesized relationships between similarity of reactions to mergers and acquisitions and cooperation are listed:

Hypothesis 19a:	Employees with similar levels of commitment are more likely to cooperate than employees with dissimilar levels of commitment.
Hypothesis 19b:	Employees with similar levels of commitment build more intensive relationships than employees with dissimilar levels of commitment.
Hypothesis 20a:	Employees with similar levels of uncertainty are more likely to cooperate than employees with dissimilar levels of commitment.
Hypothesis 20b:	Employees with similar levels of uncertainty build more intensive relationships than employees with dissimilar levels of commitment.

Table 96: Hypotheses on the effect of reactions to M&A-transactions to cooperation

In the following table, the partial models for the relationship between similarity of reaction and existence, as well as characteristics of a cooperation relationship are presented:

Summary of partial models: Similarity of reactions to M&A-transactions					
		Existence	Frequency	Importance	Strength
Standardized Beta					
Reactions to M&As					
	Similar Commitment	-.009**	-.005	-.087***	-.065**
	Similar Uncertainty	.018****	-.058*	.060*	-.030
Model statistics					
Total df		33,711	668	668	668
R²		.000	.003	.010	.005
Adjusted R²		.000	.000	.007	.002
F		6.675	1.147	3.425	1.805

**** Significant at a 0.01-level (2-sided)
*** Significant at a 0.05-level (2-sided)
** Significant at a 0.10-level (2-sided)
* Significant at a 0.15-level (2-sided)
Note: Pairwise exclusion of incomplete cases

Table 97: Partial model of similarity of reactions to M&A-transactions

5.9.4.1. Commitment similarity

According to the partial model in Table 97, similarity of commitment has a negative effect on likelihood of existence of relationships after mergers and acquisitions. This finding is not supported by the full model without control variables. However, in the full model with control variables, similarity of commitment also shows a significant negative effect on the likelihood of existence of cooperation relationships. This is opposed to the postulated effect of hypothesis 19a. Hypothesis 19a thus is not supported.

At the same time, commitment similarity shows a negative effect of importance and strength of cooperation relationships, which have been formed after the M&A-transaction. This finding is supported by the full model without control variable and the full model with control variable. Obviously, employees with dissimilar levels of commitment reduces cooperation intensity. The findings are opposed to the postulated effect in hypothesis 19b. Hypothesis 19b thus is not supported.

5.9.4.2. Uncertainty similarity

According to the partial model in Table 97, similarity of uncertainty has a positive effect on likelihood of existence of cooperation relationships between employees. This finding is supported by the full model without control variable and the full model with control variable. Obviously, employees with similar levels of uncertainty are more likely to start a cooperation relationship with each other. That means that highly uncertain employees cooperate more likely with highly uncertain employees and employees with low levels of uncertainty cooperate more likely with other employees with similar low levels of uncertainty. Hypothesis 20a thus is strongly supported.

At the same time, similar levels of uncertainty have a negative effect on frequency of cooperation. Obviously, employees cooperate less frequently with each other, if they have similar levels of uncertainty. However, the perceived importance of cooperation relationships is higher if the cooperating employees have similar levels of uncertainty. These findings are supported by the full model without control variables. In the full model with control variables, the significance of the effects of similarity of uncertainty on intensity of cooperation relationships drops below the significance level. The findings for hypothesis 20b are mixed. Hence hypothesis 20b is not supported.

5.9.5. Participation in integration measures

A number of different integration measures have been investigated on their effects on cooperation. In the table below, the hypothesized effects of participation in integration measures on cooperation relationship between employees are presented:

| Hypothesis 21a: | If employees participate in integration measures, they are more likely to form cooperation relationships with each other after mergers and acquisitions. |
| Hypothesis 21b: | There is no effect of participation in integration measures on strength of cooperation. |

Table 98: Hypotheses on the effect of participation in integration measures on cooperation

In the following table, the results of the partial models are illustrated:

Summary of partial models: Effect of participation in integration measures				
	Existence	Frequency	Importance	Strength
Standardized Beta				
Participation in integration measures	.077****	.040	.056**	.061**
Model statistics				
Total df	48,509	908	908	908
R²	.006	.002	.003	.004
Adjusted R²	.006	.000	.002	.003
F	292.274	1.444	2.885	3.345

**** Significant at a 0.01-level (2-sided)
*** Significant at a 0.05-level (2-sided)
** Significant at a 0.10-level (2-sided)
* Significant at a 0.15-level (2-sided)
Note: Pairwise exclusion of incomplete cases

Table 99: Partial model of effects of participation in integration measures at SoftCo

The partial model indicates that participation in integration measures has a strong positive effect on the likelihood of existence of cooperation relationships between employees. This finding is supported by both, the full model without control variable and the full model with control variable. Hence hypothesis 21a is strongly supported.

At the same time, the partial model in Table 99 indicates a significant positive effect of participation in integration measures on importance and strength on relationships, which have been formed after the M&A-transaction. However, in the full model without control variable, the importance of relationships of employees, which participated in active integration measures is no longer significantly higher than the importance of relationships of employees, which did not participate in such measures. Seemingly, there is some covariance between the variable for participation in integration measures and other independent variables. However, as the strength of the effect does not change and only the significance of the effect changes, it is possible that the reduced significance results from the slightly smaller research sample for the full models without control variables.

The full models with control variable show no more significant effect of participation in integration measures on intensity of cooperation. Seemingly, employees working in departments, which are connected by strong cooperation requirements, are ore likely to participate in cooperation measures. After controlling for cooperation requirements, the effect of participation in integration measures on intensity of cooperation vanishes.

With increasing scope of the models, the support of hypothesis 21b decreases. Hence hypothesis 21b is partly supported.

5.9.6. Controls

As has been discussed above, cooperation in organizations is not deliberate. Rather, structural cooperation requirements between organizational units strongly affect cooperation. In the following table, the postulated effects of structural cooperation requirements on the existence and the characteristics of the relationships two individuals are listed:

Hypothesis 22a:	The amount of cooperation relationships between two organizational units affects the probability of two individuals in each of the units to have a relationship.
Hypothesis 22b:	The intensity of cooperation relationships between two organizational units affects the intensity of relationships of two individuals in each of the units.

Table 100: Hypotheses on the effect of structural cooperation requirements on cooperation between employees

The full model in Table 89 shows very strong positive effects of cooperation requirements on the existence and characteristics of cooperation relationships between employees. While the aggregation of individual cooperation relationships to form a control variable leads to covariance of the control and the dependent variable, a minimum number of four employees limits the problem sufficiently. It is interesting to note that the weakest effect of structural cooperation requirements on characteristics of cooperation relationships is the assigned importance of a relationship. While frequency of cooperation in a cooperation relationship can easily be explained by structural cooperation requirements, it seems plausible that the individually perceived importance of a cooperation partner depends on other aspects than the average importance of cooperation between two departments. Hence the relative weakness of average importance of cooperation relationships between two departments can be seen as support for the quality of the control variable.

The findings strongly support hypothesis 22a and 22b.

5.9.7. Summary of results

In the following tables, the results presented above are summarized. For each hypothesis, the number of the hypothesis, the independent and the dependent variable are indicated. Also the direction of the expected effect is indicated. In another column, the results for the regression analyses to determine the effects of the independent variables on the existence and the intensity of relationships are indicated. Intensity of a relationship comprises frequency, importance and strength of a relationship.

For the results of the partial models, the full models without control variable and the full models with control variable three different results are possible:
- Supported: Indicates a significant statistical support for the hypothesized effect
- Not supported: Indicates a non-significant effect
- Opposite: Indicates a significant statistical effect opposite to the hypothesized effect.

The total evaluation then indicates whether the results of the partial and the full model all show support (=supported), one or two show support, one or two show no support (= partly supported), one or two show support and one or two the opposite of the postulated effect (= mixed), or one or two show insignificant effects and one, two or all models show the opposite of the postulated effect (= opposite). Summarizing the results of the findings at SoftCo, a number of findings are remarkable. In Table 101 the summary for the effects of similarity of demographic and firm-related characteristics as well as work attitudes and reaction after mergers and acquisitions are indicated.

Hypo-thesis	Independent variable	Dependent variable	Expected effect	Partial model	Full model w/o control	Full model with control	Total
12a	Similar age	Existence of relationship	+	Supp.	Supp.	Supp.	Supp.
13a	Similar gender	Existence of relationship	+	Supp.	Supp.	Not supp.	Partly supp.
14a	Similar education level	Existence of relationship	+	Supp.	Supp.	Not supp.	Partly supp.
15a	Similar education content	Existence of relationship	+	Supp.	Supp.	Supp.	Supp.
16a	Similar rank	Existence of relationship	-	Supp.	Supp.	Supp.	Supp.
17a	Similar seniority	Existence of relationship	+	Supp.	Not supp.	Not supp.	Partly supp.
18a	Similar work attitudes	Existence of relationship	+	Partly supp.	Partly supp.	Supp.	Partly supp.
19a	Similar commitment	Existence of relationship	+	Opposite	Not supp.	Opposite	Opposite
20a	Similar uncertainty	Existence of relationship	+	Supp.	Supp.	Supp.	Supp.
21a	Integration measures	Existence of relationship	+	Supp.	Supp.	Supp.	Supp.
22a	Structural requirements	Existence of relationship	+			Supp.	Supp.

Legend: Supported / Not supp. / Opposite

Table 101: Existence of new ties

As can be seen, many of the postulated hypotheses are fully supported.
- Age similarity, similarity of education content, and similarity of uncertainty show significant positive effects on likelihood of existence of new ties in all models.
- Rank dissimilarity increases the likelihood of existence of new cooperation relationships in all three models.

- Participation in integration measures increases the likelihood of the existence of a cooperation between two actors.
- Structural cooperation requirements between two departments of different merged firms show the expected positive effect on likelihood of existence of cooperation relationships between any two actors of these departments.

A number of additional hypotheses are partly supported.

- Similarity of gender shows significant positive effects on likelihood of existence of cooperation relationships in the partial model and in the full model without control variable. However, in the full model with control variable, gender similarity shows no longer a significant effect. Obviously, there are cooperation requirements between departments, which are predominantly staffed with employees of similar gender. The structural cooperation requirements thus create a spurious positive effect in the partial model and the full model without control variable, which vanishes, when the cooperation requirements are considered.
- Similarly, similarity of education level shows significant positive effects on likelihood of existence of cooperation relationships in the partial model and in the full model without control variable. However, in the full model with control variable, similarity of education level no longer a significant effect. Obviously, there are cooperation requirements between departments, which are predominantly staffed with employees of similar education level. The structural cooperation requirements thus create a spurious positive effect in the partial model and the full model without control variable, which vanishes, when the cooperation requirements are considered.
- Similarity of seniority shows a significant positive effect on likelihood of existence of cooperation relationships in the partial model. However, in the full model without control variable, the effect vanishes. Obviously, covariance with other independent variables, which have an independent effect on likelihood of existence of cooperation, create a spurious effect in the partial model. Most likely, the high correlation of seniority and rank is responsible for this spurious effect. In the full model without control variable and the full model with control variable, the spurious effect vanishes.
- Similarity of work attitudes show no significant effects in the partial model and the full model without control variables. However, when controlling for structural cooperation requirements in the full model with control variable, there is a significant positive effect of similarity of work attitudes on likelihood of existence of cooperation relationships. Obviously, there are some departments with similar work attitudes, which have higher cooperation requirements than other departments, which have equally similar work attitudes.

It is important to note that similarity of commitment yields negative effects on likelihood of existence of cooperation relationships between employees. Similarity of commitment thus shows results opposite to the postulated effect.

Cooperation intensity has been operationalized with a number of different variables. First, the frequency of cooperation within a cooperation relationship has been measured. Then, the importance, which a relationship partner assigns to a relationship, is measured. Third, the strength of a relationship is computed.

In Table 102, the results for the regression analyses to determine the effects of the independent variables on the intensity of relationships are indicated.

For the results of the partial model and the full model five different results are possible:

- Strongly supported: A hypothesis is strongly supported if at least two of the models for the dependent variables frequency, importance or strength show significant effects corresponding to the hypothesized effects.
- Partly supported: A hypothesis is partly supported, if one of the models for the dependent variables shows significant effects corresponding to the hypothesized effects.
- Not supported: A hypothesis is not supported if none of the models shows significant effects.
- Mixed: The findings for a hypothesis are mixed if the models for the different dependent variables yield contradicting results.
- Opposite: The findings for a hypothesis are opposite to the postulated effects, if at least one of the models shows a significant effect opposite to the postulated effects.

The total evaluation then indicates whether the results of the partial and the full model both show support (= strongly supported), one shows support, one shows no support (= partly supported), one shows support and one shows the opposite of the postulated effect (= mixed) and one or both show the opposite of the postulated effect (= opposite).

Hypo-thesis	Independent variable	Dependent variable	Expected effect	Partial model	Full model w/o control	Full model with control	Total
12b	Similar age	Intensity of relationship	+	Not supp.	Not supp.	Not supp.	Not supp.
13b	Similar gender	Intensity of relationship	+	Not supp.	Not supp.	Not supp.	Not supp.
14b	Similar education level	Intensity of relationship	+	Supp.	Not supp.	Not supp.	Partly supp.
15b	Similar education content	Intensity of relationship	+	Opposite	Opposite	Opposite	Opposite
16b	Similar rank	Intensity of relationship	-	Opposite	Opposite	Opposite	Opposite
17b	Similar seniority	Intensity of relationship	+	Opposite	Opposite	Opposite	Opposite
18b	Similar work attitudes	Intensity of relationship	+	Not supp.	Not supp.	Not supp.	Not supp.
19b	Similar commitment	Intensity of relationship	+	Opposite	Opposite	Opposite	Opposite
20b	Similar uncertainty	Intensity of relationship	+	Mixed	Mixed	Not supp.	Mixed
21b	Integration measures	Intensity of relationship	0	Not supp.	Partly supp.	Strongly supp.	Partly supp.
22b	Structural requirements	Intensity of relationship	+			Strongly supp.	Strongly supp.

Legend: Supported / Not supp. / Opposite

Table 102: Characteristics of new ties

Table 102 clearly shows that hardly any of the hypothesized effects can be found.

- Similarity of education level yields positive effects on intensity of cooperation in the partial model. Seemingly, employees prefer not only to form relationships with other employees of similar education level. They also prefer to cooperate more frequently and assign higher importance to their new cooperation partners, if they have a similar education level. However, in the full model without control variable and in the full model with control variable, the effects vanish. Most likely, the effect of similarity of education level on cooperation intensity is a spurious effect caused by high correlation with the independent variable rank similarity.
- Participation in integration measures has a positive effect on the intensity of cooperation relationships in the partial model. Thus the intensity of a cooperation relationship between two employees increases if they both participate in integration measures. However, in the full model without control variable, the effect decreases. In the full model with control variable, the effect completely vanishes. Obviously, employees of some departments with high cooperation requirements have experienced a higher number of integration measures. After controlling for structural cooperation requirements, the effect vanishes, supporting the postulated null effect.
- Structural cooperation requirements strongly influence the cooperation intensity of existing cooperation relationships.

However, a number of hypothesized effects are not supported or even the opposite of the postulated effect is found:
- Similarity of age does not increase the intensity of cooperation. While existence of a new relationship depends on age similarity, intensity of cooperation in new relationships does not. That means that after mergers and acquisitions, employees of all ages cooperate equally well with each other.
- Similarity of gender does not increase the intensity of cooperation. While existence of a new relationship depends on gender similarity, intensity of cooperation in new relationships does not.
- Similarity of education content even leads to lower intensity of cooperation. A possible explanation for this finding is that complementary knowledge might increase the intensity of cooperation in new relationships.
- Similarity of rank leads to increased cooperation. While it has been found that employees are more likely to cooperate with other employees of different rank, within these relationships, they cooperate more intensively with employees of the same rank.
- Similarity of seniority reduces the intensity of cooperation in new relationships. That means that older employees cooperate more intensively with younger employees and vice versa. A possible explanation for this finding might be that employees form mentoree-mentor relationships between employees of different age: employees with more experience take care of employees with less experience.
- Similarity of work attitudes yields no significant effect. Neither the partial nor the full models show significant effects of similarity of work attitudes on intensity of relationship. This is curious insofar as work attitudes are part of the culture of an organization. Cultural differences, however, have been suggested in previous research as one of the core integration barriers after mergers and acquisitions. A first explanation might be that the attitudes considered in this research are not relevant for cultural differences. A second explanation might that cultural differences are not at the root of integration problems. The significance of the findings will be discussed later.
- Employees with dissimilar commitment cooperate more intensively than employees with similar commitment. That means that employees that are less committed are cooperating more strongly with employees that are more committed.
- Uncertainty similarity yields mixed effects on cooperation intensity. While in the partial model, uncertainty similarity yields negative results on frequency of cooperation, the importance of cooperation is positively affected by uncertainty similarity. In the full model, uncertainty similarity only yields significant positive effects on importance of a relationship.

These findings indicate that the homophily that has been found to be highly effective for the likelihood of existence of cooperation relationships hardly apply for the intensity of cooperation relationships.

A first explanation for this finding might be a methodological error: For the investigation of existence of relationships, both, existing and non-existing relationships have been considered. For the investigation of intensity of relationships, only existing relationships have been considered. Hence there is a risk that existing relationships are homophilous and thus the variance of the characteristics of these relationships is not sufficient to yield significant effects of independent variables on intensity of cooperation. However, this explanation can be rejected: While the effect of homophily on likelihood of existence of cooperation relationships is highly significant, it is very weak. That means that employees do engage in numerous cooperation relationships that are not homophilous. Hence the variance of the independent variables of the existing relationships is sufficient for computing significant effects. As an example supporting this indication, Graph 16 shows the variance of age similarity for all possible relationships and for existing relationships:

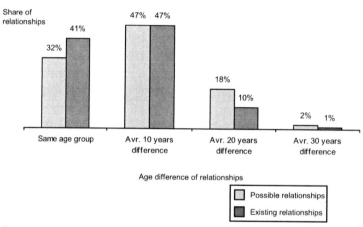

Graph 16: Age difference of existing and possible relationships

Existing relationships comprise all unilateral new relationships that have been indicated by the respondents. Possible new relationships comprise all relationships that are possible between respondents of different merged firms in the sample. The age group of relationships indicates, what the average age difference between two employees in an existing or a possible relationship is.

Obviously, there is an effect of homophily, increasing the share of existing relationships in more similar age groups compared to the possible relationships. Nevertheless, there is still a sufficiently high level of variance of the variable in the sample of existing relationships.

A second explanation for this finding might be the fact that unilateral relationships have been used and not bilateral relationships.

Summary of full models with control variable for bilateral relationships				
	Existence	Frequency	Importance	Strength
Standardized Beta				
Demographic characteristics				
Similar Age	.014***	.116* s	.204**** s	.151*** s
Similar Gender	.002	.072	.032	.052
Similar Education Level	.002	.048	-.038	.039
Similar Education Content	.011**	-.157***	-.113* s	-.159***
Firm related characteristics				
Similar Rank	-.011**	.102 ns	.036	.111*
Similar TimeInDep	-.008	-.062	-.204****	-.103
Attitudes				
Similar TaskOrientation	.009*	.022	-.085	.013
Similar Responsiveness	.010*	-.074	.093	-.023
Reactions to M&As				
Similar Commitment	-.009*	-.009	-.250****	-.109*
Similar Uncertainty	.009*	-.122* s	-.080	-.127**
Participation in integration measures	.033****	.030	.084	.060
Controls				
Cooperation requirements	.284****	.365****	.075 ns	.306****
Model statistics				
Total df	24,816	171	171	171
R²	.085	.206	.176	.188
Adjusted R²	.084	.146	.114	.126
F	191.126	3.431	2.827	3.063

**** Significant at a 0.01-level (2-sided)
*** Significant at a 0.05-level (2-sided)
** Significant at a 0.10-level (2-sided)
* Significant at a 0.15-level (2-sided)
Note: Pairwise exclusion of incomplete cases

Table 103: **Full model for existence and characteristics of new bilateral cooperation relationships at SoftCo**

In Table 103, the full models for the effects of homophily on bilateral relationships are indicated. Those effects, which differ significantly from the full model for unilateral relationships presented in Table 89, are highlighted. An "s" indicates that the analysis of bilateral relationships yields a significant effect for a variable, which only yields an insignificant effect for the unilateral relationships. An "ns" indicates that the analysis of the bilateral relationships yields an insignificant effect for a variable, which yields a significant effect for the unilateral relationships.

The table clearly shows that there is no difference between the effects of homophily in unilateral and bilateral relationships on likelihood of existence of relationships. However, the table also shows some notable differences between effects of homophily on intensity of relationships:

- A first notable effect is that age similarity yields significant positive effects on the intensity of relationships. While there is no homophily effect for age for the unilateral relationships, bilateral relationships show strong age homophily. Especially the mutually assigned importance of relationship partners is much higher in bilateral relationships.
- A second notable effect is that the effect of structural cooperation requirements on importance of relationships drops below the significance level. This indicates that importance of employees is only to a limited extent related to structure. That, however, implies that employees build their own network of highly important cooperation partners, which are not depending on structural characteristics of cooperation.
- Last but not least, a number of effects, which have been found for unilateral relationships are amplified for bilateral relationships. First, the negative effect of similarity of education content on intensity of unilateral relationships is confirmed for bilateral relationships. In addition to the negative effect of similarity of education content on frequency, there is a similar effect on mutually assigned importance in bilateral relationships. Obviously, employees estimate the importance of cooperation with new colleagues higher, if the education content is different.
The effect of rank similarity on frequency of cooperation is no longer significant. Hence the effect of rank similarity on intensity of cooperation relationships is weaker for bilateral relationships than for unilateral relationships.
Uncertainty similarity yields a negative effect on frequency and strength of bilateral relationships. While uncertainty similarity only yields a negative effect on strength of unilateral relationships, the effect that is opposite to the hypothesized effect is further supported.

Regardless of these deviations there is a high correspondence of the results for unilateral and bilateral relationships. The findings for intensity of cooperation relationships thus are not caused by a sample bias of unilateral relationships. The use of unilateral relationships is appropriate as the findings mostly coincide with the findings for bilateral relationships.

Obviously, methodological issues are not responsible for the weak findings of homophily in existing relationships. While homophily matters for the existence of relationships and thus for the initiation of relationships, the intensity of newly formed cooperation relationships seems to follow different mechanism but homophily.

In order to investigate further whether the research model errs, whether firm level variables are responsible for the findings, or whether the research model needs to be expanded to reflect the specific situation of relationship formation after mergers and acquisitions, I compare in the following paragraph old and new cooperation relationships.

5.9.8. Comparison of new ties with old ties

The differences between the effects of homophily on the existence of relationships and on the intensity of relationships are unexpected. The findings indicate that existence and characteristics of new relationships show different effects of homophily: Homophily strongly affects the likelihood of existence of new ties. That means that the likelihood of the formation of a tie between new colleagues is higher if they are similar to each other in a number of characteristics. At the same time, intensity of a relationship seems to be hardly affected by homophily.

Previous research on social networks in different settings shows homophily effects: Marsden (1988) finds homophily in core discussion networks, Verbrugge (1977, 1983) finds homophily in friendship networks, and Ibarra (1995) finds race homophily in ego-centered work-related networks. However, these studies did not consider age of a relationship. A possible explanation for the surprising findings on intensity of cooperation relationships after mergers and acquisitions might be that the investigated cooperation relationships are all relatively young. They all were formed in the aftermath of the M&A-transaction. That means that the maximum age of a cooperation relationship between employees of merged firms is 27 months (i.e. the time passed between formal integration and the gathering of the data). Many of them are younger.

In order to find out, whether homophily depends on age of relationships, I investigate relationships, which at the time of the research were older than 27 months. As the date of initiation of cooperation relationships was not gathered, the seniority of the cooperation partners is used as a proxy. The maximum age of a cooperation relationship is limited by the seniority of the less senior relationship partner. Of course, it might be possible that a cooperation relationship has been formed long after the entry of an employee in the firm. However, based on results from the exploratory interviews, it seems that most cooperation relationships were formed relatively quickly after the entry in the firm. Only relationships, which at the time of the research were 36 months or older were considered. That means that the minimum seniority of relationship partners was three years. Of course, only relationships within the previously separated firms were considered, as 36 months or longer before the research, there were no relationships between the merged firms.

In Table 104, the results for the full model with control variable for old relationships are indicated:

	Summary of full models with control variable			
	Existence	Frequency	Importance	Strength
Standardized Beta				
Demographic characteristics				
Similar Age	.050****	.016	.034	.027
Similar Gender	.011	-.054***	-.063***	-.058****
Similar Education Level	.018***	-.031*	.032	-.010
Similar Education Content	.018***	.001	-.015	-.008
Firm related characteristics				
Similar Rank	-.047****	-.004	.059***	.002
Similar TimeInDep	.006	.054***	-.027	.042***
Attitudes				
Similar TaskOrientation	.037****	.026	.053***	.039**
Similar Responsiveness	.000	.073****	.032	.062****
Controls				
Cooperation requirements	.548****	.563****	.274****	.555****
Model statistics				
Total df	8,873	1,542	1,542	1,542
R²	.313	.323	.087	.315
Adjusted R²	.312	.319	.082	.311
F	448.184	81.244	16.243	78.186

**** Significant at a 0.01-level (2-sided)
*** Significant at a 0.05-level (2-sided)
** Significant at a 0.10-level (2-sided)
* Significant at a 0.15-level (2-sided)
Note: Pairwise exclusion of incomplete cases

Table 104: Full model with control variable for existence and characteristics of old cooperation relationships at SoftCo

In order to compare the effects for old cooperation relationships with new cooperation relationships, the same independent variables need to be considered as in Table 104. Therefore, the ANOVA-analyses for the new relationships have been recalculated for the reduced number of independent variables. The results are presented in Table 105.

Summary of partial models for comparison - New Ties				
	Existence	Frequency	Importance	Strength
Standardized Beta				
Demographic characteristics				
Similar Age	.024****	-.019	.020	-.010
Similar Gender	.005	.031	.030	.029
Similar Education Level	.005	.045	.008	.039
Similar Education Content	.018****	-.086***	-.036	-.078**
Firm related characteristics				
Similar Rank	-.026****	.068*	-.008	.051
Similar TimeInDep	-.005	-.026	-.085**	-.036
Attitudes				
Similar TaskOrientation	-.021****	.010	-.006	.019
Similar Responsiveness	.009**	.001	.031	.016
Controls				
Cooperation requirements	.451****	.362****	.199****	.361****
Model statistics				
Total df	30,681	530	530	530
R²	.208	.144	.050	.140
Adjusted R²	.208	.129	.033	.125
F	896.435	9.704	3.022	9.447

**** Significant at a 0.01-level (2-sided)
*** Significant at a 0.05-level (2-sided)
** Significant at a 0.10-level (2-sided)
* Significant at a 0.15-level (2-sided)
Note: Pairwise exclusion of incomplete cases

Table 105: Full model with control variable for existence and characteristics of new cooperation relationships at SoftCo

In Table 106, the effects of the independent variables on likelihood of existence of cooperation relationships are compared for old and new cooperation relationships. In the column "Old ties", the summarized results for relationships older than three years are presented. In the column "New ties", the summarized results for new relationships are presented. There are three different results: Support of the postulated effects, no support of the postulated effects or even opposite of the postulated effects. In order to support the presentation of the results, the results are colored according to these three effects.

In the last column "Evaluation", the results are compared. Three different effects are possible: (1) The results for old ties and new ties show the same effects, (2) the results show different effects (i.e. one shows significant effects, the other shows insignificant effects) or (3) opposite effects (i.e. both show significant effects with opposite directionality).

Hypo-thesis	Independent variable	Dependent variable	Expected effect	Old ties	New ties	Total
12a	Similar age	Existence of relationship	+	Strongly supp.	Strongly supp.	✓
13a	Similar gender	Existence of relationship	+	Partly supp.	Partly supp.	✓
14a	Similar education level	Existence of relationship	+	Strongly supp.	Partly supp.	✓
15a	Similar education content	Existence of relationship	+	Strongly supp.	Strongly supp.	✓
16a	Similar rank	Existence of relationship	-	Strongly supp.	Strongly supp.	✓
17a	Similar seniority	Existence of relationship	+	Partly supp.	Partly supp.	✓
18a	Similar work attitudes	Existence of relationship	+	Partly supp.	Mixed	(.)
22a	Structural requirements	Existence of relationship	+	Supp.	Supp.	✓

■ Supported	✓	Same effect
■ Not supp.	(.)	Different effect
■ Opposite	?	Contrary effect

Table 106: Comparison of old and new relationships for the likelihood of existence of relationships

As can be seen, the effects on existence of relationships are mostly the same for old ties and for new ties. The initiation of both, old and new ties strongly depend on homophily effects. Both, old and new ties show a negative effect of similarity of rank on likelihood of existence of cooperation relationships. Obviously, relationships are more likely to exist between employees of different ranks than between employees of the same rank.

The only difference between the results for old and new ties shows the independent variable similarity of work attitudes. Similar task orientation has positive effects on the likelihood of existence of new ties, while similar responsiveness has negative effects on the likelihood of existence of new ties.

In a nutshell, both, old and new ties are more likely to exist, if there are similarities between relationship partners.

In Table 107, the effects of independent variables on intensity of cooperation relationships are compared for old and for new ties.

Hypo-thesis	Independent variable	Dependent variable	Expected effect	Old ties	New ties	Total
12a	Similar age	Intensity of relationship	+	Not supp.	Not supp.	✓
13a	Similar gender	Intensity of relationship	+	Opposite	Not supp.	(.)
14a	Similar education level	Intensity of relationship	+	Partly supp.	Partly supp.	✓
15a	Similar education content	Intensity of relationship	+	Partly supp.	Opposite	?
16a	Similar rank	Intensity of relationship	-	Opposite	Opposite	✓
17a	Similar seniority	Intensity of relationship	+	Strongly supp.	Opposite	?
18a	Similar work attitudes	Intensity of relationship	+	Strongly supp.	Not supp.	(.)
22a	Structural requirements	Intensity of relationship	+	Strongly supp.	Strongly supp.	✓

Legend:
- Supported | ✓ Same effect
- Not supp. | (.) Different effect
- Opposite | ? Contrary effect

Table 107: Comparison of old and new relationships for the intensity of relationships

As can be seen, the intensity of old ties largely depends on homophily. Only similarity of age and similarity of gender shows no homophilous effects. It is interesting to note that for old relationships, there is a difference in gender homophily between men and women. When separating male and female respondents, the two samples show different effects of gender similarity on intensity of cooperation relationships. While women show no significant effect of gender similarity on cooperation intensity, men show a strong negative effect of gender similarity on cooperation intensity. There are two different explanations for this finding: First, men were more likely to remember women colleagues when filling out the questionnaire. Second, men prefer working with women, while women do not reciprocate this preference.

New cooperation relationships hardly show effects of homophily on intensity of cooperation. Only the similarity of education level shows a partial positive effect on cooperation intensity. In two of seven independent variables, there are different effects of old and new cooperation relationships. Two other independent variables even show opposite effects for old and new relationships.

This finding indicates that the homophily principle applies for older relationships much stronger than for new relationships. While both, old and new relationships show strong effects of homophily on the likelihood of existence of cooperation relationships, only older relationships show homophily effects on intensity of cooperation.

There are two possible explanations for this finding: First, homophily might be a dynamic phenomenon, which increases with increased age of a relationship. Second, the two types of relationships cannot be compared as the new relationships are relationships between employees of different firms, formed in a post merger context, whereas the old relationships are relationships between employees of the same firm, formed in a stable environment.

In order to test these explanations, I investigate new relationships within the previously separated firms. As described in 3.1.2, SoftCo was integrated very carefully. Even more than three years after the acquisition of the two acquisition targets, SoftCo had kept brands, products as well as organizational structures mostly stable. Hence the new relationships formed within one of the previously independent firm should not suffer from the post merger integration impact as much as new cooperation relationships between employees of the previously separated firms.

In Table 108, the results for the full model with control variable for the relationships within the previously separated firms, which are younger than 3 years (i.e. young relationships) are presented.

	Summary of full models with control variable			
	Existence	Frequency	Importance	Strength
Standardized Beta				
Demographic characteristics				
Similar Age	.032****	.080****	.013	.067****
Similar Gender	.002	-.027	-.015	-.020
Similar Education Level	.026****	.016	-.001	-.000
Similar Education Content	-.002	-.007	.019	.005
Firm related characteristics				
Similar Rank	-.041****	-.015	-.058***	-.034*
Similar TimeInDep	.016**	.108****	.032	.094****
Attitudes				
Similar TaskOrientation	.002	-.029	-.029	-.035*
Similar Responsiveness	.007	.014	-.010	.001
Controls				
Cooperation requirements	.575****	.526****	.300****	.537****
Model statistics				
Total df	10,291	1,379	1,370	1,379
R^2	.335	.297	.093	.304
Adjusted R^2	.335	.293	.088	.300
F	576.614	64.385	15.697	66.614

**** Significant at a 0.01-level (2-sided)
*** Significant at a 0.05-level (2-sided)
** Significant at a 0.10-level (2-sided)
* Significant at a 0.15-level (2-sided)
Note: Pairwise exclusion of incomplete cases

Table 108: Relationships between employees within the previously separated firms younger than 3 years

In comparison with the results in Table 105, a few things are notable:
- Similarity of age increases the likelihood of existence of cooperation relationships for both types of relationships.
- Dissimilar rank increases the likelihood of existence of cooperation relationships for both types of relationships.
- The likelihood of existence of new relationships between employees of previously separated firms increases with similarity of education content, whereas the likelihood of existence of young relationships within the previously separated firms increases with similarity of education level.
- Table 105 shows mixed effects of work attitudes on likelihood of existence of new relationships, while Table 108 shows no such effects for young relationships.

Both types of relationships show only few significant effects on intensity of cooperation relationships:
- Dissimilarity of education content increases the intensity of new ties.
- Similarity of rank increases the cooperation frequency in new ties
- Dissimilarity of seniority increases the assigned importance of new relationships.
- Work attitudes show no significant effects on intensity of new relationships.
- Similarity of age and seniority increase intensity of young cooperation relationships within the previously separated firms (i.e. young cooperation relationships).
- At the same time, rank dissimilarity increases the intensity of cooperation within young cooperation relationships.
- Work attitude similarity shows a weak negative effect on strength of cooperation of young cooperation relationships.

In a nutshell, both, new relationships between previously separated firms and within the previously separated firms show homophilous effects on likelihood of existence of cooperation relationships. At the same time, both types of new relationships show much less homophilous effects than old relationships.

The findings clearly support the first explanation provided above, according to which there might be a difference between new and old relationships, because homophily is a dynamic phenomenon, which becomes stronger with age of a relationship. While it is not clear, over which time periods homophily develops, at least the results show that in both types of new relationships, i.e. new relationships between employees of the previously separated firms and young relationships between employees within the previously separated firms, homophily is much weaker than in the old relationships. Young and new relationships show hardly any demographic homophily and no attitude homophily.

According to the second explanation, there are fundamental differences between new relationships that are formed after an M&A-transaction between employees of previously separated firms and relationships that are formed within a firm. However, the second explanation cannot be discarded as there are some notable differences between the two types of new relationships, which cannot be ignored;

- First, in the full model in Table 105, three of the independent variables show the postulated effects on intensity of young relationships: Age similarity, seniority similarity as well as rank dissimilarity yield positive effects on the intensity of cooperation relationships. New relationships, however, do not show any homophily effect. Hence young relationships within the previously separated firms are more homophilous than new relationships between previously separated firms.
- Second, dissimilarity of education content and of seniority increase intensity of new cooperation relationships. This implies that complementarity of education content as well as complementarity of seniority have positive effects on new relationships. This, however, is opposed to the postulated effect. The effects of similarity of seniority are opposed for new relationships and for young relationships.
- Third, while rank dissimilarity has the proposed effects on young relationships, they have the opposite effect on new relationships. Seemingly, employees of previously separated firms prefer to cooperate more intensively with colleagues of their rank.

Based on the comparison of new cooperation relationships with old cooperation relationships, respectively with young cooperation relationships within the previously separated firms, it becomes clear that a more dynamic concept of homophily is required. While initialization of relationships, i.e. the first attraction of two potential cooperation partners, depends on homophily, later cooperation intensity does not in new respectively in younger relationships.

5.10. Methodological limitations of the research at SoftCo

Many of the conceptual limitations of the research at SpecMatCo listed in 4.9 have been considered in the research at SoftCo. The use of a full dyadic network analysis eliminated the problems, which were generated by the ego-centered network analysis at SpecMatCo:

- Almost each employee in the merged organizational unit participated in the study. Hence there was no risk of a sample effect as in the case of SpecMatCo.
- Each respondent was free to indicate as many cooperation relationships as necessary. Hence there was no bias on important cooperation relationships as in the case of SpecMatCo.
- The respondent bias on cooperation relationships is eliminated in the research at SoftCo by considering only indegree relationships, i.e. relationships that other respondents indicated to have with an individual.

The respondent bias on evaluating similarity has been eliminated by using individual level data for each respondent and assessing similarity based on this data and not based on perceived similarity. Also, the operationalization of attitudes has been done with several items and not only with single items as in the case of SpecMatCo.

However, there still are some methodological limitations, which need to be considered in order to qualify the later discussion of the results:

A first methodological limitation is the focus on one research site. Firm level variables cannot be considered quantitatively. That means that structural aspects or characteristics of the M&A-transaction can only be considered qualitatively. For example, effects of hostility or friendliness of a takeover on cooperation of employees cannot be investigated based on the research design of this study.

A second methodological limitation is the use of the top down electronic questionnaire. The use of a new data gathering approach always bears the risk of tool-related biases, which hardly can be qualified. A first problem related to the top-down approach of the electronic questionnaire is the required knowledge of the organizational structure. In the exploratory interviews, it showed that a small number of respondents did not properly know the organizational structure. These respondents did know their cooperation partners. However, they had a hard time identifying the department of their cooperation partners and thus finding their cooperation partners in the top-down structure of the questionnaire. Despite the advantages of the electronic questionnaire in handling and its reduced complexity, some relationships might not have been indicated because employees were unable to identify their cooperation partners.

This problem, however, is not considered to be very severe in the present case. The organizational structure under consideration was relatively small and simple. Hence most respondents should have been able to exhaustively identify their cooperation partners and indicate their cooperation relationships. Also, the exploratory interviews showed very few problems but hardly any failures. Hence the first usage of the electronic questionnaire should not have generated any specific biases of the gathered data.

A third methodological limitation, which needs to be considered in the discussion is the computation of the control variable. As has been mentioned several times, the use of a department-level control variable, which is based on aggregate dyadic-level measures bears a number of important limitations for this research.

- Covariance of control variable and dependent variable in small departments: Average cooperation on department level is used as a departmental-level control variable for the dependent dyadic-level measures of cooperation. For each dependent dyadic-level measure, a specific department-level dyadic variable has been computed. The covariance problem is especially virulent in small departments. In the extreme case of a department of one, all the variance of the individual level cooperation can be explained by the department level cooperation. However, by considering only departments with four or more respondents, the covariance problem is limited to a certain extent.

At the same time, the limitation of the control variable to departments with four or more respondents excludes small departments from the considerations. While the high overall response rate of the study leads on the average to high response rates in single departments, there still are some departments, which cannot be considered for the control variable effects due to the limitation to four or more respondents per department.

- Covariance of control variable and independent variables in homogeneous departments: Dyadic cooperation relationships between employees of departments, which are highly homogeneously concerning employee characteristics, can suffer from covariance of department-level cooperation and the independent variables. For example, if two departments with old employees show a high level of average cooperation, the age homophily effect covaries strongly with the control variable. For example, cooperation relationships between software hotline, which is predominantly staffed with female employees and hardware hotline, which is predominantly staffed with male employees, yields strong effects of gender dissimilarity on cooperation without considering the department-level control variable. When the department-level control variable is considered. Some or even most of the variance of cooperation, which has been explained with gender dissimilarity, will be explained with the departmental level variable.

  Nevertheless, most departments have a significantly high level of diversity concerning the independent characteristics. Data of employees of a few departments might suffer from the covariance problem, however, most of the departments are sufficiently diverse. Also, in analyzing the data, the respective models always have been computed with and without control variable. Hence the effects of covariance of the control variable can be interpreted.

A fourth limitation of the research design is the factor analytic approach for some of the independent variables. While most items of the factors have been identified conceptually and confirmed in a confirmatory factor analysis some items have been identified in an exploratory factor analysis. This, however, bears the risk of conceptual poverty. This problem is especially virulent for the work attitudes, which represent new constructs that have not been investigated in previous studies. However, as most of the items have been considered in previous research, on the item level, the conceptual uncertainty is limited.

Last but not least, the differentiation between old and new relationships bears some methodological risks. As has been described, the research design corresponds to a pre-experimental design, which, due to its specific research question can be used to simulate a longitudinal study. Hence relationships of two different types have been gathered: Old relationships and new relationships. It is assumed that old relationships are relationships between employees of the same former firm. New relationships are relationships between employees of different formerly separated firms. However, it has not been asked, since when employees cooperate with another employee. As a consequence, it might be possible that an "old" relationship is younger than a new relationship. Also, within the new relationships, there might be relationships of different age. As described above, the integration of SoftCo took place over a longer period of time. This, however, means that incrementally, employees start to cooperate. Some of the new cooperation relationships thus might date back to the early phases of the integration while other new cooperation relationships are very recent.

A second, more conceptual problem is that there are different findings for old and for new relationships. As has been said, there are at least two different explanations for the findings: First, the formation of a relationship is a dynamic process. Mature relationships therefore follow different mechanisms than new relationships. While homophily applies to some extent for mature relationships, it does not apply for new relationships. The exact mechanisms that affect intermediary stages of relationships need to be investigated in future research. A second explanation, however, might be that firm level variables or specific characteristics of the M&A-transaction are responsible for the differences between old and new relationships. In the course of this study, it cannot be clarified, to what extent either one or the other explanation apply.

Further longitudinal research on cooperation relationships is required to identify whether the differences of old and new relationships are the consequence of supra-individual variables, such as characteristics of the M&A-transaction, or whether there are different phases in the life of a relationship from initiation to maturation to termination.

6. Discussion of results for research question "Who cooperates?"

"Who cooperates?" This is the first research question of the present research. The question asks about the relationship between characteristics of individuals and their cooperation after mergers and acquisitions.
Investigating the cooperation of the employees of SoftCo after the M&A-transaction, it is possible to see significant differences in cooperation between employees. In Graph 17, all 377 employees in the research sample of SoftCo, are ranked by the sum of new ties they formed after the M&A-transaction. Each vertical bar stands for the sum of new relationships of one employee in the sample of 377 employees. The relationships are indegree-relationships, i.e. relationships that the 266 respondents, who provided relational data, indicated to have with the respective employee. The average number of new relationships is 3.2 relationships per employee. 95 employees in the sample do not have any new relationships.

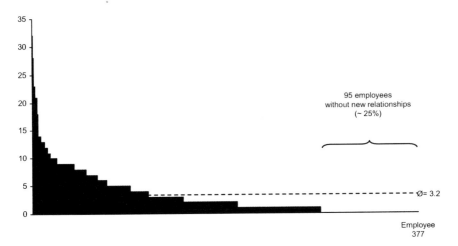

Graph 17: Number of new ties of respondents of SoftCo ranked by number of ties

As can be seen in Graph 17, the employee with the highest number of cooperation relationships with new colleagues has ten times more new relationships than the average employee at SoftCo. At the same time, roughly 25% of all employees in the research sample have no new cooperation relationship.
In order to better understand, what employees cooperate and what employees do not cooperate after mergers and acquisitions, a second question has been asked to specify the guiding research question. The second question is "What are antecedents and constraints of individual cooperation?"

Based on this question, in a first step, characteristics of employees and their effects on cooperation have been investigated. In a second step, the effects of integration measures and the effects of isomorphic forces of structural cooperation requirements on cooperation have been investigated.

The research model in 2.1.7 assumes that characteristics of employees can be separated in relatively stable characteristics on the one hand side and temporary reactions of employees after the M&A-transaction on the other side. Relatively stable characteristics are demographic characteristics, firm-related characteristics as well as attitudes of employees. Reactions of employees are commitment and uncertainty. It is further assumed that the reactions of employees are affected by both, stable characteristics of employees as well as integration measures and structural cooperation requirements.

In the following paragraphs, I will first discuss effects of independent variables on the reactions after mergers and acquisitions. Reactions are commitment and uncertainty. Then I will discuss the findings on cooperation.

6.1. Reactions of employees after mergers and acquisitions

Reactions of employees to M&A-transactions are behaviors, feelings or perceptions, which occur as a reaction to the M&A-transaction. Of course, the cross-sectional research setup is not suited to empirically identify reactions, as there is only one measurement. It is not possible to differentiate, whether a reaction is the result of the M&A-transaction or whether it is the result of other events. Hence it is only possible to conceptually identify reactions and possible antecedents, which moderate the effects of the M&A-transaction on the reactions.

In the present study, two different reactions after M&A-transactions have been investigated: First, the commitment of employees and second feelings of uncertainty of the employees.

There are different aspects that influence the reactions of employees after mergers and acquisitions: Firm level, department level as well as individual level variables. Due to methodological limitations, many of these aspects could not be considered in this research:

- Firm level variables, such as relative size of acquirer and acquisition target (e.g. Gerds, 2000; Bamberger, 1994; Kitching, 1967), performance of acquirer and acquisition target (e.g. Haunschild, Moreland, & Murrell, 1994), aspects of hostility of a takeover (e.g. Hitt, Harrison, Ireland, & Best, 1998; Haleblian & Finkelstein, 1999), or integration process (Lucks, & Meckl 2002) could not be investigated in this study due to the investigation of two research sites only

- Group level variables such as ingroup-outgroup bias (Haunschild, Moreland & Murrell, 1994) or complementarity of management (Krishnan, Miller, & Judge, 1997) neither have been considered.

At the same time, a number of individual level variables have been considered. The effects of these individual level variables on reactions after mergers and acquisitions, i.e. commitment and uncertainty, will be discussed in the following paragraphs.

6.1.1. Effects of age on reactions

6.1.1.1. Age and reactions at SoftCo

A first highly interesting finding is the positive effect of age on commitment. Kanfer, & Ackerman (2004) develop a conceptual model, which posits that older employees are less committed than their younger colleagues all other things equal, because the attractiveness of job performance decreases with increasing age. The empirical findings of this research show the opposite: Older employees are significantly higher committed, even after controlling for rank and seniority of employees.

A first explanation for this might be the higher life satisfaction of older employees (Carstensen, et. al. 1997). General life satisfaction has been found to influence work satisfaction very strongly (Schmitt, & Pulakos 1985). Similarly, Hochwarter et al. (2001) find a U-shaped relationship between age and job satisfaction. Jürges (2003) also finds a positive effect of age on job satisfaction. In addition to that, Jürges (2003) finds that older cohorts of West German Workers in general show higher levels of satisfaction than younger cohorts. According to these findings, older employees generally show higher levels of job satisfaction. In the research at SoftCo, commitment is operationalized with the help of items, which earlier have been used in previous studies for the operationalization of job satisfaction. Hence it might be possible that the lack of differentiation of commitment and satisfaction is responsible for the finding.

A second explanation to this contradiction between the conceptual model of Kanfer and Ackerman (2004) and the empirical findings of the present research might be the lack of consideration of situational factors in the conceptual model. It might well be possible that older employees are generally less committed. However, after an M&A-transaction, older employees might show higher commitment than younger employees.

While older employees show higher commitment, at the same time, there is no significant effect of age on feelings of uncertainty. While Carstensen, Fung, & Charles (2003) find that older individuals are better in handling stress and thus reach more positive psychological outcomes, Haynes, & Love (2004) find that older project managers suffer more frequently from anxiety and stress than younger project managers. However, neither of these rival findings can be supported. It might be possible that the findings of Carstensen, Fung, & Charles (2003) only hold for general emotional stress and not for uncertainty in organizations. At the same time, the findings of Haynes, & Love (2004) might be specific to project management.

6.1.1.2. Age and reactions at SpecMatCo

Similarly to the study at SoftCo, age yields a positive effect on commitment at SpecMatCo. At the same time, the research at SpecMatCo shows weak positive relationships between age and uncertainty in the partial model. However, in the full model, the effect of age on uncertainty vanishes. This indicates a spurious effect of age on uncertainty.

6.1.1.3. Synopsis of effects of age on reactions

Both studies at SoftCo and SpecMatCo thus show a positive effect of age on commitment after mergers and acquisitions. While previous studies and theoretical models assume an opposite effect, the findings indicate that older employees are even higher motivated after M&A-transactions than their younger colleagues. Further research is thus required to clarify the role of situational factors on the effects of age on commitment.

At the same time, both studies indicate that there is no significant effect of age on uncertainty. Seemingly, uncertainty is a reaction, which does not depend on age. While previous studies yield rival explanations for the effect of age on uncertainty, the present studies support neither of these hypotheses. However, when comparing these previous studies, one finds that they always focus on uncertainty in different settings and situations. It is possible that situational factors bear a moderating effect on the relationships of age and uncertainty. Maybe, older employees react more reasonably to mergers and acquisitions than younger employees, because they are more familiar with the phenomenon. Also, it is possible that institutional factors such as legal regulations affects the feeling of uncertainty of employees.

Further research is required to find out, what effects situational and institutional factors have on the relationships of age and uncertainty.

6.1.2. Effects of gender on reactions

6.1.2.1. Gender and reactions at SoftCo

Gender shows no effect on commitment of employees nor on uncertainty of employees. Female respondents at SoftCo reacted similar to their male colleagues.

6.1.2.2. Gender and reactions at SpecMatCo

At SpectMatCo, gender differences yield no effect on commitment or uncertainty. Due to the small sample size of female respondents, gender effects at SpecMatCo have to be interpreted very carefully. Therefore, the result bears no high explanatory power.

6.1.2.3. Synopsis of effects of gender on reactions

While the results at SpecMatCo have to be interpreted very carefully, it nevertheless is interesting to find that both studies show no significant effect of gender on reactions after mergers and acquisitions. Obviously, psychological reactions are not different between men and women.

In line with the hypothesized effect, the findings support Hyde (2005), who finds in a large scale meta-analysis that in very different studies, the effects for different gender are mostly similar.

6.1.3. Effects of education level on reactions

6.1.3.1. Education level and reactions at SoftCo

Education level of employees has been found to effectively reduce uncertainty. This effect has been postulated based on an institutionalist argument (Meyer & Rowan 1977, Williamson 1975). According to Williamson (1975) asset redeployability reduces uncertainty of relationship partners. Asset specificity increases uncertainty and at the same time increases the need for safeguarding. Higher education level implies that an employee holds more general knowledge, which can be redeployed in different organizational settings. At the same time, employees, who gathered their knowledge mostly within the firm have firm-specific knowledge, which devaluates strongly outside the firm. Hence higher education leads to higher redeployability of knowledge assets and thereby to lower job uncertainty. This argument has been supported by the findings at SoftCo.

A second explanation for the higher feelings of uncertainty amongst lower educated employees are restructuring measures, which took place shortly before the M&A-transaction and the lack of integration in some departments. In both acquisition targets, some 10% of the employees were laid off before the merger and acquisition took place. The lay off measures focused on support functions as well as on hotline and production departments. In these departments, the education level is rather low compared to the development, product management, sales or technical service departments, which were excluded from the restructuring measures. At the time of the research, hotlines as well as production departments still were not integrated. Exploratory interviews with employees of these functions revealed that they were afraid of what they expected to come and thus felt highly uncertain. Hence employees in these departments one the one hand side had memories of lay-offs in recent history and at the same time felt that the same thing might happen again. This might explain the higher uncertainty of employees with lower education level.

6.1.3.2. Education level and reactions at SpecMatCo

In the research at SpecMatCo, education level yields no significant effect on uncertainty. Due to the low variance of the sample concerning education content, these results have to be interpreted cautiously.

6.1.3.3. Synopsis of effects of education level on reactions

It is difficult to compare the findings at SoftCo and SpecMatCo concerning the effects of education level on uncertainty. First, the results at SpecMatCo have to be interpreted cautiously due to the sample structure. Second, there are specific firm-level effects, which have not been researched systematically. While employees of lower education levels at SoftCo faced restructuring measures and lay-offs in recent history, there were no such measures at SpecMatCo in recent history.

Hence further research is required to clarify the effects of events in recent history, affecting uncertainty of specific groups of employees. It is necessary to better understand, how individuals react in situations of high uncertainty, if they experienced similar situations before.

6.1.4. Effects of rank on reactions

6.1.4.1. Rank and reactions at SoftCo

As early as 1967 Schoennauer found that the upper management shows higher levels of commitment than the middle management. The present research confirms this finding and extends it to all levels of the hierarchy.

Also, in line with previous findings of Terry, & Callan (1997) and Schoennauer (1967), higher ranked employees feel less uncertain than lower ranked employees. It is important to note that this effect holds in the partial as well as in the full model. Hence neither age, education level, nor information asymmetries, which are strongly correlated to rank, can be held responsible for the finding. Rather, rank has an independent effect on the reduction of uncertainty. There are two possible explanations for this finding:

- At SoftCo, the structural decisions on the management levels have been taken early on in the M&A-process. The higher the rank, the earlier the decision has been taken. Hence higher ranked employees might have suffered from the same uncertainty as their subordinates. However, they experienced it earlier and therefore it has decreased stronger than the uncertainty of lower ranked respondents.
- The operationalization of uncertainty is based on three items: Job uncertainty, critique handling by supervisors and potential disadvantages if employees openly state critique. There might be a different perception of these items between employees with management responsibility and others, which have no such responsibility. Managers might not experience the same anxiety to criticize their subordinates. Hence the operationalization of uncertainty might yield a response bias depending on the rank of respondents.

Further research is required to clarify, which of the offered explanations holds for the effects of rank on uncertainty.

6.1.4.2. Rank and reactions at SpecMatCo

The findings at SpecMatCo also show a positive effect of rank on commitment after mergers and acquisitions.

At the same time, rank shows no significant effect on uncertainty. A first explanation for this finding is the lack of consideration of higher ranks in the research at SpecMatCo. Mainly respondents of the first (i.e. the operative level) and the second level of the firm have been considered. The sample contains only one employee of the third level. According to the interviews, most of the second level employees basically perform the same tasks as the first level employees. Usually, the management span of the second level employees was rather low. This might explain similar effects of different ranks on uncertainty.

6.1.4.3. Synopsis of effects of rank on reactions

Both studies confirm the postulated positive effect of rank on commitment. According to this finding, higher ranked employees are more committed after mergers and acquisitions.

The findings at SoftCo indicate that higher ranked individuals feel less uncertain than lower ranked individuals. However, it also might be possible that differences in the integration process are responsible for lower feelings of uncertainty of higher ranked individuals.

At the same time, the results at SpecMatCo show no significant effect of rank on uncertainty. The lack of significant findings might be caused by a sample effect.

The lack of consideration of firm level variables at SoftCo as well as the weak sample at SpecMatCo limit the possibilities for further explanation of the finding. Obviously, further research is required to better understand the effects of rank on uncertainty after M&As.

6.1.5. Effects of seniority on reactions

6.1.5.1. Seniority and reactions at SoftCo

Seniority does not show the expected results on commitment and uncertainty. While Social Identity Theory (Tajfel, & Wilkes 1963) predicts that seniority should increase social identity with a firm (for a review, see Hogg, & Williams 2000) and thereby increase social identity preserving behaviors as well as the fear of loosing the firm-specific social identity (Ashforth, & Mael 1989), these postulated effects cannot be confirmed: There is no significant effect of seniority on commitment and no significant effect on uncertainty. A possible explanation for this finding might be the generally low levels of seniority in the firm. As has been described above, SoftCo has been formed out of three different firms. While one of the firms is older than 20 years at the time of the mergers, the other two firms were younger than 10 years at the time of the merger. The average seniority of the respondents is only slightly above five years. It might be possible that social identity only forms after a longer period of time within one organization. It might be possible that the seniority at SoftCo is too low to generate social identity effects.

A second explanation considers cohort effects of employees. Cohort effects are effects that are relevant for a grou of individuals, which have a time-related variable such as age or seniority in common. As early as 1949, Whelpton examined different fertility rates of women of different cohorts. He finds that economic condition and birth rate are highly correlated. Cohorts of women of similar age let their birth plans strongly influence by economic conditions such as the Great Depression in the early 1930's or post war prosperity.

Jürges (2003) investigated the long-term development of work satisfaction from 1984 to 2001. He finds that older cohorts are generally happier with their work than younger cohorts. However, he also finds that employees born around 1955 are generally most unhappy. Jürges (2003) explains the decrease of job satisfaction for younger employees with an increased secular trend in job satisfaction as well as increased job uncertainty.

Transferring the cohort concept to employees of SoftCo, it is possible to identify cohort effects. In Table 109, the average commitment of employees by cohort at SoftCo is presented. The number above the columns signifies the time of employment at SoftCo. For example, the cohort "≤ 1" comprises all employees that are employed for more than 0.5 years and less or equal to 1 year. The number below the columns signifies the number of employees in each cohort. It needs to be noted that the effects are not controlled for other variables.

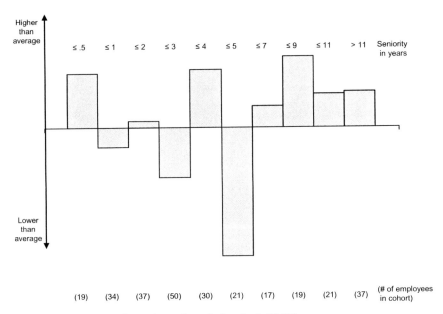

Table 109: Average values of commitment by seniority cohort at SoftCo

As can be seen, commitment is of very high amongst newly employed employees. At the same time, commitment is lower for employees in the following cohorts. Again employees that were employed between three to four years ago, indicate high commitment. Employees, which were employed four to five years ago, show the lowest level of commitment.

In order to analyze potential cohort effects, it is necessary to recall some important dates of the merger history of SoftCo:

- 45 months before the research, the acquisition of the first firm was announced
- 39 months before the research, the acquisition of the second firm was announced
- 38 months before the research, the acquisitions were put into place
- 27 months before the research, the new organizational structure was implemented

Hence employees that were employed between four to five years ago did not yet know that the merger would come. Most employees, which were employed more recently knew about the M&A-transaction and consciously chose to work for the merged firm.

The exploratory interviews revealed an important cohort effect, which is reflected in the data: Employees actively choose their employer for specific reasons. For example, size of the firm, social standards, organizational structure, business, employment certainty and other factors affect the choice of employees for a firm. Employees, who started to work for one of the separated firms before the announcement of the merger chose to work in a small firm with flat hierarchical structures, a clear single business strategy as well as relatively high job certainty. Hence they formed a social contract, which comprised these elements (for a review of literature on social contracts and violation of social contracts see Morrison, & Robinson 1997). After the merger announcement, the situation changed: The originally small firm tripled in size, the hierarchical structure became steeper and job certainty changed or at least became less transparent. Employees who just started to work for one of the firms thus felt betrayed, because their choice criteria did no longer apply. They felt that their social contract was violated. The work they performed for the firm did no longer correspond to the benefits they received in exchange (Weick 1966).

At the same time, employees who started to work after the merger announcement approximately knew what was coming. They knew that they would work in a larger company with more hierarchical structures and lower transparency. However, they felt attracted by these facts and therefore show higher commitment than their slightly more senior colleagues. Hence their social contract comprised different elements than their slightly more senior colleagues, which were not violated by the M&A-transaction.

Commitment of employees of high seniority, however, is relatively unaffected by the merger. The exploratory interviews indicated that more senior employees, who worked longer periods of time before the merger announcement for one of the firms, felt well connected within their old firm and ready for change. In the interviews, some of the employees indicated their understanding for the necessity for an M&A-transaction as a necessary step for future survival. Hence their social contract again comprised different elements than the social contracts of their younger colleagues.

While these exploratory considerations bear some superiority to the explanations provided by Social Identity Theory (Tajfel, & Wilkes 1963), they require further research. A first aspect, which requires further consideration is the dynamic of social contracts over time. Which elements are comprised by a social contract? How do they change over time? Systematic research is required in order to validate the qualitative findings of the exploratory interviews. Second, cohort effects underlie a number of additional effects. For example, in 2001 and 2002, hardly any graduates from information and decision science departments have been employed. Employees who got employed in these years probably differ from employees, who were employed during the dot.com-hype during the late 1990s. Such environmental level cohort effects need to be considered as well in order to clearly identify the effect of merger announcements on social contracts of employees and their effects on commitment of employees.

The cohort analysis for uncertainty shows results, which cannot be explained with the social contract hypothesis. In Table 110, the average values of uncertainty for the different cohorts are indicated.

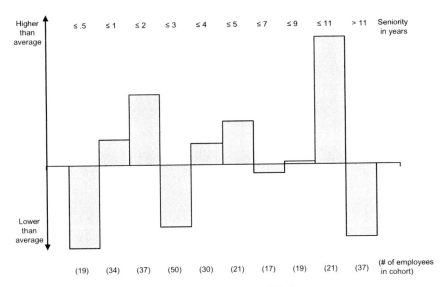

Table 110: Average values of uncertainty by seniority cohort at SoftCo

As can be seen, uncertainty for very junior employees is very low and steadily increases until two years of uncertainty. Then again, it is very low and increases for employees up to five years of uncertainty. The highest uncertainty is amongst highly senior employees. However, the cohort with the most senior employees shows very low values of uncertainty.

Again, the exploratory interviews provide some indication for these findings. First, many employees have a fixed-term contract. Most of these contracts have a duration of two years. Approaching the two year seniority level, these employees feel highly uncertain whether their contract will be prolonged or not. After the prolongation, uncertainty levels again are very low and steadily increase.

A second finding in the interviews is the fact that both firms had been downsized to some extent in the last years. In the course of the downsizing measures, some 10% of the employees have been laid off. Especially older employees were concerned by the downsizing measure. However, the employment law in Germany favors very senior employees. Therefore, the most senior cohort of employees hardly could be laid off. Hence the most senior cohort feels very certain. At the same time the second most senior cohort feels highly uncertain, because it is not yet protected by the employment law to the extent that the most senior cohort is.

Hence there are firm level and institutional level variables, which strongly affect uncertainty of employees. However, in this research, it is not possible to quantify the different effects and isolate effects of social identity. Further research is required to delineate the different effects in order to identify and quantify the different independent variables, which affect uncertainty after mergers and acquisitions.

6.1.5.2. Seniority and reactions at SpecMatCo

The findings at SpecMatCo show no significant effect of seniority on commitment. Obviously, the time that employees spent in a function is not relevant for their commitment after the M&A-transaction.
At the same time, the findings at SpecMatCo show a significant effect of seniority on uncertainty. Obviously, employees, which work for a longer time in a function perceive higher levels of uncertainty than employees, which are only shortly working in a function. This supports the effects, which were postulated based on Social Identity Theory.

6.1.5.3. Synopsis of effects of seniority on reactions

Both studies, the one on SoftCo and the one on SpecMatCo, show no significant effect of seniority on commitment. Obviously, more senior employees have no different commitment levels than younger employees. It is important to note that the findings at SoftCo show strong cohort effects on commitment. These cohort effects indicate that the social contract, which an employee has with the firm, might be crucial for the commitment to the firm after the M&A-transaction. Due to the small sample size at SpecMatCo, these cohort effects could not be replicated to further explore the findings of the SoftCo-study. However, future research is necessary to further investigate (a) the role of social contracts on commitment after mergers and acquisitions and (b) the effects of cohort effects on social contracts.

At the same time, the findings at SoftCo show a null-effect of seniority on uncertainty, while the results at SpecMatCo show a significant positive effect of seniority on uncertainty. The findings at SoftCo indicate that cohort effects caused by legal regulation might be responsible for the unsystematic effect of seniority on uncertainty. According to the exploratory interviews, the German labor legislation strongly affects feelings of uncertainty. Temporary contracts increase uncertainty of employees, if they reach the end of their contract. At the same time, highly senior employees enjoy special protection against lay-offs. These institutional factors, which are external to the firm might be stronger than the effects of social identity and thus dominate the effects of seniority on uncertainty. The respondents at SpecMatCo, however, mostly worked in countries with labor legislations, which are less regulated. Also, the practice of temporary contracts is not common at SpecMatCo As a consequence, the effects predicted by Social Identity Theory might hold in the case of SpecMatCo but not in the case of SoftCo, because they are dominated by environmental factors. Hence the differences of findings on the effect of seniority on uncertainty might be caused by institutional effects, external to the firm.

A second possible explanation for different findings on the relationship between seniority and uncertainty might be the different average seniority of the samples at SoftCo and SpecMatCo. While the employees at SoftCo on the average only work for 5.1 years in the same department, the employees at SpecMatCo work for 9.5 years in the same department. When considering the time in the firm, the difference is even more significant with an average of 5.9 years in the sample of SoftCo and 12.8 years in the sample of SpecMatCo. It might be possible that the predicted effects of Social Identity Theory only hold for more senior employees.

Hence further research is required on the dynamics of social identity to further explore how it builds over time and what effects on reactions of employees it yields over time. Also, further research is required to investigate institutional effects on reactions of employees after mergers and acquisitions.

6.1.6. Effects of task orientation on reactions

6.1.6.1. Task orientation and reactions at SoftCo

Task orientation does not show the expected effects. In the second chapter of this work, it was argued that task orientation should have no independent effect on commitment or uncertainty. However, the findings indicate that task orientation strongly increases commitment of employees. Research by Schmidt (2005) on members of music bands shows that task orientation in a wider sense (i.e. intrinsic motivation, mastery, and cooperative orientations) are related to commitment to a music band. However, the relationship between task orientation and commitment has not explicitly addressed in the research as Schmidt (2005) forms a factor, which comprises all aspects of task orientation and commitment. Also, it is unclear, how these results can be transferred from voluntary organizations to business settings.

At the same time, the findings of the present research indicate that task orientation strongly reduces uncertainty of employees. Seemingly, employees, who are strongly task oriented and focus on the work at hand, worry less about their jobs and speak up more frankly to their superiors. A possible explanation for this finding came up in the exploratory interviews: Employees with high task orientation seemed to develop some pride on their task orientation. This pride was a source of self-confidence, which reduces feelings of uncertainty.

Both, the effects of task orientation on commitment as well as on uncertainty require further research, in order to better understand how and why attitudes of employees affect reactions after mergers and acquisitions. Better theoretical conceptualization of the factors and their effects are needed to further elaborate on the role of attitudes on reactions after mergers and acquisitions.

6.1.6.2. Task orientation and reactions at SpecMatCo

Task orientation shows neither any effect on commitment nor any effect on uncertainty. Both, partial as well as full model only yield insignificant results.
At the same time, the operationalization of task orientation at SpecMatCo is problematic. The construct is operationalized with the help of a single item. This, however, bears to risk of not capturing the essence of the construct.

6.1.6.3. Synopsis of effects of task orientation on reactions

The findings at SoftCo show a significant positive effect of task orientation on commitment and a significant negative effect of task orientation on uncertainty. The findings coincide for both firms, SoftCo and SpecMatCo, for the effects of task orientation on commitment. However, the results of SpecMatCo show no significant effect for task orientation on uncertainty.

It is very difficult to compare the findings of the research at SoftCo with the findings at SpecMatCo. As has been noted in 4.9, the use of a single-item operationalization of task orientation at SpecMatCo bears strong methodological limitations. These limitations have been avoided at SoftCo with the help of a different operationalization of the construct task orientation. Despite the sameness of the name, "task orientation" has different semantic meanings in the two different studies.

6.1.7. Effects of the degree of feeling informed on reactions

6.1.7.1. Degree of feeling informed and reactions at SoftCo

The degree of feeling informed has a very strong positive effect on commitment of employees. In line with results from a previous study by Schweiger, & DeNisi (1991), the findings at SoftCo show that employees, who feel well informed are strongly committed. It is interesting to note that Schweiger, & DeNisi (1991) investigated in a field experiment the effects of communication measures, whereas in this study the effects of feeling informed are investigated. The similarity of the findings indicates that communication measures really increase the degree of feeling informed.

At the same time, the degree of feeling informed significantly reduces uncertainty. This finding again supports previous findings of Schweiger, & DeNisi (1991). Also, it confirms findings of Bordia et al. (2004), who find that communication reduces different types of uncertainty.

The degree of feeling informed thus possesses important functions as a hygiene factor: Feelings of employees after mergers and acquisitions obviously can be positively affected with the help of communication. Further research is required to identify the effectiveness and efficiency of different types of communication measures in order to translate the findings on individual perception of information to objective communication measures.

Based on the operationalization of the degree of feeling informed, it is possible to argue that the degree to which an employee feels informed is not necessarily dependent on the amount of information available but more on the perceived information requirements. It might be possible that some individuals have high information requirements and others have low information requirements. Similarly, it is possible that in some departments, there are high information requirements, whereas other departments only have low information requirements. The effects then would not be caused by objective information but by subjective information requirements.

In Table 111, the correlations between the degree of feeling informed of employees and their direct superiors are presented. In order to compute these correlation coefficients, the direct superior for each operative (i.e. non-managerial) employee has been determined. Some employees report directly to division heads, while other report to team leaders, which are two levels below the division heads. For all employees, the correlation between their own degree of feeling informed and the degree of feeling informed of their direct supervisors has been computed on a single item basis.

	Correlation matrix for items of InformationAgg of employees and direct supervisors			
	EnoughInfo Supervisor	ObjectivesKnown Supervisor	PersonalConsKnown Supervisor	DirectionKnown Supervisor
EnoughInfo Empl.	0,104	,182(*)	,151(*)	,156(*)
	0,171	0,015	0,046	0,039
	176	177	176	176
ObjectivesKnown Empl.	,344(**)	,349(**)	,368(**)	,366(**)
	0	0	0	0
	176	177	176	176
PersonalConsKnown Empl.	,198(**)	,241(**)	,280(**)	,205(**)
	0,009	0,001	0	0,006
	176	177	176	176
DirectionKnown Empl.	,273(**)	,303(**)	,298(**)	,311(**)
	0	0	0	0
	174	175	174	174

* 2-sided significance at the 0.05-level
** 2-sided significance at the 0.01-level

1st line: Pearson's correlation
2nd line Significance (2-sided)
3rd line N

Table 111: Correlation matrix for items of InformationAgg of employees and their superiors

As can be seen, the degree, to which an employee feels informed or not, strongly depends on the degree to which his direct supervisor feels informed or not. This indicates that the degree of feeling informed is intersubjective and not only subject to individual information requirements. If the degree, to which employees feel informed was purely subjective and caused by individual information requirements, there would be no significant correlations, unless the individual information requirements of employees and supervisors were identical. However, this case is rather unlikely.

At the same time, there are two distinct explanations for the findings: First, it might be that within a department, employees have similar information requirements as their supervisors due to departmental level variables, which have not been captured in this research. While this case cannot be excluded based on the empirical investigation, it still seems unlikely. Rather, the findings indicate that direct supervisors are an important source of information for employees. This indication bears important implications for further research on information flow after mergers and acquisitions.

6.1.7.2. Degree of feeling informed and reactions at SpecMatCo

The degree of feeling informed shows no significant effect on the commitment of employees at SpecMatCo. The partial as well as the full model both show positive effects. However, they both stay above the relevant significant level.

At the same time, the findings at SpecMatCo indicate a negative effect of the degree of feeling informed on uncertainty. Obviously, employees at SpecMatCo feel less uncertain if they feel better informed.

6.1.7.3. Synopsis of effects of the degree of feeling informed on reactions

The findings for commitment are different for SoftCo and SpecMatCo. While the employees at SoftCo are more committed if they feel better informed, there is only an insignificant positive effect at SpecMatCo. Nevertheless, these findings indicate that the degree of feeling informed has positive effects on commitment after mergers and acquisitions.

At the same time, both studies indicate that uncertainty of employees is lower if they feel well informed.

Both research sites thus confirm the positive effects of information as a hygiene factor. Employees react more positively if they feel well informed. Positive reaction thereby means they are more committed and at the same time feel less uncertain than employees, who lack information.

It is important to note that based on the results in Table 111, the degree of feeling informed is a valid measure to capture the amount of information that an employee has received. More information leads directly to higher commitment and lower uncertainty of employees.

6.1.8. Effects of participation in integration measures on reactions

6.1.8.1. Participation in integration measures and reactions at SoftCo

Participation in integration measures yields no effect neither on commitment nor on uncertainty. It has been argued in chapter 2 that participation in integration measures should increase commitment, because employees participate more actively in the integration of the merging firms. Harrison, & Freeman (2004) argue that participation increases commitment of employees. However, in the current research, no significant effect of participation in integration measures on commitment has been found. Similarly, the hypothesized negative effect of participation in integration measures on uncertainty could not be confirmed. Obviously, participation in integration measures does not affect reactions of employees after mergers and acquisitions.

According to the findings, information thus can increase commitment and reduce uncertainty, while participation in integration measures has no such effect. Hence integration measures are most effective, if they are linked to high levels of information.

6.1.8.2. Participation in integration measures and reactions at SpecMatCo

The research at SpecMatCo shows no significant effect of participation in integration measures on commitment. Neither the partial nor the full model yield significant effects.

At the same time, participation in integration measures yields a positive effect on uncertainty in the partial model, which vanishes in the full model. This indicates that the effect might be a spurious effect, caused by covariance with other independent variables.

Nevertheless, there might an alternative explanation, which was indicated by some of the respondents during the exploratory interviews: It is possible that uncertainty and participation in integration measures both are caused by high restructuring efforts in a department. Such high restructuring efforts could result from structural decisions, implying stronger integration in some departments than in other departments. Integration efforts then might cause uncertainty on the one hand side as employees experience sever changes of work structures and social structures of their department. On the other hand side, strong integration efforts might be accompanied by an increased application of integration measures.

However, these qualitative interpretations require further research. The relationship between integration requirements as well as the relationship between execution of integration measures and uncertainty need to be further explored to clarify cause and effect.

6.1.8.3. Synopsis of effects of participation in integration measures on reactions

Both studies do not support the hypothesis that participation in integration measures is supposed to increase commitment of employees. Obviously, participating in exchange programs, kick-off meetings as well as integration teams by itself yields no positive effect on commitment.

Similarly, there hardly is an effect of participation in integration measures on uncertainty. While it was expected that participation in integration measures should reduce the uncertainty of employees, the findings at SpecMatCo indicate that even the opposite could be the case. However, the effect is weak and most likely spurious.

6.1.9. Summary for reactions of employees after mergers and acquisitions

Commitment and uncertainty concern the feelings of employees after mergers and acquisitions. There is not much research on feelings of employees in the aftermath of an M&A-transaction (for one of the few exceptions see Schweiger & DeNisi 1991).

In two different firms, I investigated the effects of demographic and firm-related characteristics, as well as the effect of different attitudes of employees and the effects of communication and participation in integration measures on commitment and feelings of uncertainty of employees after mergers and acquisitions. In Table 112, the results are summarized. For each hypothesis, the number of the hypothesis, the independent and the dependent variable as well as the expected effect is indicated. Also, the summarized findings at SpecMatCo and SoftCo are presented. The last column shows, whether the findings in both firms coincide ("✓"), are significant in one firm and non-significant in the other firm ("(.)") or opposite in the two firms ("?"). Green color indicates that the findings support the hypothesis. Light green color indicates no significant findings and red color indicates opposite findings.

It needs to be noted that the variable "commitment" is operationalized in two different ways in the study at SpecMatCo and in the study at SoftCo. However, despite the different operationalization of the dependent variables, the postulated effects show a high degree of robustness. This supports the findings not only from an empirical level but also increases the validity of the findings.

As can be seen in Table 112, the findings at SpecMatCo and at SoftCo are highly similar. Only task orientation and the degree of feeling informed yield different results. The findings for task orientation cannot be compared due to strongly differing operationalization of the variables. The degree of feeling informed yields a positive but insignificant effect at SpecMatCo. Hence the findings there are similar as well. In a nutshell, the findings in the two research sites show the following effects:

- Age shows a positive effect on commitment, which is opposite to the postulated effect
- Gender differences show no significant effect on commitment as hypothesized
- Rank shows a significant positive effect on commitment: Higher ranked employees are more committed than lower ranked employees
- Seniority shows no significant effect on commitment. The respective hypothesis is not supported
- Task orientation shows mixed findings. Further conceptual grounding of the construct is necessary to clarify the existence and the directionality of the effects.
- The degree of feeling informed positively effects the commitment of employees, supporting the respective hypothesis
- Participation in integration measures yields no significant effect on commitment. The respective hypothesis thus is not supported.

Hypothesis	Independent variable	Dependent variable	Expected effect	SpecMatCo	SoftCo	Total
1c	Age	Commitment	-	Opposite	Opposite	✓
2	Gender	Commitment	0	Supp.	Supp.	✓
4b	Rank	Commitment	+	Supp.	Partly supp.	✓
5b	Seniority	Commitment	-	Not supp.	Not supp.	✓
6b	Task orientation	Commitment	0	Supp.	Not supp.	(.)
9a	Degree of feeling informed	Commitment	+	Not supp.	Supp.	(.)
10b	Integration measures	Commitment	+	Not supp.	Not supp.	✓

Supported		✓	Same effect
Not supp.		(.)	Different effect
Opposite		?	Contrary effect

Table 112: Summary of findings at SoftCo and SpecMatCo on commitment

The findings for uncertainty differ significantly between the two firms. In Table 113, the results for uncertainty for SpecMatCo and SoftCo are presented.

While findings in both firms indicate that gender has no effect on uncertainty, and that a higher degree of feeling informed effectively reduces uncertainty, the findings of the other variables differ between SoftCo and SpecMatCo. However, when investigating the effects in more detail, some of the differences can be explained:

- The significant positive effects of age on uncertainty can only be found in the partial model at SpecMatCo. The effect vanishes in the full model, indicating that it is spurious.
- The null-effect of education level on uncertainty at SpecMatCo might be caused by the low variance of the sample. 70% of the respondents have a diploma. Most other respondents mostly studied, are a master craftsmen or even own a doctoral degree.
- In the case of rank it is unclear whether the positive effect found at SoftCo is caused by specific characteristics of the integration process or not.
- The effect of seniority on uncertainty might differ between the different countries due to different work legislations. At SpecMatCo, the work legislation has less impact on different cohorts, whereas at SoftCo, clear cohort effects can be identified and linked to the work legislation.
- Task orientation is operationalized very differently. The findings therefore cannot be compared.
- The negative effect of integration measures on uncertainty found at SpecMatCo most likely is spurious.

Hypo-thesis	Independent variable	Dependent variable	Expected effect	SpecMatCo	SoftCo	Total
1c.1	Age	Uncertainty	-	Opposite	Not supp.	(.)
1c.2	Age	Uncertainty	+	Partly supp.	Not supp.	(.)
2	Gender	Uncertainty	0	Supp.	Supp.	✓
3b	Education level	Uncertainty	-	Not supp.	Supp.	(.)
4c	Rank	Uncertainty	-	Not supp.	Supp.	(.)
5c	Seniority	Uncertainty	+	Supp.	Not supp.	(.)
6b	Task orientation	Uncertainty	0	Supp.	Not supp.	(.)
9b	Degree of feeling informed	Uncertainty	-	Supp.	Supp.	✓
10c	Integration measures	Uncertainty	-	Opposite	Not supp.	(.)

Legend:
- Supported
- Not supp.
- Opposite
- ✓ Same effect
- (.) Different effect
- ? Contrary effect

Table 113: Summary of findings at SoftCo and SpecMatCo on uncertainty

Considering these explanations, a number of findings are supported in both studies:

- Age hardly shows an effect of uncertainty. Hence it can be concluded that older employees in general do not react with higher levels of uncertainty than their younger colleagues. Hence the respective hypotheses are not supported
- Gender shows no significant effect on uncertainty, confirming the postulated effects
- The more informed employees feel, the less uncertain they are

All other findings at present show mixed results and require further research in order to better understand the origins of the differences of the findings at SpecMatCo and at SoftCo.

Three findings are especially interesting: First, older employees react more positively to mergers and acquisitions than younger employees. In general, they are more committed and mostly show the same level of uncertainty as their younger colleagues.

The degree of feeling informed shows very positive effects on commitment and very negative effects on uncertainty. Obviously, information is the key for positive reactions of employees after mergers and acquisitions.

Participation in integration measures has no significant effect on reactions after mergers and acquisitions.

When considering the results on commitment and uncertainty, it needs to be considered that the M&A-transaction took place a while ago. Some important restructuring measures have been initiated already. It might be possible that due the time, which has passed between integration and research, the effects of the M&A-transaction on reactions have faded already. This implies the possibility that some of the effects of demographic and firm related characteristics, attitudes, as well as integration measures are no longer connected to the M&A-transaction.

Many of the findings had to be qualified with the help of group level, firm level or even environmental level variables. Obviously, some of these variables yield important moderating effects on the relationships of individual level variables on reactions after mergers and acquisitions. It is interesting to note that some of the higher level variables, which have been mentioned above, have been investigated in previous research on mergers and acquisitions. For example, the structure of the integration process has been found to affect success of mergers and acquisitions (Lucks & Meckl 2002). They argue that it is important to get the management structure ready and identify the responsibles as soon as possible. However, based on the results of this study, it is possible to interpret the findings: Early decisions on the management structure might reduce uncertainty of manager. Less feeling of uncertainty reduces dysfunctional behaviors. Hence the merger is more successful.

Hence further research is required to investigate the effects of demographic, firm related as well as attitudinal effects on reactions after mergers and acquisitions. Especially, research is necessary, which tracks the development of reactions after mergers and acquisitions over time in order to identify the effects and their dynamics more clearly. Also, future research needs to link group, firm and environmental level variables, which have been considered in previous studies on M&A-success, to cooperation. By doing so, some of the ambiguous or even contradicting effects found in different studies might be explained by considering the key moderating variable cooperation.

Future research thus needs to bridge the gap between cooperation and group, firm and environmental level variables in order to further validate the macro-micro-framework of M&A-success.

6.2. Cooperation of employees after mergers and acquisitions

In this study, cooperation is considered to be the key moderating variable for the realization of an abstract synergy potential. Cooperation thus moderates the generation of synergies.

Previous studies never investigated cooperation as an independent variable. Rather, they investigated different independent variables as well as M&A-success as dependent variable. These independent variables, however, often affected cooperation and not the synergy potential. In the present study, some of these independent variables and their effects on cooperation are considered. Due to the research design, firm level variables such as relative size of acquirer and acquisition target (e.g. Gerds, 2000; Bamberger, 1993; Kitching, 1967), performance of acquirer and acquisition target (e.g. Haunschild & Murrell, 1994), aspects of hostility of a takeover (e.g. Hitt, Harrison, Ireland, & Best 1998; Haleblian & Finkelstein 1999), or integration process (Lucks, & Meckl 2002) could not be investigated. As the focus of this study is on individual level variables, only two different research sites have been considered. Group level variables such as ingroup-outgroup bias (Haunschild & Murrell, 1994) or complementarity of management (e.g. Krishnan, Miller, & Judge, 1997) neither have been considered.

At the same time, a number of individual level variables have been investigated. The individual level variables comprise demographic characteristics, firm-related characteristics, attitudes as well as reactions after mergers and acquisitions. With the help of this data, some answers could be generated for the research question "Who builds cooperation relationships after mergers and acquisitions?"

In addition to the individual level variables, the effects of communication as well as the effects of integration measures have been considered. Last but not least, the isomorphic forces of structural cooperation requirements have been considered.

6.2.1. Effects of age on cooperation

6.2.1.1. Age and cooperation at SoftCo

While previous findings of Lansford, Sherman, & Antonucci (1998) and Carstensen, Isaacowitz, & Charles (1999) as well as earlier theorizing of Carstensen (1991, 1992, 1993) indicate that older employees have smaller social networks and higher intensity of social networks, the findings of this research indicates that these findings only to some extent apply for the specific case of cooperation networks. Obviously, older employees cooperate as intensively with new colleagues as younger employees. It is interesting to note that the average intensity of new relationships of older employees is higher than the average intensity of new relationships of younger employees. This supports the argumentation of Carstensen, Issacowitz, & Charles (1999), who claim that older individuals focus their attention on less relationships, which are more intense than those of younger individuals.

These findings have been supported by the exploratory interviews. Obviously, older employees are quicker to identify competent and similar others than their younger colleagues. The cooperation relationships with these selected colleagues are more intense.

It is important to note that the effect is stable in all models. Hence eve after controlling for rank as well as for seniority, the effects are stable.

While the findings of Socioemotional Selectivity Theory have been found to apply in different social contexts, the theory needs to be revisited in order to apply to organizational contexts. Seemingly, cooperation relationships follow different mechanisms than other types of social relationships, such as friendship or communication patterns.

6.2.1.2. Age and cooperation at SpecMatCo

While Carstensen et al. (1997) argue that older employees form less and more intensive relationships, the findings at SpecMatCo speak a different language. Regardless of their rank or seniority, older employees have been found to cooperate more with employees of the other previously separated firm than their younger colleagues. While older employees cooperate in the sum more intensively, the findings at SpecMatCo indicate no difference of intensity of single relationships.

6.2.1.3. Synopsis of effects of age on cooperation

In the integration of SpecMatCo as well as in the integration of SoftCo older employees only played a marginal role in the integration plans. They were hardly considered in integration teams, and they were hardly awarded with new roles unless they already had been in management positions before the M&A-transactions.

Despite this practical neglect of older employees, both studies show the same surprising results: Older people are not cooperating less than younger employees. The results at SpecMatCo show that they even cooperate more than their younger colleagues. The results at SoftCo indicate that they cooperate differently, insofar as they build more intensive relationships.

Obviously, while the predictions of Socioemotional Selectivity Theory have been confirmed for friendship and other social relationships, they do not apply for cooperation relationships. Therefore, further research is required to confirm the findings of this study. With the help of these findings then Socioemotional Selectivity Theory can be expanded to cooperation relationships. In addition to that, it is necessary to investigate, whether the effects of age on cooperation only hold after mergers and acquisitions, or whether they are generally true for cooperation relationships of older employees.

6.2.2. Effects of gender on cooperation

6.2.2.1. Gender and cooperation at SoftCo

A second surprising finding is that gender does have an effect on cooperation. Simmons, King, Tucker, & Wehner (1986) find that gender has no effect on choice between cooperation and competition. However, their research is based on narratives of students. Therefore, the validity of the results is hard to assess. Similarly, Stackman, & Pinder (1999) find that gender has no effect on work related relationships.

The results of this research indicate that gender does have a significant effect on cooperation:

- Women cooperate more than their male counterparts. It is important to note that the partial model shows mixed findings, which indicates only weakly the higher cooperation intensity of women. However, when controlling for departmental level effects, the findings show clearly a positive relationship between female gender and cooperation intensity. This indicates that women more often work in departments with little structural cooperation requirements and men more often work in departments with high structural cooperation requirements. Research, which does not control for structural effects, therefore comes to the conclusion that there is no difference between women and men.
- While women in sum cooperate more intensitvely than men, they have lower average intensity of new cooperation relationships. As there is no significant effect of the differences of average frequency, importance and strength of old and new

relationships (DelAvFreq, DelAvImp, DelAvStren), it can be concluded that women have weaker old relationships with colleagues from the old company as well. This finding is supported by Ibarra (1992), who finds that women tend to have weaker relationships that reach farther within the organization. However, while Ibarra (1992) finds that after controlling for structural and demographic characteristics, the effects of gender vanish, the present research shows that they become even stronger. The finding deserves special attention, because it suggests that there is a gender difference, and that women are cooperating more with new colleagues after mergers and acquisitions.

6.2.2.2. Gender and cooperation at SpecMatCo

In the partial model of the research at SpecMatCo, gender has been found not to have any effects on amount or quality of cooperation of employees in the partial model. At the same time, the full model shows positive effects of female gender on cooperation.
As has been noticed in 4.6, the findings for gender need to be considered carefully. Especially the null-findings might result from the small number of female respondents in the sample.

6.2.2.3. Synopsis of effects of gender on cooperation

Both studies show that female gender has, when controlling for other independent variables, positive effects on cooperation. The findings indicate that women often work in departments, with relatively low cooperation requirements. As a consequence, they seem to cooperate less than their male colleagues. However, when controlling for structural cooperation requirements, female gender shows positive effects on cooperation.
At the same time, the results of Ibarra (1992) have been replicated, which finds that women on the average have weaker instrumental ties than men. Hence her conceptual considerations can be expanded to the formation of new ties after mergers and acquisitions as well.
While Hyde (2005) finds that studies on gender differences hardly show significant differences, his argument that gender yields no differences on most dependent variables does not apply for cooperation. Further research thus is required to confirm the findings of female cooperation after mergers and acquisitions and to further identify specific differences between mal and female cooperation behaviors.

6.2.3. Effects of education level on cooperation

6.2.3.1. Education level and cooperation at SoftCo

In the partial model, the findings at SoftCo indicat a positive effect of education level on cooperation. However, the full model with control variable shows opposite effects, indicating that when considering structural cooperation requirements, higher education effectively reduces cooperation. This indicates that higher educated employees usually work in departments with higher structural cooperation requirements. However, within these departments, they cooperate less than their less educated colleagues. Most of the new cooperation ties have been formed between the development departments and the product management departments. Most employees in these departments are highly educated. This might explain the departmental level effects.

It is interesting to note that higher education does not confirm the findings of Klein et al. (2004) who find that higher education level increases centrality in advice as well as in friendship networks. Obviously, cooperation relationships follow different mechanisms than advice ties.

Nevertheless, there is no obvious explanation for this finding. Hence further research is required to confirm the finding and clarify the mechanisms that underlie the effects.

6.2.3.2. Education level and cooperation at SpecMatCo

The findings at SpecMatCo partly show the postulated positive effect of education level on cooperation. However, the more detailed analysis of the findings shows that higher educated employees do not cooperate more, but differently: They differ less between old and new colleagues.

6.2.3.3. Synopsis of effects of education level on cooperation

While the findings at SpecMatCo indicate that higher educated employees are more cooperative than employees with lower education, the results at SoftCo are mixed. Departmental level effects might account for some of the unexpected findings. However, further research is required to identify departmental level and firm level variables, which might account for the different findings.

6.2.4. Effects of rank on cooperation

6.2.4.1. Rank and cooperation at SoftCo

Higher rank clearly shows a positive effect on cooperation. Previous findings of Bovasso (1993) and Schoennauer (1967) show that higher management cooperates more after mergers and acquisitions than lower management. While Bovasso (1993) and Schoennauer (1967) only focused on cooperation of employees of the management levels, this research extends the findings to the operative levels as well.

6.2.4.2. Rank and cooperation at SpecMatCo

Rank has been found to strongly affect reactions of employees after mergers and acquisitions as well as cooperation at SpecMatCo. This is interesting to note insofar, as rank is a structural characteristic of individuals. Regardless of personality traits such as demographic characteristics or psychological factors, rank has been found to bear strong effects.

6.2.4.3. Synopsis of effects of rank on cooperation

Both studies show very strong positive effects of rank on cooperation of employees. Higher ranked employees cooperate more intensively than their lower ranked colleagues. At the same time, they cooperate differently as they have more balanced relationships portfolios. Even after controlling for different individual characteristics, the effects are stable and strong.

It is interesting to note that rank is an individual trait, which is caused by the formal structure of organizations. Hence higher ranked employees play an important role in bonding merged firms. Building on this finding, it is necessary to investigate in further detail, how different leadership styles affect the cooperation of higher ranked employees. Especially, it might be interesting what situational leadership styles (e.g. Gumpert & Hambleton 1979) might be most successful in initiating and manifesting cooperation between merged firms.

6.2.5. Effects of seniority on cooperation

6.2.5.1. Seniority and cooperation at SoftCo

While the predicted effects of Social Identity Theory do not hold for commitment and uncertainty, the results show a strongly negative effect of seniority on cooperation. As predicted by Social Identity Theory, cooperation with new colleagues decreases with higher seniority of employees. The more detailed analysis of cooperation strength by cohort in Table 114 shows that more senior employees cooperate much stronger with their old colleagues and somewhat weaker with new colleagues than their less senior employees.

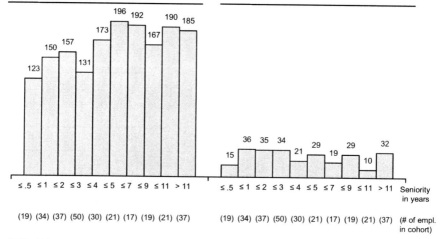

Table 114: Average cooperation strength by seniority cohort at SoftCo

This effect is mainly driven by a much higher number of cooperation relationships to old colleagues and only slightly driven by a higher average cooperation to old colleagues. As can be seen in Table 115, there is a very strong difference in number of ties with old colleagues amongst more senior and less senior employees. At the same time, there is only a slight difference in number of ties with new colleagues amongst more senior and less senior employees.

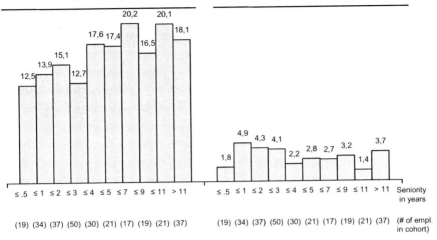

Table 115: **Average number of old and new cooperation relationships by seniority cohort at SoftCo**

In Table 116, the average strength of cooperation relationships for the different seniority cohorts is presented.

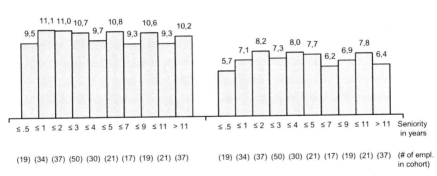

Table 116: **Average cooperation strength of old and new cooperation relationships by seniority cohort at SoftCo**

As can be seen, cooperation strength with new colleagues is generally lower than for old colleagues. However, there hardly is a difference amongst different seniority cohorts.

It is important to note that the results presented in Table 114, Table 115 and Table 116 are not controlled for effects of other independent variables. Therefore, they are not fully comparable to the results of the ANOVA-analyses for seniority.

Nevertheless, the findings of these additional analyses support the postulated hypothesis. Obviously, Social Identity Theory applies for cooperation of employees after mergers and acquisitions.

6.2.5.2. Seniority and cooperation at SpecMatCo

Seniority has been found to show to some extent the expected negative effects on cooperation. Previous work of Hogg, & Williams (2000) finds that longer group affiliation increases social identity. Mergers and acquisitions represent severe threats to the existing social identity of employees. Ashforth, & Mael 1989 find that threats to social identity evokes identity preserving behaviors. Identity can best be preserved by avoiding contact to the new colleagues. The findings support the argument that higher seniority leads to decreased cooperation with new colleagues. The qualitative impressions of the 39 interviews confirm this finding: More senior employees more frequently questioned the meaning of the M&A-transaction. Also, they more strongly felt that "the others" had different work styles and different ideas of how to do the business. At the same time, the interviews showed some remarkable exceptions: Some of the more senior employees knew each other and had learned to appreciate each other as competitors. These employees were even more effective in bonding with new colleagues.

6.2.5.3. Synopsis of effects of seniority on cooperation

Both studies support the hypothesis that more senior employees cooperate less than junior employees. Hence in both studies, the hypothesized negative effects of seniority on cooperation have been found. It is important to note that the predictions of Social Identity hold for cooperation as a dependent variable but not for commitment and uncertainty after mergers and acquisitions. Further research thus is required to identify the reasons, why Social Identity Theory applies for cooperation, and why it does not apply for commitment and uncertainty.

6.2.6. Effects of attitudes on cooperation

6.2.6.1. Attitudes and cooperation at SoftCo

Task orientation hardly shows a significant effect on number of cooperation relationships, frequency, importance or strength of cooperation. In the full model with control variable, it even shows a negative effect on the sum of cooperation frequency, cooperation importance and cooperation strength. Obviously, there are some departments with highly task oriented employees and high structural cooperation requirements.

However, it shows a consistent positive effect on cooperation quality. Obviously, highly task oriented employees get along better with their new colleagues than employees with low task orientation. In the exploratory interviews, those employees, who had a strong focus on the problems at hand and the daily work often got along well with their new colleagues. They frequently indicated that cultural differences or individual differences do not matter very much if work gets done well.

Further research is required to support these findings. Especially, it is necessary to develop valid and reliable scales for the standardized measurement of attitudes in order to identify further individual attitudes, which affect cooperation.

6.2.6.2. Attitudes and cooperation at SpecMatCo

While task orientation has no effect on reactions after mergers and acquisitions, task orientation has been found to strongly affect cooperation of employees. In line with Harringthon (2002: J5), the study at SpecMatCo shows that highly task oriented employees build more cooperation relationships and cooperate more frequently with new colleagues. However, the single item operationalization of task orientation bears limitations to the construct validity of the findings on the conceptual level. Further research is necessary to confirm the findings at SpecMatCo.

6.2.6.3. Synopsis of effects of attitudes on cooperation

The results of the studies at SpecMatCo and SoftCo cannot be compared due to the different operationalization of task orientation.

Despite the differences in operationalization, the two studies show that attitudes (i.e. task orientation and responsiveness in the case of SoftCo and task orientation and rule orientation in the case of SpecMatCo) have an effect on cooperation of employees after mergers and acquisitions. Hence there might be more attitudes, which yield an effect on cooperation.

Further research is necessary to identify and confirm further attitudes of employees, which affect cooperation after mergers and acquisitions.

6.2.7. Effects of commitment on cooperation

6.2.7.1. Commitment and cooperation at SoftCo

Commitment has been found to have a strongly positive effect on cooperation in the partial model and in the full model without control variables at SoftCo. At the same time, the full model with control variables shows no significant effects of commitment on cooperation. Basically, this indicates that highly committed employees are working in departments with high structural cooperation requirements.

There are different explanations for this finding:

- Commitment of employees really has a strong positive effect on cooperation as postulated in hypothesis 7.
- Mason & Griffin (2005) find that group task satisfaction is strongly correlated to individual task satisfaction. Task satisfaction in their study is similarly operationalized as commitment in the present study. This means that individual commitment strongly depends on group commitment. Hence employees within one department have highly similar levels of commitment. Assuming that commitment really has a positive effect on cooperation as postulated in hypothesis 7, high levels of departmental commitment thus should result in high levels of departmental cooperation, whereas low levels of departmental commitment result in low levels of departmental cooperation. In this study, departmental cooperation is taken as a proxy for structural cooperation requirements. Controlling for structural cooperation requirements thus eliminates the significant effect of commitment on cooperation. The lower the variance of commitment within a department, the weaker the effect of commitment on cooperation is after controlling for structural cooperation requirements.
- A second explanation might be that despite the conceptual reasoning commitment in reality depends on cooperation. Hence employees who cooperate more are more committed than colleagues who cooperate less. Due to the cross-sectional research design used in this study, it is not possible to test this explanation.

Van der Vegt, Emans, and Van de Vliert (2001) find that task interdependence in groups increases both, job as well as team satisfaction. According to their findings, both explanations offered above can be true. However, Van der Vegt, Emans, and Van de Vliert (2001) used a cross-sectional research design. While cross-sectional research designs can show the relationship between variables, they cannot empirically test the directionality of the relationship. As a consequence, neither the findings of Van de Vegt, Emans, and Van de

Vliert (2001) nor the findings of the present study can finally state the direction of the relationship between commitment and cooperation.

6.2.7.2. Commitment and cooperation at SpecMatCo

The findings at SpecMatCo similarly show strong positive effects of commitment on cooperation in the partial model and insignificant positive effects in the full model. This indicates that the commitment is strongly correlated to other variables.

6.2.7.3. Synopsis of effects of commitment on cooperation

Both studies show highly similar effects of commitment on cooperation. In the partial models, both studies show highly significant positive effects of commitment on cooperation. However, after controlling for structural cooperation requirements, the effect becomes insignificant.

A first explanation for the findings assumes that low intra-departmental variance of commitment leads to insignificant effects of commitment on cooperation after controlling for structural cooperation requirements. A second explanation assumes that cooperation is not a dependent but an independent variable for commitment. Hence commitment is the consequence of high levels of cooperation.

Therefore, longitudinal research on the relationship of commitment and cooperation is required to further explore and test these explanations. With the help of several measurements, it will be possible to identify the directionality of the effects between commitment and uncertainty.

6.2.8. Effects of uncertainty on cooperation

6.2.8.1. Uncertainty and cooperation at SoftCo

In the partial model, uncertainty shows a strong effect on cooperation: Highly uncertain employees cooperate less than employees, which do not feel uncertain. However, in the full model without control variables, this effect vanishes. This indicates covariance with other significant independent variables, which creates a spurious effect in the partial model. For example, uncertainty is strongly negatively correlated with rank. Rank shows a significant positive effect on cooperation in the full model. Hence the joint consideration of rank and uncertainty eliminates the effect of uncertainty on cooperation.

Still, this indicates that highly uncertain employees cooperate less, confirming the findings of Hogg and Terry (2000) as well as the findings of Schweiger and DeNisi (1991).

6.2.8.2. Uncertainty and cooperation at SpecMatCo

The findings at SpecMatCo indicate a positive effect of uncertainty on cooperation, which is opposite to the postulated effect. In the partial as well as in the full model, uncertainty is positively related to cooperation.

This result requires further consideration. Basically, there are three possible explanations for these findings:

- Uncertainty might not be the antecedent but the result of cooperation with new colleagues. According to this explanation, employees that have more cooperation relationships and that cooperate more frequently with new colleagues experience higher levels of uncertainty.
- Uncertainty might effectively lead to higher cooperation. Despite previous empirical findings and theoretical predictions, uncertainty might increase cooperation with new colleagues. A possible explanation for this unexpected finding might be that employees cooperate actively to reduce their uncertainty, following the saying that attack is the best form of defense. Buono, & Bowditch (1989) suggest that one coping strategy after M&A-transactions is benign-positive. However, benign-positive reactions are not linked to high levels of perceived uncertainty. Other researchers also suggest proactive coping strategies (Larsson, & Finkelstein 1999, Terry, & Callan 1997). However, these scholars do not investigate, whether the choice of a proactive coping strategy is linked to high levels of uncertainty. In the course of the study at SpecMatCo, this explanation can neither be supported nor be rejected.
- Uncertainty might affect the answers of respondents. A social desirability bias of respondents might motivate especially respondents with high uncertainty to answer according to socially acceptable behaviors. In the case of mergers and acquisitions, the socially acceptable behavior is cooperation. Hence the use of personal interviews to gather data on ego-centered networks might suffer from a strong respondent bias. This bias, however, can neither be quantified nor eliminated in the study at SpecMatCo.

6.2.8.3. Synopsis of effects of uncertainty on cooperation

The findings on the effects of uncertainty on cooperation strongly differ between SpecMatCo and SoftCo. While the findings at SoftCo support the postulated effect and show a negative effect of uncertainty on cooperation, the opposite is the case at SpecMatCo.

Three different explanations have been offered for the findings at SpecMatCo. The first explanation assumes that uncertainty is the consequence of higher levels of cooperation. This explanation can be ruled out with the help of the data found at SoftCo: In the partial model, the results at SoftCo show an effect, opposite to this explanation. In the full model, the effect is insignificant. Both findings do not support the first explanation.

The second explanation similarly can be rejected based on the findings. Again, the postulated effects are opposite to the findings at SoftCo.

The third explanation cannot be rejected. It might be possible that in the case of uncertainty, there is a respondent bias caused by social desirability (Edwards 1957).

Further research is required to investigate how employees react to structural cooperation requirements. Especially, longitudinal research is required to determine empirically the directionality of the effects of uncertainty and cooperation.

6.2.9. Effects of participation in integration measures on cooperation

6.2.9.1. Participation in integration measures and cooperation at SoftCo

Participation in integration measures shows a very strong positive effect on cooperation intensity. Employees who participated in integration measures show a strong increase in cooperation for all different measures of new cooperation relationships. In Graph 18, the effects of participation in integration measures on cooperation are listed. Four different dependent variables have been considered: Number of new ties, sum of frequency of new ties, sum of importance of new ties as well as sum of strength of new ties. For each dependent variable, the x-axis shows the number of integration measures that an employee participated in. Only one employee indicated participation in all six integration measures. This employee has not been considered as an outlier. On the y-axis, the average value for the respective cooperation measure is indicated. As can be seen, the most significant difference of participation in integration measures is between two and three participated integration measures. The number of new ties almost triples if employees participate in two instead of one integration measure. Similarly, the sum of frequency of new ties more than doubles as does the sum of importance and strength of new ties. Hence integration measures yield a strong effect mainly after the participation in the second integration measure.

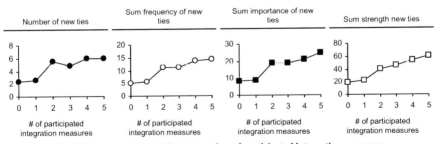

Graph 18: Cooperation intensity depending on number of participated integration measures

While increased participation in integration measures increases the cooperation of employees significantly, this analysis does not show, which effect specific integration measures yield on cooperation.

Six different types of integration measures have been considered in the research (see 5.4.2.4). In Graph 19, the different integration measures and their effects on different dependent variables of cooperation are indicated. For each dependent variable, the effects of participation in a specific cooperation measure are indicated. The percentage indicates the increase of cooperation if an employee indicates participation in a specific integration measure compared to other employees, who did not participate in this integration measures.

As can be seen, the most efficient integration measures are visits to other locations. Employees, who visit other locations cooperate more than two times as much with employees, who did not visit other locations. However, it needs to be noted that the values are not corrected for structural cooperation requirements and other independent variables.

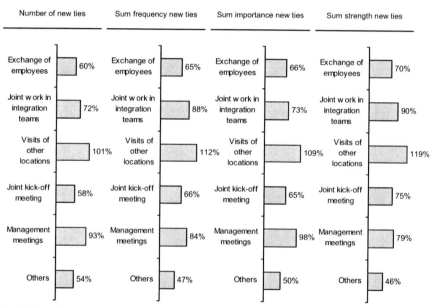

Graph 19: Change of cooperation after participation in integration measures (compared to non-participation)

Obviously, integration measures yield a very strong effect on cooperation. While of course some of these effects are spurious and caused by highly correlated independent variables such as rank or structural cooperation requirements, the full model with control variable still shows very strong effects of integration measures on cooperation.

6.2.9.2. Participation in integration measures and cooperation at SpecMatCo

Participation in integration measures shows a positive effect on cooperation in the research at SpecMatCo. In the partial as well as in the full model, the effects are partly supported. Closer examination of the sample structure at SpecMatCo show the reasons for the weak findings. One of the respondents transferred after the integration to the location of the other previously separated firm. There, he worked in a management position. However, all employees in the department, he was heading were from the other previously separated firm. Hence his most important coworkers almost exclusively were new colleagues. At the same time, this respondent did not participate in any integration measures. Hence his data strongly affects the findings. In Graph 20, the x-axis shows the number of participated integration measures. Two employees in the sample participated in no integration measure, 13 participated in one type of integration measure, ten participated in two integration measures, five in three integration measures, five participated in four integration measures and one employee participated in five different types of integration measures. On the y-axis, the cooperation with new colleagues is indicated for NumNewTies, SumFreqNew, SumImpNew, and SumStrenNew. The solid line links the averages of the employees, which participated in the same number of integration measures. The dotted line shows the value, if the data indicated by employee, who was relocated, is not considered.

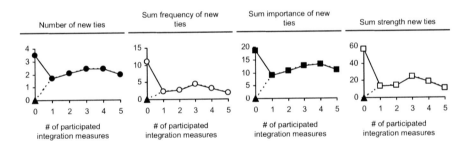

Graph 20: Cooperation intensity depending on number of participated integration measures at SpecMatCo

As can be seen, the relationship at SpecMatCo also shows a positive effect of integration measures on cooperation. However, due to the small sample of respondents, one employee strongly distorts the results. When considering the sample structure of the research at SpecMatCo, participation in integration measures similarly show strongly significant effects.

There is a second sample effect. As can be seen in 4.4.2.4, most respondents at SpecMatCo participated at least in one integration measure. Only two respondents did not participate in integration measures compared to roughly 50% of the respondents at SoftCo. It is possible that the marginal utility of integration measures strongly decreases after the first integration measure. In this case, the weak effect of integration measures on cooperation intensity would be the result of a sample bias.

6.2.9.3. Synopsis of effects of participation in integration measures on cooperation

Both studies show positive effects of participation in integration measures on cooperation. Considering the sample effects at SpecMatCo, it is even possible to say that participation in integration measures strongly increases cooperation of employees. With the help of the data gathered at SoftCo, it is even possible to rank the different integration measures according to effectiveness.

However, the research does not provide any insights on situational factors, which make the use of one or another integration measure advisable. For example, it might be that in specific situations, such as a hostile takeover, it might not be advisable to organize visits of the other locations. Further research thus is required to determine such firm level effects in order to determine the actual effect of different integration measures.

6.2.10. Effects of structural cooperation requirements on cooperation

6.2.10.1. Structural cooperation requirements and cooperation at SoftCo

Structural cooperation requirements strongly affect cooperation of employees. Employees, who work in departments with high structural cooperation requirements are more likely to cooperate more intensively than other employees, who work in departments with low structural cooperation requirements. Hence formal structure effectively shapes the cooperation of employees as argued by proponents of the organizational design school (e.g. Galbraith, 1974; Arrows, 1967) and as newer research on social networks indicates (e.g. Stackman & Pinder, 1999).

Structural cooperation requirements show very strong effects on cooperation. Formal structure channels cooperation relationships of employees effectively. In departments with high cooperation requirements, employees are very likely to also cooperate intensively.

The methodological limitations of the variable used to operationalize structural cooperation requirements cannot be neglected. However, in the case of the present research, the use of an aggregate measure to control for structural cooperation requirements is conceptually justified. The limitation to the computation of the control variable to departments of four or more employees effectively limits the covariance problem.

6.2.10.2. Structural cooperation requirements and cooperation at SpecMatCo

Structural cooperation requirements have been found to significantly affect individual cooperation. While structural cooperation requirements hardly affect the absolute values of cooperation, it does affect the relation of cooperation with old and new colleagues. Employees, who work in departments, which have lower shares of cooperation with old departments are most likely to similarly yield lower shares of cooperation with old colleagues. There are two methodological explanations why integration measures yield no stronger effects:

- In order to gather information on structural cooperation, a complete list of all departments of the organization has been presented to the respondents. The list comprised 94 different departments and top line managers of the two previously separated firms, with whom they could indicate departmental cooperation. However, in the ego-centered analysis, they were only asked to indicate their most important coworkers. As a consequence, there is a strong bias on strong individual level relationships, while on the departmental level, weak cooperation relationship is considered as well. Hence the relationship between individual level and departmental level cooperation is only based on strong individual relationships. Weak individual relationships are not considered for computing the effects. As a consequence of the measurement of individual level and departmental level cooperation, the relationship necessarily is lower than in reality.

- The data on cooperation relationships on the department level has been gathered with the help of key informants. The use of key informants to gather information on cooperation of departments suffers from a lack of overview of the cooperation activities of all employees in a department. First, it is difficult to observe cooperation relationships because they can only be observed in the moment of the transaction. Second, it is difficult to overview all transactions of colleagues within a department with other colleagues from other departments. As a consequence, it is highly likely that respondents answer according to their own cooperation situation. Hence the use of key informants to gather information on departmental cooperation bears a significant risk of a strong respondent bias. The measurement of cooperation requirements thus is questionable.

While the problems of the operationalization of the dependent and the control variable and a possible respondent bias cannot be discarded, structural cooperation requirements still play an important role for cooperation after mergers and acquisitions. Further research is required to address the methodological limitations of the control variable.

6.2.10.3. Synopsis of effects of structural cooperation requirements on cooperation

Both studies show significant positive effects of structural cooperation requirements on cooperation. In both studies, the effects of the control variables are much stronger than the effects of the other independent variables.

Cooperation relationships thus are not deliberate as other types of social relationships (e.g. friendship or romantic relationships). Rather, structure provides a framework for cooperation, within which, employees according to their individual characteristics cooperate. However, the degrees of freedom for cooperation are strongly constrained by structural cooperation requirements. As argued by Galbraith (1974) formal structure thus channels cooperation and provides boundaries, within which cooperation emerges.

Hence after mergers and acquisitions, employees most likely cooperate in line structural cooperation requirements. However, individual level factors influence a significant share of the variance of cooperation within these structures.

It is important to note that despite the methodological limitations of each of the control variables, both show highly similar results. This indicates that structural cooperation requirements really affect cooperation.

The two operationalizations used in this research only considered actual group level cooperation as a proxy for target structures. Further research is required to deal with the methodological problems of the measurement of structural cooperation requirements. Especially, it is necessary to further investigate, to what extent formal structures, which have been developed as part of the structural decision in the integration process, become implemented in the integration process, i.e. it is necessary to further explore the relationship between target structure and actual structure of individuals.

6.2.11. Summary for cooperation of employees after mergers and acquisitions

Cooperation is the key moderating variable for the generation of synergies. However, cooperation on the individual level never has been investigated in previous studies. As a consequence, there are no studies, which investigate the effects of individual level variables on cooperation after mergers and acquisitions. Also, there are no studies, which investigate the effects of information, integration measures as well as structural cooperation requirements on cooperation after mergers and acquisitions.

In this study, the question "Who builds cooperation requirements after mergers and acquisitions?" has been investigated at the example of two different firms, SoftCo and SpecMatCo. In Table 117, the summary of the effects is presented.

As can be seen, there are some differences in the findings at SpecMatCo and at SoftCo. When investigating the effects in more detail, some of the differences can be explained:

- Age in both studies does not show the expected effects. Both studies indicate that older employees cooperate either more (at SpecMatCo) or have more intensive cooperation relationships (at SoftCo)
- Gender in both studies also does not show the expected null effect. While the findings at SpecMatCo partly show null effects, the full model shows positive effects of female gender on cooperation. At SoftCo, all models show that women cooperate more than men and at the same time, have weaker relationships than men
- Education level shows positive effects at SpecMatCo and mixed findings at SoftCo
- The effects of task orientation cannot be explained due to the different operationalizations of the variable at SpecMatCo and SoftCo
- Uncertainty yields positive effects on cooperation, which most likely is generated by a respondent bias caused by social desirability.

These considerations and a number of similar findings yield insights, which can help to answer the research question:

- Older employees cooperate equally well or even more than their younger colleagues
- Women cooperate more after mergers and acquisitions after controlling for structural cooperation requirements
- Higher ranked employees clearly cooperate more than employees in lower ranks
- More senior employees cooperate less than their junior colleagues
- Higher commitment of employees increases cooperation after mergers and acquisitions
- Participation in integration measures strongly fosters the cooperation after mergers and acquisitions
- Structural cooperation requirements dominate all individual level effects strongly. Mostly, employees cooperate with employees, which are structurally connected to them

Hypo-thesis	Independent variable	Dependent variable	Expected effect	SpecMatCo	SoftCo	Total
1a	Age	Cooperation intensity	-	Opposite	Not supp.	(.)
1b	Age	Average intensity of ties	+	Not supp.	Partly supp.	(.)
2	Gender	Cooperation intensity	0	Partly supp.	Not supp.	(.)
3a	Education level	Cooperation intensity	+	Partly supp.	Mixed	(.)
4a	Rank	Cooperation intensity	+	Strongly supp.	Strongly supp.	✓
5a	Seniority	Cooperation intensity	-	Partly supp.	Strongly supp.	✓
6a	Task orientation	Cooperation intensity	+	Strongly supp.	Mixed	?
7	Commitment	Cooperation intensity	+	Partly supp.	Partly supp.	✓
8	Uncertainty	Cooperation intensity	-	Opposite	Partly supp.	?
10a	Integration measures	Cooperation intensity	+	Partly supp.	Strongly supp.	✓
11	Structural requirements	Cooperation intensity	+	Strongly supp.	Strongly supp.	✓

Supported		✓	Same effect
Not supp.		(.)	Different effect
Opposite		?	Contrary effect

Table 117: Summary of findings at SoftCo and SpecMatCo on cooperation

By summarizing the findings, a number of additional conclusions can be drawn:
- Cooperation strongly depends on structural variables: Rank and structural cooperation requirements all both structural variables. Rank is an individual level variable, which is structurally determined. Structural cooperation requirements are caused by the formal structure of the firm. In addition to these two variables, participation in integration measures represents a variable, which strongly affects cooperation after mergers and acquisitions. While integration measures are not determined by organizational structures, they are determined by the management.
- A significant share of the explained variance depends on individual characteristics of employees: Demographic characteristics, as well as seniority and reactions after mergers and acquisitions have been clearly identified as significant factors for the level of cooperation of employees after mergers and acquisitions.
  It is especially notable that older employees show similar cooperation or even more cooperation as their younger colleagues. Also women cooperate more intensively than their male colleagues.

Due to the exploratory nature of this study, most of the findings require further conceptualization, replication and refinement. First, conceptualization is needed for the factors, which have been established with the help of a mix of exploratory and confirmatory factor analyses. With the help of more theoretically grounded factors, it is possible to increase the construct validity of this research. Second, the replication of the results is needed to test the reliability of the findings. Insights on individual level variables on the one hand side are easy to use in practical context. On the other hand, there is a risk of generalizing findings, which are not yet confirmed in different settings. Third, refinement is needed to further explore contextual variables, which affect the individual level variables.

A more general finding is the fact that many concepts and findings of previous research on social relationships cannot easily be transferred to cooperation relationships. For example, while Socioemotional Selectivity Theory is well established and tested for friendship or advice, it does not hold for cooperation. Hence existing theories need to be expanded to apply for cooperation as well.

Also, the findings indicate a number of effects of independent variables on cooperation after mergers and acquisitions, which previous studies on mergers and acquisitions partly have considered before. However, none of these studies investigated cooperation as a key moderating variable. Therefore, future research on mergers and acquisitions needs to (a) consider cooperation as a moderating variable and (b) conceptualize the effects of independent variables correctly as effects on value creation potential and as effects on the moderating variable cooperation. By doing so, it is possible to separate effects on the synergy potential, respectively the value creation potential and the moderating effect of cooperation on the realization of the value creation potential.

Last but not least, further research on group level and firm level variables is needed to understand, how such contextual variables influence the cooperation after mergers and acquisitions. The present study only focused on individual level variables and structural cooperation requirements as a group level variable. However, other firm level variables most certainly affect cooperation. These effects need to be investigated more closely to further understand the role of cooperation in the generation of synergies and thus the success of mergers and acquisitions.

7. Discussion of results for research question "Who cooperates with whom?"

"Who cooperates with whom after mergers and acquisitions?" This question has two answers: A simple one and a more complex one. The simple one is: „Colleagues within previously separated firms do, colleagues from different previously separated firms don't."

Theoretically, every employee can have a cooperation relationship with every other employee in the merged firm. In reality, only a small percentage of the theoretically possible number of relationships exists and has been indicated in this research. The ratio of indicated and possible relationships between employees of previously separated firms is very low: Only 1.9% of all possible unilateral cooperation relationships between employees of previously separated firms have been formed. That means that more than 98% of all possible relationships have not been formed after the M&A-transaction. The number becomes even more dramatic, when it is compared to the relationships within the previously separated firms: 13.8% of all possible unilateral cooperation relationships within the previously separated firms exist. This is more than seven times the number of new relationships.

Now one might argue that SoftCo was only recently integrated, and that it takes more time to build relationships. Then it is possible to compare the new relationships between the previously separated firms with the relationships within the previously separated firms, which both have been formed after the M&A-transaction. The relationships within the previously separated firms can be differentiated by age: Assuming that most cooperation relationships are formed only shortly after the entry of an employee in the firm, it is possible to use seniority as a proxy for the age of relationships: The age of a relationship is determined by the seniority of the less senior relationship partner. For example, if one of the relationship partners entered the firm five years before the research and the second relationship partner entered the firm two years before the research, the maximum age of the cooperation relationship is two years. Hence based on this proxy, the maximum age of relationships can be determined. While it is not possible to determine the exact minimum age of cooperation relationships with the help of this proxy, it still can be assumed that most cooperation relationships are formed after a short time.

The relationships within the previously separated firms can thus be classified in two groups: The first group contains relationships, which potentially have been formed before the M&A-transactions. These relationships are three years or older. The second group contains relationships, which must have been formed after the M&A-transaction. For each group, the number of indicated relationships and the number of theoretically possible relationships can be determined.

While the ratio of indicated to possible unilateral relationships, which potentially existed before the M&A-transaction is 15.3%, the ratio of relationships within the previously separated firms, which have been formed after the M&A-transaction still is 12.7%. This indicates that there are some differences caused by age of cooperation relationships. The older a potential relationship is, the more likely it is that it becomes an existing relationship.

In addition to the scarcity of relationships between the previously separated firms, the average intensity of new relationships between the previously separated firms is significantly weaker than that of relationships within the previously separated firms. In Table 118, the intensity of the different types of relationships is indicated for both, the new relationships at SoftCo and SpecMatCo as well as the old relationships at SoftCo and SpecMatCo. In the fields to the left, the characteristic of the relationships as well as the possible range of values are indicated. In the first column, the average values for indicated relationships between employees of different previously separated firms are indicated. In the next column, the average values for all indicated relationships between employees of the same previously separated firm are presented. In the third and fourth column, these relationships are grouped by their maximum age. The first group comprises all relationships, which potentially were formed before the M&A-transaction. The second group of relationships comprises all relationships, which were certainly formed after the M&A-transaction. In the fifth and sixth column, the results for SpecMatCo are indicated.

	SoftCo				SpecMatco	
	Between previously separated firms	Within previously separated firms			Between previously separated firms	Within previously separated firms
		All	≥ 3 years	< 3 years		
Average frequency (1 to 5)	2.17	2.60	2.52	2.67	1.98	3.29
Average importance (1 to 5)	3.71	3.73	3.72	3.74	3,76	3.97
Average strength (1 to 25)	8.62	10.23	9.96	10.65	7.62	13,40

Table 118: Intensity of cooperation relationships within and between previously separated firms at SoftCo and SpecMatCo[9]

As can be seen in both studies, cooperation frequency and thus cooperation strength is higher within the previously separated firms than between the previously separated firms. It is

---

[9] The values for frequency, importance and strength have been recalculated to match the scales used in the SoftCo-research. Hence the four-point scale for frequency has been expanded to five points by multiplying the score with 5/4. The seven-point scale for importance has been reduced to five points by multiplying the score with 5/7. The 28-point scale for strength has been reduced by multiplying the score with 25/28.

interesting to note that the new relationships within the previously separated firms at SoftCo are even slightly stronger than the older relationships. At the same time, the average importance of cooperation relationships hardly shows differences.

The results for both, existence as well as intensity of cooperation relationships, indicate that cooperation after mergers and acquisitions is difficult to achieve. While newcomers seem to be fully integrated after three years, it obviously is more difficult to integrate employees of previously separated firms.

The more complex answer to the question "Who cooperates with whom?" requires asking the second part of the research question as formulated in 1.6.3: "What are antecedents and constraints of cooperation relationships?"

This question again can be split in two questions: The first question asks about the antecedents and constraints, which influence the likelihood of existence of a cooperation relationship between any two employees of previously separated firms. Answers for this question are generated based on the findings of the research at SoftCo. Due to methodological limitations, there are no findings on likelihood of existence of relationships in the study at SpecMatCo.

The second question asks about the antecedents and constraints, which influence the cooperation intensity of an existing cooperation relationship. Answers for this question are generated based on the findings of the research at SoftCo and at SpecMatCo. Due methodological limitations of the research at SpecMatCo, some of the analysis in the next sections can only be generated for the data collected at SoftCo.

7.1. Likelihood of existence of cooperation relationships

The answer for the first question is relatively easy: Based on the findings of the empirical investigation at SoftCo, there are a number of different factors influencing the likelihood of existence of cooperation relationships. A first important factor is homophily between employees. The second important set of factors consists of isomorphic forces, formed by structural constraints affecting the cooperation between employees.

"Homophily is the principle that a contact between similar people occurs at a higher rate than among dissimilar people" (McPherson, Smith-Lovin, & Cook 2001). Berscheid, & Reis (1998) point out that mutual attraction is especially important for the initiation of relationships. Mutual attraction, however, is strongly based on homophily. Relationships between individuals, which feel attracted to each other are thus more likely to exist.

In this research, similarity of demographic characteristics such as age, gender, education level and education content, similarity of seniority, similarity of work attitudes, as well as similarity of reactions after the M&A-transaction were assumed to increase the likelihood of existence of cooperation relationships. The results in Table 101 show that all but one aspect of similarity yield a positive effect on the likelihood of existence of relationships. The different characteristics of employees, whose similarity increases the likelihood of existence of relationships are:

- Age similarity
- Gender similarity
- Education level similarity
- Education content similarity
- Seniority similarity
- Work attitudes similarity
- Uncertainty similarity.

However, similarity of commitment is the only characteristic of employees, whose similarity does not increase the likelihood of existence of relationships. The explanation for this finding is the fact that commitment of employees is the necessary condition for the formation of relationships. Similarity of commitment then is a contingent factor, which increases the likelihood of formation between two specific individuals. Highly committed employees are more likely to build relationships than little committed employees. Hence if two employees are highly committed, it is very likely that they form a cooperation relationship. However, if two employees are poorly committed, they are unlikely to form relationships at all. Hence it is unlikely that they form a relationship despite their similarity. The assumed effects of similarity of commitment and likelihood of existence of a relationship are presented in Illustration 41. On the right side of Illustration 41, the assumed effects of commitment of two employees on likelihood of existence of relationships are presented. On the right side, the empirical results are presented. Employees are classified as demonstrating high commitment, when their score for commitment exceed the median of all investigated employees. Low commitment thus is below the median of commitment. The percentage in each of the four fields describes the ratio of the indicated unilateral relationships and the possible number of relationships for the respective constellation of commitment of pairs of employees. In brackets, the maximum possible number of relationships in the respective fields is indicated.

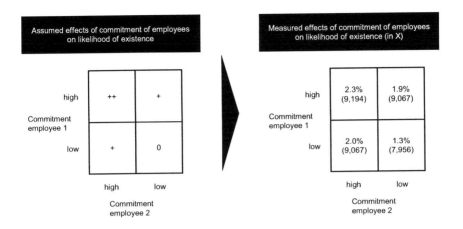

Illustration 41: Effects of commitment similarity and sum of commitment on likelihood of existence of relationships

As can be seen, in line with the argument elaborated above, high commitment from both employees strongly increases the likelihood of existence of ties. However, at the same time low commitment from both employees strongly reduces the likelihood of existence of ties. The ratio of indicated and possible relationships of employees with high/high and low/low commitment is lower than the ratio of indicated and possible relationships of employees with high/low and low/high commitment. As a consequence, dissimilar commitment results in higher likelihood of cooperation than dissimilar commitment. Hence the unexpected effect for similarity of commitment is a result of different motivational stances and not of homophily.

A second set of factor, which increases the likelihood of existence of cooperation relationships are isomorphic forces at the workplace (Lazega, Duijin (1997). Isomorphic forces are external constraints such as formal organizational structures, which strongly influence network structures. In this research, isomorphic forces consist of structural positions of employees as well as of management interventions:
- Dissimilar rank increases the likelihood of existence of new cooperation relationships. Obviously, employees quickly build relationships to their supervisors, respectively to their subordinates in line with the formal reporting structure.
- Structural cooperation requirements strongly affect the likelihood of existence of cooperation relationships. While the ratio of indicated cooperation relationships to possible relationships is very low, the likelihood of existence of cooperation relationships strongly increases with increasing structural cooperation requirements. This indicates that structure strongly dominates the cooperation networks of firms.

The strong effect of structural cooperation requirements also indicates that there are hardly any cooperation relationships form between employees of different previously separated firms at random without cooperation requirements.
- Participation in integration measures strongly increases the likelihood of existence of a cooperation relationship between employees.

In a nutshell, the likelihood of existence of relationships depends on homophily and on structure. While homophily yields a number of significant effects, structure strongly dominates likelihood of existence of cooperation to a large extent: Participation in integration measures can fully compensate for effects of demographic dissimilarities. According to Table 89, participation of both employees in integration measures can almost compensate for maximum dissimilarities of demographic characteristics[10].

7.2. Intensity of cooperation relationships

The answer for the second question is more complex.

Previous research on social networks in different settings shows homophily effects not only on existence of relationships but also on relationship intensity: Marsden (1988) finds homophily in core discussion networks, Verbrugge (1977, 1983) finds homophily in friendship networks, and Ibarra (1995) finds race homophily in ego-centered cooperation networks. These researchers did not control for age of relationships. However, the findings of this study indicate that homophily shows different effects at different ages of cooperation relationships. Based on the research setup of Marsden (1988), Verbrugge (1977, 1983) and Ibarra (1995), it is very likely that they investigated mostly mature relationships.

While previous studies investigated effects of ingroup-outgroup effects on integration after mergers and acquisitions (e.g. Marks 1988; Buono, & Bowditch 1989; Haunschild, Moreland, & Murrell 1994), there are no studies, which investigated homophily effects after mergers and acquisitions. Hence age of cooperation relationships as well as effects of mergers and acquisitions need to be considered as explorative explanations for the findings on intensity of cooperation relationships.

In Table 119 the findings on intensity of cooperation relationships after mergers and acquisitions gathered in the research at SpectMatCo and in the research at SoftCo are presented.

---

[10] The variable age similarity can take values between 0 and 3. The variable gender similarity can take values of 0 and 1. The variable of education level similarity can take values from 0 to 4. The variable education content similarity can take values from 0 to 1. The variable participation in education content can take values from 0 to 2. Looking at the different regression coefficients in Table 89, it is possible to calculate the maximum effects of dissimilarity of demographic characteristics and the maximum effect participation in integration measures. According to this calculation, maximum dissimilarity creates a negative effect of 0.118, while participation in integration measures creates a positive effect of up to 0.092.

Hypo-thesis	Independent variable	Dependent variable	Expected effect	SpecMatCo	SoftCo	Total
12b	Similar age	Intensity of relationship	+	Not supp.	Not supp.	✓
13b	Similar gender	Intensity of relationship	+	Not supp.	Not supp.	✓
14b	Similar education level	Intensity of relationship	+		Partly supp.	
15b	Similar education content	Intensity of relationship	+		Opposite	
16b	Similar rank	Intensity of relationship	-		Opposite	
17b	Similar seniority	Intensity of relationship	+		Opposite	
18b	Similar work attitudes	Intensity of relationship	+	Mixed	Not supp.	(.)
19b	Similar commitment	Intensity of relationship	+		Opposite	
20b	Similar uncertainty	Intensity of relationship	+		Mixed	
21b	Integration measures	Intensity of relationship	0	Strongly supp.	Partly supp.	✓
22b	Structural requirements	Intensity of relationship	+	Partly supp.	Strongly supp.	✓

Legend: Supported / Not supp. / Opposite — ✓ Same effect / (.) Different effect / ? Contrary effect

Table 119: Synopsis of results for findings at SpecMatCo and SoftCo

As can be seen, most of the findings in the different studies are similar. Despite the differences of the research designs, both studies yield similar effects. Only similarity of work attitudes shows mixed findings at SpecMatCo. There are two explanations for this finding. First, work attitudes are operationalized highly differently in the SpecMatCo-study than in the SoftCo-study. In the SpecMatCo-study, respondents are asked to indicate, how similar the work attitudes of their important coworkers and their own work attitudes are. In the SoftCo-study, work attitudes of respondents are gathered and the similarity of the work attitudes is computed based on the information provided by each respondent. Also, similarity of work attitudes only yields positive effects on quality of cooperation relationships, which have not been considered in the SoftCo-study. For frequency, importance and strength of cooperation, the findings at SpecMatCo yield no significant effect similar to the SoftCo-study.

While the homophily principle holds for the likelihood of existence of new cooperation relationships after mergers and acquisitions, it hardly holds for an explanation of the intensity of cooperation relationships.

- Age homophily is not supported in both studies
- Gender homophily is not supported in both studies

- Homophily of education level is partly supported in the partial model. However, in the full model without control variable and the full model with control variable do not show any effects in the SoftCo-study
- Education content similarity shows negative effects on cooperation intensity in the SoftCo-study. This implies that employees with different educational background are more likely to cooperate than employees with the same educational background
- Similarity of seniority also shows negative effects on cooperation intensity in the SoftCo-study. Hence junior employees are more likely to cooperate with employees of senior levels than with employees on their level
- Work attitude homophily is not supported in both studies
- Similarity of commitment shows negative effects on intensity of cooperation in the SoftCo-study
- Similarity of uncertainty shows mixed effects: Some aspects of intensity are positively, some are negatively affected in the SoftCo-study.

While homophily hardly affects intensity of new cooperation relationships, structural position of employees and management measures do.

- Rank similarity yields positive effects on cooperation intensity in the SoftCo-study. This means that employees of similar rank cooperate more intensively than employees of different ranks. The findings in the SoftCo-study indicate that the higher intensity is mainly caused by higher frequency of cooperation. Hence employees of similar rank cooperate more frequently in relationships, which were formed between previously separated firms.
- Participation in integration measures shows positive effects on intensity of cooperation in both studies
- Structural cooperation requirements show positive effects on intensity of cooperation in both studies despite different operationalizations.

In a nutshell, while homophily strongly affects likelihood of existence of cooperation relationshisp, it does not affect the cooperation intensity. A number of similarities between employees even show effects opposite to homophily effects. Also, rank similarity yields results opposite to the postulated effects of isomorphic forces.

7.2.1. Explanations for findings on intensity of cooperation relationships

A number of different explanations are offered in the following paragraphs, why homophily does not effect the intensity of cooperation relationships. A first explanation assumes that homophily might only apply for existence of relationships but not necessarily for intensity of cooperation. A second explanation assumes that homophily is a dynamic concept, which increases over time. Hence new relationships should show less homophilous effects than old relationships. A third explanation assumes that there are fundamental differences between relationships, which are formed within a firm and others, which are formed between employees of different merged firms.

7.2.1.1. Explanation 1: "Homophily only applies for existence but not for intensity of relationships"

According to the first explanation, homophily does not apply for intensity of cooperation relationships. Until today, only few studies investigated intensity of cooperation relationships. One example of a study on networks at the workplace is Ibarra's investigation of racial and gender effects on social networks at the workplace (Ibarra 1995). In this study, she gathered ego-centered network data. Intensity was measured as frequency. She measured homophily "… as the proportion of same-race contacts mentioned among total citations across the five network questions" (Ibarra 1995: 686). She finds that minorities have more heterogeneous social networks than members of the majority. However, as she gathers the data with the help of ego-centered networks without controlling for the actual availability of same race and other-race relationship partners, her research is not conclusive about effects of homophily on intensity of relationships. Similarly, Lazega, & Van Dijn (1997) investigate cooperation relationships between employees of a law firm. While they operationalized homophily appropriately and measured the effects with the help of a logistics regression model, they only investigated the existence of relationships and not the intensity of relationships. Bacharach, Bamberger, Vashdi (2005) also investigated only existence of ties when examining supportive relationships at the work place.

Due to the lack of conclusive findings in previous studies, the existence of effects of homophily on intensity of cooperation relationships has been tested with the help of the data gathered in the SoftCo-study. In order to test, whether homophily exists for intensity of cooperation relationships, all indicated relationships within the previously separated firms, which have been formed before the M&A-transaction have been investigated. The results show significant homophilous effects for education level, education content, seniority and work attitudes. Also, the results show homophily for rank, which is opposite to the postulated effects. However, the results do not show effects of homophily for age as well as gender. From these findings, it can be concluded that homophily effects on intensity of cooperation relationships exist. The first explanation can be discarded, because there are effects of homophily on intensity of cooperation.

7.2.1.2. Explanation 2: "Homophily increases over time"

"Homophily is considered by many to be a law of social relationships" (Reagans 2005: 1381). This means that homophily should apply in all contexts and for all types of relationships. However, according to the second explanation, homophily is a dynamic phenomenon and depends on time. The second explanation thus needs to be tested by comparing old and new relationships within the previously separated firms. In order to do that, all relationships, which potentially have been formed previously to the M&A-transaction are compared to relationships, which have certainly be formed in the aftermath of the M&A-transaction. In Table 108, the full model with control variables is presented for relationships, which have been formed after the M&A-transaction within the previously separated firms. As can be seen, the full model shows strong support of age homophily as well as homophily for seniority. However, effects of gender homophily, education level homophily as well as education content homophily cannot be found.

Rank dissimilarity yields positive effects on new cooperation relationships within the previously separated firms. This indicates that less senior employees quickly build intensive cooperation relationships with their supervisors. Also, structural cooperation requirements strongly influence the intensity of cooperation relationships.

Compared to the full models with control variable for old relationships in Table 104, the results for new relationships within the previously separated firms show some notable differences:

- The new relationships within previously separated firms show significant effects of age homophily, while there is no such effect for older relationships.
- The new relationships show no effect of gender similarity on cooperation intensity, while the older relationships show an unexpected negative effect of gender similarity on cooperation intensity. As analyzed in 5.9.8, the negative effects of gender similarity are caused by male respondents, who indicated more female cooperation relationship partners. Female respondents show no homophilous effects.
- The new relationships show weak negative effects of work attitude similarity on cooperation intensity, while older relationships show strong positive effects of work attitudes similarity in cooperation intensity. This indicates that attitude similarity one emerges after a longer period of cooperation. It seems likely that repeated interaction is necessary to recognize attitude similarities and translate the gathered knowledge about the attitudes of relationship partners into different intensity of cooperation relationships. It further is interesting that attitude similarity has no effect on intensity of new cooperation relationships between previously separated firms. Attitudes are elements of culture. According to many studies, cultural differences have a negative effect on integration or merger success (Cartwright, & Cooper 1993b, Hambrick, & Cannella 1993, Chatterjee et al. 1992. See also 1.5.3.2.3). However, the findings

indicate that similarity of attitudes only longer periods after mergers and acquisitions affect the cooperation intensity.
- While new relationships show significant negative effects of rank similarity, older relationships show significant positive effects of rank similarity on intensity of cooperation relationships.

Obviously, there are some notable differences between new and old relationships. These differences indicate that homophily might develop over time and change during the process. While for new relationships more obvious similarities such as age homophily matter, more implicit characteristics such as the similarity of work attitudes matter for older relationships. Hence the second explanation cannot be discarded. Homophily effects in older relationships are different from homophily effects in newer relationships.

7.2.1.3. Explanation 3: "There are fundamental differences between relationships within and between firms"

According to the third explanation, homophily effects in relationships formed after M&A-transactions are different from homophily effects in relationships formed regularly between newcomers in a firm and their more senior colleagues.

In order to test this explanation, newly formed relationships within the previously separated firms were compared to newly formed relationships between the previously separated firms.

Hypo-thesis	Independent variable	Dependent variable	Expected effect	New ties within prev. sep. firms	New ties between prev. sep. firms	Total
12a	Similar age	Intensity of relationship	+	Strongly supp.	Not supp.	✓
13a	Similar gender	Intensity of relationship	+	Not supp.	Not supp.	(.)
14a	Similar education level	Intensity of relationship	+	Not supp.	Not supp.	✓
15a	Similar education content	Intensity of relationship	+	Not supp.	Opposite	?
16a	Similar rank	Intensity of relationship	-	Opposite	Opposite	✓
17a	Similar seniority	Intensity of relationship	+	Strongly supp.	Opposite	?
18a	Similar work attitudes	Intensity of relationship	+	Opposite	Not supp.	(.)
22a	Structural requirements	Intensity of relationship	+	Strongly supp.	Strongly supp.	✓

Supported	✓	Same effect
Not supp.	(.)	Different effect
Opposite	?	Contrary effect

Table 120: Comparison of full models with control variable for intensity of new relationships within and between previously separated firms

In Table 120, the results for the full models with control variable for intensity of cooperation relationships for new ties within and for new ties between previously separated firms are presented.

Both types of relationships show low levels of homophily. This further supports the finding that new relationships differ from old relationships, because homophily is dynamic and emerges over time. However, there are some differences between new relationships between previously separated firms and new relationships within previously separated firms.

- While new cooperation relationships within the previously separated firms show strong effects of age homophily on intensity of cooperation relationships, this effect is not found for new ties between previously separated firms.
- While similarity of education content has no effect on intensity of cooperation relationships within previously separated firms, similarity of education content yields negative effects on intensity of cooperation relationships between previously separated firms.
- While similarity of seniority yields positive effects on cooperation intensity of new relationships within previously separated forms, it yields negative effects on cooperation intensity of new relationships between previously separated firms.
- While similarity of work attitudes show a weak negative effect on intensity of cooperation relationships, it show no effect on new cooperation relationships between previously separated firms. This finding is especially interesting, because many studies on mergers and acquisitions emphasize the importance of cultural differences as integration barriers (e.g. Cartwright, & Cooper 1993b).

A number of different explanations are offered for the differences between relationships, which have been formed within the previously separated firms and between employees of previously separated firms. First, employees of previously separated firms at SoftCo work in different locations. Previous research by Van den Bulte, & Moenaert (1998) indicates that collocation enhanced the cooperation between R&D-teams. Earlier, Bochner, Duncan, Kenney, & Orr (1976) have found that social interaction in high rise buildings strongly depends on proximity. Hence it is likely that there are differences between relationships formed between previously separated firms from different locations and within firms in one location. Being in different locations might be one firm-level explanation for the generally low levels of cooperation between employees of previously separated firms. At the same time, being in the same location increases the number of opportunities for social interaction. In social interactions, however, homophily might yield stronger effects than in mere instrumental cooperation interactions. This might explain, why relationships in the same location show effects of age homophily, and gender homophily on intensity of cooperation relationships.

A second explanation for different findings for new relationships between the previously separated firms and within the previously separated firms are ingroup-outgroup effects. Research on mergers and acquisitions shows that employees experience "we against them"-feelings, leading to devaluation of outsiders and appreciation of insiders (Marks 1988; Buono, & Bowditch 1989; Haunschild, Moreland, & Murrell 1994; compare also 1.5.3.3).

While ingroup-outgroup effects can explain the generally lower levels of intensity of cooperation relationships between employees of previously separated firms (see Illustration 41), they cannot explain why employees from previously separated firms, who work in different locations show significant effects on cooperation, which are not homophilous. First, dissimilarity of education content increases intensity of cooperation. Second, dissimilarity of seniority increases cooperation. Hence both explanations, the physical proximity hypothesis as well as the ingroup-outgroup explanation can be discarded. While it is well possible that physical proximity moderates the strength of cooperation intensity, it seems unlikely that it moderates the directionality of the effects of homophily on cooperation relationships as well. Also, if the ingroup-outgroup explanations would apply, there should be no positive effects of dissimilarity on cooperation intensity either.

An alternative explanation for the positive effects of dissimilarity of education content on cooperation intensity might be the complementarity of knowledge. According to Nielsen (2005), relational embeddedness of knowledge is a full mediator for the creation of knowledge based synergies in alliances. However, it is highly unlikely that different educational backgrounds should generate synergies after M&A-transactions. Educational background consists of knowledge, which can be acquired outside the firm. Hence it is not necessary to engage in mergers and acquisitions to integrate employees with other educational backgrounds into the firm. Complementarity effects can be discarded as explanation for the effects of dissimilarity of education content on cooperation intensity.

Dissimilarity of seniority might be explained with specific mentoree-mentor relationships, which emerge after M&A-transactions. As Kram (1983) points out, mentor-mentoree relationships are especially effective in times of development of roles and of role confusion. Stokes (1994) point out that "The experienced person communicates information, insight, knowledge, tips, techniques, and advice and counsel about the culture of the organization, its key players, their strategies and the strategies of the enterprise, and the politics of how work gets accomplished" (Stokes 1994: 34). After mergers and acquisitions, employees need to learn about the merged firm. Hence employees might seek mentors to learn about the new organization. The most utile mentors, however, are employees with high seniority. The most thankful mentorees are employees with low seniority. However, if mentoring was a main driver for the intensity of cooperation relationships, the effect should be similar in the case of young relationships within the previously separated firms. This is not the case. Therefore, mentoring as an explanation for the positive effects of dissimilarity on cooperation intensity has to be discarded as well.

A better explanation for the findings is offered by Burt's concept of structural equivalence. Burt (1992) argues that structural equivalence of actors in social networks means that actors with similar relational characteristics are structurally equivalent. According to Burt (1992), structurally equivalent actors often share similar individual traits such as education, age, and other characteristics.

Structurally equivalent actors are less likely to cooperate with each other, because they are in direct competition. Focusing the concept on demographic characteristics, similarity of education content and similarity of seniority might generate a structural equivalence situation for actors, which reduces their cooperation intensity. Especially employees within a merged department should feel the competitive pressure more than employees of different functions. Therefore, employees of different merged firms might prefer to cooperate more intensively with colleagues, with whom they are not in direct competition. However, newcomers do not show this effect of structural equivalence with cooperation relationships within the same firm. As they arrive newly in a department, there hardly can be competition between employees of similar seniority. This explanation is further supported by findings of Reagans (2005). He finds that homophily depends on the number of employees with similar traits in an organizational unit. The findings of Reagans "… indicate that being the same tenure has a positive effect on communiation frequency, but that positive effect becomes less positive as the number of people like the focal respondent increases" (Reagans 2005: 1379). In the case of the SoftCo merger, the number of similar others in each department doubled or even tripled. As a consequence, homophilous effects should strongly decrease according to Reagans' (2005) argumentation.

Further research is required to understand the effects of structural equivalence on cooperation after mergers and acquisitions. It is necessary to understand, what context variables influence the effects of structural equivalence. Furthermore, it is necessary to understand, at what point the effects of structural equivalence vanish and homophily effects dominate. Last but not least, it is necessary to investigate, how these effects can either be compensated with the help of additional integration measures, or how these effects can be used in designing integration processes and integration measures after mergers and acquisitions.

7.3. Summary for cooperation relationships after mergers and acquisitions

"Who cooperates with whom?", "What are antecedents and constraints of cooperation relationships?", "How do structural cooperation requirements influence cooperation after mergers and acquisition?"

These research questions have been tackled in the previous paragraphs. The findings at SoftCo show that generally, the ratio of existing to possible cooperation relationships within the previously separated firms is much higher than between the previously separated firms. Hence employees prefer to work with colleagues of their old firm. Different firm level variables such as different locations as well as ingroup-outgroup effects might be responsible for this finding.

The more detailed answer to the question "Who cooperates with whom?" investigates relationships, which have been formed between employees of the previously separated firms. It shows that likelihood of existence of cooperation relationships strongly depends on homophily and isomorphic forces. While homophily is based on similarity of traits of employees, isomorphic forces are based on hierarchical position of employees, their participation in integration measures and the cooperation requirements between departments. It shows that homophily has significant weaker effects on likelihood of existence of relationships between previously separated firms than isomorphic forces.

At the same time, the intensity of existing relationships between employees of previously separated firms also depends on isomorphic forces. However, there are hardly effects of homophily. Even a number of effects opposite to homophily have been found. A number of explanations for the findings had to be discarded. However, structural equivalence leading to competition between employees might be a possible explanation for the surprising positive effects of dissimilarity of education content as well as dissimilarity of seniority.

Further research is required to investigate, whether and when the effects of homophily will begin to hold for new relationships between employees of previously separated firms. Even if the effects of homophily in cooperation relationships between previously separated firms begin to converge to the effects shown by relationships within previously separated firms after a certain period of time, it is necessary to investigate the reasons, why new cooperation relationships between previously separated firms show different effects than new cooperation relationships within previously separated firms. While structural equivalence and competition between employees due to increased numbers of similar others might be possible explanations for the findings on new cooperation relationships, further research is required to investigate the factors, which cause the contra-intuitive effects.

8. Implications for practitioners

Most mergers and acquisitions fail. While most mergers and acquisitions are initiated with the objective to create value through synergy generation, these objectives are often missed (e.g. Kitching, 1974; Porter, 1987; Bühner, 1990a, b; Agrawal, Jaffe, & Mandelker, 1993). Failure of mergers and acquisitions can have different reasons:

- There is no synergy potential
- The structural decisions are not suited to capture the synergy potential
- The deal was too expensive, i.e. the premium paid exceeds the synergy potential
- The synergy potential has not been realized

(Sirower, 1997: 44ff.)

M&A-success thus is the result of a sequence of different preconditions: If there is no synergy potential, there is no possibility to create value unless the acquisition target can be bought cheaper than it actual value (Bühner, 1990a; Sirower, 1997). If there is synergy potential and the structural decision does allow capturing the synergies, there is no possibility for value creation. If there is synergy potential and the structural decision allows capturing the synergies, value cannot be generated, if the premium paid exceeds the synergy potential. If there is synergy potential and the premium does not exceed the synergy potential and there is no cooperation between employees, the synergy potential cannot be realized and there is no value creation.

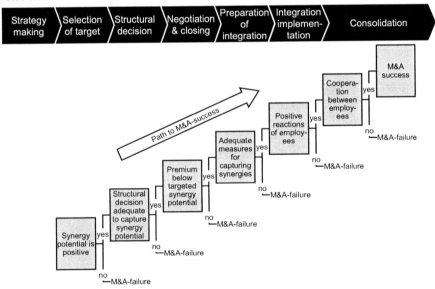

Illustration 42: Path to M&A-success

Hence the success of an M&A-transaction cannot be explained by investigating only one aspect of the sequence of these different success factors. The illustration abovew shows how different subsequent steps lead to M&A-success.

In this chain of necessary conditions for M&A-success, cooperation plays a central role (Larsson, & Finkelstein, 1999: 6). Knowledge about factors that influence cooperation can help practitioners to identify potential hazards for cooperation and to address them in managerial decisions.

The present study is the first study to generate detailed knowledge about cooperation after mergers and acquisitions and its antecedents. There are four important findings for practitioners generated by this study:

- Individual disposition of employees determines cooperation after mergers and acquisitions. Some employees cooperate more and some employees cooperate less. The individual disposition for cooperation depends on a number of different characteristics of employees, such as demographic characteristics as well as attitudes and reactions after the M&A-transaction.
- Cooperation barriers on the individual level are only effective for the initiation of relationships. However, in existing relationships, there are no cooperation barriers caused by dissimilar characteristics or attitudes of employees.
  Employees prefer to initiate cooperation relationships with new colleagues, who are similar to themselves. However, in existing relationships, employees have no preferences, which affect the intensity of cooperation.
- Structural characteristics of the merged firm strongly determine cooperation. Rank as well as cooperation requirements within and between departments strongly affect who cooperates and who cooperates with whom.
- Integration measures can help to overcome integration barriers between employees. Integration measures further can compensate for a cooperation-averse individual disposition. In addition to that, quality of cooperation as well as commitment of employees can be secured with the help of information. Information also reduces feelings of uncertainty of employees.

Individual disposition of employees as well as cooperation barriers represent given constraints for cooperation after mergers and acquisitions. Structural characteristics and integration measures represent managerial levers, which can significantly affect cooperation.

Based on this knowledge, practitioners can increase the likelihood of cooperation after mergers and acquisitions and thereby the likelihood of M&A-success significantly. In a first step, they can identify the synergy potential of an M&A-transaction. Based on the assessment of the synergy potential, they can identify the cooperation requirements between employees of the merging firms. Cooperation requirements exist wherever synergies effects are targeted. Then they can identify cooperation constraints in those areas with high cooperation requirements. Last but not least, they can identify management levers, which help to fulfill the cooperation requirements under given constraints.

Illustration 43 shows these steps, in a sequential order. Following these four steps, practitioners can address potential cooperation hazards in success-critical parts of the organization with the help of targeted measures to ensure and facilitate cooperation. Such targeted measures can be structural decisions as well as integration measures.

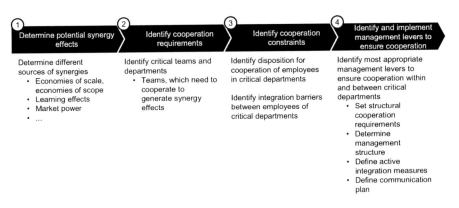

Illustration 43: Management measures based on the current study

In the following paragraphs, I will elaborate each of these steps. First, I will show the different aspects of a step. Then I will illustrate them at the example of SoftCo.

Last but not least, I will investigate to what extent the findings of the current research can be used not only in the integration phase but also in the pre-closing phase for evaluating later integration barriers as well as necessary integration measures.

8.1. Determine potential synergy effects

According to Koegeler (1991) synergy effects can accrue in sales and marketing, research and development, in production, in procurement and logistics as well as in the administration. In addition to that, financial synergies can be generated by pooling liquidity, by tax effects and by higher capital turnover (Koegeler, 1991: 47 – 63).

Each of these synergy effects requires employees of specific functions to cooperate with each other. In the following table, a number of exemplary synergy effects are listed.

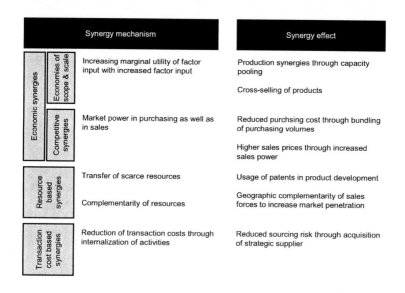

Table 121: Potential synergy effects after mergers and acquisitions

Depending on the characteristics of the merging firms, different synergy effects are possible. An acquiring firm or merging firms can determine the type and amount of synergies they can expect from joining the firms.

Case example SoftCo:
The main products of SoftCo are ERP (Enterprise Resource Planning)-products for a specific industry. Before the acquisition by SoftCo, the two acquired firms both had a solid market share in the industry. However, the next generation of the ERP-products could not be developed by either of the two firms. The necessary investments and software development capacity exceeded the means of both firms. SoftCo had both, financial strength as well as significant software development capacities. By cross-exploiting the financial resources and the software development capacities, positive effects for the future market position of SoftCo in the ERP-market were expected.

A second lever, which was planned after the finalization of the new product, is the integration of the sales force and the integration of the service units. Both units today have traveling time of 60% or more. More customers and a larger sales and service force can reduce the area covered by a sales person or a service person and thus reduce travel time and cost.

Summarizing, SoftCo expected synergy effects from two different levers: Pooling of development capacities as well as integration of sales and service force.

8.2. Identify cooperation requirements

The generation of synergy effects requires cooperation. However, the generation of specific synergy effects only requires cooperation between specific functions. Hence it is possible to determine the cooperation requirements in the merged firm based on the expected synergy effects. In the following table, a number of different synergy effects and the subsequent cooperation requirements are listed.

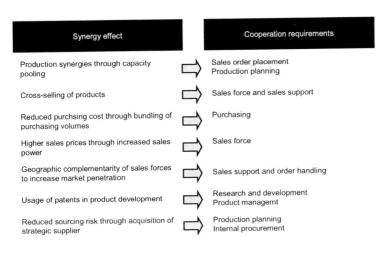

Table 122: Synergy effects and resulting cooperation requirements

For example, production synergies through capacity pooling can only be generated, if the Production planning of the merged firms is integrated. Also, the Sales order placement and the subsequent demand planning in Production planning need to be integrated. If these functions are not integrated, it is not possible to allocate sales orders in different production sites in a way that maximizes the efficiency of the production network of merging firms.

Case example SoftCo:
SoftCo aimed for significant synergy effects in the development of a new software. As a consequence, Software development as well as Product management needed to cooperate most tightly. At the same time, synergy effects in sales and service were planned only for the time after the new product was developed. Therefore, both sales forces as well as the sales support functions remained mostly separated and continued to sell the former products. Also, the service units remained separate: The expertise, which is necessary to install and maintain an ERP-system, is too broad to be able to know about two different systems. Hence the

cooperation requirements for capturing the expected synergy effects accrued mainly in Software development and in Product management.

8.3. Identify cooperation constraints

Basically, there are two different cooperation constraints: First, there is the individual disposition of employees to cooperate with colleagues from the previously separated firms after mergers and acquisitions. Second, there are integration barriers between employees of the previously separated firms.

After having identified the departments, which are required to cooperate in order to capture the expected synergy effects, managers can investigate the individual disposition for cooperation of employees within these departments. Depending on the availability of information, different characteristics of employees can be considered, which affect their propensity to cooperate.

Also, for those departments of previously separated firms, which are required to cooperate to capture expected synergies, the integration barriers between employees of these departments can be determined. Again, depending on availability of data, different types of integration barriers can be determined.

In the following table, effects of individual disposition for cooperation as well as integration barriers between employees are listed.

Individual disposition for cooperation		Integration barriers based on similarity of employees	
Age:	No effect	Age dissimilarity:	Increases integration barriers
Gender:	Female positive, male negative	Gender dissimilarity:	Increases integration barriers
Education level:	No effect	Education level dissimilarity:	Increases integration barriers
Seniority:	Negative	Education content dissimilarity:	Increases integration barriers
Task orientation:	Positive	Rank dissimilarity:	Decreases integration barriers
Commitment:	Positive	Seniority dissimilarity:	Increases integration barriers
Uncertainty:	Negative	Work attitude dissimilarity:	Increases integration barriers

Table 123: Individual disposition for cooperation and integration barriers

As can be seen in Table 123, there are characteristics of employees, which have positive or negative effects on cooperation. For example, highly senior employees cooperate less after mergers and acquisitions than less senior employees.

Also, there are integration barriers between employees, which decrease if employees share the same characteristics. For example, employees of similar age are more likely to cooperate after mergers and acquisitions than employees of dissimilar age. The more dissimilar the age of two employees, the less likely they are to cooperate.

Based on individual disposition of employees and based on cooperation barriers between employees of critical departments, which need to cooperate to capture synergies, it is possible to determine, whether cooperation deficits can be expected or not.

8.4. Identify and implement management levers to ensure cooperation

Depending on the expected cooperation deficits, it might be necessary to enforce and facilitate cooperation between departments of the merging firms. In departments that are critical for synergy realization, which show a high likelihood of cooperation deficits, management levers can be used to ensure cooperation.

A first managerial lever is the decision on the organizational detailing. Within departments, cooperation is generally higher than between departments. Hence it might be advisable to integrate activities of two departments, which are likely to show cooperation deficits within one department. Also, it is possible to ensure cooperation between departments with the help of supervisors. Supervisors are more likely to cooperate. By adding additional hierarchical levels, it is possible to enforce cooperation between departments.

Structural cooperation requirements are most effective to ensure cooperation. Structural cooperation requirements can be generated by centralizing selected functions. Departments of the merged firms thus are required to cooperate with the centralized function. Also, it is possible to specialize mirroring departments in a way that forces employees of the previously separated firms to cooperate. For example, it is possible to create a customer oriented sales force. Customers of the merging firms are then allocated according to specific characteristics and not according to previous sales contacts.

A second managerial lever is integration measures. If potential cooperation deficits are recognized in functions, which are required to cooperate tightly, integration measures can increase the likelihood of cooperation. In Graph 21, the effect of participation in different integration measures on cooperation intensity is illustrated.

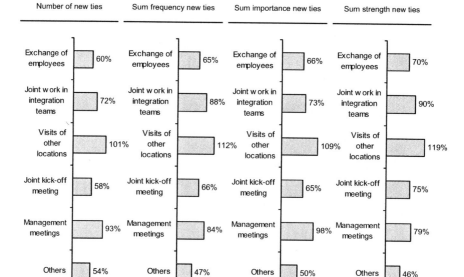

Graph 21: Effects of integration measures on cooperation at SoftCo

As can be seen, participation in integration measures has very strong effects on cooperation of employees. Participation in a single integration measure can increase cooperation up to 110% compared to employees, which did not participate.

It should be noted that managers can also influence the reactions of employees on mergers and acquisitions: Information can effectively reduce uncertainty of employees after mergers and acquisitions. Uncertainty again has a strong negative effect on cooperation.

This means that managers of merging firms can choose appropriate and effective integration measures to foster cooperation between employees of critical departments of previously separated firms and to reduce dysfunctional reactions of employees.

8.5. Relevance of findings for the evaluation of acquisition targets

Managers can use the findings of this research not only to focus integration measures on most relevant areas of the merged firm after closing, they also can use the findings for the target evaluation. It is possible to determine the synergy effects, the resulting cooperation requirements and, based on the results of a human resources due diligence (Krystek, 1992), it is possible to anticipate potential cooperation deficits. In a fourth step, it is then possible to determine potentially appropriate integration measures and their potential cost. If the integration barriers are deemed to be too high in a critical department, or if the integration costs for establishing cooperation within a critical department are higher than the expected synergies, it is possible to adjust the evaluation of the M&A-target. In the course of an iterative process, it is thus possible to adjust the expected synergies, revise organizational decisions and the integration plan by considering potential integration barriers and necessary integration measures. Illustration 44 shows, how firms can use knowledge about characteristics of employees and potential cooperation deficits and integration barriers.

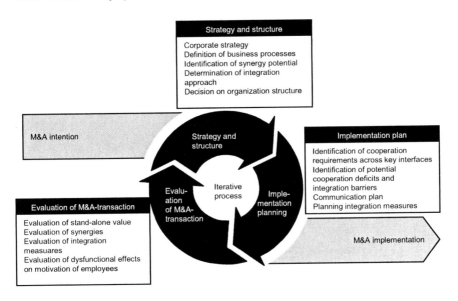

Illustration 44: Use of findings in the iterative evaluation of acquisition targets

Upfront knowledge about later integration problems thus can help to reduce the risk of not being able to capture the expected synergy potential. The advantage of the findings of the present study in doing this is that they are based on easily accessible data. While full cultural audits to determine potential integration hindrances are difficult to conduct in a pre-merger phase, information about demographic characteristics of employees as well as seniority can easily be gathered.

8.6. Summary of implications for practitioners

The present research yields bad new and good news for practitioners.

The bad news is that cooperation between employees of different firms suffers from different hindrances: Some employees cooperate more and others cooperate less after mergers and acquisitions. Individual characteristics thus can cause cooperation deficits. Furthermore, differences in characteristics and attitudes of employees create cooperation barriers. As a consequence, employees do not initiate cooperation relationships. Both, potential cooperation deficits as well as cooperation barriers can cause cooperation problems in the integrated firm.

The good news is that cooperation barriers are only relevant for the initiation of cooperation relationships. When cooperation relationships are in place, differences of characteristics no longer matter. When the management of the merged firm manages to initiate relationships between employees of previously separated firms, they do not have to expect further cooperation problems.

The good news further is that managers can strongly influence cooperation after mergers and acquisitions:
- Structural decisions can consider possible cooperation barriers as well as potential cooperation deficits. Wherever cooperation problems are likely, managers can detail the formal structure in a way to avoid cooperation between employees.
- The installation of joint supervisors can initiate cooperation between previously separated departments if cooperation is required.
- The use of active integration measures can strongly foster cooperation between employees. First, active integration measures overcome cooperation barriers. Second, active integration measures can compensate for cooperation-averse individual disposition.

Based on the findings of this research, managers thus can sharpen their awareness for cooperation barriers and tackle them more effectively.

Last but not least, the findings of the present study can be used in combination with a human resource due diligence in the pre-closing phase to identify potential cooperation problems and evaluate the necessary integration barriers.

9. Academic contribution and implications for further research

M&A-research still is mostly driven by phenomenological questions and not by theoretical considerations. "While there is no shortage of literature available in the area of M&As, until recently few if any of the investigations of M&A processes and outcomes were theory driven" (Hogan, & Overmyer-Day 1994: 274). The lack of theoretical foundation implies borrowing from other academic fields. As a consequence, the results of the current research contribute not only to M&A-research but also to other academic fields, which were used to formulate the hypotheses under investigation. Similarly, implications for further research can be distinguished by different fields as well.

In the following paragraphs, I will highlight three different areas to which the present research contributes and calls for future research: M&A-research, psychology, especially Socioemotional Selectivity Theory, as well as research on social networks.

9.1. Contributions to M&A-research and implications for future research

A first contribution of this work to M&A-research is the generation of an integrative framework, which addresses the process character of M&A-transactions, the multi-level character of the success factors for M&As as well as the importance of cooperation as a key moderating variable for the realization of synergies.

Based on an extensive literature review, I developed a framework, which allows a new perspective on conflicting evidence of prior M&A-research. Hardly any prior framework for the investigation of M&A-success explicitly considered the process character of M&A-transactions (for exceptions see Gerds 2000; Larsson, & Finkelstein 1999; Hogan, & Overmyer-Day 1994).

- Success factors of early phases constrain success factors of later phases. Without consideration of this endogeneity problem, M&A-research yields necessarily conflicting evidence. Directing attention to the endogeneity problem is a significant contribution of the present research. Future M&A-studies need to consider endogeneity more strongly than it has been the case in the past
- A number of success factors, which have been investigated in the past only indirectly affect M&A-success. Rather, they affect the moderating variable cooperation, which moderates the realization of synergy potential. In order to really understand the impact of different factors on M&A-success, it is necessary to consider both, synergy potential as well as synergy realization, which depends strongly on cooperation between employees of the merging firms

A second contribution of this work is the investigation of different factors influencing cooperation after mergers and acquisitions. While previous "... M&A prescriptions are directed to top management ..." (Buono, & Nurick 1992: 31), a number of individual level and group level variables could be identified, which affect cooperation after mergers and acquisitions on all hierarchical levels of a firm. Illustration 45 shows a summary of the different factors, which have been investigated in the course of this research.

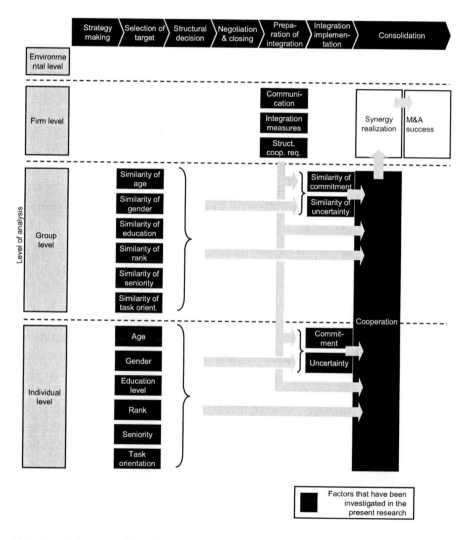

Illustration 45: Summary of investigated factors within research framework

Especially, reactions after mergers and acquisitions seem to depend not only on firm level variables but also on individual level variables. A better understanding of these factors will yield important insights in assessing the fit of merging companies not only from a strategic perspective but also from a social perspective (compare Buono, & Bowditch 1989; for a review see Hogan, & Overmyer-Day 1994).

A third contribution for M&A-research are the findings on structure and management interventions as two important firm-level levers for strengthening cooperation after mergers and acquisitions. While previous studies mostly focused on characteristics of the integration process, only few studies investigated the role of discrete integration measures (e.g. Gerds 2000: 136ff.; for the importance of structural and soft integration measures see Gerds, & Schewe 2004: 54ff.).

A fourth contribution for M&A-research has only been identified qualitatively: A finding in both studies, at SpecMatCo as well as at SoftCo is the fact that cooperation emerges only slowly after mergers and acquisitions. Both sites showed significant cooperation deficits even after years of structural integration. As a consequence, current thinking about the timeframe of realization of synergies needs to be reviewed. Obviously, synergy effects do not apply after the finalization of the implementation phase. Rather, it takes longer periods of time until cooperation between employees of previously separated firms has emerged and has become equally strong as cooperation within the previously separated firms.

Besides these contributions, the framework for success factors for mergers and acquisitions shows a clear research gap, which needs to be addressed in future research: While there seems to be general agreement amongst researchers that cooperation is the key moderating variable for realization of synergy effects, it is necessary to investigate the relationship of cooperation and synergy realization in future research. Two potential research questions arise:
1. Does cooperation in specific activities of firms generate synergy effects in these activities?
2. What is the optimal level of cooperation in both, scope and depth to maximize synergy generation while minimizing integration costs?

A second set of questions for future research result from the approach taken in the present research: The focus on individual and group level factors limits the understanding of factors on the firm level, which influence reactions of employees as well as cooperation of employees. Further research is required to identify variables on the firm level, which influence cooperation to better understand, how the structure of mergers and acquisitions influences cooperation and thereby M&A-success.

Additional cross-sectional research tackling these questions is required better understand the interrelationships between different levels of success factors.

Last but not least, a third question for future research concerns the dynamic of synergy realization. "The paucity of existing research on acquisition implementation provides excellent opportunities for meaningful future research ..." (Datta 1991: 294). The present research indicates that cooperation between previously separated firms only emerges over long time periods, systematic research of the timelines for synergy realization is needed. As Sirower (1997) points out, acquisitions easily get overpaid if expected synergy effects are not realized timely. Knowledge on the times needed to translate a synergy potential into actual synergy effects could change the way M&A-transactions are done today.

- If the realization of synergies takes longer than usually expected, it is necessary to review the premiums paid or even M&A-transactions in general. Otherwise, M&A-transactions destroy value for owners of the firm
- The implementation of integrated structures would need to be reviewed as well. Synergy effects in different functions need to be evaluated separately by reviewing the time needed for realization, the cost of implementation of the new structure as well as the value effects of the expected synergy effects. This could change the scope and depth of integration, because the trade-off between integration cost and synergy effects would need to be reconsidered.

Summarizing, the contributions of the present research mainly consist of emphasizing cooperation as a key moderating variable for M&A-success as well as the examination of factors affecting cooperation. As a key implication for further research, the dynamics of synergy realization depending on cooperation between employees of previously separated firms need to be investigated more thoroughly to overcome the static view on synergies.

9.2. Contributions to Socioemotional Selectivity Theory and implications for future research

One of the main theories to hypothesize about the effects of individual characteristics on cooperation behaviors has been Socioemotional Selectivity Theory (Carstensen 1992, 1993, 1995). According to Socioemotional Selectivity Theory, older people should have less social relationships and be less committed to work (Kanfer, & Ackerman 2004; Lansford, Sherman, & Antonucci 1998; Lang Carstensen 2002). Previous empirical studies focus on social relationships such as friendship or communication. A first study looking after the relationship building of newcomers in firms depending on age by Finkelstein, Kulas, & Dages (2003) only considers a small sample with a low response rate, providing weak support of the age-commitment and age-relationship building hypotheses. The current research suggests based on the investigation of a large sample that both hypotheses do not apply for cooperation relationships within organizations after mergers and acquisitions. Findings even show in the opposite direction.

A first implication for research in the field of Socioemotional Selectivity Theory is the need for differentiation between different types of social relationships. Prior findings in the field of friendship relationships could not be replicated for cooperation relationships.

A second implication is the need for reconsidering motivational issues at the workplace after mergers and acquisitions. According to the findings of the present research, older employees are not less committed to their work. Even the opposite is the case. It is important to note that this effect holds even after controlling for seniority within the firm. However, as has been noted above, the low average age of the employees in the sample might have yielded a sample bias, which cannot be validated.

Future research in the field of Socioemotional Selectivity Theory should investigate different types of relationships. Based on the findings of this study, it might well be possible that the theoretical predictions have to differentiate between different types of relationships.

Also, future research needs to reconsider the theoretical predictions for motivational structures of people. First, it is necessary to replicate the findings of this research with a more balanced sample. If the effects still hold, the theoretical predictions of Socioemotional Selectivity Theory need to be reconsidered.

9.3. Contributions to social network research and implications for future research

The present research yields two different types of contributions for the field of social network research. First, the approach used for the research at SoftCo is highly innovative and opens new opportunities for future research on large social networks. Second, the empirical findings bear important implications for answering one of the most contested questions in social network research: "Where do networks come from?" (e.g., Gulati, & Gargiulo 1999).

9.3.1. Methodological contributions

Before computers became easily accessible in most research settings, social network analysis had to be made with paper and pencil interrogation methods. Physically, this limits the size of the social networks that can be investigated (see also Wasserman, & Faust 1994: 33). Larger populations only have been investigated with the help of ego-centered network analyses. These, however, bear a high probability of being incomplete.

In this research, I developed an innovative top-down network analysis tool, which allows covering a large sample while at the same time reducing the risk of incompleteness and of respondent biases. At least to my knowledge, this is the first questionnaire of its kind. It opens a new field for large sample network analyses in discrete populations.

9.3.2. Contributions to social network research

There are three major contributions of this research to social network research, especially to the question "Where do networks come from?" A first contribution is the investigation of a large sample of new relationships. A second, more organization specific contribution is the consideration of structural cooperation requirements as a control variable. A third contribution concerns the examination of the dynamics of homophily.

Social network analysis has been trapped for years between micro and macro theories. While macro theoretical considerations emphasize structural characteristics of social networks and its effects on individuals in social networks, micro theoretical considerations emphasize individual characteristics of actors in the social networks and their effects on the network structure. However, being a typical chicken-egg problem, none of the sides really gained an explanatory advantage. Consequently, Burt (2000) strongly emphasizes that there is a need for better understanding of the origins of social networks.

The present research represents an innovation in the field of social network research as it examines newly formed relationships between individuals. Due to the very nature of an M&A-transaction, it is certain that employees of different firms did not have cooperation relationships before the M&A-transaction. If they have a relationship after the M&A-transaction, it is certainly a new one.

Also, as there has not been any structure between the merging firms before the M&A-transaction, there is no network structure, which influences the formation of these new relationships, it is clearly the individual characteristics of the employees and not characteristics of the network structure that affects the formation of relationships.

As a consequence, the findings on effects of individual characteristics on the formation of social relationships are definitely the result of individual level variables and not of structural characteristics of the network structure.

Future social network research needs to identify further opportunities to investigate the formation of new ties unrelated to existing network structures in order to confirm the exploratory findings of this study. Also, future research should aim for more longitudinal research to capture the dynamics of social relationships. This also would allow a better understanding of the relationship between individual characteristics and the formation of relationships.

Closely linked to this contribution is the control for structural cooperation requirements. Previous studies considered affiliation to functions as a control variable. However, cross functional cooperation requirements have not been considered in previous studies. In order to better understand structural cooperation requirements and their impact on informal cooperation structures it is necessary to identify all cooperation requirements and isolate them. Only by doing so, the impact of individual characteristics on cooperation relationships as well as the impact of homophily on the choice of cooperation partners can be clearly identified in organizational context.

This seems especially important considering the low ratio of existing cooperation relationships to potential relationships. To my knowledge, the present study is the first large sample social network analysis, which considers the full sample. Hence it is the first study, which yields a ratio of existing to possible relationships. This ratio is surprisingly low with roughly 12% within the previously separated firms and less than 2% between the previously separated firms. Such low numbers of cooperation relationships indicate (a) that structural cooperation requirements are dominating individual cooperation behaviors strongly and (b) that structural cooperation requirements can be used actively to create cooperation requirements.

Future research should aim to verify the used measure for structural cooperation requirements and aim for a creative advancement of the concept. By doing so, our understanding on the impact of structural cooperation requirements can be expanded.

A third important contribution of this work is the discovery of first indications of a dynamic dimension of homophily. This is especially important, as homophily in the past has been seen as a universal law of social structures. However, only recently, researchers point out the need for dynamic data to investigate the effects of homophily on tie formation and tie dissolution (e.g. McPherson et al. 2001).

The findings of the present research indicate that homophily requires a more differentiated conceptualization. The findings indicate that homophily depends on the level of mutual knowledge. If relationship partners do not know very much from each other, they seem to focus rather on obvious criteria to identify similar others such as age or gender. However, when having more time to get to know each other, similarity of attitudes has a significant effect on intensity of cooperation relationships.

Further research is needed to investigate how different characteristics are subject to homophily over time. Such knowledge could bear important implications for a better understanding of social dynamics in groups or larger social entities.

9.4. Final remarks on the social side of mergers and acquisitions

Research on mergers and acquisitions has highlighted different aspects of acquisitions. Researchers have extensively looked after the financial aspects of mergers and acquisitions. Others have investigated in detail the strategic implications of mergers and acquisitions. Again others investigated motivation and reactions of employees in M&A-transactions, i.e. the "human side of mergers and acquisitions" (Buono, & Bowditch 1989). Until today, cooperation between employees of merging firms, i.e. the social side of mergers and acquisitions has mostly neglected. However, it is people and it is their relationships that ultimately make an M&A-transaction work.

The present research aims to contribute to a sharpening of the consciousness that mergers and acquisitions are ultimately social phenomena and that they should be dealt with as such. Generating more knowledge on the social side of mergers and acquisitions might modify the current practice of mergers and acquisitions:

First, managers might be able to consider social aspects of the M&A-transaction in the strategy making, the target selection as well as the evaluation and the integration of mergers and acquisitions and thus avoid costly ventures.

Second, and even more importantly, employees and their needs to build new cooperation relationships could be considered more thoroughly in implementation plans. This would reduce dysfunctional effects for employees after mergers and acquisitions. Thereby, the social side of mergers and acquisitions could bear important effects on the human side.

References

Agrawal, Anup, Jaffe, Jeffrey F., & Mandelker, Gershon N. (1992). The Post-Merger Performance of Acquiring Firms: A Re-examination of an Anomaly. **Journal of Finance**, 47(4): 1605 - 1621.

Allport, Gordon W. (1954). **The nature of prejudice.** Cambridge, MA: Addison-Wesley

Althauser, Ulrich, & Tonscheidt-Göstl, Dagmar (1999). Kultur Due Diligence: Erfolgsfaktor bei Fusionen und Akquisitionen. **Personalwirtschaft**, 8 (1999): 40 -46.

Ansoff, Igor H. (1957). Strategies for diversification. **Harvard Business Review**, 35 (2): 113 – 124.

Ansoff, Igor H. (1965). **Corporate Strategy: an analytic approach to business policy for growth and expansion.** New York.

Asch, Solomon E. (1946). Forming impressions of personality. **Journal of Abnormal and Social Psychology**, 41: 258 - 290.

Ashforth, Blake. E., & Mael, Fred (1989). Social Identity Theory and the Organization. **Academy of Management Review**, 14 (1): 20 - 39.

Bain, Joe S. (1954). Economies of Scale, Concentration, and the condition of Entry in Twenty Manufacturing Industries. **American Economic Review**, 44 (1): 15 - 39.

Bain, Joe S. (1959). **Industrial Organization.** New York: Wiley.

Balloun, James, & Gridley, Richard (1990). Post-merger management, Understanding the challenges. **The McKinsey Quarterly**, 26 (4): 91-102.

Bamberger, Burkhard (1994). **Der Erfolg von Unternehmensakquisitionen in Deutschland: Eine theoretische und empirische Untersuchung.** Dissertation, Universität Bamberg, Köln.

Bacharach, Samuel B., Bamberger, Peter A., & Vashdi, Dana (2005). **Academy of Management Journal**, 48 (4): 619 - 644.

Bark, Cyrus, & Kötzle, Alfred (2001). Integrations-Controlling: Das PMI-Dashboard als Instrument zur Steuerung von Post-Merger-Integrations-Prozessen. **Controlling**, 7: 337 - 346.

Barley, Stephen R. (1990b). The alignment of technology and structure through roles and networks. **Administrative Science Quarterly**, 35: 61 - 103.

Barney, Jay B. (1991). Firm Resources and Sustained Competitive Advantage. **Journal of Management**, 17 (1): 99 - 120.

Barney, Jay B. (1988). Returns to bidding firms in mergers and acquisitions: Reconsidering the relatedness hypothesis. **Strategic Management Journal**, 9: 71 - 78.

Barney, Jay B. (1986). Strategic factor markets. **Management Science**, 42: 1231 - 1241.

Bazerman, Max H., & Samuelson, William F. (1983). The Winner's Curse: An Empirical Investigation. In: Reinhard Tietz (ed.), **Aspiration Levels in Bargaining and Economic Decision Making**, Lecture Notes in Economics and Mathematical Systems, 213, Berlin/Heidelberg: Springer Verlag.

Berkowitz, Steven D. (1982). **An Introduction to Structural Analysis: The Network Approach to Social Research**. Toronto: Butterworths.

Berscheid, Ellen, & Reis, Harry R. (1998). Attraction and close relationships. In: Giblert, Daniel T., Fiske, Susan. T., & Lindzey, Gardner (Eds.) (1998). **The Handbook of Social Psychology**. New York: McGraw-Hill.

Berscheid, Ellen & Ammazzalorso, Harry (1999). Emotional Experience in Close Relationships. In: Hewstone, M., & Brewer, M. (eds.) (in preparation): **Blackwell Handbook of Social Psychology** (Vol. 2: Interpersonal Processes), Oxford, UK: Blackwell Publishers.

Berthold, Christian (2004). **Unternehmenskultur, strukturelle Voraussetzungen und Erfolg von Unternehmenszusammenschlüssen**. Dissertation, Berlin.

Bittlingmayer, George (1985). Did Antitrust Policy Cause the Great Merger Wave?. **Journal of Law and Economics**, 28 (1): 77 - 118.

Blake, Robert R., & Mouton, Jane Srygley (1985). How to Achieve Integration on the Human Side of the Merger. **Organizational Dynamics**, 13: 41 - 56.

Bochner, Stephen, Duncan, Robert, Kennedy, Elizabeth, & Orr, Fred (1976). Acquaintance links between residents of a high rise building: An application of the 'small world' method. **Journal of Social Psychology**, 100 (2): 277 - 284.

Bordia, Prashant, Hobman, Elizabeth, Jones, Elizabeth, Gallois, Cindy, & Callan, Victor J. (2004). Uncertainty during organizational change: Types, consequences, and management strategies. **Journal of Business & Psychology**, 18 (4): 507 - 532.

Bortz, Jürgen & Döring, Nicola (2003). **Forschungsmethoden und Evaluation für Human- und Sozialwissenschaftler**. Berlin: Springer.

The Boston Consulting Group (2003). **Winning through mergers in weak times**.

Bovasso, Gregory (1993). A structural analysis of the formation of a network organization. **Group & Organization Management**, 17 (1): 86 - 106.

Bower, Joseph L. (2001). Not All M&As Are Alike--and that Matters. **Harvard Business Review**, 79 (3): 92 - 101.

Bradley, Michael, Desai, Anand, & Kim, Han E. (1983). The rationale behind interfirm tender offers: Information or synergy. **Journal of Financial Economics**, 11: 182 - 206.

Brass, Daniel J., & Burkhardt, Marlene E. (1992). Centrality and power in Organizations. In: Nohria, Nitin, & Eccles, Robert G. (eds). **Networks and Organizations**. Boston, MA: Harvard Business School Press, 1: 191 - 215.

Brass, Daniel J., & Burkhardt, Marlene E. (1993). Potential power and power use: An investigation of structure and behavior. **Academy of Management Journal**, 36 (3): 441 - 470.

Bryson, Jane (2003). Managing HRM risk in a merger. **Employee Relations**, 25 (1): 14 - 30.

Bühner, Rolf (1990c). Reaktion des Aktienmarktes auf Unternehmenszusammenschlüsse. **Schmalenbachs Zeitschrift für betriebswirtschaftliche Forschung**, 4: 295 - 316.

Bühner, Rolf, (1990d). Der Jahresabschlusserfolg von Unternehmenszusammenschlüssen. **Zeitschrift für Betriebswirtschaft**, 12: 1275 -1294.

Bühner, Rolf (1990b). **Erfolg von Unternehmenszusammenschlüssen in der Bundesrepublik Deutschland.** Stuttgart: Poeschel.

Bühner, Rolf (1990a). **Unternehmenszusammenschlüsse: Ergebnisse empirischer Analysen.** Stuttgart: Poeschel.

Buono, Anthony F., & Bowdich, James L. (1989). **The human side of mergers and acquisitions: managing collisions between people, cultures and organizations.** San Francisco: Jossey-Bass.

Buono, Anthony F., & Nurick, Aaron J. (1992). Intervening in the Middle: Coping Strategies in Mergers and Acquisitions. **Human Resource Planning,** 15: 19-33.

Burkhardt, M. E., & Brass, D. J. (1990). Changing patterns or patterns of change: The effects of a change in technology on social network structure. **Administrative Science Quarterly,** 35: 104 - 127.

Burt, Ronald S. (1982). **Towards a structural theory of action.** New York: Academic Press.

Burt, Ronald S. (1987). Social contagion and innovation: Cohesion versus structural equivalence. **American Journal of Sociology,** 92: 1287 - 1335.

Burt, Ronald S. (1992). **Structural Holes.** Cambridge, MA: Harvard University Press.

Burt, Ronald S. (2000). Decay functions. **Social Networks,** 22: 1 - 28.

Byrne, Donn (1971). **The attraction paradigm.** New York: Academic Press.

Webb, Eugene J., Campbell, Donald T., Schwartz, Richard D., & Sechrest, Lee (1966). **Unobtrusive Methods: Nonreactive Research in the Social Sciences.** Chicago: Rand McNally.

Cannella, Albert A. Jr., & Hambrick, Donald C. (1993). Effects of executive departures on the performance of acquired firms. **Strategic Management Journal,** 14: 137 - 152.

Carstensen, Laura L., Fung, Helene H., & Charles, Susan T. (2003). Socioemotional Selectivity Theory and the Regulation of Emotion in the Second Half of Life. **Motivation and Emotion,** 27 (2): 103 - 123.

Carstensen, Laura L. (1992). Social and emotional patterns in adulthood: Support for socioemotional selectivity theory. **Psychology and Aging**, 7: 331-338.

Carstensen, Laura L. (1993). Motivation for social contact across the life span: A theory of socioemotional selectivity. In: J. E. Jacobs (Ed.), **Nebraska Symposium on Motivation: Vol. 40. Developmental perspectives on motivation—Current theory and research in motivation** (pp. 209-254). Lincoln: University of Nebraska Press.

Carstensen, Laura L. (1995). Evidence for a life-span theory of socioemotional selectivity. **Current Directions in Psychological Science**, 4: 151-156.

Carstensen, Laura L., & Isaacowitz, Derek M. (1999). Taking Time Seriously. **American Psychologist,** 54 (3): 165.

Cartwright Sue, & Cooper, Cary L. (1993b). The psychological impact of merger and acquisition on the individual: A study of building society managers. **Human Relations**, 46 (3): 327 - 347.

Cartwright, Sue, & Cooper, Cary L. (1992). **Mergers & Acquisitions: The Human Factor**. Oxford: Butterworth-Heinemann.

Cartwright, Sue, & Cooper, Cary L. (1993a). Of mergers, marriage, and divorce. **Journal of Managerial Psychology**, 8 (6): 7 - 10.

Cartwright, Sue, & Cooper, Cary L. (1993c) The role of culture compatibility in successful organizational marriage. **Academy of Management Executive**, 7 (2): 57 - 70.

Casstevens, Reber E. (1979). An Approach to Communication Model Building. **Journal of Business Communication**, 16 (3): 31 - 40.

Caves, Richard E., & Porter, Michael E. (1977). From Entry Barriers to Mobility Barriers: Conjectural Decisions and Contrived Deterrence to New Competition. **Quarterly Journal of Economics**, 91 (2): 241 - 262.

Chandler, Alfred D. (1977). **The Visible Hand: The Managerial Revolution in American Business**. London, UK: Belknap Press.

Chandler, Alfred D. (1962). **Strategy and Structure: Chapters in the History of the American Industrial Enterprise.** Cambridge, MA: MIT Press.

Chatterjee, Sayan (1986). Types of synergy and economic value. The impact of acquisitions on merging and rival firms. **Strategic Management Journal**, 7: 119 - 140.

Chatterjee, Sayan (1991). Gains in vertical acquisitions and market power: Theory and evidence. **Academy of Management Journal**, 34 (2): 436 - 448.

Chatterjee. Sayan, Lubatkin, Michael H., Schweiger, David M., & Weber, Yaakov (1992). Cultural differences and shareholder value in related mergers: Linking equity and human capital. **Strategic Management Journal**, 13 (5): 319 - 334.

Child, John (1975). Managerial and organizational factors associated with company performance - Part II: A contingency analysis. **Journal of Management Studies**, 12 (1): 12 - 27.

Choi, Ivan C, & Comstock, George W. (1975). Interviewer Effect on Responses to a Questionaire relating to Mood. **American Journal of Epidemology**, 101 (1): 84 - 92.

Coase, Ronald (1937). The nature of the firm. **Economica**, 4 (16): 386 - 405.

Coleman, James S. (1990). **Foundations of social theory**. Cambridge, Mass.: Harvard University Press.

Cross, Rob, Borgatti, Stephen P., & Parker, Andrew (2002). Making Invisible Work Visible: Using Social Network Analysis to Support Strategic Collaboration. **California Management Review**, 44: 25 - 46.

Datta, Deepak, Pinches, George E., & Narayanan, Rajesh P. (1992). Factors influencing wealth creation from mergers and acquisitions: a meta-analysis. **Strategic Management Journal**, 13 (1): 67 - 84..

Datta, Deepak (1991). Organizational Fit and Acquisition Performance: Effects of Post-Acquisition Integration. **Strategic Management Journal**, 12: 281 - 297.

Davis, Gerald F., & Stout, Suzanne K. (1992). Organization theory and the market for corporate control: A dynamic analysis of the characteristics of large takeover targets. **Administrative Science Quarterly**, 37: 605 - 633.

Dicken, André J. (2000). Erfolg von Unternehmensfusionen aus aktueller Sicht. **Betriebswirtschaftliche Forschung und Praxis**, 4: 358 - 372.

Dierickx, Ingemar, & Cool, Karel (1989). Asset Stock Accumulation and Sustainability of competitive Advantage. **Management Science**, 35 (12): 1504 - 1511.

DiMaggio, Paul J., & Powell, Walter W. (1983). The Iron Cage Revisited: Institutional Isomorphism and Collective Rationality in Organizational Fields. **American Sociological Review**, 48 (2): 147 - 160.

Donaldson, Lex (2001). **The contingency theory of organizations.** Thousand Oaks, CA: Sage Publications.

Duch, Karl C. (1985). Zauber der Kultur - oder Kulturzauber? - Unternehmenskultur auf dem Prüfstand. **Personalwirtschaft**, 11: 427 - 436:

Edmonds, Christopher C. (1923). Tendencies in the Automobile Industry. **American Economic Review**, 13 (3): 422 - 441.

Eisenhardt, Kathleen M. (1989a). Agency theory: An assessment and review. **Academy of Management Review**, 14 (1): 57- 74.

Eisenhardt, Kathleen M. (1989b). Building theory from case study research. **Academy of Management Review**, 14 (4): 532 - 550.

Emerson, Karen S., & Cook, Richard M. (1978). Power, Equity and Commitment in Exchange Networks. **American Sociological Review**, 43 (5): 721 - 739.

Festinger, Leon (1957). **A theory of cognitive dissonance.** Stanford, Ca: Stanford University Press.

Festinger, Leon (1962). Cognitive dissonance. **Scientific American Magazin**, 207: 93 - 102.

Finkelstein, Lisa M., Kulas, John T., & Dages, Kelly (2003). Age differences in proactive newcomer Socialization Strategies in two Populations. **Journal of Business & Psychology**, 17 (4): 473 - 502.

Finkelstein, Sydney (1986). **The Acquisition Integration Process**. Working Paper, Columbia University.

Finkelstein, Sydney, & Haleblian, Jebayr (2002). Understanding Acquisition Performance: The Role of Transfer Effects. **Organization Science: A Journal of the Institute of Management Sciences**, 13: 36 - 47.

Fischer, Claude S. (1977). **Networks and places: social relations in the urban setting**. New York: Free Press.

French, John R.P. Jr., & Raven, Bertram (1959). The bases of social power. In: D. Cartwright (eds), **Studies in social power** (pp. 150-167). Ann Arbor: University of Michigan Press.

Friedrichs, Jürgen (1980). **Methoden empirischer Sozialforschung**. Opladen: Westdeutscher Verlag.

Fuller, Richard B. (1975). **Synergetics**. New York: MacMillan Publishing Co.

Galbraith, Jay R. (1974). Organization design: An information processing view. **Interfaces**, 4 (3): 23 - 36.

Galpin, Timothy J., & Herndon, Mark (1999). **The complete guide to mergers and acquisitions. Process tools to support M&A integration at every level**. San Francisco: Jossey-Bass Inc..

Gerds, Johannes (2000). **Post Merger Integration**. Wiesbaden: Deutscher Universitätsverlag.

Gerpott, Thorsten J. (1993). **Integrationsgestaltung und Erfolg von Unternehmensakquisitionen**. Stuttgart: Schäffer-Poeschel.

Gerpott, Torsten J. (1994). Abschied von der Spitze: Eine empirische Studie zur Höhe und zu Determinanten der Ausscheidungsquote von Top Managern akquirierter deutscher Unternehmen. **Zeitschrift für die betriebswirtschaftliche Forschung**, 46 (1): 4 - 31.

Goold, Michael, & Campbell, Andrew (1999). Synergien suchen - um jeden Preis?. **Harvard Business Manager**, 2: 65 - 77.

Greenwood, Royston, Hinings, C. R., & Brown, John (1994). Merging professional service firms. **Organization Science**, 5 (2): 239 - 257.

Gulati, Ranjay, & Gargiulo, Martin (1999). Where do interorganizational networks come from? **American Journal of Sociology**, 104 (5): 1439 - 1493.

Gutknecht, John E., & Keys, Bernard J. (1993). Mergers. acquisitions and takeovers: Maintaining morale of survivors and protecting employees. **Academy of Management Executive**, 7: 26 - 36.

Hackman, J. Richard (1987). The design of work teams. In: J.W. Lorsch (eds), **Handbook of organizational behavior**. Englewood Cliffs, NJ: Prentice-Hall.

Haleblian, Jebayr, & Finkelstein, Sydney (1999). The Influence of Organizational Acquisition Experience on Acquisition Performance: A Behavioral Learning Perspective. **Administrative Science Quarterly, Administrative Science Quarterly**, 44: 29 - 56.

Harrigan, Kathryn R. (1984). Formulating vertical integration strategies. **Academy of Management Review**, 8: 638 - 652.

Harrington, Brooke (2002). The pervasive Effects of Network Content. **Academy of Management Proceedings**, J1.

Harrison, Jeffrey S., Hitt, Michael A., Hoskisson, Robert, & Ireland, R. Duane (1991). Synergies and Post-Acquisition Performance: Differences versus Similarities in Resource Allocations. **Journal of Management**, 17: 173 - 191.

Harvard Business Review 1922: 11 - 15.

Haspeslagh, Philippe C., & Jemison, David B. (1991). **Managing acquisitions: Creating value through corporate renewal**. New York, NY: The Free Press.

Haunschild, Pamela R., Moreland, Richard L., & Murrell, Audrey J. (1994). Sources of resistance to mergers between groups. **Journal of Applied Social Psychology**, 24 (13): 1150 - 1178.

Haynes, Natasha S., & Love, Peter E.D. (2004). Psychological adjustment and coping among construction project managers. **Construction Management & Economics**, 22(2): 129-140.

Hayward, Mathew L. A., & Hambrick, Donald C. Hambrick (1997). Explaining the Premiums Paid for Large Acquisitions: Evidence of CEO Hubris. **Administrative Science Quarterly**, 42(1): 103-129.

Hitt, Michael A., Harrison, Jeffrey S., Hoskisson, Robert E., & Ireland, R. Duane (2001). Resource complementarity in business combinations: Extending the logic to organizational alliances. **Journal of Management**, 27 (6): 679 - 691.

Hitt, Michael A., & Harrison Jeffrey S., Ireland, R. Duane, & Best, Aleta (1998). Attributes of Succesful and Unsuccessful Acquisitions of US Firms. **British Journal of Management**, 9 (2): 91 - 104.

Hitt, Michael A., & Hoskisson, Robert E. (1989). Acquisitive Growth Strategy and Relative R&D Intensity: The Effects of Leverage, Diversification, and Size. **Academy of Management Proceedings**, 1: 22 - 26.

Hitt, Michael A., Hoskisson, Robert E., Ireland, R. Duane, & Harrison, Jeffrey S. (1991). Are acquisitions a poison pill for innovation?. **Academy of Management Executive, Academy of Management**, 5 (4): 22 - 34.

Hochwarter, Wayne A., Ferris, Gerald R., Perrewé, Pamela L., Witt, L. Alan, & Kiewitz, Christian (2001). A Note on the Nonlinearity of the Age-Job-Satisfaction Relationship. **Journal of Applied Social Psychology**, 31 (6): 1223 - 1237.

Hofstede, Geert (1984). **Cultures and Consequences**. London: Sage Publications.

Hogan, Eileen A. & Overmyer-Day, Leslie (1994). The psychology of mergers and acquisitions. **International Review of Industrial and Organizational Psychology**, 9: 247 - 281.

Hogg, Michael A., & Terry, Deborah J. (2000). Social Identity and Self-Categorization Processes in Organizational Contexts. **Academy of Management Review** 25(1): 121-140.

Hogg, Michael A., & Williams, Kip D. (2000). From I to We : Social Identity and the Collective Self. **Group Dynamics: Theory, Research, and Practice**, 4(1): 81 - 97.

Hubbard, Nancy (1999). **Acquisition -- Strategy and Implementation**. New York: Palgrave.

Hughes, Alan, & Müller, Dennis C. (1980). **Hypotheses about Mergers**. Cambridge: University of Cambridge.

Hui, Chun, & Lee, Cynthia (2000). Moderating effects of organization-based self-esteem on organizational uncertainty: Employee response relationships. **Journal of Management**, 26 (2): 215 - 232.

Huston, Ted L., &. Levinger, George (1978). Interpersonal Attraction and Relationships. **Annual Review of Psychology**, 29: 115 - 156.

Hyde, Janet S. (2005). The Gender Similarities Hypothesis. **American Psychologist**, 60 (6): 581 - 592.

Ibarra, Herminia (1993a). Personal networks of women and minorities in management: A conceptual framework. **Academy of Management Review**, 18: 56 - 87.

Ibarra, Herminia (1993b). Network centrality, power and innovation involvement: Determinants of technical and administrative roles. **Academy of Management Journal**, 36: 471 - 501.

Ibarra, Herminia (1995). Race, opportunity, and diversity of social circles in managerial networks. **Academy of Management Journal**, 38 (3): 673 - 703.

Ibarra, Herminia (1992). Homophily and Differential Returns: Sex Differences in Network Structure and Access in an Advertising Firm. **Administrative Science Quarterly**, 37 (3): 422 - 447.

Ivancevich, John M., Schweiger, David M., & Power, Frank R. (1987b). Strategies for managing human resources during mergers and acquisitions. **Human Resource Planning**, 10 (1): 19 - 35.

Jürges, Hendrik (2003). Age, Cohort, and the Slump in Job Satisfaction among West German Workers. **LABOUR: Review of Labour Economics & Industrial Relations**, 17: 489 - 518.

Jemison, David B., & Sitkin, Sim B. (1986a). Corporate acquisitions: A process perspective. **Academy of Management Review**, 11 (1): 145 - 163.

Jemison, David B., & Sitkin, Sim B. (1986b). Acquisitions: The process can be the problem. **Harvard Business Review**, 64: 107 - 116.

Jensen, Michael C. (1986). Agency costs of free cash flow, corporate finance and takeovers. **The American Economic Review**, 76: 323 - 329.

Kanfer, Ruth, & Ackerman, Phillip L. (2004). Aging, adult development, and work motivation. **Academy of Management Review**, 29: 440 - 458.

Karnani, Aneel, & Wernerfelt, Birger (1985). Multiple Point Competition. **Strategic Management Journal**, 6 (1): 87 - 96.

Keila, Parambir S., & Skillicorn, David (2005). Structure in the Enron Email Dataset. **Computational & Mathematical Organization Theory**, 11 (3): 183 - 199.

Keith, Nina ,& Frese, Michael (2005). Self-Regulation in Error Management Training : Emotion Control and Metacognition as Mediators of Performance Effects. **Journal of Applied Psychology**, 90 (4): 677 - 691.

Keul, Alexander G. (1993). Soziales Netzwerk - System ohne Theorie. In: Laireiter, A. (1993). **Soziales Netzwerk und soziale Unterstützung: Konzepte, Methoden und Befunde**. Bern: Huber.

Keupp,Heiner (1987). Soziale Netzwerke - Eine Metapher des gesellschaftlichen Umbruchs?. In: Keupp, Heiner, & Röhrle, Bernd (Hrsg.) (1987). **Soziale Netzwerke**. Frankfurt: Campus Verlag.

Kieser, Alfred, & Kubicek, Herbert (1992). Organisation. New York: de Gruyter.

Kitching, John (1967). Why do mergers miscarry?. **Harvard Business Review**, 11 (12): 84 - 101.

Kitching, John (1974). Winning and losing with European acquisitions. **Harvard Business Review**, 52: 124 - 136.

Klein, Katherine J., Lim, Beng-Chong, & Mayer, David M. (2004). How do they get there? An Examination of the Antecedents of Centrality in Team Networks. **Academy of Management Journal**, 47 (6): 952 - 963.

Knop, Oliver C. (1993). Die Bewertung internationaler Unternehmensakquisitionen in der modernen Finanztheorie. In: Frank, Gert M., & Stein, Ingo (eds). **Management von Unternehmensakquisitionen**. Stuttgart: Schäfer-Poeschel.

Koch, Thomas (2001). Koordination von Integrationen. In: Jansen, Stephan A., Picot, Gerhard, Schiereck, Dirk (Hrsg.). Internationales Fusionsmanagement: **Erfolgsfaktoren grenzüberschreitender Unternehmenszusammenschlüsse**. 1. Auflage. Stuttgart, 87 - 102.

Koch, Thomas (2000). Post-Merger Management. In: Picot, Gerhard (Ed.). **Mergers & Acquisitions: Planung, Durchführung, Integration**. Stuttgart: Schäfer-Poeschel.

Kode, G. V. M., Ford, J. C., & Sutherland, M. M. (2003). A conceptual model for evaluation of synergies in mergers and acquisitions: A critical review of the literature. **South African Journal of Business Management**, 34 (1): 27 - 38.

Koegeler, Ralf (1991). **Synergiemanagement im Akquisitions- und Integrationsprozess von Unternehmungen**. Dissertation, Universität Basel.

Krackardt, David, & Kilduff, Martin (1990). Friendship patterns and culture. **American Anthropologist**, 92 (1): 142 - 154.

Krackhardt, David & Porter, Lyman W. (1986). The snowball effect: Turnover embedded in communication networks. **Journal of Applied Psychology**, 71 (1): 50 - 55.

Kram, Kathy E. (1983). Phases of the Mentor Relationship. **Academy of Management Journal**, 26 (4): 608 - 625.

Krishnan, Hema A., Miller, Alex, & Judge, William Q. (1997). Diversification and top management team complementarity: Is performance improved by merging similar or dissimilar teams?. **Strategic Management Journal**, 18 (5): 361 - 374.

Kroeber-Riel, Werner, & Weinberg, Peter (1996). **Konsumentenverhalten**. München: Vahlen Verlag.

Krug, Jeffrey, & Hegarty, W. Harvey (2001). Predicting who stays and leaves after an acquisition: A study of top managers in multinational firms. **Strategic Management Journal**, 22 (2): 185 - 196.

Krüger, Wilfried (1988). Management von Akquisitionsprojekten: Probleme, Erfolgsfaktoren und Aufgaben bei der Durchführung von Unternehmenszusammenschlüssen. **Zeitschrift für Organisation**, 6 (1988): 371 - 377.

Krystek, Ulrich (1992). Unternehmenskultur und Akquisition. **Zeitschrift für die Betriebswirtschaft**, 62 (5): 539 - 565.

Kuranel, Piraye (2005). Benefits in bank mergers. **International Financial Law Review**, 24 (4): 107 - 108.

Kusewitt, John B. (1985). An exploratory study of strategic acquisition factors relating to performance. **Strategic Management Journal**, 6 (2): 151 - 169.

Laatz, Wilfried (1993). **Empirische Methoden : ein Lehrbuch für Sozialwissenschaftler**. Thun: H. Deutsch.

Lang, Frieder R., & Carstensen, Laura L. (2002). Time Counts : Future Time Perspective, Goals, and Social Relationships. **Psychology and Aging**, 17 (1): 125 - 139.

Lansford, Jennifer E., Sherman, Aurora M., & Antonucci, Toni C. (1998). Satisfaction with social networks: an examination of socioemotional selectivity theory across cohorts. **Psychology and Aging**, 13 (4): 544 - 552.

Larsson, Rikard, & Finkelstein, Sydney (1999). Integrating strategic, organizational, and human resource perspectives on mergers and acquisitions: A case survey of synergy realization. **Organization Science**, 10 (1): 1 - 26.

Laumann, Edward O. (1994). Sexual networks. In: Lauman, Edward O., Gagnon, John H., Michael, Robert T., & Michaels, Stuart (eds). **The Social Organization of Sexuality: Sexual Practices in the United States**. Chicago, IL: University of Chicago Press. Chapter 6.

Lawrence, Paul R., & Lorsch, Jay W. (1967). Differentiation and Integration in Complex Organizations. **Administrative Science Quarterly**, 12 (1): 1 - 47.

Lazega Emmanuel, & Van Duijn, Marijtje A.J. (1997). Position in formal structure, personal characteristics and choices of advisors in a law firm : a logistic regression model for dyadic network data. **Social Networks**, 19 (4): 375 - 397.

Learned, Edmund P. (1930). Mergers in the Cotton Industry. **Harvard Business Review**, 8 (4): 501.

Lee, Sharon K., & Pawlukiewicz, James E. (2000). Poison pills: 1980s vs. 1990s. **American Business Review**, 18 (1): 28 - 31.

Liedtka, Jeanne M. (1998). Synergy Revisited: How a "Screwball Buzzword" can be Good for the Bottom Line. **Business Strategy Review**, 9 (2): 45 - 55.

Lloyd, Bruce (1976). Economies of scale: A primer. **Merger & Acquisitions**, 10 (4): 4 - 14.

Lorsch, Jay W., & Allen, Stephen A. (1973). **Managing diversity and interdependence: An organizational study of multidivisional firms**. Boston: Harvard University.

Louch, Hugh (2000). Personal network integration: transitivity and homophily in strong-tie relations. **Social Networks**, 22: 45 - 64.

Lubatkin, Michael (1987). Merger strategies and stockholder value. **Strategic Management Journal**, 8: 39 - 53.

Lubatkin, Michael (1983). Mergers and the performance of the acquiring firm. The **Academy of Management Review**, 8 (2): 218 - 225.

Lubatkin, Michael, & O'Neill, High M. (1987). Merger strategies and capital market risk. **Academy of Management Journal**, 30 (4): 665 - 684.

Lubatkin, Michael, & Schulze, William S., Mainkar, Avinash, & Cotterill, Ronald W. (2001). Ecological Investigation of Firm Effects in horizontal Mergers. **Strategic Management Journal**, 22 (4): 335 - 357.

Lubatkin, Michael, & Schweiger, David, & Weber, Yaakov (1999). Top Management Turnover in Related M&A's: An Additional Test of the Theory of Relative Standing. **Journal of Management**, 25 (1): 55-73.

Lubatkin, Michael, Srinivasan, Narasimhan, & Merchant, Hemant (1997). Merger strategies and shareholder value during times of relaxed antitrust enforcement: The Case of Large Mergers During the 1980s. **Journal of Management**, 23 (1): 59 - 81.

Lucks, Kai, & Meckl, Reinhard (2002). **Internationale Mergers & Acquisitions: Der Prozessorientierte Ansatz**. Berlin: Springer.

Malatesta, Paul H. (1983). The wealth effects of merger activity and the objective functions of the merging firms. **Journal of Financial Economics**, 11: 155 - 181.

Marks, Mitchell L. (1988). The merger syndrome. The human side of the corporate combination. **Journal of Buyouts and Acquisitions**, 1: 18 - 23.

Marks, Mitchell L., & Mirvis, Philip H. (1997c). **Joining forces - Making one plus one equal three in mergers, acquisitions and alliances**. San Francisco: Jossey-Bass.

Marsden, Peter V. (1988). Homogeneity in confiding relations. **Social Networks**, 10: 57 - 76.

Marsden, Peter V. (1987). Core Discussion Networks of Americans. **American Sociological Review**, 52 (1): 122 - 131.

Mason, Claire M., & Griffin, Mark A. (2005). Group Task Satisfaction. **Group Organization Management**, 30 (6): 625 - 652.

Mathieu, John E., & Kohler, Stacey S. (1990). A Cross-Level Examination of Group Absence Influences on Individual Absence. **Journal of Applied Psychology**, 75: 217 - 220.

McPherson, Miller, & Smith-Lovin, Lynn (2001). Birds of a Feather: Homophily in Social Networks. **Annual Review of Sociology**, 27 (1): 415 - 444.

Mealiea, Laird W., & Lee, Dennis (1979). An Alternative To Macro-Micro Contingency Theories: An Integrative Model. **Academy of Management Review**, 4 (3): 333 - 345.

Mehra, Ajay, Kilduff, Martin, & Brass, Daniel J. (1998). At the margins: A distinctiveness approach to the social identity and social networks of underrepresented groups. **Academy of Management Journal**, 41 (4): 441 - 452.

Messick, David M., & Mackie, Diane M. (1989). Intergroup Relations. **Annual Review of Psychology**, 40: 45 - 81.

Meyer, John W., & Rowan, Brian (1977). Institutionalized Organizations: Formal Structure as Myth and Ceremony. **American Journal of Sociology**, 83: 340 - 363.

Milholland, John E. (1964). Theory and Techniques of Assessment. **Annual Review of Psychology**, 15: 311 - 318.

Mintzberg, Henry (1979). **The Structuring of Organizations**. Englewood Cliffs, NJ: Prentice-Hall.

Mirvis, Philip H., & Marks, Mitchell Lee (1992). The Human Side of Merger Planning: Assessing and Analyzing "Fit". **Human Resource Planning**, 15 (3): 69-92.

Möller, Wolf-Peter (1983). **Der Erfolg von Unternehmenszusammenschlüssen. Eine empirische Untersuchung**. München: Minerva.

Morrison, Elizabeth W., & Robinson, Sandra L. (1997). When employees feel betrayed: A model of how psychological contract violation develops. **Academy of Management Review**, 22 (1): 226 - 256.

Moore, Frederick T. (1959). Economies of Scale: Some statistical Evidence. **Quarterly Journal of Economics**, 73 (2): 232 - 245.

Mossholder, Kevin W., & Bedeian, Arthur G. (1983). Cross-level inference and organizational research: Perspectives on interpretation and application. **Academy of Management Review**, 8 (4): 547 - 558.

Mussweiler, Thomas, & Strack, Fritz (1997). Explaining the Enigmatic Anchoring Effect: Mechanisms of Selective Accessibility. **Journal of Personality and Social Psychology**, 73: 437 - 446.

Myers, Stewart C., & Malhuf, Nicholas S. (1984). Corporate financing and investment decisions when firms have information that investors do not have. **Journal of financial Economics**, 13 (2): 187 - 221.

Nahavandi, Afsaneh, & Malekzadeh, Ali R. (1988). Acculturation in Mergers and Acquisitions. **Academy of Management Review**, 13 (1): 79 - 90.

Olbrich, Rainer, Alves, Rudolf, & Reinke, Bodo (1996). Akquisitions- und Integrationsmanagment von Handelskonzernen, Strategien des externen Wachstums im Handel und ihre organisatorischen Gestaltungserfordernisse. **Zeitschrift für Organisation**, 5: 6-13.

Pablo, Amy L. (1994). Determinants of acquisition integration level: A decision-making perspective. **Academy of Management Journal**, 37 (4): 803 - 836.

Pauly, John (1977). The case for a new model of business communication. **Journal of Business Communication**, 14 (4): 11 - 23.

Pausenberger, Ehrenfried (1989). Zur Systematik von Unternehmenszusammenschlüssen. **Das Wirtschaftsstudium**, 11: 621 - 626.

Peteraf, Margaret A. (1993). The Cornerstones of Competitive Advantage: A Resource-Based View. **Strategic Management Journal**, 14 (3): 179 - 191.

Pfeffer, Jeffrey, & Salancik, Gerald R. (1978). **The external control of organizations : a resource dependence perspective**. New York: Harper & Row.

Piderit, Sandy Kristin (2000). Rethinking resistance and recognizing ambivalence: A multidimensional view of attitudes toward an organizational change. **Academy of Management Review**, 25 (4): 783 - 794.

Piske, Reiner (2002). German acquisitions in Poland: an empirical study on integration management and integration success. **Resource Development International**, 5 (3): 295 - 312.

Popper, Karl (1959). **The Logic of Scientific Discovery**. UK: Routledge.

Porter, Michael E. (1980). **Competitive Strategy**. New York, NY: The Free Press.

Porter, Michael E. (1985). **Competitive Analysis**. New York, NY: The Free Press.

Porter, Michael E. (1987). From competitive advantage of corporate strategy. **Harvard Business Review**, 65 (3): 43 - 59.

Prahalad, CK, & Hamel, Gary (1990). The Core Competence of the Corporation. **Harvard Business Review**, 68 (3): 79 - 91.

Pribilla, Peter (2000). Personelle und kulturelle Integration. In: Picot, Gerhard (Ed.). **Mergers & Acquisitions: Planung, Durchführung, Integration**. Stuttgart: Schäfer-Poeschel.

Puranam, Panish, Singh, Harbir, & Zollo, Maurizio (2003). A bird in the hand or two in the bush? Integration trade-offs in technology-grafting acquisitions. **European Management Journal**, 21 (2): 179 - 184.

Ramaswamy, Kannan (1997). The performance impact of strategic similarity in horizontal mergers: Evidence from the U.S. banking industry. **Academy of Management Journal**, 40 (3): 697 - 715.

Reagans, Ray (2005). Preferences, Identity, and Competition: Predicting Tie Strength from Demographic Data. **Management Science**, 51 (9): 1374 - 1383.

Rentsch, Joan R., & Schneider, Benjamin (1991). Expectations for postcombination organizational life: A study of responses to merger and acquisition scenarios. **Journal of Applied Social Psychology**, 21 (3): 233 - 252.

Rhodes-Kropf, Matt, Robinson, David T., & Viswanathan, S. (2005). Valuation waves and merger activity: The empirical evidence. **Journal of Financial Economics**, 77 (3): 561 - 603.

Rice, Linda E., & Mitchell, Terence R. (1973). Structural Determinants of Individual Behavior in Organizations. **Administrative Science Quarterly**, 18 (1): 56 - 70.

Roethlisberger, Fritz J. (1941). **Management and morale**. Cambridge, Mass.: Harvard University Press.

Roll, Richard (1986). The hubris hypothesis of corporate takeovers. **Journal of Business**, 59 (2): 197 - 216.

Rusbult, C. E. (1980a). Commitment and satisfaction in romantic associations: A test of the investment model. **Journal of Experimental Social Psychology,** 16: 172 - 186.

Rusbult, Caryl E. (1980b). Satisfaction and commitment in friendships. **Representative Research in Social Psychology**, 11: 96 - 105.

Salancik, Gerald R. (1995). WANTED: A good network theory of organization. **Administrative Science Quarterly**, 40: 345 - 349.

Salecker, Jürgen, & Müller-Stewens, Günter (1991). Kommunikation - Schlüsselkompetenz im Akquisitionsprozess. **Absatzwirtschaft**, 10: 104 - 113.

Sarason, Irwin G., Sarason, Barbara R., & Pierce, Gregory R. (1995). Social and personal relationships: Current issues, future directions. **Journal of Social and Personal Relationships**, 12: 613 - 619.

Scheck, Christine L., & Kinicki, Angelo J. (2000). Identifying the antecedents of coping with an organizational acquisition: a structural assessment. **Journal of Organizational Behavior**, 21: 627 - 648.

Schein, Edgar H. (1990). Organizational Culture. **American Psychologist**, 45 (2): 109 - 119.

Scheiter, Dietmar (1989). **Die Integration akquirierter Unternehmen**. Dissertation Nr. 1117, Hochschule St. Gallen. Bamberg: difo-druck Schmacht.

Scherer, Frederic M. (1980). **Industrial Market Structure and Economic Performance**, 2nd ed. Chicago, IL: Rand McNally.

Schmitt, Neal , & Pulakos, Elaine D. (1985).Predicting job satisfaction from life satisfaction: Is there a. general satisfaction factor?. **International Journal of Psychology**, 20: 155 - 167.

Schoennauer, Alfred W. (1967). Behavior Patterns of Executives in Business Acquisitions. **Personnel Administration**, 30: 27 - 31.

Schubbe, Marcus (1999). **Der Einfluss von Unternehmenskulturen auf den Integrationsprozess bei Unternehmenszusammenschlüssen.** Dissertation, Freiburg im Breisgau.

Schuman, S. C., & Alpert, S. B. (1960). Economies of Scale: Some Statistical Evidence: Comment. **Quarterly Journal of Economics**, 74 (3): 493 - 497.

Schweiger, David M., & DeNisi, Angelo S. (1991). Communication with employees following a merger: A longitudinal field experiment. **Academy of Management Journal**, 34 (1): 110 - 135.

Schweiger, David M., & Goulet, Philip K. (2002). Explaining acquisition integration effectiveness through cultural learning: A longitudinal field experiment. **Academy of Management Proceedings**,1: 1 - 6.

Schweiger, David M., & Lee, Cynthia (1993). Longitudinal effects of merger and behavioral interventions on job security. **Academy of Management Proceedings**, 1: 262 - 267.

Schweiger, David M., & Walsh, James P. (1990). Mergers and acquisitions: An interdisciplinary view. **Research in Personnel and Human Resources Management**, 8: 41 - 107.

Schweiger, David M., Csiszar, Ernst N., & Napier, Nancy K. (1993). Implementing international mergers and acquisitions. **Human Ressource Planning**, 16 (1): 53 - 71.

Schweiger, David M., Ivancevich, John M., & Power, Frank R. (1987). Executive actions for managing human resources before and after acquisition. **Academy of Management Executive**, 1 (2): 127 - 138.

Seth, Anju (1990). Sources of value creation in acquisitions: An empirical investigation. **Strategic Management Journal**, 11 (6): 431 - 446.

Shah, Pri (1998a). **Network Destruction: The Structural Implications of Downsizing**. Draft.

Shaver, Myles J. (1998). Accounting for endogeneity when assessing strategy performance: Does entry mode choice affect Fdi Survival?. **Management Science**, 44 (4): 571 - 586.

Shelton, Lois M. (1988). Strategic Business fits and corporate Acquisition: Empirical Evidence. **Strategic Management Journal**, 9 (3): 279 - 287.

Sherif, Muzafer, & Sherif, Carolyn W. (1969). Social psychology. New York: Harper & Row.
Sherman, Roger (1972). How Tax Policy induces conglomerate Mergers. **National Tax Journal**, 25 (4): 521-529.

Shrivastava, Paul (1986). Postmerger Integration. **Journal of Business Strategy**, 7: 65 - 76.

Simmons, Carolyn H., King, Cheryl S., Tucker, Suzette S., & Wehner, Elizabeth A. (1986). Success Strategies: Winning Through Cooperation or Competition. **Journal of Social Psychology**, 126 (4): 437-445.

Simon, Herbert A. (1957). **Models of Man**. New York: Wiley.

Simon, Hermann (1999). Kollision der Kulturen. **Manager Magazin**, 6: 96 - 98.

Singh, Harbir, & Montgomery, Cynthia A. (1987). Corporate Acquisition Dtrategies and Economic Performance. **Strategic Management Journal**, 8 (4): 377 - 386.

Singleton, Royce A., Straits, Bruce C., & Straits, Margaret M. (1993). **Approaches to Social Research**, 2nd ed. New York: Oxford University Press.

Sirower, Mark L. (1997). **The synergy trap: how companies lose the acquisition game**. New York, NY: The Free Press.

Slusky, Alexander R., & Caves, Richard E. (1991). Synergy, Agency, and the Determinants of Premia Paid in Mergers. **Journal of Industrial Economics**, 39 (3): 277 - 296.

Smidts, Ale, Pruyn, Ad Th. H., & Riel, Cees B. M. van (2001). The Impact of Employee Communication perceived external Prestige on Organizational Identification. **Academy of Management Journal**, 49 (5): 1051 - 1062.

Sommer, Stefan (1996). **Integration akquirierter Unternehmen: Instrumente und Methoden zur Realisierung von leistungswirtschaftlichen Synergiepotentialen**. Dissertation, Göttingen.

Spitzberg, Brian H. (1998). Sexual Coercion in Courtship Patterns. In: Spitzberg, Brian H., & Cupach, William R. (1998). **The Dark Side of Close Relationships**. New Jersey: LEA.

Stackman, Richard W., & Pinder, Craig C. (1999). Context and sex effects on personal work networks. **Journal of Social & Personal Relationships**, 16 (1): 39 - 65.

Stahl, Günter K., & Voigt, Andreas (2004). Meta-Analyses of the Performance Implications of Cultural Differences in Mergers and Acquisitions. **Academy of Management Proceedings**, 5: 1 - 5.

Stearns, Linda B., & Allan, Kenneth D. (1996). Economic behavior in institutional environments: The corporate merger wave of the 1980s. **American Sociological Review**, 61 (4): 699 -718.

Steel, Robert P., Rentsch, Joan R., & Hendrix, William H. (2002). Cross-Level Replication and Extension of Steel and Rentsch"s (1995) Longitudinal Absence Findings. **Journal of Business and Psychology**, 16 (3): 447 - 456.

Stevenson, William B., & Gilly, Mary C. (1991). Information processing and problem solving: The migration of problems through formal positions and networks of ties. **Academy of Management Journal**, 34 (4): 918 - 928.

Stokes Jr., Stewart L. (1994). Networking with a human face. **Information Systems Management**, 10 (2): 73 - 77.

Sumner, William G. (1906). **Folkways : a study of the sociological importance of usages, manners, customs, mores, and morals Folkways**. New York: Ginn.

Tajfel, Henri (1985). **Psychology of Intergroup Relations**. Cambridge, UK: Cambridge University.

Tajfel, Henri, & Wilkes, Al (1963). Classification and quantitative judgement. **British Journal of Psychology**, 54: 101 - 114.

Tajfel, Henri (1982). Social Psychology of Intergroup Relations. **Annual Review of Psychology**: 1 - 33.

Teece, David J., Pisano, Garry, & Shuen, Amyet al. (1997). Dynamic Capabilities and Strategic Management. **Strategic Management Journal** 18(7): 509-533.

Tenter, Christina G., & Müller, Sylvia (2000). Unternehmenskultur - Problem- oder Erfolgsfaktor bei Fusionen. In: Henckel v. Donnersmarck, & Schatz, R. (3. Aufl.) (2000). **Fusionen: Gestalten und Kommunizieren**. Bonn: InnoVatio Verlag.

Terry, Deborah J., & Callan, Victor J. (1997). Employee adjustment to large-scale organizational change. **Australian Psychologist**, 32 (3): 203 - 210.

Terry, Deborah J., & O'Brien, Anne T. (2001). Status, Legitimacy, and Ingroup Bias in the Context of an Organizational Merger. **Group Processes & Intergroup Relations**, 4 (3): 271.

Tetenbaum, Toby J. (1999). Beating the Odds of Merger & Acquisition Failure: Seven Key Practices That Improve the Chance for Expected Integration and Synergies. **Organizational Dynamics**, 28 (2): 22 - 35.

The Boston Consulting Group (2004). **Volumes of M&A-transactions**. Internal working paper.

Thibaut, John W., & Kelley, Harold H. (1959). **The Social Psychology of Groups**. New York, NY: John Wiley & Sons, Inc..

Town, Robert J. (1992) Merger waves and the structure of merger and acquisition time-series. **Journal of Applied Econometrics**, 7 (4): 83 - 100.

Trzicky, Nico (2000). Stakeholder einer Fusion und deren Feindbilder. In: Henckel von Donnersmarck, & Schatz, Roland (Eds.). **Fusionen. Gestalten und Kommunizieren**. Fribourg: InnoVatio.

Tsai, Wenpin, & Goshal, Sumantra (1998). Social capital and value creation: The role of intrafirm networks. **Academy of Management**, 41 (4): 464 - 476.

Van De Ven, Andrew H. (1976). A Framework for Organization Assessment. **Academy of Management Review** 1(1): 64.

Van den Bulte, Christophe, & Moenart, Rudy K. (1998). The Effects of R&D Team Co-location on Communication Patterns among R&D, Marketing, and Manufacturing. **Management Science**, 44 (11): 1 - 18.

Verbrugge, Lois M. (1983). A Research Note on Adult Friendship Contact: A Dyadic Perspective. **Social Forces**, 62 (1): 78 - 83.

Verbrugge, Lois. M. (1977). The Structure of Adult Friendship Choices. **Social Forces**, 56 (2): 576 - 597.

Very, Philippe, & Schweiger, David M. (2001). The Acquisition Process as a Learning Process: Evidence from a Study of Critical Problems and Solutions In Domestic and Cross-Border Deals. **Journal of World Business, Elsevier Science Publishing Company,** 36: 11 - 31.

Wasserman, Stanley, & Faust, Katherine (1994). **Social Network Analysis.** New York, NY: Cambridge University Press.

Weber, Max (1922). **Wirtschaft und Gesellschaft.** Tübingen

Weber, Roberto A., & Camerer, Colin F. (2003). Cultural conflict and merger failure: An experimental approach. **Management Science,** 49 (4): 400 - 415.

Weber, Yaakov, & Shenkar, Oded (1996). National and corporate cultural fit in mergers/acquisitions: An exploratory study. **Management Science,** 42 (8): 1215 - 1227.

Weber, Yaakov (1996). Corporate cultural fit and performance in mergers and acquisitions. **Human Relations,** 49 (9): 1181 - 1202.

Weick, Karl E. (1966). The Concept of Equity in the Perception of Pay. **Administrative Science Quarterly,** 11 (3): 414 - 439.

Wernerfelt, Birger (1984). A resource-based view of the firm. **Strategic Management Journal,** 5 (2): 171 - 180.

White, Harrison C. (1992). **Identity and control : a structural theory of social action.** Princeton, N.J. : Princeton University Press.

Williamson, Oliver E. (1975). **Markets and Hierarchies: Analysis and Anti-trust Implications.** New York: Free Press.

Yunker, James A. (1983). **Integrating Acquisitions: Making Corporate Marriages Work.** Greenwood Publishing Group.

Zaheer, Akbar, Castaner, Xavier, & Souder, David (2005 forthcoming). **To integrate or not to integrate? Complementarity, similarity and acquisition value creation.**

Zimmermann, Rainer (2000). Interne und externe Kommunikation. In: Picot, Gerhard (Ed.). **Mergers & Acquisitions: Planung, Durchführung, Integration**. Stuttgart: Schäfer-Poeschel.

Appendix I – IV

See www.tim.tu-berlin.de

Deutscher Universitäts-Verlag
Ihr Weg in die Wissenschaft

Der Deutsche Universitäts-Verlag ist ein Unternehmen der GWV Fachverlage, zu denen auch der Gabler Verlag und der Vieweg Verlag gehören. Wir publizieren ein umfangreiches wirtschaftswissenschaftliches Monografien-Programm aus den Fachgebieten

- ✓ Betriebswirtschaftslehre
- ✓ Volkswirtschaftslehre
- ✓ Wirtschaftsrecht
- ✓ Wirtschaftspädagogik und
- ✓ Wirtschaftsinformatik

In enger Kooperation mit unseren Schwesterverlagen wird das Programm kontinuierlich ausgebaut und um aktuelle Forschungsarbeiten erweitert. Dabei wollen wir vor allem jüngeren Wissenschaftlern ein Forum bieten, ihre Forschungsergebnisse der interessierten Fachöffentlichkeit vorzustellen. Unser Verlagsprogramm steht solchen Arbeiten offen, deren Qualität durch eine sehr gute Note ausgewiesen ist. Jedes Manuskript wird vom Verlag zusätzlich auf seine Vermarktungschancen hin geprüft.

Durch die umfassenden Vertriebs- und Marketingaktivitäten einer großen Verlagsgruppe erreichen wir die breite Information aller Fachinstitute, -bibliotheken und -zeitschriften. Den Autoren bieten wir dabei attraktive Konditionen, die jeweils individuell vertraglich vereinbart werden.

Besuchen Sie unsere Homepage: *www.duv.de*

Deutscher Universitäts-Verlag
Abraham-Lincoln-Str. 46
D-65189 Wiesbaden